YOUTH AT RISK

A Prevention Resource for Counselors, Teachers, and Parents

Fifth Edition

This book is due elors, Teachers, and Parents
Failure to ·
in a·

Edited by

David Capuzzi and Douglas R. Gross

AMERICAN COUNSELING ASSOCIATION
5999 Stevenson Avenue
Alexandria, VA 22304
www.counseling.org

YOUTH AT RISK

A Prevention Resource for Counselors, Teachers, and Parents

Fifth Edition

10 9 8 7 6 5 4 3 2

AMERICAN COUNSELING ASSOCIATION
5999 Stevenson Avenue
Alexandria, VA 22304

Director of Publications ▓ Carolyn C. Baker

Production Manager ▓ Bonny E. Gaston

Copy Editor ▓ Elaine Dunn

Editorial Assistant ▓ Catherine A. Brumley

Cover and text design by Bonny E. Gaston

LIBRARY OF CONGRESS CATALOGING-IN-PUBLICATION DATA
Youth at risk: a prevention resource for counselors, teachers, and parents / edited by David Capuzzi, Douglas R. Gross. — 5th ed.
        p. cm.
  Includes bibliographical references and index.
  ISBN 978-1-55620-275-9 (alk. paper)
  1. Youth with social disabilities—United States. 2. Youth—Counseling of—United States. 3. Deviant behavior. 4. Adolescent psychopathology—United States. 5. Adolescent psychotherapy—United States. 6. Dropout behavior, Prediction of. I. Capuzzi, David. II. Gross, Douglas R.

HV1431.Y68 2007
  362.74—dc22   2007014940

Dedication

To: Kevin and Keith Capuzzi

Your supportiveness and quick wit made this book possible.
You are wonderful role models, each in your own way,
for other young people.

To: Lola Gross

With love all is possible.

Table of Contents

Preface

Youth at Risk: A Prevention Resource for Counselors, Teachers, and Parents is a revision of the 2004 fourth edition. In this fifth edition, major emphasis has again been placed on prevention efforts with at-risk populations as well as practical guidelines for successful intervention with behaviors most often identified as placing youth at risk. Selected chapters include case studies that explore prevention efforts from individual, family, school, and community perspectives. Every effort has been made to address the complexities of working with vulnerable youths in a way that provides professionals, as well as parents, with an information base and guidelines for working within the parameters of the prevention–intervention paradigm. This text differs from similar texts because of the attention placed on counseling and systems applications with youth at risk.

The text is developmental in orientation. Part One presents information dealing with population identification, definition, and behaviors and causal factors descriptive of youth at risk. Information is also included that serves as a foundation for understanding the prevention–intervention paradigm. Part One also addresses prevention from the point of view of identification and promotion of resilience in our youth.

Part Two of the text deals with parameters that often serve as causal factors for the development of at-risk behaviors. Included in this section are chapters dealing with the effects of a dysfunctional family, low self-esteem, depression, mood disorders, and stress and trauma. Each chapter in this section not only identifies various aspects of the causal factors but also presents information related to prevention strategies designed to deal with these factors and adaptations for diversity

Part Three of the text deals with issues and behaviors most often identified as placing youth at risk. A new chapter, "I'll Cry Tomorrow": Diverse Youth and the Scars That Don't Show, has been added to deal with such issues as racial and ethnic identity and acculturation and diversity, as these affect not only at-risk youth but also those who work with them. The behaviors in Part Three include those that lead to eating disorders, suicide, gang membership, counseling queer youth, violence on campus, substance abuse, homelessness, and the school dropout. New in this edition is a combining of two former chapters into one titled "A Future in Jeopardy: Sexuality Issues in Adolescence," covering such topics as teen pregnancy, sexually transmitted diseases, rape and date rape, and sexual predation. Each chapter in Part Three provides definitive information related to the specific issue or behavior, includes a case study to illustrate the information presented, and provides approaches to prevention and intervention from individual, family, school, and community perspectives. Adaptations for diversity are also addressed because prevention and intervention efforts usually need to be modified to meet the needs of minority and disenfranchised youth served by the schools, communities, and mental health practitioners.

Every effort has been made by the editors and contributors to provide the reader with current and relevant information in each of the 17 areas of focus. We hope that this new edition of *Youth At Risk: A Prevention Resource for Counselors, Teachers, and Parents* will prove to be an invaluable resource for individuals committed to assisting young people in the often difficult transition between adolescence and adulthood.

Acknowledgments

We would like to thank the 25 authors who contributed their expertise, knowledge, and experience in the development of this text. We would also like to thank our families, who provided the freedom and encouragement to make this endeavor possible. Our thanks are also directed to staff at the American Counseling Association for their encouragement and assistance with copyediting and ultimately the production of the book.

Meet the Editors

David Capuzzi, PhD, NCC, LPC, is affiliate professor in the Department of Counselor Education, Counseling Psychology, and Rehabilitation Services at The Pennsylvania State University. He is professor emeritus at Portland State University. He is a past president of the American Counseling Association (ACA; formerly the American Association for Counseling and Development). Prior to his affiliation with The Pennsylvania State University, he served as scholar in residence at Johns Hopkins University.

From 1980 to 1984, Dr. Capuzzi was editor of *The School Counselor*. He has authored a number of textbook chapters and monographs on the topic of preventing adolescent suicide and is coeditor and author with Dr. Larry Golden of *Helping Families Help Children: Family Interventions With School-Related Problems* (1986) and *Preventing Adolescent Suicide* (1988). He coauthored and edited *Youth at Risk: A Prevention Resource for Counselors, Teachers, and Parents* (1989, 1996, 2000, 2004); *Introduction to the Counseling Profession* (1991, 1997, 2001, 2005); *Introduction to Group Counseling* (1992, 1998, 2002, 2006); and *Counseling and Psychotherapy: Theories and Interventions* with Douglas R. Gross (1995, 1999, 2003, 2007). He also edited *Suicide Across the Life Span* (2004), *Approaches to Group Work: A Handbook for Practitioners* (2003), and *Sexuality Counseling* (2002), the latter coauthored and edited with Larry Burlew. *Career Counseling: Foundations, Perspectives, and Applications* (2006) and *Foundations of Addictions Counseling* (2008), both edited with Mark D. Stauffer, are his two most recent textbooks. He has authored or coauthored articles in a number of ACA-related journals.

A frequent speaker and keynoter at professional conferences and institutes, Dr. Capuzzi has also consulted with a variety of school districts and community agencies interested in initiating prevention and intervention strategies for adolescents at risk for suicide. He has facilitated the development of suicide prevention, crisis management, and postvention programs in communities throughout the United States; provides training on the topics of youth at risk, grief and loss, group work, and using meditation and mindfulness to increase therapeutic presence in counseling; and serves as an invited adjunct faculty member at other universities as time permits. He is the first recipient of ACA's Kitty Cole Human Rights Award and also a recipient of the Leona Tyler Award in Oregon.

■

Douglas R. Gross, PhD, NCC, is professor emeritus at Arizona State University, Tempe, where he served as a faculty member in counselor education for 29 years. His professional work history includes public school teaching, counseling, and administration. He is currently retired and living in Michigan. He has been president of the Arizona Counselors Association, president of the Western Association for Counselor Education and Supervision, chairperson of the Western Regional Branch Assembly of the ACA, president of the Association for Humanistic Education and Development, and treasurer and parliamentarian of the ACA.

Dr. Gross has contributed chapters to eight texts: *Counseling and Psychotherapy: Theories and Interventions* (1995, 1999, 2003, 2007); *Youth at Risk: A Resource Guide for Counselors, Teachers, and Parents* (1989, 1996, 2000, 2004); *Foundations of Mental Health Counseling* (1986, 1996); *Counseling: Theory, Process and Practice* (1977); *The Counselor's Handbook* (1974); *Introduction to the Counseling Profession* (1991, 1997, 2001, 2005); and *Introduction to Group Counseling* (1992, 1998, 2002, 2006). His research has appeared in the *Journal of Counseling Psychology; Journal of Counseling & Development; Association for Counselor Education and Supervision Journal; Journal of Educational Research, Counseling and Human Development; Arizona Counselors Journal; Texas Counseling Journal;* and *AMHCA Journal.*

For the past 13 years, Dr. Gross has provided national training in the areas of bereavement, grief, and loss.

■

Meet the Authors

Lisa Lungfuss Aasheim, PhD, is the coordinator of the school counseling master's program at Portland State University and the director of the community counseling clinic at Portland State. She specializes in clinical supervision and enjoys teaching courses in clinical supervision, addictions counseling, couples and family counseling, and practicum and internship. Her research interests focus primarily on clinical supervision in agency settings, counselor education and skill development, and the therapeutic alliance. She especially enjoys being surrounded by her knowledgeable colleagues and eager, delightful counseling students who share in her passion and profound belief in the change process.

Elva E. Blanks, PhD, is a recent graduate of the counseling psychology program at Arizona State University. She is currently working as a counselor at the Counseling and Consultation Center within Arizona State University. She has focused both her clinical work and research attention on areas of disordered eating and other risky behaviors of gifted/talented young women.

Sonja C. Burnham, EdD, has been a counselor educator in Mississippi for the past 14 years. She began her professional life as a public school teacher in Louisiana and Mississippi and taught for 7 years. While working with students with disabilities at the university level, she implemented federal grants that promoted transition from school to work. Since that time, she has written and worked in the area of career counseling and supervision while educating and supervising school counselors. Her publications deal with issues related to school and school counseling. She was named Outstanding Teacher of the Year for 2002 and served as program coordinator for counselor education in the Department of Leadership and Counselor Education at the University of Mississippi. Dr. Burnham recently retired from the University of Mississippi.

Cass Dykeman, PhD, is an associate professor of counselor education at Oregon State University. He is a national certified counselor, master addictions counselor, and national certified school counselor. Dr. Dykeman received a master's in counseling from the University of Washington and a doctorate in counselor education from the University of Virginia. He served as principal investigator for two federal grants in the area of counseling. In addition, he is the author of numerous books, book chapters, and scholarly journal articles. Dr. Dykeman is past president of both the Washington State Association for Counselor Education and Supervision and the Western Association for Counselor Education and Supervision. He is also past chair of the School Counseling Interest Network of the Association for Counselor Education and Supervision. His current research interests include addiction counseling and psychopharmacology.

Jeannie Falkner, PhD, MSSW, has over 25 years of clinical experience in private practice working with individuals, children, adolescents, and groups. She is currently an assistant professor of social work at Delta State University. Dr. Falkner has presented numerous national and regional workshops on the role of money in group counseling and financial wellness for counselors. Her research interests include integrated health and mental health and resiliency in African American families in the Mississippi Delta.

Abbé Finn, PhD, is a licensed professional counselor and an associate professor in the counseling program at Florida Gulf Coast University. She earned a BA and MEd from Tulane University, an MS from Loyola University in New Orleans, and a PhD from the University of New Orleans. Dr. Finn has a variety of clinical experiences in crisis management and the prediction of violence. She worked as an employee assistance professional with U.S. Postal Service workers for 6 years. She was a team leader on the National Crisis Response Team. Dr. Finn spent a week in New York City counseling survivors following the destruction of the World Trade Center and 2 weeks with the Red Cross as a counselor working with survivors of Hurricane Katrina. While working for the U.S. Postal Service in New Orleans, she initiated the management training in violence prevention. She has also worked with the New Orleans Fire Department, training captains and district chiefs in the prevention of workplace violence. Dr. Finn has written and lectured on numerous occasions regarding the importance of school crisis response plans and the identification of students most at risk for harming others, and identification and management of employees at risk for harming others.

Lea R. Flowers, PhD, is an assistant professor in counselor education at Georgia State University. She is a nationally certified counselor and a licensed professional counselor. Dr. Flowers has had a wide range of experiences in counseling in community agencies and school settings. Her specific research interests are primarily around ethics and leadership, group work, socialization, women's developmental and career issues across the life span, and advocacy for special populations in school settings. She has presented at local, state, national, and international conferences on her specialty areas. Her most recent publication was a coauthored book chapter in *Introduction to Group Work* (2006). She earned both a master's degree and a doctorate in counselor education from the University of New Orleans. Dr. Flowers also has a bachelor of science degree in speech language pathology from Xavier University in New Orleans, Louisiana and worked for 7 years as a speech language pathologist, primarily with at-risk students and special needs populations in the Palm Beach County School System in West Palm Beach, Florida, and the Cobb County School System in Marietta, Georgia.

Camea J. Gagliardi-Blea, PhD, is an assistant professor of clinical psychology at New Mexico Highlands University. She began her work with at-risk youth as a high school English teacher in the Colorado Public Schools. She completed her doctorate of philosophy in counseling psychology at Arizona State University.

Her clinical training has focused on health and family and includes an internship at the Barrow Neurological Institute in Phoenix, Arizona, and an internship at the Department of Veterans Affairs in Albuquerque, New Mexico. Her research interests include academic persistence, creativity, and family/community reinforcement and psychoeducational models of treatment.

Fernando J. Gutierrez, EdD, JD, is a life and organizational coach and an attorney in inactive status in Miramar, Florida. He is also an adjunct faculty member at Sistema Universitario Ana G. Mendez, the first accelerated discipline-based, dual-language immersion university in the United States. He teaches courses in the master's program in guidance and counseling, undergraduate education and psychology courses, and law courses in the department of criminal justice. He is coeditor of *Counseling Gay Men and Lesbians: Journey to the End of the Rainbow* (1992), published by the American Counseling Association (ACA), and a special issue of the *Journal of Counseling & Development* on lesbian, gay, and bisexual issues. Dr. Gutierrez was named inaugural Legacy Fellow of the Association for Gay, Lesbian, and Bisexual Issues in Counseling in 2007. In 1999, Dr. Gutierrez received the Joe Norton Award from the Association for Gay, Lesbian, and Bisexual Issues in Counseling, a division of ACA. Dr. Gutierrez has presented at local, state, national, and international conferences on issues of lesbians, gays, and bisexuals; Hispanics and ethnic minorities; chemical dependency; and domestic violence. Additionally, he has taught courses in family dynamics, chemical dependency, and college student development.

Melinda Haley, PhD, received her doctorate in counseling psychology from New Mexico State University in Las Cruces, New Mexico and completed her internship at Texas Women's University in Denton, Texas. She currently works for South Texas Rural Health Services, which is a non-profit organization dedicated to providing medical, dental, and mental health services to the economically disadvantaged clients. Dr. Haley has written numerous book chapters and multimedia presentations on topics as diverse as group psychotherapy and counseling, school counseling, career counseling, counseling theory, single-parenting, teen sexuality, technology in counseling, and the risks and protective factors associated with suicide. She has extensive applied experience working with adults, adolescents, inmates, domestic violence offenders, and culturally diverse populations in the areas of assessment, diagnosis, treatment planning, crisis management, and intervention. Her planned therapeutic specialties include mood disorders, personality disorders and multicultural issues in therapy. Dr. Haley's research interests include multicultural issues in counseling, personality development over the life span, personality disorders, psychology of criminal and serial offenders, trauma, and posttraumatic stress disorder, bias and racism, and social justice issues.

Mary A. Hermann, JD, PhD, is an assistant professor at Virginia Commonwealth University. She holds a JD in law and a PhD in counselor education. She is a licensed attorney, a licensed professional counselor, a national certified counselor, and a certified school counselor. Dr. Hermann has coedited a book on legal and ethical issues in school counseling and written numerous journal articles and book chapters. She regularly presents at national, regional, and state conferences.

Rolla E. Lewis, EdD, NCC, is an associate professor of educational psychology and school counseling coordinator at California State University, East Bay. His research and scholarship interests include developing ecological models to guide school counseling practice, promoting resilience in school communities, using structured narratives in counseling and supervision, and creating university–community collaborations that place counselors-in-training in service to high-need youth and families. He has been recognized in his efforts to create local knowledge and community service. Dr. Lewis has published numerous chapters and articles and has received Portland State University's Civic Engagement Award two times. He was awarded the Oregon Counseling Association's Leona Tyler Award for outstanding contributions to professional counseling.

Rebecca B. McCathren, PhD, is an associate professor of special education at the University of Missouri–Columbia. Her research interests include early communication and language development for young children with disabilities and early identification and intervention for young children with autism. She is also interested in young children at risk and strategies for supporting and enhancing their development.

Benedict T. McWhirter, PhD, is an associate professor of counseling psychology at the University of Oregon. He teaches courses related to working with at-risk youth, helping skills, prevention and community interventions, and counselor supervision. His primary research focuses on the factors that contribute to risk and resilience and interventions and outcomes for late adolescents to early adults, including youth who are at risk for problem behavior and college students. He is also interested in ethnic identity as a protective factor and the development of multicultural competencies among counseling professionals. His publications include *At Risk Youth: A Comprehensive Response* (4th ed., 2007) by J. Jeffries McWhirter, Benedict T. McWhirter, Ellen Hawley McWhirter, and Robert J. McWhirter. For each year since 1995, he has visited and worked in Peñalolén, Chile, a low-income community of Santiago, where, with his spouse, Dr. Ellen Hawley McWhirter, he has conducted pro bono training workshops for couples on conflict resolution, family communication, parenting, and group leadership skills. He was named a Fulbright Scholar to Chile in 2004 to conduct research on Chilean adolescents and he has extended his research on Chilean youth in poor, urban schools with support of the Spencer Foundation (2007–2009). He currently continues his international research, service, and teaching activities.

Sandra S. Meggert, PhD, is president of The Unfinished Business and is an adjunct professor at Antioch University in Seattle, Washington. She has presented over 900 Creative Humor at Work seminars throughout the United States and Europe for counselors, educators, businesses, and various civic groups. She also does assessments of adults with learning disabilities at a private learning center. She received her PhD in counselor education/counseling psychology from Arizona State University and has taught in counselor education programs, counseled, and consulted for several years. Dr. Meggert has written articles on career guidance and humor and developed career guidance materials. She is currently writing a book about humor titled *Creative Humor at Work: Living the Humor Perspective.*

Russell D. Miars, PhD, is an associate professor in the counselor education program at Portland State University. Previously, Dr. Miars was director of the Counseling and Student Development Center and adjunct associate professor in clinical psychology at Indiana University of Pennsylvania. His research and scholarly interests include counselor supervision, legal and ethical issues in counseling, life span human development, and assessment in counseling. An emphasis in all his work is translating theory and research into effective clinical practice.

Jane E. Rheineck, PhD, is currently an assistant professor in counseling at Northern Illinois University. Dr. Rheineck has worked with children and adolescents as a mental health counselor in a variety of settings that included inpatient residential treatment, outpatient counseling, and as a mental health counselor in the schools. Her research interests not only include counseling issues pertaining to children and adolescents, but concerns that affect the lesbian, gay, bisexual, and transgendered community. Dr. Rheineck received her PhD in counselor education from the University of Arkansas and is a licensed counselor in Illinois as well as being a national certified counselor.

Sharon E. Robinson Kurpius, PhD, received her doctoral degree in counseling and in education inquiry methodology from Indiana University in 1978. Since that time she has been a professor of counseling and counseling psychology at Arizona State University. She has a special interest in at-risk adolescents and has been the coprincipal investigator on several large grants focusing on working with talented, at-risk teenage girls. She has designed and taught specialized courses on counseling at-risk youth. In addition, she has extensively researched these factors and published both conceptual and empirically based articles in this area.

Crystal Rofkahr, MA, is currently a doctoral student in counseling psychology at Arizona State University. She received her master's degree from the community counseling program at West Virginia University. Her research interests include health issues, women's issues, and children and adolescents.

Laura R. Simpson, PhD, is an assistant professor of counselor education at Delta State University in Cleveland, Mississippi. A licensed professional counselor, Dr. Simpson also maintains a small private counseling practice. Dr. Simpson moved into academia following 15 years of work in a community mental health setting and has a particular interest in supervision, secondary traumatic stress, and spirituality. She has published articles for a variety of journals and authored chapters in several books.

Melissa A. Stormont, PhD, is an associate professor of special education at the University of Missouri–Columbia. Her research interests include characteristics and support needs of young children who are at risk for failure in school and supporting teachers in their implementation of supports in school settings. She has recently written a book titled *Fostering Resilience in Young Children at Risk for Failure: Strategies for Grades K–3.*

Jason Vasquez, MA, is a 2nd-year doctoral student in the counseling psychology program at New Mexico State University, Las Cruces. He has experience counseling a variety of populations in outpatient counseling, including high school students, college students, domestic violence offenders, and older adult populations. His professional interests include mentoring, identity development, multicultural issues, sex therapy, and social justice issues.

Karrie P. Walters, MEd, MA, received her MEd in special education from the University of North Texas and her MA in counseling psychology from the University of Minnesota. She is currently completing her PhD in counseling psychology at the University of Oregon. Over the past 10 years, she had worked as a teacher for youths with behavioral disorders, a therapist for children with autism, and a counselor for young offenders. In her work as an educational consultant, she was especially successful at building bridges between school administrators, teachers, and parents. Her research interests include studying the connection between identity and behavior, especially as it relates to conflict resolution and peace education, and learning more about the factors involved in effective prevention and intervention programs for youth at risk for behavior problems. Her other interests include multiculturalism; issues concerning the lesbian, gay, bisexual, transgender, and questioning community; advocacy; and social justice. Her additional research and practice activities focus on increasing multicultural competence among educators and practitioners in the human services profession.

Dana J. Weber, BA, is a doctoral student in the counseling psychology program at Arizona State University. She received her bachelor's degree in psychology and sociology from the University of Wisconsin–Milwaukee. Her research interests include substance abuse prevention, marital discord, child maltreatment, stress and coping, and inmate recidivism.

Kimberly Wright, PhD, is a licensed psychologist who has worked with a full range of clients with eating disorders at several universities. She earned her bachelor's and master's degrees from California State University, Long Beach, and her doctorate in counseling psychology from Indiana State University. For the last 13 years, she served as the co-coordinator of eating disorder treatment at Arizona State University (ASU), coordinating a multidisciplinary team of counseling and health center providers. She has also served as adjunct faculty for the counselor education department at ASU. She recently resigned from ASU's Counseling and Consultation Center in order to devote more time to private practice.

■

PART ONE

■

Introducing the Problem

Any person who either works with or lives with youth becomes increasingly aware of the potential that exists for the development of at-risk behaviors. This awareness is enhanced by media coverage, educational reform, mental health programming, governmental mandates, and law enforcement reporting. This ongoing bombardment of the vulnerability of youth provides a call to action for all persons involved with this population. Prior to taking such action, however, one must understand not only the demographics of this population but also current definitions, at-risk behaviors, generic causal factors, and prevention and intervention approaches to dealing with youth at risk. Part One of this text provides the reader with this foundational information. Chapter 1, Defining Youth At Risk, introduces the topic of *at-riskness* by providing the reader with foundational information related to definitions, at-risk behaviors, and causal factors that enhance the development of at-risk behaviors. The chapter concludes with an introduction to the concept of resilience and the prevention and crisis-management paradigm.

Building on this foundation, Chapter 2, Prevention: An Overview, lays the groundwork for understanding the various strategies incorporated in the term *prevention*. Information presented in this chapter includes goals and purposes of prevention; primary, secondary, and tertiary concepts related to prevention; and program examples to illustrate prevention's place in the broad spectrum of helping. Some discussion of the schools' efforts to develop tragedy response plans is included. The chapter concludes with an explanation of how to plan prevention and intervention strategies.

Chapter 3, Resilience: Individual, Family, School, and Community Perspectives, adds dimension to the prevention paradigm by offering counselors, teachers, and parents an alternative view that sees youth "at promise" rather than "at risk." This chapter provides key research, definitions, effective practices, and professional possibilities. It sets forth ideas for practices promoting resilience that establishes a framework for seeing youth as having innate self-righting capacities for changing their life trajectories, a landscape that defines risks in ecosocial contexts rather than people, and an outlook that asks people to slow down enough to listen deeply to the stories embedded in everyday lives.

These first three chapters provide a necessary foundation for all persons wishing to reduce the vulnerability of youth for the future development of at-risk behaviors.

CHAPTER 1

■

Defining Youth at Risk

Douglas R. Gross and David Capuzzi

As John Patron sat down at the large table in the conference room, he hoped that something positive could come from this meeting, perhaps something finally could be done to help some of the students in his classroom. He knew that he had been instrumental in forcing Ms. Callis, his principal, to call this meeting. He hoped that all of his colleagues attending shared his view on the urgency for taking some positive action.

This was John's third year of teaching, and each day he was confronted with problems in his classroom. The problems were not those of math, his subject area, but problems that he observed and that were reported to him by many of his students. The problems covered a wide range of areas, including pregnancy, gangs, drugs and alcohol, violence, eating disorders, and dropping out of school. Certainly, he was not the first to notice these problems or the only teacher in whom students confided. If these problems were so obvious to him, why hadn't something been done to deal with them? Most of his students were now juniors in high school, and he was sure that the problems did not have their origins in attaining junior status.

He did the best he could, but he was not trained to handle these issues. In seeking direction, he talked with the school counselor, the school psychologist, and Ms. Callis. Although all of the people contacted wanted to help, they were also overwhelmed by the demands on their time. John's questions for the most part went unanswered. If he was correct that these problems did not begin during the junior year in high school, why hadn't something been done earlier? Hadn't former school personnel recognized the difficulties these students were having? Hadn't parents asked for help with their children? Why hadn't something been done to prevent these problems from developing? John hoped that answers would be forthcoming at the meeting.

After the meeting John sat in his classroom and reflected on what had happened. He was very pleased that he was not alone in his concern about the students and that his colleagues had raised many of the same questions that plagued him. He was also pleased that many of his colleagues saw a need for adding trained personnel to work with teachers, students, and parents in developing strategies to intervene in the disrupted lives of many of the students before it was too late. John felt that several helpful outcomes resulted from the meeting. The first of these was that of exploring the development of prevention strategies aimed at early identification of problem behaviors and establishing programs directed at impeding their development. This outcome generated much discussion centering around such questions as "What constitutes prevention?" "How does prevention differ from crisis management?" "What have other schools tried and what has worked?" "Do we need to go beyond the school to build a prevention program?" and "What part will the community and parents play in the prevention program?"

The second outcome dealt with the identification of other at-risk issues, such as suicide, increased sexual activity and the danger of sexually transmitted diseases including AIDS, and the impact of homelessness on a small percentage of the students. This outcome led to a discussion of the questions, "Are there community resources we can use to aid us in better dealing with these identified problems?" and "Where in the community can we find suicide prevention/intervention programs, AIDS education, and services to aid the homeless?"

A third outcome dealt with the concept of resilience and the related questions, "What makes some young people resilient to high-risk environments while others succumb to these same environments?" and "What are the characteristics of both the individual and his or her environment that make him or her resistant to these high risks?" John had not thought much about resilience and was excited over finding answers to these questions. He sensed that the questions came more easily than would the answers.

The major directives that came from the meeting were (a) the establishment of a committee to investigate what is currently being done by other schools to develop an approach to prevention, (b) the development of a list of community mental health services that could be utilized by the school to supplement the work currently being done by the school staff, and (c) the collection of data relating to the concept of resilience and how these data would affect the development of a prevention program. John had volunteered to serve as chairperson of the committee investigating current programs and to assist in gaining more information about the issue of resilience. He looked forward to the next meeting that was scheduled in 2 weeks.

■

This hypothetical situation has been repeated over and over in school districts across the United States as teachers, counselors, administrators, community leaders, and parents attempt to better understand what needs to be done to provide effective programs to help with the growing numbers of young people who are labeled *at risk* because of their involvement in certain destructive behaviors and to help prevent the development of these destructive behavioral patterns. The question these concerned citizens are striving to answer is, "Do we continue to deal with the problem behaviors of young people from a crisis-management perspective, or do we take a preventive approach to attempt to stop these problem behaviors from developing?"

The answer to both parts of this complex question is yes. With the growing numbers of young people entering the educational systems identified as at risk, it is not possible to say no to continuing the crisis-management strategies. Because of these increasing numbers, however, most educational systems are not equipped to address this problem from a purely crisis-management perspective. Therefore, steps must be taken to attempt to stop its development. Such steps are usually described in terms of prevention modalities aimed at providing programs that will identify young people with the highest potential for developing at-risk behaviors, prevent these destructive behaviors from developing, and work to identify individual and environmental characteristics that enhance the resilience of the individual and his or her environment. Thus, we must continue to intervene at the points of crisis and at the same time set into place prevention programs that will eventually reduce the need for crisis intervention.

This chapter first provides a foundational perspective on at-risk youth by presenting definitions, identifying the population, and describing the population's behavioral and causal characteristics. The chapter then introduces the concept of resilience and concludes with a discussion of a prevention and crisis-management paradigm.

A FOUNDATIONAL PERSPECTIVE

Many problems are encountered in attempting to understand the concepts and issues that surround the term *at-risk youth*. Such problems center on defining cause and effect, calculating and determining the population, and developing and implementing both prevention and crisis-management programs that have an impact on the various destructive behaviors that place youth at risk. According to Conrath (1988), "Principals and teachers have known at risk youth for a long time. They have recently been discovered by policy makers and budget sculptors" (p. 36). Simple answers and agreed-on definitions do not currently exist. The best we have at this time are experimental programs; a host of opinions, definitions, and population descriptors; and a high motivation to find workable solutions. The concepts that surround the students at risk and the most effective ways to deal with this at-riskness are complex, filled with frustration for those who attempt to understand them, filled with despair for those who attempt to affect them, and often filled with tragedy for the individuals so labeled.

Overwhelming statistics place the concepts and issues surrounding at-risk youth high on the priority lists of educators, mental health workers, counselors, social workers, psychologists, parents, and community leaders. According to Capuzzi and Gross (2004), the Centers for Disease Control and Prevention (2000), Finn (2004), Gibeaut (1998), the National Center for Education Statistics (1997, 2002), and Sedlak and Broadhurst (1996), approximately

- 3,800,000 youths drop out of high school each year.
- 500,000 youths give birth each year.
- 27,000,000 youths live in poverty.
- 14,000,000 youths are being raised by a single parent.
- 1,500,000 youths are referred for some form of abuse each year.
- 3,000,000 youths and teachers are victims of crime each year.
- 665,000 youths belong to gangs.
- 500,000 youths are homeless.
- 4,000 youth suicides are reported each year.

It is important to keep in mind that each day steps are being taken to reduce these staggering numbers. Educational, psychological, sociological, governmental, and community-based entities are developing and applying prevention and crisis-management strategies directed toward a society at risk. This book has as its major purpose providing these entities with information and direction in meeting their difficult tasks.

The Definition

Tracing the exact origins of the term *at risk* as it applies to education and youth is impossible, but during the past 35 years, the term has appeared frequently in educational literature, federal reports, and legislative mandates from the individual states. In 1988, *Education Week* reported that three out of four states either have adopted or are preparing a definition of their populations determined to be at risk (Minga, 1988), and although current data are not available, it is assumed that all states have by now established legislative parameters for their at-risk populations. A review of the known definitions reveals not only a lack of clarity and consensus but also that the term is explained most often from an educational perspective and indicates individuals at risk of dropping out of the educational system. The characteristics of at-risk youth presented in these definitions include the well-known risk factors of tardiness, poor grades, low math and reading scores, and failing one or more grades (Dynarski & Gleason, 2002; Hermann, 2004; Walker & Sprague, 1999).

A more interesting listing of characteristics was adopted by the Montana State Board of Education in April 1988. This definition (reported by Minga, 1988) is as follows:

> At-risk youths are children who are not likely to finish high school or who are apt to graduate considerably below potential. At-risk factors include chemical dependence, teenage pregnancy, poverty, disaffection with school and society, high-mobility families, emotional and physical abuse, physical and emotional disabilities and learning disabilities that do not qualify students for special education but nevertheless impede their progress. (p. 14)

This definition speaks directly to the confusion that surrounds the issue of being at risk and somewhat indirectly addresses concerns regarding cause versus effect. From this definition, it could be concluded that behaviors such as tardiness, truancy, and low grades are the effects of identified causal factors, for example, chemical dependency, teenage pregnancy, and poverty (Aruffo, Gottlieb, Webb, & Neville, 1994; Donmoyer & Kos, 1993; Homebase, 1993).

If programs dealing with at-risk youth first attempt to deal with factors such as tardiness, truancy, and low grades, they may be placing the proverbial cart before the horse. If the desired effects are to reduce tardiness and truancy and to improve grades, with the ultimate aim of reducing the dropout rate, perhaps more attention needs to be directed toward such identified causal issues as are listed by the Montana State Board of Education. Underlying much of the confusion surrounding at-risk youth is the amount of emphasis placed on either cause or effect (behavior) or both. Whichever position is selected often determines both definition and strategies to operate within that definition. For example, if we approach this area from an effect (behavior) point of view, then what we need to do is identify the behaviors that place the individual at risk and develop strategies to change these behaviors. Or if we approach this area from a causal perspective, then we must try to determine what caused the development of the effect (behavior) and attempt to develop strategies that eliminate the causal factors, thereby stopping the development of the effect (behavior). If we approach from both cause and effect perspectives, then we must develop strategies both to identify and eliminate the causal factors and at the same time put into motion programs that will change the behavior.

This last approach—from both cause and effect perspectives—forms the basis for our definition of at risk. In this book, the term *at risk* encompasses a set of causal/effect (behavioral) dynamics that have the potential to place the individual in danger of a negative future event. This definition not only considers the effect (behavior) that may lead to a negative future event but also attempts to trace the causal factors that led to the development of the effect (behavior). For example, with school-age persons, one of these negative future events may be that of dropping out of school. The causal/behavioral approach identifies not only the behaviors that led to this event but also the myriad causal factors that aided in the development of this behavior. This definition speaks directly to the need for programs to change existing negative behaviors and for prevention programs to tackle the precipitating events that serve as causal factors in the development of the negative behavior. When viewed from the causal/effect (behavioral) perspective, the concept of being at risk broadens, and dropping out is only one of many possible outcomes. Other risks include, but are not limited to, graduating without an education, without goals and objectives, without direction for what comes next, without an understanding of potentials and possibilities, without appreciation for self, or without a knowledge of one's place in the larger society.

When viewed from this causal/effect (behavioral) perspective, the concept of being at risk takes on new dimensions and places the emphasis on individual and systemic dynamics that may or may not lead to a wide range of destructive outcomes. Such a viewpoint emphasizes the vulnerability of all youth to be at risk and provides a strong rationale for the development of prevention programs directed toward stemming the negative impact of certain individual and systemic dynamics. This viewpoint directs attention to a set of causal issues and resultant behaviors that often have proved to be significantly related to the development of many personal and educational dilemmas faced by today's youth. Any one of these dilemmas could result in personal and educational impairment. In combination, the results could be both personally and educationally fatal. This book uses the causal/effect (behavioral) definition of being at risk and presents both information and strategies to deal with at-riskness from a preventive perspective.

The Population

One of the basic issues confronting those wishing to work in the area of at-risk youth centers on the identification of the population. Who are these youths identified as being at risk? Is it possible to identify young people who, by behavior or circumstance, are more at risk than others? Are not all young people, based on behaviors, environments, and developmental patterns, at risk? Specific answers to these questions are not readily available. The research literature in this area is replete with more opinion and supposition than fact. Interest in this population is recent. Population identification may be possible only after the fact, as exemplified by the studies that deal with placing the label of at-risk youth on those who drop out of school, abuse alcohol and/or drugs, become involved in gangs, and attempt and/or complete suicide. In such studies, the population is identified by the specific behaviors manifested. Such an approach to identification, although interesting, limits the identification process of at-riskness to those who currently manifest the specified behaviors.

Another factor that may hinder gaining a comprehensive perspective on the population of at-risk youth is the fact that the terms *at-risk youth* and *adolescence* are used somewhat interchangeably. It seems that to be at risk is to be between the ages of 13 and 18. Such parameters are understandable when we realize that most of the behaviors that are used to describe at-risk youth are those that coincide with the turbulent and exploratory developmental period of adolescence. Factors such as sexual experimentation, first-time drug and alcohol utilization, ego and self-concept development, and peer inclusion or exclusion are descriptive of both adolescence and of the population labeled *at-risk youth*. Such age-specific parameters, however, are limiting and often rule out a large segment of youth, namely, those younger than 13, who also need to be a focus in any discussion of at-risk youth.

According to Stevens and Griffin (2001), it is alarming to realize the age at which youths begin to engage in risk behaviors. Large numbers of children ages 9 through 12 experiment with chemical substances. Stevens and Griffin reported that, based on a 1996 report, 32.4% of those who reported having had at least one drink in their lifetime were under 13 years of age, 7.6% had tried marijuana, and 9% had become sexually active. It is easy to see that such early behavior choices put young people at risk for poor outcomes in later life.

If we limit our identification process of at-risk youth to adolescence, we may also limit issues of cause and effect. From this perspective, both causal and behavioral dynamics are correlated with entrance into and exit from the developmental stage termed *adolescence*. On the basis of the definition of at-risk youth stated earlier and knowledge of human development, we take a somewhat different viewpoint in identifying this population and view adolescence as simply the emerging period for behaviors that have been developing over a much longer period of time.

In keeping with this definition and viewpoint, the population identified as at risk includes all youth regardless of age. All young people have the potential for the development of at-risk behaviors. The key words in this statement are *potential for*. All young people may move in and out of at-riskness depending on personal, social, educational, and family dynamics. No one can be excluded.

By expanding the at-risk population to include all youth, the doors are open to begin work with this population at a much earlier age, to identify causal factors in the individual's environment that may either encourage or impede the later development of at-risk behaviors, and to develop prevention programs for all youth regardless of age or circumstance. If all youth have the potential for the development of at-risk behaviors, preventive steps can be taken to see that the young person does not reach his or her at-risk potential. If this population also includes those who have achieved their at-risk potential, then crisis-management steps can be taken to reduce the level of at-riskness and return them to a level more descriptive of "potential for."

Behaviors and Causal Factors

Based on the assumption that all youth have the potential for at-riskness, how then are we able to identify both behaviors and causal factors that make these behaviors reality? Is it possible to spell out a direct cause–effect relationship, or is this relationship much more indirect and circular in nature? The answers to these questions are at best speculative and perhaps best understood by looking at the developmental period that describes this population and then by identifying the behaviors and causal factors related to this population from school, mental health, and home perspectives.

The developmental period from childhood through adolescence is characterized by rapid physical change, striving for independence, exploration and implementation of new behaviors, strengthening peer relationships, sexual awakening and experimentation, and seeking clarity relating to self and one's place in the larger society. Pressures exerted by family, school, peers, and society to conform or not conform to established standards contribute to the highly charged environment in which this developmental process takes place and the degree of vulnerability that exists within it for the individual. Ingersoll and Orr (1988), in an article about adolescents at risk, discussed G. Stanley Hall's 1904 view of adolescence as a phase of "storm and stress" and painted a graphic picture of this developmental process in which adolescence is simply the emerging period for behaviors that have been developing over a much longer period of time:

> Still, for those who deal with adolescents in a therapeutic context, there remains a subgroup that does experience storm and stress, whose transition to adulthood is marked by turmoil and trial. Further, only a recluse could be unaware of the statistics that show an upsurge in adolescent suicide, pregnancy, and venereal disease, as well as continued patterns of drug and alcohol use and abuse, school dropouts, and delinquency. For some young people, adolescence is an extended period of struggle; for others the transition is marked by alternating periods of struggle and quiescence. During periods of stress and turmoil, the latter group's ability to draw on effective adaptive coping behaviors is taxed. The resulting maladaptive behavior risks compromising physical, psychological, and social health. These young people are at risk. (p. 1)

Terms such as *turmoil, trial, struggle, compromise,* and *stress* lend credence to the difficulty that surrounds this developmental period of youth. Research dealing with this developmental period includes but is not limited to such factors as eating disorders (Anderson, 2002; Beaumont, 2002; K. S. Wright, 2004), homelessness (McMorris, Tyler, Whitbeck, & Hoyt, 2002; Stormont, 2004), sexual behaviors (Haley & Sherwood-Hawes, 2004; Kirby, 2001; O'Donnell, O 'Donnell, & Stueve, 2001), abuse (Appleton & Dykeman, 2004; Friedrich, 2002; Rencken, 1996), affective disorders (Capaldi & Stoolmiller, 1999; Lewinsohn, Rohde, Klein, & Seeley, 1999; McGee & Williams, 2000; Meggert, 2004), substance use and abuse (Burrow-Sanchez, 2006; Gagliardi, Gloria, Robinson-Kurpius, & Lambert, 2004; Inaba & Cohen, 2000), pregnancy (Blake & Bentov, 2001; Haley & Sherwood-Hawes, 2004), suicide and suicide ideation (Borowsky, Ireland, & Resnick, 2001; Capuzzi & Gross, 2004; Maples et al., 2005; National Institute of Mental Health, 2002), and violence (Fernandez, 2000; Finn, 2004; Finn & Remley, 2002; Furlong & Morrison, 2000; Ross, 2003). Each of these factors is descriptive of either behaviors or causal factors that can be identified from the perspective of the school, the mental health community, and the home. The behaviors and causal factors are separated for purposes of discussion only. Many items could appear in each perspective's listing.

From a School Perspective

At-risk behaviors. From an educational perspective, there seems to be a good deal of consistency regarding the behaviors of youth who fall within the parameters of the at-risk population. According to Brooks, Schiraldi, and Ziedenberg (2000), Hermann (2004), Jimerson, Anderson, and Whipple (2002), Mayer and Leone (1999), and Walker and Sprague (1999), the following behaviors are red flags for those at risk:

- tardiness,
- absenteeism,
- poor grades,
- truancy,
- low math and reading scores,
- failing one or more grades,
- rebellious attitudes toward school authority,
- verbal and language deficiency,
- inability to tolerate structured activities,
- dropping out of school, and
- aggressive behaviors or violence.

Causal factors. Behaviors such as those just listed, viewed either individually or in combination, aid in the identification process. However, this type of identification focuses on existing behaviors that need crisis-management strategies to attempt to change them. A different approach, and one we support, identifies the causal factors that lead to these behaviors and suggests prevention programs that may keep these behaviors from developing.

Ekstrom, Goertz, Pollack, and Rock (1986) attempted to address these causal issues in their analysis of data from the U.S. Department of Education's High School and Beyond national sample of 30,000 high school sophomores and seniors. The researchers looked at sophomores in 1980 and 1982 and concentrated on the differences between graduates and nongraduates. Their findings indicated that behavior problems and low grades were major determinants of dropping out. Other determinants included family circumstances with few educational supports and parents uninvolved in the ongoing process of their child's education. Further, students who dropped out tended to have close friends whose attitudes and behaviors also indicated alienation from school.

In a study of a comprehensive high school in upper Manhattan, Fine (1986) concluded that the structural characteristics that may lead to dropping out include a school that has a disproportionate share of low-achieving students and insufficient resources to provide for this population; overcrowded classrooms; teachers who are predominantly White, leading to poor communication with minority students and a lack of understanding; and teaching styles based more on control than conversation, authority than autonomy, and competition than collaboration.

Barber and McClellan (1987) and Paulu (1987) addressed the dropout problem from the students' perspective and reported that the reasons students gave for leaving school included personal reasons such as family problems, pregnancy, and academic problems. Other reasons that spoke directly to problems inherent in the educational structure included the absence of individual help, challenging classes, smaller classes, consistent discipline, and understanding, support, and help by teachers, as well as the presence of boredom and communication problems with teachers, counselors, and administrators.

According to Garnier, Stein, and Jacobs (1997) and Rumberger (1993), socioeconomic status plays a large role in adolescent dropout rates from school, with the highest dropout rate stemming from those in the lowest 20th percentile of income. Dropping out was also seen as a gradual disengagement from school activities that begins in childhood.

Hermann (2004) and Kushman, Sieber, and Heariold-Kinney (2000), reporting on studies of early warning signs, have identified a variety of school and personal factors that aid in predicting dropping out. These factors are described by the following four categories: (a) poor academic performance (low grades, low test scores, behind in grade); (b) behavior problems (disruptive classroom behavior, acting out, truancy, suspension); (c) affective characteristics (poor self-concepts, alienation); and (d) personal circumstances (teen pregnancy, teen parenting, having to work, caring for family members).

From a Mental Health Perspective

At-risk behaviors. Today, more and more young people are seen by mental health agencies either in terms of clients who present for treatment or through the mental health agency's consulting relationships with schools. Regardless of the nature of the involvement, the following behaviors are most often presented:

- drug and alcohol use and abuse,
- eating disorders,
- gang membership,
- pregnancy,
- suicide or suicide ideation,
- depression,
- sexual acting out,
- aggression,
- withdrawal and isolation,
- low self-esteem,
- school-related problems, and
- family problems.

Causal factors. On the basis of the behaviors identified, it is easy to realize that no single causal factor provides the answer as to why such behaviors develop. The answer probably is better understood in terms of combinations of causal factors leading to somewhat predictable behaviors. Often listed as causal factors for many of the behaviors just identified are dysfunctional family dynamics, peer group pressure for inclusion/exclusion, lack of positive adult models, an uninspired educational system, learning difficulties that go untreated, increased violence within the community and the school, homelessness and economic hardship, single-parent households, living in a highly stressed society, and physical, sexual, or psychological abuse (Beaumont, 2002; Ember, 2001; Embrey, Stoep, Evens, Ryan, & Pollock, 2000; Flannery, Singer, & Wester, 2001; Friedrich, 2002; Salmon & Bryant, 2002; Stennard, 2000)

From the Perspective of the Home

At-risk behaviors. Parenting in today's society presents many challenges, not the least of which is attempting to understand children and the various factors that have an impact on them. Parents do not have the objective, somewhat clinical, viewpoint of at-risk behaviors as do either school personnel or members of the mental health profession. Because of the parents' close relationship with their children, the following is descriptive of what parents might list if asked to identify behaviors that place their children at risk:

- failing to obey rules or directives,
- avoiding taking part in family activities,

- spending a great deal of time alone in their room,
- being secretive about friends and activities,
- not communicating with parents or siblings,
- displaying values and attitudes different from family,
- resisting going to school or discussing school activities,
- arguing about everything, and
- staying away from home as much as possible.

Causal factors. As the family and its dynamics are generally viewed as one of the major contributors (causal factors) to at-risk behaviors, what does the family identify as causal factors and where do they look for explanations? Families must look inside the family structure as well as to entities outside the family to arrive at causal factors. These include the educational system, the peer group, the media, the economic conditions that necessitate both parents working, the lack of time for family interaction, the absence of extended family, the availability of drugs and alcohol, the lack of funds or governmental support for child care, and the violence so common in the community, the school, and the society at large (Appleton & Dykeman, 2004; Capuzzi & Gross, 2004; McWhirter, McWhirter, Hart, & Gat, 2000; Shields & Cicchetti, 2001).

Origins of Causal Factors

The three perspectives illustrate not only the differing behaviors identified but also the differing opinions as to the origins of the causal factors that aid in the development of these behaviors. Is one perspective more accurate than the other two? Does one provide a better answer than the other two? Are all three perspectives accurate? The answer to all three of these questions could be yes depending on the setting, the perspective of the person in the setting, and the individual under evaluation. No one single factor can explain the development of at-riskness; only in combination are we able to understand the impact these factors have on the developmental process. For example, the young person growing up in a dysfunctional family often internalizes aspects of this dysfunction. Such internalization may stem from physical, sexual, or psychological abuse and may result in low self-esteem, poor school performance, drug and alcohol use, or gang membership. The causal factors stem both from the degree of dysfunctionality within the family and how the young person reacts to that dysfunctionality. We know that not all young people who live in a dysfunctional family environment achieve at-risk status. We do know, however, that the potential for at-riskness in this type of environment is high.

This same situation exists when we move from the family environment to the school environment. The child who enters school for the first time may find this environment both frightening and difficult. So much depends on what is done to recognize these reactions in the child and to develop programs to aid the child in making the transition from home to school. First impressions can have a far-reaching impact on this child's movement though the educational system—an impact that has the potential for such future behaviors as poor grades, lack of interest in learning, disruptive behaviors, and eventually dropping out of the educational system.

Aligned closely with the school environment is the developing pressured environment of the peer group. Part of the developmental process from childhood through adolescence is the growing importance of the peer group and the need to conform or to belong. The peer group affects youths in areas such as self-identification, self-esteem and self-worth, interactive styles, attitudes, values, and beliefs. As youths develop, the peer group is like a magnet that continually pulls them away from family and often encourages behaviors that are decidedly different from those espoused by the family. Young people attempting to find their place in the world are faced with making choices, choices that for the most part place them at odds with one of two pulling forces: the family or the peer group. The ensuing stress demands the use of coping strategies and decision-making skills, both of which are often not part of the young person's behavioral repertoire. Unless something is done to relieve this pressure, the young person may develop a wide range of emotional reactions or behavioral dynamics in an attempt to relieve the stress, including depression, aggressiveness, use of alcohol and drugs, eating disorders, and suicide or suicide ideation. Any one of these classifies the young person as being at risk.

Society provides a further environment that has the potential for causing at-riskness in young people. One influencing element within today's society is conflicting standards for youth. On one hand, through legislative actions, persons under the age of 18 have few rights. Decisions regarding many aspects of their lives are made by parents or other adults. The message is clear: You are too young to make these important decisions. On the other hand, the media, which permeate so much of society, provide and promote all types of models that encourage youths to be more adult in terms of behaviors, clothes, physical appearance, and relationships. The pull that the media hold for youth is like that of the peer group. The only difference is that the pull may be even stronger and again may encourage youths to move away from the demands of the family, culture, racial and/or ethnic orientations, and religious teachings.

A second influencing element on youths in today's society is best summed up in the term *violence*. It is difficult to read a newspaper or view a news program without being confronted with stories detailing robbery, rape, assault, murder, drive-by shootings, gang-related retaliations, and terrorism. In the late 1990s, schools in Pearl, Mississippi; Paducah, Kentucky; Jonesboro, Alabama; Edinboro, Pennsylvania; Springfield, Oregon; Green River, Wyoming; and Littleton, Colorado made national headlines as armed students killed or wounded both peers and school personnel. All of these involved young people and took place in environments generally thought of as safe, elementary and high school playgrounds and campuses. The terrorist attack of September 11, 2001, added yet another layer of violence, and again this took place in an environment generally viewed as safe, "America." Faced with vivid examples of such violent responses together with the death of family, friends, peers, and teachers, young people experience a great deal of uncertainty about their future. Such uncertainty creates stress, frustration, and often an attitude of hopelessness and helplessness. Any one of these enhances the at-riskness potential of youth; in combination, they almost assure it (Shafii & Shafii, 2001; U.S. Department of Health and Human Services, 2001). Because of the growing significance of violence in schools, we again devote an entire chapter (Chapter 14) to a discussion of the issues surrounding violence in schools together with prevention information from an individual, family, school, and community perspective.

Within these four environments—the family, the school, the peer group, and society—are found most of the causal factors that lead to at-riskness in youth. However, the individual's internal environment (what the individual brings to and takes from these environments) needs also to be considered in terms of its place in this causal paradigm. What part does the individual play in response to these various environments? Are youths simply the victims without recourse, or do they play an active role in determining their own at-riskness? Answers to these questions may be found in the growing body of research surrounding the concept of resilience.

Resilience

The term *resilience*, when applied to at-risk youth, describes certain skills, abilities, personal qualities, or attributes that enable certain youths who are exposed to significant stress and adversity to cope with and even thrive in spite of the stress and adversity. These youths, unlike many of their peer counterparts, do not succumb to the stresses and adversities present in their environment and in fact may develop strength and positive coping strategies from the exposure (Bernard, 1997, 2004; Friesen & Brennan, 2005; Goldstein & Brooks, 2006; Werner, 2006).

The research on resilience (Bernard & Marshall, 2000a, 2000b; Cosden, 2001; Deater-Deckard, Ivy, & Smith, 2006; Kaplan, 2006; Krovetz, 1999; Marshall, 2004; Unger, 2004, 2005) identifies various sets of characteristics that, when present in youth, provide a screening device that allows them to adjust to and cope with the negative conditions within their environments. Such listings often include but are not limited to the following:

- approaching life's problems in an active way;
- constructively perceiving pain, frustration, and negative experiences;
- gaining positive attention from others;
- having a view of life as both positive and meaningful;
- possessing positive self-esteem;
- comprehending, appreciating, and producing humor;
- willing to risk and accept responsibility;
- being proactive;
- being adaptable; and
- being competent in the school, social, and cognitive dimensions.

There are no data to indicate what percentage of youths fit this profile. Based on the staggering figures presented earlier, it seems that the percentage is perhaps small. The research on resilience, however, does provide direction for those working with at-risk youth (Bernard, 2004; Bradley, Parr, & Gould, 1999; Brodsky, 1999; Marshall, 2004; Vaillant, 2002; Werner & Smith, 2001; M. O. Wright & Masten, 2006). Based on our view of its growing importance in prevention programming, we have devoted an entire chapter (Chapter 3) to a discussion of resilience and its application to prevention programs for at-risk youth.

PREVENTION AND CRISIS-MANAGEMENT PARADIGM

The descriptions of at-risk youth in terms of causal factors, behaviors, and factors of resilience provide a logical entry into a discussion of the prevention and crisis-management paradigm as this relates to developing programs that will assist in preventing the development of the problem behaviors, treating the problem behaviors that have developed, or enhancing resilience factors.

Prevention

Two basic criteria underlie the development of effective prevention programs for at-risk youth: the causal factors that lead to at-riskness can be enumerated, and the population of young people who are affected by these factors can be identified. Causal factors are enumerated for a variety of identified problems in this chapter and the chapters that follow, and there seems to be a good deal of similarity across these factors. The population of young people affected by these factors is also identified in this chapter: All young people have the potential for at-riskness. With these two basic criteria established, prevention programs can be developed to keep the identified population from achieving its at-risk potential.

Prevention programs can be and have been developed for a wide range of potential at-risk behaviors. The theory behind prevention is simply "stop certain behaviors from developing." Prevention programming for at-risk youth applies this theory but in a somewhat more comprehensive manner. Effective prevention programs directed at at-risk youth are generally viewed as multidisciplinary and are developed based on the knowledge and expertise of several publics. For example, a prevention program directed at alcohol and drug abuse might involve not only school personnel (teachers, counselors, administrators) but also parents, students, community leaders, religious leaders, police, and representatives from various human service organizations. A multidisciplinary approach assures the widest range of expertise, involvement of those most likely to be affected by the program, and a commitment from the community in making the program work. It enhances the physical and financial resources of the proposed program and alerts young people to the fact that this is not just a school-based program but one that has the backing of both their parents and the community. Because the program has prevention as its purpose, as opposed to crisis management, information will be provided regarding alcohol and drug use, redesigning environments to remove the availability of alcohol and drugs, changing existing policies and procedures within the educational system to enhance the prevention of alcohol and drug use, changing parenting styles and rules and regulations within the home to better accommodate the needs of the young person, designing alternative activities for young people that do not include alcohol and drug use, and providing peer mentoring systems to allow young people to learn from each other. These are just examples. One of the key factors in prevention program development is individualizing the programs to better meet the unique needs of the targeted population, the school, and the community.

According to Conyne (1994), many of the identified problems of at-risk youth are preventable. What is needed are well-designed programs that take into consideration such factors as knowledge and understanding of the concepts that define prevention, local assessments to define target population, information regarding existing programs both locally and nationally, and the selection of multiple strategies for implementation of the program. This is best done through a team composed of many individuals representing a broad spectrum of the community. This broadened base not only expands the knowledge and skill base of the program but also assures financial and personal commitment from the many publics affected by the program, including students, parents, school personnel, and members of the community (Brown & Simpson, 2000; Keys, Bemak, Carpenter, & King-Sears, 1998; Keys, Bemak, & Lockhart, 1998; Shelley, 2001). Once the program is designed, it can be piloted and then restructured as needed. When the team is satisfied that the program is ready, formal implementation can take place. Evaluation is continual, and the program is revised as necessary. A more in-depth discussion of prevention is found in Chapter 2, and each of the chapters that follow present prevention programming with a problem-specific focus.

Crisis Management

Although crisis management is not the main thrust of this book, it is important to understand the basic differences between prevention and crisis management. Whereas prevention programs have as one of their basic goals reducing the at-risk potential for youth, crisis-management programs have as their basic goals eliminating existing at-risk behaviors and providing new behaviors, coping skills, and knowledge that will keep the at-risk behaviors from reoccurring. In the first, we attempt to stop something before it begins (primary prevention), and in the second, we attempt to stop something from continuing (secondary and tertiary prevention). Underlying the development of either secondary or tertiary prevention programs is the fact that many of the behaviors discussed in this chapter are currently present in a large percentage of youths and that steps need to be taken to change or remediate these behaviors. It is too late to prevent these behaviors from developing; they are present. Therefore, programs are designed to eliminate or reduce the behaviors that have placed the individual at risk. In so doing, programs that may be aimed at either individuals or groups of individuals identify the problematic behavior(s), identify the individual(s) operating within this behavioral pattern, design programs based on current knowledge or select existing programs that have proved to be effective, implement strategies, and then evaluate the results of the implementation.

Similarities between programmatic aspects of primary prevention and secondary and tertiary prevention are obvious. Differences also exist. Secondary and tertiary prevention often occur in a structured setting such as a treatment center, mental health clinic, or school counseling office. In these settings, counseling/therapy is provided to address specific problem behaviors and varies according to identified problem behaviors, theoretical orientation of the counselor/therapist, institutional/organization policies, parameters of insurance reimbursement, and the willingness of the individual to take part in the process. Secondary and tertiary prevention are often of a more immediate nature than primary prevention because of the severity of the presenting at-risk behavior. Programs aimed at preventing youths from developing suicidal behaviors do not have the same immediacy as programs developed to deal with youths who have attempted suicide. Primary prevention programs tend to deal with healthy individuals or those with the potential for at-risk behaviors, whereas secondary and tertiary prevention programs tend to deal with individuals who have moved from healthy lifestyles to unhealthy lifestyles. A final difference is that primary prevention programs tend to be group or population based, whereas secondary and tertiary prevention programs focus more on the individual and his or her place in the larger group. Similarities and differences among these differing levels of prevention will become clearer in the chapters that follow.

SUMMARY

This chapter provided a working definition of at-risk youth, information pertaining to the causal factors and behaviors that are descriptive of this population, factors of resilience, and general information related to the similarities and differences between prevention and crisis management. Such information could have helped our hypothetical teacher, John Patron. It could have provided some foundational material to aid him in better understanding the various parameters that surround the students in his classroom. It could have provided him with directives as he began to seek out information regarding what is currently being done to develop approaches to prevention, community resources that could be utilized by the school, and insight into factors of resilience. If John had the opportunity to read this book, he could be in a much better place in terms of answering the many questions raised at the meeting. For those who share some of John's concerns, have questions similar to John's, and feel the need to know more about the areas of at-risk youth and prevention, this book can be of great assistance. The true benefit of the knowledge gained will be not only better service for those youths who have a potential for developing at-risk behavior but also better preparation for dealing with those youths whose behaviors currently place them at risk.

REFERENCES

Anderson, A. E. (2002). Eating disorders in males. In C. G. Fairburn & K. D. Brownell (Eds.), *Eating disorders and obesity* (pp. 188–192). New York: Guilford Press.

Appleton, V. E., & Dykeman, C. (2004). The impact of dysfunctional family dynamics on children and adolescents. In D. Capuzzi & D. R. Gross (Eds.), *Youth at risk: A prevention resource for counselors, teachers, and parents* (4th ed., pp. 69–92). Alexandria, VA: American Counseling Association.

Aruffo, J., Gottlieb, A., Webb, R., & Neville, B. (1994). Adolescent psychiatric inpatients: Alcohol use and HIV risk-taking behavior. *Psychosocial Rehabilitation Journal, 17,* 150–156.

Barber, L. W., & McClellan, M. C. (1987). Looking at America's dropouts. *Phi Delta Kappan, 69,* 264–267.

Beaumont, P. J. V. (2002). Clinical presentation of anorexia nervosa and bulimia nervosa. In C. G. Fairburn & K. D. Brownell (Eds.), *Eating disorders and obesity* (pp. 162–170). New York: Guilford Press.

Bernard, B. (1997). Changing the condition, place, and view of your people in society: An interview with youth development pioneer Bill Lofquist. *Resiliency in Action, 2*(1), 7–18.

Bernard, B. (2004). *Resiliency: What we have learned.* San Francisco: WestEd.

Bernard, B., & Marshall, K. (2000a). *Competence and resilience research: Lessons for prevention.* Minneapolis: University of Minnesota, National Resilience Resource Center and the Center for the Application of Prevention Technologies.

Bernard, B., & Marshall, K. (2000b). *Protective factors in individuals, families, and schools: National longitudinal study on adolescent health.* Minneapolis: University of Minnesota, National Resilience Resource Center for the Application of Prevention Technologies.

Blake, B. J., & Bentov, L. (2001). Geographical mapping of unmarried teen births and selected sociodemographic variables. *Public Health Nursing, 18,* 33–39.

Borowsky, I. W., Ireland, M., & Resnick, M. D. (2001). Adolescent suicide attempts: Risks and protectors. *Pediatrics, 107,* 485–493.

Bradley, L., Parr, G., & Gould, L. J. (1999). Counseling and psychotherapy: An integrative perspective. In D. Capuzzi & D. R. Gross (Eds.), *Counseling and psychotherapy: Theories and interventions* (2nd ed., pp. 459–480). Englewood Cliffs, NJ: Merrill.

Brodsky, A. E. (1999). Making it: The components and process of resilience among urban, African-American, single mothers. *American Journal of Orthopsychiatry, 69*, 148–160.

Brooks, K., Schiraldi, V., & Ziedenberg, J. (2000). *School house hype: Two years later.* Washington, DC: Justice Policy Institute.

Brown, E. J., & Simpson, E. M. (2000). Comprehensive STD/HIV prevention education targeting US adolescents: Review of an ethical dilemma and proposed ethical framework. *Nursing Ethics, 7*, 339–349.

Burrow-Sanchez, J. (2006). Understanding adolescent substance abuse: Prevalence, risk factors, and clinical implications. *Journal of Counseling & Development, 84*, 283–290.

Capaldi, D. M., & Stoolmiller, M. (1999). Co-occurrence of conduct problems and depressive symptoms in early adolescent boys: III. Prediction to young-adult adjustment. *Development and Psychopathology, 11*, 59–84.

Capuzzi, D., & Gross, D. R. (2004). *Youth at risk: A prevention resource for counselors, teachers, and parents* (4th ed.). Alexandria, VA: American Counseling Association.

Centers for Disease Control and Prevention. (2000). *Adolescent pregnancy.* Atlanta, GA: Author.

Conrath, J. (1988). A new deal for at-risk students. *NAASP Bulletin, 14*, 36–39.

Conyne, R. K. (1994). Preventive counseling. *Counseling and Human Development, 27*, 21–28.

Cosden, M. (2001). Risk and resilience for substance abuse among adolescents and adults with L.D. *Journal of Learning Disabilities, 34*, 352–359.

Deater-Deckard, K., Ivy, L., & Smith, J. (2006). Resilience in gene–environment transactions. In S. Goldstein & R. Brooks (Eds.), *Handbook of resilience in children* (pp. 49–64). New York: Springer Science+Business Media.

Donmoyer, R., & Kos, R. (1993). *At-risk students: Portraits, policies, programs, and practices.* Albany: State University of New York Press.

Dynarski, M., & Gleason, P. (2002). How can we help? What we have learned from recent federal dropout prevention evaluations. *Journal of Education for Students Placed at Risk, 7*, 43–69.

Ekstrom, R. R., Goertz, M. E., Pollack, J. M., & Rock, D.A. (1986). Who drops out of school and why: Findings from a national study. *Teachers College Record, 87*, 356–373.

Ember, N. (2001). *Self-esteem: The costs and causes of low self-esteem.* York, England: York Publishing Services.

Embrey, L. E., Stoep, A. V., Evens, C., Ryan, K., & Pollock, A. (2000). Risk factors for homelessness in adolescents released for psychiatric residential treatment. *Journal of the American Academy of Child and Adolescent Psychiatry, 39*, 1293–1299.

Fernandez, M. D. (2000). School violence: Implications for school counselor training programs. In D. S. Sandhu & C. B. Aspy (Eds.), *Violence in American schools: A practical guide for counselors* (pp. 371–386). Alexandria, VA: American Counseling Association.

Fine, M. (1986). Why urban adolescents drop into and out of public high school. *Teachers College Record, 87*, 393–409.

Finn, A. (2004). Death in the classroom: Violence in schools. In D. Capuzzi & D. R. Gross (Eds.), *Youth at risk: A prevention resource for counselors, teachers, and parents* (4th ed., pp. 353–371). Alexandria, VA: American Counseling Association.

Finn, A., & Remley, T. P. (2002). Prevention of school violence: A school and community response. In D. Rea & J. Bergin (Eds.), *Safeguarding our youth: Successful school and community programs* (pp. 19–27). New York: McGraw-Hill.

Flannery, D., Singer, M., & Wester, K. (2001). Violence exposure, psychological trauma, and suicide risk in a community sample of dangerously violent adolescents. *Journal of the American Academy of Child and Adolescent Psychiatry, 40,* 435–442.

Friedrich, W. N. (2002). *Psychological assessment of sexually abused children and their families.* Thousand Oaks, CA: Sage.

Friesen, B. J., & Brennan, E. (2005). Strengthening families and communities: System building for resilience. In M. Ungar (Ed.), *Handbook for working with children and youth: Pathways to resilience across cultures and contexts* (pp. 295–312). Thousand Oaks, CA: Sage.

Furlong, M., & Morrison, G. (2000). The school in school violence: Definitions and facts. *Journal of Emotional and Behavioral Disorders, 8*(2), 71–82.

Gagliardi, C. J., Gloria, A. M., Robinson-Kurpius, S. E., & Lambert, C. (2004). "I can't live without it": Adolescent substance abuse. In D. Capuzzi & D. R. Gross (Eds.), *Youth at risk: A prevention resource for counselors, teachers, and parents* (4th ed., pp. 373–400). Alexandria, VA: American Counseling Association.

Garnier, H. E., Stein, J. A., & Jacobs, J. K. (1997). The process of dropping out of high school: A 19-year perspective. *American Educational Research Journal, 34,* 395–419.

Gibeaut, J. (1998). Gang busters. *American Bar Association Journal, 84,* 64–69.

Goldstein, S., & Brooks, R. B. (2006). *Handbook of resilience in children.* New York: Springer Science+Business Media.

Haley, M., & Sherwood-Hawes, A. (2004). Children having children: Teenage pregnancy and parenthood. In D. Capuzzi & D. R. Gross (Eds.), *Youth at risk: A prevention resource for counselors, teachers, and parents* (4th ed., pp. 211–242). Alexandria, VA: American Counseling Association.

Hermann, M. (2004). "This isn't the place for me": School dropout. In D. Capuzzi & D. R. Gross (Eds.), *Youth at risk: A prevention resource for counselors, teachers, and parents* (4th ed., pp. 425–440). Alexandria, VA: American Counseling Association.

Homebase. (1993). *Reaching and teaching children without housing: Improving educational opportunities for homeless children and youth.* San Francisco: Author.

Inaba, D. S., & Cohen, W. (2000). *Uppers, downers, and all arounders: Physical and mental effects of psychoactive drugs.* Ashland, OR: CNS Publications.

Ingersoll, G., & Orr, D. (1988). Adolescents at risk. *Counseling and Human Development, 20,* 1–8.

Jimerson, S. R., Anderson, G. E., & Whipple, A. D. (2002). Winning the battle and losing the war: Examining the relation between grade retention and dropping out of school. *Psychology in the Schools, 39,* 441–457.

Kaplan, H. B. (2006). Understanding the concept of resilience. In S. Goldstein & R. Brooks (Eds.), *Handbook of resilience in children* (pp. 39–48). New York: Springer Science+Business Media.

Keys, S. G., Bemak, F., Carpenter, S. L., & King-Sears, M. E. (1998). Collaborative consultant: A new role for counselors serving at-risk youths. *Journal of Counseling & Development, 76,* 123–133.

Keys, S. G., Bemak, F., & Lockhart, E. J. (1998). Transforming school counseling to serve the mental health needs of at-risk youth. *Journal of Counseling & Development, 76,* 381–388.

Kirby, D. (2001). Understanding what works and what doesn't work in reducing adolescent sexual risk-taking. *Family Planning Perspective, 33,* 276–281.

Krovetz, M. L. (1999). Resiliency: A key element for supporting youth at-risk. *Clearing House, 73,* 121–124.

Kushman, J. W., Sieber, C., & Heariold-Kinney, P. (2000). This isn't the place for me: School dropout. In D. Capuzzi & D. R. Gross (Eds.), *Youth at risk: A prevention resource guide for counselors, teachers, and parents* (3rd ed., pp. 353–381). Alexandria, VA: American Counseling Association.

Lewinsohn, P. M., Rohde, P., Klein, D. N., & Seeley, J. R. (1999). Natural course of adolescent major depressive disorder: I. Continuity into young adulthood. *Journal of the American Academy of Child and Adolescent Psychiatry, 38,* 56–63.

Maples, M. F., Packman, J., Abney, P., Daugherty, R. F., Casey, J., & Pirtie, L. (2005). Suicide by teenagers in middle school: A postvention team approach. *Journal of Counseling & Development, 83,* 397–405.

Marshall, K. (2004). Resilience research and practice: National Resilience Resource Center bridging the gap. In H. C. Waxman, Y. N. Padron, & J. P. Gray (Eds.), *Educational resiliency: Student, teacher and school perspectives* (pp. 63–86). Greenwich, CT: Information Age.

Mayer, M. J., & Leone, P. E. (1999). A structural analysis of school violence and disruption: Implications for creating safer schools. *Education and Treatment of Children, 22,* 333–358.

McGee, R., & Williams, S. (2000). Does low self-esteem predict health compromising behaviours among adolescents? *Journal of Adolescence, 23,* 569–582.

McMorris, B. J., Tyler, K. A., Whitbeck L. B., & Hoyt, D. R. (2002). Familial and "on-the-street" risk factors associated with alcohol use among homeless and runaway adolescents. *Journal of Studies on Alcohol, 63,* 34–44.

McWhirter, B. T., McWhirter, J. J., Hart, R., & Gat, I. (2000). Depression in childhood and adolescence: Working to prevent despair. In D. Capuzzi & D. R. Gross (Eds.), *Youth at risk: A prevention resource for counselors, teachers, and parents* (3rd ed., pp. 137–165). Alexandria, VA: American Counseling Association.

Meggert, S. S. (2004). "Who cares what I think": Problems of low self-esteem. In D. Capuzzi & D. R. Gross (Eds.), *Youth at risk: A prevention resource for counselors, teachers, and parents* (4th ed., pp. 93–115). Alexandria, VA: American Counseling Association.

Minga, T. (1988). States and the "at-risk" issues: Said aware but still "failing." *Education Week, 8*(3), 1–16.

National Center for Education Statistics, Fast Response Survey System. (1997). *Principal/school disciplinarian survey on school violence* (FRSS 63). Washington, DC: U.S. Department of Education.

National Center for Education Statistics. (2002). *Dropout rates in the United States: 2000.* Retrieved November 16, 2003, from http://nces.ed.gov/pubs2002/droppub_2001/

National Institute of Mental Health. (2002). *Suicide facts.* Retrieved November 21, 2002, from http://www.nimh.nih.gov/research/suifact.htm

O'Donnell, L., O'Donnell, C. R., & Stueve, A. (2001). Early sexual initiation and subsequent sex-related risks among urban minority youth: The Reach for Health Study. *Family Planning Perspectives, 33,* 268–275.

Paulu, N. (1987). *Dealing with dropouts: The urban superintendents' call to action.* Washington, DC: Office of Educational Research and Improvement, U.S. Department of Education.

Rencken, R. H. (1996). Body violation: Physical and sexual abuse. In D. Capuzzi & D. R. Gross (Eds.), *Youth at risk: A prevention resource for counselors, teachers, and parents* (2nd ed., pp. 59–80). Alexandria, VA: American Counseling Association.

Ross, D. (2003). *Childhood bullying, teasing, and violence: What school personnel, other professionals, and parents can do* (2nd ed.). Alexandria, VA: American Counseling Association.

Rumberger, R. W. (1993). Chicano dropouts: A review of research and policy issues. In R. Valencia (Ed.), *Chicano school failure and success: Research and policy agendas for the 1990's* (pp. 64–89). London: Falmer Press.

Salmon, K., & Bryant, R. A. (2002). Posttraumatic stress disorder in children: The influence of developmental factors. *Clinical Psychology Review, 22*, 163–188.

Sedlak, A., & Broadhurst, D. (1996). *Third National Incidence Study of Child Abuse and Neglect: Final report*. Washington, DC: U.S. Department of Health and Human Services, Administration of Children and Family.

Shafii, M., & Shafii, S. L. (2001). *School violence: Assessment, management, and prevention*. Washington, DC: American Psychiatric Association.

Shelley, J. F. (2001). Controlling violence: What schools are doing. In S. G. Kellam, R. Prinz, & J. F. Shelley (Eds.), *Preventing school violence: Plenary papers for the 1999 Conference on Criminal Justice Research and Evaluation—Enhancing Policy and Practice Through Research* (Vol. 2, pp. 37–57). Washington, DC: U.S. Department of Justice, National Institute of Justice.

Shields, A., & Cicchetti, D. (2001). Parental maltreatment and emotion dysregulation as risk factors for bullying and victimization in middle childhood. *Journal of Clinical Child Psychology, 30*, 349–364.

Stennard, R. P. (2000). Assessment and treatment of adolescent suicidality. *Journal of Mental Health Counseling, 22*, 204–217.

Stevens, P., & Griffin, J. (2001). Youth high-risk behaviors: Survey and results. *Journal of Addictions and Offender Counseling, 22*, 31–47.

Stormont, M. (2004). Nowhere to turn: Homeless youth. In D. Capuzzi & D. R. Gross (Eds.), *Youth at risk: A prevention resource for counselors, teachers, and parents* (4th ed., pp. 401–424). Alexandria, VA: American Counseling Association.

Unger, M. (2004). *Nurturing hidden resilience in troubled youth*. Toronto, Ontario, Canada: University of Toronto Press.

Unger, M. (Ed.). (2005). *Handbook for working with children and youth: Pathways to resilience across cultures and contexts*. Thousand Oaks, CA: Sage.

U.S. Department of Health and Human Services. (2001). Youth violence: A report of the Surgeon General—Executive summary. *American Journal of Health Education, 32*, 169–174.

Valliant, G. E. (2002). *Aging well: Surprising guideposts to a happier life from the landmark Harvard study of adult development*. Boston: Little, Brown.

Walker, H. M., & Sprague, J. R. (1999). The path to school failure, delinquency, and violence: Causal factors and some potential solutions. *Intervention in School and Clinic, 35*(2), 67–73.

Werner, E. E. (2006). What can we learn about resilience from large-scale longitudinal studies? In S. Goldstein & R. Brooks (Eds.), *Handbook of resilience in children* (pp. 91–106). New York: Springer Science+Business Media.

Werner, E. E., & Smith, R. S. (2001). *Journeys from childhood to midlife: Risk, resilience and recovery*. Ithaca, NY: Cornell University Press.

Wright, K. S. (2004). The secret and all-consuming obsessions: Eating disorders. In D. Capuzzi & D. R. Gross (Eds.), *Youth at risk: A prevention resource for counselors, teachers, and parents* (4th ed., pp. 167–209). Alexandria, VA: American Counseling Association.

Wright, M. O., & Masten, A. S. (2006). Resilience processes in development. In S. Goldstein & R. Brooks (Eds.), *Handbook of resilience in children* (pp. 17–38). New York: Springer Science+Business Media.

CHAPTER 2

■

Prevention: An Overview

David Capuzzi and Douglas R. Gross

The number of children and adolescents who engage in behaviors (e.g., unprotected sex, substance use and abuse, abnormal eating patterns, suicide attempts) and are exposed to environmental factors (e.g., abuse, violence, homelessness) that place them at risk for adverse mental and physical health consequences is increasing at alarming rates (Hovell, Blumberg, Liles, Powell, & Morrison, 2001; Kazdin, 1993; Popenhagen & Qualley, 1998; Reddy & Richardson, 2006). In addition, many children and adolescents are experiencing serious psychological and emotional impairment. Because the impairments that youths experience can persist and increase in severity across the life span, the importance of early prevention and intervention efforts has increased in significance.

Conyne (1994) emphasized the significance and importance of early prevention efforts by offering examples of some of the problems that characterize contemporary residents of the United States:

- There are 20 million illiterate adults. This amounts to 13% of the U.S. population.
- Nineteen percent of the population (or 43 million adults) have been identified as experiencing some type of mental disturbance.
- The number of youths dropping out of school each year has reached 1 million, or 25% of those enrolled in K–12 settings.
- AIDS has become one of the leading causes of death among the 15- to 24-year age group.
- Nearly 5,000 infants are born each year with fetal alcohol syndrome.
- Adolescent suicide ranks second or third in most reports of the leading causes of death in the 11- to 24-year age group.
- First marriages end in divorce 50% of the time, and 50%–75% of child mental health referrals are for children affected by divorce.
- Almost 18.5 million Americans abuse alcohol, and over 100,000 alcohol-related deaths occur annually.
- Increasing numbers of women—3 to 4 million annually—are physically assaulted by intimate male partners.

Dryfoos (1997) summarized data supplied by the U.S. Bureau of the Census, the Centers for Disease Control and Prevention, the U.S. Department of Justice, and the National Center for Education Statistics with respect to the prevalence of at-risk behaviors of the 14- to 17-year-old population. The data indicate that 25% of all the young people in this age range are behind in grade and that 5% have already dropped out. Between 18% and 48% are involved in some form of substance abuse, and 53% are sexually active. More than 9% have been adjudicated as delinquents, 22% carry some form of weapon, and 21% have frequently been truant. About 25% of this population report that they have been preoccupied with suicidal thoughts, and 9% report that they have made suicidal attempts. Similar data have been reported by Astor, Meyer, Benbenishty, Marachi, and Rosemond (2005), Collins et al. (2002), Fetro, Coyle, and Pham (2001), and King (2001).

The cost associated with these examples in terms of economics is staggering. Approximately $273 billion was spent in 1990 in treatment and social services associated with alcohol, drug abuse, and mental illness (Horner & McElhaney, 1993). These costs do not include those associated with teenage pregnancy, AIDS, eating disorders, suicide, homelessness, and school dropout (Astor et al., 2005; Reddy & Richardson, 2006). When these additional areas are taken into consideration, the estimated figure increases to incomprehensible levels. As significant as these dollar amounts are, however, they do not include the immeasurable costs associated with human loss and suffering and the concomitant issues related to grief and loss.

In the wake of the need for counseling and therapy created by conditions in the North American culture, the availability of counselors, social workers, psychiatric nurses, psychologists, and psychiatrists pales by contrast (Conyne, 1994). Mandates connected with managed care and the understaffing of social service agencies further compound the difficulties experienced by children, adolescents, and adults in need of assistance from the professionally prepared, licensed helper.

Prevention is based on a different approach to help giving than that associated with prevalent diagnostic/prescriptive approaches. Prevention is not focused on dysfunction and associated remediation; it is focused on a proactive approach designed to empower the individual, change systemic variables, and forestall the development of dysfunction. Prevention is also based on awareness of the risk factors that researchers have identified as the most common antecedents of at-risk behaviors (Dryfoos, 1997; Hallfors et al., 2006):

1. Parents' ability to provide nurturing and support is closely connected to a child's ability to mature and develop. Parents who are unable to parent in ways that convey a sense of nurturing and support create barriers to optimal development.
2. The schooling experience is a significant precursor to maturation and development. Poor grades, deficits in basic skills, low academic expectations, and repeated school discipline problems are predictors of involvement in at-risk behavior.
3. Peer influences are strong determinants of youth behavior during the middle school years and sometimes earlier. Youths who engage in high-risk behaviors lack ability to resist joining their friends in experimenting with drugs, sex, and other delinquent behavior.
4. Young people who are depressed or have conduct disorders (e.g., engaging in multiple problem behaviors such as truancy, stealing, cheating, running away, arson, cruelty to animals, unusually early sexual intercourse, and ex-

cessive fighting prior to the age of 15) are extremely vulnerable to making choices that are far from responsible and productive.

5. Life in a low-income family and an impoverished neighborhood also increases the probability of at-risk behavior because economically disadvantaged youths often lack access to quality education and safe environments.

6. Race and ethnicity are also factors effecting youth's vulnerability not because of race and ethnicity alone, but because African American, Hispanic, and Native American youth may be at a disadvantage economically and live in poorer, less safe neighborhoods.

DEFINING QUALITIES OF PREVENTION

As noted by the American Academy of Pediatrics (2004), Conyne (1994), Dryfoos (1997), Gilliland and James (1993), Janosik (1984), Kadish, Glaser, Calhoun, and Ginter (2001), and Reddy and Richardson (2006), prevention efforts focus on averting human dysfunction and promoting healthy functioning. The emphasis in prevention is on enhancing optimal functioning or well-being in psychological and social domains and on the development of competencies. This emphasis is in contrast to an emphasis on the identification and diagnosis of various disorders or maladaptive behavioral patterns in individuals and the provision of treatment to lessen impairment (Kazdin, 1993). Prevention efforts are characterized by a number of defining qualities:

1. *Prevention efforts are proactive.* Prevention initiatives address individual and systemic strengths and further develop those strengths so that dysfunction either does not develop or does not manifest itself to the point that impairment occurs. This contrasts with reactive approaches that are designed to intervene after problems have developed (Brooks, 2006; King, 2001).

2. *Prevention efforts focus on functional people and those who are at risk.* As noted by Conyne (1994), prevention services (e.g., classroom guidance, individual or small group counseling) focus on those who are healthy and coping well so that strengths may be identified and enhanced and additional skills can be learned. Prevention efforts are also directed to those known to be at risk, such as children of divorce, children of alcoholics, or the homeless. The purpose is to provide proactive intervention so that future difficulties are avoided (Bosworth, Espelage, DuBay, & Daytner, 2000).

3. *Prevention efforts are cumulative and transferable.* When professionals help others through prevention, every effort is made to point out relationships and to assist clients to master a hierarchy of skills. For example, elementary-age children who have participated in groups designed to enhance self-esteem may, at a later date, feel good enough about themselves to participate in assertiveness training. Ability to use assertiveness skills may be useful in the context of refusing drugs; these same skills may prevent a youth from being victimized in some other situation.

4. *Prevention efforts are used to reduce incidence* (Astor et al., 2006; Conyne, 1994; King, 2001). Prevention activities are used before the fact so that problems do not develop. They may also be used to reduce the incidence of a new dysfunction.

5. *Prevention efforts promote peer helping.* When elementary, middle school, and high school youths learn to enhance communication, assertiveness, problem solving, and other related abilities, they are better able to help peers,

encourage friends to seek professional assistance, and participate in supervised peer-helper programs. In many instances, the power of a member of the peer group outdistances that of a concerned adult in terms of providing encouragement, support, and straightforward feedback (Dryfoos, 1997; King, 2001).

6. *Prevention efforts can be population based, individually based, or group based.* Many prevention efforts are focused on at-risk populations (e.g., information and discussion about the HIV virus or hepatitis B may be shared with sexually active adolescents, or victims of abuse may be assisted so that they do not develop lifelong dysfunctional patterns). Prevention may also be focused entirely on an individual so that suicidal preoccupation can be eliminated or depression can be overcome. When larger populations are reached through prevention programming, it is possible to affect the life space of large numbers of people (Conyne, 1994; Reddy & Richardson, 2006).

7. *Prevention efforts can be used early in the life span.* We know that children who are homeless or who have been physically or sexually abused may develop traits and self-concepts that put them at risk during adolescence and adulthood. Early prevention efforts can effect changes in self-esteem, behavior, feelings, and thinking so that these children are not at risk of substance abuse, prostitution, depression, and suicide at a later time (Brooks, 2006; Buckley, 2000; Dryfoos, 1997; Reddy & Richardson, 2006).

8. *Prevention efforts target more than a single system.* Because each person must simultaneously interact in a variety of environments, practitioners do not emphasize one system to the exclusion of others. Healthy individuals must learn to cope with the demands of several systems on a daily basis (Dryfoos, 1997; King, 2001; McGowan, 2006).

9. *Prevention efforts are sensitive to the needs of diverse populations.* No constellation of services or approach to prevention can make equal impact on all groups. Diverse populations present unique challenges; what one population finds acceptable may be totally incompatible with the needs of another. Practitioners must be sensitive to the traditions, needs, and differences presented by subcultures in North America (Brown & Simpson, 2000; Conyne, 1994; Dryfoos, 1997; Kitts, 2005; Shaughnessy, Doshi, & Jones, 2004).

10. *Prevention efforts are collaborative.* As noted by Conyne (1994), prevention efforts can be complex and must be conducted in concert with professionals from a number of disciplines. For example, a counselor working with an adolescent who is depressed may need the assistance of a psychiatrist or nurse practitioner if medication is needed along with counseling to control a body-chemistry-related bipolar pattern of depression. Often the expertise needed to assist an individual, a family, or a larger population may require input and teaming among professionals from several disciplines.

11. *Prevention efforts are applicable in more than one context.* Faculty and staff in a school setting, for example, may seek the assistance of someone who can provide staff development, train a crisis team, and provide input on to a written crisis-management plan. Such efforts may be focused, initially, on substance use and abuse prevention or suicide prevention. After the adults connected with a particular school or school district have been prepared with respect to one particular at-risk population, they can usually apply the same principles and process to providing prevention services to another at-risk group.

12. *Prevention efforts are empowering.* Empowerment should be the primary goal of all prevention efforts (Brooks, 2006; Conyne, 1994). This empowerment should apply not only to the recipients of prevention efforts but also to the providers of prevention services. When those receiving assistance build on strengths and learn new coping skills, they feel better about themselves and their ability to make responsible, healthy decisions. As professionals increase their ability to enrich the lives of others, they, too, feel productive, competent, and capable of impacting change.

13. *Prevention efforts involve parents.* Inviting parents to be in responsible roles in their children's schools, such as paid or volunteer classroom aides or voting members of school reorganization initiatives, results in more positive outcomes for children and adolescents. Establishment of parent centers in schools for parents and youths for whom English is a second language or for whom assistance with health and social services, transportation, child care or meals is needed has been found to be effective (Brooks, 2006; Dryfoos, 1997; Reddy & Richardson, 2006).

14. *Prevention efforts make connections to the world of work.* Many at-risk youths have little exposure to the world of work and may not have adult role models who are consistently employed. When these youths are exposed to curricula that provide career information, skills training, and opportunities for volunteer or paid work experience, their involvement in at-risk behaviors decreases (Dryfoos, 1997).

15. *Prevention efforts include social and life skills training.* Improving social, decision-making, and assertiveness skills leads to more positive outcomes. Research also demonstrates that consistency of participant involvement and opportunity for "booster" sessions are required to maintain long-term effects (Beautrais, 2005; Dryfoos, 1997).

16. *Prevention efforts include in-service training for both faculty and staff.* Prevention efforts rarely succeed unless time and money are committed to the in-service training necessary to provide the adults in the school with the insight, skills, and motivation needed to successfully implement initiatives aimed at aspects of systemic reform.

17. *Prevention efforts include the presence of dedicated adults.* Successful prevention programs are usually the result of the efforts of adult role models who have a great deal of empathy and provide high levels of support for young people who have risk factors in their lives that predispose them to engaging in at-risk behaviors. It is very difficult to implement new programs and policies in a school in which the faculty and staff are not receptive to new ways of enhancing the school climate and are unreceptive to the needs of youths who may be quite different from themselves.

APPROACHES TO PREVENTION

A number of experts in contemporary prevention strategies have identified prevention as primary, secondary, or tertiary (Buckley, 2000; Hadge, 1992; Janosik, 1984; King, 2001; McWhirter, McWhirter, McWhirter, & McWhirter, 1998, 2007; Roberts, 1991). As practitioners consider prevention strategies for possible implementation with an individual, a family, a school, or a community, it is important to be able to assess needs and identify strategies in relation to whether these strategies can be categorized as primary, secondary, or tertiary.

Primary Prevention

Primary prevention involves proactive planning of strategies and activities to keep specific problems or crises from developing in the first place (Gilliland & James, 1993). In primary prevention, the purpose is to reduce the incidence of future problems by reinforcing internal coping ability, modifying external variables, or both. Primary prevention provides assistance prior to the development of problems through counseling, teaching, or other services that emphasize anticipatory planning. Through anticipatory planning, individuals of all ages are given the opportunity to select and practice behaviors that are helpful in both present and future circumstances.

Examples of primary prevention include parent education programs to prevent child neglect and abuse and educational programs on university campuses to prevent sexual harassment, date rape, or violation of affirmative action guidelines. School programs for teenage boys and girls regarding the consequences of teenage pregnancies, the impact of school dropout, or the importance of effective communication skills are additional examples of primary prevention. Entire communities might also benefit from primary prevention efforts. For example, a series of mental health education seminars might be offered, free of charge, to residents of a community and might be collaboratively planned by representatives from the local schools, mental health services, and business sectors. Television and radio journalists might provide coverage of the services offered by women's and children's shelters or local crisis hotlines. Whatever the emphasis, the focus is always on preventing future and, more often than not, long-term pain or impairment.

Chapter 3 of this edition of our text presents valuable, additional information on primary prevention from a resilience point of view. This provides an additional perspective that may prove helpful to those whose practice focus is working with children and adolescents.

Secondary Prevention

Secondary prevention consists of early intervention with people in crisis for the purpose of restoring equilibrium as soon as possible and reducing the impact of the distress. During periods of crisis, people are aware that the situation is out of control, and they may feel helpless. Unless secondary prevention is made available, a crisis may escalate to the point at which it may be difficult to contain or consequences may be irreversible. For example, a suicidal adolescent who does not obtain assistance may attempt suicide, survive, and be left with lifelong physical impairment and emotional turmoil that overlay the traits and characteristics that precipitated the suicidal crisis in the first place. When individuals, families, schools, or communities recognize the parameters connected with a crisis situation, they may be quite motivated and extremely receptive to secondary prevention efforts.

Examples of secondary prevention include support groups for students who are experiencing the grief and loss associated with the unexpected death of a peer, school and community collaborative efforts to provide child care and alternative education opportunities for teenage parents, residential or outpatient treatment for teenagers who abuse alcohol, or counseling services established to stop battering or other violent behavior. During the secondary prevention process, emphasis should be placed on individual, family, school, and community resources and abilities. Preoccupation with defeat and negative consequences seldom results in the management of a particular crisis situation and the reestablishment of equilibrium.

It is important to note, at this juncture, that more and more school districts are writing *tragedy response plans* for the purpose of planning and coordinating efforts of school personnel who are suddenly presented with a sudden crisis situation. The reason for doing so is to prevent the systemic chaos and resultant negative impact on individuals and groups on a school campus at the time an unanticipated crisis occurs. These tragedy response plans usually delineate not only the roles of members of the crisis team but also the roles of all other school personnel as well as the roles of individuals or groups in the community that the school may need to call on in the midst of a crisis. Developing plans in advance has a number of advantages, including the opportunity to have such plans evaluated by experts in crisis management and by the school or district's legal team in advance so that modifications and additions can be made.

Tragedy response plans usually outline crisis responses to natural disasters (earthquakes, tornados, release of airborne toxins, etc.), fire, death, accidents, child abduction, violence, and other events that need to be addressed immediately and may not have been anticipated. These plans are usually quite comprehensive and include guidelines for possible evacuation, transportation, contacting parents, responding to the inquiries of journalists, and working with police and disaster relief workers from the community, among others. Many school districts are beginning to publish their plans on the Internet, and we encourage school/community groups planning to commence work on tragedy response plans to read what other school/community groups have developed and to contact representatives from schools that have experience in this area. Making such contacts can provide opportunities for collaborative sharing and evaluation and can eliminate the necessity to start from scratch.

Tertiary Prevention

Tertiary crisis prevention attempts to reduce the amount of residual impairment that follows the resolution of some crisis. Adolescents who complete residential or outpatient programs for substance abuse may benefit through participation in weekly support groups, facilitated by a professional, for the purpose of providing the reinforcement and support needed to prevent relapse. These same adolescents may need to participate concurrently in individual counseling or therapy to address the unmet needs that led to the use and abuse of a substance in the first place, because emotional development and coping skills are usually arrested about the time substance use begins. Victims of sexual abuse may participate in either group or individual (or both) counseling or therapy long after the abuse has ceased for the purpose of repairing damaged self-esteem and rebuilding the capacity to trust and share intimacy with significant others.

As emphasized by Janosik (1984), crisis in contemporary society is so prevalent that it is not possible for all those experiencing crisis to access the help of professionals. It is possible, however, to identify factors that place individuals, families, schools, and communities at risk. Thus, it is of paramount importance to reduce emotional pain, residual impairment, and cost to society as a whole through judicious use of prevention, whether primary, secondary, or tertiary in nature.

TYPES OF PRIMARY PREVENTION

The youth of today are faced with coping amidst a society that is more populated, more connected by advanced communication technology, and more complex with respect to a variety of psychosocial stressors. This edition of *Youth at Risk* places more emphasis on prevention with respect to causative factors (such as low self-esteem, stress, depression) and a number of at-risk behaviors (such as drug abuse, unprotected sex, eating disorders, suicidal preoccupation, gang membership). The chapters that follow Chapter 3 highlight secondary and tertiary prevention efforts. This chapter provides information on primary prevention efforts based on the types described by McWhirter et al. (1998, 2007) and further addressed by Buckley (2000), Collins et al. (2002), Hovell et al. (2001), Kadish et al. (2001), and Watts (2000). These include developing life skills, enhancing interpersonal communication, learning strategies for cognitive change, achieving self-management and self-control, and coping with stress.

Developing Life Skills

Life skills can be defined as the ability to make use of personal resources for the purpose of expressing needs and positively influencing the environment. Such skills influence the formation of relationships and friendships, nonviolent methods of conflict resolution, and communicating with adults (Beautrais, 2005; McWhirter et al., 1998, 2007). Developing life skills can be accomplished through education and training in life skills, school peer mediation, peer tutoring, and peer facilitation.

Education and training in life skills involve developing and incorporating instructional modules into the curriculum at elementary, middle, and high school levels. Also involved is the collaborative input of a variety of professionals (counselors, nurses, physicians, social workers, psychologists, physical educators, and classroom teachers) for the purpose of teaching skills needed by most individuals on a day-to-day basis. The format for teaching any targeted skill should, ideally, contain the following components: teach, model, role-play, provide feedback, and assign homework. Almost any skill can be taught within this paradigm, and the fact that implementation is most often effected in the classroom means that entire populations can be accessed so that more and more young people can master skills that can help them avoid future problems.

School peer mediation, peer tutoring, and peer facilitation all involve training and supervising students to perform interpersonal helping tasks. School peer mediation requires trained peer mediators who work in partnerships with other students for the purpose of facilitating problem solving between disputing students. As noted by McWhirter et al. (1998, 2007), peer mediation ensures that both peer mediators and peer disputants increase experience with critical thinking, problem solving, and self-discipline.

Peer tutors are students who teach other students in both formal and informal learning situations. Peer tutoring can provide a cost-effective means of meeting individual needs, developing better ownership of the value of the educational experience, and enhancing self-esteem and motivation.

Peer facilitation, sometimes called peer helping, is a process in which students are trained to listen, paraphrase, support, and provide feedback to other students in the school. Peer facilitation is an effective way to empower children and adolescents and to provide adjunct support to the professional counselor or other human services specialist.

Enhancing Interpersonal Communication

Interpersonal communication skills are primary factors in the development of mutually beneficial relationships. Most programs designed to enhance interpersonal communication skills offer training in verbal and nonverbal communication, creation of constructive friendships, avoidance of misunderstanding, and the development of long-term relationships with significant others (Brooks, 2006; McWhirter et al., 1998, 2007). Lack of ability to communicate well with others can lead to lowered self-esteem, isolation, and the development of future at-risk behaviors. Assertiveness training and resistance and refusal training are often important components of training in interpersonal communication.

Assertiveness training is most often accomplished in the context of small groups. It can include providing assistance with expressing positive and negative feelings; the ability to initiate, maintain, and end conversations; and practice on setting limits. Nonverbal communication is an important component of assertiveness training because the manner in which something is communicated—body language, eye contact, personal distancing, and voice tone—can influence the message as much as the context of the message itself.

Resistance and refusal training is provided to help children and adolescents resist peer pressure or other negative social influences. Students are taught to label and recognize various forms of pressure and develop behavior to resist such pressure and influence. Both assertiveness training and resistance and refusal training provide numerous modeling, role-play, feedback, and reinforcement opportunities during the process of acquiring such interpersonal communication skills so that new behaviors are more likely to be used in day-to-day interactions with peers.

Learning Strategies for Cognitive Change

Because cognition mediates both behavior and affect, cognitive restructuring can be an effective primary prevention strategy. Techniques used in problem solving and decision making, self-management and self-control, and cognitive restructuring are among the primary prevention strategies that can be taught to children and adolescents.

All young people have the potential to problem solve and make decisions. At times, however, the emotional components connected with a particular problem, the egocentric focus commonly associated with the early years of human growth and development, and the lack of experience with systematically approaching problem-solving situations provide barriers to effective problem solving and decision making (Beautrais, 2005; McWhirter et al., 1998, 2007). Instruction can be provided, however, in each step of the problem-solving and decision-making process. Teaching children and adolescents how to resolve problematic situations can help them enhance self-esteem, overcome feelings of being helpless, and promote a generalized sense of empowerment.

Calling their model the DECIDE model, McWhirter et al. (1998, 2007) suggested that the following components be taught:

1. *Define the problem.* The problem is defined as clearly as possible and is stated as a goal to be achieved. This goal is assessed by asking the following questions: Does it meet the underlying needs? If it is attained, does it help the individual achieve satisfaction?

2. *Examine variables.* The specifics of the total situation are examined. Background issues and environmental factors are considered, so it may be necessary to gather and appraise additional information. It is particularly important to identify the feelings and thoughts of the youth at this step. Often earlier maladaptive responses must be modified. In both this step and Step 1, questions and suggestions from other students in the classroom or the group are useful.

3. *Consider alternatives.* Various means of solving the problem are considered. The strengths and weaknesses of each possibility are evaluated. Again, the teacher or counselor may call for brainstorming to generate ideas from other students about alternatives and strategies.

4. *Isolate a plan.* The alternatives are gradually narrowed down until what seems like the best response or solution remains. A plan for carrying out this alternative is prepared, and the potential consequences are considered in more detail.

5. *Do action steps.* After a plan is decided on, action must be taken to implement it. Thus, youngsters are systematically encouraged to follow through on the necessary steps to carry out their plan. They perform the behaviors that make up the solution plan.

6. *Evaluate effects.* Finally, youngsters need to evaluate the effectiveness of the solution. It is important to teach them to look for effects in their thoughts and feelings. They analyze and evaluate the outcome, review the decision, and, if necessary, develop another plan to achieve their goal.

McWhirter et al. reported that this model is effective for teaching problem solving and decision making.

Achieving Self-Management and Self-Control

Self-management means that self-control has been achieved. It implies that individuals can develop the ability to control, to a great extent, their thoughts, feelings, and behaviors. Teaching children and adolescents the techniques of self-management and self-control can result in outcomes similar to those connected with teaching problem solving and decision making, enhanced self-esteem, overcoming feelings of being helpless, and a sense of empowerment. Teaching self-management and self-control involves teaching children and adolescents self-assessment, self-monitoring, and self-reinforcement (McWhirter et al., 1998, 2007). Self-assessment means that the individual learns to evaluate his or her own behaviors against a standard that has personal meaning to determine whether the behavior is adequate. Self-monitoring requires that the individual observes his or her own behavior and records it. Record keeping may involve notation of contingencies in the environment prior to and immediately following the behavior. Self-reinforcement involves supplying one's own consequences for a given behavior (e.g., self-praise, buying something of personal significance). Generally, children and adolescents who master the techniques of self-management and self-control feel energized, motivated, and positive about themselves.

Coping With Stress

The term *coping with stress* is particularly significant in contemporary society. There are so many potential stressors encountered on a day-to-day basis that it behooves the adults in society to teach children and adolescents as much as possible about stress and stress management. It is an important primary prevention strategy. Chapter 7, Stress and Trauma: Coping in Today's Society, addresses this topic fully through discussion and analysis of perspectives on stress, including stimulus-oriented views, response-oriented views, stress as a transaction between person and environment, life event stressors, daily stress, home and family stress, school stress, and developmental stress.

PLANNING PREVENTION PROGRAMS

Laudatory prevention efforts of schools and communities have failed because planning efforts have not included important steps or because a group of concerned adults has moved to the implementation stage and shortchanged the entire planning process. The following steps, which are based on our experience in a variety of school and community settings, will help ensure success:

1. *Read the research on prevention programs.* There are excellent reviews and monographs on approaches to prevention (American Academy of Pediatrics, 2004; Astor et al., 2005; Collins et al., 2002; Dryfoos, 1997; Gager & Elias, 1997; Goldston, Yager, Heinicke, & Pynoos, 1990; Kadish et al., 2001; Reddy & Richardson, 2006; Romano, 1997; Weisberg, Caplan, & Harwood, 1991). Often practitioners, who are anxious to implement programs and services, do not take the time to learn about and build on the successes and failures of others. On the basis of numerous outcome studies, a number of generalizations can be made:
   - Prevention programs directed to the early years (e.g., pre- and postnatal parents and children during preschool years) can reduce factors that increase risk for maladaptive behaviors. Most of these efforts are focused on primary prevention and reduce the incidence of dysfunction in childhood and adolescence (Lally, Mangione, & Honig, 1988; Reddy & Richardson, 2006).
   - Prevention programs that involve parents, connect to the real world of work, incorporate social and life skills training, incorporate staff development, and involve dedicated role-model adults seem to have the most lasting and positive impact (Brooks, 2006; Dryfoos,1997).
   - School-based programs targeting adolescents have improved prosocial competence and decreased at-risk behaviors (such as the behaviors discussed in Part Three of this book; Schinke, Botvin, & Orlandi, 1991; Schneider, Attili, Nadel, & Weisberg, 1989).
   - Broad-based programs aimed at several causative factors or at-risk behaviors seem to be the most successful because youth at risk usually present with a number of conditions (Astor et al., 2005; Caplan & Weisberg, 1989).
   - Occasionally programs have not been effective or have made problems escalate (Bangert-Drowns, 1988). Finding out why could be extremely important to practitioners prior to implementing any prevention effort (Collins et. al., 2002).
2. *Assess needs.* Sometimes the professional helper fails to target the right population, the best combination of causative factors, or the at-risk behaviors of most concern to children, adolescents, and their families. It is important to touch base with the population being served prior to doing much planning. Children and adolescents, families, school faculty and staff, and compo-

nents of the community (e.g., hospitals, businesses, churches, social service agencies) should be asked about their view of factors creating risk, problematic behaviors, and skill deficits. Prevention programming should always be designed to address needs and concerns identified by recipients of future services.

3. *Meet with administrators, elected officials, and business owners.* Prevention efforts take time, commitment, and money to implement. Numerous prevention programs have met with failure because planners failed to obtain the input and support of those in positions to reinforce efforts and keep programs and services funded and in place on a long-term basis. This is a critical step in planning for program support.

4. *Establish a broad-based planning group.* Educators, parents, youths, administrators, mental health professionals, physicians, nurses, and police should all be included in planning efforts for prevention programming. The more interdisciplinary and representative the group, the richer the input. The best prevention efforts have been based on the collaborative teaming of members of the community to be served.

5. *Target the population, the causative factors, or the at-risk behaviors.* Often, planning groups are too ambitious with respect to goals and expectations. There is always more to be accomplished than can be realized with respect to a given prevention program. It is important to use the results of a needs assessment to target initial efforts so that initiatives are well planned and supported by adequate resources. Once a focus has been established, findings of research conducted relative to similar populations, risk factors, or at-risk groups should be utilized so that problems can be circumvented and past successful practices can be used.

6. *Identify existing prevention programs and resources.* Sometimes planning groups recreate programs, services, or resources that already exist and could be built on or used as adjuncts to newly created programs. It is important to identify existing prevention programs and assess them in terms of whether they offer primary, secondary, or tertiary prevention. Planning groups can then determine how to focus new initiatives (i.e., primary, secondary, or tertiary) and do a better job of effectively utilizing newly committed funding and resources.

7. *Carefully describe policies and procedures.* Before implementing a new program, it is extremely important to draft a description of all policies and procedures to be followed. This ensures that everyone involved in the program can be clear about roles and responsibilities. A written description also provides opportunity for input, revision, and refinement. Program descriptions can (and should) be checked in advance of implementation for legal and ethical implications.

8. *Plan variations for diversity.* For many young people, minority status is associated with low socioeconomic status, poor living conditions, fragmented families, and a variety of critical cultural, ethnic, and racial differences. All human service specialists must be flexible about making adaptations in prevention programming in a way that shows sensitivity and respect for diversity. Variations for diversity are addressed throughout this edition of *Youth at Risk*.

9. *Plan staff development.* Whether prevention programming is centered in school or community settings, all staff need to be educated, supervised, and prepared in advance of program implementation. Adults working on behalf of children and adolescents need to be carefully prepared and provided with opportunities to have their questions answered and their concerns addressed.

10. *Make sure adjunct services and referral options have been identified*. Those working on behalf of children and adolescents often need the assistance of other medical and social service professionals. Identifying adjunct services and referral options and acting as a liaison with employees in those settings, in advance, should never be overlooked.

11. *Plan evaluation procedures prior to program implementation*. Practitioners often neglect the evaluative component of prevention programming efforts. Evaluation procedures should be preplanned and data collection should be an integral part of efforts on behalf of youth. Data can be used to modify and improve the services offered and can provide justification for continued funding and commitment of other needed resources.

SUMMARY

Our overview of prevention has provided introductory material highlighting the problems that underscore the need for escalation of prevention efforts; defined the qualities of prevention programming; described the differences among primary, secondary, and tertiary prevention and noted the need for additional primary prevention programs; and suggested guidelines and steps for prevention programming. We hope that this information provides an enriched perspective with which to approach the material in the chapters that follow. The context of this chapter is reflective of our belief that more emphasis needs to be placed on proactive prevention efforts so that, as time passes, individuals, families, schools, and communities can lessen the amount of time and energy directed toward remediation and containment of impairment and dysfunction.

REFERENCES

American Academy of Pediatrics. (2004). Policy statement: School-based mental health services. *Pediatrics, 113*, 1839–1845.

Astor, R. A., Meyer, H. A., Benbenishty, R., Marachi, R., & Rosemond, M. (2005). School safety interventions: Best practices and programs. *Children and Schools, 27*, 17–32.

Bangert-Drowns, R. L. (1988). The effects of school-based substance abuse education: A meta-analysis. *Journal of Drug Education, 18*, 243–264.

Beautrais, A. L. (2005). National strategies for the reduction and prevention of suicide. *Crisis, 26*, 1–3.

Bosworth, K., Espelage, D., DuBay, T., & Daytner, G. (2000). Preliminary evaluation of a multimedia violence prevention program for adolescents. *American Journal of Health Behavior, 24*, 268–280.

Brooks, J. E. (2006). Strengthening resilience in children and youths: Maximizing opportunities through the schools. *Children and Schools, 28*, 69–76.

Brown, E. J., & Simpson, E. M. (2000). Comprehensive STD/HIV prevention education targeting US adolescents: Review of an ethical dilemma and proposed ethical framework. *Nursing Ethics, 7*, 339–349.

Buckley, M. A. (2000). Cognitive–developmental considerations in violence prevention and intervention. *Professional School Counseling, 4*, 60–70.

Caplan, M. Z., & Weisberg, R. P. (1989). Promoting social competence in early adolescence: Developmental considerations. In B. H. Schneider, G. Attili, J. Nadel, & R. P. Weisberg (Eds.), *Social competence in developmental perspective* (pp. 371–385). Norwell, MA: Kluwer Academic.

Collins, J., Robin, L., Wooley, S., Fenley, D., Hunt, P., Taylor, J., et al. (2002). Programs-that-work: CDC's guide to effective programs that reduce health-risk behaviors of youth. *Journal of School Health, 72,* 93–99.

Conyne, R. K. (1994). Preventative counseling. *Counseling and Human Development, 27,* 1–10.

Dryfoos, J. D. (1997). Adolescents at risk: Shaping programs to fit the need. *Journal of Negro Education, 65,* 5–18.

Fetro, J. V., Coyle, K. K., & Pham, P. (2001). Health-risk behaviors among middle school students in a large majority–minority school district. *Journal of School Health, 71,* 30–37.

Gager, P. J., & Elias, M. J. (1997). Implementing prevention programs in high-risk environments: Application of the resiliency paradigm. *American Journal of Orthopsychiatry, 67,* 363–373.

Gilliland, B. E., & James, R. K. (1993). *Crisis intervention strategies.* Pacific Grove, CA: Brooks/Cole.

Goldston, S. E., Yager, J., Heinicke, C. M., & Pynoos, R. S. (Eds.). (1990). *Preventing mental health disturbances in childhood.* Washington, DC: American Psychiatric Association.

Hadge, C. (1992). *School-based prevention and intervention program: Clearinghouse fact sheet* (Report No. CG 025 63 1). Piscataway, NJ: Rutgers University, Center of Alcohol Studies. (ERIC Document Reproduction Service No. ED 372 329)

Hallfors, D., Brodish, P. H., Khatapoush, S., Samchez, V., Cho, H., & Steckler, A. (2006). Feasibility of screening adolescents for suicide risk in "real world" high school settings. *American Journal of Public Health, 96,* 282–287.

Horner, J., & McElhaney, S. (1993). Building fences. *American Counselor, 2,* 17–21, 30.

Hovell, M. F., Blumberg, E. J., Liles, S., Powell, L., & Morrison, T. C. (2001). Training AIDS and anger prevention social skills in at-risk adolescents. *Journal of Counseling & Development, 79,* 347–355.

Janosik, E. H. (1984). *Crisis counseling: A contemporary approach.* Monterey, CA: Wadsworth Health Sciences.

Kadish, T. E., Glaser, B. A., Calhoun, G. B., & Ginter, E., J. (2001). Identifying the developmental strengths of juvenile offenders: Assessing four life-skills dimensions. *Journal of Addictions & Offender Counseling, 21,* 85–95.

Kazdin, A. E. (1993). Adolescent mental health: Prevention and treatment programs. *American Psychologist, 48,* 127–141.

King, K. A. (2001). Developing a comprehensive school suicide prevention program. *Journal of School Health, 71,* 132–137.

Kitts, R. L. (2005). Gay adolescents and suicide: Understanding the association. *Adolescence, 40,* 621–628.

Lally, R., Mangione, P. L., & Honig, A. S. (1988). The Syracuse University Family Development Research Program: Long-range impact on an early intervention with low-income children and their families. In D. Powell (Ed.), *Parent education as early childhood intervention: Emerging directions in theory, research, and practice* (pp. 79–104). Norwood, NJ: Ablex.

McGowan, M. (2006). Assessing "risk" versus promoting resilience. *Therapy Today, 17,* 27–28.

McWhirter, J. J., McWhirter, B. T., McWhirter, A. M., & McWhirter, E. H. (1998). *At-risk youth: A comprehensive response* (2nd ed.). Pacific Grove, CA: Brooks/Cole.

McWhirter, J. J., McWhirter, B. T., McWhrter, E. H., & McWhirter, R. J. (2007). *At risk youth: A comprehensive response* (4th ed.). Pacific Grove, CA: Brooks/Cole.

Popenhagen, M. P., & Qualley, R. M. (1998). Adolescent suicide: Detection, intervention, and prevention. *Professional School Counseling, 1*(4), 30–36.

Reddy, L. A., & Richardson, L. (2006). School-based prevention and intervention programs for children with emotional disturbance. *Education and Treatment of Children, 29*, 379–404.

Roberts, A. R. (Ed.). (1991). *Contemporary perspectives on crisis intervention and prevention.* Englewood Cliffs, NJ: Rutgers University Center of Alcohol Studies.

Romano, J. L. (1997). School personnel training for the prevention of tobacco, alcohol, and other drug use: Issues and outcomes. *Journal of Drug Education, 27*, 245–258.

Schaughnessy, L., Doshi, S. R., & Jones, S. E. (2004). Attempted suicide and associated health risk behaviors among Native American high school students. *Journal of School Health, 74*, 177–182.

Schinke, S. P., Botvin, G. J., & Orlandi, M. A. (1991). *Substance abuse in children and adolescents: Evaluation and intervention.* Newbury Park, CA: Sage.

Schneider, B. H., Attili, G., Nadel, J., & Weisberg, R. P. (Eds.). (1989). *Social competence in developmental perspective.* Norwell, MA: Kluwer Academic.

Watts, G. F., Sr. (2000). Attitude toward sexual intercourse and relationship with peer and parental communication. *American Journal of Health Studies, 16*, 156–163.

Weisberg, R. P., Caplan, M., & Harwood, L. (1991). Promoting competent young people in competence-enhancing environments: A systems-based perspective on primary prevention. *Journal of Consulting and Clinical Psychology, 55*, 542–549.

CHAPTER 3

■

Resilience: Individual, Family, School, and Community Perspectives

*Rolla E. Lewis**

The literature on resilience provides an alternative view that sees youth at promise rather than at risk and offers counselors, teachers, and parents positive and viable resources for promoting the well-being of youth. The models, methods, and data emerging from education, prevention, and counseling fields about resilience do not represent a singular point of view, however. There is diversity that results in debate and controversies about resilience, but there is agreement that the family of phenomena referred to as resilience challenges the negative assumptions found in deficit-focused models. Resilience results from good outcomes in spite of exposure to risk. There is no denial that risk exists. The issue becomes one of creating healthy systems that invite youths to participate in meaningful activities rather than repairing individuals who have been damaged by risks.

This chapter looks at resilience literature and practices not to synthesize but rather to call attention to different pathways counseling and teaching professions can follow to construct healthy systems and climates that support positive youth development. Additionally, this chapter calls for creating collaborative efforts between professionals and community members to help all youths grow toward their greatest potential in just and caring communities. The resilience literature cited in this chapter refers to the evolving multidisciplinary research and practices that have emerged from the prevention, counseling, education, social work, and youth development fields (Benard, 1991, 1997, 2004; Benard & Marshall, 2001a, 2001b;

*The author wishes to thank Kathy Marshall for her review of an earlier draft and clarification regarding *A Framework for Practice: Tapping Innate Resiliency* (Benard & Marshall, 1997). The author would also like to thank Jeanne Slingluff for sharing her expertise and knowledge about her work in the schools and Linda Hennessey for reviewing the chapter and her dialogue about ecology and careers.

Friesen & Brennan, 2005; Goldstein & Brooks, 2006; Jennings, 2001, 2003; Kaplan, 2006; Luthar, Cicchetti, & Becker, 2000a, 2000b; Marshall, 1998, 2004; Masten, 2001; Ungar, 2004, 2005; Werner, 2006). Although it is beyond the scope of this chapter, the resilience and wellness constructs have much in common (Goldstein & Brooks, 2006; Myers & Sweeney, 2005; Prilleltensky & Prilleltensky, 2005). This chapter concentrates on how the resilience literature moves primary prevention perspective and practices away from short-term, individual interventions and toward long-term, comprehensive interventions designed to foster positive youth development in and beyond the school and into the community (Benard, 1997, 2004; Benard & Marshall, 1997, 2001a, 2001b; Brooks, 2006; Duncan, 2005; Friesen & Brennan, 2005; Jennings, 2001; Luthar et al., 2000a; Matsen, 2001; Taub & Pearrow, 2006; Ungar, 2004, 2005). The key difference between preventionists and resilience researchers should be noted. Preventionist efforts usually represent disease avoidance, whereas resilience researchers concentrate on "wellness in addition to the absence of dysfunction" (Luthar et al., 2000b, p. 574). In many ways, the resilience literature offers school counselors one pathway back to and forward from the counseling profession's roots in human development and education, back to and forward from the assumption that growth and development are human imperatives. In following the development pathway, this chapter is guided by key research, effective practices, and professional possibilities.

1. *Key research.* Key research points to resilience as an evolving construct that is understood in multiple ways (Benard, 2004; Benard & Marshall, 2001a, 2001b; Deater-Deckard, Ivy, & Smith, 2006; Kaplan, 2006; Luthar et al., 2000a, 2000b; Marshall, 1998, 2001, 2004; Masten, 2001; Ungar, 2004, 2005; Vaillant, 2002; Werner, 1989, 1996, 1998; Werner & Smith, 1982, 1992, 2001; Wright & Masten, 2006). A notable body of resilience research and practice has at its heart the radical notion that "Resilience is a capacity all youth have for healthy development and successful learning" (Benard, 2004, p. 4). Such a view shifts the professional perspective to see youth as having the developmental resources and self-righting capacities they need to navigate through life. Counselors, teachers, and parents are in a position to help youths realize this, but core providers must perceive their own self-righting capacities if they are going to help youths understand their own health. In other words, to promote the health of youths at risk, helpers are advised to recognize their own resilience and health.

Most of the practices found in this chapter begin with the assumption that resilience is a self-righting capacity fostered transactionally in the presence of certain environmental variables. Resilience is an end product of buffering processes that do not eliminate risk (Werner & Smith, 2001). As such, risk should be considered in broader socially constructed and ecologically embedded contexts whereby poverty, racism, and injustice are rooted in social practices. Resilience can then be viewed as a dynamic process associated with global factors like affiliation with caring adults. Metaphorically, youths are like diverse seeds with great potential, like acorns with the capacity to become oak trees but dependent on adequate ecological variables such as soil, water, and sun. Resilience practices can guide school counselors, teachers, and parents to appreciate the true meaning of education (*e-ducare*, a Latin word, means to lead out rather than put in) by advocating for environments where students draw out their own self-righting capacities under the mentorship of caring adults.

2. *Effective practices.* What makes counseling practice effective? Four common factors have been proposed as the principal elements accounting for effective change in clients: (a) Client/extratherapeutic factors account for 40% of successful out-

comes, (b) relationship factors account for 30% of outcomes, (c) hope and expectancy account for 15%, and (d) model/technique accounts for 15% (Hubble, Duncan, & Miller, 1999).

Client/extratherapeutic factors are those factors attributed within the client or the client's life circumstances (i.e., what the client brings to therapy and what influences the client outside of therapy), pointing perhaps to their self-righting capacities growing out of community support. Relationship factors are such qualities as caring, empathy, and acceptance, found in any effective family, classroom, or community. Hope and expectancy deal with both the counselor's and the client's belief in the possibility of change and are found in any meaningful, goal-oriented activity (Duncan, 2005; Snyder, Feldman, Shorey, & Rand, 2002). Model/technique includes those interventions counselors use to motivate clients to take actions to help themselves; these are the skills such as the miracle question that counselors learn in graduate school. De Shazer (1988, p. 5) described the classic miracle question: "Suppose that one night there is a miracle and while you are sleeping the problem that brought you into therapy is solved. How would you know? What would be different?"

The effective practices fostering resilience described in this chapter point to creating supportive systems, helping clients tap the qualities within themselves, and recognizing alternative stories within their experiences (Benard & Marshall, 1997; Bertolino & O'Hanlon, 2002; Monk, Winslade, Crocket, & Epston, 1997). In a narrow sense, effective practices fostering resilience draw on extratherapeutic factors, relationship factors, hope and expectancy factors, and finally technique factors. Fostering resilience has less to do with technique and more with taking a positive and affirming stance with others. Coupled with taking a positive and affirming stance, it is vital for counselors, especially those working in the schools, to develop research agendas, to determine what works in their schools, and to use the results to help all students (Whiston, 2002).

3. *Professional possibilities.* Practices promoting resilience can guide school counselors and teachers in their efforts to foster success for all students' personal, social, academic, and career development. Masten (1994) pointed out, "Fostering resilience is an attempt to deflect a developmental pathway in a more positive direction" (p. 21). Schools and communities offer numerous possibilities for helping youths recognize their self-righting capacities and for shifting school systems to support youths in defining their life trajectories along positive pathways. Pathways that include instilling a sense of hope and recognizing self-righting capabilities are fundamental. As Werner and Smith (1992) concluded in their longitudinal study, "The central component in the lives of the resilient individuals . . . which contributed to their effective coping in adulthood appeared to be a confidence that the odds can be surmounted. Some of the luckier ones developed such hopefulness early in their lives, in contact with caring adults" (p. 207).

Begin by being an ally to youth. Allies see youths as resources, and professional efforts open pathways for youths to perceive their own ability to spring back from adversity, to realize their own self-righting capacities, to understand their own ability to learn, and to fulfill their own power to engage passionately in meaningful activities. Teachers and counselors model these capacities by showing how part of learning to live has to do with individuals' ability to get up after they have been knocked down, to have heart, gumption, determination, and compassion. Youths and adults experience the world in different ways. Life can be rocky at any developmental or life stage; life demands participation and engagement. As such, life offers opportunities for adults to explore and join with youths to grasp the role of thought in interpreting experience (Mills, 1995; Sedgeman, 2005; Shure & Aberon, 2006). Learning to learn is related to individuals' ability to learn from difficulties and failures, and from their capacity to struggle with uncertainty and let solutions and deeper wisdom emerge (Bruner, 1986, 1990; Claxton, 1997, 1999; Clinchy, 1996; Langer, 1997; Shure & Aberson, 2006). Learning to learn is also concerned with helping all students develop competencies and finding adults who will nurture capabilities in meaningful contexts (Brooks, 1994, 1997, 2006; Masten & Coatsworth, 1998). Learning to work is connected to individuals' ability to adjust to the ongoing and continual changes in their livelihoods as students and adults. More important, learning to work is connected to finding one's capacity to be passionate about the work one chooses to do and doing things one finds meaningful (Quattrociocchi & Peterson, 1997). Promoting resilience begins with wellness and seeing youth as having resources and providing opportunities for youth and adults to find healthy pathways to learn to live, learn to learn, and learn to work.

RESILIENCE DEFINED

Given the diversity within the resilience literature, this chapter defines resilience as a dynamic developmental process (Luthar et al., 2000a) of healthy human development growing out of nurturing relationships that support social, academic, and vocational competence and the self-righting capacity to spring back from exposure to adversity and other environmental stressors. This self-righting capacity does not occur in a social vacuum; it may emerge at different developmental stages and frequently entails having a caring teacher or an adult mentor available (Werner & Smith, 2001). Global factors associated with resilience include possessing cognitive and self-regulation skills, having positive views of self and the motivation to be effective, and connecting with competent and caring adults (Masten, 2001). Luthar et al. (2000a) pointed out that although resilience is a dynamic process, it is frequently misrepresented as a narrow trait that makes some youth "have what it takes" to overcome the odds and others "not have" those special qualities. According to Masten (2001), "Resilience does not come from rare and special qualities, but from the everyday magic of the ordinary, normative human resources in the minds, brains, and bodies of children, in their families and relationships, and in their communities" (p. 235). Resilience is not extraordinary; it is the "power of the ordinary." Helping all youth tap this power of the ordinary is the fundamental challenge facing all adults who care about kids.

Benard and Marshall (1997) argued that it is easier to teach health if it is known or embodied in one's own life. To foster the self-righting capacity for healthy human development in youth, counselors, teachers, parents, and others must recognize their own resilience. "Resilience is an inside-out process that begins with one person's belief and emanates outward to transform whole families, classrooms, schools and communities. . . . It means we shift from a focus on fixing individuals to creating healthy systems" (Benard & Marshall, 1997, p. 1). Teachers, counselors, and parents who begin with their own well-being foster resilience.

Because diverse professional fields contribute to the evolving resilience literature, there are a variety of perspectives about resilience that lead to misunderstandings (Kaplan, 2006). On the one hand, as Masten (1994) pointed out, "Studies of resilience suggest that nature has provided powerful protective mechanisms for human development. . . .When adversity is relieved and basic human needs are restored, then resilience has a chance to emerge. Rekindling hope may be an important spark for resilience processes to begin their restorative work" (pp. 20–21). On the other hand, one of McWhirter, McWhirter, McWhirter, and McWhirter's (1998) concerns is that "the justice system has used the term resiliency to help punish offenders—contending that a violent and abrasive upbringing provides no explanation for violent behavior because some youth who grow up in the same type of environment do not engage in violence" (p. 80). Such practices by those in the justice system totally misunderstand the research and practices emerging from resilience literature. As made clear by Werner (1998), "As long as the balance between stressful events and protective factors is favorable, successful adaptation is possible even for youngsters who live in 'high risk' conditions. However, when stressful life events outweigh the protective factors in a child's life, even the most resilient individual can develop problems" (p. 8).

As diverse as it is, the resilience literature does not support institutionalizing ways to blame individuals in need of help, creating policies that fail to support children and families, and spending more money on trying to fix serious coping problems rather than promoting prevention (Werner & Smith, 2001). Such practices are contrary to the assumptions guiding the diverse resilience practices cited in this chapter; the imperative for growth and development unfolds naturally when certain environmental attributes are present.

"Resilience is not the cheerful disregard of one's difficult and traumatic life experiences; neither is it the naive discounting of life's pains. It is rather the ability to bear up in spite of these ordeals" (Saleebey, 1997, p. 9). Blum (1998) offered a perspective regarding what should be done in response to the positive findings in the resilience research:

> Rather than viewing the findings from resiliency research as a rationale for inaction, we should redouble our efforts. The good news is that for those reared in adversity, the outcomes are not necessarily bleak. . . . It is likewise clear that, as the African proverb states, "it takes a community to rear a child." (p. 374)

To embody this proverb, individuals can learn to draw on their own resilience, foster resilience in others, and work within their schools and communities to encourage collaborative and systemic approaches that foster resilience in youth.

RESILIENCE: FACTORS, PERSPECTIVES, AND PRACTICES

There are multiple factors influencing the developmental trajectories of youth and many explanations for the difficulties they face (Benard & Marshall, 2001a, 2001b; Luthar et al., 2000a; Masten & Coatsworth, 1998; Ungar, 2004; Wright & Masten, 2006). Merely identifying risks and causal factors does not always work. Benard's (2004) and Benard and Marshall's (2001a, 2001b) research synthesis is useful in showing that identifying risks does not translate into strategies for reducing those risks. This section explores how resilience promotion efforts viewed in the broader social contexts shift how we see why some children are not damaged or spring back from deprivation and adversity. Rather than attempting to capture the scope of the literature and prevention efforts, this section highlights key longitudinal resilience research that reveals the self-righting capacity in people and the need to create structures to support those people. Research spanning over 40 years conducted by Emmy E. Werner and her colleagues that describes protective factors within youth, within the family, and within the community is discussed (Werner, 1989,

1996, 1998, 2006; Werner & Smith, 1982, 1992, 2001); then additional research that profiles qualities of resilient youth and three protective factors that enhance student resilience in the schools are examined (Benard, 1991, 1997, 2004; Benard & Marshall, 1997, 2001a, 2001b).

Emmy E. Werner: The Mother of Resilience

The life span, cross-cultural studies, such as those exemplified in the longitudinal studies of Emmy E. Werner and her colleagues, have concluded that resilience is the natural human capacity for self-righting (Werner, 1996, 2006; Werner & Smith, 1982, 1992, 2001). Werner and Smith's (1992) transactional–ecological model of human development posits that people are active, self-righting organisms continuously adapting to their environment and have an imperative for growth and development. Their influential resilience research used a prospective, developmental, and longitudinal design to assess how youth at various stages of development grow in high-risk conditions and respond to risk factors (Werner, 1989, 1996, 1998, 2006; Werner & Smith, 1982, 1992, 2001). Werner and Smith (1992) stated, "prospective longitudinal studies have fairly consistently shown that even among children exposed to potent risk factors it is unusual for more than half to develop serious disabilities or persistent problems" (p. 4). Essentially, the longitudinal perspective has resulted in a change in what researchers find, including that most delinquent youths do not develop into career criminals (Werner, 1996, 1998, 2006; Werner & Smith, 1992, 2001). That their research design changed how they discerned the individuals being studied over time deserves explanation. The prospective design is different from the retrospective design. Researchers using prospective designs study groups of youth over time, whereas researchers using retrospective design are more likely to investigate risk factors linked to the history of a person with identified difficulties. Prospective design offers researchers different possibilities in describing youth who grow up in high-risk environments, whereas retrospective designs focus on events that lead to or interventions that are devised to diminish pathology. Longitudinal research offers an alternative way of understanding and learning about human self-righting capacities.

This hopeful and optimistic view needs to be explained in the context of research, commentary, and life stories supporting inborn, self-righting capacities. Werner and her colleagues' study (Werner, 1989; Werner, Bierman, & French, 1971; Werner & Smith, 1977, 1982, 1992, 2001) has extended more than 40 years and has found there are protective factors within youth, the family, and the community. Beginning with the entire population of 698 youths born in 1955, the study on Kauai, Hawaii, has followed 505 individuals from the prenatal stage to the adult stage of development. Data have been collected from cohort members in the prenatal period, at birth, and at ages 1, 2, 10, 18, 32, and 40. By birth, one third of the group was considered at risk because of four or more factors: significant poverty, being reared by parents with little formal education, moderate to severe perinatal stress, family discord, divorce, alcoholism, or mental retardation. One third of these high-risk youths did not develop difficulties as a result of the exposure to risk, and another one third rebounded as they reached adulthood to become competent adults (Werner, 1998; Werner & Smith, 1992, 2001).

- *The Children of Kauai* (Werner et al., 1971) documented development from birth to age 10 and the cumulative effects of poverty, perinatal stress, and disorganized caretaking.

- *Kauai's Children Come of Age* (Werner & Smith, 1977) analyzed the likelihood of persistent problems into childhood by examining learning disorders, mental health problems, and antisocial behavior of high-risk youths in their teens.
- *Vulnerable but Invincible* (Werner & Smith, 1982) documented vulnerable and stress-resistant youths up to the transitional phase when they were about to leave high school.
- *Overcoming the Odds* (Werner & Smith, 1992) traced the long-term effects of childhood adversity and examined the protective factors that led most of the youths to adapt successfully as adults.
- *Journeys From Childhood to Midlife* (Werner & Smith, 2001) continued documenting the stability of resilience from childhood to adulthood and the ability of high-risk individuals to bounce back later in life.

Werner and Smith (1992) found that resilience is not something that is fixed and concrete but a quality that is enhanced by protective buffers that appear to transcend ethnic, social class, and geographical boundaries. Individual variability had to be taken into account, but the majority of resilient youths in the Kauai study had a variety of internal or external protective factors (Werner, 1996). Those youths who overcame the odds were described as resilient, and as Werner and Smith (1992) pointed out, "they began to perceive themselves as movers of their destiny rather than as pawns in a power game played by outsiders" (p. 21).

The vast majority of delinquent youths in the study did not become adult career criminals. The majority of chronic criminals from the study cohort consisted of a small group who had averaged four or more arrests before becoming 18 years old. Those who did become persistent offenders needed remedial educational help (usually reading) prior to age 10, were considered troublemakers by their fifth-grade teachers and parents, and had grown up in homes in which significant caregivers were absent for extended periods of time during adolescence (Werner & Smith, 1992). Youth "exposed to adversities in early childhood are not predestined to grow into adults with failed marriages, criminal records, or psychiatric disorders. At each developmental stage, there is an opportunity for protective factors (personal competencies and sources of support) to counterbalance the negative weight exerted by adverse experiences" (Werner & Smith, 1992, p. 171).

"Second chance" opportunities were usually found at major life transitions. Such opportunities enabled high-risk individuals to rebound and are frequently found in adult education programs, military service, active participation in a church community, or a supportive friend or spouse.

Werner and Smith (1992) asserted that the protective factors within the individual, family, and community have a more profound impact on the lives of youth than risk factors. Key protective factors pointed out by Werner and Smith (1992) and expanded by Werner (1998) are worthy of note for professionals working with youth:

1. *Within the individual:* Resilient individuals were characterized by their caregivers as
   - being active, affectionate, cuddly, good-natured, and easy to deal with in infancy;
   - having effective reading skills by age 10 or Grade 4;
   - having communication and reasoning skills;
   - being responsible and achievement oriented and having competence and self-efficacy as general hallmarks;
   - being more nurturant, compassionate, and socially perceptive;

- being more socially mature and possessing an internalized set of values;
- having a special interest or hobby;
- being liked by peers and adults;
- being reflective rather than having an impulsive dominant cognitive style;
- having an internal locus of control, believing that they can influence the environment around them;
- being flexible in coping strategies when dealing with adversity; and
- setting career and job success as high priorities as adults.

2. *Within the family:* Resiliency is enhanced when
   - There are different child-rearing practices for boys and girls. Resilience is fostered in households with male role models who encourage the expression of emotion for boys and in households with an emphasis on risk taking and independence for girls, with a tendency not to overprotect and reliable emotional support from another woman, such as a mother, grandmother, older sister, or aunt.
   - There are affectional ties with alternative caregivers. Caring, nonjudgmental adults who are not necessarily family members are crucial in fostering resiliency.
   - Youths from chaotic families have an association with friends and other individuals from stable households.
   - There is an emphasis on youths being helpful. Chores and domestic responsibilities prove to be sources of competence and strength.
   - There is faith that provides a sense of coherence and rootedness that gives youths a sense of meaning and compassion.

3. *Within the community:* Resilience is enhanced when
   - Youths are able to make and keep friends. Resilient youths keep friends into adulthood and look to them for emotional support.
   - There is a favorable attitude toward school.
   - There is structure and clear limits for boys and the opportunity to take independent action for girls.
   - There is positive mentoring at school. Those remembering one or more teachers are more resilient (the most frequently identified role models are favorite teachers). The impact of positive mentoring may last a lifetime.

Werner and Smith (1992) concluded that the protective factors

appear to transcend ethnic, social class, geographical, and historical boundaries. Most of all, they offer a more optimistic outlook than the perspective that can be gleaned from the literature on the negative consequences of perinatal trauma, caregiving deficits, and chronic poverty. They provide us with a corrective lens—an awareness of the self-righting tendencies that move children toward normal adult development under all but the most persistent adverse circumstances. (p. 202)

Counselors, teachers, parents, and other core providers can foster the protective buffers that support positive life trajectories for youth in which competence, confidence, and ability to care for others will flourish, but those helpers must believe in youth if this is going to happen. According to Werner and Smith (1992), "The life stories of the resilient youngsters now grown into adulthood teach us that competence, confidence, and caring can flourish, even under adverse circumstances, if children encounter persons who provide them with the secure basis for the development of trust, autonomy, and initiative" (p. 209).

Kitashima (1997), a youth from the Kauai study, has embodied this point in sharing what made a difference in her life growing up in a high-risk household. Kitashima found caring and supportive people in school significant contributors to her success. At the same time, she found some professionals in the school made her a target of racism and put-downs. She described a time when her fifth-grade math teacher told her, "You are a good-for-nothing Hawaiian and will never amount to anything." In contrast, her school principal told her, "You are Hawaiian, and you can be anything you choose to be" (Kitashima, 1997, p. 34). At age 16, when she became pregnant and had a child, another school principal supported her desire to stay in school. As with many youths from the Kauai study, the protective factors counterbalanced the risks, and Kitashima went on to become a successful adult.

One factor having a profound impact on her resilience was her faith in something greater than herself. Her faith in something greater led Kitashima (1997) to conclude, "Treasures exist in each one of our children—be they our own or somebody else's—and we need to be patient until they realize their promise. . . . Never give up on kids" (p. 36). Kitashima's guiding beliefs and comments open a larger question: the growing discussion about spirituality in public education. Palmer (1998/1999) wrote,

> I advocate any way we can find to explore the spiritual dimension of teaching, learning, and living. By "spiritual" I do not mean the creedal formulation of any faith tradition. . . . I mean the ancient and abiding human quest for connectedness with something larger and more trustworthy than our egos—with our own souls, with one another, with the worlds of history and nature, with the invisible winds of the spirit, with the mystery of being alive. (p. 6)

Such discussion and position should cause counselors and teachers to pause because they place professionals in a position where they must wrestle with complex issues regarding "the spirit of education" in which educators can "neither ignore religion nor proselytize a particular belief" (Scherer, 1998/1999, p. 5). Ultimately, as Kitashima's experience and beliefs show, the act of believing in youth "becomes a concern of the spirit" (Wesley, 1998/1999, p. 42). Counselors and teachers thinking about spiritual issues are forced to recognize and appreciate the issues raised and how beliefs foster resilience.

Changing Perspectives and Practices

Early research regarding resilience concentrated on understanding the personal qualities found in resilient individuals. As research evolved, resilience has been acknowledged to derive from factors outside of the youth and to be the result of underlying protective processes rather than protective factors (Luthar et al., 2000a, 2000b). There is an interplay between the self-righting qualities inherent in the individual and the protective processes fostering resilience. Benard's (2004) review of the resilience research described personal and environmental sources of healthy development and informs prevention efforts that balance the self-righting qualities inherent in the individual and the need to create systems that support protective processes fostering resilience.

Drawing on the transactional–ecological model of human development, Benard (1997) stated that "personality and individual outcomes are the result of a transactional process between self, agency, and environmental influences. To be successful, prevention interventions must focus on enhancing and creating positive environmental contexts—families, schools, and communities that, in turn, reinforce positive behaviors" (p. 69). The individual traits include social competence, problem-solving skills, autonomy, and a sense of purpose and belief in a bright future. These resilience traits and protective factors support the self-righting tendencies within the person (Benard, 2004). Youth with a positive sense of well-being demonstrated the following (Benard, 2004):

- *Social competence:* responsiveness, flexibility, empathy and caring, communication skills, and a sense of humor.
- *Problem-solving skills:* thinking abstractly and reflectively, planning skills, and flexibility.
- *Autonomy:* internal locus of control, sense of power, self-discipline, and adaptive distancing.
- *Sense of purpose and future:* healthy expectations, goal-directedness, success orientation, educational aspirations, persistence, hopefulness, hardiness, belief in bright or compelling future, and a sense of coherence or meaning.

Protective factors were also needed. Environmental characteristics or protective factors that support positive youth development include the following:

- *Caring relationships:* Having a connection with at least one caring person is the single most important factor in fostering resilience in youth. Relationships noted for stable care, affection, attention, intergenerational social networks, and a basic sense of trust foster climates of care and support.
- *High expectations:* These imply that adults see strengths and assets more than problems and deficits, and they recognize the potential for maturity, responsibility, self-discipline, and common sense in youth. Providing structure, order, clear expectations, and cultural traditions; being valued; and promoting social and academic success foster resilience in youth.
- *Opportunities to participate and contribute:* These grow naturally from relationships based on caring and high expectations (Benard, 2004). Participation connects youth to other people, to interests, and to valuing life itself. Being valued participants, having socially and economically useful tasks, having responsibilities for decision making, planning, and helping others are the essence of meaningful participation.

Benard (2004) indicated that prevention efforts must "focus on our belief in young people's innate resilience and developmental wisdom" (p. 113). Such a focus shifts perspective from risk to resilience, a shift that occurs by focusing on strengths and helping "caregivers of our youth recognize their own resilient nature" (Benard, 2004, p. 114). To assess student, school, and community strengths, Benard has been involved in developing the California Health Kids Survey (HKS; see http://www.wested.org/hks/). The HKS instrument enables local school leaders to assess their own systems, to develop plans for helping all students become more connected with their schools, and to generate ongoing developmental plans for fostering resilience within school communities.

Like solution-focused, narrative, and other competency-based counseling approaches, resilience practices build on strengths. Professionals, such as school counselors, are challenged to create supportive systems and work as partners in collaborating to help people to draw on the power to help themselves (Benard,

2004; Bertolino & O'Hanlon, 2002; De Jong & Berg, 2002; Duncan, 2005; Monk et al., 1997; Parry & Doan, 1994; Saleebey, 1997; White & Epston, 1990; Winslade & Monk, 1999, 2000). Seeing people as inherently possessing power shifts the professional role away from authority, expert, and director to that of collaborator working with others who have resources, expertise in their own lives, and the capacity to recognize their own well-being. Problems are defined as external to the person. Both Benard (1991) and narrative counselors (White & Epston, 1990) have stated that the person is not the problem; the problem is the problem. To begin solving problems, professionals are challenged to enter into dialogues with individuals, families, and communities who are seeking assistance in wrestling with problems. The next section explores problems influencing professional and personal discourses, developing dialogues, and how understanding resilience as transactional processes informs professional discourses related to risk, racism, poverty, and career development.

DISCOURSES OF RISK, RACISM, POVERTY, AND CAREERS

Like fish in water, people and cultures exist in language. We are biological, social, and psychological beings embedded in discourses that describe our ecosocial experience, understanding, and actions. Such discourses are culturally and ecologically embedded and define the taken-for-granted world in which we exist. Those being helped and those helping exist in complex ecosocial networks found in multiple bioregional, community, cultural, familial, and personal contexts that are described in various discourses, including a "discourse of disorder" (Bowers, 1997, 2000, 2001; Capra, 2002; Gergen & McNamee, 2000). As such, professionals are challenged to reflect critically on the discourses that shape their own taken-for-granted assumptions about the world, education, social situations, and their professional roles (Atkinson & Claxton, 2000; Felner, 2006; Lott, 2002; Payne, 2003; Winslade & Monk, 2000). Reflecting on discourses defining the taken-for-granted world forces professionals to recognize a need to come as partners into dialogues shaping courses of action taken in systems, such as schools, or as helpers working with others who may exist in separate cultural discourses.

Looking at discourse patterns allows a number of professional possibilities, but this chapter focuses on two things. First, exploring discourse patterns enables counselors to understand how both clients and professionals are shaped by a variety of discourses in their lives. Numerous discourses shape the way they experience the world and the language registers they use at home, school, work, and so on to describe that experience to multiple audiences. For instance, Payne (2003) pointed out that the middle class use formal-register discourse patterns that go straight to the point, whereas among many poor and underrepresented people casual-register discourse patterns go around and around. The formal-register discourse pattern is valued more in school and in middle-class venues and leads to the categorization of groups of people into upper and lower strata, thus allowing those with the valued discourse patterns to maintain their power and ability to "maneuver in the society they control" (Lott, 2002, p. 101). "Power, defined as access to resources, enables the group with greatest access to set the rules, frame the discourse, and name and describe those with less power" (Lott, 2002, p. 101).

Second, understanding discourses opens the opportunity for teachers and counselors to launch themselves out beyond their taken-for-granted world by listening to learn and by hearing people as experts of their own experiences. Understanding multiple discourses opens opportunities to develop collaborative dialogues between and among people in specific contexts at specific points in time. Everyone sees, experiences, and tells stories about the world from certain perspectives and uses language in different ways, and counselors and teachers are challenged to enter into collaborative dialogues, to describe power, and to invite the less powerful to access tools to fully participate. Such a stance moves the image of helping from having an expert above the client who is charged with removing the problem from the client to placing two people side-by-side viewing the problem together, knocking the problem out of the way, or working together to resolve it.

Risk Discourse

The discourse regarding troubled families, schools, and communities binds problems to individuals composing those families, schools, and communities that are at risk. An alternative discourse would not place the problem in people; rather problems would be described as interactive processes constructed in specific ecosocial locations. Benard (1994) pointed out, "Labeling youths, their families, and their communities as at risk means we are acting on stereotypes, on unquestioned assumptions about who people really are. . . . In contrast, resilience research focuses on learning . . . individual stories and truths, on studying the individual variation within groups having risk status" (p. 4). Fostering resilience means recognizing social ecology and the discourses that we participate in as people and professionals because risk factors rarely occur in isolation (Wright & Masten, 2006). Jennings (2001) asserted, "Unfortunately, children and their families who are considered to be 'at risk' (for what is rarely identified) are frequently assumed to be minority, poor, and passively victimized" (p. 153).

Swadener and Lubeck (1995), who seemed unfamiliar with the resilience literature, stated that describing youth "at risk" creates an "ideology of risk, which has embedded in it interpretations of children's deficiencies or likelihood of failure due to environmental, as well as individual variables. The problem of locating pathology in the victim is the most objectionable tenet of much of the dominant rhetoric of risk" (p. 18). In other words, describing youth at risk creates political consequences that result in the victims of social injustice being blamed for the results of that injustice. For Swadener and Lubeck, the need to confront structural injustices is lost when professional conversations and actions focus on fixing youth at risk. According to Fine (1995),

> "Youth at risk" is an ideological and historical construction. While numbers and their skewed class and racial distributions are intolerable, and the academic and economic consequences are severe, we must remember that today more students graduate from high school than was true fifteen years ago. . . . Fundamentally, the notion of "risk" keeps us from being broadly, radically, and structurally creative about transforming schools and social conditions for all of today and tomorrow's youth. (p. 90)

Although Swadener and Lubeck (1995) and Fine (1995) did not locate themselves in the counseling profession or even in prevention work, such perspectives should prompt counselors, teachers, parents, and others to pause and think. By taking advantage of the deconstruction of the at-risk construct, counselors and teachers can critically reflect on their own practice and open up possibilities for different kinds of professional practice to help youths move beyond victim-focused identities (Jennings, 2001).

Doing something about it. Counselors can offer alternative discourses. On the one hand, as Saleebey (1997) wrote, we might be a

> culture obsessed with, and fascinated by, psychopathology, victimization, abnormality, and moral and interpersonal aberrations. A swelling conglomerate of businesses and professions, institutions and agencies, from medicine to pharmaceuticals, from the insurance industry to the mass media turn handsome profits by assuring us that we are in the clutch (or soon will be) of any number of emotional, physical, or behavioral maladies. (p. 4)

On the other hand, counselors can participate in discourses that build on the traditions that foster resilience, emphasize health and competence, and communicate hope to and faith in youth.

Racism Discourse

Robinson and Ginter (1999) captured how people's lives are woven into stories that illustrate racism's toxic effects in counselors' personal and professional lives. Professionals and those they serve are woven into a racist social fabric. Euro American counselors and African American counselors experience the world in different ways; one might walk down the street sensing that there is no racism in the United States, whereas the other might experience racist remarks or more subtle forms of marginalization while walking down the same street. As Kitashima's (1997) earlier account above demonstrates, racism infects both individual and environmental attributes fostering resilience; most counselors and teachers recognize not every youth has the personal and environmental attributes Kitashima had when faced with racism at school. Youths need allies to advocate for safe space and equity.

Counselors, teachers, parents, and other core providers are challenged to understand how dominant discourses affect how their clients' stories are heard, understood, and responded to. Robinson (1999) stated, "Counselors must avoid attributing certain occupations, attitudes, and experiences to their clients due to the visibility of their race, gender, and other identities. Making judgments about people's humanity and its quality due to established criteria is to rely on tried but extremely powerful discourse steeped in oppression" (p. 78). Counselors have to know stereotypes, themselves, their privilege, the cultural context in which they meet others, and be able to listen deeply to the story of others without judgment if they are to engage in profoundly human conversations. Robinson argued that if counselors' practice takes a constructionist perspective, they do not assume a preferred position in any dialogue; a constructionist perspective allows for a plurality of ways for viewing the world and shows how power, privilege, and disadvantage do not have to be deemed as absolute and fixed.

Doing something about it. In the above example of the two counseling professionals, if the African American described feeling marginalized by some experience on the street or at a conference, the Euro American might be curious about the colleague's experience and listen to learn from the experience being described. There are separate realities that open themselves up to being shared and experiences that simply have to be understood. A Chinese American graduate student described an incident in Portland, Oregon, where he was told, "Why don't you go back to where you came from." Having been born in the United States, he was where he came from—a country where racism is woven into the social fabric. When he conveyed his story to the predominantly Euro American class, the group recognized that such comments are not part of their day-to-day experience, their White privilege shields them from such day-to-day hostility, but their responsibility is to make their community safe for all. Rather than merely saying "thanks for sharing," the Euro American students were challenged to describe ways they could take hold of the loom and weave stories that recognize and appreciate diversity, as well as the need to advocate for the basic right for all people to be able to walk safely in their communities. A diverse community is a resilient community.

Poverty Discourse

While recognizing there are multiple dimensions to poverty besides having financial need, the poverty discourse reveals social distancing (Felner, 2006; Lott, 2002; Payne, 2003; Ungar, 2004). Look at poverty and children. In the United States, 17.8% of all children are poor; by race, 14.9% (over 8.6 million) of White non-Hispanic children, 30.9% (over 4.0 million) of Black children, and 28.0% (over 4.1 million) of Hispanic children are poor (Children's Defense Fund, 2005). All poor children experience various forms of social distancing, and all need multiple resources for overcoming poverty.

The nonpoor distance themselves from the poor in a variety of ways that result in exclusion, separation, devaluing, discounting, and classist discrimination (Lott, 2002). Such discrimination allows for the conscious and unconscious marginalization of the poor as expendable and undeserving individuals who are viewed as uneducated, unmotivated, lazy, unpleasant, angry, and stupid. As an individual problem, poverty can be described as resulting from behaviors rather than from the social and economic structures perpetuating poverty. For instance, schools perpetuate classism; the most profound memories a group of low-income women could recall about school were those of being treated with disdain and not being encouraged by teachers and school officials (Lott, 2002). Lott asserted that the middle-class discourse blames the poor for their position and maintains social policies that maintain distance from the poor. Class distancing includes within-race status groupings as well; for instance, some upper-strata Whites distance themselves from poor Whites by referring to them derogatorily as "White trash," "hillbillies," and so on.

Doing something about it. As important as financial resources are, poverty involves more than mere financial resources. Other resources include emotional, mental, spiritual, and physical support systems; relationship/role models; and knowledge of hidden rules (Payne, 2003). Understanding the hidden rules is one area that helps professionals foster collaborative dialogues with children, parents, and families. As mentioned earlier, middle-class formal-register discourse patterns are different from casual-register discourse patterns frequently used by the poor. In accounting for events, students, families, and communities using casual-register discourse patterns tell their stories in different, less direct ways. Listen, learn, and appreciate the richness found in the casual-register discourse patterns. At the same time, formal-register discourse patterns are given status by those in power in such settings as schools and some places of employment. For counselors and teachers, understanding the formal-register discourse pattern is privileged. This means entering collaborative dialogues with students, parents, and the community who use casual-register discourse patterns to let them in on a secret; learning the formal-register discourse pattern is one pathway for access to education and entrance into certain careers. This does not mean imposing middle-class values and forcing formal-register discourse patterns on all students; it means respectfully providing access to the resources necessary to enter into contexts that require a certain way of speaking. Fostering resilience requires flexibility and working with individuals, families, and communities to make choices as well as helping them to access and develop multiple resources to address their poverty.

Careers Discourse

A meaningful careers dialogue begins with hopes and dreams. Quattrociocchi and Peterson (1997) pointed to the need for parents, counselors, and teachers to see that hope emerges from finding passion for work and meaning embedded in those activities one chooses to do. Encouraging passion and meaningful participation can serve as guides when teachers, counselors, and parents collaborate their efforts in designing developmental comprehensive counseling and guidance programs that focus on helping youths to become aware, explore, and make decisions about possible career pathways (Herring, 1998; Silva & Radigan, 2004).

Yet, it is crucial for teachers, counselors, and parents to recognize that embedded in any careers discourse are assumptions about the nature of work, career opportunities, corporate power, political power, social comparisons, material accumulation, consumerism, leisure, and so on (Bowers, 2000, 2001; Schor, 1992, 1998). For instance, consider consumerism. Bowers (2001) pointed out,

> The more people rely on consumerism, the more they have to work in order to pay for their expanding dependencies: food preparation, entertainment, transportation, clothes, leisure time, health care, and so forth. And the more people have to work, the less time they have for parenting and involvement in activities that strengthen the reciprocal networks within the community. (p. 10)

Youth are developing career pathways in a historic period when the world and its diverse nations grapple with finite resources such as oil, communities face business upheaval such as jobs being outsourced to other countries, and individuals confront career uncertainty such as being laid off when businesses downsize. Given the changing nature of the world in which we live, fostering passion, hope, and career resilience is crucial to offer alternative discourses that empower youth with a sense of their competence and capacity to make it in an uncertain world (Brooks, 1994; Quattrociocchi & Peterson, 1997).

Doing something about it. Maintaining hope and passion is a challenge facing both adults and youth, and youth need models for finding passion and meaning in the activities they engage. First, start with fundamental questions: Why are we doing this? What are we trying to accomplish? Second, find role models who can show students how to maintain passion and find meaning in what they do. One model is the Edible Schoolyard concept that found root at Martin Luther King Jr. Middle School in Berkeley, California, a project that grew out of a relationship between nationally recognized chef, Alice Waters of Chez Panisse Restaurant, and the school principal, Neil Smith (Capra, 2002; Lappe & Lappe, 2002). The project also involves the Berkeley-based Center for Ecoliteracy and its cofounder, Fritof Capra (2002), who argued that resilient communities are ecologically and socially diverse communities that extend learning beyond the classroom. Those involved with the Edible Schoolyard see the project as an opportunity to integrate natural and human systems, as well as for youth to learn that life is about social and ecological connections, changes, and challenges (see http://www.edibleschoolyard.org or http://www.ecoliteracy.org/index.html).

The Edible Schoolyard integrates middle school classroom learning and competence, relationships developed among students and adults, and processes involved in growing and preparing food they will eat at school; in other words, the project is guided by a tradition that teaches the head, the heart, and the hand. If the plants get eaten by pests, students must use their heads to find out what happened, have heart not to be discouraged, and use their hands for replanting and maintaining viable solutions for controlling the pests. Thus, the students learn to work together to get up after they are knocked down and to find the resources necessary to overcome real-life problems. Students also learn that work is related to community practices that foster passion and hope. Obviously, when it comes to weeding, there might not be much passion, but when it comes to learning how to grow, prepare, serve, and share food, there is the hope that the results will taste good and be appreciated by others in the school community. By taking on a number of roles and responsibilities that result from participating in processes that range from mulching the soil to planting the seed to clearing the table in projects like the Edible Schoolyard, middle school students are taught fundamental skills related to career and life success. Fostering resilience means exposing youth to different career discourses, providing youth with the resources and opportunities to make connections, helping them to get back up after getting knocked down, experiencing competence in context, and making work-related adjustments in an ever-changing world.

APPROACHES TO FOSTERING RESILIENCE

This section discusses approaches that exemplify resilience practices. The approaches were selected because they illustrate how resilience practices support processes that begin with believing in individuals, families, schools, and communities. Each approach shows how fostering resilience is a collaborative process, respectful of multicultural perspectives, and hopeful about engaging youth as resources. Each approach shows the importance that significant relationships develop over time and include just hanging around, listening to another person's story, struggling with difficult tasks, and being alive in the moment with another person. Because a caring adult is the single consistent known factor fostering resilience found across the resilience literature (Benard, 2004; Benard & Marshall, 1997, 2001a, 2001b; Goldstein & Brooks, 2006; Gregg, 1996; Resnick et al., 1998; Reynolds, 1998; Ungar, 2004, 2005; Werner, 1996; Werner & Smith, 1982, 1992), these approaches describe ways caring adults can foster relationships with youth.

Structured Narrative

Youth have abundant opportunities to create stories of success or stories of woe. Because schools are one of those places where youths create stories regarding their abilities to learn to live, to learn to learn, and to learn to work, much of this section focuses on a written counseling intervention that can be adapted in different school contexts. The structured narrative intervention described here was developed in an effort to address the cold efficiencies necessitated from school counselor-to-student ratios that had been as high as 600:1 in the school in which the study took place.

The writing intervention was designed to help individual students cultivate positive stories about their possibilities for renewal and redirection and to provide normally anonymous students with voices during the critical transition into high school (Berliner, 1993; Lewis, 1995). Students had space to tell their stories and knew someone would take time to "listen" to every story by reading them. As a written approach, structured prompts help students to clarify or redefine personal narratives and to see possibilities for living with greater hope and power (Lewis, 1999, 2002).

As an intervention, the structured narrative grows out of a tradition that uses narrative and writing in counseling (Bruner, 1986, 1990; Desetta & Wolin, 1998; L'Abate, 1992, 1994; Lewis, 1999, 2002; Lifton, 1993; Monk, 1997; Monk et al., 1997; Riordan, 1996; White & Epston, 1990; Winslade & Monk, 1999, 2000). The nature of narrative is nonnormative and can be optimistic because every person has numerous possibilities for describing any experience. Structured narrative lessons may be used in a number of ways from lessons designed to enhance transition into high school to lessons created to enhance the mindful practice required by graduate students in the teaching and counseling professions. Such lessons orient individuals to requirements defined by organizations such as schools or prompt individuals to explore narrative possibilities that entering the teaching and counseling professions provide. The lessons may also be used to assess individuals who might need additional help in developing their writing skills, making connections with caring adults, or reaching personal and professional goals.

"A Write Way," consisting of six structured narrative lessons, was used to help youths during their transition into high school (Lewis, 1995, 1996, 1999). The prompts are formatted on a page to limit the length of responses, to make responding more attractive to reluctant writers, and to focus respondents on time-limited tasks (Lewis, 1999). The prompts must be adapted to local needs and range from closed-ended questions to short essays that provide opportunities for creative responses. For instance, in a study focusing on youths transitioning into high school, youths were asked the closed-ended question: "Do you plan to graduate from high school? Yes or No." They were also given the prompt: "Describe a time when you were a positive leader or participant at home, school, or elsewhere" (Lewis, 1995). The study concluded that creating structures helps students understand high expectations, but caring and supportive face-to-face relationships are equally important in helping students succeed (Lewis, 1995, 1999).

One purpose of "A Write Way" lessons was to help youths see possibilities for viewing or rewriting their school story in a positive way by assisting them to become oriented to the organizational demands of the school, document their own perspective about learning, and open them up to see more possibilities for living and learning in themselves. Prompts were designed to explore developmental possibilities and not leap to conclusions about themselves as learners or as people because drawing conclusions too quickly might close off possibilities for discovering the world and themselves anew (Claxton, 1997; Langer, 1997).

Structured narratives assist individuals in seeing that their life trajectories are not set by the stars or fates: People can change their life stories by discovering the possibilities inherent in coexisting alternative stories, and the vast majority of youths do become successful adults. Structured narratives attempt to give youths greater agency in describing their lives and are especially useful when youths see their life stories in the context of other life stories. In the end, stories supporting positive relationships or overcoming the odds are critical to children, and these stories encourage students to take action in constructing more satisfying personal stories about their experiences. Resilience is fostered by taking action developing one's own ever-changing story and by listening to the success stories of others. At the same time, as Parry and Doan (1994) stated, "No one ever fully becomes the author of her/his own story; any such assumption can only lead back to the illusions of control, individual autonomy, isolated selfhood, and single truth. The person goes forth instead to join with others in the universal human action of multiple authorship" (p. 43). The structured narrative and other active approaches facilitate youth in becoming agents in their own life narratives, and reflective approaches like bibliotherapy facilitate youth in valuing the stories of others (Brooks, 1997; Fredericks, 1997; Gladding, 1997; Rockwell, 1998). Stories can focus on individual youth in organizational contexts, but what is frequently called for is to change the beliefs guiding the organization.

Tapping Resilience: A Framework for Practice

Tapping resilience is an "inside-out process" according to Benard and Marshall (1997), who posited that individual change can be encouraged and successfully tapped with systems change and education rather than risk-focused therapeutic interventions. Benard, senior associate for development at WestEd, a nonprofit research, development, and service agency based in California, and Marshall, executive director at the University of Minnesota National Resilience Resource Center, have developed a tool for guiding school community systems change initiatives designed to foster resilience in children, youth, adults, and organizations. Successful systemic interventions, according to Benard and Marshall, are not quick fixes but require 3 to 5 years to implement. The framework is only one part of their comprehensive approach to establishing a resilience-operating philosophy in major systems, such as school districts. Ultimately, the purpose is to help adults foster the resilience of individuals by first learning to discover and tap their own resilience.

The planning framework encourages planners to focus on four areas: (a) the beliefs planners hold about the natural resilience and promise of human beings, (b) conditions for empowerment revealed in research and best practice, (c) program strategies to create these conditions that tap resilience, and (d) individual and societal outcomes to be evaluated as part of the process. This framework cuts new ground. It directs planners to explore their fundamental beliefs about human functioning and how it is fully realized. Traditional prevention planning guides, for example, have primarily focused on needs assessment, as well as community assets and deficits as precursors to poor youth outcomes. Staff development and technical assistance services offered by the National Resilience Resource Center use the framework for tapping resilience to shift the local focus from "at risk" to "at promise." Benard and Marshall suggested that our beliefs about the capacity of youth determine the degree to which youth are ultimately able to realize their own potential.

Belief is the foundation of the planning framework. Adults must "see how conditioned thoughts prevent us from recognizing students' natural strengths" (Benard & Marshall, 1997, p. 2). Understanding the power of conditioned, limiting beliefs and learning how to tap one's own resilience—the health of the helper—are of paramount importance. The key questions in the early planning phase include the following: What do we believe about the capacity for resilience in all people? Is it natural and inborn in all human beings even though it is not always realized or manifested in behaviors, skills, and characteristics? If we look through behaviors, can we discern health? Is it there waiting to be tapped?

With the framework, planners also study resilience research and best practices. What creates the conditions of empowerment? What taps resilience? What evidence supports our beliefs about human resilience? This phase of program development unites common sense, research, and program evaluation. What do we know works? Where is more study needed?

In simplest terms, Benard (2004) categorized the conditions of empowerment as three protective factors: caring relationships, high expectations, and meaningful opportunities for participation and contribution. The challenge is how to prepare adults to provide these critical protective factors: to be caring, to believe youth can succeed, and to invite genuine participation, even when behavior is highly problematic, past performance meager, and social behavior completely obnoxious or even personally threatening.

Based on an understanding of both beliefs and evidence, planners are guided to develop or select strategies that will tap resilience. After an exhaustive search for effective prevention and youth development strategies, Benard and Marshall (1997) settled on the health realization approach as one of the most efficient and effective ways school and community representatives could be taught to foster resilience. The experiences of a district student assistance director trained by the National Resilience Resource Center using this system's change approach in fostering resilience are described later.

The framework also pushes planners to think about evaluation from the very beginning.

Key questions to address include the following:

- What will it look like if a young person realizes his or her resilience?
- How will it look in adults?
- How does resilience look in a school, family, neighborhood, and community?
- Do we know what we are looking for and trying to make happen?
- Will we know healthy human functioning when we see it?

Resilience is not about labels. According to Benard and Marshall (1997), "To label a child, family, community or culture resilient—or not resilient—misses the mark. Labeling one child resilient implies another is not and contradicts the resilience paradigm in which resilience is part of the human condition and the birthright of all human beings" (p. 4).

Benard and Marshall (1997) called for a systems change that shakes traditional prevention, special education, and mental health services at the very core. Are human beings capable by nature? As professionals, can we teach healthy functioning and in an organized fashion tap resilience? Can school counselors be most effective if they point students to their health rather than cementing student, parent, and professional thoughts about diagnosis, labels, problems, risks, and looming danger and failure? The framework for tapping resilience can assist counselors, teachers, and parents in encouraging school leaders to begin a systematic paradigm shift to health rather than dysfunction. The next section builds on the approach that has reported success in challenging environmental contexts such as inner-city housing projects and other environments like public schools.

Health Realization: The Psychology of Resilience

Health realization begins with the assumption that every person has the innate capacity for mental health, common sense, and living in a mature and responsible manner regardless of their past and current circumstances (Mills, 1995). As a prevention and education approach, health realization focuses on inside-out change and innate resilience (Health Realization Institute, 2001; Mills, 1995; G. S. Pransky, 1998; J. Pransky & Carpenos, 2000; Sedgeman, 2003, 2005). This section shares the principles and the impact the health realization approach had on a high-risk public housing site in Miami, Florida, and concludes with stories from a district student assistance director from St. Cloud, Minnesota, who uses health realization to guide her work with youth.

Health realization's three guiding principles are described as providing a basis for the renaissance of psychology (G. S. Pransky, 1998). Mind, thought, and consciousness are described as the source of human experience and psychological functioning (Mills, 1995; G. S. Pransky, 1998; Sedgeman, 2003, 2005). *Mind* is defined as the source of thought and consciousness (G. S. Pransky, 1998). Like physicists' use of the terms *energy* or *life force*, mind is the power that makes thought and consciousness possible. "Thought as a function originates beyond our individual psychological personage just as the life force originates beyond our individual physical personage" (G. S. Pransky, 1998, p. 38). The brain processes thoughts moment to moment, giving each person a different experience of reality. "The function of thinking, the ability to think is universal, but the content of that thinking is determined by each person" (G. S. Pransky, 1998, p. 38). Consciousness is the process of experiencing our thinking through our senses. "If you mistakenly thought you were in extreme danger, you would have a sensory experience of being in danger" (G. S. Pransky, 1998, p. 39).

Mills (1995) and G. S. Pransky (1998) saw individual problems as emerging from the way people think about themselves, and well-meaning efforts that focus on symptom reduction usually fail to point people toward the principle of thought. Because individuals construct their personal realities, health realization focuses on those qualities of thought that elicit a sense of well-being in the moment and do not explore the psychic damage resulting from past trauma. Mills (1995) found that "people's ability to change their outlook, and the quality of their lives, varied directly in relation to their understanding of thought" (p. 61). The counseling process is approached as educational (Mills, 1995, 1996; G. S. Pransky, 1998). "We concluded that we could help people much more by teaching them to elicit their own intrinsic health, rather than encouraging them to explore their dysfunctions" (Mills, 1995, p. 53). Psychological difficulties were approached as products of thoughts rather than as existing independently and having a life of their own. The intervention shifted to eliciting and teaching people to understand the source of their mental health. Individuals were helped to understand moment-to-moment thought.

"People who understand what mental health is . . . live effortlessly in mental well-being" (G. S. Pransky, Mills, Sedgeman, & Blevens, 1997, p. 412). Innate resilience is accessed when individuals recognize that reality is formed from moment-to-moment thought, and that the trajectory of a life story can be changed by recognizing the role of thought in creating that story (Mills & Spittle, 1998, 2001). Teaching individuals about thought, coupled with community- building activities, has resulted in impressive preliminary results.

The model was used as a community intervention at the Modello-Homestead Gardens Project in Metro-Dade County, Florida. Staff were initially trained in health realization prior to conducting outreach activities. Outreach activities for project residents included initiating PTA meetings, parenting classes, and individual and family counseling sessions. Residents were taught about how their thinking formed their outlook and behavior, and to recognize the difference between their learned or conditioned thinking from the past and their more free-flowing, here-and-now, commonsense thinking. All staff contact with the residents was respectful, and residents were viewed as being resilient and healthy.

After 3 years, the program served 142 families and 600 youths. Resident surveys after 3 years revealed the following (Mills, 1997, p. 2):

- 87% of parents reported that their children were more cooperative and reported significantly less frustration with or less hostility toward their children.
- Over 60% of residents involved in programs became employed, from a baseline of 85% on public assistance.
- School discipline referrals and suspensions decreased by 75% from baseline at the middle school level.
- Attendance improved and school truancy rates improved around 80%.
- Parent involvement in schools improved by 500%.
- School failure dropped from 50% to 10%.
- Middle school teen pregnancy dropped 80%.
- The Homestead police reported that they had not had any calls for drug trafficking or criminal activities such as stolen cars of burglaries for almost a year.

In addition, parents reported they stopped hitting their children, they got more involved with schools, and the children improved their school performance. The community became a better place to live for both adults and youth. With communities typically defined as at risk, the health realization approach has been helpful in promoting positive individual and community outcomes. Other communities and programs reporting successes using health realization range from the South Bronx in New York to the Avalon Gardens in South Central Los Angeles (Mills, 1995). The work is not merely directed toward high-risk communities.

Jeanne Slingluff, the district student assistance director in St. Cloud, Minnesota, was trained in health realization by the National Resilience Resource Center to improve the performance of student assistance teams, committees of teachers, principals, social workers, counselors, and others who focus on improving the performance of at-risk youth. Slingluff initially found that some teams met on a regular basis and others did not and that their success could be improved. Two pilot schools with staffs of 15–20 were selected for health realization training.

Staff were taught to talk about innate resilience and to teach youth the source of thought. One teacher used peanut M&Ms to move youths along; there were many different colors but a common interior. Youths were taught about the "busy mind" during a group exercise designed to help them "get quiet" and "clear their minds" on their own. The exercise used the following steps:

- Students were told they had been given a call slip to the office to talk to the principal and to write down their thoughts on a half sheet of paper.
- After writing, the students broke into groups and summarized their thoughts on post-its.
- Then, individually and in small groups the students were asked to put their post-its on their teacher's glasses as she sat in front of the class. It was only moments before the teacher's glasses were covered with post-its and soon her nose and other parts of her face were covered as well. The teacher said, "When you have a busy mind, you can't see." A busy mind can lead to problems.

- Next, the teacher posed some questions: "What would happen if this student had to go to a test after meeting with the principal? How would the student perform?"
- Finally, the teacher asked: "What can you do to clear your thoughts?" The students offered suggestions and strategies for getting quiet. Some suggestions were as simple as to close one's eyes or to picture something relaxing.

Once the students have the concept, they know how to quiet their minds. Slingluff recommended that when the class starts to get overly busy, the teacher can simply tell the class in a respectful way, "Put your heads down just for a minute to clear your heads." The students stop and clear their minds. According to Slingluff, this occurs because teachers, counselors, and administrators believe in students' innate capacities. To illustrate her point, she shared the story of a young man who was sent to her after he expanded a one-paragraph assignment about conflict into a five-page catharsis that described his experience being sexually abused and having substance-abusing parents. The teacher was concerned that the student was suicidal. Slingluff said she normally would think in terms of getting an ambulance, but this time she decided to clear her own mind before meeting the young man and to listen deeply to him without letting her mind get busy. She listened to the child as he told his story. He brought in a friend when they met, and the three of them talked about strengths that could be found in the story he told. From there, he generated options and a plan for taking care of himself.

The data and the stories point to a variety of possibilities for the health realization model. As more schools experiment with the approach and more research studies are conducted, there will be more opportunities to assess the impact the approach has on individuals and organizations. The West Virginia Initiative for Innate Health at the Robert C. Byrd Health Sciences Center at West Virginia University has initiated a variety of research projects (see http://www.hsc.wvu.edu/wviih/). The next section discusses how practices that foster resilience have been directed toward youth with special needs.

RESILIENCE AND YOUTH WITH DISABILITIES

Youth with disabilities may require specific interventions in addition to enhancing schoolwide protective processes, such as designing multidisciplinary and multimodal teams to address the needs of the whole person. Counselors may be designated on those teams as strengths advocates and define an important role for looking for strengths. In fact, individualized educational programs (IEPs) can identify and maximize strengths without eliminating the need to detect and accommodate weaknesses that add to risk, and remediation efforts can be directed toward building up youth competence (Arman, 2002; Gregg, 1996; Mather & Ofiesh, 2006).

"Children with ADHD [attention-deficit hyperactivity disorder] exhibit many characteristics attributed to creativity and giftedness," according to Gregg (1996, p. 6). These children need help with their social skills, but more important, they need the unconditional support of at least one "prosocial adult who believes in the child" (Gregg, 1996, p. 6). Three conditions must be present to help foster resilience in youth with disabilities: (a) giving opportunity for bonding to take place; (b) increasing academic skills, social skills, and self-esteem to assist youth in successful bonding; and (c) recognizing and reinforcing accomplishments in a consistent and systematic manner (Gregg, 1996).

One responsible and caring adult—teacher, counselor, administrator, relative, or other core provider—can help a youth with disability to become more prosocial. Providing disabled youths with coaches or mentors is one way to help them initiate the bonding relationship. Supporting all facets of each youth's education from art to athletics to reading helps them to find and express possible talents and encourages them to work effectively with others. Developing creative "alternatives to suspension and expulsion—like community service—for all but the most serious offences, to keep from further isolating and alienating" youth enables them to remain attached to the school culture (Gregg, 1996, p. 9). Helping youths find something meaningful to do at school is critical to their future success. Besides the critical skill of reading (there is a high correlation between reading and income), youths must be encouraged to develop a passion for what they do.

In a similar vein, Brooks (1997) said it is vital to identify and reinforce a youth's strengths, because "every person possesses at least one small 'island of competence,' one that is, or has the potential to be, a source of pride and accomplishment" (p. 391). Teachers who are taught to show personal interest in youth by spending a few extra moments or writing words of encouragement on papers or in notes foster resilience in youth. Brooks (1997) stated, "Adults must constantly walk a tightrope when discipline is concerned, maintaining a delicate balance between rigidity and permissiveness, striving to blend warmth, nurturance, acceptance, and humor with realistic expectations, clearcut regulations, and logical and natural consequences" (p. 393). To foster resilience, schools must be made places where youth experience a growing sense of competence and resulting self-esteem (Brooks, 1994; Brooks & Goldstein, 2001).

ADAPTATIONS FOR DIVERSITY

Diversity is integral to resilience theory and practice because listening deeply to the experience of others opens up possibilities for relationships grounded in understanding and compassion. Each section in this chapter has raised concerns that call on counselors, teachers, parents, and others to become aware of their personal and professional discourse, to wrestle with the scourge of racism and poverty, and to listen deeply to the stories of their clients. Illustrated below, in an intervention integrating special needs and culturally appropriate practice, is an approach that sees the strengths in clients, that recognizes the self-righting capacities in all people, and that understands that resilience approaches are ultimately about empowerment.

Macfarlane (1998) developed an approach for Maori special education students in New Zealand that used culturally appropriate practice. "In New Zealand it is the dominant culture that provides the guidelines for conventional and special education, as well as the majority of professionals determining 'who is the problem'" (Macfarlane, 1998, p. 2). Like underrepresented youth in the United States, Maori youth frequently find themselves alienated from school. Macfarlane's (1998) bicultural approach begins with a meeting, or what the Maori refer to as *hui*, during which school officials and Maori youths could "speak with each other about difficult things in a way that avoids sliding back into the dynamics that gave rise to the problems in the first place" (p. 3). By moving away from punitive and judgmental discourse, the *hui* was designed to promote culturally appropriate alternatives to suspension-based community partnerships with the school. The conference was embedded in a culturally appropriate discourse that drew on Maori culture and values, such as the four principles of consensus, reconciliation, examination, and harmony. The conference started by saying in Maori and English, "I am who I am. You are who you are. Let us move together in tandem" (Macfarlane, 1998, p. 11). The youngsters were introduced to a new school discourse that placed their values and culture central to finding solutions to the problems being faced at school. The youths experienced discourse in school that embedded Maori students' success and well-being. It is an approach that does not leave youths out on their own but calls on adults and youths to move together in tandem. To foster resilience within all youth, we need to create systems that support the well-being of all youth (Rivera, 2004; Topf, Frazier-Maiwald, & Krovetz, 2004).

SUMMARY

The resilience literature offers counselors, teachers, parents, and other core providers a path back to their roots in education and development that takes into account ecosocial contexts. Resilience research supports an optimistic, longitudinal view of the person and offers a proactive approach for enhancing human development. Most radically, resilience adherents see people as having innate self-righting capacities for changing their life trajectories, a landscape that defines risks in ecosocial contexts rather than people, and an outlook that asks people to slow down enough to listen deeply to the stories embedded in everyday lives. Resilience-promoting interventions are primarily systemic; link individual, family, school, and community; and require counselors, teachers, parents, and others to consider the ground they stand on.

At the very least, fostering resilience in the schools is vital to the well-being of youth. Counselors, teachers, parents, and others can look to prevention and practices designed to foster resilience to help youth learn to live, learn to learn, and learn to work (Goldstein & Brooks, 2006; Ungar, 2004, 2005; Waxman, Padron, & Gray, 2004). Benard and Marshall (1997), Mills (1995), and G. S. Pransky (1998) offered approaches for teaching students to recognize their healthy thinking. Lewis (1996, 1999) offered a tool for helping students make successful transitions at predictable developmental points, such as the move from middle to high school, and pointed youths toward developing more empowering learning stories. Gregg (1996) and Brooks (1997, 2006) reminded counselors, teachers, parents, and others that every youth has a gift or an "island of competence" that can be tapped if one looks. Indeed, the resilience literature calls on counselors, teachers, parents, and others to see that all people have the innate capacity for self-righting and well-being and need support to tap it.

REFERENCES

Arman, J. F. (2002). A brief group counseling model to increase resiliency of students with mild disabilities. *Journal of Humanistic Counseling, Education, and Development, 41,* 120–128.

Atkinson, T., & Claxton, G. (2000). *The intuitive practitioner: On the value of not always knowing what one is doing.* Philadelphia: Open University Press.

Benard, B. (1991). *Fostering resiliency in kids: Protective factors in the family, school, and community.* Portland, OR: Northwest Regional Educational Laboratory.

Benard, B. (1994, December). *Applications of resilience: Possibilities and promise.* Paper presented at the Conference of the Role of Resilience in Drug Abuse, Alcohol Abuse, and Mental Illness, Washington, DC.

Benard, B. (1997). Changing the condition, place, and view of young people in society: An interview with youth development pioneer Bill Lofquist. *Resiliency in Action, 2*(1), 7–18.

Benard, B. (2004). *Resiliency: What we have learned.* San Francisco: WestEd.

Benard, B., & Marshall, K. (1997). *A framework for practice: Tapping innate resiliency.* Minneapolis: University of Minnesota, Center for Applied Research and Educational Improvement, College of Education and Human Development. Retrieved August 16, 2006, from http://education.umn.edu/CAREI/Reports/Rpractice/Spring97/framework.html

Benard, B., & Marshall, K. (2001a). *Competence and resilience research: Lessons for prevention.* Minneapolis: University of Minnesota, National Resilience Resource Center and the Center for the Application of Prevention Technologies. Retrieved August 17, 2006, from http://www.cce.umn.edu/pdfs/NRRC/capt_pdf/competence.pdf

Benard, B., & Marshall, K. (2001b). *Protective factors in individuals, families, and schools: National longitudinal study on adolescent health,* Minneapolis: University of Minnesota, National Resilience Resource Center for the Application of Prevention Technologies. Retrieved August 16, 2006, from http://www.cce.umn.edu/pdfs/NRRC/capt_pdf/protective.pdf

Berliner, B. A. (1993). *Adolescence, school transitions and prevention: A research-based primer.* San Francisco: Far West Regional Educational Laboratory.

Bertolino, B., & O'Hanlon, B. (2002). *Collaborative, competency-based counseling and therapy.* Boston: Allyn & Bacon.

Blum, R. W. (1998). Healthy youth development as a model for youth health promotion. *Journal of Adolescent Health, 22,* 368–375.

Bowers, C. A. (1997). *The culture of denial: Why the environmental movement needs a strategy for reforming universities and public schools.* Albany: State University of New York Press.

Bowers, C. A. (2000). *Let them eat data: How computers affect education, cultural diversity, and the prospects of ecological sustainability.* Athens: University of Georgia Press.

Bowers, C. A. (2001). *Educating for eco-justice and community.* Athens: University of Georgia Press.

Brooks, R. B. (1994). Children at risk: Fostering resilience and hope. *American Journal of Orthopsychiatry, 64,* 545–553.

Brooks, R. B. (1997). A personal journey: From pessimism and accusation to hope and resilience. *Journal of Child Neurology, 12,* 387–396.

Brooks, R. B. (2006). The power of parenting. In S. Goldstein & R. Brooks (Eds.), *Handbook of resilience in children* (pp. 297–314). New York: Springer Science+Business Media.

Brooks, R. B., & Goldstein, S. (2001). *Raising resilient children.* Lincolnwood, IL: Contemporary Books.

Bruner, J. (1986). *Actual minds, possible worlds.* Cambridge, MA: Harvard University Press.

Bruner, J. (1990). *Acts of meaning.* Cambridge, MA: Harvard University Press.

Capra, F. (2002). *The hidden connections: Integrating the biological, cognitive, and social dimensions of life into a science of sustainability.* New York: Doubleday.

Children's Defense Fund. (2005). *The state of America's children, 2005.* Retrieved August 15, 2006, from http://cdf.convio.net/site/DocServer/Greenbook_2005.pdf?docID=1741

Claxton, G. (1997). *Hare brain, tortoise mind: Why intelligence increases when you think less.* London: Fourth Estate.

Claxton, G. (1999). *Wise up: The challenge of lifelong learning.* New York: Bloomsbury.

Clinchy, B. M. (1996). Connected and separate knowing. In N. R. Goldberger, J. M. Tarule, B. M. Clinchy, & M. F. Belenky (Eds.), *Knowledge, difference, and power: Essays inspired by women's ways of knowing* (pp. 205–247). New York: Basic Books.

Deater-Deckard, K., Ivy, L., & Smith, J. (2006). Resilience in gene–environment transactions. In S. Goldstein & R. Brooks (Eds.), *Handbook of resilience in children* (pp. 49–64). New York: Springer Science+Business Media.

De Jong, P., & Berg, I. K. (2002). *Interviewing for solutions* (2nd ed.). Pacific Grove, CA: Brooks/Cole.

Desetta, A., & Wolin, S. (1998). Youth communication: A model program for fostering resilience through the art of writing. *Resiliency in Action, 3*(1), 19–23.

de Shazer, S. (1988). *Clues: Investigating solutions in brief therapy.* New York: Norton.

Duncan, B. (2005). *What's right with you: Debunking dysfunction and changing your life.* Deerfield Beach, FL: Health Communications.

Felner, R. D. (2006). Poverty in childhood and adolescence. In S. Goldstein & R. Brooks (Eds.), *Handbook of resilience in children* (pp. 125–148). New York: Springer Science+Business Media.

Fine, M. (1995). The politics of who's "at risk." In B. B. Swadener & S. Lubeck (Eds.), *Children and families "at promise": Deconstructing the discourse of risk* (pp. 76–94). Albany: State University of New York Press.

Fredericks, L. (1997). Why children need stories: Storytelling and resiliency. *Resiliency in Action, 2*(3), 26–29.

Friesen, B. J., & Brennan, E. (2005). Strengthening families and communities: System building for resilience. In M. Ungar (Ed.), *Handbook for working with children and youth: Pathways to resilience across cultures and contexts* (pp. 295–312). Thousand Oaks, CA: Sage.

Gergen, K. J., & McNamee, S. (2000). From disordering discourse to transformative dialogue. In R. A. Neimeyer & J. D. Raskin (Eds.), *Constructions of disorder: Meaning-making frameworks for psychotherapy* (pp. 333–349). Washington, DC: American Psychological Association.

Gladding, S. T. (1997). Stories and the art of counseling. *Journal of Humanistic Education and Development, 36,* 68–73.

Goldstein, S., & Brooks, R. B. (2006). *Handbook of resilience in children.* New York: Springer Science+Business Media.

Gregg, S. (1996). *Preventing antisocial behavior in disabled and at-risk students: Policy briefs.* Charleston, WV: Appalachia Educational Laboratory.

Health Realization Institute. (2001, July). *The understanding behind health realization, a principle-based psychology: Summary of clinical, prevention, and community empowerment applications. Documented outcomes.* Saratoga, CA: Author.

Herring, R. D. (1998). *Career counseling in schools: Multicultural and developmental perspectives.* Alexandria, VA: American Counseling Association.

Hubble, M. A., Duncan, B. L., & Miller, S. D. (1999). *The heart and soul of change: What works in therapy.* Washington, DC: American Psychological Association.

Jennings, R. G. (2001). Transformation of "at-risk" identity: Parental involvement and resiliency promotion. In L. Ramirez & O. Gallardo (Eds.), *Portraits of teachers in multicultural settings: A critical literacy approach* (pp. 153–165). Needham Heights, MA: Allyn & Bacon.

Jennings, R. G. (2003). An exploration of meaningful participation and caring relationships as contexts for school engagement. *California School Psychologist, 8,* 43–52.

Kaplan, H. B. (2006). Understanding the concept of resilience. In S. Goldstein & R. Brooks (Eds.), *Handbook of resilience in children* (pp. 39–48). New York: Springer Science+Business Media.

Kitashima, M. (1997). Lessons from my life: No more "children at risk". . . all children are "at promise." *Resiliency in Action, 2*(3), 30–36.

L'Abate, L. (1992). *Programmed writing: A paratherapeutic approach for intervention with individuals, couples, and families.* Pacific Grove, CA: Brooks/Cole.

L'Abate, L. (1994). *A theory of personality development.* New York: Wiley.

Langer, E. J. (1997). *The power of mindful learning.* Reading, MA: Addison-Wesley.

Lappe, F. M., & Lappe, A. (2002). *Hope's edge: The next diet for a small planet.* New York: Jeremy P. Tarcher/Putman.

Lewis, R. E. (1995). *A Write Way: Programmed writing effects on high school math students' attendance, homework, grades, and attributions.* Unpublished doctoral dissertation, University of San Francisco.

Lewis, R. E. (1996). Writing changes lives: Counselors and English teachers working together. *Oregon English Journal, 18,* 8–12.

Lewis, R. E. (1999). A Write Way: Fostering resiliency during transitions. *Journal of Humanistic Education and Development, 37,* 200–211.

Lewis, R. E. (2002). The structure narrative exercise. In G. McAuliffe & K. Eriksen (Eds.), *Teaching strategies for constructivist and developmental counselor education* (pp. 55–58). Westport, CT: Bergin & Garvey.

Lifton, R. J. (1993). *The protean self: Human resilience in an age of fragmentation.* New York: Basic Books.

Lott, B. (2002). Cognitive and behavioral distancing from the poor. *American Psychologist, 57,* 100–110.

Luthar, S. S., Cicchetti, D., & Becker, B. (2000a). The construct of resilience: A critical evaluation and guidelines for future work. *Child Development, 71,* 543–562.

Luthar, S. S., Cicchetti, D., & Becker, B. (2000b). Research on resilience: Response to commentaries. *Child Development, 71,* 573–575.

Macfarlane, A. H. (1998, November). *Hui: A process for conferencing in schools.* Paper presented at the Western Association for Counselor Education and Supervision Conference, Seattle, WA.

Marshall, K. (1998). Reculturing systems with resilience/health realization. In *Fourteenth Annual Rosalyn Carter Symposium on Mental Health Policy: Promoting positive and healthy behaviors in children* (pp. 48–58). Atlanta, GA: The Carter Center.

Marshall, K. (2001). *Bridging the resilience gap: Research to practice.* Minneapolis: University of Minnesota, National Resilience Resource Center and the Center for the Application of Prevention Technologies. Retrieved August 17, 2006, from http://www.cce.umn.edu/pdfs/NRRC/capt_pdf/bridge.pdf

Marshall, K. (2004). Resilience research and practice: National Resilience Resource Center bridging the gap. In H. C. Waxman, Y. N. Padron, & J. P. Gray (Eds.), *Educational resiliency: Student, teacher, and school perspectives* (pp. 63–86). Greenwich, CT: Information Age Publishing.

Masten, A. S. (1994). Resilience in individual development: Successful adaptation despite risk and adversity. In M. C. Wang & E. W. Gordon (Eds.), *Educational resilience in inner-city America: Challenges and prospects* (pp. 3–25). Hillsdale, NJ: Erlbaum.

Masten, A. S. (2001). Ordinary magic: Resilience processes in development. *American Psychologist, 56,* 227–238.

Masten, A. S., & Coatsworth, J. D. (1998). The development of competence in favorable and unfavorable environments. *American Psychologist, 53,* 205–220.

Mather, N., & Ofiesh, N. (2006). Resilience in children with learning disabilities. In S. Goldstein & R. Brooks (Eds.), *Handbook of resilience in children* (pp. 239–256). New York: Springer Science+Business Media.

McWhirter, J. J., McWhirter, B. T., McWhirter, A. M., & McWhirter, E. H. (1998). *At-risk youth: A comprehensive response—For counselors, teachers, psychologists, and human service professionals.* Pacific Grove, CA: Brooks/Cole.

Mills, R. C. (1995). *Realizing mental health: Toward a new psychology of resiliency.* New York: Sulzburger & Graham.

Mills, R. C. (1996, August). *Empowering individuals and communities through health realization: Psychology of mind in prevention and community revitalization.* Paper presented at the 104th Annual Convention of the American Psychological Association, Toronto, Ontario, Canada.

Mills, R. C. (1997). *Comprehensive health realization community empowerment projects: List of completed and current projects.* Long Beach, CA: R. C. Mills & Associates.

Mills, R. C., & Spittle, E. B. (1998). *A community empowerment primer.* Long Beach, CA: R. C. Mills & Associates.

Mills, R. C., & Spittle, E. B. (2001). *The wisdom within.* Renton, WA: Lone Pine.

Monk, G. (1997). How narrative therapy works. In G. Monk, J. Winslade, K. Crocket, & D. Epston (Eds.), *Narrative therapy in practice: The archaeology of hope* (pp. 3–31). San Francisco: Jossey-Bass.

Monk, G., Winslade, J., Crocket, K., & Epston, D. (Eds.). (1997). *Narrative therapy in practice: The archaeology of hope.* San Francisco: Jossey-Bass.

Myers, J. E., & Sweeney, T. J. (Eds.). (2005). *Counseling for wellness: Theory, research, and practice.* Alexandria, VA: American Counseling Association.

Palmer, P. J. (1998, December/1999, January). Evoking the spirit in public education. *Educational Leadership, 56,* 6–11.

Parry, A., & Doan, R. E. (1994). *Story re-visions: Narrative therapy in the postmodern world.* New York: Guilford Press.

Payne, R. K. (2003). *A framework for understanding poverty* (3rd ed.). Highlands, TX: aha! Process.

Pransky, G. S. (1998). *The renaissance of psychology.* New York: Sulzburger & Graham.

Pransky, G. S., Mills, R. C., Sedgeman, J. A., & Bleven, J. K. (1997). An emerging paradigm for brief treatment. In L. Vandecreek, S. Knapp, & T. L. Jackson (Eds.), *Innovations in clinical practice: A source book* (Vol. 15, pp. 401–420). Sarasota, FL: Professional Resource Press.

Pransky, J., & Carpenos, L. (2000). *Healthy thinking/feeling/doing from the inside out: A middle school curriculum and guide for the prevention of violence, abuse and other problem behaviors.* Brandon, VT: Safer Society Press.

Prilleltensky, J., & Prilleltensky, O. (2005). Beyond resilience: Blending wellness and liberation in the helping professions. In M. Ungar (Ed.), *Handbook for working with children and youth: Pathways to resilience across cultures and contexts* (pp. 89–104). Thousand Oaks, CA: Sage.

Quattrociocchi, S. M., & Peterson, B. (1997). *Giving children hope and skills for the 21st century.* Olympia, WA: WOIS/The Career Information System.

Resnick, M. D., Bearman, P. S., Blum, R. W., Bauman, K. E., Harris, K. M., Jones, J., et al. (1998). Protecting adolescents from harm: Findings from the National Longitudinal Study on Adolescent Health. *Journal of the American Medical Association, 278,* 823–832.

Reynolds, A. J. (1998). Resilience among Black urban youth: Prevalence, intervention effects, and mechanisms of influence. *American Journal of Orthopsychiatry, 68*, 84–100.

Riordan, R. J. (1996). Scriptotherapy: Therapeutic writing as a counseling adjunct. *Journal of Counseling & Development, 74*, 263–269.

Rivera, H. H. (2004). Resilient communities: The interplay between community development and child development through effective school reform. In H. C. Waxman, Y. N. Padron, & J. P. Gray (Eds.), *Educational resiliency: Student, teacher, and school perspectives* (pp. 227–246). Greenwich, CT: Information Age Publishing.

Robinson, T. L. (1999). The intersections of dominant discourses across, race, gender, and other identities. *Journal of Counseling & Development, 77*, 73–79.

Robinson, T. L., & Ginter, E. J. (1999). Introduction to the *Journal of Counseling & Development*'s special issue on racism. *Journal of Counseling & Development, 77*, 3.

Rockwell, S. (1998). Overcoming four myths that prevent fostering resilience. *Reaching Today's Youth, 2*(3), 14–17.

Saleebey, D. (Ed.). (1997). *The strengths perspective in social work practice* (2nd ed.). White Plains, NY: Longman.

Scherer, M. (1998, December/1999, January). Linking education with the spiritual. *Educational Leadership, 56*, 5.

Schor, J. B. (1992). *The overworked American: The unexpected decline of leisure.* New York: Basic Books.

Schor, J. B. (1998). *The overspent American: Why we want what we don't need.* New York: Harper Perennial.

Sedgeman, J. A. (2003). *The principles underlying life experience: The beauty of simplicity.* Morgantown: West Virginia University, Robert C. Byrd Health Sciences Center, Sydney Banks Institute for Innate Health. Retrieved August 17, 2006, from http://www.hsc.wvu.edu/wviih/pdfs/sedgeman/principlesRevised1-03.pdf

Sedgeman, J. (2005). Health realization/innate health: Can a quiet mind and a positive feeling state be accessible over the lifespan without stress-relief techniques? *Medical Science Monitor, 11*(12), 47–52.

Shure, M. B., & Aberon, B. (2006). Enhancing the process of resilience through effective thinking. In S. Goldstein & R. Brooks (Eds.), *Handbook of resilience in children* (pp. 373–396). New York: Springer Science+Business Media.

Silva, R., & Radigan, J. (2004). Achieving success: An agentic model of resiliency. In H. C. Waxman, Y. N. Padron, & J. P. Gray (Eds.), *Educational resiliency: Student, teacher, and school perspectives* (pp. 113–136). Greenwich, CT: Information Age Publishing.

Snyder, C. R., Feldman, D. B., Shorey, H. S., & Rand, K. L. (2002). Hopeful choices: A school counselor's guide to hope theory. *Professional School Counseling, 5*, 298–307.

Swadener, B. B., & Lubeck, S. (Eds.). (1995). *Children and families "at promise": Deconstructing the discourse of risk.* Albany: State University of New York Press.

Taub, J., & Pearrow, M. (2006). Resilience through violence prevention in schools. In S. Goldstein & R. Brooks (Eds.), *Handbook of resilience in children* (pp. 357–372). New York: Springer Science+Business Media.

Topf, R. S., Frazier-Maiwald, V., & Krovetz, M. L. (2004). Developing resilient learning communities to close the achievement gap. In H. C. Waxman, Y. N. Padron, & J. P. Gray (Eds.), *Educational resiliency: Student, teacher, and school perspectives* (pp. 205–226). Greenwich, CT: Information Age Publishing.

Ungar, M. (2004). *Nurturing hidden resilience in troubled youth.* Toronto, Ontario, Canada: University of Toronto Press.

Ungar, M. (Ed.). (2005). *Handbook for working with children and youth: Pathways to resilience across cultures and contexts*. Thousand Oaks, CA: Sage.

Valliant, G. (2002). *Aging well: Surprising guideposts to a happier life from the landmark Harvard Study of Adult Development*. Boston: Little, Brown.

Waxman, H. C., Padron, Y. N., & Gray, J. P. (Eds.). (2004). *Educational resiliency: Student, teacher, and school perspectives*. Greenwich, CT: Information Age Publishing.

Werner, E. E. (1989). Children of the garden island. *Scientific American, 260,* 106–111.

Werner, E. E. (1996). How children become resilient: Observations and cautions. *Resiliency in Action, 1*(1), 18–28.

Werner, E. E. (1998). Resilience and the life-span perspective: What we have learned—so far. *Resiliency in Action, 3*(4), 1, 3, 7–9.

Werner, E. E. (2006). What can we learn about resilience from large-scale longitudinal studies? In S. Goldstein & R. Brooks (Eds.), *Handbook of resilience in children* (pp. 91–106). New York: Springer Science+Business Media.

Werner, E. E., Bierman, J. M., & French, F. E. (1971). *The children of Kauai*. Honolulu: University of Hawaii Press.

Werner, E. E., & Smith, R. S. (1977). *Kauai's children come of age*. Honolulu: University of Hawaii Press.

Werner, E. E., & Smith, R. S. (1982). *Vulnerable but invincible: A longitudinal study of resilient children and youth*. New York: McGraw Hill.

Werner, E. E., & Smith, R. S. (1992). *Overcoming the odds: High risk children from birth to adulthood*. Ithaca, NY: Cornell University Press.

Werner, E. E., & Smith, R. S. (2001). *Journeys from childhood to midlife: Risk, resilience, and recovery*. Ithaca, NY: Cornell University Press.

Wesley, D. C. (1998, December/1999, January). Believing in our students. *Educational Leadership, 56,* 42–45.

Whiston, S. C. (2002). Response to the past, present and future of school counseling: Raising some issues. *Professional School Counseling, 5,* 148–155.

White, M., & Epston, D. (1990). *Narrative means to therapeutic ends*. New York: Norton.

Winslade, J., & Monk, G. (1999). *Narrative counseling in schools: Powerful and brief*. Thousand Oaks, CA: Corwin Press.

Winslade, J., & Monk, G. (2000). *Narrative mediation: A new approach to conflict resolution*. San Francisco: Jossey-Bass.

Wright, M. O., & Masten, A. S. (2006). Resilience processes in development. In S. Goldstein & R. Brooks (Eds.), *Handbook of resilience in children* (pp. 17–38). New York: Springer Science+Business Media.

PART TWO

■

Examining the Causes

Building on the foundational information in Part One, the four chapters that compose Part Two provide the reader with current and comprehensive information regarding the factors generally considered to be causal to the development of at-risk behaviors. It is important to keep in mind that it is impossible to draw a direct cause–effect relationship between any one of the four factors identified and any of the 10 issues or behaviors identified in Part III of this text. Authors in Part Two understand this and caution their readers to view these causal factors as both cumulative and cyclical. This perspective enhances the awareness that, taken separately, any one of these causal dimensions enhances the likelihood of at-riskness in youth. When viewed from a cumulative and cyclical perspective, the development of at-risk behaviors is almost inevitable.

Chapter 4, The Impact of Dysfunctional Family Dynamics on Children and Adolescents, spells out the various gradations of family dysfunctionality and couples this with case examples to enhance the readers' understanding. The author elaborates on five causal factors within the family dynamic that enhance the possibility of at-riskness in youth. In this presentation, the following areas are discussed: at-risk adults parenting, parental conflict, family denial, parentification of children, and serious illness and disability within the family. Again, case examples highlight these explanations. After presenting information on the incidence and impact of abuse and neglect, the chapter ends with a discussion of prevention approaches aimed at ameliorating the identified causal factors.

Chapter 5, "Who Cares What I Think": Problems of Low Self-Esteem, touches on a causal factor that permeates any discussion of at-risk behaviors. The information in this chapter includes not only definitions and indicators of low self-esteem but also causal factors from parental, social, psychological, physical, environmental, and cultural perspectives. Prevention approaches are presented from individual, family, school, community, and global perspectives. The case study, Project Reach, provides a realistic application of the approaches described.

Chapter 6, Preventing and Treating Mood Disorders in Children and Adolescents, approaches the topic by illuminating the complex issues of both definition and diagnosis. The case study of Esteban provides a central theme around which the authors present information dealing with causal factors from biological, psychodynamic, behavioral, cognitive, family systems, and interpersonal relationships models. Individual, family, school, and community-based prevention and treatment programs are presented. The chapter ends with a case summary and a discussion of "Teencourt," a program developed by the authors and utilized by first-time juvenile offenders between the ages of 8 and 17 who have committed a misdemeanor offense, status offense, or minor traffic violation.

Chapter 7, Stress and Trauma: Coping in Today's Society, begins by presenting the confusion surrounding the definition of stress and delineates the following perspectives on stress and traumatic stress: (a) stimulus-oriented views, (b) response-oriented views, (c) stress as a transaction between the person and the environment, and (d) trauma and posttraumatic stress. From this foundation, the authors present 13 factors that may have a causal relationship to the development of at-risk behaviors. Approaches to prevention from individual, family, school, and community perspectives are presented. A discussion of adaptations for diversity concludes the chapter.

CHAPTER 4

■

The Impact of Dysfunctional Family Dynamics on Children and Adolescents

Cass Dykeman

In their influential work on high-risk youth in schools, Pianta and Walsh (1996) defined the term *at-risk status* as the likelihood that a given youth will attain a specific outcome, given certain conditions. The specific outcomes of concern for this book were presented in Chapter 1. The present chapter explores dysfunctional family dynamics as the certain condition. In addition, the chapter also provides readers with some practical ways to prevent at-risk status in youth.

The level of dysfunction in families can vary widely. Moreover, severity of at-risk status runs parallel to severity of family dysfunction. Thus, in this chapter the multilevel nature of family dysfunction is defined and the causal factors are examined, that is, the specific family situations that both precede and fuel at-risk behaviors. The final section considers prevention at the individual, family, school, and community levels.

DEFINITIONS OF FAMILY DYSFUNCTION LEVELS

When examining the level of dysfunction in family dynamics, it is possible to classify families at either the moderate dysfunction level or the severe dysfunction level. This classification is important because severity level determines the appropriate interventions to be used. This section defines the distinctions between the moderate and severe levels of dysfunction to enable the reader to better understand family dynamics when planning work with youth and parents.

Moderate Dysfunction

In families at the moderate dysfunction level, each parent presents an appropriate image to the outside world. Hence, it is difficult to believe that there may be severe problems with one of the children. However, below the surface and hidden from the community views are problems that the family is not willing to reveal. The at-risk youth becomes the not-so-popular messenger, letting the community know that the family has secrets and is not perfect. The advantage of working with families at the moderate dysfunction level is that the adults are competent in dealing with the basic aspects of life (e.g., working, providing food). The following case study fleshes out how a family at this level of dysfunction may present itself:

CASE STUDY

Derek Jones was a high school junior who was failing several classes. In addition, he appeared quite depressed at times. Mr. and Mrs. Jones were college-educated professionals who were well known in the local community. In terms of family dynamics, Mr. Jones had a very bad temper and engaged in frequent arguments with Derek. When these arguments happened, Mrs. Jones always sided with Derek against his father. Mrs. Jones's consistent siding with Derek caused significant problems between Mr. Jones and Mrs. Jones. The tension in the Jones family came to a head when Derek's failing quarter grades were posted. After these grades were posted, Derek's counselor, Mr. Dykeman, called together Derek, his parents, and his teachers for a before-school conference.

At the start of the conference, Mr. and Mrs. Jones voiced their concern and willingness to do what was necessary to have Derek be more successful and happy. However, as the conference proceeded, the dysfunctional patterns of communication noted above appeared. In the middle of the conference, an intense argument on TV privileges broke out between Mr. Jones and Derek. After a few minutes of arguing, Derek broke down in tears. Derek's sadness led Mrs. Jones to put her arm around him and cry as well. At this point, the school bell rang, signaling 5 minutes until the start of first period for Derek and his teachers. The teachers immediately got up and headed for their classes. After his tears had stopped, Derek was given a hall pass and left for first period.

With Derek gone, Mr. Jones expressed his remorse for fighting with Derek and his frustration that Mrs. Jones did not enforce the TV rules when he was gone. Mr. Dykeman first empathized with Mr. Jones's remorse and frustration as well as Mrs. Jones's sadness. Then he noted that the Joneses had problems that were common to parents of teenagers and that were fixable. Mr. Dykeman referred the Joneses to Ms. Macintosh, a local family counselor known for brief and effective treatment of families with communication problems. Because Mr. Dykeman couched his description of the Joneses' difficulties as both normative and fixable, the Joneses were able to consider his advice without further loss to their self-esteem or self-efficacy. Indeed, the Joneses appeared grateful for Mr. Dykeman's suggestions as well as his confidence in their ability to heal their family.

In family therapy, Mr. and Mrs. Jones began to understand the need for cooperation between them if there was to be any change in Derek. After a few weeks, Mr. Jones began to simply talk with Derek rather than yell. Mrs. Jones no longer took Derek's side during arguments and did not undercut Mr. Jones's attempts to enforce appropriate rules. Derek eventually quit using one parent against the other to get his way. Moreover, Derek and his father were able to establish a satisfying relationship with each other.

Severe Dysfunction

In the family at the severe dysfunction level, one or more adults may exhibit many at-risk behaviors such as substance abuse. In work with severely dysfunctional families, adults may often be found to be functioning at a less capable level than their children. This collapse of adult–child differentiation in functioning limits the extent to which one can effectively intervene in the life of an at-risk child. The following case study illuminates this difficulty:

CASE STUDY

Susan Smith was a high school junior with a long history of school attendance problems. She lived with her mother, Ms. Baker, and her mother's new live-in boyfriend, Mr. Green. Susan has never met her biological father. Both Ms. Baker and Mr. Green currently abuse alcohol and marijuana. On more than one occasion, Susan and her mother smoked marijuana together. Ms. Baker and Mr. Green are both currently unemployed and live on public assistance. The relationship between Ms. Baker and Mr. Green has been conflictual since he moved in 6 months ago. The two have frequent battles over money, friends, and drugs.

In the summer between her sophomore and junior year, Susan lived with her Aunt Joan and her older cousin Katie in a town on the other side of the state. Susan was impressed by how Katie seemed to have her life all together. When Susan moved back home at the end of the summer, she vowed to get her act together. In contrast to previous years, Susan's attendance during the first quarter of her junior year was excellent. She was well liked by both teachers and peers and maintained a B average. Susan dreamed of going to the local community college to study fashion merchandising like her older cousin Katie. However, as winter quarter began, the fighting at home between Ms. Baker and Mr. Green worsened exponentially. As Susan sought to escape this fighting by smoking marijuana, her attendance began to slide.

Concerned about the slip in attendance of a talented fashion design student, Susan's consumer and family life teacher asked if the school counselor, Mr. Dykeman, would talk to Susan. Mr. Dykeman called Susan into his office and expressed the concern everyone at school had about Susan's sliding attendance. Susan claimed that she had been feeling ill lately and that other than that, everything was fine. She rebuffed all of Mr. Dykeman's gentle invitations to talk about the issues that concerned her. After the conference with Susan, Mr. Dykeman attempted to call Ms. Baker. However, Ms. Baker's phone had been disconnected. Mr. Dykeman sent a letter to Ms. Baker asking her to contact him. However, she never responded to that letter. By the middle of winter quarter, Susan had stopped coming to school completely.

CAUSAL FACTORS

Before working with at-risk youth, one must understand how dysfunctional family dynamics can lead to specific destructive behavioral patterns in youth. Dysfunctional family dynamics create a noxious emotional atmosphere for at-risk youth. Such an atmosphere produces severe personal stress and emotional upheaval. Moreover, this highly charged emotional atmosphere causes the at-risk youth to accommodate his or her behavior in such a way as to reduce the internal stress and upheaval. Accommodating the stress and upheaval creates problem behaviors such as poor school performance depression, anorexia, loss of control, and myriad other at-risk behaviors. This section first examines specific family factors that lead to these problem behaviors and then the incidence and impact of abuse, neglect, and poverty.

Specific Family Factors

Several specific family factors contribute to youth at-riskness. These factors include at-risk adults who become parents, parental conflict, family denial, parentification of children, and serious illness and disability.

At-Risk Adults Parenting

We can gain critical insight on the direction and depth of the problems exhibited by an at-risk youth through cultivating an awareness of the problems of the youth's parents. The problematic behaviors of the at-risk youth and his or her at-risk parents may differ, but the end goal of these separate behaviors typically runs parallel. The following case study illustrates this point.

CASE STUDY

Bob Adams was a 45-year-old father of two who had been married for 24 years to Tern. Both were professional people with highly responsible jobs. Bob had a severe drinking problem that had affected the family for years. In addition, Bob had been consistently impervious to suggestions that he address his problem. Bob and Tern's two daughters, ages 17 and 19, were both high achievers in high school. Despite Bob's problems, the Adamses appeared as a "picture-perfect" family to other members of the community. However, the family's underlying dysfunction emerged when the oldest daughter Mary left for college.

Although initially excited to go off to college, Mary soon found herself consumed with worries about her family; she had always been the one to smooth over conflicts between her parents. She found that these worries left her little time for peers or academics. She returned home after passing only one course during the fall quarter.

After being home for the entire year, she applied to another college and went off to school once again. Needless to say, she could not stay at the new college either, returning home after only a few weeks. At about this time, Bob had a severe alcoholic episode, having to be brought home in a taxi one evening because of his drunkenness. He fought with his wife and destroyed the house before being hospitalized for several days. He checked out of the hospital before treatment was completed and against medical advice.

Mary's reaction to all of the confusion in her life was to take a bottle of pills. Her attempt at suicide was a cry for help, one that almost cost Mary her life. In trying to fix her parents and their marriage, she became unable to manage her own life.

This case demonstrates several important points. First, the father's severe drinking problem both produced and directed his daughter's at-risk behavior. Second, by never getting her life together, Mary avoided leaving home and abandoning her parents for whom and to whom she felt responsible. As many family counselors would conclude, Mary rescued the marriage and family by putting herself at risk.

Thus, if a counselor attempted to work with Mary's suicidal feelings independent of her family role as the rescuer, the counseling would be doomed to fail.

One final note of importance needs to be mentioned. The transmission of at-risk tendencies from parent to child is much easier to see in families at the severe dysfunction level. Families at the moderate level generally possess the skills to hide problems. The at-risk behaviors in youth from families at this level can appear to exist without cause. However, rarely does an at-risk youth emerge *sui generis* (i.e., self-generated). While keeping mindful that exceptions do exist, one should always seek to understand the underlying family aspects of a youth's at-risk behavior. Otherwise, work with at-risk youth may never amount to more than the bandaging of symptoms.

Parental Conflict

If parents are having difficulty processing conflict between them, the situation is likely to deteriorate into communication problems between the parents. This problem also extends to communication problems between parents and children. Secrets begin to exist between the parents. In the conflict between parents, children often become the emotional pawns in the intensified atmosphere of the home. Moreover, a direct relationship exists between both verbal and nonverbal parent conflict and at-risk behavior in children (Amato & Cheadle, 2005; Cummings, Goeke-Morey, & Papple, 2004).

Conflict between parents also leads to power struggles in parenting children. Each parent attempts to structure his or her relationship with the child as an individual instead of as a member of the marital unit. Loyalty issues are pressed onto the child. For example, a teenager comes home after curfew and is grounded for a week by the father. However, after 2 days the mother allows the teenager to visit friends but says, "Don't tell Dad!" This pattern of deceit between parents empowers the at-risk youth in two ways. First, the youth learns not to follow rules, and second, the youth learns to be deceitful. As family functioning begins to deteriorate, the youth will begin to demonstrate increasingly maladaptive behavior (Sourander et al., 2006). The following case study concretizes this process.

CASE STUDY

James Cooper was a 10-year-old fourth grader who was in frequent difficulties at school and in the community. His teacher reported him to be an aggressive, high-energy boy with a low attention span. However, his level of inappropriate conduct was never very severe until the day he assaulted another student on the playground during recess. The student he assaulted had to go to the emergency room for four stitches. At that time, James's parents were forced to enter counseling to assist him with his anger management program. Completion of this anger management program was the main prerequisite for the school district's lifting of James's suspension. In the family counseling part of the anger management program, it was immediately evident that Mr. and Mrs. Cooper had a very long history of marital and parental discord. Mr. Cooper was upset with Mrs. Cooper over numerous issues, which included an affair, overspending, poor discipline of the children, and meddling in-laws. Both Mr. and Mrs. Cooper reported that their fighting had escalated recently. Given the parents' marital trauma, the assault incident can be viewed as the inevitable act of a high-energy, aggressive boy who needed to create a major problem to bring his parents back together.

This brief example demonstrates several important points about the struggles faced by at-risk youth. First, it is difficult to discipline a youth having severe difficulties without complete cooperation between the parents. One parent undercutting the effectiveness of the other makes it impossible to bring about change in the family and creates a situation in which the youth can become at risk. Second, loyalty issues between family members can create severe problems if the loyalty lines are inappropriately drawn (Visher & Visher, 1996). A youth who is dependent on one parent can become angry with the other parent and attempt various at-risk behaviors. In other words, Parent A will fight Parent B through the at-risk behavior of their children.

Third, a youth's temperament will shape the at-risk behaviors the youth uses to heal family trauma. For example, an aggressive youth may choose fighting, whereas a depressed youth may choose a self-destructive act such as a suicide attempt. Finally, parental conflict can lead to divorce. To oversimplify a difficult and complex problem, let us say that a divorce happens when two people fail to communicate and resolve conflicts. Following divorce, if a youth exhibits at-risk behaviors, it usually takes a significant problem to force the parents to face the gravity of the issues. Amato and Cheadle (2005) reported that parental conflict after divorce is a significant problem for children—a problem because youth give voice to their concerns over parental conflict through at-risk behaviors.

Family Denial

Denial is the defense mechanism whereby problems and their intensity are ignored or redirected. Denial is acted out in two ways within families. The first way denial is enacted is by burying one's head in the sand, that is, ignoring the reality of the situation. The second way denial is enacted is by finger pointing, that is, blaming other people or events for one's problems. Both methods of using denial lead to youth becoming at risk. The following case study illustrates the effect of denial on the development of at-risk youth.

CASE STUDY

Kathy was a 17-year-old senior who had become increasingly defiant with her parents. The parents attributed the defiance to Kathy's boyfriend of the past 8 months. She began to stay out beyond her assigned curfew, her grades at school declined, and her attitude at home became progressively negative. At various times over the end of her junior year and the beginning of her senior year, Kathy would become ill and was unable to work or attend school. Her parents suspected that she was pregnant, but Kathy denied that she was. Throughout this period of time, the parents were concerned about Kathy's relationship with her 20-year-old boyfriend. They had frequent violent arguments with Kathy about her need to see him less or break off the relationship.

During the 2nd month of her senior year, Kathy had a baby. The parents never knew she was pregnant until the night Kathy's water broke at home. After being rushed to the hospital, Kathy gave birth to a baby with numerous disabilities who lived only several months. During this time, the parents and Kathy continued to battle over the relationship with the baby's father.

This tragic case study presents the ultimate example of denial of a major problem while focusing on a serious but tangential problem. Kathy's parents ignored the issue of the pregnancy even though they strongly suspected something was physically wrong with their daughter. Rather than having their daughter examined by a physician, the parents went along with Kathy's denial. Instead of directly confronting issues with children, parents tend to allow them to have the power over major decisions in their lives. Kathy's parents wanted to believe that she was fine but knew in their own minds she was not. Therefore, not wanting to risk a battle with Kathy, they denied that anything was wrong and placed their daughter in the at-risk category.

If Kathy's parents had become involved earlier in the process, a tragedy could have been avoided. Because the parents could only focus on Kathy's relationship, they could not see the larger picture. Kathy's relationship with her boyfriend was symbolic of the gap in the relationship between herself and her parents. Specifically, Kathy's parents had lost control of their relationship with Kathy, and they could not face their responsibility in having let this loss occur. Kathy's parents used denial to avoid examining the problems they had and placed all the blame on the boyfriend. Because of their strong denial, they placed Kathy at risk.

Parentification of Children

One dysfunctional pattern of family dynamics that begins in the early years of childhood is parentification of children. This pattern occurs when parents give responsibilities and privileges to younger children that would be more appropriate for older children or adults. Young children, by their actions and requests, maintain the control of the household and frequently dictate the mood of the entire family. Parents, fearful of disrupting the family calm, refrain from effective discipline techniques. Thus, the children gain control of the family.

Parentified children are placed in situations in which they are given the power to make decisions that belong with the parents. The parents, by giving the power to the child, abdicate their responsibility for protecting the child from potentially dangerous situations. The following case study helps demonstrate this parentification process.

CASE STUDY

Ray, a 10th grader, was referred by a student to Mrs. Wall, an English teacher and the Natural Helpers adviser. Ray was referred by the student because he was overheard saying that he wanted to die. After talking with Ray, his school counselor assessed that Ray was at moderate risk for suicide and thus immediately contacted Ray's parents. The school counselor referred Ray's parents to three private practice counselors known for their strong skills with adolescents. Ray objected to the counseling and said he would not go to see anyone. The parents contacted one of the referred counselors and asked for a suggestion as to how they could get him into counseling. The counselor told them to tell Ray that he had no choice in the matter and that he had to go to counseling. This approach worked, and Ray and his family appeared at the counselor's office for help.

Ray was seen for three sessions alone and for one family session. After these sessions, the counselor provided the family with his feedback, suggesting that Ray remain in counseling to deal with his depression, mood swings, and suicidal tendencies. The parents were told that some family counseling would help them to deal more effectively with Ray. After the feedback session, the mother and father said they would let Ray decide because the counseling was for him! Even though they were told about Ray's depression and suicidal ideation, they felt Ray had to make the decision because they did not want to have to "fight" with him to get him to attend counseling sessions.

In this instance, the parents left the well-being of the child with the child rather than taking control of the situation. By permitting the child to make such decisions, the at-risk status increases significantly. The parentification process not only affects dramatic issues such as suicide but also accelerates the at-risk status of youth confronting common teenage problems such as academic failure or alcohol use.

This parentification is a common by-product of divorce. As the conflict between divorcing parents escalates, more and more self-care is left with the child. In addition, some very young children are even expected to carry the burden for maintaining the well-being of the parents during the separation and divorce process. Life is fine as long as the child is behaving, giving attention to the parents, and causing no apparent difficulty. The burden can become intense as the child grows and matures. It is very tiring to always be happy, provide love for a parent, care for other children, and be adultlike. In these cases, the parents often report that the child has never been a difficulty but the ideal child who always took care of everything.

Children and youth want to be in control of the decisions that affect their lives and will take every opportunity to gather more power. Parents must be encouraged to involve their children in the decision-making process but be reminded that involvement is different from making a final decision. Final decisions belong to the parents, not the children. When the child makes the choices alone, at-risk status is inevitable.

Serious Illness and Disability Within the Family

Serious illness and disability can catapult a family into a trauma response and affect their ability to maintain healthy coping. Consider an example in which the father has a newly diagnosed heart condition but denies his symptoms to his family. He might fear his role as the provider would be questioned. If the parents are unable to discuss the issue with each other or with the children, the family members are left more vulnerable to fears and fantasies about how bad the situation is. As secrecy or even dishonesty or deceit increases, these families become more at risk and sensitive at home, work, or school.

Kazak, Christakis, Alderfer, and Coiro (1994) discussed the impact of illness in families. They suggested that (a) family members tend to overreact to simple problems, (b) parents are protective of the children, and (c) in general, the entire family is acutely sensitive. In an attempt to cope with this sensitivity, the family will focus on less serious problems and concerns. Thus, denial becomes a major risk aspect. This denial can be considered dysfunctional. However, it can also be understood as an expected part of the reaction to trauma (Aguilera & Messick, 1986).

Typically, families will go through a series of stages in coping with the shock of the diagnosis of an illness, disability, hospitalizations, and treatment. There is a movement from defensive coping strategies such as denial or anger toward more functional ways of coping. The families at greatest risk are those unable to move toward the last stage. They remain mired in defensive coping patterns that affect all members in negative ways. The following case study illustrates the high at-risk status of families unable to address a child's suffering.

CASE STUDY

Jeff Stone was a 7-year-old brought to the Riverbend Pediatric Hospital for rehabilitation surgery. The surgery was for a hand deformed at birth that left it shrunken and twisted. All Stone family members referred to this appendage as the "paw." When Jeff experienced anxiety about reconstructive surgery, the Stones were unable to discuss the hand with him, because this issue had been avoided from the time of Jeff's birth. Mr. and Mrs. Stone felt tremendous guilt over their boy's disability. The consulting counselor to the surgery unit, Mrs. Appleton, supervised a counseling intern to develop an initial assessment of the boy's view of the situation. Because it is often easier to draw a problem than to discuss it, using art materials is an effective method for assessment and offers a rich symbolic view of the patient's experience of hospitalization and trauma (Appleton, 2001). The counseling intern suggested that Jeff draw a person. Jeff drew an image of a teddy bear with a deformed paw. During the family interactions, Mrs. Appleton also observed the defensive nature of the family coping.

After the initial assessment, Mrs. Appleton worked with the counseling intern to create a plan that would increase family communications and address denial. In supervision, they invented a game called "Secrets." In this game, the family members examined the names they gave things that bothered them at home, school, or work. While playing the game, Mrs. Stone was able to disclose that the "paw" was her way to avoid discussing the boy's disability or embarrassing him or the other family members. Mrs. Stone hoped that the reference to a "paw" was easier on Jeff and the family. When this issue arose, the father and siblings spoke of the "paw" disparagingly. With the intern's assistance, Jeff was able to share his feelings of inferiority in the family and of feeling like a nonperson (or stuffed bear). Through these disclosures, it was clear no one in the family was comfortable with the term "paw."

In follow-up counseling, medical staff members were accessed for a discussion about the diagnosis and plans for rehabilitation of Jeff's weak hand. Mrs. Appleton and the intern discussed the ways the hospital team might help the family to discuss the disability openly during medical and counseling interventions. In this way, the multidisciplinary team of doctors, nurses, physical therapists, counselor, and intern shared methods to encourage the family to practice more open communication during and after the surgery process. This support proved effective, and the Stones began to learn a new way to cope with difficult issues by discussing them together and with others.

As the case example demonstrates, the family faced with an illness or disability must handle many emotionally charged issues. Because there is relatively little support in the medical setting for such issues, multidisciplinary teams that include counselors and appropriate referral are critical. In most instances, problematic family issues that existed before the medical crisis are exaggerated during the trauma of illness, loss of function, surgery, and other medical interventions. Fortunately, diagnosis and medical intervention also provide an opportunity for change. In states of crisis and trauma, otherwise rigid or resistant families may be responsive to psychosocial resources. In this way, the danger of the illness can provide new opportunities for change in the communication and coping systems within the family.

The Incidence and Impact of Abuse and Neglect

Atrocities of violence against children are among the most difficult to discuss. However, abuse is a historical problem that does not go away. In fact, as professionals are trained to understand and report abuse, the number of reported cases has risen dramatically. A consideration of the incidence of abuse and neglect will help us recognize those children who are at the highest risk for maltreatment.

In 1973, the Child Abuse Prevention and Treatment Act (Public Law 93-247) defined the legal responsibilities of health care providers encountering child abuse or neglect. Intervention is defined as social, legal, medical, or any combination of the aforementioned. Congress declared that child abuse and neglect means the physical and mental injury, sexual abuse, negligent treatment, or maltreatment of a child under age 18 by a person who is responsible for the child's welfare under circumstances that indicate the child's health or welfare is thereby harmed or threatened. Every state now has within its statutes a legal definition of abuse.

Incidence

The United States Congress mandated a report documenting the incidence of child abuse and neglect in this country. This report is called the National Incidence Study of Child Abuse and Neglect (NIS). Professionals across a spectrum of schools and agencies act as sentinels and gather data about abuse incidences. In this way, the NIS estimates provide a more complete measure of the scope of child abuse and neglect known to community professionals that may not be included in official statistics. The most recent NIS study is NIS-3 (Sedlak & Broadhurst, 1996).

NIS-3, which covered a 7-year period, reported an alarming increase in the incidence of child abuse and neglect. This report revealed that the number of abused and neglected children had nearly doubled. An estimated 1.5 million children in the United States were abused or neglected. Physical abuse had almost doubled, and sexual abuse more than doubled. The number of children seriously injured and endangered had quadrupled.

The NIS-3 study also discovered there were specific characteristics of the abused and neglected children and families in which these behaviors occurred most often. The factors that contributed to the highest incidence of abuse included the child's age, the child's gender, and the child's family in terms of income and other family demographics. Race was not a significant factor in the incidence of maltreatment or injury.

Child's age. There is little reporting of sexual abuse in children from age 1 to 3, but the number of children vulnerable to sexual abuse is consistent from age 3 onward, with reports of sexual abuse distributed evenly across these children. This flattening of the age differences is provocative and suggests a broad range of vulnerability for sexual abuse starting in preschool. In terms of neglect, there is a near linear comparison between the child's age and risk for maltreatment. However, the lower incidence of reported abuse in young children might reflect undercoverage of these children. As children mature, they are involved with an increasing number of community professionals who can observe them and make appropriate investigations. They may also be better able to escape, retaliate, or ask for help.

Child's gender. Girls are most vulnerable to sexual abuse, at a rate three times higher than boys. Because serious injury can accompany sexual abuse, this accounts for higher incidence rates for injury among girls. Boys are at greater risk for other forms of maltreatment and are 24% more likely than girls to be emotionally neglected and to suffer serious injury resulting in death.

Child's family. The demographics of the family are also linked to incidences of child maltreatment (Sedlak & Broadhurst, 1996). Children of single parents have a 77% greater risk of being harmed by physical abuse and an 87% higher risk of physical neglect than children living with both parents. Children in the largest families are physically neglected at about three times the rate of those who are single children. Children in poverty (annual family income of less than $15,000) are 25 times more likely to suffer some form of maltreatment than children in families who earn more than $30,000 per year. Moreover, poverty is directly linked with the incidence of sexual abuse and serious harm. Children in the lowest income families are more likely to be sexually abused and suffer serious injury from maltreatment.

Impact

Abuse is an issue of control and power, whether it is perpetrated within or outside of the family. The impact of physical and sexual abuse is directly related to intensity, the amount of coercion, and level of conflict involved. Webb and Terr (1999) distinguished between two kinds of trauma. A single traumatic event in an otherwise normal life is called Type I trauma, and the effects of prolonged and repeated trauma are called Type II trauma. Within families, children are more likely to suffer Type II trauma and endure repeated and anticipated pain, violence, and chaos. The Type II syndrome, according to Webb and Terr, includes coping mechanisms of denial, psychological numbing, self-hypnosis, dissociation, and extreme shifts between rage and passivity.

When observing children suspected of being maltreated, one needs to understand the form their trauma and symptoms take. According to Gil (1996), children will exhibit the impact of abuse and neglect through either internalized or externalized behaviors. Children who cope through internalized behavior negotiate the pain by themselves. They are likely to avoid interaction and appear depressed, joyless, phobic, hypervigilant, and regressed. Given the stress of coping without help, these children manifest physical symptoms including sleep disorders and somatic problems (e.g., headaches and stomachaches). Additionally, they withdraw emotionally and may appear overly compliant. In more severe cases they disassociate, self-mutilate, and become suicidal. They are also likely to use drugs to numb both the physical and emotional pain of abuse. Conversely, children who cope through externalized behavior direct their pain outwardly and toward others. They express emotions that are often hostile, provocative, and violent. They may kill or torture animals, destroy property through fire settings, and exhibit sexualized behaviors. However, the effects are not, for the most part, multigenerational.

Physical abuse effects. Physically abused children have deficits in gross motor development, speech, and language. The impact of physical abuse includes psychic trauma, chaos, rejection, deprivation, distorted parental perceptions, and unrealistic expectations. Further disruptions of family life occur with hospitalizations, separation, foster placement, and frequent home changes.

At a minimum, children hurt by others suffer an impaired capacity to enjoy life. When the abuse is more extreme, psychiatric symptoms will appear (e.g., enuresis, hyperactivity, and bizarre behavior). In school, abused children who exhibit more internalized behaviors will present learning problems, compulsiveness, hypervigilance, and suicidal tendencies. Children who cope with abuse through more externalized behaviors are oppositional. Typically, these children have problems managing aggressive behavior and cannot establish relationships with other children (Kereste & Milanovi, 2006).

Sexual abuse effects. The impact of child sexual abuse can be measured along a continuum from neutral to very negative (Friedrich, 2002). At its extreme, the effects of sexual abuse manifest in dissociation. The term *dissociation* refers to a disturbance in the normal functions of identity, memory, and consciousness (American Psychiatric Association, 2000). Dissociation occurs when the child is exposed to overwhelming events that result in extreme feelings of helplessness. In the traumatic situation, the child attempts to cope by dissociating the self from the act being perpetrated. This dissociation becomes part of the child's development and results in long-term difficulties. In this way, internalized behaviors such as eating disorders, substance abuse, and depression can be understood as behavioral read-outs of dissociation. Externalized behaviors accompanying sexual abuse include school difficulties, anger, running away, delinquency, and sexualized behaviors.

Sexualized behavior is an externalized behavior that is shaped by sexual experiences, feelings, and attitudes that occur in the abuse process (Finkelhor, 1984). Early and manipulated exposure to sex may result in a child's excessive or preoccupying interest in it. There is a difference between normal sexual curiosity and sexualization. Unlike other children, the sexualized child (a) completes intercourse without coercion, (b) is not inhibited about masturbating, and (c) exhibits focused sexual behavior in front of others. This lack of inhibition can extend to play, art, or conversation that is imitative of adult sexual relationships.

The sexualized child is clearly at risk for developmentally inappropriate sexual behavior as well as pregnancy, sexually transmitted diseases, and prostitution. Thus, it is critical for the professional to understand and differentiate what is normal sexual development in children from behaviors that indicate trauma.

Neglect effects. The dynamics of neglect differ markedly from those of physical or sexual abuse. The main difference is the attention received by the parents. The attention associated with abuse is inappropriate, excessive, harsh, and damaging, but the parent is still involved with the child. Neglecting parents do the opposite. For example, they fail to stimulate or interact on an emotional or a physical level. In extreme cases, it is as though the parent does not know the child exists.

The effects of child neglect and deprivation occur across all levels of development, including social, affective, physical, emotional, behavioral, and cognitive. We can expect to see internalized behaviors, including a lack of affect (feelings), social detachment, and impaired empathy, as well as externalized behaviors, including violence and delinquency. Neglected youth can be identified by behaviors that convey low self-esteem, a negative worldview, and internalized or externalized anxieties or aggressions. Because of the lack of nurturance, there is typically poor intellectual development, developmental disabilities, and developmental delays. In addition, neglected children are seriously bereft of personal or family resources for care.

Stress resistance. Some abused and neglected children appear relatively less traumatized than others do. Garbarino, Guttman, and Seeley (1986) proposed the concept of "stress-resistant children" who become prosocial and competent despite harsh or even hostile upbringing. It is speculated that these children receive compensatory psychological nurturance and sustenance. This nurturance may come from home, school professionals, neighbors, or family friends. Perhaps the experience of even minimal care enables the child to cope better and to develop social competence. With a basis of social competence, the child's view of the world and his or her role within it remain more positive. In a time when counseling is reduced to a bare minimum of contact with at-risk youth, school professionals might examine what is the good-enough intervention to promote the natural adaptability of young people. For a further examination of methods that are designed to increase the natural adaptability and resilience of children, see Chapter 3 in this volume.

Continuing effects/youth sex offenders. It is not inevitable that sexual abuse victims become youth sex offenders (Righthand, 2005), and there is no singular cause for a sexual abuse victim to enter the victim-offender cycle. Lambie, Seymour, Lee, and Adams (2002) reported that when compared with a whole population of sexual abuse victims, those who enter this cycle were more likely to have (a) fantasized and masterbated about the abuse, (b) reported deriving pleasure from the abuse, (c) had infrequent social contact with peers, and (d) lacked family and nonfamily support during childhood.

What do the homes of youth sex offenders look like? With these youth, Concepcion (2004) noted the presence of (a) broken families, (b) substance abuse, (c) multigenerational abuse, (d) high rates of poverty, (e) witnessing of domestic violence by children, (f) lack of positive anger management, (g) blurred privacy boundaries, and (h) denial of responsibility by family members.

What do the youth sex offenders look like? Let us examine three recent articles on this topic. Oxnam and Vess (2006) found that youth sex offenders fell into one of three distinct personality groups: antisocial, inadequate, and normal. They noted that members of the *antisocial* group tend to act out in an aggressive and unpredictable manner with a propensity to dominate and abuse others' rights. They described the *inadequate* group as youths who are chronically insecure and avoidant of interpersonal contact. Finally, they found a group with no distinguishing personality features that they labeled *normal*. Richardson (2005) studied the interpersonal schemas of youth sex offenders. He found three maladaptive schemas prominent in these youth: emotional inhibition, social isolation/alienation, and mistrust/abuse. Farr, Brown, and Beckett (2004) studied both the ability to empathize and the masculinity levels in youth sex offenders. They found youth sex offenders far less able to empathize than a comparison nonoffender group of youths. In terms of masculinity, two subscales of the measure they used differentiated youth sex offenders from nonoffenders. These subscales were (a) callous sexual attitudes toward females and (b) adversarial attitudes toward females and sexual minorities. The youth sex offenders scored far higher on both subscales.

One theme emphasized by many of the authors cited in this subsection was the need for family-based interventions for youth sex offenders. It is amazing that little research has been done on family-based interventions for youth sex offenders. One promising approach is the use of multifamily group therapy. A detailed description of this approach to treating youth sex offenders appears in Nahum and Brewer (2004). The reported benefits of this approach included economical use of clinician resources, family-to-family transfer of knowledge and mentoring, community-based resourcefulness, and accelerated catalyzing of emotions.

APPROACHES TO PREVENTION

The preceding section reviewed a number of dysfunctional family situations and some of the youth at-risk behaviors that could flow from such family situations. The impact of physical and sexual abuse on youth was also explored. However, when faced with at-risk youth, professionals need more than knowledge; they need to be armed with practical ways to help these youths. Such arming is the goal of this section.

Pianta and Walsh (1996) posited that three forms of prevention operate in work with at-risk youth: primary prevention, secondary prevention, and tertiary prevention. Table 4-1 contains the focus and timing aspects of all three forms of prevention. An example of primary prevention is Washington State's HIV/AIDS Education Law (RCW 28A.230.020). This law mandates that all students in all common schools receive HIV/AIDS prevention education each year. The law represents primary prevention because it is directed to all students before the period when at-risk behaviors (e.g., IV drug use) begin. A transition-to-middle-school

Table 4-1

■

Form, Focus, and Timing of Prevention Activities

	Form		
Focus and Timing	*Primary*	*Secondary*	*Tertiary*
All students	✓		
Potential at-risk students		✓	
At-risk students			✓
Before at-risk status is obtained	✓	✓	
After at-risk status is obtained			✓

support group for students with low grades is an example of secondary prevention because it is directed at a specific population before it obtains at-risk status (e.g., school dropout). An example of tertiary prevention is a school-based aftercare group for students who have recently returned from a stay at a drug rehabilitation center. The goal of tertiary prevention is to remediate students who have already obtained an at-risk status.

With the forms of prevention defined, attention now turns to the levels of prevention: individual, family, school, and community.

Individual

Counseling

Individual counseling can be a secondary or tertiary prevention activity. Counselors who work with at-risk youth must exemplify the importance of well-defined rules and responsibilities. In working with the at-risk youth, the counselor must be sure to follow the rules of the counseling process. Just as the at-risk youth attempts to alter the rules in other settings for personal gain, the youth will attempt to have the counselor alter and ignore the rules of the counseling process.

For example, the youth may have a simple request, such as asking the counselor to write an excuse that would allow him or her to miss a class at school or be permitted to miss detention. Other, more critical violations of the rules may be requests for emergency appointments late at night or over the weekend. One counselor from a rural district spent 6 hours with a youth along a country road following a phone call requesting her help. It was considerate of the counselor but also very risky and ethically questionable. The youth did not follow the rules of counseling—attending the counseling session—in the appropriate location. One way to decrease the at-risk behavior is to define upfront the role of the counselor and the rules of the counseling process.

Another aspect of prevention within the individual counseling process is the determination of the severity of the at-risk youth's actions and interactions. Whether the youth is abusing alcohol, is pregnant, or is a runaway, the counselor needs to determine the extent of danger to the well-being of the youth. The prudent counselor takes few chances with an at-risk youth. Risk taking on the part of the counselor is ill advised because these youths tend to be impulsive in their actions and prone to hurting themselves physically.

In determining severity, the counselor needs to be highly aware of the concept of duty to warn. This is prevention of the highest order. At the initiation of counseling, both the at-risk youth and the family are informed that any suspicious or questionable behaviors will be reported. Both confidentiality and at-risk status are clearly defined early in the process, reinforcing the professional's responsibility to follow the rules.

If there are questions about the level of severity of the behavior the youth exhibits, professionals need to follow a cautious route and involve the parents. Following the rules may mean having a crisis team available to give the youth the appropriate treatment, including the possibility of hospitalization. If the youth is suicidal, a coordinated professional effort may need to be utilized to resolve the problem. The sooner the at-risk youth is involved in treatment, the greater the opportunity for successful resolution and prevention of problems.

In principle, the counselor should always involve a family in at-risk prevention planning. However, there are situations in which individual counseling with an at-risk student should be emphasized over family counseling. These situations include (a) when the relationship between the parents is questionable, (b) the parenting skills are almost nonexistent, (c) one parent is an alcoholic, and (d) the parents are frequently absent from the home.

An emphasis on individual counseling places even more responsibility on the counselor to follow the rules. To treat effectively the myriad of difficulties of an at-risk youth, the professional must maintain a high level of confidence. Treating the at-risk youth can be a substantial test of a counselor's self-confidence. Thus, appropriate attention to the counselor's own self-care against stress and anxiety is warranted. This self-care is the best antidote to counselor burnout.

Abuse Prevention

Providing care. It is critical that professionals who work with the difficult issues of child abuse and neglect are trained in the specifics of these issues. Hurt children evoke complex responses in caregivers. At some point, the most skilled practitioner wants to rescue the child from trauma. Therefore, a support system and professional contact base are essential in this work. Also, specific resources for reporting, legal issues, safe housing, and community support services are necessary for effective interventions to occur.

Clarification of roles, empowerment, and the stages of intervention. Given the issues of control and coercion in child abuse, it is particularly important for the counselor to define his or her role with the young person. For example, Herman (1997) suggested that at the outset of working together, the counselor and the client must be able to name the problem. To debate the story or the existence of an abuse report undermines the potential for recovery. By acknowledging the story, the counselor and the client begin to form an alliance. This alliance is critical because abused and neglected children have poor and often brutalized experiences with trust and intimacy. When hearing the story, the young person must understand that he or she is the survivor, not merely a victim. Further, the young person needs to know that he or she carries no responsibility for the abuse.

At the first stages of intervention, the counselor can work to develop small steps of self-care, plans for safety, and other support resources. The young person must be told at the outset that the counselor must report the threat of harm to self or others. Depending on the severity of the abuse or neglect, the later stages of counseling will direct the young person toward self-care and independence. In this way, the counselor can help the young person toward the future. This process cannot be rushed and will depend on the young person's internal, familial, and other support resources. As gains are made in a transfer of learning to the world outside counseling, prevention and education become important. When intention is delayed, group counseling is a valuable approach. Mutual support is critical and can reinforce affective awareness and empowerment.

Empowerment also occurs through mastery. As seen in other developmental sequences, children develop a sense of mastery by practicing. Nonverbal processes give an outlet for raw emotion and a place to practice or work through the trauma impact. The following case study of a child's abuse reflects the complexity of issues surrounding at-risk families:

CASE STUDY

Janet Firwood, age 13, was brought to the intensive care burn unit of a local pediatric hospital for reconstructive surgery. This surgery was for burns sustained when she was age 3. She had been burned while jumping over a candlestick, igniting her nightgown. Janet lived with her mother. Her father was the mother's boyfriend. This man had an intact family with a wife and several children and lived separately from Janet and her mother. Her mother was molested by this man when she was babysitting for him at age 17, and their relationship had continued since then.

The hospital's counselor began the assessment by talking with the medical staff and school personnel. A nurse reported seeing Janet holding hands with a 22-year-old patient during movie night. The hospital's schoolteacher also reported provocative behavior in class. In fact, Janet had shown other children her burn scars, including removing her underpants, if they gave her money. This pattern of premature sexual behavior, such as flirting with an older man and exhibitionism, is an indicator of sexual abuse.

The counseling intervention started at the first step by naming the problem. Janet did not see herself as having a problem. However, she was happy to have attention from the counselor. Eventually, through artwork, Janet portrayed her feelings of powerlessness and of being divided by her loyalties to her mother and father, who fought with one another. Before discharge, she revealed that her father sexually abused her. The referral to the local child abuse agency resulted in investigation and incarceration of the father. Unfortunately, Janet's case is one in which serious identity and role confusion for the survivor resulted. This confusion was the product of delayed identification of abuse and the lack of social services. Besides identity and role confusion, Janet also exhibited characteristics of the youthful offender discussed earlier in this chapter. These characteristics included exhibitionism and peer coercion. Intensive counseling and support services were necessary to help Janet and her mother begin to resolve the chaos of their lives.

Family

The Family Role of the At-Risk Youth

When an at-risk youth is identified, much attention is often given directly to the youth without commensurate attention to the entire family. This inattention is unfortunate because at-risk behavior is simply a behavioral readout of family dysfunction. In other words, the youth's at-risk behavior is not *sui generis* but rather the acting out of a script provided by the family system.

One common script is that of the identified patient. The family of the at-risk youth asserts that all in the family is well except for the at-risk youth. In truth, the at-risk youth's behaviors are merely the symptoms of family dysfunction. The greater the difficulties demonstrated by the youth, the larger the number of issues that need attention within the family. It is inappropriate to assume that the identified problem child is the only family member with mental health needs or the only family member who may be at risk. The case of Justin illustrates the identified-problem role.

CASE STUDY

Justin, a 14-year-old high school freshman, was referred for counseling by his school counselor following the interception of a suicide note. Two of Justin's friends found a letter describing how he planned to shoot himself. Justin, along with his mother and father, came to counseling. It was apparent in the initial session that Justin did not want to be there. He was rude, obnoxious, and embarrassing to his parents. His mother was tearful, while his father remained stoic. Both parents were obviously shaken by Justin's recent behaviors. The counselor attempted to understand the relationship between the issues Justin expressed and the problems that the family faced, but no clear correlation emerged. Justin's behaviors were so disruptive that it was difficult to have his parents in the counseling session. Although several more counseling appointments were set up, the mother called the next day and canceled them. Two weeks later, the counselor received a call from the mother asking for help. Her husband had been placed in the psychiatric unit of the local hospital. She explained that her husband had been laid off from work for the last 6 months and was becoming increasingly withdrawn. He seemed devastated by the problems with Justin. In despair, he pulled out his shotgun and threatened to kill himself. Justin's mother called the police, and eventually her husband was placed in inpatient psychiatric care.

Impact of Malevolent Family Dynamics

Once a youth demonstrates at-risk behaviors, family dynamics play a significant role in whether the at-risk behaviors will escalate or decline. If the dysfunctional aspects of the family dynamics are not identified, discussed, and changed, the behaviors of the at-risk youth will continue to escalate. Moreover, parental conflict has a compounding effect for the at-risk youth (Ehrensaft et al., 2003). Thus, involvement of the family is vital to prevent at-risk behaviors from escalating.

Families and Change of At-Risk Behavior

The involvement of the family of the at-risk youth in assessment, diagnosis, and treatment planning is essential. The counselor provides a model of behavior to the parents, and the parents provide a wealth of information, spoken or unspoken, to the counselor. Many counselors wonder which family members should be involved in the counseling process. It is important to consider all members of the household as potential participants in the work with at-risk youth.

Frequently, one of the most effective treatment modalities to bring about change in youths is parents' counseling. If the parents can commit to working on their relationship, along with being willing to learn different parenting approaches with their children, the chances of successfully assisting an at-risk youth increase significantly. However, as demonstrated throughout the case studies, there frequently is much disarray in the relationship between the parents. Such disarray makes it understandable why the youth may be having emotional difficulty. Also, parents provide an inappropriate model for the developing youth when they work too much, drink too much, or allow their lives to be out of control (Coldwell, Pike, & Dunn, 2006). Once parents can be taught to reorient and redirect some of their energies, the positive changes in youths are absolutely astounding. Therefore, parents' counseling along with family counseling can produce remarkable changes in dysfunctional family structures.

Thus, family counseling must be part of the intervention and prevention plan for at-risk youth. In working with the family, the counselor must maintain a neutral position and avoid a position of being on someone's side. The youth and the parents will attempt to enlist the counselor's support in their efforts to maintain the dysfunctional family system. Phone calls by the youth or a parent, bringing damaging evidence to the session to demonstrate someone's problems, or asking for additional sessions are all situations that represent some of the influence peddling family members try. It is important to remember that the goal is not to fix the at-risk youth but rather to support the development of a new and functional family interaction system.

Postabuse Family Intervention

The critical issue for children not removed from their families is monitoring the risk factors for the child and his or her parents. Any postabuse plan must assess and ensure a safe environment by evaluating parental abuse proneness, the vulnerability of the child, and environmental stresses that trigger abuse (Green, 1988). The counselor will also need to assess the family's level of coping and complexity. At-risk families are typically ones with multiple problems, poor ability to cope with stress, and few resources for help internally or in the community. Therefore, it is important for the counselor to devise realistic goals. Postabuse counseling will be a process of mediating the need for the family members to express their feelings and safety from punishment or retaliation for this behavior at home. Self-help groups such as Daughters & Sons United, Parents Anonymous, and Parents United may be helpful to families as well.

School

Preservice/In-Service Needs

School counselors and teachers are the frontline soldiers in the war against at-risk behaviors. To be capable soldiers, school counselors and teachers need to possess adequate knowledge in the following areas: parent consultation, referral and networking, and professional comportment.

Parent consultation. All school professionals need to be comfortable with the principle of parent consultation. If a school professional does not contact parents regarding at-risk behaviors, the professional is maintaining too much responsibility for the at-risk youth. Parents need to be encouraged to take responsibility for their at-risk children and to become actively involved in the prevention process as soon as possible.

Providing an effective consultation with the parents will assist the family in understanding the necessary steps of the helping process. It is important for the school professional making the initial contact with the family to understand the critical nature of his or her role. It is essential to provide the family with a clear understanding of the helping process. The initial consultation should be used to encourage and assist the family in receiving the most effective services possible. If the initial consultation is a positive experience, more than likely the family will be ready to pursue the necessary steps of the treatment process.

Referral and networking. Another necessary knowledge area for school counselors and teachers is referral and networking. If school professionals cannot provide the at-risk youth with appropriate services, they must refer the at-risk youth and the family to an appropriate agency, institution, or private practitioner. Frequently, the at-risk youth is identified by school professionals, but the services required for treatment are offered elsewhere. Thus, schools must link their efforts for at-risk youths with the efforts of local agencies, practitioners, and hospitals.

Maintaining a comprehensive referral network of helping professionals is probably one of the most important aspects of prevention as well as a major responsibility for school professionals treating at-risk youth. The network should include both medical and nonmedical mental health service providers. Specifically, referral sources need to include psychiatrists, drug and alcohol counselors, mental health counselors, clinical psychologists, marriage and family specialists, and clergy. School professionals treating at-risk youths must have a thorough knowledge of the variability and comprehensiveness of various services in the community.

Professional comportment. Critical to proper professional comportment is knowledge on how to act in an ethical and legal manner when working with at-risk youth. One key ethical and legal concern in working with at-risk youth is the issue of confidentiality. Too often school professionals maintain confidentiality without considering the ramifications to the youth as well as to themselves. Being direct and upfront with the youth about the types of information and behavior that are treated in a confidential manner versus those to be reported to the parents helps avoid potential problems later.

School counselors and teachers often serve as the primary connection between at-risk youth and their families. Thus, it is essential for school professionals to possess knowledge of parental consultation, referral and networking, and proper professional comportment. Using professional colleagues for support and consultation, making effective and necessary referrals of particularly difficult cases, and seeking personal counseling when the stress becomes too great are some ways a school counselor or teacher can maintain a high level of self-confidence and effectiveness.

Curriculum-Based Interventions

When people think of school counselors working with at-risk youths, they usually think of school counselors performing secondary and tertiary prevention activities, for example, school counselors facilitating support groups or conducting individual counseling. However, school counselors have an important role to play in the primary prevention of at-risk status in youth.

In 1997, the American School Counselor Association published national standards for school counseling programs. The model program contained K–12 guidance curriculum goals in three areas: personal/social development, career development, and academic development. Lapan, Gysbers, and Sun (1997) found that full implementation of a guidance program serves as a powerful antidote to at-risk status. Students in schools with a more fully implemented guidance program reported that (a) they earned higher grades, (b) their education was better in preparing them for the future, (c) their school made more career information available to them, and (d) their school had a more positive climate. School guidance programs are not the sole domain of counselors. In fact, because of their small numbers, the main role of the school counselor in the guidance program is that of facilitator. The key deliverer of the curricular parts of the guidance program is the teacher. Thus, the student outcomes just noted are possible only if school counselors and teachers work in concert.

School counselors are not the only education professionals with a curriculum that serves as an at-risk primary prevention activity. Family and consumer sciences teachers have also published a national curriculum. This curriculum aims to help young people develop the social skills and decision-making skills that can serve as a protection against at-risk behaviors. In addition, this curriculum contains standards on parent training for youth. There is no better example of primary prevention activity than giving people parenting skills before they become parents! Thus, national curricula exist in the United States that directly address the skill deficits that can lead to an at-risk status for youth. Such curricula have been shown scientifically to be efficacious. Unfortunately, none of these curricula are universal in U.S. schools.

Mentoring Programs

To prevent the development of at-risk behaviors may mean that the child needs to find other role models and mentors in his or her own day-to-day experiences. At-risk youths sometimes find their own ability to develop appropriate roles and responsibilities from interactions with peers, schoolteachers, neighbors, and other community leaders. For at-risk youths to change their pattern of behavior means that they need to see an alternative way to life.

Physical and Sexual Abuse Education for Children

The NIS-3 report (Sedlak & Broadhurst, 1996) stressed that schools play a central role in identifying and helping abused and neglected young people. School professionals are the frontline observers who form relationships of care with young people. Rencken (1989) advocated three axes of prevention for abuse that are useful at the school and community levels: empowerment, sex education, and gender equity. The first axis includes teaching assertiveness and the ability to say no from a foundation of self-esteem, responsibility, and age-appropriate control. The second axis is sex education to remediate ignorance for young people and their families. The third axis is a discussion of gender role differences between males and females in society and the development of equitable power arrangements.

It is clear that physically abused and neglected children are not always helped even with reporting. Child protection agencies and the court system are already seriously overworked. Often they are unable to follow up on cases except where there is threat of fatality. To address this problem, grassroots support systems are being developed. Schools and mental health agencies are teaming together to develop individualized and tailored care that uses the natural support systems in communities to help protect children. These support systems include safe places for children to go after school, neighborhood police stations, child mentorship, and after-school activities such as tutoring and gym nights. Schools can become a place to provide support to at-risk youth and their families. Grants and donations of time and money are typically used by schools and agencies to development these support resources.

Community

Parent Education

A powerful prevention activity is parent education. Both schools and community agencies can sponsor such an activity for minimal cost. If only one activity could be selected to prevent at-risk status in youth, it should be parent education. Nothing provides more bang for the buck.

Two parent education activities that have solid research support are systematic training for effective parenting (STEP) and parent monitoring. It is important to note that these activities can be easily sponsored and led not only by school personnel but also by local community agencies or churches. Neither is the kind of fancy, complex activity that garners media attention. Rather, they are doable, proven at-risk prevention activities that can make a difference in the lives of youths and their parents. As such, they merit the considerations of anyone looking for ways to address the at-risk youth problems they encounter in their workplace or in their community.

STEP program. STEP is a widely used parent education program. The STEP program curriculum presents practical ideas for parents based on Adlerian psychology. There are a wide variety of STEP modules, including those for parents of young children, parents of teens, Christian parents, and Latino parents. Although designed for the average parent, there is even evidence of STEP's effectiveness with parents who have previously abused their children (Fennell & Fishel, 1998).

The STEP program is well laid out with clear lesson plans and appropriate participant activities. There is also a training facilitator's handbook for support (Dinkmeyer, 1997). A person who has had some previous training in developmental psychology and in communication skills would do an excellent job of facilitating STEP training.

Parent monitoring. Although it may sound like an incredibly simplistic solution, extensive research supports the idea that at-risk behaviors can be substantially decreased by increasing parental monitoring of youth. Murray, Kelder, Parcel, and Orpinas (1998) developed a parent education program that taught parents practical monitoring skills of middle school students. They identified four skills that are essential in building competent monitoring in parents:

1. Parents will ask their child where he or she is going.
2. Parents will obtain a list of telephone numbers of their child's friends.
3. Parents will call parents of their child's friends.
4. Parents will visit their child's school.

Learning objectives are identified for each skill. For example, one of the learning objectives for the second skill is "parents will be able to recognize most of their child's friends on the street and know their names" (Murray et al., 1998, p. 50).

Community Capacity Building

At-risk behaviors of youth do not wreak havoc in just families and schools. The social and economic costs of such behaviors affect every community. As such, building the capacity of communities to prevent at-risk behaviors benefits all citizens. Given the central role of schools in most communities, school personnel can be key instigators of a community's focusing on at-risk prevention. In terms of communitywide prevention efforts, school personnel should work toward two goals: education on family dynamics and communitywide networking.

Education on family dynamics. One key community prevention goal is educating the general public about the variation in family structures and individual differences. It is still difficult for many local institutions such as churches, hospitals, and other community organizations to make allowances for the various family structures such as blended families, single-parent families, interracial families, and dual-career families. Moreover, if at-risk youths are to find surrogate role models in the community, it is important for the potential role models to understand the dysfunctional and nontraditional aspects of family life in the current culture.

Communitywide networking. Another key community prevention goal is the successful networking of school personnel with other professionals in the community who serve at-risk youth. These professionals include private practice counselors, community agency counselors, probation officers, law enforcement officers, and pediatricians. This networking is necessary given the multifaceted nature of youth at-risk status. For example, substance abuse may lead to both academic and health problems. Given this multifacetedness, school professionals must have an effective network of other professionals to offer the youth and the family the best services possible. The network should include knowledge of runaway shelters, crisis intervention teams, support groups, hospitals, and outpatient services.

ADAPTATIONS FOR DIVERSITY

Poverty among minority families is an underrecognized and poorly addressed factor that leads to family dysfunction and the development of at-risk behaviors in youth. For example, 34% of African American children in the United States live below the poverty level (U.S. Census Bureau, 2006). For a single parent with no money, the effect of the chronic stressors often overwhelms efforts to cope with the demands of raising children. Single parents carry the greatest load of pressure in society, often raising their children without economic or social resources to provide for basic needs and safety. A counseling approach that supports single parents understands that these parents often feel they should not ask for assistance, believing that they alone are responsible for their families. Reaching out in a nonjudgmental way is a critical first step toward changing the family dysfunction and at-risk behaviors of the children who live in poverty.

The American Psychological Association created a Minority Fellowship Program to support doctoral students in research that increases the knowledge of and studies about ways to improve the quality of mental health and substance abuse services delivered to ethnic minority populations. Their mission is consistent with Healthy People 2010, the Surgeon General's Report on Mental Health, and other federal initiatives to reduce health disparities. Outcomes from this program include the examination of an innovative approach known as multidimensional family therapy (MDFT). MDFT has been shown empirically to provide an effective treatment for impoverished youth of color who have drug and alcohol behavior problems (Liddle, Rowe, Dakof, Ungaro, & Henderson, 2004). The strategy of MDFT is strengths based, wherein the counselor listens to and validates the parent's and the child's stories about the family while working to bring the parent and the youth into an increasing amount of involvement with one another. Additionally, the counselor must earn the trust of the parent by acknowledging the stereotypes of being representative of the system and find ways to nurture the nurturer.

As noted earlier in this chapter, the causes of at-risk behavior are directly linked to the parent's view of the child, the level of communication established in the family, and the ability to build positive relationships of support within the family. Among multiethnic families with delinquent inner-city youth, parents often believed that the cause of their family problems and at-risk youth behaviors was due to the level of discipline (Madden-Derdich, Leonard, & Gunnell, 2002). These parents saw themselves as needing to continually monitor their children's behavior and for their children to comply with their wishes or face harsh consequences. This parenting style has been associated with the development of antisocial behavior. In contrast, the children believed that poor communication, interpersonal conflict, lack of parental concern, and drug use were the factors that interfered with positive change in the family and their own behaviors. The youths saw the real problem. The counseling approach of choice in this situation is structural family therapy. Structural family therapy encourages the family to stop blaming the member who is in the identified-problem role (i.e., the child) and assists parents to gain control by taking responsibility for creating positive family communication and interactions. Acknowledging the rich heritage of ethnicity is critical to the success of this counseling intervention.

SUMMARY

This chapter provides an overview of how dysfunctional family dynamics both precede and fuel at-risk behavior. In addition, the chapter provides some ideas about how to best provide a program of prevention to assist at-risk youth and their families. Several points need to be emphasized for those charged with working with at-risk youth.

First, there is no more difficult population to serve than at-risk youth. They tend to be more professionally demanding, emotionally draining, and behaviorally unpredictable than youth in general. Professionals assigned to work with this population must learn to be direct and honest with the youth as well as his or her family. As mentioned in the discussion of prevention, these same professionals must learn to follow the rules in serving these youths.

Second, the at-risk family is a special entity and needs tremendous amounts of attention to keep it functioning without tragedy. A professional working with an at-risk individual has to always be aware of the remaining family members to make sure that another member does not manifest a severe behavioral difficulty. Consultation with other important adults surrounding the family members is necessary to effectively work with the at-risk family. This is a responsible approach for counselors working with any family and is particularly important when these community persons reflect the culture of the family that is different from the counselor's own cultural background or identity.

Finally, treating at-risk youth mandates that professionals be involved with families and community agencies. There is no place in work with at-risk youth for the professional Lone Ranger. The biggest mistake made by caring professionals is to assume too much individual responsibility for the at-risk youth and his or her family. Find a support system to assist in the treatment process, and be sure to have a support system available for you. Maintaining physical energy and emotional balance is as important as any decision the professional can make.

REFERENCES

Aguilera, D. C., & Messick, J. M. (1986). *Crisis intervention: Theory and methodology*. St. Louis, MO: Mosby.

Amato, P. R., & Cheadle, J. (2005). The long reach of divorce: Divorce and child well-being across three generations. *Journal of Marriage and Family, 67*, 191–206.

American Psychiatric Association. (2000). *Diagnostic and statistical manual of mental disorders* (4th ed., Text Revision). Washington, DC: Author.

Appleton, V. B. (2001). Avenues of hope: Art therapy and the resolution of trauma. *Art Therapy: Journal of the American Art Therapy Association, 18*, 6–13.

Coldwell, J., Pike, A., & Dunn, J. (2006). Household chaos: Links with parenting and child behaviour. *Journal of Child Psychology and Psychiatry, 47*, 1116–1122.

Concepcion, J. I. (2004). Understanding preadolescent sexual offenders. *The Florida Bar Journal, 78*(7), 30–37.

Cummings, E. M., Goeke-Morey, M., & Papple, L. M. (2004). Everyday marital conflict and child aggression. *Journal of Divorce and Remarriage, 32*, 191–202.

Dinkmeyer, D. (1997). *Systematic training for effective parenting: Leaders resource binder.* Circle Pines, MN: American Guidance Service.

Ehrensaft, M., Wasserman, G., Verdelli, L., Greenwald, S., Miller, L., & Davies, M. (2003). Maternal antisocial behavior, parenting practices, and behavior problems in boys at risk for antisocial behavior. *Journal of Child and Family Studies, 12*, 27–41.

Farr, C., Brown, J., & Beckett, R. (2004). Ability to empathise and masculinity levels: Comparing male adolescent sex offenders with a normative sample of non-offending adolescents. *Psychology, Crime and Law, 10*, 155–167.

Fennell, D. C., & Fishel, A. H. (1998). Parent education: An evaluation of STEP on abusive parents' perceptions and potential abuse. *Journal of Child and Adolescent Psychiatric Nursing, 11*, 107–121.

Finkelhor, D. (1984). *Child sexual abuse.* New York: Free Press.

Friedrich, W. M. (2002). *Psychological assessment of sexually abused children and their families.* New York: Sage.

Garbarino, J., Guttman, E., & Seeley, J. W. (1986). *The psychologically battered child.* San Francisco: Jossey-Bass.

Gil, E. (1996). *Treating abused adolescents.* New York: Guilford Press.

Green, A. H. (1988). The abused child and adolescent. In C. J. Kestenbaum & D. J. Williams (Eds.), *Handbook of clinical assessment of children and adolescents* (Vol. 2, pp. 841–863). New York: New York University Press.

Herman, J. L. (1997). *Trauma and recovery.* New York: Basic Books.

Kazak, A. E., Christakis, D., Alderfer, M., & Coiro, M. J. (1994). Young adolescent cancer survivors and their parents: Adjustment, learning problems, gender. *Journal of Family Psychology, 8*, 74–84.

Kereste, G., & Milanovi, A. (2006). Relations between different types of children's aggressive behavior and sociometric status among peers of the same and opposite gender. *Scandinavian Journal of Psychology, 47*, 477–483.

Lambie, I., Seymour, F., Lee, A., & Adams, P. (2002). Resiliency in the victim-offender cycle in male sexual abuse. *Sexual Abuse: A Journal of Research and Treatment, 14*, 31–48.

Lapan, R., Gysbers, N. C., & Sun, Y. (1997). The impact of more fully implemented guidance programs on the school experiences of high school students: A statewide evaluation study. *Journal of Counseling & Development, 75*, 292–302.

Liddle, H. A., Rowe, C. L., Dakof, G. A., Ungaro, R. A., & Henderson, C. E. (2004). Early intervention for adolescent substance abuse: Pretreatment to posttreatment outcomes of a randomized clinical trial comparing multidimensional family therapy and peer group treatment. *Journal of Psychoactive Drugs, 36*, 49–63.

Madden-Derdich, D. S., Leonard, S. A., & Gunnell, G. A. (2002). Parents' and children's perceptions of family processes in inner-city families with delinquent youths: A qualitative investigation. *Journal of Marital and Family Therapy, 28*, 355–369.

Murray, N., Kelder, S., Parcel, G., & Orpinas, P. (1998). Development of an intervention map for a parent education intervention to prevent violence among Hispanic middle school parents. *Journal of School Health, 68,* 46–53.

Nahum, D., & Brewer, M. M. (2004). The use of multi-family group therapy for sexually abusive youth. *Journal of Child Sexual Abuse, 13,* 215–243.

Oxnam, P., & Vess, J. (2006). A personality-based typology of adolescent sexual offenders using the Millon Adolescent Clinical Inventory. *New Zealand Journal of Psychology, 35,* 36–44.

Pianta, R. C., & Walsh, D. J. (1996). *High-risk children in schools.* New York: Routledge.

Rencken, R. H. (1989). *Intervention strategies for sexual abuse.* Alexandria, VA: American Counseling Association.

Richardson, G. (2005). Early maladaptive schemas in a sample of British adolescent sexual abusers: Implications for therapy. *Journal of Sexual Aggression, 11,* 259–276.

Righthand, S. (2005). *Report of the committee to prevent sexual abuse: State of Maine.* Retrieved December 1, 2006, from http://maine.gov/dhhs/bcfs/report2005.doc

Sedlak, A., & Broadhurst, D. (1996). *Third national incidence study of child abuse and neglect: Final report.* Washington, DC: U.S. Department of Health and Human Services, Administration of Children and Family.

Sourander, A., Pihlakoski, L., Aromaa, M., Rautava, P., Helenius, H., & Sillanpää, M. (2006). Early predictors of parent- and self-reported perceived global psychological difficulties among adolescents. *Social Psychiatry and Psychiatric Epidemiology, 41,* 173–182.

Visher, E. B., & Visher, J. S. (1996). *Therapy with stepfamilies.* New York: Brunner/Mazel.

U.S. Census Bureau. (2006). *Current population survey: 2006 annual social and economic supplement.* Washington, DC: Author. Retrieved December 1, 2006, from http://pubdb3.census.gov/macro/032006/pov/new05_100_06.htm

Webb, N. B., & Terr, L. (1999). *Play therapy with children in crisis.* New York: Guilford Press.

CHAPTER 5

■

"Who Cares What I Think": Problems of Low Self-Esteem

Sandra S. Meggert

As counselors, we observe many adolescents in pain. We see many with negative attitudes or low self-esteem and suspect there are many more. Many researchers believe that one of the major causes of deviant or potentially destructive behavior is low self-esteem (Hazler, Carney, & Granger, 2006; Kaplan, 1975; Maternal and Child Health Branch, Hawaii State Department of Health, 1991). A review of the literature supports the belief that negative self-esteem affects behavior in negative or destructive ways (Aronson & Mettee, 1968; Burrow-Sanchez, 2006; Graf, 1971; Kaplan, 1975; Kaplan, Martin, & Johnson, 1986; Lorr & Wunderlich, 1986; Weinburg, 2001). Kaplan (1976) stated that poor self-esteem or "negative self-attitudes increase the probability of later adoption of each of a range of different types of deviant responses" (p. 788). Low self-esteem is a critical factor in at-risk behavior. Eskilson, Wiley, Meuhlbauer, and Dodder (1986) reported that adolescents who feel excessive demands to succeed academically are apt to disclose involvement in deviant activities, to have low self-esteem, and to feel inadequate and unable to fulfill their families' aspirations for them. Aronson and Mettee (1968) used college students as participants in a study on dishonesty. They hypothesized that students with "low self-esteem are more likely to engage in immoral behavior" (p. 74). Results showed that 87% of the students with induced low self-esteem cheated on a test as compared with 60% of the neutral group and 40% of the induced high self-esteem group. In a similar study, Graf (1971) reported that 40% of those with induced low self-esteem, 17% of the neutral group, and 14% of the group with induced high self-esteem engaged in dishonest behavior.

Kaplan's (1976) theory suggests that low self-esteem influences a person to adopt delinquent or other behaviors that are deviant from the norm. The theory identifies two routes that negative self-attitudes may take to influence deviant behavior. One is that these attitudes make conformity to membership group patterns painful or distressing, the other is "by influencing the person's need to seek alternatives to the disvalued normative patterns in order to satisfy the self-esteem motive" (p. 788). The

Maternal and Child Health Branch of the Hawaii State Department of Health (1991) collected data on adolescent health in Hawaii and found that adolescents with low self-esteem were more likely to exhibit high-risk behaviors than were their peers with high self-esteem.

The results of a study of adolescents at risk for compulsive overeating (Marston, Jacobs, Singer, Widaman, & Little, 1988) showed that students designated at risk perceived their life quality as poor, and the authors hypothesized that this meant the students were getting along poorly with the person to whom they felt closest. Because esteem is closely tied to perceived evaluations from significant others, the quality of significant relationships is a crucial ingredient of self-esteem. The research findings of Yanish and Battle (1985) supported the importance of significant others to adolescents. They found depression in adolescents to be more strongly affected by the relationship with parents than with peers. Masche's (2000) longitudinal study of 54 intact families tentatively concluded that the self-concept of adolescents was influenced by the quality of both the parent–adolescent and marital relationships. A longitudinal study by Cohen, Burt, and Bjorck (1987) indicated that low self-esteem and depression, an indicator of low self-esteem, are positive predictors of controllable negative events, for example, expulsion from school. Portes and Zady (2000) studied cultural differences in self-esteem and adaptation of Spanish-speaking second-generation adolescents. They concluded that parent–child conflicts and depression were common predictors of self-esteem for this population and noted this was similar to samples from the dominant culture labeled *mainstream*. Hazler and Mellin (2004) noted there are symptoms of depression in adolescents that differ from those in adults, and these must be addressed. Drawing on the work of Moreau (1996), Mufson and Moreau (1997), and Stanard (2000), they identified these symptoms as "excessive boredom, substance abuse, family problems, insubordination, symptoms of conduct disorder, and eating disorders" (Hazler & Mellin, 2004, p. 19) and explained that with adolescents, the stages of depression are "followed by stages of improved functioning which reflect the more episodic nature of adolescent depressive disorders" (p. 19). They focused on depression in adolescent females and described specific issues important to work on in this population: the "internal feeling of belonging and the external knowledge of interactions and conflicts with others that cause social isolation or loneliness and require specific interpersonal, culturally appropriate approaches to treatment for adolescent females" (p. 22). The most observable symptoms of depression with female adolescents are "eating disorders, dissatisfaction with one's body, and weight loss" (p. 20), also symptoms of low self-esteem.

Simmons, Burgeson, Carlton-Ford, and Blyth (1987) stated that young people who encounter several important life events at the same time they are adjusting to the changes of adolescence are expected to be at greater risk than those who have longer periods of time to adjust to adolescence. Findings in this study showed that girls suffer loss of self-esteem, and both boys and girls show declines in grade point average and participation in extracurricular activities. For girls, each subsequent life change brings more difficulty with coping. Simmons et al. suggested that, in terms of self-esteem, this group of young adolescents does better if one aspect of their life is comfortable. If this is accomplished, then the timing and pacing of major changes are of primary importance. Kelly, Lynch, Donovan, and Clark (2001) found that low self-esteem and family dysfunction in adolescent girls diagnosed with at least one mental disorder were found to be predictors of suicidal ideations.

As discussed in the many preceding examples, adolescents who exhibit signs of low self-esteem may be considered at risk for adopting or experimenting with deviant or potentially destructive behaviors. These young people may or may not be responding to life situations with deviant behaviors currently. However, when the signs indicate low self-esteem, interventions designed to improve self-esteem are important to help these youths avoid at-risk behaviors.

This chapter examines low self-esteem as one of the primary causes of the at-risk behaviors just described and delineates strategies and programs to prevent low levels of self-esteem. Self-esteem is defined in relation to at-risk youth, and behavioral descriptions frequently linked to low self-esteem are discussed. The chapter also presents causal factors that influence the development of self-esteem, as well as prevention strategies that can be used by the parents, individual, schools, and communities to make young people feel valued and significant participants in making their environment a satisfying, safe, and rewarding place. A case study describes a successful experimental program with at-risk students that has brought about changes that reflect improved levels of self-esteem.

DEFINITIONS OF SELF-ESTEEM

Self-esteem refers to subjective evaluations of worth. These value judgments develop through personal success or failure experiences, interactions with others, maturation, heredity, and social learning and are formulated from an individual's perspective. Kaplan (1975, 2006) discussed the self-esteem motive as being an individual's need to optimize positive feelings about self while reducing negative feelings. It is the process of increasing feelings of self-respect, approval, worth, and esteem. When the balance is on the negative side, a person is said to feel self-rejection, self-derogation, and, in many cases, self-hate.

Self-esteem is also a function of perceived evaluation by significant others. Mack and Ablon (1983) believed that no human is ever totally independent of the evaluation of others, and everyone retains "to some degree, a dependence upon connectedness with others for validation of our worth" (p. 10). A person's self-evaluation is referred to as self-esteem (Robison-Awana, Kehle, & Jenson, 1986) and is influenced by the individual's feelings of competence and efficacy. Carlock (1999) summed up various definitions compiled from Cantor and Bernay (1992), McDowell (1984), and Satir (1981) and described self-esteem as

> how you feel about yourself, how highly you regard yourself. That degree of regard is based on your sense of how lovable and special you believe you are, how wanted you feel and your sense of belonging, how special or unique you believe you are, how competent you feel and how well you fulfill your potential, how willing you are to take risks and face challenges and how able you are to set goals, make choices, and fulfill your goals and dreams. (p. 5)

Guindon (2002) described self-esteem as being both "general (global) and selective (specific or situation)" (p. 206) and pointed out the ambiguity or uncertainty this may cause when selecting appropriate interventions to build self-esteem. She maintained a client may have positive general self-esteem but have low self-esteem in a specific area depending on the situation and expectations. She provided the following definitions:

1. *Self-esteem*. The attitudinal, evaluative component of the self; the affective judgments placed on the self-concept consisting of feelings of worth and acceptance that are developed and maintained as a consequence of awareness of competence, sense of achievement, and feedback from the external world.
2. *Global self-esteem*. An overall estimate of general self-worth, a level of self or respect for oneself, a trait or tendency relatively stable and enduring, composed of all subordinate traits and characteristics within the self.
3. *Selective self-esteem*. An evaluation of specific and constituent traits or qualities or both within the self, at times situationally variable and transitory, that are weighted and combined into an overall evaluation of self, or global self-esteem. (p. 207)

Guindon emphasized that using these definitions can help the counselor design interventions focused on the specific areas of self-esteem that need improvement. She explained that working on the specific areas of self-esteem that need improvement may ultimately affect the global self-esteem.

Two other terms are sometimes used interchangeably with self-esteem: self-concept and self-acceptance. *Self-concept* refers to the perception individuals have about their personal attributes and the roles they fulfill. Some of these perceptions are accurate, and some are not. According to Beane and Lipka (1980), people receive feedback about the roles they play and internalize information about the character and quality of their role performance: "Self-concept refers to the valuative assessment of those descriptions" (p. 3). For example, individuals have an academic self-concept, a social self-concept, or a physical appearance self-concept. Elliott (1988) maintained that anyone with low self-esteem has an unstable self-concept. The term *self-acceptance* pertains to the degree to which people are comfortable with their self-concept (Frey & Carlock, 1984).

For purposes of this discussion, self-esteem is defined as the pattern of beliefs an individual has about self-worth. It is the subjective part of self-concept, the evaluation of self and behaviors based on an individual's perceptions of personal experiences and feedback from significant others. It is expressed in feelings of power or helplessness, called efficacy, or in beliefs about personal control.

INDICATORS OF LOW SELF-ESTEEM

Beliefs about self develop as a result of perceptions and evaluations of success and failure experiences. In this process, an individual forms some beliefs about personal control (internal vs. external) and personal effectiveness (self-efficacy).

Locus of control refers to a person's belief about outcomes. Locus of control is the conviction that success or failure at a task is internally determined by one's own actions or ability, or that the outcome is due to external influences such as luck, fate, or chance. According to D. S. Johnson (1981), "internal attributions for success are associated with higher levels of self-esteem," and low self-concept "was predicted independently and significantly by internal attribution for failure and external attribution for success" (p. 174). Abramson, Seligman, and Teasdale (1978) suggested that low-achieving students ascribe any failures to internal causes and all successes to external causes. Personal effectiveness, or *self-efficacy*, as defined by Benoit and Mitchell (1987), has four essential elements: awareness of required behavior to bring about success, expectation that this behavior will be successful, belief that there is a relationship between behavior and outcome and that this behavior will have an impact, and belief that the outcome will provide something valued.

Evidence supports the fact that an individual with low self-esteem does most likely believe in luck (external control) rather than ability (internal control) to achieve success. However, failure is attributed to personal shortcomings (internal control). Because self-esteem judges whether such an individual can, in fact, succeed at a given task, the lack of belief in self makes it likely that someone with low self-esteem will also exhibit feelings of helplessness or powerlessness, in other words, low levels of self-efficacy. In this case, a possible defense might be to deny that the outcome of the behavior has any value and to withdraw or drop out.

Individuals with low self-esteem often find it necessary to develop defenses. People who have low self-esteem hurt. To avoid this hurt, their tendency is either to shun experiences they believe will bring additional pain or to change these experiences in some way. They erect barriers or defenses. At times they may be hostile, critical, or suspicious of others or lack identification with others. Sometimes retreating defenses are exhibited when a person avoids coming to grips with problems or denies reality (Kaplan, 1975, 2006). A person might retreat into an "I don't care" stance or simply resist trying. It is too much of a risk for someone with feelings of poor self-worth to be exposed to additional hurt or situations in which failure is expected.

People with low self-esteem may be distractible, timid, shy, withdrawn, inhibited, anxious, less academically able, and have a narrow range of interests (see, e.g., Domino & Blumberg, 1987). They are more likely to daydream and to want to find jobs in which they have little or no supervision and in which there are minimal amounts of competition. From their perspectives, an ideal situation is one in which they have no supervision because then no one can confirm their failure. Generally, they express the idea that they do not really want to get ahead in life. This could be because they will not place themselves in a position in which they expect to fail. This too is a defense.

Individuals with low self-esteem have few coping strategies. They often feel a lack of control over life events. They do not feel connected and have few, if any, expectations of future success. They lack a sense of belonging. Possibly, dropping out is a defensive way of demonstrating some power, self-defeating though it may be. Chapman and Mullis (1999) studied the connection between coping strategies and self-esteem in adolescents. Their data showed that adolescents who had lower self-esteem and boys used more avoidance coping strategies compared with girls, who typically used spiritual and social support.

Low self-esteem can cause emotional distress as well. Many individuals who question their worth are sad, lethargic, tense, anxious, and angry. Some of these feelings stem from concurrent feelings of helplessness and powerlessness. Physically, they may exhibit sleeplessness, headaches, or nightmares. McGee and Williams (2000) found that levels of global self-esteem predicted reports of suicidal ideation, problem eating, and multiple compromising behaviors by adolescents in New Zealand.

Those who have low self-esteem are generally dissatisfied with themselves and their lives, contemptuous of self, and have low levels of self-respect. Typically, they are fearful of new experiences and have a poor physical appearance and a low energy level. Apologizing, criticizing others, showing an interest in material things, and bragging are all indicators of low self-esteem.

CAUSAL FACTORS

Parental, individual, social, psychological, physical, environmental, and cultural influences affect self-esteem. They all contribute to the development of self-esteem to the extent that each or all of these are valued or devalued by significant others who provide feedback. This feedback is both verbal and nonverbal, overt and covert, and dramatically affects how adolescents see themselves.

Parental Influences on Self-Esteem

Frey and Carlock (1984) identified a representative list of "psychological pathogens" to self-esteem (pp. 25–31). Many of these are associated with parental influences. These pathogens may persist throughout life and, if so, may consistently keep self-esteem low unless someone or something intervenes. Among the pathogens they identified and the problems that might arise when these are present during childhood are the following:

- *Expecting perfection.* Nobody has achieved this state of perfection yet, but many people try. A burden of always trying to be perfect throughout childhood guarantees failure. Those who set idealistic or unrealistic goals for themselves are constantly frustrated, critical, and impatient with themselves and others, always trying harder and never quite feeling successful. Negative self-evaluations, which are formulated by the young person from perceptions of adult reactions, deeply affect his or her feelings about self. Unless a person learns to set realistic goals and acknowledge small steps along the way, self-esteem remains low because the person never feels adequate.
- *Inconsistency and failure to set limits.* Although some people believe consistency is a myth, children often search for consistency and limits, apparently seeking the security that structure and predictability provide. When that is missing, the result is anger, insecurity, and hostility.
- *Failure to give positive feedback.* Many parents and significant others assume that children know that positive behavior is appreciated and only respond to negative or improper behavior. Being constantly reminded or punished when behavior is inappropriate and seldom being appreciated when behavior is appropriate create feelings of inadequacy and inferiority.
- *Failure to listen.* Failing to listen to a child indicates a lack of respect and communicates that the child or what the child is trying to communicate is not important. When this feeling is carried through childhood, it fosters additional feelings of inferiority and inadequacy that are sometimes expressed in anger or hostility.
- *Rejection.* Consistent rejection critically affects an individual's self-esteem. The rejected child's basic needs are not being met, in some cases deliberately. The child may view death, divorce, severe illness, or ignoring the child as rejection, with the ensuing feelings of inadequacy, guilt, self-hate, or self-rejection.
- *Being a maladjusted role model.* Children who model their behavior after an adult who is maladjusted often end up disliking themselves because of those behaviors. Their self-esteem is greatly diminished in such cases.
- *Failure to help children adapt.* Societal and cultural values are being questioned more now than ever before. It is difficult for children to feel adequate in a society in which values are shifting or unclear. It becomes even more difficult

when children try to adapt to a different culture and experience conflict in values.

- *Forcing children into a pattern.* Sometimes parents try to fit children into certain behaviors or patterns that may restrict their unique development or be beyond their capacity. This is sometimes called living vicariously and creates frustration, feelings of worthlessness, and inadequacy in both parent and child.
- *Allowing and supporting procrastination.* Believing that one does not have the self-discipline necessary to complete a task contributes to poor self-esteem. The longer the child procrastinates, the more the feelings of inadequacy and worthlessness multiply. Concurrently, there is a loss of self-respect.

Frey and Carlock (1984) listed several additional pathogens and observed that "one can be the recipient of several of these dynamics" (p. 31). Each of these, or a combination of several, is detrimental to a child's self-esteem.

Parents have significant impact on the self-esteem of their children. Parental attitudes and behaviors have been shown to affect children (Appleton & Dykeman; 2004; Lord, Eccles, & McCarthy, 1994). A study by Lord et al. (1994) that focused on the number of divorces and remarriages and the child's subsequent adjustment found some evidence of a "negative linear relationship" (p. 28) between these variables. Buri and Dickinson (1994) reported that although parental authority was predictive of self-esteem, these behaviors were less important than overgeneralization, particularly in female adolescents. The authors described overgeneralization as the inclination for a person to view a failure as an indication of his or her general inadequacy.

A consequence of the dynamics just described is that young people today feel unimportant or even irrelevant in their families (Glenn & Nelson, 1989). Many believe that they are important only when they are doing what someone else wants them to do. Glenn and Nelson speculated that this is one impetus for early sexual involvement. Sex becomes a strategy to make young people believe themselves to be significant in the eyes of someone else. For girls, the irony is that if she has a child, she is automatically treated as an adult when, in fact, there are now two children.

The need to feel significant is also a powerful motivator to become a gang member. News stories report daily regarding the initiation rites to join a gang. Some young people want so badly to belong that they lose their lives during the initiation process.

Note that many of the pathogens identified are behaviors found in extremely inexperienced parents who may use the child to satisfy personal needs not previously filled. The child will not feel valued, may be confused, and most likely will develop low self-esteem. The cycle will remain unbroken unless there is some type of intervention.

Using self-esteem and psychosocial competence as indicators, Sim (2000) studied the role of parental regard on Singaporean adolescents' psychosocial competence. Results indicated adolescents' regard for parents was positively related to self-esteem and negatively associated with antisocial susceptibility. Regard for parents was also found to mediate the relationship between parental monitoring and antisocial susceptibility.

Individual Influences on Self-Esteem

People learn about themselves as they interact with their environment and receive feedback on how well or how poorly they do things. Young children learn about their capabilities and their limits or strengths from others and form beliefs about their own competence. If a child receives negative feedback consistently, he or she will learn to believe in his or her own inferiority. This, in turn, could affect attitudes and outlook on life and leave the child with a sense of not "fitting in" or not belonging and being powerless.

These beliefs about self are powerful and form a lens through which a person views the world. This view will have an influence on the experiences the individual chooses to undertake and probably outcomes as well. Building self-esteem includes a measure of being realistic about one's abilities. When most feedback is negative, a child's view of his or her competence often becomes unrealistic, and the child makes choices based on what he or she believes to be true about self. Carlock (1999) stated that "it is important for young children not just to learn specific skills and behaviors but to acquire an overall belief in their ability to affect their world" (p. 291).

Social Influences on Self-Esteem

A basic assumption in social psychology is that self-concepts are heavily influenced by social contexts (Bachman & O'Malley, 1986). Each of us has a long history of dependency in infancy and childhood during which we need to receive positive responses from adults. We are motivated to behave in ways that increase the likelihood of receiving these positive responses. As children, we internalize adult standards in this manner, and we attempt to regulate our own behavior and react with positive or negative self-feelings at the perceived evaluations/reactions of significant adults (Kaplan, 1976, 2006).

Kaplan (1976) further noted that low self-esteem is thought to be caused by self-perceptions that either one's behavior or characteristics do not meet personal standards valued by the social system, by self-perceptions that one is not valued positively or perhaps even negatively by significant others, or that one might not have developed "normatively acceptable coping mechanisms" that could protect one from the effect of "self-perceptions of failure or rejection by others" (p. 790). A person with a history of being devalued is most likely to have low self-esteem. This can be said to evolve from two sources: (a) an individual's history of negative self-evaluation and perception and (b) perceptions of highly valued others in the environment responding to the individual with less than positive attitudes (Kaplan, 1975). An individual is more likely to value the attitudes of those persons "who were associated with need gratification or deprivation" (p. 37).

Society imposes strong gender-based role behaviors that continue their impact on self-esteem long after adolescence. A study by Burnett, Anderson, and Heppner (1995) demonstrated that masculine bias is still strong in the United States. Masculinity, defined as having high levels of traditional masculine behaviors (such as competitiveness, decisiveness, and independence) as opposed to feminine characteristics (such as focus on relationships and nurturing), has been shown to be "significantly correlated with self-esteem for both men and women, but individual femininity was not significantly related to self-esteem in either sex" (Burnett et al., 1995, p. 325).

Even though masculine behaviors are clearly valued in the United States, they are not generally characteristic of at-risk youth. If they are evident in some, they are not generally evident in socially acceptable ways. For example, aggressiveness and rebelliousness might substitute for independence and competitiveness. Enns (1992) stated that "there is some evidence that the socialization process is even more stringent for men than it is for women, and that boys and men experience higher costs for straying from traditional gender roles than do girls and women" (p. 11). There is the possibility that absence of masculine skills in boys, and to some extent girls, has the potential of contributing to low self-esteem. Bower (1993) reported that development of self-esteem in males and females is different because of societal pressures that dictate male and female role behaviors. Some research has also indicated that teenage girls have lower self-esteem than teenage boys (Dwyer, 1993). A *U.S. News & World Report* article surveyed research regarding self-esteem of adolescent girls (Saltzman, 1994). After examining several research studies, Saltzman concluded that social science has no conclusive answers and that parents have to assess and address the needs of their daughters individually.

Many of the social changes are high-risk changes. As young people are alienated from society and practice more violent methods to feel significant and powerful, many die or become incapacitated. Wars are fought on TV, and children feel threatened. Technology has changed the world of work, and many parents or parental figures are unemployed. Divorce is common, and homes are broken. Values are lost. Young people hear of others their own age dying from the variety of perils to which they are exposed. Many of them believe that they will live short lives. No one has prepared them for the choices they have to make.

Psychological Influences on Self-Esteem

Mack and Ablon (1983) wrote that it is "questionable, indeed, whether human beings can deeply experience positive self-worth except as the result of a relationship" (p. 9). Everyone knows two basic truths about the self. One is that the self is alone and private, and the other is "that one is a real self only to the extent that caring and reaching beyond the self continue" (Yankelovich, 1981, p. 240). Therefore, an important psychological determinant of self-esteem is the individual's feelings about the level of success within relationships.

The whole notion of connectedness or belonging to someone is central to the development of self-esteem. Belonging to a family, a culture, a community, or a school provides a connection to aid in sustaining a sense of worth. Lacking such a feeling, a person is likely to feel not valued and retreat into a defensive posture to protect the self from the pain of feeling isolated, hopeless, worthless, and unconnected. According to Mack and Alblon (1983), "Virtually all maladaptive defensive patterns in childhood, adolescence, and adult life have as at least one major purpose, protection of the pain associated with lowered self-esteem" (p. 38).

Television has become a psychological determinant of self-esteem (Glenn & Nelson, 1989). Young people receive messages about the society in which they live in a passive manner. They do not have to participate to learn. In the past, people learned about functioning in society while they were actively involved in living and working. The learning might be trial and error, role modeling, or direct teaching, but individuals were active. Glenn and Nelson referred to this as on-the-job training. Today, with the use of television, children's reality becomes distorted. Within a short time, they see problems solved through miracles, violence, various medications, sex, and drinking. According to Glenn and Nelson (1989), young people learn the following:

1. In productive and desirable social interactions, drinking or substance abuse is necessary.

2. Pain, fatigue, listlessness, and boredom are all dispelled through self-medication.
3. Indiscriminate or uninvolved sexual encounters are appropriate ways to communicate.
4. Problems can be resolved instantly through manipulation, violence, and breaking the law.
5. Deferred gratification, hard work, and personal initiative are unacceptable, and drinking and self-medication can help a person avoid these stresses. Any stressful situation can be alleviated by using specific products and/or services. (pp. 42–43)

These "truisms" are further complicated by some parents who foster the belief that most material possessions can be obtained in ways other than hard work. So because things come easy, there is no respect for possessions and no positive messages about the purpose of life. It is easy to speculate that if no active role modeling or teaching of healthier, more productive attitudes dispute these claims, young people may feel alienated, angry, and confused. When they use these same behaviors that work on television to solve their problems, they get into trouble. The nonacceptance of their behaviors confirms their sense of worthlessness and insignificance. The only way they can feel any sense of worth is when they are with others who feel and think as they do.

Physical Influences on Self-Esteem

Inherited physical characteristics, such as physique, appearance, and disabilities, also may influence self-esteem. The physical attributes that an individual has inherited can affect others' perceptions and behavior. Others may respond negatively to an individual's disabled condition or physical appearance, thus affecting that individual's self-esteem, even though the individual's initial self-perception may not have been negative.

Others' reactions are also influenced by maturational rates. Adults treat children differently at differing maturation levels. Children who mature early are quite often treated as adults and develop positive self-esteem. Those who mature later and continue to be treated as children tend to develop low self-esteem. Even when this latter group matures, they often maintain old self-perceptions and the corresponding low self-esteem. Maturation also affects mastery of developmental tasks. Social disapproval, maladjustment, and increased difficulty in mastering higher level developmental tasks are all possible results of delayed maturation (Frey & Carlock, 1984).

Environmental Influences on Self-Esteem

It is difficult to define the effect environment plays in the development of low self-esteem. A person learns values and has needs satisfied within the environment through social interaction with significant others, and if needs are not met and the expressions of beliefs and values meet with disapproval within the environment, self-esteem is likely to be damaged.

An additional aspect of environment has to do with the groups within the environment with which the person identifies. Each member of a group is evaluated by every other member. If the group is significant to an individual, these evaluations affect self-esteem. For example, if a person's perception is one of not being valued by the group, low self-esteem is probable. Esteem is related to one's rank in a group rather than rank of the group when compared with other groups (Rosenberg, 1965).

As the U.S. population has moved from rural to city areas, the environment in which children had built-in networks and role models has diminished and, in many cases, been lost. In the past, grandparents, aunts, uncles, cousins, neighbors, and friends were available to help educate and advise young people, and that was a given. In the absence of such an array of support, young people have turned to their peers for guidance and approval. In doing so, they use peer norms, created out of lack of experience, for evaluating behavior rather than the collective experience and wisdom of a network of adult role models (Glenn & Nelson, 1989).

Parents have also suffered a loss of support. In most cases, the parents have no network of relatives nearby to assist in parenting, they have to depend on themselves to make the right choices, and they have no experience being parents. Because both parents usually work, they parent part-time. In single-parent families, even part-time parenting is shared with other stresses involved in survival. So now there are time factors as well as inexperienced parents as well as the challenges presented to children in today's world. It becomes easier to see why parents use the same stress reducers as their children.

APPROACHES TO PREVENTION

The pervasive distress and too frequent demise of our young people seem to be out of control. Jason et al. (1993) reported that in Chicago schools, "more than 40% of children do not graduate high school" (p. 69). They believed that the problems leading to dropout often begin in the elementary schools. It is clear that some interventions and prevention strategies targeting low self-esteem must be integrated into every level of the community. Smith and Sandhu (2004) concurred, noting that interventions must occur at an early age on multiple levels. In this section, specific approaches for individuals, parents, schools, and communities are discussed. No one segment of the population is solely responsible for providing prevention. All groups should overlap, and building and maintaining high levels of self-esteem should become an integral part of the total community structure. Although parents are charged with the initial environment for the child, they too are part of a community and have need of resources from the community. A global approach that could be utilized by the entire community is described at the end of this section.

Individual

Self-esteem develops as a result of interaction with and feedback from others. It is doubtful whether an individual can build self-esteem in a vacuum. If the feedback is negative, either verbal or nonverbal, the individual internalizes negative feelings about self and has poor feelings of worth. If feedback is positive and the individual feels successful, self-esteem is enhanced. An individual who feels valued and worthwhile has high self-esteem and responds to others in a manner that communicates this level of self-esteem.

It is difficult, perhaps impossible, for someone suffering from low self-esteem to undertake a prevention program alone. Most of the feedback that builds or destroys self-esteem comes either directly or indirectly from others. An individual is influenced by role models and can be encouraged to learn skills and attitudes that will lead to success experiences. As self-esteem is raised, a person may seek out avenues that will bring more success.

Volunteering, learning to be assertive, learning to cope with anger and conflict constructively, attending workshops and special classes to learn life skills, and entering programs that are specifically designed for young people are all ways an individual can build self-esteem. In each of these possibilities, external guidance is often necessary for a person with low self-esteem.

Family

The environment in which a child is raised has a significant impact on the child's self-esteem (Barber, Chadwick, & Orter, 1992; Benard & Marshall, 2001; Blake & Slate, 1993; Cerezo & Frias, 1994; M. Harvey & Byrd, 1998; Shek, 1997). Historically, children were born into an intact family, and that was the primary environment in which the child learned about being an adult. Today, families vary in structure. Households in which both parents work outside the home are common. Single parenting, step-parenting, joint parenting, parenting by someone other than the biological parent, and homelessness have altered family structures and added to the pressures young people face as they grow into adulthood. Many who find themselves in parenting roles have no idea how to accomplish this and fall back on personal experience. They feel the loss of assistance and experience that an extended family provides, so they parent as they were parented, as best as they can remember. They may have low self-esteem as a result of their own childhood experiences and perpetuate their own feelings of low self-worth in their children. Their own parental role models may not have had the wisdom of the extended family experience either, and this lack of parenting skills continues from one generation to the next.

In terms of prevention, steps must be taken to teach parents how to parent. Recognizing and admitting the need to learn parenting is a primary step in the process of building self-esteem. Sensitivity to cultural norms for parenting is essential in approaching parents. Today's parents have access to parenting classes and special support groups to help them learn to work with their children. These groups are sponsored by school specialists as well as churches and agencies in the community. Joining a class or support group serves a dual purpose. The parents learn skills at the same time that they are increasing their network of support. Getting to know neighbors is another excellent way to extend the support network and can serve as a means to check perceptions of neighborhood situations.

Citing the work of Patterson, Reid, and Dishion (1992) and Reid, Patterson, and Snyder (2002), Smith and Sandhu (2004) described a program that "teaches parents prosocial behaviors, alternatives to aggression as a discipline strategy, and problem-solving skills. In addition, parents are taught to nurture and communicate effectively with children, to establish and negotiate family rules and consequences, and to reward prosocial behavior" (p. 288). This curriculum has been successful in "reducing family conflict and increasing a sense of family unity. Long term effects include a stronger sense of connectedness among family members with a greater likelihood of positive social interactions" (p. 288). Another program prepares parents to be emotional coaches, who, rather than ignoring or discouraging negative emotional reactions such as anger or unhappiness, views the enactment of such emotions as opportunities for the child to develop a deeper understanding of self and others, particularly regarding these potentially troubling feelings (Gottman & DeClair, 1997; Gottman, Katz, & Hooven, 1996).

From a multicultural perspective, parents must understand their own needs for success, status, and control as these needs relate to their child-rearing practices. They must be able to put these needs aside and respond to each child as a unique person and to recognize and accept the contributions their children make in the family. There may have to be conscious efforts made to include each child and to discover ways in which each child can successfully contribute to the well-being of the family. Taking out the garbage can become significant if a child understands that his or her contribution is important to the family. When a parent asks a child for assistance with a task or project, one that cannot be done alone, the child learns that his or her contribution is an integral part in the task completion. In this case, it is essential that the child understands his or her help is not gratuitous but essential. For example, if the family pet has a thorn in a paw, it is difficult for one person to hold the animal, examine or probe the paw, and extract the thorn. It is much easier if someone else holds the animal. Asking for the child's assistance, and pointing out that this task is difficult or impossible for one person to do alone, validates the value of the child's contribution.

Another way to prevent low self-esteem is to allow children to do what they can do and not do it for them. Often adults, who can do things faster or better, become impatient and complete tasks for the children. This indicates a lack of respect for the child and gives negative messages about the child's abilities and worth. These negative messages are both overt and covert and have a powerful effect on self-esteem. Though it may be difficult, allowing a child to complete a task more slowly and in a different manner or to make a mistake brings greater opportunities for learning. Using the mistake as a teachable moment is of greater value than scolding, punishing, or doing it for them.

Spending time with the child, talking or playing, gives positive messages about the child's importance. Letting children know that they are valued is critical in building self-esteem. Ironically, this is often the most difficult prevention technique; it takes time and is the first date to be canceled when schedules get tight. During regularly scheduled time together, bonds are cemented, relationships are nurtured, and both parent and child feel important. In using this strategy, parents must listen carefully, suspend judgment, and be accepting of the child's point of view. Children will discuss serious topics if they believe what they say will be heard and valued. They also learn from the role modeling.

Many families hold regularly scheduled meetings to discuss family matters. These meetings are used to resolve conflicts, plan outings, make decisions about the household, test out new ideas, and involve the whole family in a variety of discussions. Again, these should not be canceled except with solid reasons. If meetings are canceled too often, their usefulness diminishes. The interesting effect of using preventative measures is that the parents' or parental figures' self-esteem grows as well. When parent–child interactions are positive and productive, both participants feel valued.

School

Everyone needs to feel connected to others and to feel supported and accepted. Drawing on the work of Elias et al. (1994) and Eron, Gentry, and Schlegel (1994), Smith and Sandhu (2004) noted children who were "well liked by peers are happier at school, better adjusted both psychologically and emotionally, and considerably less likely to engage in aggressive and violent behaviors" (Elias et al., 1994, p. 289).

Because every child has the opportunity to attend school, this is an ideal place to continue the low-self-esteem prevention programs. Hamachek (1995) noted that school performance and "self-attitudes" (i.e., self-esteem) are interactive. D. W. Johnson, Johnson, and Taylor (1993) reported higher levels of self-esteem achievement and cohesion in fifth graders who participated in cooperative learning environments. Strategies for improving school performance cannot be developed without attending to methods to "help students feel better about themselves" (p. 422). Educators have long been aware of the need for students to feel good about themselves and what they can do. Many schools have peer-tutoring or lower-grade-tutoring programs, peer helpers, and student aides. In such tutoring programs, students are paired with students for teaching or coaching. The tutored students are either peers or, in many cases, younger students in elementary schools. Peer helper programs train selected young people in listening skills and have them talk with and listen to their peers. Student aides assist teachers and office staff. Some of these programs tend to exclude the high-risk populations.

In school, students labeled as high risk are frequently referred to the counselor, who can work on self-esteem issues with students individually or in groups. Lemoire and Chen (2005) believe the conditions that are present in a person-centered approach to counseling are important when working with individuals with low self-esteem, specifically lesbian, gay, bisexual, and transgender (LGBT) adolescents. Unconditional positive regard, acceptance, and empathy combine to provide a safe environment and appear to "hold some promise in addressing the psychological distresses of LGBT adolescents" (Lemoire & Chen, 2005, p. 148). Although the researchers identified a specific group of adolescents, their reasoning seems applicable to a broader range of students as they noted, "the counseling process highlights and strengthens a positive sense of self by allowing the client the firsthand experience of self-exploration and self-understanding" (p. 149). Burrow-Sanchez (2006) agreed. He described motivational interviewing, which uses person-centered counseling strategies, as an effective method to reduce a "client's ambivalence toward change while increasing his or her motivation to engage in the behavior-change process" (p. 286). The counselor supports client behaviors that are congruent with the desired changes and uses reflection, reframing, and active listening to make the client feel understood and accepted.

Guindon (2002) suggested that if counselors understand the definitions of self-esteem (global or selective), he or she can select the type of intervention best suited to the clients' needs at the time and will understand that if the need is for global self-esteem, it may not be readily changeable. However, as with "mountains made of teaspoons of dirt, global self-esteem is made up of numerous facets of selective self-esteem which can be addressed individually and ultimately affect the whole or global self-esteem" (Guindon, 2002, p. 207). Shechtman (2002) placed low-performing children in one of two groups: one group received concentrated academic help and the other group received therapy. After 6 months, those who received therapy showed improvements in "grades, self-esteem, social status, and self-control" (p. 295). These improvements were still present at follow-up. The recommendation was that more therapy groups are needed in schools.

Myers, Sweeney, and Witmer (2000) developed a model for wellness that has been used successfully in many contexts with "young-to-older adults." Their Wheel of Wellness includes six life tasks—spirituality, self-direction, work, leisure, love, and friendship (p. 253)—and identifies a sense of worth as one of the 12 subtasks under self-direction. Using this wheel, professionals can assess an individual on 16 characteristics of wellness, either formally or informally, and design an individualized program to improve or enhance any deficiencies.

Reasoner (1994) described several programs that have been successful in improving self-esteem and reducing crime and violence. A Florida high school program that focused on positive advisor–advisee relationships reported that, within 3 weeks, grade point averages and attendance, both indicators of levels of self-esteem, improved (Testerman, 1996). Still another study (McCormick & Wold, 1993) found positive changes in self-concept of gifted and talented female students who had exhibited underachievement in science and math after exposure to a program describing nontraditional career choices.

Hains (1994) reported on the effectiveness of a cognitive stress management program that showed high school participants made significant improvement in anxiety, self-esteem, depression, and anger. In another cognitive restructuring program, participants either were exposed to a computer-based program that targeted irrational beliefs or a relaxation training program. Those participating in the computer-based program improved self-esteem (Horan, 1996).

A mediation intervention program was piloted at a middle school in Georgia where results indicated a decrease in suspensions, a school morale improvement, and an increase both in requests for peer mediation and the belief that it works (Thompson, 1996). Edmondson and White (1998) found significant improvement in the self-esteem of students who participated in both a tutorial and a counseling program. Conclusions drawn from a 3-year longitudinal study of urban children in Georgia stress the importance of both early and developmentally specific interventions (Spencer, 1991). Kraizer (1990) discussed skills that children need to master the stresses of development. She identified a list of life skills essential to successful passage into adolescence, then advocated early and continuing intervention to prevent development of inappropriate behaviors.

Because schools are community institutions and have the most contact with children, and because many services were available to families but delivery was fragmented or crisis oriented, the West Virginia Education Association and Appalachia Educational Laboratory (1993) surveyed the existing school–community partnerships in that state. In this survey process, the researchers gathered information about problems inherent in school-linked services and about additional school-linked service possibilities. With these data, the research team developed profiles for each of these social service programs and made recommendations for changes at the school, district, and policymaking levels.

Bernard Haldane (1989) developed the Dependable Strengths Articulation Process in 1948, initially for use with returning military personnel who wanted to change careers after World War II. The program has evolved and is being used with high school students in Washington State (Forester, 2004). The Dependable Strengths Assessment Training (DSAT) encouraged students "to articulate their strengths and use those strengths when making their most important plans" (p. 1). Participants in a 2002 DSAT training workshop have adopted the assessment with middle school, junior, and senior high school students with success. Using a prescribed set of activities, students are directed to identify strengths, get feedback from peers about strengths, prioritize them, test them for reliability, and use them when making plans. Although there were no formal data gathered from these experiences using DSAT, users indicated students were more positive and more successful in school (conversations with participants, June 17–21, 2002, University of Washington, Seattle).

One of the warning signs of adolescent suicide is low self-esteem. Maples et al. (2005) identified the need for suicide prevention and intervention programs for schools. They advocated for the need for partnerships among schools, community, and families to educate everyone to the warning signs and interventions for prevention. Simpson (1999, p. 28) noted several strategies that have worked successfully in several educational settings:

- *School gatekeeper training:* in-service training for school staff on identifying students at risk for suicide and where to refer them for help.
- *Community gatekeeper training:* training similar to school gatekeeper training but designed for parents, recreation staff, and other community members.
- *General suicide education:* school-based program for students geared to help them identify the warning signs of suicide and to build self-esteem and coping skills.
- *Screening programs:* programs to identify high-risk youth for targeted assistance.
- *Peer support programs:* programs to foster peer relationships, competency development, and social skills among high-risk youth.
- *Crisis centers and hotlines:* emergency counseling for those who may be suicidal.
- *Means restrict:* activities designed to restrict student access to firearms, drugs, and other means of committing suicide.

With such a program in place, at-risk students can be targeted, and strategies to help them build self-esteem and provide support and connection to their community can be implemented with the hope of ultimately preventing suicide. Writing after a middle school student committed suicide, Maples et al. (2005) suggested a postvention program needs to be in place as well to help everyone deal with the aftermath of a suicide. They advocated a team approach developed by Roberts, Lepkowski, and Davidson (1998) that includes counselors, administrators, parents, and teachers. The program, called TEAM, has four components: developing a team (T), establishing procedures (E), arranging supports (A), and monitoring progress (M). The authors recommended this approach along with appropriate training be in place before any crisis occurs. Further recommendations include the following by the West Virginia Education Association and Appalachia Educational Laboratory (1993):

School and District-Level Recommendations
- The responsibilities of schools should include serving as a focal point to connect families with health and social service providers.
- The mission of the school should include health and social services provision.
- Educational focus should be on prevention and early intervention.
- Schools should provide training to staff to teach them to work effectively with health and social service problems of students.
- Research and evaluation should be undertaken regularly to assess program success and recommend any needed improvements.
- Districts should establish foundations whose funds would be used to develop programs to benefit children and families. Independent sources would donate these funds. (p. 36)

Policy Recommendations

- Funding for programs for at-risk populations should be provided for in the budget, which would serve to standardize school-linked programs. These programs should be protected from budget cuts.
- Early intervention and prevention programs should be given priority.
- Operational procedures of schools and service providers should be examined and changed if these procedures interfere with effective delivery of services. (p. 37)

The recommendations reflect the belief that no one group or institution is totally responsible for bringing health and social services to those community members who need them. The philosophy is that the entire community must work as a team, with the school being the common link between service providers and families.

Jones and Watson (1990) studied high-risk students in higher education. Several of their findings can be considered for earlier educational experiences as well. Recommended prevention programs and strategies include the following:

- Market the benefits of persistent, positive student behaviors.
- Provide career information beginning at an early age. Encourage goal identification.
- Use low-achieving college students to tutor students K–12. This raises self-esteem of each participant.
- Encourage and market counseling services as part of the curriculum. Involve teachers in the referral process.
- Provide in-class programs designed to teach positive attitudes and skills that would include acceptance of others, for example, high-risk students.
- Use peer advisers.
- Enlist school organizations to develop programs to assist fellow students.
- Provide educational programs to teach teachers how to teach. Provide opportunities for teachers to learn alternative teaching techniques and ways to empower students.
- Evaluate testing materials to see that needs of high-risk students are being assessed effectively.
- Develop orientation programs addressing the needs of high-risk populations.
- Acknowledge school personnel who work with high-risk students by reducing class loads.
- Develop methods to assure high-risk students an in-school support system. Using local businesses, provide opportunities for high-risk students to do visits, internships, or part-time work in the community. Many schools invite business people into the classroom to work with students.
- Provide programs for teachers and school personnel to examine their attitudes toward minorities, women, and other high-risk populations. (pp. 85–88)

Community

If we accept the philosophy that at-risk students and families and the school are all part of the total community, any of the just-listed strategies can be offered throughout the community and sponsored by any business or agency. The following are examples of programs that have been developed in a major metropolitan area that may be similar to programs available in other areas.

YMCA (1994) Teen Services

- *County Youth Initiative* provides opportunities for leadership training, public speaking, project planning and delivery of community services, and employment.
- *Earth Service Corps* provides opportunities for environmental education and action, leadership development, and project planning and implementation.
- *The Manifesto Newspaper* provides an opportunity, through a youth-produced countywide newspaper, for teenagers to share their ideas and creativity with members of the community.
- *Y-Zone* provides a safe, alternative environment for youths to participate in activities and special events on a weekend night. This has expanded in adjacent communities to being available both weekend nights.
- *Youth Employment* sponsors a youth-run espresso cart at a local YMCA. The youths are hired and trained before they begin working this cart.

Central Area Youth Association (1992)

- *TeenPATH (Teen Parent Assistance and Transitional Housing Program)* provides assistance to homeless or near-homeless teen parents under the age of 18. The program's goal is to provide assistance to teen parents to break out of the poverty cycle. Through TeenPATH, stable, safe housing is found. In return, the teen parent(s) are required to complete high school, get work training and/or employment, and be responsible parents.
- *Mentorship* assigns role models who offer companionship, guidance, and support and who help empower participants to be free of gang and drug involvement.
- *STARS (Special Tutor for At-Risk Students)* provides one-on-one tutorial services to at-risk students in Grades K–8. Tutors are available both in school and after school in churches, libraries, and community centers.
- *Sports Program* provides adult role models who focus on team work, mental health, physical health, and individual and group responsibilities.
- *4-H Challenge* teaches participants, particularly minority males, coping skills, communication skills, problem-solving skills, and decision-making skills.
- *Introduction to Challenge* places youths in support groups and introduces rules, concepts, and benefits of the Challenge program.
- *Boot Camp/National Guard* introduces youths to orderly, disciplined environments and provides opportunities for building self-esteem.
- *Job Power* allows youths to explore assets and liabilities with regard to employment.
- *Ropes Course* provides outdoor activities to help adult and youth participants learn and develop problem-solving, goal-setting, and communication skills while experiencing total commitment.
- *I'll Take Charge* provides opportunities for youths to take responsibility for their choices.
- *Self-Determined Projects* allow members to determine, with guidance, their own projects that might not be available otherwise.
- *Multimedia* teaches students techniques and technology involved in video production while exposing them to drama, music, and arts.
- *Job Readiness* helps youths to create contacts without turn-downs, teaches them job interviewing skills, and brings the community together to help youths become productive, responsible members of society.

- *Elite Boxing* provides a meaningful outlet for physically aggressive youths in a positive, acceptable manner.
- *BALANCE (Beautiful, Ambitious Ladies Able to Negotiate With Commitment to Self-Esteem and Excellence)* provides weekly support groups for young women, through which substance abuse education and services are provided.

STARS I and II

Two community-based programs for African American youth, STARS I and II, targeted at-risk youth ages 6–10 years and 11–17 years and their parents or guardians. In STARS I, "sessions focused on cultural legacy family communication, the role of the extended family, and decision making" (Dabrowski, Avery, Gyger, & Emshoff, 1993, p. 4). The program for the older children focused on drug education, assertiveness, resisting peer pressure, raising self-esteem, and family communication. Program outcomes showed improvement in all areas for both adults and the children.

Other Community Programs

Nassar-McMillan and Cashwell (1997) offered adventure-based counseling as an intervention to foster self-esteem. Kennison (1996) described a similar wilderness program for youth with diagnosed attention-deficit hyperactive disorder (ADHD) in which activities are built to address the characteristic behaviors of this population. Another special population program, Camp Elsewhere, provided a program for adolescent females with eating disorders, who reported the program had a positive impact on them (Tonkin, 1997). According to participants, a university-sponsored, 2-week residential leadership education program for adolescent girls positively affected self-confidence (Taylor & Rosselli, 1997).

The HAWK Federation focuses on issues unique to Black adolescent males and is rooted in African traditions. Initial reports indicate that those who participated in the program improved their academic achievement (Nobles, 1989). Delgado (1997) described a substance abuse program for Puerto Rican teenagers. Another program with a cultural focus is MAAT Center for Human and Organizational Enhancement Inc., a rites-of-passage program for Egyptian adolescents (A. R. Harvey & Coleman, 1997).

Additional community programs include volunteer chore services; training to become volunteers; volunteer opportunities in social service agencies, churches, and community agencies; and community projects sponsored by individual clubs and organizations, for example, Junior Chamber of Commerce and Boys and Girls Clubs. Many of these offer training and provide built-in support and networking sources.

A Global Approach to Prevention

Glenn and Nelson (1989, pp. 48–49) identified seven tools that are critical to the parenting process and building of self-esteem. These tools can also be used in schools, in the community, and by individuals. The authors noted that they discovered these tools, which are basic to survival in times of change, while they were studying failure, not success. These tools, referred to by the authors as the "significant seven," include the following:

- perceptions of personal capabilities
- perceptions of personal significance

- perceptions of personal power or influence over life
- intrapersonal skills
- interpersonal skills
- systemic skills
- judgmental skills

Perception, as described by Glenn and Nelson (1989), is "the conclusion we reach after we have had time to reflect on that experience" (p. 51). Perception guides our attitudes and behaviors, and as we mature, we become more and more creatures of perception. Perceptions include four components: "The experience, what we interpret as significant about the experience, why it is important, and how we generalize the experience" (p. 55). Because perceptions change as we mature and because they are unique to each individual, it is important that the four components reflect the perceiver's point of view. Even if an experience is shared, perceptions of the experience differ for each person. It is significant to each person in different ways and important to each person for different reasons, and the experience is generalized individually. In terms of building self-esteem, the learner must see the personal importance and value of an experience for himself or herself. As teachers or role models, we have to suspend our own perceptions, judgments, and beliefs and genuinely and respectfully listen to the learner's perspective.

In teaching the first tool and helping young people develop a strong idea about their personal capabilities, there are some critical behaviors we have to give up (Glenn & Nelson, 1989). We must give up assuming that we know how someone else will react in situations and acting as if that were true. We no longer need to rescue or explain, expect attainment of perfection, or dominate and control. Instead, we must learn to listen and hear individual perceptions; check out assumptions; be open to, accepting, and respectful of a young person's thoughts and feelings; and be encouraging and celebrate successes. These changes in adult behaviors will help young people begin to feel valued and respected in the community.

As noted earlier, in the past each family member used to feel that his or her contributions were essential to the family's maintenance and survival. For the most part, this reality has been lost. What has not been lost is the need to be needed. The individual's perception of personal significance is of primary importance. To develop this second tool, we must find ways to acknowledge each individual's personal worth, to help the person see that the family is richer because this person is contributing his or her uniqueness. This can be done by listening, understanding, and accepting another's perspective, by soliciting ideas and perceptions from young people, by having frequent personal contact, and by providing a loving, warm family climate.

The third tool, the individual's belief in his or her ability to influence life, refers to the earlier discussion of internal versus external locus of control. Adults can help children build this internal power by establishing firm boundaries for behavior. One of the purposes for maladaptive behavior is to see if limits are real. If an adult cares enough to set limits and to adhere to them, the child learns that he or she is valued and loved and knows the parameters within which to make decisions about behavior. At the same time, he or she also learns about the natural or logical consequences of stepping outside of these parameters. Children will learn from their mistakes if allowed to do so. They will build a belief system that says they have influence over their world. As already noted, adults have to be good listeners so there can be continued discussions with the child as he or she matures and encounters new decision-making opportunities.

Intrapersonal skills, the fourth tool, refer to an individual being able to understand and express feelings, to exercise self-control and self-discipline (Glenn & Nelson, 1989). As a child learns to make decisions within established boundaries, in new situations he or she can consider available responses and choose appropriately. The parent who does not allow the child to make a decision and does it for the child is a primary interference here. A better intervention is to provide a list of alternatives, discuss with the child the consequences of each action (from the child's perspective), and allow the child to decide.

Interpersonal skills, the fifth tool, refer to those skills that allow people to communicate with each other. The extent to which a young person learns these skills is closely related to how well the child gets along with others. Adults can teach these skills through modeling and talking with children.

The systemic and judgmental skills, identified by Glenn and Nelson (1989) as the sixth and seventh tools, are not always specifically taught. They are based on, composed of, and the result of earlier lessons learned. Understanding how the system in which we live works is to become aware of the connection between what we do and the result of our actions. By becoming aware of cause and effect, we learn to predict outcomes and are able to set attainable, realistic goals. We learn to be flexible and to take responsibility for our actions because we know the possible outcomes or consequences. For children to learn and increase these skills, adults must provide information about behavior in a caring, respectful climate. Helping an individual to develop good judgment skills requires adults to allow the person most affected by the decision to make it, to provide opportunities for young people to make decisions and experience the consequences, and to collaborate with them during the process. As part of the learning process, we also need to help them evaluate their decisions.

ADAPTATIONS FOR DIVERSITY

Self-esteem develops within the cultural environment in which an individual lives (Hales, 1990; McCarthy & Holliday, 2004). Culture defines how roles will be played by members. One's success or failure in fulfilling cultural role expectations influences self-esteem. Success brings with it a feeling of belonging to a group, of being an important contributing member of that culture, and of feeling good about self. Failure, of course, brings the opposite.

A problem occurs when at-risk youths belong to a nondominant culture and are faced with living in another culture, one with new or different expectations. Conflict is inevitable. A person who is respected for specific behaviors in one culture and chastised or punished for the same behavior in another culture could easily develop lowered self-esteem. Evidence of this is seen in at-risk youth today. Brentro, Brokenleg, & Van Bockern (1990) suggested a feeling of competence is one aspect essential to the development of self-esteem, and in the above scenario an individual may not feel competent.

According to Phinney (1992), continuing to identify with one's own culture as well as with the main culture is an important component of high self-esteem. Problems arise if the cultural or national group is not viewed as esteemed by other cultures or nations. Those identifying with the original culture or group may suffer low self-esteem. It becomes difficult when minorities identify with their own culture, are accepted and develop positive feelings of worth and belonging within that culture, and do not receive the same positive responses in the new culture. Ishiyama (1995) referred to this phenomena as *cultural dislocation*. This is particularly painful when the culture of origin does not appear to be valued in the new culture, and the beliefs and values of the two cultures are divergent. We see this occurring with minorities when they experience difficulty assimilating another culture's values.

Another issue was highlighted in a recent discussion with immigrants to the State of Washington (personal communication, 2000). Conflicts have emerged between those children who were born and lived in another country and culture before emigrating with their parents and those who were born in the United States after the move. Members of the same family are conflicted, some wanting to retain what is known and familiar and some wanting to "fit in" and not be associated with the "old" culture. Whatever the resolution of the conflict, it will be a direct threat to self-esteem.

Sheets (1995) and Washington (1989) discussed the impact of school culture on self-esteem. Describing different ethnic cultures, they both agreed that teaching and programs that are culturally appropriate can help minorities maintain a positive level of self-esteem and self-validation.

To add to any existing conflicts between dual cultures, norms, and values, Kumamoto (1997) explained that people's views of self and culture are changing because of the massive changes in the world today. The changing, or perhaps conflicting guidelines for roles for everyone, regardless of culture, affect members of both the dominant and the minority cultures. With the resulting confusion, the success or failure in adapting to new ways of acting and interacting creates an additional assault on self-esteem.

In previous generations young people had roles to play that confirmed their value as important contributors to the welfare of the family and community. This gave them a meaningful role in their community and ensured the transfer of cultural beliefs and values (Glenn & Nelson, 1989). In contemporary society, with single-parent families and population mobility, that is less likely to occur. Changes in society have provided more passive ways for values to be transmitted to the young. Roles that are depicted in the media often do not reflect appropriate cultural beliefs and values, and many young people do not have multiple adult role models who can correct inappropriate perceptions of behaviors and beliefs illustrated in the media.

CASE STUDY: PROJECT REACH

Project Reach is an alternative program for at-risk students in the Socorro School District in Texas (Heger, 1992). Students in this program were in serious trouble in school and had reached the stage where the next step was expulsion. Health education, drama, group therapy, and computer-assisted instruction were blended in a program designed to prevent dropouts or expulsions and to assist in the reintegration of these at-risk students into the mainstream.

The curriculum was a traditional curriculum delivered in a nontraditional way, through computers. In the remaining time during the school day, students participated in health and drug education, drama, and personal log writing. The psychological part of the program is described as similar to "Tough Love" and "Boot Camp," which are highly structured programs that leave no doubt as to limits and consequences of misbehavior.

The school day started at 11 a.m. and continued into early evening, and admission was for an undetermined length of time. Students had levels of tasks to complete, and when these stages were accomplished, they were readmitted into the mainstream. The pace of progress was individualized.

Evaluators found dramatic results. Attrition rates went from 84% in 1990–1991 to 2.9% in 1992–1993. At the same time, 76% of the students reported better grades. Students were surveyed periodically, and 86% believed the program was helpful to them. The longer they were in the program, the more helpful they reported it to be.

Success of this program is attributed to the design, the staff, and the execution. Staff members were from nontraditional backgrounds, and many had turned to teaching after trying other occupations. Some were not fully certified, but all had prior experience in helping people in nontraditional curricula.

SUMMARY

In our society, young people daily exhibit deviant behaviors. There is evidence everyday that there are many more adolescents demonstrating characteristics that are understood to be at risk. These young people are considered at risk because unless they are helped to succeed, they will become part of the deviant subculture. Research has shown that there is a connection between how a person feels about himself or herself and how that person acts (Kaplan, 1975, 2006; Kaplan et al., 1986; Marston et al., 1988). Self-esteem is an issue that must be confronted as a cause of at-risk behaviors.

This chapter identifies specific symptoms of low self-esteem, factors that influence self-esteem, and prevention programs and strategies for parents, individuals, schools, and communities. The activities and programs designed to be used with at-risk youth are not extensive. We must look within our own communities to discover available and successful youth programs. Additional information and resources may also be found in popular magazines (Corbett in *Essence*, 1995; Cordes in *Parenting*, 1994; Herman in *Utne Reader*, 1992; McMahon in *Cosmopolitan*, 1994; McMillan, Singh, & Simonetta in *Education Digest*, 1995; Tafel in *McCalls*, 1992). Carlock's book, *Enhancing Self-Esteem* (1999), identifies many publications and educational audiotapes and videotapes that focus on building self-esteem. The goal is to reach all adolescents, particularly those at risk, and give them a chance to succeed and feel worthwhile.

REFERENCES

Abramson, L. Y., Seligman, M. E. P., & Teasdale, J. D. (1978). Learned helplessness in humans: Critique and reformulation. *Journal of Abnormal Psychology, 87*, 49–74.

Appleton, V., & Dykeman, C. (2004). The impact of dysfunctional family dynamics on children and adolescents. In D. Capuzzi & D. R. Gross (Eds.), *Youth at risk: A prevention resource for counselors, teachers, and parents* (4th ed., pp. 69–92). Alexandria, VA: American Counseling Association.

Aronson, M., & Mettee, S. (1968). Dishonest behavior as a function of differential levels of induced self-esteem. *Journal of Personality and Social Psychology, 9*, 121–127.

Bachman, J. G., & O'Malley, P. M. (1986). The frog's pond revisited (again). *Journal of Personality and Social Psychology, 50*, 35–46.

Barber, B. K., Chadwick, B. A., & Orter, R. (1992). Parental behaviors and adolescent self-esteem in the United States. *Journal of Marriage and Family Therapy, 54*, 128–141.

Beane, J. A., & Lipka, R. P (1980). Self-concept and self-esteem. A construct differentiation. *Child Study Journal, 10*, 1–6.

Benard, B., & Marshall, K. (2001). *Competence and resilience research: Lessons for prevention.* Minneapolis: University of Minnesota, National Resilience Resource Center and the Center for the Application of Prevention Technologies. Retrieved September 13, 2006, from http://www.cce.umm.edu/pdfs/NRRC/capt_pdf/protective.pdf

Benoit, R. B., & Mitchell, L. K. (1987). Self-efficacy: Its nature and promise as an approach to dealing with high school dropout among minorities. *CACD Journal, 8,* 31–38.

Blake, P. C., & Slate, J. R. (1993). A preliminary investigation into the relationship between adolescent self-esteem and parental verbal interaction. *The School Counselor, 41*(2), 81–85.

Bower, B. (1993). Gender paths wind toward self-esteem: Gender differences in self-esteem development. *Science News, 143,* 308.

Brentro, L. K., Brokenleg, M., & Van Bockern, S. (1990). *Reclaiming youth at-risk: Our hope for the future.* Bloomington, IN: National Education Service.

Buri, J. R., & Dickinson, K. A. (1994, May). *Comparison of familial and cognitive factors associated with male and female self-esteem.* Paper presented at the annual meeting of the Midwestern Psychological Association, Chicago, IL.

Burnett, J. W., Anderson, W. P., & Heppner, P. P. (1995). Gender roles and self-esteem: A consideration of environmental factors. *Journal of Counseling & Development, 73,* 323–326.

Burrow-Sanchez, J. J. (2006). Understanding adolescent substance abuse: Prevalence, risk factors, and clinical implications. *Journal of Counseling & Development, 84,* 283–290.

Cantor, D., & Bernay, T. (1992). *Women in power: The secrets of leadership.* Boston: Houghton Mifflin.

Carlock, C J. (Ed.). (1999) *Enhancing self-esteem.* Philadelphia: Accelerated Development.

Central Area Youth Association. (1992). *A history and overview* [Paper and brochures]. (Available from CAYA, 119 23rd Ave., Seattle, WA 98122)

Cerezo, M., & Frias, D. (1994, November). Emotional and cognitive adjustment in abused children. *Child Abuse and Neglect: The International Journal, 18,* 23–32.

Chapman, P. L., & Mullis, R. L. (1999). Adolescent coping strategies and self-esteem. *Child Study Journal, 29,* 69–77.

Cohen, L. H., Burt, C. E., & Bjorck, J. P. (1987). Life stress and adjustment: Effect on life events experienced by young adolescents and their parents. *Developmental Psychology, 23,* 583–592.

Corbett, C. (1995). The winner within: A hands-on guide to healthy self-esteem. *Essence, 26*(2), 56–70.

Cordes, H. (1994). Resources: Groups, books, magazines, and other tools for building girls' self-esteem. *Parenting, 8*(3), 96.

Dabrowski, R. M., Avery, M. E., Gyger, R. L., & Emshoff, J. G. (1993, March). *Community based, family-focused prevention of youth substance use.* Paper presented at the Southeastern Psychological Association, Atlanta, GA.

Delgado, M. (1997). Strengths-based practice with Puerto Rican adolescents: Lessons from a substance abuse prevention project. *Social Work in Education, 19,* 101–112.

Domino, G., & Blumberg, E. (1987). An application of Gough's conceptual model to a measure of adolescent self-esteem. *Journal of Youth* and *Adolescence, 16*(2), 87–90.

Dwyer, V. (1993). Eye of the beholder: Young women have self-image problems. *Maclean's, 106*(8), 46–47.

Edmondson, J. H., & White, J. (1998). A tutorial and counseling program: Helping students at risk of dropping out of school. *Professional School Counseling, 1*(4), 43–47.

Elias, M. J. K., Weissberg, R. P., Hawkins, J. D., Perry, C. L., Zins, J. E., Dodge, K. A., et al. (1994). The school-based promotion of social competence: Theory, research, practice, and policy. In R. J. Hagerty, N. Garmezy, M. Rutter, & L. Sherrod (Eds.), *Stress, risk and resilience in children and adolescence: Processes, mechanisms, and interventions* (pp. 269–315). New York: Cambridge University Press.

Elliott, G. C. (1988). Gender differences in self-consistency: Evidence from an investigation of self-concept structure. *Journal of Youth and Adolescence, 17*, 41–57.

Enns, C. (1992). Self-esteem groups: A synthesis of consciousness-raising and assertiveness training. *Journal of Counseling & Development, 71*, 7–13.

Eron, L. D., Gentry, J. H., & Schlegel, P. (Eds.). (1994). *Reason to hope: A psychosocial perspective on violence and youth*. Washington, DC: American Psychological Association.

Eskilson, A., Wiley, G., Meuhlbauer, G., & Dodder, L. (1986). Parental pressure, self-esteem, and adolescent reported deviance: Bending the twig too far. *Adolescence, 21*, 501–515.

Forester, J. R. (2004). Your best plans must use your best strengths. In S. Mygatt-Wakefield (Ed.), *Unfocused kids: Innovative practices to help students focus on their plans after high school; a resource for educators*. Greensboro: ERIC/CAPS and the American Counseling Association.

Frey, D., & Carlock, C. J. (1984). *Enhancing self-esteem*. Muncie, IN: Accelerated Development.

Glenn, H. S., & Nelson, J. (1989). *Raising self-reliant children in a self-indulgent world*. Rocklin, CA: Prima.

Gottman, J., & DeClair, J. (1997). *The heart of parenting: Raising an emotionally intelligent child*. New York: Simon & Schuster.

Gottman, J., Katz, L., & Hooven, C. (1996). *Meta-emotion: How families communicate emotionally, links to child peer relations and other developmental outcomes*. Mahwah, NJ: Erlbaum.

Graf, R. C. (1971). Induced self-esteem as a determinant of behavior. *Journal of Social Psychology, 85*, 213–217.

Guindon, M. H. (2002). Toward accountability in the use of the self-esteem construct. *Journal of Counseling & Development, 80*, 204–214.

Hains, A. A. (1994). The effectiveness of a school-based, cognitive–behavioral stress management program with adolescents reporting high and low levels of emotional arousal. *School Counselor, 42*, 114–125.

Haldane, B. (1989, March). *The dependable strengths articulation process: How it works*. Paper presented at the annual convention of the American Association for Counseling and Development, Boston, MA.

Hales, S. (1990, Winter). Valuing the self: Understanding the nature of self-esteem. *The Saybrook Perspective*, 3–17.

Hamachek, D. (1995). Self-concept and school achievement: Interaction dynamics and a tool for assessing the self-concept component. *Journal of Counseling & Development, 73*, 419–123.

Harvey, A. R., & Coleman, A. A. (1997). An Afrocentric program for African American males in the juvenile justice system. *Child Welfare, 76*(1), 197–211.

Harvey, M., & Byrd, M. (1998). The relationship between perceptions of self-esteem, patterns of familial attachment and family environment during early and late phases of adolescence. *International Journal of Adolescence and Youth, 7*(2), 93–111.

Hazler, R. J., & Mellin, E. A. (2004). The developmental origins and treatment needs of female adolescents with depression. *Journal of Counseling & Development, 82,* 18–24.

Hazler, R. J., Carney, J. V., & Granger, D. A. (2006). Integrating biological measures into the study of bullying. *Journal of Counseling & Development, 84,* 298–307.

Heger, H. K. (1992, October). *Retaining Hispanic youth in school: An evaluation of a counseling-based alternative school program.* Paper presented at the annual conference of the Rocky Mountain Educational Research Association, Stillwater, OK.

Herman, E. (1992, January/February). Are politics and therapy compatible? A lesson from the self-esteem movement. *Utne Reader,* 97–100.

Horan, J. J. (1996). Effects of computer-based cognitive restructuring on rationally mediated self-esteem. *Journal of Counseling Psychology, 43,* 371–375.

Ishiyama, F. I. (1995). Culturally dislocated clients: Self-validation and cultural conflict issues and counseling implications. *Canadian Journal of Counseling, 29,* 262–273.

Jason, L. A., Weine, A. M., Johnson, J. H., Danner, K. E., Kurasaki, K. S., & Warren-Sohlberg, L. (1993). The school transition project: A comprehensive preventative intervention. *Journal of Emotional and Behavioral Disorders, 1,* 65–70.

Johnson, D. S. (1981). Naturally acquired learned helplessness: The relationship of school failure to achievement behavior, attributions, and self-concept. *Journal of Educational Psychology, 73,* 174–180.

Johnson, D. W., Johnson, R. T., & Taylor, B. (1993). Impact of cooperative and individualistic learning on high-ability students achievement, self-esteem, and social acceptance. *Journal of Social Psychology, 133,* 839–844.

Jones, D. J., & Watson, B. C. (1990). *High-risk students and higher education.* Washington, DC: George Washington University, Clearinghouse on Higher Education.

Kaplan, H. B. (1975). *Self-attitudes and deviant behavior.* Pacific Palisades, CA: Goodyear.

Kaplan, H. B. (1976). Self-attitude and deviant response. *Social Forces, 54,* 788–801.

Kaplan, H. B. (2006). Understanding the concept of resilience. In S. Goldstein & R. Books (Eds.), *Handbook of resilience in children* (pp. 39–48). New York: Springer Science+Business Media.

Kaplan, H. B., Martin, S. S., & Johnson, R. J. (1986). Self-rejection and the explanation of deviance: Specification of the structure among latent constructs. *American Journal of Sociology, 92,* 384–411.

Kelly, T. M., Lynch, K. G., Donovan, J. E., & Clark, D. B. (2001). Alcohol use disorders and risk factor interactions for adolescent suicidal ideation and attempts. *Suicide and Life-Threatening Behavior, 32,* 181–193.

Kennison, J. A. (1996). Therapy in the mountains. In *Proceedings of the 1995 International Conference on Outdoor Recreation and Education.* Boise, ID: Association of Outdoor Recreation and Education.

Kraizer, S. (1990). Skills for living: The requirement of the 90s. In *Critical issues in prevention of child abuse and neglect: Adolescent parenting life skills for children* (pp. 131–139). Austin: Children's Trust Fund of Texas.

Kumamoto, C. C. (1997, March). *Unison in variety, congeniality in difference: Sifting beyond the multicultural sieve.* Paper presented at the annual meeting of the Conference on College Composition and Communication, Phoenix, AZ.

Lemoire, S. J., & Chen, C. P. (2005). Applying person-centered counseling to sexual minority adolescents. *Journal of Counseling & Development, 83,* 146–154.

Lord, S., Eccles, J. S., & McCarthy, K. A. (1994). Surviving junior high school transition: Family processes and self-perceptions as protective and risk factors. *Journal of Early Adolescence, 14*, 162–199.

Lorr, M., & Wunderlich, R. A. (1986). Two objective measures of self-esteem. *Journal of Personality Assessment, 50*, 18–23.

Mack, J. E., & Ablon, S. L. (Eds.). (1983). *The development and sustenance of self-esteem in childhood.* New York: International Universities Press.

Maples, M. F., Packman, J., Abney, P., Daugherty, R. F., Casey, J. A., & Pirtle, L. (2005). Suicide by teenagers in middle school: A postvention team approach. *Journal of Counseling & Development, 83*, 397–405.

Marston, A. R., Jacobs, D. F., Singer, R. D., Widaman, K. F., & Little, T. D. (1988). Characteristics of adolescents at risk for compulsive overeating on a brief screening test. *Adolescence, 23*, 59–72.

Masche, J. G. (2000, March/April). *Does a happy marriage make positive parent–adolescent relationships and self-satisfied children?* Paper presented at the biennial meeting of the Society for Research on Adolescence, Chicago, IL.

Maternal and Child Health Branch, Hawaii State Department of Health. (1991). *Adolescent health in Hawaii: The Adolescent Health Network's teen health advisor report.* Rockville, MD: Health Resources and Services Administration.

McCarthy, J., & Holliday, E.L. (2004) Help-seeking and counseling within a traditional male gender role: An examination from a multicultural perspective. *Journal of Counseling & Development, 82*, 25-30.

McCormick, M. E., & Wold, J. S. (1993). Programs for gifted girls. *Roeper Review, 16*(2), 85–88.

McDowell, J. (1984). *Building your self-image.* Wheaton, IL: Living Books.

McGee, R., & Williams, T. (2000). Does low self-esteem predict health compromising behaviors among adolescents? *Journal of Adolescence, 23*, 569–582.

McMahon, S. (1994). Let us now praise me. *Cosmopolitan, 217*(2), 6–70.

McMillan, J. H., Singh, J., & Simonetta, L. G. (1995). Self-oriented self-esteem self-destructs. *Education Digest, 60*(7), 9–12.

Moreau, D. (1996) Depression in the young. In J. A. Sechzer, S. N. Pfafflin, F. L. Denmark, A. Griffin, & S. J. Blumenthal (Eds.), *Women in mental health* (pp. 31–44). New York: New York Academy of Sciences.

Mufson, L., & Moreau, D. (1997). Depressive disorders. In R. T. Ammerman & M. Hersen (Eds.), *Handbook of prevention and treatment with children and adolescents* (pp. 403–430). New York: Wiley.

Myers, J. E., Sweeney, T. J., & Witmer, J. M. (2000). The Wheel of Wellness counseling for wellness: A holistic model for treatment planning. *Journal of Counseling & Development, 78*, 251–266.

Nassar-McMillan, S. C., & Cashwell, C. S. (1997). Building self-esteem of children and adolescents through adventure based counseling. *Journal of Humanistic Education and Development, 36*(2), 59–67.

Nobles, W. W. (1989). *The HAWK Federation and the development of Black adolescent males: Toward a solution to the crises of America's young Black men.* Testimony before the Select Committee on Children, Youth and Families in the Congressional Hearings on America's Young Black Men: Isolated and in Trouble, Washington, DC.

Patterson, G. R., Reid, J. B., & Dishion, T. J. (1992). *Antisocial boys: A social interactional approach* (Vol. 4). Eugene, OR: Castalia.

Phinney, J. S. (1992). Acculturation attitudes and self-esteem among high school and college students. *Youth and Society, 23*, 299–312.

Portes, P. R., & Zady, M. F. (2000, April). *Cultural differences in the self-esteem and adaptation of Spanish-speaking second generation adolescents.* Paper presented at the annual meeting of the American Educational Research Association, New Orleans, LA.

Reasoner, R. W. (1994). *Self-esteem as an antidote to crime and violence.* Port Ludlow, WA: National Council for Self-Esteem.

Reid, J. B., Patterson, G. R., & Snyder, J. (2002). *Antisocial behavior in children and adolescents: A developmental analysis and model for intervention.* Washington, DC: American Psychological Association.

Roberts, R., Lepkowski, W., & Davidson, K. (1998). Dealing with the aftermath of a student suicide: A T.E.A.M. approach. *NAASP Bulletin, 82,* 53–59.

Robison-Awana, P., Kehle, T. J., & Jenson, W. R. (1986). But what about smart girls? Adolescent self-esteem and sex role perceptions as a function of academic achievement. *Journal of Educational Psychology, 78,* 179–183.

Rosenberg, M. (1965). *Society and the adolescent self-image.* Princeton, NJ: Princeton University Press.

Saltzman, A. (1994). Schooled in failure? Fact or myth—teachers favor boys; girls respond by withdrawing. *U.S. News and World Report, 117,* 88–93.

Satir, V. (1981, June). Paper presented at the AVANTA Process Community Conference, Park City, UT.

Schectman, Z. (2002). Child group psychotherapy in the school at the threshold of a new millennium. *Journal of Counseling & Development, 80,* 293–299.

Sheets, R. H. (1995). From remedial to gifted: Effects of culturally centered pedagogy. *Theory Into Practice, 34,* 186–193.

Shek, D. T. L. (1997). Family environment and adolescent psychological well-being, school adjustment and problem behavior: A pioneer study in a Chinese contest. *Journal of Genetic Psychology, 153,* 113–128.

Sim, T. N. (2000). Adolescent psychological competence: The importance of role and regard for parents. *Journal of Research on Adolescence,10,* 49–64.

Simmons, R. C., Burgeson, R., Carlton-Ford, S., & Blyth, D. A. (1987). Impact of cumulative change in early adolescence. *Child Development, 58,* 1220–1234.

Simpson, M. (1999). Student suicide: Who's liable? *NEA Today, 17,* 25–29.

Smith, D. C., & Sandhu, D. S. (2004). Toward a positive perspective on violence prevention in schools: Building connections. *Journal of Counseling & Development, 83,* 287–293.

Spencer, M. B. (1991). *Adolescent African American male self-esteem: Suggestions for mentoring program content* (Mentoring Program Structures for Young Minority Males conference paper series). Washington, DC: Urban Institute.

Stanard, R. P. (2000). Assessment and treatment of adolescent depression and suicidality. *Journal of Mental Health Counseling, 22,* 204–217.

Tafel, R. (1992). How your self-esteem affects your child's. *McCalls, 119*(6), 40–42.

Taylor, E. L., & Rosselli, H. (1997, March). *The effect of a single gender leadership program on young women.* Paper presented at the annual meeting of the American Educational Research Association, Chicago, IL.

Testerman, J. (1996). Holding at-risk students. *Phi Delta Kappan, 77,* 364–365.

Thompson, S. M. (1996). Peer mediation: A peaceful solution. *School Counselor, 44,* 151–154.

Tonkin, R. S. (1997). Evaluation of a summer camp for adolescents with eating disorders. *Journal of Adolescent Health, 20,* 412–413.

Washington, E. D. (1989). A componential theory of culture and its implications for African-American identify. *Equity and Excellence, 24*(2), 24–30.

Weinburg, N. Z. (2001). Risk factors for adolescent substance abuse. *Journal of Learning Disabilities, 34*, 343–351.

West Virginia Education Association and Appalachia Educational Laboratory. (1993). *Schools as community social-service centers: West Virginia programs and possibilities* (Available from Appalachia Educational Laboratory, P. O. Box 1348, Charleston, WV 25325)

Yanish, D. L., & Battle, J. (1985). Relationship between self-esteem, depression, and alcohol consumption among adolescents. *Psychological Reports, 57*, 331–334.

Yankelovich, Y. D. (1981). *New rules: Search for self-fulfillment in a world turned upside down*. New York: Random House.

YMCA. (1994). *YMCA teen services* [Flyer]. Seattle, WA: Author.

CHAPTER 6

■

Preventing and Treating Mood Disorders in Children and Adolescents

Benedict T. McWhirter and Karrie P. Walters

The incidence, nature, and treatment of depression, bipolar disorders, and other mood disorders during childhood and adolescence have been topics of extensive research in recent years (Birmaher, Ryan, Williamson, Brent, & Kaufman, 1996; Kovacs & Devlin, 1998; Lewinsohn, Rohde, & Seeley, 1998; Michael & Crowley, 2002; Wagner & Ambrosini, 2001). Currently, for instance, depression in youth is viewed as a significant problem, with 4%–8% of adolescents and 2%–5% of younger children experiencing depression in any given year (Costello et al., 2002). In fact, one in five youths report a minimum of one episode of major depression by the age of 18 (Lewinsohn, Hops, Roberts, Seeley, & Andrew, 1993). Furthermore, the prevention of mood disorders in childhood and adolescence is critical to reducing the high cost of treating this disorder among adults (King, 1991), as follow-up studies with depressed adolescents have found an increased risk for recurrence in adulthood (Costello et al., 2002). Therefore, child and adolescent mood disorders are a major phenomenon and deserves the full attention of mental health and educational professionals.

This chapter focuses on the problem of child and adolescent depression and bipolar disorder. We first present some of the diagnostic issues in child and adolescent mood disorders. Next, we tell the story of Esteban, a Latino adolescent who is struggling with depression, which illustrates some of its causes and related intervention strategies. We then discuss some of the causal factors associated with mood disorders and some of the prevention and treatment models and strategies that have been found to be effective for children and adolescents suffering from depression and bipolar disorder. The strategies we discuss include interventions at the individual, family, school, and community levels. We conclude this chapter with a section on adaptations for diversity, exploring how the various prevention and treatment strategies discussed can be combined to form a responsible and comprehensive response to diverse young people experiencing depression, bipolar disorder, and other affective problems.

DIAGNOSTIC ISSUES

Until recently, depression in childhood and adolescence was not well addressed in the psychological literature. Bipolar disorders among youth have only recently received the clinical and research attention that it merits. Current research clearly supports that depression and bipolar disorders in childhood and adolescence are important clinical problems. Today, for example, adolescents seen in mental health centers are most frequently diagnosed with an affective disorder (Marcotte, 1997). Because of extensive research designed to understand the course of depression in children and adolescents and to find efficacious treatment, it is now known that depression is not typically transitory but fairly chronic: Youths who have experienced depression are likely to have another episode of depression within a few years of their first experience (Costello et al., 2002; Kovacs & Devlin, 1998; Lewinsohn et al., 1998). Bipolar disorders diagnosed in childhood and adolescence typically have a lifelong course, implying the need for effective intervention early in a young person's life. As such, clearly and precisely diagnosing depression, bipolar disorders, and other affective problems among youth is critical.

The *Diagnostic and Statistical Manual of Mental Disorders*, now in its fourth edition and having recently undergone a text revision (*DSM IV–TR*; American Psychiatric Association, 2000), divides mood disorders into three major categories: depressive disorders, bipolar disorders, and mood disorders due to a general medical condition. The depressive disorders include major depressive disorder, characterized by one or more depressive episodes without history of mania, and dysthymic disorder, characterized by conditions indicating mood disturbance that has been chronic or intermittent for at least 2 years but without the degree of severity to warrant a diagnosis of major depressive disorder. Bipolar disorders include Bipolar I disorder, Bipolar II disorder, and cyclothymic disorder. The bipolar disorders are distinguished by the presence of a manic episode. Bipolar II, for instance, indicates depression with hypomania, a milder form of and presence of manic episodes. Cyclothymia, of course, is a milder form of bipolar disorder. The final category includes mood disturbances judged to be of medical etiology. This condition is found with increasing frequency among younger populations. The *DSM–IV–TR* also includes specifiers such as seasonal pattern indicators (e.g., seasonal affective disorder) in which people become more depressed during certain times of the year. Practitioners should also pay attention to adjustment disorders that may be accompanied by depressed mood as another important diagnostic category. Additionally, in some cases, youths may experience related affective problems concurrently; for example, many children diagnosed with bipolar disorder also experience the effects of seasonal affective disorder.

Although core symptoms of depression are the same in both adults and children, the *DSM–IV–TR* addresses important differential aspects of adolescent depressive symptomatology. For example, instead of weight loss, children may not meet expected weight gain. It appears that in childhood the rates of depression are relatively equal between boys and girls, and not until adolescence do girls have increased rates closely paralleling the gender differences found in adulthood (Birmaher, Ryan, Williamson, Brent, Kaufman, Dahl, et al., 1996; Kazdin, 1994; Lewinsohn et al., 1998). Further symptom delineation can be seen between prepubescent children and adolescents. Young children are much more likely to experience irritability instead of a depressed mood, in addition to somatic complaints and social withdrawal. In contrast, adolescents are more apt to display psychomotor retardation and hypersomnia. Furthermore, depression is comorbid in childhood and adolescence more often than in adulthood (Lewinsohn, Rohde, Klein, & Seeley, 1999). Prepubertal children typically display major depressive episodes in conjunction with disruptive behavior disorders, attention-deficit disorders, and anxiety disorders (American Psychiatric Association, 2000; Costello et al., 2002; Kovacs & Devlin, 1998). Adolescent depression is more commonly associated with anxiety, disruptive behavior disorders, attention-deficit disorders, substance-related disorders, and eating disorders (American Psychiatric Association, 2000; Birmaher, Ryan, Williamson, Brent, & Kaufman, 1996; Costello et al., 2002). In addition, the depressed adolescent is likely to have a depressotypic cognitive style, negative body image, less social support (peer and familial), and more conflictual family interactions than nondepressed peers. The unique symptomatology and additional comorbidity found in childhood and adolescent depression make thorough assessment and careful diagnosis of this population all the more essential.

Although the central focus of this chapter is on depressive disorders, we note that bipolar disorder is a serious mental condition that can negatively affect the normal functioning of children and adolescents. Young people suffering from this disorder may experience extreme episodes of mania and depression that switch frequently. On the basis of the limited epidemiological data available, it appears that bipolar disorder is more prevalent in children after puberty (see James & Javaloyes, 2001). For example, available evidence suggests that the rates of mania in adolescence is similar to the rates in adulthood (i.e., approximately 1%; Lewinsohn, Klein, & Seeley, 1995). Reported prevalence rates also vary depending on how strictly DSM–IV–TR criteria were applied, but the range of children and adolescents diagnosed with bipolar disorder are from 1% to 2% of the population (James & Javaloyes, 2001).

Much of the information on bipolar disorder in childhood and adolescence has been extrapolated from the adult literature. For example, this disorder is diagnosed for young people using the same DSM criteria as used for adults. Using the same criteria, however, has presented difficulties in diagnosing children. For example, although both types of bipolar disorder (i.e., Bipolar I and II) can be experienced in a rapid cycling fashion (i.e., rapidly changing episodes of manic and depressive symptoms), DSM–IV–TR criteria require a hypermanic episode to last at least 4 days. Research findings suggest that young children and adolescents with bipolar disorder may experience cycling (from depression to mania) several times a day. So, as opposed to adult bipolar disorder, which presents with clear periods of relapse and recovery, child bipolar disorder often presents as chronic and remitting (Costello et al., 2002).

Bipolar disorder is often misdiagnosed in children and adolescents. In addition to the above complications using DSM–IV–TR criteria, Sanchez, Hagino, Weller, and Ronald (1999) suggested that misdiagnosis partially stems from (a) a low rate of occurrence of the disorder in child and adolescent populations and (b) the fact that many symptoms overlap with other common childhood disorders such as attention-deficit hyperactivity disorder (ADHD) and conduct disorder. Additional differential diagnostic issues and comorbid conditions for the practitioner to consider include language disorders, oppositional defiant disorder, sexual abuse, schizophrenia, and substance abuse (Geller & Luby, 1997). At a minimum, James and Javaloyes (2001) suggested that an accurate diagnosis will include clinical interviews with relevant individuals from the child's family and school environments. In addition, they suggested complete physical and biochemical examinations for the child or adolescent because certain medical conditions such as neurological diseases, Cushing's syndrome, use of antidepressants, and substance abuse can produce symptoms of mania. Several factors have been found to correlate with later bipolar disorder, including an early onset of depression, the presence of psychotic features in the initial depression, antidepressant-related hypomania, and a family history of bipolar disorder (Costello et al., 2002).

The clinical presentation of bipolar disorder varies depending on the age of the child. For example, younger children may present with disruptive behaviors, impulsivity, inattention, and overall moodiness (Sanchez et al., 1999). To complicate matters, periods of manic and depressive symptoms may cycle so rapidly that discrete episodes can be difficult to determine in children (Sanchez et al., 1999). In contrast, adolescents present with symptoms that are more similar to the adult presentation of the disorder. Specifically, some adolescents may experience psychotic features (e.g., hallucinations, delusions, thought disorders) that are associated with adult bipolar disorder (Sanchez et al., 1999). We encourage readers to refer to Craney and Geller (2003) for a more complete review of the clinical presentation of this disorder in children and adolescents.

CASE STUDY

Esteban was a 15-year-old Mexican American high school sophomore who was referred to counseling at a community mental health center by his mother after he threatened to kill her with a kitchen knife. He had straight black hair that was long on top and shaved from one inch above his ears on down. He had several facial piercings, crooked teeth, jeans that were fashionably oversized and that hung lower than his bottom, and an untucked flannel shirt. Esteban attended an ethnically mixed high school, but the majority of students were European American from middle-class backgrounds. In our first session, Esteban sat silently and played with his hands while his mother provided information about the family and described her concerns.

Esteban had two sisters, Reynalda ("Reina"), age 16, and Catalina, 13. His mother, Irma, and his father, Reynaldo, were married when they were 18 and 20, respectively. According to Irma, Reynaldo began a series of extramarital affairs shortly after Esteban was born. He had always been a heavy drinker and lost his job with the mining company after "too many Monday flus." The family environment described by Irma included harsh and inconsistent discipline by Reynaldo and guilt-induced permissiveness by Irma, in a context of poverty, frequent moves, and anxiety regarding Reynaldo's next binge. On several occasions, Reynaldo hit Irma in front of the children and was frequently verbally abusive toward her. Irma had finally divorced Reynaldo 3 years ago, and within 2 months he was remarried to an 18-year-old. Currently, Irma was working the 3–11 p.m. shift at a factory. Reynaldo has had intermittent contact with his children since the divorce. Reina and Esteban "hated" their father's new wife, Tina, and Reynaldo refused to spend time with them apart from Tina.

Irma described Esteban as a sweet little boy who had grown into a monster like his father. When he entered high school last year, his grade average began slipping, he started to smoke, and he skipped classes. Whenever Irma confronted him, she reported that Esteban would use the same verbally abusive language that his father used, such as "It's none of your business, you dirty whore." He refused to help out around the house and spent most of his time locked in his room listening to rap and hip-hop CDs with "a girl who dresses like a boy." When asked whether she had concerns about sexual activity between Esteban and this young woman, Irma said scornfully, "Even if she did want it—and that girl don't want it—he wouldn't know what to do." Esteban visibly flinched as she said this, his first overt reaction since arriving in the office.

Irma made the appointment for Esteban after an argument in which he shouted, "If you don't leave me alone I'm going to come after you with that big ol' knife! Everybody hates you, and if I killed you they would laugh." Irma said that although she didn't think Esteban would kill her or even attempt to hurt her, she was frightened by the hatred in his voice. When asked what she hoped counseling would accomplish, she said, "Find my sweet little boy and bring him back to me."

The remainder of that first session was spent alone with Esteban. As soon as his mother left, he asked if he could smoke. That was his only question and his only spontaneous communication. It quickly became obvious that he was painfully shy, embarrassed, and very nervous. His brief answers to questions did not seem to convey hostility or resentment but a profound sense of frustration and inadequacy. Additional information slowly emerged in the one-on-one meeting. His mother had a string of boyfriends, none of whom he liked; he communicated very little with his siblings and knew nothing of how they felt; he had only one friend— the aforementioned "girl who don't want it"—who did, in fact, "want it" but so far had only permitted him to lie in bed naked with her. This they did regularly while listening to CDs and smoking cigarettes. When asked how he felt toward others— his mother, teachers, people at school—he stated, unconvincingly, that he hated them. He frequently stated, more convincingly, that he didn't care or didn't know about much of what was going on around him most of the time.

In subsequent sessions, Esteban began to communicate more openly, using longer sentences and asking more questions. It was clear that Esteban lacked many basic social skills. He spent much of his time at home while his mother worked. Often, her current boyfriend would hang out there while she worked. He didn't like this, but it was the only time that he would talk with his sisters, because they would hang out in his room to avoid their mother's boyfriends. There were no indications of any attempted sexual contact between any of the boyfriends and the three children. Esteban indicated that he was embarrassed to ask his teachers for help and so he never tried to talk to them. He also reported that he felt responsible for his father's behavior, that if he wasn't the way that he was, his father would not have been a drunk and been so violent.

Esteban seemed to hate himself as much, if not more, than others around him. He was clearly experiencing a great deal of pain, frustration, guilt, and depression. Although he did not want to feel so isolated from others, he felt stuck and had never been taught the skills to move forward.

CAUSAL FACTORS

Esteban is clearly feeling depressed, among other things, and this affects his life in major ways. Esteban's depression could have been caused by any number of factors. In this section, we describe some of the more central causal and conceptual models of depression and mood disorder—biological, psychodynamic, behavioral, cognitive, family systems, and interpersonal relational—and how each of these models might apply to Esteban. In the next section, we discuss how these causal models flow into effective prevention and treatment from an ecological perspective that responsibly considers all aspects of Esteban's environment—and not just Esteban—in treatment.

Biological Models

Biological models of depression can be divided into two main categories: those that focus on the role of genetic factors and those that emphasize biochemical aspects of depression. There is a strong genetic component in the risk of depression and bipolar disorders (Kovacs & Devlin, 1998). Based on adult twin and adoption research and recent meta-analysis of epidemiological studies, genetic factors account for approximately 30%–50% of the variance in the transmission of mood disorders (Sullivan, Neale, & Kendler, 2000). Children of depressed parents are three times more likely to have a major depressive episode at some point during their lives (Williamson et al., 2004); this likelihood increases when the parent has had multiple depressive episodes (Garber & Robinson, 1997). Moreover, in studies of children with depression, 25% to 54% of first-degree relatives and approximately 15% of second-degree relatives were found to have major depression (Kovacs & Devlin, 1998). These biological factors seem to have an even greater impact when the individual lives in a stressful environment or experiences stressful life events (Wurtman, 2005). The diathesis-stress model suggests that individuals have a biological predisposition to a disorder that is activated and exacerbated by a major stressful experience and/or the cumulative effects of environmental stress (e.g., family violence, abuse, etc.) over time. The specific nature of genetic transmission has not been determined, and further studies using children and adolescents may help to clarify the genetic contributions to the onset and maintenance of mood disorders.

Another biological model of depression focuses on biochemical processes such as growth hormones, serotonergic systems, hypothalamus-pituitary-adrenal axis, and so forth (Birmaher, Ryan, Williamson, Brent, & Kaufman, 1996). Neurotransmitter actions and their interactions with antidepressant medications have been the focus of much biochemical research on depression. Whether a primary cause of depression or a secondary component, evidence suggests that abnormalities in the metabolism of neurotransmitters are present in people who are depressed. These can be counteracted with antidepressant drugs. We present findings on antidepressant treatments for depression in the Approaches to Prevention and Treatment section of this chapter.

In Esteban's case, evidence suggests that both of his parents may have experienced depression. His mother's patterns of developing relationships and his father's alcoholism and abusiveness both support the notion that they suffered from a lack of coping skills and poor self-esteem, which is almost always a concomitant of depression. The weakness of this model in explaining Esteban's depression is that it does not attend to the profound impact of Esteban's environment in forming his behavior and feelings about himself and others.

Psychodynamic Models

Psychodynamic models of depression focus on the loss of meaning or satisfaction in one's life and its effect on self-esteem regulation (Bemporad, 1988; Wolf, 1988). Depression is generally expressed in one of two ways: anger turned inward or feelings of emptiness and loss.

Heightened self-blame and rejection, often linked with the failure to live up to an idealized view of oneself, are viewed as reflections of anger turned inward (Wolf, 1988). Low self-esteem develops because it is impossible to meet the standards of this idealized view of self. In contrast, the latter expression of depression relates to the loss of something important in one's life (e.g., relationship, job, academic achievement) without which one feels worthless or empty (Bemporad, 1988). This type of depression is viewed as a result of never being valued or accepted when young, so one's positive self-esteem does not develop. In this person, self-esteem depends on external sources rather than an internal sense of worth, so when the external source is lost the person is unable to maintain his or her self-worth. The reliance of these theories on untestable, intrapsychic constructs has prevented their validation, but these perspectives provide important conceptualizations of depression that can be useful for practitioners. The caveat to this model is that it fails to consider the impact of the multiple contexts of Esteban's life (e.g., school, family, peers) and risks pathologizing him.

In Esteban's case, for example, it is likely that he did not feel valued while younger, so he did not learn to value himself. After the loss of his father, he may feel no one will ever love him because he is unworthy of being loved. He may also believe that if only he was a better person, his father would not have left. His realization that he will never be perfect then becomes anger that is directed inward because he is unable to achieve perfection. Over time, these feelings have severely damaged Esteban's self-esteem. According to this model, in order for Esteban to resolve his depression, he must learn to value himself and accept realistic expectations for himself instead of trying to live up to an unachievable ideal.

Behavioral Models

Behaviorists view depression as a result of significant loss (Kovacs & Beck, 1977; Schwartz & Johnson, 1985) and the consequence of inadequate or insufficient reinforcement (Ferster, 1973, 1974). Lewinsohn's social learning theory provides a concise behavioral model of depression. This theory suggests that depressive behaviors are determined by the presence or absence of reinforcers and maintained through the reduction of response-contingent reinforcing events (Lewinsohn & Hoberman, 1985). Depression may be the result of limited positive reinforcement for the individual, which is determined by the number of potentially reinforcing events, the number of these events available in the environment, and the individual's social skills to elicit accessible reinforcers (Levitt, Lubin, & Brooks, 1983). Depression may also result from excessive punishment, especially when it occurs at high rates, when the individual is highly sensitive to punishment, and when necessary coping skills to terminate punishment are limited (Lewinsohn & Hoberman, 1985). Unfortunately, the depressive behaviors stimulated by inadequate reinforcement are further reinforced by the concern or sympathy expressed by significant others. Eventually, though, others avoid the depressed person because of the nature of his or her depressive behaviors, which minimizes positive reinforcement and further exacerbates the depression (Lewinsohn & Hoberman, 1985).

In Esteban's case, Esteban receives almost no positive reinforcement, except perhaps from his female friend. Further, his lack of social skills does nothing to elicit positive reactions from others. On the contrary, his surly manner elicits negative reactions from others so that he never receives the social reinforcement that he so desperately needs to help lift his feelings of depression. He feels more and more isolated, less liked by others, and subsequently more depressed.

Cognitive Models

Research has also supported the role of cognition in depression (Beck, 1967; Rehm, 1977; Seligman, 1974, 1975). The following cognitive models of depression are helpful in understanding this perspective.

The first model, proposed by Beck (1967), suggests that cognition and affect are interactive and that the prior occurrence of cognition will determine a person's affective response to an event. If cognitions are distorted or inaccurate, the individual's emotional response will be inappropriate. Dysphoria may be the affective response of one's tendency to interpret experiences and events as negative or self-devaluative, indicating a cognitive role in the experience of depression.

Beck, Rush, Shaw, and Emery (1979) pointed to three cognitive components central to depression: the cognitive triad, schemas, and cognitive errors. The cognitive triad includes three negative thought patterns: a negative view of self, of the world, and of the future. Schemas, like personality traits, represent a stable cognitive pattern that individuals create to organize and evaluate information and events. People who experience depression develop schemas that distort environmental stimuli to coincide with a derogatory self-image. These dysfunctional or negative schemas are often created and exacerbated by faulty information processing or consistent errors in logic, called *cognitive errors*. The person suffering from depression uses these automatic cognitive errors to evaluate events, often leading to negativistic, categorical, absolute, and judgmental thinking (Levitt et al., 1983; Lewinsohn & Hoberman, 1985).

The second model of depression, Seligman's (1974, 1975) learned helplessness model, contends that depression exists in people who perceive that they have no control over their environment. They develop self-defeating attributions. They make internal (feeling responsible for an event), stable (the causes of an event remain constant), and global (event outcomes affect all areas of life) attributions for failure. In contrast, they attribute successful outcomes to external (caused by others), unstable (causes of events are transitory), and specific (situation specific) causes (Kaslow & Rehm, 1983). According to this model, this self-defeating attributional style results in the lowered motivation and reduced self-esteem common in clients with depression (Kaslow & Rehm, 1983). Self-defeating attributional style has been correlated with depression (Garber & Robinson, 1997; Lewinsohn & Hoberman, 1985). It is interesting to note that having a positive attribution style seems to serve as a protective factor for depression for boys but not for girls (Lewinsohn, Rohde, Seely, Klein, & Gotlib, 2000). Abela (2001) found that, beginning in early adolescence, attributional style moderates the effects of negative life events. This same study also noticed a self-critical tendency in girls that was not seen in boys, with the author suggesting that this could open up "an additional pathway" for girls that could account for some of the later gender differences found in depressed adults. Cole, Martin, and Powers (1997) proposed a similar, competency-based model of depression. Their model links a child's perceived helplessness, pessimism, and depression to a negative self-construct based on a lack of competence across five important domains within his or her life (school, attractiveness, social, conduct, and athleticism). Thus, if the child is unable to master tasks in one or more of these domains, he or she forms negative self-constructs leading to depression and helplessness.

Rehm's (1977) self-control theory represents the third cognitive model of depression. Problems of self-control are manifested through deficits in three cognitive processes: self-monitoring, self-reinforcement, and self-evaluation. Clients who are depressed fail to view situations with an orientation to the future and tend to concentrate on immediate consequences of events (Gilbert, 1984). They selectively attend to negative outcomes and focus on immediate reinforcements, a negative view of the self, the environment, and the future results. Similarly, depressed individuals tend to have negative attribution styles in which events are seen as being due to either external causes beyond their control or internal, unchangeable skill deficits. They tend to set high standards for positive self-evaluation, while at the same time have low standards for negative self-evaluation (Lewinsohn, Clarke, Rohde, Hops, & Seeley, 1996; Stark, Swearer, Kurowski, Sommer, & Bowen, 1996). They are likely to take credit for failures but not successes.

In accord with these models, cognitions play a key role in Esteban's depression. For example, Esteban maintains the faulty belief that he is responsible for his father's behavior and for the breakup of his family. Likewise, he attributes negative outcomes to deficiencies in himself (a negative internal attribution) instead of to the dysfunctional family and unstable economic environment around him.

Family Systems Models

A family systems approach to understanding the development of childhood and adolescent depression attends to family dynamics and the family environment. These dynamics are of considerable importance. Proponents of this perspective suggest that young people who experience depression are "symptoms" of family malfunction. The homeostasis of a maladaptive family system is maintained when a child or adolescent performs the role of the "sick" family member. This person is often referred to as the identified patient. In accord with this model, other family members often resist any positive change in the adolescent because it risks upsetting the homeostasis of the family. This reality necessitates the involvement of the entire family system in treatment interventions (Guttman, 1983; Nichols & Schwartz, 1995).

This approach requires Esteban's entire family be involved in the treatment process. Although Esteban's concerns may be more acute right now, his sisters are both also at risk for a variety of behavioral problems. Family intervention may help to not only resolve his issues but also prevent future problems from being expressed by his siblings. Furthermore, the behaviors and messages of Esteban's mother and father must be explored for each family member to recognize the resulting consequences. It is clear that the ideal is for Esteban's mother and father to be involved in treatment and to make changes. But if his father is no longer involved with the core family, then at least Esteban's mother needs to understand and modify her patterns of communication and behavior. It is also important that the entire family receives support and validation in treatment, especially given the economic marginalization and racial victimization they experience. According to this model, if family members are unwilling to be involved in treatment or if counselors and other interventionists are not willing to engage the family in the intervention, any individual treatment focused solely on Esteban is likely to be ineffective. While this point has been argued elsewhere (J. J. McWhirter, McWhirter, McWhirter, & McWhirter, 2007), more recently, scholars suggest that interventions for children and youth that fail to include and involve the family in some major way are not only ineffective but also fundamentally unethical (e.g., see Dishion & Stormshak, 2006).

Models Focusing on Interpersonal Relationships

Models focusing on interpersonal relationships are similar to family systems models but highlight the importance of all interpersonal relationships (with parents, siblings, peers, teachers, and other important persons) in a young person's life as centrally linked to the development—and therefore resolution—of problems. In relation to mood disorders, models focusing on interpersonal relationships suggest that the effect of many poor relationships is additive; that is, the number of dysfunctional relationship patterns that a young person has with parents, peers, and others leads to an increase in depressive symptoms (Allen et al., 2006). In some cases, these relationship influences have been found to vary between boys and girls. For girls, parental rejection and conflict with parents increase depressive symptoms (Lewinsohn et al., 2000; Oldehinkel, Venstra, Ormel, de Wintr, & Verhulst, 2006). In other cases, for both boys and girls, parental overprotection increases depressive symptoms, especially in preadolescents who were already experiencing high levels of frustration. (Oldehinkel et al., 2006).

Negative interactions with peers can also powerfully influence the experience of depression. For youths who are particularly anxious, high levels of early peer exclusion has been found to increase depressive symptoms (Gazelle & Lad, 2003). Depressive symptoms that are related to peer relationships seem to continue until later ages. For example, research has found that children experiencing poor peer relationships and subsequent mood problems as early as kindergarten continue to experience depressive symptoms and relationship problems through the fourth grade (Gazelle & Lad, 2003).

Additionally, youths who report feeling depressed also often report a higher level of being around youths who engage in delinquent behavior (e.g., Connell & Dishion, 2006). More than a simple co-occurrence, this suggests a pattern of relationships and sequence of events. It points to a pattern in which depressed youths are rejected by peers, become socially isolated, and then begin to display problem behaviors themselves and "hang out" with deviant peers to reduce their feelings of loneliness and isolation. This sequence of events and pattern of relationships, in turn, increases depressive symptoms and delinquent behavior itself (Beyers & Loeber, 2003; Connell & Dishion, 2006). The interpersonal relational model suggests that youths experience the greatest risk when both family and peer relationships are poor and that risk is even higher when different relationship systems interact negatively (e.g., when parents fail to communicate with teachers or engage in conflictual communications with teachers, when parents and peers reject each other, etc.).

In the case of Esteban, his dysfunctional family relationship patterns, association with a girlfriend who herself seems to be very disconnected from school and appears to be isolated, his anxiety, and his lack of social skills to improve relationships all increase his social isolation and marginalization. These, in turn, may likely draw him to other similar peers who are at risk and augment his experience of depression. According to this model, it would be critical to know about and understand his peer relationships in and outside of school. It would be important to know how the makeup of Esteban's school population affects his peer relationships and his own behavior to understand how the relationships in his environment increase his social isolation.

In the next section, we discuss how these causal models of depression flow into effective prevention and treatment. We begin by presenting a conceptual framework for discussing intervention. As before, we follow Esteban's treatment as a way of highlighting the practical aspects of the prevention and treatment strategies presented.

APPROACHES TO PREVENTION AND TREATMENT

Elsewhere, we have proposed a conceptual model for understanding and intervening with at-risk youth (J. J. McWhirter et al., 2007). This model is based on two key assumptions: (a) Being at risk for problematic behavior reflects not only a current condition but also an element of prediction for future problems, and (b) at-riskness must be viewed not so much as discrete and unitary but rather as a series of steps along a continuum. This continuum begins with youths who are at minimal risk for problematic behavior, proceeds through remote risk, high risk, and imminent risk, and ends with those already engaged in category activity. Category activity refers to participation in one or more destructive behaviors such as drug use, delinquent activity, and sexual promiscuity, and so forth. A child or adolescent's placement along the at-risk continuum is mediated by demographics, family and school environments, psychosocial stressors, and his or her personal characteristics (J. J. McWhirter et al., 2007). This model suggests that prevention, early intervention, and treatment must involve the family, school, and community. In short, interventions must attend to current problems, to the potential for future difficulty, and to multiple aspects of a young person's life.

According to J. J. McWhirter et al.'s (2007) model, for example, Esteban would be considered at imminent risk. He lives in a very negative family environment, comes from a poor socioeconomic background, experiences a great deal of psychosocial stressors including subtle and direct racial discrimination, and does not have effective coping skills or clear goals for his future. Furthermore, he has already developed "gateway behaviors," such as smoking, being sexually explorative, and having violent outbursts, which highly predict future category behavior. Esteban needs treatment focused specifically on his depression and on its root causes as well as treatment focused on helping him develop skills for dealing with future problems across a wide range of areas. Esteban would benefit greatly from individual cognitive and behavioral strategies, by school intervention programs designed to help kids develop social and communication skills and connect with others in positive ways, and by community-based treatment approaches to help his family. Interventions are clearly required for his entire family to improve communication, safety, monitoring, and parenting.

Bronfenbrenner's (1979) ecological model is one way to conceptualize treatments across a variety of domains. He described four systems within a person's life: the micro-, meso-, exo-, and macrosystems. Each system represents a level of interaction of the person within his or her multiple contexts, from the immediate family to the political structures that organize society. We refer to this model when discussing subsequent interventions. At the most basic level of the ecological model is the microsystem, which is composed of the individual and his or her interactions within small contexts such as the family, classroom, and friends. Esteban's microsystems include his sibling relationships, relationship with his mother, family interactions, his classes, and his peers. Next is the mesosystem, in which interactions become more complex. This system involves the interactions of the individual and significant others across microsystems, such as a conference with Esteban, Irma, and one of his teachers. The exosystem is the even larger systems that indirectly influence the child. It would not include the direct interaction of the youth. This could refer to a school in-service that the teacher attends that may indirectly affect the child. Finally, the macrosystem represents the larger societal influences that distantly relate to the individual. Government educational policies, race relations, and economic barriers within a person's community all play a role in mental health. For example, a recent epidemiology study (Gilman, Kawachi, Fitzmaurice, & Buka, 2002) found that participants growing up in low socioeconomic status families during the first 7 years of life were at greater risk for depression in adulthood. Using this model helps counselors and others to examine the direct and indirect influences on a youth's depression and can illuminate possible ways to prevent or intervene.

In the following sections, we discuss how the core components of prevention as well as more specific treatment strategies might be applied to youth at risk for depression. We describe these prevention and treatment strategies with a focus on the individual, family, school, and community, and we conclude by discussing a comprehensive intervention that reaches across domains.

Individual

Individual approaches include individual cognitive–behavioral interventions and interpersonal psychotherapy as well as pharmacological treatment. Individual approaches vary, and practitioners should follow their own orientation in attending to child and adolescent depression. Frequently, individual approaches involve both individual and family sessions, with the focus remaining on the depressed child or adolescent.

Exercise, nutrition, and additional self-care habits are often ignored in prevention efforts but can be easily incorporated into a variety of individual approaches. One study (Tomson, Pangrazi, Friendman, & Hutchison, 2003) found the risk for depressive symptoms in inactive children were 2.8–3.4 times higher than for active children. In a study by Brown, Welsh, Labbe, Vitulli, and Kulkarni (1992), a group of psychiatrically institutionalized adolescent boys and girls were assigned to a 9-week aerobic exercise program. The treated girls showed lower incidence of depression, anxiety, hostility, confused thinking, and fatigue, and both the adolescent boys and girls in the aerobics program showed improved vigor and self-efficacy. The added benefits of using exercise and nutritional strategies with youth are multifold because forming healthy habits early in life is easier than changing habits later in life. Similarly, utilizing stress reduction techniques such as relaxation training, biofeedback, autogenic training, meditation, affirmations, and guided visual imagery may also be helpful in preventing or reducing depression among children and adolescents.

Cognitive–Behavioral Interventions

We focus on cognitive–behavioral interventions that can be used to prevent and treat mood disorders because they have demonstrated proven effectiveness. For instance, Reinecke, Ryan, and DuBois (1998) conducted a meta-analysis of cognitive–behavioral therapy for depression and dysphoria. All of the 24 studies they included demonstrated positive results in the treatment and alleviation of depression in adolescents because of the cognitive–behavioral interventions used. Similarly, Rossello and Bernal (1996) modified a cognitive–behavioral treatment for Puerto Rican adolescents with depression, and their preliminary findings showed positive results for its use with this population. One must be cautioned that in young children (more or less before fifth grade) a cognitive focus may not be as effective because higher order thinking is not as well developed. We highlight below a description of individual cognitive–behavioral interventions as well as a description of interpersonal psychotherapy, followed by a discussion of pharmacological treatment.

Cognitive–behavioral treatments for depression flow directly from the cognitive and behavioral models described earlier. For example, Beck et al. (1979) developed a therapy with both behavioral and cognitive components designed to reduce automatic negative cognition with the goal of challenging the assumptions that maintain these faulty cognitions. Because clients often have difficulty utilizing cognitive tasks, behavioral strategies should be used first in the therapeutic process. These strategies include scheduling pleasant activities, relaxation training, graduated task assignments, social skills training, role-plays, and behavioral rehearsal (Lewinsohn et al., 1996, Reinecke et al., 1998). Behavioral strategies increase an individual's activity level and, therefore, the frequency of potentially rewarding activities, which may also increase the level of response-contingent reinforcement. During depression, there is a tendency to withdraw from activities and interactions with others. Behavioral strategies directly address withdrawal behaviors and encourage children and adolescents to be active, which in turn lessens the attention to and perseverance of depressogenic cognitions. Behavioral interventions appear appropriate for Esteban. Unless he becomes more involved in more positive peer interactions and in pleasant activities, he may have great difficulty in improving his depressed mood and in learning more positive cognitions about himself and his environment.

After these strategies are utilized successfully, emphasis is moved to cognitive interventions that emphasize identifying, testing, and modifying cognitive distortions. Strategies that have been used successfully include (a) recognizing the connection between cognition, affect, and behavior; (b) monitoring negative automatic thoughts; (c) examining evidence related to distorted automatic cognition; (d) substituting more realistic interpretations for distorted cognitions; (e) learning to identify and modify irrational beliefs; (f) altering biased attentional processes; (g) affect regulation; and (h) impulse control (Brent et al., 1996; Ellis, 1962; Ellis & Bernard, 1983; Marcotte, 1997; Reinecke et al., 1998).

Such strategies could be implemented with Esteban as part of individual treatment to address his cognitions and their relation to his mood and behavior. Of course, these strategies could be used as part of a prevention program in the school setting as well, which we discuss later.

Another cognitive–behavioral approach for depression is based on Rehm's (1977) self-control model. This intervention has been described as a primary prevention method, useful in teaching the skills necessary to avoid depression (Kaslow & Rehm, 1983). Kolko (1987) recommended that treatment in self-control involve specific training in monitoring positive events and self-statements, engaging in positive behaviors and cognitions, emphasizing long-term positive consequences, developing more realistic and achievable goals, making more legitimate attributions, and creating more frequent self-reinforcements. Consistent with this, one cognitive–behavioral technique is to help search for positive assets that a child or adolescent has or believes about himself or herself. The task of the counselor is to help develop positive assets from typical behaviors that the young person may not see himself or herself (often involving reframing experiences and responses). Then, ask the child or adolescent to repeat a standard, positive phrase, such as "I am a good person," "I am an honest and decent person," and "I am attractive and caring," every time he or she takes out a pen from his or her backpack, for example. This simple type of intervention may prove helpful to Esteban, who clearly needs to augment his positive self-statements. Although cognitive–behavioral approaches have been shown to be effective for many youths, it is important to note that intervention may not necessarily need to focus on cognitions to be effective. A recent meta-analysis by Weisz, McCarty, and Valeri (2006) revealed that the results of noncognitive treatments were as robust and effective as the cognitive–behavioral interventions.

Interpersonal Psychotherapy

Another individual approach that has demonstrated positive results in alleviating depression among children and adolescents is interpersonal psychotherapy (IPT). This approach has received promising empirical support (Mufson, Weissman, Moreau, & Garfinkel, 1999; Mufson et al., 2004; Rossello & Bernal, 1996). For instance, in a comparison of programs, Rossello and Bernal (1996) found IPT to be as efficacious as a cognitive–behavioral intervention. IPT has also been shown to be an effective school-based intervention (Mufson et al., 2004; Oswald & Mazefsky, 2006). With appropriate cultural modifications, IPT has been shown to be successful with some adolescents of color as well, such as Latino and Puerto Rican adolescents with depression (Mufson et al., 1999; Rossello & Bernal, 1996). IPT conceptualizes depression as conflict taking place in the context of interpersonal relationships (Mufson, Moreau, & Weissman, 1996). There are five areas that form the problem areas and treatment goals in IPT: grief, interpersonal role disputes, role transitions, interpersonal deficits, and single-parent families (this is a modification for use with adolescents).

Goals in IPT are to reduce depression and address the underlying conflict that was associated with the depression. Examples of techniques used in this approach include exploratory questioning, linking affect and events, clarifying conflicts and communication patterns, and applying behavior modification strategies. In the case of Esteban, IPT would focus on his grief over his parents' divorce, interpersonal deficits (poor social skills), and coping in a single-parent family. Role transitions around adolescence and increasing independence may also be an area on which to focus.

Pharmacological Treatment

Although pharmacological interventions are commonly and successfully used with adults, the results with youth are mixed (Ambrosini, 2000; Birmaher, Ryan, Williamson, Brent, Kaufman, Dahl, et al., 1996; Michael & Crowley, 2002; Wagner & Ambrosini, 2001; Ziervogel, 2000). To date, most medication trials have used tricyclic antidepressants (TCA; e.g., amitriptyline, imipramine) and have failed to demonstrate significant differences between the active medications and the placebos (Ambrosini, 2000; Emslie & Mayes, 2001; Michael & Crowley, 2002). Michael and Crowley (2002), for instance, reviewed 11 studies using TCA and 2 studies using selective serotonin reuptake inhibitors (SSRIs) for youth who are depressed. They found TCAs to have serious side effects and did not perform significantly better than placebo. Studies with SSRIs have found less negative side effects and more promising results in treating depression, but limited research exists in this area for young populations (Ambrosini, 2000; Hamrin & Scahill, 2005; Michael & Crowley, 2002; Wagner, 2005; Wagner & Ambrosini, 2001; Ziervogel, 2000). After reviewing recent research, Wagner (2005) concluded that whereas some medications in the class of SSRIs (such as citalopram, fluoxetine, and sertraline) have proved to be efficacious with children and adolescents, other classes of antidepressants have not proved to be as beneficial. Results from the Treatment for Adolescent Depression Study (TADS;

2004) demonstrated that adolescents treated with fluoxetine (Prozac) had better outcomes than those in the placebo control group, with the adolescents who participated in a cognitive–behavioral intervention along with the fluoxetine having the most positive treatment response (TADS, 2004). Despite these promising results, some important cautions remain. After a review of the literature, conducted in September 2004, a U.S. Food and Drug Administration advisory committee concluded that antidepressants can cause an increased risk in suicide for some pediatric patients (Wagner, 2005). SSRIs have been associated with increased risk of behavioral activation and self-harm behavior (Goodman, Murphy, & Lazoritz, 2006; Hamrin & Scahill, 2005). It is essential for clinicians to be especially alert for adverse behavioral changes during the initial or transitional stages of medication use (Hamrin & Scahill, 2005).

Further investigation is warranted to determine appropriate use of antidepressants with children and adolescents (Ambrosini, 2000; Birmaher, Ryan, Williamson, Brent, Kaufman, Dahl, et al., 1996; Michael & Crowley, 2002; Wagner & Ambrosini, 2001). Although frequently used in the clinical setting, the effectiveness of antidepressant medication for children and adolescents has not yet been firmly established through controlled research (Ambrosini, 2000; Brent et al., 1996; Michael & Crowley, 2002; Wagner & Ambrosini, 2001).

In the case of bipolar disorders, use of pharmacological interventions is probably essential. Controlled pharmacological studies for the treatment of bipolar disorder have received much less attention with child and adolescent samples compared with adult samples (Geller & Luby, 1997; James & Javaloyes, 2001). In fact, much of the information known about the treatment of bipolar disorder with medication comes from the adult literature. However, the limited research findings in this area indicate that mood stabilizers such lithium, sodium valproate, and carbamazapine may be effective in managing this disorder in young populations (James & Javaloyes, 2001; Kowatch et al., 2000; Sanchez et al., 1999). The use of lithium is especially risky for children living in chaotic families, however, because children's lithium levels and renal and thyroid functioning must be constantly monitored (Geller & Luby, 1997). Additional medications of enzodiazepines and atypical antipsychotics (e.g., risperidone, olanzapine) have been used when indicated for agitation and psychotic features, respectively (Frazier et al., 2001; James & Javaloyes, 2001). In only the most severe and treatment-resistant bipolar cases are medications such as clozapine and methods such as electroconvulsive treatment used (James & Javaloyes, 2001). Of course, during a severe manic episode, the behavior often causes problems that result in hospitalization. With adolescents, counselors and other practitioners need to be attentive to less severe mood swings or problems with a view to referral. Although the existence of a bipolar disorder does not seem probable in Esteban's situation, a medical referral for his depression may still be important.

Traditionally, pharmacotherapy has been the primary treatment for bipolar disorder in adults, and such practices have been extrapolated to children and adolescents. James and Javaloyes (2001) recommended the use of individual and family psychoeducational approaches but indicated that little empirical research exists on the efficacy of such treatments for this disorder in young populations. Given the severity of this disorder, it is clear that possible treatment approaches could be implemented on many levels. For example, individual and family psychoeducation approaches could be used to assist the family in dealing with this disorder. In addition, comorbid disorders (e.g., ADHD, substance abuse) must be accurately identified and effectively treated.

Family

The role of the family in the successful treatment of the depressed child or adolescent is crucial. As mentioned previously, there are strong correlations between depression and family interactions, such as parent–child conflict and overprotectiveness. As such, to be successful, clinicians need to be prepared to work with all family members, especially parents. In Esteban's family, for example, if his mother and sisters are not engaged in treatment and assisted to change some of their family dynamics, Esteban will likely continue to suffer from the same environment that contributed to his depression in the first place.

Although many options for family systems therapy serve many different types of families, one promising intervention is attachment-based family therapy (ABFT). Although more research is needed to demonstrate effectiveness, current results are promising (Diamond, Siqueland, & Diamond, 2003; Oswald & Mazefsky, 2006). ABFT is a manualized treatment designed for depressed adolescents and their families. It focuses on repairing ruptured relationship between parents and adolescents and includes factors such as building competency, trust, and family alliance.

In many circumstances, parent training for enhancing communication can benefit the family and help prevent depression and other problems. Parent training workshops can be particularly useful and cost-effective, especially those that focus on developing communication skills, enhancing family interactions, and sharing information about common issues (such as birth control, signs of drug use, and so forth). Workshops also offer parents a forum for discussing fears, concerns, and frustrations with other parents and with a professional facilitator, who can increase parental confidence and comfort with discussing issues with their children. In families with greater dysfunction, therapeutic programs attending to child abuse and neglect, parental dysfunction, and family violence may also be required and beneficial.

Parent training may also be utilized as a prevention measure. Although a variety of effective parent training programs exist, one effective program is family effectiveness training (FET; Szapocznik, Santisteban, Rio, Perez-Vidal, & Kurtines, 1986b, 1989), a preventative training model for Latino families of preadolescents at risk for future drug abuse. FET is designed to address three problems that often serve as antecedents to adolescent behavior problems: maladaptive family interactions, intergenerational conflict, and intercultural conflict. It is one of few empirically tested programs that directly address cultural differences in intervention. The model has three components.

The first component, family development, helps the family to negotiate the transition from childhood to adolescence. All family members learn constructive communication skills and take increased responsibility for their own behaviors. Parents become educated about drugs so that they can teach their children; they also learn the skills to become democratic rather than authoritarian leaders.

The second component, bicultural effectiveness training (BET; Szapocznik, Santisteban, Kurtines, Perez-Vidal, & Harris, 1984; Szapocznik, Santisteban, Rio, Perez-Vidal, & Kurtines, 1986a), is designed to bring about family change by (a) temporarily placing the blame for the family's problems on the cultural conflict within the family and (b) establishing alliances between family members through the development of bicultural skills and mutual appreciation of the values of both cultures. The family learns to handle cultural conflicts more effectively and reduces the likelihood that such conflicts will occur. BET represents an excellent parent training program in and of itself. This program would be particularly helpful for Esteban's family, who contends with acculturation issues as well as overt and covert racism on a daily basis.

The third component of FET is the implementation of brief strategic family therapy. Based on the work of Minuchin (1974), this component involves a series of family therapy sessions and is the most experiential aspect of this didactic–experiential model. The entire training consists of 13 sessions that last from 1.5 to 2 hours; the entire family is present for each session. Finally, FET can be modified to deal specifically with other child and adolescent behavior problems.

This program represents one of the effective parent training programs useful for preventing depression. Other extensive, empirically based, parent training programs have been developed for working with families in the home and school environments. For example, Carolyn Webster-Stratton and colleagues have developed and evaluated parent training programs that primarily target children with conduct disorders (see Reid & Webster-Stratton, 2001; Webster-Stratton & Hancock, 1998; Webster-Stratton, Reid, & Hammond, 2001). Others have developed additional parent training models (see Dinkmeyer & McKay, 1989), and, often, parenting resources are available at local community counseling centers on a variety of topics, including behavior management and discipline, nutrition, family budgeting, and preventing chemical dependency.

Parent training programs could help Esteban, but because he already shows clear signs of depression, direct therapeutic intervention with the whole family is indicated. Helping Irma and her children communicate more effectively with each other and clarifying roles and boundaries have the potential of creating a great deal of change in the family. In addition, helping each of the children to see their value and importance in the family is important. The family can become a primary source of support and encouragement if family members can share their needs, wants, and feelings more effectively.

School

The occurrence of depression among children and adolescents has been linked to increased environmental and family stressors, as well as social isolation and peer exclusion. These findings support the need for early prevention that can be effectively provided in school settings. Schools are an ideal setting for preventive interventions because children and adolescents can be reached and because skills training, such as problem resolution skills and communication skills, can be taught as an integral part of a school-based curriculum. Training in life skills, which we discuss below, can reduce existing problems and prevent others.

In responding to depression, school-based prevention programs should engage in multiple strategies, including enhancing their skills in assessing depression. To be effective, assessment should consider a child's cognitive and affective characteristics, environment, life stressors, and relationships with others (e.g., Vernon, 2005). School interventions should include a mixture of affective, cognitive, and behavioral strategies that focus on self-acceptance, problem solving, decision making, social skills development, and enhancing interpersonal relationships (Vernon, 2005). Further, group interventions are central to many school-based prevention programs because of their ability to reach a large number of children, adaptability to the classroom format, and relative cost-effectiveness. Unfortunately, small group intervention programs for depression and other psychosocial problems have not often been rigorously evaluated in school settings, but existing outcome studies indicate positive results. For example, in a study consisting of five school-based mental health clinics, adolescents treated with interpersonal psychotherapy demonstrated significant reduction of depressive symptoms and improved social functioning as compared with adolescents in the treatment-as-usual control group (Mufson et al., 2004).

In another example of a group intervention, Lewinsohn et al. (1996) described an 8-week cognitive–behavioral group intervention called the Adolescent Coping With Depression Course (CWD-A). This psychoeducational structured intervention incorporates cognitive–behavioral techniques such as skill development, mood enhancement, problem solving, and role-playing (Lewinsohn et al., 1996). The groups are facilitated by therapists over an 8-week time frame with approximately 10 or fewer adolescents experiencing depression. In addition, there is a parallel parent group that meets with a therapist to teach parents how to support their adolescents in treatment. The CWD-A has been empirically evaluated over a number of studies, and successful outcomes for adolescents experiencing depression has been found (Lewinsohn, Clarke, Hops, & Andrews, 1990; Lewinsohn et al., 1996, 1998). While success for the CWD-A group intervention has been demonstrated in clinical settings (see Lewinsohn et al., 1996, 1998), its individual sessions are presented in a classlike manner and thus it may be adaptable to school settings. Although results of very structured group work with youth are promising, more research on school-based depression interventions is needed.

Early prevention in the schools can take the form of educational programs focused on forming friendships (social skills), nonviolent conflict resolution, assertiveness training, and skills for relating to adults, dealing with peer pressure, and improving critical school competencies such as basic academic skills and academic survival skills (McWhirter et al., 2007). Broad-based skills training programs such as these not only prevent depression but also help to prevent other critical problems, such as early and unsafe sexual activity and drug use. In Esteban's case, such programs may provide the social skills training that he did not receive at home as well as assistance in mastering academic survival skills that he may have missed because of his frequent moves.

The core components of good life skills prevention programs include interpersonal communication, strategies for cognitive change, coping with stress, and managing health (J. J. McWhirter et al., 2007). Life skills are those that involve behaviors and attitudes necessary for coping with academic challenges, communicating with others, forming healthy and stable relationships, and making good decisions. Life skills training programs emphasize the acquisition of generic social and cognitive skills. The theoretical foundation of life skills training includes Bandura's (1977) social learning theory and Jessor and Jessor's (1977) problem behavior theory. In accord with these perspectives, children and adolescents are not blamed for causing their problems but are viewed as capable of learning new ways to behave that reduce the likelihood of future problems. Counselors and other mental health professionals can all be involved in teaching life skills. Three broad skill categories are usually included in basic life skills programs: (a) interpersonal communication skills, including assertiveness and refusal skills; (b) cognitive change strategies, including problem-solving, decision-making, self-control and self-management skills, and cognitive–behavioral restructuring approaches; and (c) anxiety coping approaches, including relaxation, imagery training, and exercise.

Learning effective social skills is core to life skills training because it improves and increases the positive feedback and reinforcement that is received from others

(Spence, 2003; Zimmerman, 2002). Treatment here focuses on the improvement of interpersonal style and on the development of skills, such as peer etiquette and group entry (Frankel, Cantwell, & Myatt, 1996). Modeling, feedback, role-playing, instruction, situation logs, and homework practice are all used to help augment social skills and minimize the depression caused by an inability to elicit positive consequences. Although generalizability from group to external environments has had mixed results (Frankel et al., 1996), recent reviews of research suggest that social skills training has stronger long-term effectiveness when it is used as part of a multimodal intervention (Spence, 2003; Zimmerman, 2002). Focusing on improving social skills seems especially appropriate for Esteban. Given the fact that he has had relatively little peer group interaction and prefers to be by himself, it appears that he has not developed effective social skills with his peer group. Indeed, he seems unable to cope with the responses of his classmates and family. Thus, social skills training would appear to be a useful strategy to help lift his depression.

Community

Thus far, we have reviewed individual, family, and school approaches for the prevention and treatment of childhood and adolescent depression. Many of the interventions discussed in this chapter could easily be used by counselors, psychologists, social workers, and other mental health professionals who work in community agencies. But approaches that specifically involve the larger community acknowledge the role of the larger context in which depression and other problems of childhood and adolescence emerge. Given the high correlation between delinquency and depression (J. J. McWhirter et al., 2007), the community program described below can be seen as both a treatment and a prevention measure for depression and other concerns.

Teencourt (J. J. McWhirter, McWhirter, McWhirter, & McWhirter, 1998) is an example of a community program used in many counties in many U.S. states for first-time juvenile offenders between the ages of 8 and 17 who have committed a misdemeanor offense, status offense, or minor traffic violation. The Teencourt program incorporates leadership skills, critical thinking, career exploration, responsibility taking, and influencing peer norms. Youths referred to Teencourt have a choice of (a) pleading guilty, participating in the program, and keeping their record clean, or (b) going through the traditional juvenile court system. Teencourt sentencing is designed to fit the offense and usually includes community service, tutoring, attending workshops, or traffic survival school.

Each session of Teencourt lasts 4 months and involves six attorneys, 20 jurists, one court clerk, and three bailiffs, all of whom are trained high school students. Thus, offenders passing through Teencourt are tried by their peers; the judge is the only adult representative of the legal system. All defendants are required to serve a term of jury duty after their own sentencing. This is consistent with the goals of Teencourt, which include the prevention of repeat offenses among those who are tried; the prevention of first-time offenses among the many students who voluntarily participate as attorneys, bailiffs, and so on; the education of adolescents about the legal system; and the use of peer pressure to evoke conformity to positive behaviors. The recidivism rate for Teencourt participants is well below both state and national averages (E. H. McWhirter, 1994). This program models an empowerment philosophy as defined by E. H. McWhirter (1994) because it not only prevents future problems but also helps young people develop skills for helping others and for changing their communities.

Thus far, Esteban has not been accused of any legal violation, although he does smoke before the legal age. However, his involvement in some offense would not be surprising given his current alienation, anger, and apathy. Participation in a program such as Teencourt as an offender and then a jury member could have a considerable positive effect on Esteban. Teencourt's philosophy of empowerment is manifested in a variety of ways: by increasing adolescents' awareness of the legal system, providing specific skills training as well as the broader experience of leadership and citizenship, utilizing peers of equal power status rather than adults, involving adolescents with community organizations, tailoring sentences to individual offenses, and emphasizing responsibility for behavior (E. H. McWhirter, 1994). In the context of Seligman's (1974, 1975) model of learned helplessness, the Teencourt program addresses many of the deficiencies and apathetic responses from which Esteban suffers.

ADAPTATIONS FOR DIVERSITY

We have discussed the issues of individual, family, school, and community interventions, but we are still confronted with a very depressed 15-year-old who needs support. The comprehensive model we propose here is built on the foundation of a solid interpersonal relationship between the depressed child or adolescent and the helpers in his or her environment: counselors, teachers, and parents. This relationship, although necessary and yet not sufficient for fully treating depression, must incorporate the basic conditions of empathy, genuineness, warmth, and respect for differences. It must also incorporate multicultural awareness and sensitivity. In the case of Esteban, multicultural competency and sensitivity involves more than knowledge of Mexican American cultural norms; it must include awareness of the effects of racism, economic marginalization of people of color, and the nature of the community in which his family lives. While we have integrated attention to cultural issues and have highlighted culturally competent intervention considerations throughout this chapter, we wish to briefly highlight points for adapting this chapter content to diverse clientele.

Given the complexity of Esteban's present problems and the threat of future overtly violent behaviors, and taking into consideration our earlier discussion of Bronfenbrenner's (1979) ecological model, we recommend the use of a comprehensive treatment strategy that addresses Esteban's different contexts (micro- and mesosystems), his cognitions, behaviors, and affect, as well as attending to larger environmental issues (exo- and macrosystems). The nature and severity of his depression should be assessed thoroughly, via a family intake interview with measures of anxiety, depression, anger, and self-esteem. In sum, to be accurate and clinically useful, Esteban's comprehensive assessment needs to include individual factors as well as contextual and interpersonal ones such as family dynamics, poor school performance, fear of interaction with others, peer rejection, and overt and covert racism that he experiences regularly. This type of comprehensive assessment cannot be completed quickly, either in one session or by talking to one person. An ecologically based assessment requires the clinician to gather information from Esteban himself, his family, and most likely his teachers, being sure to take exo- and macrosystemic context into account throughout this assessment.

After this ecologically based assessment, an intervention should be collaboratively developed with Esteban and his family. As with the assessment, the intervention should be based in the principals of the ecological model and multicultural competence. This plan should be responsive to Esteban's degree of risk along the continuum that we presented earlier. He is currently depressed, but a skill-building intervention—which is core to any prevention program—can prevent future depressive episodes and other problems. Effective intervention for Esteban should include the following components: behavioral interventions of life skills training and increasing age-appropriate pleasurable activities; cognitive interventions designed to identify, test, and modify his dysfunctional beliefs about himself, his family, and his future; family interventions designed to improve the communication within the family and to improve his mother's parenting consistency; and school interventions designed to attend to his poor performance and relationships with peers. In addition, some understanding and potential use of biological and pharmacological interventions may be necessary if his depression does not remit.

Finally, the importance of client empowerment cannot be understated. E. H. McWhirter (1994) defined empowerment as

> the process by which people, organization, or groups who are powerless or marginalized become aware of the power dynamics at work in their life text; develop the skills and capacity for gaining some reasonable control over their lives, which they exercise, without infringing upon the rights of others, and which coincides with the active support of empowering others in the community. (p. 12)

In future work, Esteban may choose to become active in Mexican American groups at school or within the community. Esteban should be supported in both this and other important aspects of the empowerment process, including helping Esteban recognize how he is affected by the exo- and macrosystemic context that surround him (racism, educational disparities, opportunity access, etc.) and encouraging him to gain more control over his life choices.

SUMMARY

Depression and bipolar disorders are significant and complicated mental health problems among children and adolescents. Mood disorders manifest differently in adolescence and especially in childhood than they do in adults. They have been linked to other risk factors such as suicide, school attrition, substance use, and delinquency, further augmenting the difficulty in accurately diagnosing the problem and in recommending and implementing effective intervention. Current research supports several treatment approaches as being equally successful in remitting depression and other mood disorders. Future research should continue to examine the active ingredients in depression prevention and intervention to improve efficacy as well as further our understanding of depression among children and adolescents. In light of effective medications for treating adult depression, but less effective results with youth, pharmacological research for mood disorders in children and youth is especially recommended.

What is very clear is that depression and other affective problems can have a catastrophic effect on children and adolescents and on those around them. This is true for young Esteban. The interventions described above that involve the individual, family, school, and community could all be used in a comprehensive way to help tackle the depression that Esteban, and many young people, experience. Parents, counselors, teachers, and other school personnel who play primary roles in the lives of children and adolescents must be especially aware of and responsive to the symptoms, causes, and problems associated with depression. Recognizing and re-sponding quickly to depression and to its root causes are especially important in avoiding the potentially devastating effects of this disorder on the young people with whom we live and work.

REFERENCES

Abela, J. (2001). The hopelessness theory of depression: A test of the diathesis-stress and causal mediation components in third and seventh grade children. *Journal of Abnormal Child Psychology, 29,* 241–254.

Allen, J. P., Insabella, G., Porter, M. R., Smith, F. D., Land, D., & Phillips, N. (2006). A social–interactional model of the development of depressive symptoms in adolescence. *Journal of Consulting and Clinical Psychology, 74,* 55–65.

Ambrosini, P. J. (2000). A review of pharmacotherapy of major depression in chil-dren and adolescents. *Psychiatric Services, 51,* 627–633.

American Psychiatric Association. (2000). *Diagnostic and statistical manual of mental disorders* (4th ed., Text Revision). Washington, DC: Author.

Bandura, A. (1977). Self-efficacy: Toward a unifying theory of behavioral change. *Psychological Review, 84,* 191–215.

Beck, A. T. (1967). *Depression: Causes and treatment.* Philadelphia: University of Pennsylvania Press.

Beck, A. T., Rush, A. G., Shaw, B. F., & Emery, G. (1979). *Cognitive therapy of depres-sion.* New York: Guilford Press.

Bemporad, J. R. (1988). Psychodynamic treatment of depressed adolescents. *Journal of Clinical Psychiatry, 49*(9, Suppl.), 26–31.

Beyers, J., & Loeber, R. (2003). Untangling developmental relations between de-pressed mood and delinquency in male adolescents. *Journal of Abnormal Child Psychology, 31,* 247–266.

Birmaher, B., Ryan, N. D., Williamson, D. E., Brent, D. A., & Kaufman, J. (1996). Childhood and adolescent depression: A review of the past 10 years. Part II. *Journal of the American Academy of Child and Adolescent Psychiatry, 35,* 1575–1583.

Birmaher, B., Ryan, N. D., Williamson, D. E., Brent, D. A., Kaufman, J., Dahl, R. E., et al. (1996). Childhood and adolescent depression: A review of the past 10 years. Part I. *Journal of the American Academy of Child and Adolescent Psychiatry, 35,* 1427–1439.

Brent, D. A., Roth, C. M., Holder, D. P., Kolko, D. J., Birmaher, B., Johnson, B. A., & Schweers, J. A. (1996). Psychosocial interventions for treating adolescent suici-dal depression: A comparison of three psychosocial interventions. In E. D. Hibbs & P. S. Jensen (Eds.), *Psychosocial treatments for child and adolescent disorders: Empirically based strategies for clinical practice* (pp. 187–206). Washington, DC: American Psychological Association.

Bronfenbrenner, U. (1979). *The ecology of human development: Experiments by nature and design.* Cambridge, MA: Harvard University Press.

Brown, S. W., Welsh, M. C., Labbe, E. E., Vitulli, W. F., & Kulkarni, P. (1992). Aerobic exercise in the psychological treatment of adolescents. *Perceptual and Motor Skills, 74,* 555–560.

Cole, D. A., Martin, J. M., & Powers, B. (1997). A competency-based model of child depression: A longitudinal study of peer, parent, teacher, and self-evaluations. *Journal of Child Psychology and Psychiatry, 38,* 505–514.

Connell, A. M., & Dishion, T. (2006). The contribution of peers to monthly variation in adolescent depressed mood: A short-term longitudinal study with time-varying predictors. *Development and Psychopathology, 18*, 139–154.

Costello, E. J., Pine, D. S., Hammen, C., March, J. S., Plotsky, P. M., Weissman, M. M., et al. (2002). Development and natural history of mood disorders. *Biological Psychiatry, 52*, 529–542.

Craney, J. L., & Geller, B. (2003). A prepubertal and early adolescent bipolar disorder-I phenotype: Review of phenomenology and longitudinal course. *Bipolar Disorder, 5*, 243–256.

Diamond, G. S., Siqueland, L., & Diamond, G. M. (2003). Attachment-based family therapy for depressed adolescents: Programmatic treatment development. *Clinical Child and Family Psychology Review, 6*, 107–127.

Dinkmeyer, D., & McKay, G. D. (1989). *Systematic training for effective parenting* (3rd ed.). Circle Pines, MN: American Guidance Service.

Dishion, T. J., & Stormshak, E. A. (2006). *An ecological approach to child and family intervention.* Washington, DC: American Psychological Association.

Ellis, A. (1962). *Reason and emotion in psychotherapy.* New York: Stuart.

Ellis, A., & Bernard, M. E. (Eds.). (1983). *Rational-emotive approaches to the problems of childhood.* New York: Plenum.

Emslie, G. J., & Mayes, T. L. (2001). Mood disorders in children and adolescents: Psychopharmacological treatment. *Biological Psychiatry, 49*, 1082–1090.

Ferster, C. B. (1973). A functional analysis of depression. *American Psychologist, 28*, 857–870.

Ferster, C. B. (1974). Behavioral approaches to depression. In R. J. Friedman & M. M. Katz (Eds.), *The psychology of depression: Contemporary theory and research* (pp. 29–53). New York: Winston-Wiley.

Frankel, F., Cantwell, D. P., & Myatt, R. (1996). Helping ostracized children: Social skills training and parent support for socially rejected children. In E. D. Hibbs & P. S. Jensen (Eds.), *Psychosocial treatments for child and adolescent disorders: Empirically based strategies for clinical practice* (pp. 595–618). Washington, DC: American Psychological Association.

Frazier, J. A., Beiderman, J., Tohen, M., Feldman, P. D., Jacobs, T. G., Toma, V., et al. (2001). A prospective open-label treatment trial of olanzapine monotherapy in children and adolescents with bipolar disorder. *Journal of Child and Adolescent Psychopharmacology, 11*, 239–250.

Garber, J., & Robinson, N. S. (1997). Cognitive vulnerability in children at risk for depression. *Cognition & Emotion, 11*, 619–635.

Gazelle, H., & Ladd, G. (2003). Anxious solitude and peer exclusion: A diathesis-stress model of internalizing trajectories in childhood. *Child Development, 74*, 257–278.

Geller, B., & Luby, J. (1997). Child and adolescent bipolar disorder: A review of the past 10 years. *Journal of the American Academy of Child and Adolescent Psychiatry, 36*, 1168–1176.

Gilbert, P. (1984). *Depression: From psychology to brain state.* London: Erlbaum.

Gilman, S. E., Kawachi, I., Fitzmaurice, G. M., & Buka, S. L. (2002). Socioeconomic status in childhood and the lifetime risk of major depression. *International Journal of Epidemiology, 31*, 359–367.

Goodman, W. K., Murphy, T. K., & Lazoritz, M. (2006). Risk of suicidality during antidepressant treatment of children and adolescents. *Primary Psychiatry, 13*(1), 43–50.

Guttman, H. A. (1983). Family therapy in the treatment of mood disturbance in adolescence. In H. Golombek & B. Garfinkel (Eds.), *The adolescent and mood disturbance* (pp. 263–272). New York: International Universities Press.

Hamrin, V., & Scahill, L. (2005). Selective serotonin reuptake inhibitors for children and adolescents with major depression: Current controversies and recommendations. *Issues in Mental Health Nursing, 26,* 433–450.

James, A. C. D., & Javaloyes, A. M. (2001). The treatment of bipolar disorder in children and adolescents. *Journal of Child Psychology and Psychiatry and Allied Disciplines, 42,* 439–449.

Jessor, L. C., & Jessor, S. L. (1977). *Problem behavior and psychosocial development: A longitudinal study of youth.* New York: Academic Press.

Kaslow, N. J., & Rehm, L. P. (1983). Child depression. In R. J. Morris & T. R. Kratochwill (Eds.), *The practice of child therapy* (pp. 27–51). New York: Pergamon.

Kazdin, A. E. (1994). Psychotherapy for children and adolescents. In A. E. Bergin & S. L. Garfield (Eds.), *Handbook of psychotherapy and behavior change* (4th ed., pp. 543–594). New York: Wiley.

King, S. R. (1991). Recognizing and responding to adolescent depression. *Journal of Health Care for the Poor and Underserved, 2,* 122–129.

Kolko, D. J. (1987). Depression. In M. Herson & V. Van Hassalt (Eds.), *Behavior therapy with children and adolescents: A clinical approach* (pp. 137–183). New York: Wiley.

Kovacs, M., & Beck, A. T. (1977). An empirical–clinical approach toward a definition of childhood depression. In J. G. Schulterbrandt & A. Raskin (Eds.), *Depression in childhood: Diagnosis, treatment, and conceptual models* (pp. 1–25). New York: Raven Press.

Kovacs, M., & Devlin, B. (1998). Internalizing disorders in childhood. *Journal of Child Psychology and Psychiatry, 39,* 47–63.

Kowatch, R. A., Suppes, T., Carmody, T. J., Bucci, J. P., Hume, J. H., Kromelis, M., et al. (2000). Effect size of lithium, divalproex sodium, and carbamazepine in children and adolescents with bipolar disorder. *Journal of the American Academy of Child and Adolescent Psychiatry, 39,* 713–720.

Levitt, E. E., Lubin, B., & Brooks, J. M. (1983). *Depression: Concepts, controversies, and some new facts.* Hillsdale, NJ: Erlbaum.

Lewinsohn, P. M., Clarke, G. N., Hops, H., & Andrews, J. (1990). Cognitive–behavioral treatment for depressed adolescents. *Behavior Therapy, 21,* 385–401.

Lewinsohn, P. M., Clarke, G. N., Rohde, P., Hops, H., & Seeley, J. R. (1996). A course in coping: A cognitive–behavioral approach to the treatment of adolescent depression. In E. D. Hibbs & P. S. Jensen (Eds.), *Psychosocial treatments for child and adolescent disorders: Empirically based strategies for clinical practice* (pp. 109–135). Washington, DC: American Psychological Association.

Lewinsohn, P. M., & Hoberman, H. M. (1985). Depression. In A. S. Bellack, M. Herson, & A. E. Kazdin (Eds.), *International handbook of behavior modification and therapy* (Student ed., pp. 173–207). New York: Plenum Press.

Lewinsohn, P. M., Hops, H., Roberts, R., Seeley, J. R., & Andrew, J. (1993). Adolescent psychopathology: I. Prevalence and incidence of depression and other *DSM–III–R* disorders in high school students. *Journal of Abnormal Psychology, 102,* 183–204.

Lewinsohn, P. M., Klein, D. N., & Seeley, J. R. (1995). Bipolar disorders in a community sample of older adolescents: Prevalence, phenomenology, comorbidity, and course. *Journal of the American Academy of Child and Adolescent Psychiatry, 34,* 454–463.

Lewinsohn, P. M., Rohde, P., & Seeley, J. R. (1998). Major depressive disorder in older adolescents: Prevalence, risk factors, and clinical implications. *Clinical Psychology Review, 18,* 765–794.

Lewinsohn, P. M., Rohde, P., Klein, D. N., & Seeley, J. R. (1999). Natural course of adolescent major depressive disorder: I. Continuity into young adulthood. *Journal of the American Academy of Child and Adolescent Psychiatry, 38,* 56–63.

Lewinsohn, P. M., Rohde, P., Seely, J. R., Klein, D., & Gotlib, I. H. (2000). Natural course of adolescent major depressive disorder in a community sample: Predictors of recurrence in young adults. *American Journal of Psychiatry, 157,* 1584–1591.

Marcotte, D. (1997). Treating depression in adolescence: A review of the effectiveness of cognitive–behavioral treatments. *Journal of Youth and Adolescence, 26,* 273–283.

McWhirter, E. H. (1994). *Counseling for empowerment.* Alexandria, VA: American Counseling Association.

McWhirter, J. J., McWhirter, B. T., McWhirter, A. M., & McWhirter, E. H. (1998). *At risk youth: A comprehensive response* (2nd ed.). Pacific Grove, CA: Brooks/Cole.

McWhirter, J. J., McWhirter, B. T., McWhirter, E. H., & McWhirter, R. J. (2007). *At risk youth: A comprehensive response* (4th ed.). Pacific Grove, CA: Brooks/Cole.

Michael, K. D., & Crowley, S. L. (2002). How effective are treatments for child and adolescent depression? A meta-analytic review. *Clinical Psychology Review, 22,* 247–269.

Minuchin, S. (1974). *Families and family therapy.* Cambridge, MA: Harvard University Press.

Mufson, L., Dorta, K. P., Wickramaratne, P., Nomura, Y., Olfson, M., & Weissman, M. M. (2004). A randomized effectiveness trail of interpersonal psychotherapy for depressed adolescents. *Archives of General Psychiatry, 61,* 577–584.

Mufson, L., Moreau, D., & Weissman, M. M. (1996). Focus on relationships: Interpersonal psychotherapy for adolescent depression. In E. D. Hibbs & P. S. Jensen (Eds.), *Psychosocial treatments for child and adolescent disorders: Empirically based strategies for clinical practice* (pp. 137–156). Washington, DC: American Psychological Association.

Mufson, L., Weissman, M. M., Moreau, D., & Garfinkel, R. (1999). Efficacy of interpersonal psychotherapy for depressed adolescents. *Archives of General Psychiatry, 56,* 573–579.

Nichols, M. P., & Schwartz, R. C. (1995). *Family therapy: Concepts and methods* (3rd ed.). Boston: Allyn & Bacon.

Oldehinkel, A. J., Venstra, R., Ormel, J., de Wintr, A. F., & Verhulst, F. C. (2006). Temperament, parenting, and depressive symptoms in a population sample of preadolescents. *Journal of Child Psychology and Psychiatry, 47,* 684–695.

Oswald, D., & Mazefsky, C.A. (2006). Empirically supported psychotherapy interventions for internalizing disorders. *Psychology in the Schools, 43,* 439–449.

Rehm, L. P. (1977). A self-control model of depression. *Behavior Therapy, 8,* 787–804.

Reid, M. J., & Webster-Stratton, C. (2001). The Incredible Years parent, teacher, and child intervention: Targeting multiple areas of risk for a young child with pervasive conduct problems using a flexible, manualized treatment program. *Cognitive and Behavioral Practice, 8,* 377–386.

Reinecke, M. A., Ryan, N. E., & DuBois, D. L. (1998). Cognitive–behavioral therapy of depression and depressive symptoms during adolescence: A review and meta-analysis. *Journal of the American Academy of Child and Adolescent Psychiatry, 37,* 26–34.

Rossello, J., & Bernal, G. (1996). Adapting cognitive–behavioral and interpersonal treatments for depressed Puerto Rican adolescents. In E. D. Hibbs & P. S. Jensen (Eds.), *Psychosocial treatments for child and adolescent disorders* (pp. 157–186). Washington, DC: American Psychological Association.

Sanchez, L., Hagino, O., Weller, E., & Ronald, W. (1999). Bipolarity in children. *Psychiatric Clinics of North America, 22,* 629–648.

Schwartz, S., & Johnson, J. H. (1985). *Psychopathology of childhood* (2nd ed.). New York: Pergamon Press.

Seligman, M. E. (1974). Depression and learned helplessness. In R. J. Friedman & M. M. Katz (Eds.), *The psychology of depression: Contemporary theory and research* (pp. 83–125). New York: Wiley.

Seligman, M. E. (1975). *Helplessness: On depression, development, and death.* San Francisco: Freedman.

Spence, S. H. (2003). Social skills training with children and young people: Theory, evidence and practice. *Child and Adolescent Mental Health, 8*(2), 84–96.

Stark, K. D., Swearer, S., Kurowski, C., Sommer, D., & Bowen, B. (1996). Targeting the child and family: A holistic approach to treating child and adolescent depressive disorders. In E. D. Hibbs & P. S. Jensen (Eds.), *Psychosocial treatments for child and adolescent disorders: Empirically based strategies for clinical practice* (pp. 207–238). Washington, DC: American Psychological Association.

Sullivan, P. F., Neale, M. C., & Kendler, K. S. (2000). Genetic epidemiology of major depression: Review and meta-analysis. *American Journal of Psychiatry, 157,* 1552–1562.

Szapocznik, J., Santisteban, D., Kurtines, W. M., Perez-Vidal, A., & Harris, O. (1984). Bicultural effectiveness training: A treatment intervention for enhancing intercultural adjustment in Cuban-American families. *Hispanic Journal of Behavioral Sciences, 6,* 317–344.

Szapocznik, J., Santisteban, D., Rio, A., Perez-Vidal, A., & Kurtines, W. M. (1986a). Bicultural effectiveness training (BET): An experimental test of an intervention modality for families experiencing intergenerational/intercultural conflict. *Hispanic Journal of Behavioral Sciences, 8,* 303–330.

Szapocznik, J., Santisteban, D., Rio, A., Perez-Vidal, A., & Kurtines, W. M. (1986b). Family effectiveness training (FET) for Hispanic families. In H. P. Lefley & P. B. Pedersen (Eds.), *Cross-cultural training for mental health professionals* (pp. 245–261). Springfield, IL: Charles C Thomas.

Szapocznik, J., Santisteban, D., Rio, A., Perez-Vidal, A., & Kurtines, W. M. (1989). Family effectiveness training: An intervention to prevent drug abuse and problem behaviors in Hispanic adolescents. *Hispanic Journal of Behavioral Sciences, 11,* 4–27.

Tomson, L. M., Pangrazi, R. P., Friendman, G., & Hutchison, N. (2003). Childhood depressive symptoms, physical activity and health related fitness. *Journal of Sport and Exercise Psychology, 25,* 419–439

Treatment for Adolescents With Depression Study Team. (2004). Fluoxetine, cognitive–behavioral therapy, and their combination for adolescent with depression. *Journal of the American Medical Association, 292,* 807–820.

Vernon, A. (2005). *Assessment and intervention with children and adolescents: Developmental and multicultural approaches* (2nd ed.). Alexandria, VA: American Counseling Association.

Wagner, K. D. (2005). Pharmacotherapy for major depression in children and adolescents. *Progress in Neuropsychopharmacology and Biological Psychiatry, 29,* 819–826.

Wagner, K. D., & Ambrosini, P. J. (2001). Childhood depression: Pharmacological therapy/treatment (pharmacotherapy of childhood depression). *Journal of Clinical Child Psychology, 30*(1), 88–97.

Webster-Stratton, C., & Hancock, L. (1998). Training for parents of young children with conduct problems: Content, methods, and therapeutic processes. In C. E. Schaefer & J. M. Briesmeister (Eds.), *Handbook of parent training* (pp. 98–152). New York: Wiley.

Webster-Stratton, C., Reid, M. J., & Hammond, M. (2001). Preventing conduct problems, promoting social competence: A parent and teacher training partnership in Head Start. *Journal of Clinical Child Psychology, 30*, 283–302.

Weisz, J. R., McCarty, C. A., & Valeri, S. M. (2006) Effects of psychotherapy for depression in children and adolescents: A meta-analysis. *Psychological Bulletin, 132*, 132–149.

Williamson, D. E., Ryan, N .D., Birmaher, B., Dahl, R. E., Kaufman, J., Rao, U., & Puig-Antich, J. (2004). *Journal of the American Academy of Child & Adolescent Psychiatry, 43*, 291–297

Wolf, E. S. (1988). *Treating the self: Elements of clinical self-psychology.* New York: Guilford Press.

Wurtman, R. J. (2005). Genes, stress, and depression. *Metabolism, 54*(5), 16–19.

Ziervogel, C. F. (2000). Selective serotonin re-uptake inhibitors for children and adolescents. *European Child and Adolescent Psychiatry, 9*(Suppl. 15), 120–126.

Zimmerman, D. P. (2002). Research and practice in social- and life-skills training. *Residential Treatment for Children and Youth, 20*(2), 51–75.

CHAPTER 7

■

Stress and Trauma: Coping in Today's Society

Jane E. Rheineck and Russell D. Miars

Multiple demands including time conflicts, social and economic factors, and the complex and ever-changing nature of technology and the world of work characterize the society in which we live. As a result, coping with stress has become synonymous with modern adult life. It is interesting, however, that the image of a carefree childhood void of stress and trauma has dominated the U.S. cultural view of youth for most of the 20th century. Since the mid-1980s, however, there has been an increasing awareness not only that children and adolescents experience stress and trauma (Bagdi & Pfister, 2006; Dinicola, 1996; Humphrey, 1988; La Greca, Silverman, Vernberg, & Roberts, 2002; McMahon, Grant, Compas, Thurm, & Ey, 2003; Osofsky et al., 2004) but also that in complex ways yet to be understood, the numerous stresses and trauma youth actually do experience are linked to the alarming rise in at-risk behavioral difficulties many youths display (Gottlieb, 1991; Kim, Conger, Elder, & Lorenz, 2003; Raghavan & Kingston, 2006; Wilburn & Smith, 2005). There is also an increasing interest in the role trauma (extreme stress) and posttraumatic stress play in at-risk behaviors and mental health problems of youth (Berthold, 2000; Kilpatrick & Williams, 1998; Lahad, Shacham, & Niv, 2000; Parson, 1995). In addition, catastrophes such as the September 11, 2001, terrorist attack and Hurricane Katrina have presented new and additional concerns for mental health professionals to consider when assessing and treating stress and trauma.

PROBLEM DEFINITION

Paradoxically, although youths and adults alike seem to know what it means to be stressed (e.g., being under pressure; being tense or anxious about problems at work, school, or in family), there has yet to emerge a uniformly agreed-on definition of the stress concept by researchers. This problem of definition in the literature complicates any discussion of stress and coping in youth. Trauma is more consistently defined in the literature as a form of stress that is extreme, overwhelming, and subjectively experienced as uncontrollable or unpredictable (Allen, 1995). Research on stress has historically focused more on the consequences of stress for organismic functioning (Selye, 1993) than on how stress is aroused (Pearlin, 1993) and subsequently coped with at the emotional and behavioral level (Moos & Schaefer, 1993; Sandler, Wolchik, MacKinnon, Ayers, & Roosa, 1997).

Until recently, an additional complication in understanding stress in youth has been that most research has been conducted exclusively with adults (J. H. Johnson, 1986; Lazarus, 1991, 1999; Sherr, Bergenstrom, & McCann, 1999). It is doubtful, however, that stress and coping in adults is the same, or directly similar, to stress and coping in youth (J. H. Johnson, 1986; Sherr et al., 1999). In fact, several authors (Dise-Lewis, 1988; Humphrey, 1988; Kruczek & Salsman, 2006; Sandler et al., 1997) are quite clear that stress in youth must be regarded as distinct. Kruczek and Salsman (2006) also reported that a child's age and developmental level affect the response and recovery of stress and trauma and should be accounted for in both assessment and treatment.

In this chapter we examine what is currently known about human stress, trauma, and coping processes in general, giving special attention to causes and prevention of stress in youth. We first review the predominant ways stress and trauma have been conceptualized over the past three decades and then concentrate on causal factors (the sources of stress and trauma) with consideration of how developmental stages interact with the experience of stress and the coping strategies used by youth when faced with stress and trauma. Next we address approaches to prevention of stress and trauma from individual, family, school, and community perspectives. We conclude with a brief consideration of stress and trauma from a cultural perspective. In this chapter the term *children* refers to youths who are preschool to age 10, whereas *adolescents* refers to youths who are ages 11 to 19. As used here, the term *youth* is inclusive of preschool to age 19.

PERSPECTIVES ON STRESS AND TRAUMATIC STRESS

Historically, the stress concept has been conceptualized from three major perspectives: stimulus-oriented views, response-oriented views, and stress as a transaction between person and environment (J. H. Johnson, 1986). These three perspectives, however, do not include the special attention that is given in the research literature to trauma and posttraumatic stress. For this reason, trauma and posttraumatic stress are included below as a fourth perspective on the stress concept.

Stimulus-Oriented Views

From a stimulus-oriented perspective, the focus is on stress as a specific stimulus: "Stress is seen as resulting from experiencing any of a number of situations that are noxious or threatening or that place excessive demands on the individual" (J. H. Johnson, 1986, p. 16). Research that has defined stress from a life events perspective (e.g., divorce, death in the family) falls under this view. This perspective alone is limiting in that it cannot account for why some individuals experience potential stressors negatively whereas others experience the same stressor as a positive challenge (J. H. Johnson, 1986; Undergraff & Taylor, 2000).

Response-Oriented Views

Up until the 1960s, stress was almost exclusively defined from a stimulus perspective. Embedded in this framework was an engineering analogy of stress in which an external force created a strain on the object and deformed it in proportion to the pressure of the stressor (Lazarus, 1993b). After several decades of work around the stress concept, Hans Selye (1974, 1993) asserted that stress is the organism's physiological response to external stressors. Selye's (1974, 1993) work popularized a physiological version of the engineering analogy by conceiving stress as having three distinct phases: alarm, resistance, and exhaustion. This sequence was termed the *general adaptation syndrome* (GAS) and refers to the "manifestations of stress in the whole body" (Selye, 1974, p. 139).

In the alarm reaction phase, the organism responds with a series of complex biochemical alterations, such as increased breathing and blood sugar release through the discharge of hormones preparing the body for fight or flight (Selye, 1993). Because a state of alarm cannot be maintained continuously, a second phase, the stage of resistance, ensues. If the stressor continues to impinge on the organism, its limited adaptational energy is focused more singularly on resisting further the threat presented by the stressor. Unfortunately, when the organism's adaptational energy is focused on selected stressors in an ongoing fashion, it leaves itself vulnerable to other ensuing stressors (Ivancevich & Matteson, 1980). This biological stress syndrome (Selye, 1974, 1993) is how numerous stress studies have successfully linked various stressors with the onset of psychiatric (Rabkin, 1993) and somatic disease processes (Creed, 1993; Holmes & Rahe, 1967; Selye, 1993).

The final phase is the stage of exhaustion. Selye (1993) emphasized that the body is limited in the amount of adaptational energy available to withstand stress. Once the adaptational energy has been expended, significant efforts at restoration must follow. If the body cannot engage in replenishment and restore itself to the level of resistance, a phase of burnout (Pines, 1993) may occur. Most adults have had some experience with burnout in terms of their involvement with work, career, or other prolonged life events. We tend to forget, however, that because of the incredible energy that youngsters expend in multiple spheres of activity, they too, by their very developmental nature, are equally vulnerable to burnout (Youngs, 1985).

Stress as a Transaction Between Person and Environment

This view of stress has been most fully developed by Lazarus (Lazarus & Folkman, 1984). How the person views the stressfulness of the environmental event, whether the event is seen as threatening or nonthreatening, desirable or undesirable, controllable or uncontrollable, and if the person believes coping resources are readily available for dealing with the events are significant in this perspective. From this perspective, Lazarus and Folkman (1984) offered their definition of stress: "Psychological stress is a particular relationship between the person and the environment that is appraised by the person as taxing or exceeding his or her resources and endangering his or her well-being" (p. 19). The emphasis in this definition is on the psychological processes (cognitive and mediational variables) in the person's experience of stress.

Lazarus (1993b, 1999) argued that stress should be seen as a subset of emotion. This view is adopted for two reasons. First, knowing that a person is experiencing "emotions resulting from harms, losses and threats" (anger, anxiety, fear) or from "emotions resulting from benefits" (joy, pride) in response to stress is useful and says a lot more about how a troubled person–environment relationship is being coped with than when the subjective experience of emotion is omitted (p. 24). As Houston (1987) noted, "an event cannot be regarded as a stressor without reference to the affective response it elicits" (p. 379). Second, the more striking issue in understanding stress is the person's various coping responses to stressors, not just the body's physiological response and adaptation to stress.

Trauma and Posttraumatic Stress

Trauma is the extreme stress reaction that results from the experience of a threatening and overwhelming (traumatic) life event (American Psychiatric Association, 2000). The diagnostic criteria of the American Psychiatric Association (2000, pp. 469–472) defines a traumatic stress event to include both the witnessing and/or involvement in a threatening (to self or others) situation (including death or serious injury) and the person's psychological response of intense fear, helplessness, or horror. Posttraumatic stress includes the "generalized reaction pattern to traumatic events, which is predetermined by the limited response range of affective, cognitive and behavioral responses that humans have to overwhelming stress" (McFarlane & de Girolamo, 1996, pp. 129–130). Only since the 1980s has it been acknowledged that exposure to trauma, over and beyond stress in general, is a widespread human experience. Like adults, youths are exposed to traumas of various types (Costello, Erkanli, Fairbank, & Angold, 2002; Tolin & Foa, 2006) and are vulnerable to posttraumatic stress reactions including the most severe form, posttraumatic stress disorder (PTSD). PTSD is a syndrome that includes three clusters of symptoms: hyperarousal, reexperiencing the trauma, and avoidance or numbing (American Psychiatric Association, 2000). Although PTSD can be construed (paradoxically) as a form of adaptation to trauma (Allen, 1995), its dysfunctional and self-damaging nature causes maladaptive functioning in the person's present life experience. PTSD symptoms may be acute (less than 3 months duration) or chronic (more than 3 months), and for some traumas (e.g., war-related, rape) the disorder can occur and/or recur weeks, months, or even years after exposure to the traumatic event (American Psychiatric Association, 2000; Carty, O'Donnell, & Creamer, 2006; Freedy & Donkervoet, 1995; Voelker, 2005). Children and youth frequently show posttraumatic stress symptoms and PTSD from such traumas as child sexual/physical abuse, domestic violence, criminal violence, and any number of natural or man-made (caused) disasters.

CAUSAL FACTORS

Exact causal factors relating stress to certain emotional or behavioral outcomes are exceedingly difficult to show in the stress field (J. H. Johnson, 1986). Part of the difficulty is that it is now known that the experiences of stress and traumatic stress are multiply determined by personality characteristics and contextual factors (Allen, 1995; Peterson, Kennedy, & Sullivan, 1991) that are compounded even further by the idiosyncratic range of individual response variation around any one given source of stress (Lazarus, 1991, 1993b). This is particularly true for children and adolescents because developmental changes interact with stressors to produce varied outcomes in coping responses (Compas & Phares, 1991; Kruczek & Salsman, 2006). In the following subsections, we present 13 factors that may have a causal relationship to the development of stress and at-risk behaviors.

Life Event Stressors

Life event scales have been developed for children (Coddington, 1972) similar to those originally developed for adults (Holmes & Rahe, 1967). The key feature of these scales is that they index the source and the amount of change demanded by the occurrence of specific events that are common across the developmental age range of youth. Each stress event has its own rated level of life change units that varies across the preschool to senior high school age range.

Two problems arise with the life events approach to the causes of stress in children and adolescents. One is that the external view of raters such as parents, teachers, and other adults is questionable in terms of whether the ratings would actually correspond well with children's self-ratings of the same events (J. H. Johnson, 1986). The other is that life events are regarded as stressful (i.e., negative) without consideration of their desirability (e.g., getting married). An alternative approach to address these issues, and one that may be more useful in practice settings, is to ask the child to indicate events as either good or bad and then provide self-ratings of the extent of impact of the event (e.g., ranging from *none* to *great*) in the child's life (Gray, 2004; J. H. Johnson, 1986). The child or adolescent's evaluation and subjective perspective are thus preserved and may be more valid indicators of childhood stress. J. H. Johnson (1986) summarized a number of studies that show that child/adolescent adjustment and life stress scores, using either measurement approach, have shown a significant relationship between increased levels of life stress and difficulties with self-esteem, delinquent behavior, poor school performance, and overall level of psychiatric symptomatology. This includes such specific psychological problems as suicidal tendencies and anorexia nervosa. The implication of these studies was that the accumulation of unchecked stressful life events may set the stage for vulnerability and possible development of at-risk emotional and behavioral problems in youth. Further, when the coping resources of youths are strained or depleted, they are particularly vulnerable to traumatic stress reactions when faced with trauma (Gaffney, 2006; Hobfoll, Dunahoo, & Monnier, 1995).

Traumatic Stress

The most extreme and disruptive stressors youth face are traumatic events that result from some human action such as violence or a natural disaster. The defining characteristics of trauma are that the event is perceived as a potential threat to survival and that, on a subjective level, the event is experienced as uncontrollable or unpredictable (American Psychiatric Association, 2000; Friedman & Marsella, 1996). Many traumas are possible from manmade and natural sources, but those affecting youth the most are likely to be violence or violent crimes, domestic violence, physical abuse, sexual abuse, life-threatening illness or severe accidental injury, or one of numerous natural disasters. Traumatic stress from any of these sources differs from challenging or painful stress in that an acute or chronic posttraumatic stress condition results when normal coping resources are ineffective or depleted (Hobfoll et al., 1995). Therefore, it becomes imperative that mental health professionals understand and can distinguish the difference between normal developmental coping skills and those that impair the healthy developmental process.

The key to whether a traumatic event leads to a posttraumatic stress condition is based on a complex matrix of preexisting genetic factors (proneness to anxiety), developmental factors (disruption of attachment), and coping style (resilience) that interact with length of exposure to the traumatic experience, the perceived intensity of the traumatic experience, and posttrauma factors such as quickness of treatment intervention, strength of the person's social support (especially family), and overall coping resources. When extreme or negative levels of these factors converge in one person's experience and coping fails, the clinical syndrome of

PTSD is the likely outcome. PTSD can be acute or chronic, and as a diagnosable psychiatric condition includes symptoms of intrusive recollection (flashbacks), emotional numbing to avoid the trauma-based memories, and hyperarousal (e.g., generalized anxiety, insomnia, irritability; American Psychiatric Association, 2000). PTSD requires clinical diagnosis and intervention at the individual and family level as the condition rarely resolves on its own (Allen, 1995) and may actually induce secondary traumatic stress in spouses, children, and other family members (Steinberg, 1998).

Natural Disasters

In addition to financial losses, natural disasters have an effect on children that affect both their personal growth and development. Some of the potentially devastating costs include missed school, a decrease in academic function, missed social opportunities, and exposure to life stressors such as divorce, domestic violence, and substance abuse (La Greca et al., 2002).

Hurricane Katrina has been identified as the most devastating natural disaster in U.S. history (Weisler, Barbee, & Townsend, 2006) and with that has come an unprecedented need for mental health care that may take years to measure (Voelker, 2005). After the initial emergency response, it was anticipated that there would be a dramatic increase in incidents of PTSD, depression, anxiety, and substance abuse for both adults and youth. A survey conducted in 2006 by Ronald Kessler of the Harvard Medical School has indicated that the prevalence of serious mental health concerns after Hurricane Katrina rose from 6.1% to 11.3%, whereas moderate to mild mental health problems increased from 9.7% to 19.9% (Kessler, 2006). Factors that set Katrina apart from other natural disasters included the (a) vast expanse of geographic destruction, (b) displacement of thousands of people, and (c) intense civil unrest (Voelker, 2005). In a survey conducted by the Centers for Disease Control and Prevention (CDC), approximately 44% of the children victimized by Hurricane Katrina, as reported by their caregivers, had symptoms of new mental health problems that included depression, anxiety, and sleep disturbances (Weisler et al., 2006).

Terr (1991) described traumatic events as falling into two categories. Type I are typically short-term, single events that usually involve a quick recovery. Type II events are defined as prolonged abuse, sexual victimizations, and natural disasters such as Hurricane Katrina. According to Terr, children who experience a Type II trauma experience severe stress and more difficulty with adjustment. Events such as terrorism or natural disasters take on even more complex symptomatology. These events can have catastrophic consequences involving multiple issues and losses. Voelker (2005) reported that symptoms may not show up for 6 to 12 months and the effects produce an "impact pyramid" (p. 1600), with those directly affected being the tip and those indirectly affected such as family, friends, rescue workers, and the community at large forming the foundation. To exacerbate the losses, those who usually assist the child back to precrisis stability are also reeling from the effects and may not be able to provide the support needed (Gaffney, 2006).

The September 11, 2001, terrorist attack has provided some insight to the needs of children who experience Type II trauma. Gaffney (2006) reported that the most helpful approach was giving support systems such as family, peers, and teachers the language to effectively communicate; in effect, training others to work with those affected by a natural disaster. They learned not only the supportive language but also the appropriate emotional responses: "Compassion building became a part of every therapeutic intervention for children, families, in the classrooms and with adults" (p. 1002).

Although the long-term effects of Hurricane Katrina are still unknown, there is sufficient evidence that psychological debriefing and psychoeducational programming are beneficial in response to natural disasters (Kruczek & Salsman, 2006). These researchers suggested that the most effective format of intervention with children and adolescents is group work that includes caregivers and teachers. After symptoms of acute stress or PTSD are present, Kruzcek and Salsman recommended cognitive–behavioral interventions to help the youths manage their symptoms either in an individual or group environment. As with all levels of intervention, caregivers' involvement in this stage can also facilitate and stabilize adaptive coping skills.

Home and Family Stress

Home and family are important contexts for understanding stress in children and adolescents and represent a large portion of the types of stressors youths experience (Humphrey, 1988). Numerous studies have identified significant relationships between the extent of parental stress and levels of child distress (Compas & Phares, 1991; Jones & Prinz, 2005; Low & Stocker, 2005; Steinberg, 1998). Many of these studies show that as one or both parents' stress and maladjustment increase, so does the level of stress and maladjustment in the child or adolescent. Discussions of child abuse, divorce and marital dissolution, family economic problems, and adolescent–parent conflict are considered to illustrate how home and family stress can be strong sources of stress for many youths.

Child Abuse

Physical, sexual, emotional, and negligent abuse of children is of enormous concern in society, and despite the increased effort to combat child abuse over the past half century, the true incidence and damaging consequences of abuse (including later posttraumatic reactions in adults) are still not fully known or understood (Adams, 2006; Irving & Ferraro, 2006; C. F. Johnson & Cohn, 1990). Typically, the stress youth experience from the abuse is not expressed as such, but rather is expressed through a wide range of posttraumatic-linked emotional and behavior difficulties such as anger, apathy, delinquency, school problems, shame, or eating disorders (Scheeringa, Wright, Hunt, & Zeanah, 2006; Stoddard et al., 2006; Widom, 1991). C. F. Johnson and Cohn (1990) provided a comprehensive list of reported effects. It is interesting to note that the typical runaway is likely to have come from an abusive family and may regard life on the street as less stressful than the home environment (Farber, Kinast, McCoard, & Falkner, 1984; Tyler, Cauce, & Whitbeck, 2004). This is just one example of how the ongoing effects of the stress of child abuse can be displaced in the form of other at-risk coping strategies in youth.

Divorce and Marital Dissolution

Because of the high incidence of divorce in the United States, researchers have expanded their concern about the effects of divorce from a more singular life event readjustment to the chronic effects of divorce on children's mental, emotional, social, and academic development (Houseknecht & Hango, 2006; Kalter, 1987; McMahon et al., 2003; Wertlieb, 1991). The antecedents (emotional conflict and diminished support) and aftermath of divorce are now considered as more inclusive aspects of the actual stress youths experience from marital dissolution (Arnold & Carnahan, 1990). These researchers have also summarized a number of studies that showed interactions among sex, age, time of divorce in the youth's life, and the stress of readjustment. In general, boys appear to experience the stress of divorce more intensely at the elementary school level, whereas girls at this age fair about as well as those in intact families. Later, however, adolescent girls of divorcing parents show significantly increasing problems with self-esteem and, later still, in heterosexual relationships that later affect their parenting styles and increase stress levels in their children (Nair & Murray, 2005). Overall, one of the better ways to understand divorce as a source of stress for youth is to recognize the significant loss/change in access to parents the experience usually represents. Diminished access to parents can significantly reduce the felt social support youths receive from parents at times when they may need it most. It is only when parents are free from the trauma themselves that they can provide a positive influence on their children's adjustment to divorce (Taylor, 2004). As noted further in the section on prevention approaches, for a variety of life events and chronic stressors, social support plays a critical role in buffering the negative effects of stress (Gottlieb & Wagner, 1991; Taylor, 2004).

Economic Stress

No discussion of home and family stress is complete without mentioning the chronic and often devastating effects of economic stress in the family (Committee for Economic Development, 2002; McMahon et al., 2003). Poverty creates an overall psychological environment in the family that is stressful for parents and youth alike and is linked to the incidence of numerous mental health adjustment issues of children, such as child abuse and its associated stresses. But economic stress is not limited to those families struggling to make ends meet. Occupational stress in adults has been associated with a number of health and psychological adjustment variables (Ahola et al., 2006; Holt, 1993; Wang, 2006), contributing to the overall level of stress in the family. The dual roles of career and parent, especially for women, but increasingly for men as well (Zunker, 2002), create stress in the form of daily hassles, such as child-care arrangements, and strain in the parenting role. Finally, job loss, career change, and being a displaced worker are all stresses deriving from economic change/uncertainty and the stress inherent in the rapid change to a technology and service-based economy (Zunker, 2002).

School Stress

All aspects of the school experience challenge youth to adapt to the stresses of the educative process. Sears and Milburn (1990, p. 225) listed 25 common school-age stressors. These include anxiety about going to school, changing schools, competitiveness (including fear of failure and fear of success), conflict with teachers, failing an exam, worrying about taking tests, and peer teasing.

Although school is a major source of stress for some youths, for others school can be a source of motivational challenge and stress relief (Elias, 1989). Thus, when assessing the stress experienced by a child or adolescent, the nature and impact of the stress can only be ascertained in the context of the child's whole life space, such as background, home life, school life, age, and gender (Humphrey, 1988).

For many youths, and possibly increasing numbers of youths, the school experience is not the benign academic learning experience it was once regarded to be (Elias, 1989; Hemphill, Toumbourou, Catalano, & Mathers, 2004; Skinner & Wellborn, 1997). School reform pressures, which overemphasize academic success at the expense of psychosocial learning and development, may be contributing to "debilitating student stress" in up to 30% of the student population (Elias, 1989, p. 394). Rather than providing a balance between academics and preparation of students for adult citizenship, social competence, and the world of work, schools are under tremendous pressure from parents who are "looking to the schools to guarantee their children's future success" (Elias, 1989, p. 395). As this singular pressure for academic success and test score performance has increased, so has the stress level of students, to the point that for some the stress is debilitating. Students display the effects of this debilitating stress through physical symptoms of fatigue, headaches, and nausea; a sense of alienation from satisfaction gained through effectiveness and success; and delinquent and antisocial behavior, such as substance abuse or gang involvement, as means of coping with the stress of thwarted expectations for a positive future (Elias, 1989; Oaten & Cheng, 2006).

Sexual Identity/Gender Expression

Although supportive peer relationships assist in minimizing stress-related responses for all youth, they appear to be particularly important for sexual minorities (Diamond & Lucas, 2004). The stigma associated with nonconformity to both gender expression and sexual identity often creates fear of parental disapproval and even rejection (Savin-Williams, 1998), which may result in greater investment in peer relationships. This investment or need may also paradoxically establish increased levels of stress for the same reasons as parental disapproval: the fear of losing or maintaining close ties with peers because of their minority status (Diamond & Lucas, 2004).

In Diamond and Lucas's (2004) study, mixed results were found. Higher levels of depression, anxiety, and physical symptomatology were found in the sexual minority (gay, lesbian, bisexual, and unlabeled) group, yet these participants reported no higher perceived stress or lower self-esteem. They did report smaller peer networks but did not report less connectedness with their friends or fewer romantic relationships. This body of work continues to support previous research regarding the stigmatization and victimization of sexual minority youths but also recommended further investigation into the more normative and mundane aspects of daily adolescent life that are critical to understanding the differences between sexual minorities and heterosexual youths' psychosocial well-being (Diamond & Lucas, 2004).

Developmental Stress/Biological Changes

Puberty is the most dramatic of all the developmental transitions in the human life span (Peterson et al., 1991; Sigelman & Rider, 2003). Biological changes in early adolescence leading to adult appearance and size, reproductive capacity, and internal endocrine changes produce challenges and stresses in the intrapersonal and social adaptation spheres of adolescent functioning. Issues of sexuality and sexual behavior emerge as a result of these biological changes and can be very stressful for early adolescents and their parents. This observation supports the belief that there is a downward age trend for today's youth in the timing of the stress of emerging sexuality.

Cognitive–Emotional Changes

The increase in cognitive and emotional complexity required for expanding from concrete experiences of the world to a capacity for abstract thinking and emotion (Piaget & Inhelder, 1969) is a developmental stressor of enormous implications in the transition from childhood to adolescence. Larson and Asmussen (1991) reported data that show there is an increase in the experience of negative emotion (e.g., anger, worry, hurt) from preadolescence to adolescence. In a certain sense, maturing cognitive and emotional capacities set the stage for adolescence to be the first major confrontation with the existential issues of choice, responsibility, and freedom in the life span (Bugental, 1981; Sigelman & Rider, 2003). As is commonly recognized, the inherent stress of this developmental transition can be overwhelming for many youths.

Gender Differences

Gender socialization has emerged as a significant variable in the experience of stress in youth (Burton, Stice, & Seeley, 2004; Gore & Colten, 1991; Tolin & Foa, 2006). Some of the conclusions emerging from the literature in this area are extremely relevant to our understanding of the sources of stress in youth, particularly in older adolescents. For example, Peterson et al. (1991) concluded from a number of studies that although in early adolescence there is only one gender divergence (for body image with girls showing a decline), by late adolescence there is marked gender divergence across all measures of self and negative affect, with girls becoming markedly more depressed as adolescence proceeds. The available evidence suggests that girls "amplify" negative moods as a form of coping with developmental stressors, whereas boys are "more likely to distract themselves from a depressed mood" (p. 105). Thus, girls' coping responses to stress change along gender lines during adolescence (suggesting they become more vulnerable to various stressors), but boys' coping responses appear to remain the same. Paradoxically, girls' coping responses to developmental stress in adolescence may set a lifelong pattern of coping with stress with depressive affect. Similarly, the pattern of boys' coping may be protective for gender-based functioning in instrumental and achievement spheres, but it may also be quite maladaptive for future interpersonal relationships that require emotional intimacy (Peterson et al., 1991).

Interpersonal Stress

Interpersonal relationships increasingly become a source of stress for youth as they progress from childhood to early adolescence and through late adolescence. This appears to be true for both girls and boys, but adolescent girls report greater interpersonal stress than adolescent boys (Compas & Wagner, 1991). Compas and Wagner (1991) also noted that when stressful life events occur in an adolescent's life, they are likely to be "directly related to others in their social networks, especially their parents" (p. 75). In a study that directly examined adolescent–parent conflict, Smetana, Yau, Restrepo, and Braeges (1991) found that conflict, although stressful, provides a context for debates over the extent of adolescents' developing autonomy and thus serves an adaptive function. However, when the interaction style between parent and adolescent is negative (i.e., devaluing or judging), adolescent development is inhibited (causing further intrapersonal stress and interpersonal conflict).

Another significant finding was that adolescent–parent conflict is greater in married than divorced families, and that children and adolescents who have had to deal with the stress of parental divorce may actually increase their coping competence and resilience to future life stress (Smetana et al., 1991). Finally, Compas and Wagner noted that interpersonal stress shows a reliable developmental variation: In junior high, negative family interaction is the predominant source of interpersonal stress, whereas by senior high, conformity and concerns about acceptance by the peer group are the dominant interpersonal stressors. Stress arising from dependency on the peer group subsides by later adolescence, and with entry into college, academic events become the predominant source of stress.

APPROACHES TO PREVENTION

Both primary and secondary prevention strategies are important in reducing stress in youth. Primary prevention consists of attempts to minimize youths' vulnerability to stress or actually prevent its occurrence, whereas secondary prevention consists of teaching vulnerable youth the therapeutic coping skills they need to know (Lazarus, 1991). Tertiary prevention consists of clinical treatment of stress and posttraumatic stress after the damage has occurred, and although not preventive in an absolute sense, such intervention can prevent the exacerbation of traumatic stress as well as lessen the secondary traumatic stress of family members of the traumatized individual (Steinberg, 1998).

Because so many stressors of youths (especially in children) are outside of their control and related to situations with parents, other family members, teachers, or socioeconomic conditions (Ryan-Wenger, 1992; Salmon & Bryant, 2002), it is particularly relevant to approach the prevention of stress in youth from a systemic perspective. At the same time, many life and traumatic stressors are unavoidable for youths or stem from normal developmental challenges. Given this, an additional prevention strategy becomes maximizing the coping resources of youths so that the negative effects of stress are buffered to the greatest extent possible (Gottlieb, 1991; Sandler et al., 1997). This latter strategy reflects the current research emphasis on understanding individual coping processes (Lazarus, 1991, 1993a, 1993b, 1999) and psychosocial protective factors (Kimchi & Schaffner, 1990; Roosa, Wolchik, & Sandler, 1997) when the person is under stress. In this overview of approaches to prevention in the individual, family, school, and community, consideration is given to possible systemic prevention of stress as well as various coping and protective factors that appear to buffer the effects of stress and trauma in youth.

Individual

As already noted, secondary prevention of stress consists of teaching therapeutic stress and coping skills to the individual in hopes that the negative effects of stress will not escalate. This may be done in a remedial fashion once the need for stress reduction has been identified, or more broadly and in advance through coping skills training (Elias, 1989; Sandler et al., 1997). Because children, and to a certain extent adolescents, are less able to identify the sources of stress or know how to cope with a variety of stressors (Ryan-Wegner, 1992), adults in the lives of youths must facilitate the referral of youths for remedial stress reduction and anticipate the need for and benefits of coping training (Folkman, Chesney, McKusick, Ironson, & Coates, 1991). Stress reduction strategies and techniques that rely on progressive muscle relaxation, visual imagery, and biofeedback have been shown to be effective for both adults (Girdano, Everly, & Dusek, 1990) and children (Humphrey, 1988; Romano, 1997; Youngs, 1985). Stress reduction in children might best focus on the aspects of body relaxation, nutrition, and exercise to counter the effects of stress (Humphrey, 1988); as cognitive development increases, cognitive, emotional, and social support coping skills training are additional forms of preventive intervention for adolescents (Folkman et al., 1991). However, Romano (1997) found that cognitive coping strategies were being used in the school environment by children as early as the fourth and fifth grades.

With respect to coping, researchers have identified conceptual frameworks that relate to the present discussion of coping effectiveness in the individual as a preventive measure against stress (Carlson & Dalenberg, 2000; Ebata & Moos, 1991). The approach–avoidance coping model (Lazarus & Folkman, 1984) distinguishes between active approach-oriented coping (toward threat) versus passive or avoidance-oriented coping (away from threat). Approach coping includes efforts to change ways of thinking about a problem (stressor) as well as behavioral attempts to resolve or address the problem. Avoidant coping includes cognitive attempts to deny or minimize threat and behavioral attempts to avoid or get away from the problem. Research has shown that adolescents who use more approach coping than avoidance coping are better adjusted and less distressed (Ebata & Moos, 1991). Further, Ebata and Moos (1991) concluded that adolescents who show a pattern of avoidance coping may be at greater risk for poorer adjustment to subsequent life stressors and crises. Through coping skills training, adolescents can be shown the positive value of approach coping and be encouraged to engage in approach coping behavior when faced with life events and developmental stressors.

An additional way to think about stress prevention for the individual from a coping perspective is highlighted by the problem-focused versus emotion-focused distinction (Lazarus, 1993a, 1999). In this framework, coping efforts can be focused on modifying the stressor itself (problem-focused coping) or on attempts to regulate the emotional responses that accompany the stressor (emotion-focused coping). Ebata and Moos (1991) reported research that suggests adolescents who used more problem-focused coping with interpersonal stressors, such as talking with the other person, reported fewer stressful emotional and behavioral reactions than those who used emotion-focused strategies, such as ignoring the situation or yelling at the other person. Ebata and Moos summarized several studies that examined the relationship between family and peer support, active coping strategies, and substance use in adolescents. In general, adolescents who used active behavioral and cognitive coping as well as the seeking of adult support showed less substance use, whereas those adolescents who relied more on peers and acting out to cope showed more substance use. Other authors (e.g., Gottlieb, 1991; Hendron, 1990) have also noted that attachment, support, and guidance from at least one adult figure (teacher, coach, parent, or school counselor) in an adolescent's life can buffer the effects of stress and facilitate approach and problem-focused coping.

The prevention of traumatic stress can take two additional forms. First, preliminary research has shown that when trauma occurs, immediate crisis intervention and critical incident stress debriefing can minimize the risk of posttraumatic stress reactions in many individuals (Saylor, Belter, & Stokes, 1997). This type of prevention applies more to singular events (e.g., natural disasters, catastrophic accidents, violent crime) than it does to repeated or more hidden traumas (e.g., child sexual abuse, domestic violence). In the latter case, posttraumatic symptoms or PTSD often show a delayed onset in the individual and require corrective therapy in the form of psychological and/or pharmacological therapies (Allen, 1995). In all cases of traumatic stress in the individual, crisis intervention is likely to be preventive of an intensification of posttraumatic stress reactions (Sorenson, 2000). Thus, community efforts to have services in place in advance of trauma, whether in disaster agencies, hospitals, schools, or clinics, are the best prevention when traumatic events inevitably occur in the lives of youths (Saylor et al., 1997).

Family

From a larger systems perspective, services that reduce stress in family life can directly prevent stress in children that may interfere with normal development (La Greca et al., 2002; Wagner, 1994) or cause secondary traumatic stress reactions in children (Steinberg, 1998). Peterson et al. (1991) observed that when such a strategy can be implemented from childhood to early adolescence, and through adolescence, a positive trajectory of coping with the stress of developmental transitions is set in motion. The earlier and the more consistent the support is from parents in this process, the more positive is the overall mental health of the child. Further, Peterson et al. noted that positive mental health in children and adolescents (higher self-esteem) is related to greater internal coping resources when youths are faced with unexpected life event stressors. Given this overall picture, school-based mental health services (Sleek, 1994) that can provide family support (Gottleib, 1991) in the form of integrated social, health, and mental health services may be one of the most effective means of decreasing family stress, and as a result, preventing stress in youth.

A more direct way in which the family plays a role in the prevention of stress in youth is through the family's function as an informal social support network (Sandler et al., 1997; Willis, 1987). This idea has also been advanced for posttraumatic stress reactions (Dinicola, 1996). Although the caregivers of traumatized youths may also be at risk for developing secondary traumatic stress reactions (Steinberg, 1998), research still indicates that family support may be the most important buffer in mitigating the effect of trauma (Gaffney, 2006; Wasserstein & LaGreca, 1998), whereas the absence of family support can have a detrimental effect on traumatized youths. Dimensions of family support, which appear to make a real difference in buffering the negative effects of stress, are esteem support (e.g., emotional and confidant support), informational support (e.g., problem-solving steps), motivational support (e.g., encouragement), and instrumental support (e.g., material aid such as money). In contrast, one of the reasons child abuse is so likely to have posttraumatic stress features is that the various forms of family support are so lacking in the abusive family. Other family factors that appear to be protective of stress in youth are noted by Kimchi and Schaffner (1990) and include such dimensions as adequate rule setting and structure, family cohesion, lower parental conflicts, open communication, warmth toward the child, and being patient in parenting style. As noted earlier, the family can be a powerful source of stress in youth; likewise, it can be a powerful buffer to stress when functioning effectively.

School

Gottlieb (1991) emphasized the benefits of social support interventions. Because inclusion, acceptance, and approval from one's peer group are so important in adolescence, peer counseling programs in schools can materially increase the social support adolescents feel. Humphrey (1988) suggested that stress from academic competition needs to be offset by an increased emphasis on cooperative learning experiences. With such added peer/social support, the stressful aspects of school and the challenges of developmental changes can be minimized.

Klingman (2001) developed a five-level approach to school-based intervention that was developed as a response to large-scale traumatic events. The first level, *anticipatory guidance,* is to prepare schools for a large-scale event prior to any event occurring. This involves the development of disaster plans, emergency procedures, and collaboration with community agencies. The second level, *primary preventive interventions,* are programs integrated into schools that have already experienced large-scale events. Some of these programs include psychological debriefing and psychoeducational services. *Early indicated preventive interventions* describe the third level. This may involve interventions such as mass screenings to identify those children who are exhibiting acute stress symptoms. Those identified in the third level then move to the fourth level, *indicated prevention programming.* This level provides the identified students with counseling to explore their traumatic events, begin the development of coping skills, and assist in the prevention of PTSD. The final level, *tertiary preventive interventions,* provides relapse prevention for those students who already have PTSD.

School personnel can be especially helpful because the schools are often the first point of contact for children. They can be instrumental in identifying students who demonstrate impairments in multiple areas (e.g., social, family, and academics) and collaborate with appropriate outside agencies.

Community

Wagner (1994) observed that the povertization of childhood is the single largest threat to the welfare of children today. It is clear that poverty is stressful for parents and families and plays a large role in the chronic stress that many youths experience in the family, school, and community. In addition, poverty may also be associated with more frequent witnessing of violent crime by many youths, serving as a source of traumatic stress and its associated risks (Parson, 1995). There are no simple or direct ways to prevent poverty, but communities can advocate for changes in public policy that empower children, protect their rights, and facilitate access to social and mental health services to reduce stress (Stern & Newland, 1994). Such efforts, when successful, can go a long way in preventing stress in youth while benefiting all children as a social group.

The stress associated with violence in the schools can be another important target of community prevention. The threat of violence in schools affects nearly all students, and the fear that results can inhibit a sense of industry, achievement, and self-confidence (Christie & Toomey, 1990). Further, posttraumatic reactions and PTSD are likely for those in immediate proximity to a violent crime at school or a school shooting. Given that schools are embedded in the larger community, the stress of violence must be prevented by community-based programs. Because much of the violence in schools may be related to the problems of drugs and gangs in and around schools (in the inner city and suburbs alike), school–community prevention strategies that address these issues reduce an aspect of chronic stress in youth.

In addition, the community can play a preventive role in reducing stress in youth by publicly supporting the continuing efforts of schools to integrate psychosocial education and other at-risk intervention programs into the schools (see

Elias, 1989). McWhirter, McWhirter, McWhirter, and McWhirter (1994) identified "five Cs of competency" that distinguish high and low risk youth: *critical* school (academic) competencies; *concept* of self and self-esteem; *communication* with others; *coping* ability; and *control* over decision making, delay of gratification, and purpose in life. Adults in the community can help prevent stress in youth by teaching and valuing these coping competencies that are so necessary to deal with a rapidly changing world.

ADAPTATIONS FOR DIVERSITY

Considering stress, traumatic stress, and coping from an ethnocultural perspective is the most recent development in the stress field (deVries, 1996; Marsella, Friedman, Gerrity, & Scurfield, 1996; Nader, Dubrow, & Stamm, 1999). Cross-cultural applicability is an important question and begins with whether the stress concept (including posttraumatic stress) validly applies to children, adolescents, and adults from other cultures (de Vries, 1996). On the basis of the available research, Marsella et al. (1996) concluded that PTSD is a valid and clinically meaningful diagnosis in non-Western cultures. These authors cautioned, however, that in most cases there are culture-specific responses to trauma not captured in the universal aspects of the diagnosis. Similarly, deVries (1996) and Perren-Klinger (2000) supported the concept that traumatic stress is valid cross-culturally but added that a person's unique culture or ethnic subculture may offer protective responses to stress that are integrated into the culture's existing framework for holding problems and illnesses, including stress/traumatic stress

From the same perspective, Gonzales and Kim (1997) indicated that the available literature on stress, coping, and overall mental health of youth also requires specific consideration of cultural factors. Hispanic and African American children and adolescents appear to be at an increased risk for PTSD and are less likely to show a decrease in symptoms over time (Kruczek & Salsman, 2006). Poverty and social oppression, especially in urban environments, are likely to exacerbate the risk of traumatic events that may lead to PTSD (Kruczek & Salsman, 2006). In addition to all the life stress and coping adaptation concepts outlined in the literature, working with ethnic minority youth requires consideration of their cultural ecology, which includes the stress-related variables of socioeconomic status, neighborhood context, migration/acculturation, and ethnic/racial discrimination. Gonzales and Kim's (1997) cultural ecological process model for ethnic minority children provides a comprehensive picture of how ethnicity and cultural protective factors interact to produce varied stress and coping outcomes.

SUMMARY

In this chapter, stress was discussed from three perspectives: stimulus-oriented view, response-oriented view, and person–environment transaction view. In addition, trauma and posttraumatic stress were considered as extreme stress and significant challenges to coping. Recent research and theory emphasize the person–environment transactional model in which both the perception of stress and coping responses to stress play an active role in the stress phenomenon (including traumatic stress). Only since the mid-1980s has research focused specifically on stress and coping in youth, and only in the past two decades has a fuller appreciation of trauma and posttraumatic stress in youth, especially ethnocultural considerations, emerged in the literature. Causal factors for stress and trauma in youth are multiple, varied, and complexly interwoven with the developmental challenges of childhood and adolescence. Life events, daily hassles, traumatic stress, family stress, child abuse, divorce, economic factors, school stress, and developmental challenges are highlighted as causal factors for stress in youth. Approaches to prevention are considered across individual, family, school, and community from a larger systems perspective as well as from individual coping skills and social support factors that are preventive of stress in youth. Important ethnocultural factors are also highlighted as they relate to the cross-cultural validity of posttraumatic stress and stress and coping in ethnic minority youth.

REFERENCES

Adams, C. M. (2006). The consequences of witnessing family violence on children and implications for family counselors. *Family Journal, 14*, 334–341.

Ahola, K., Honkonen, T., Kivimäki, M., Virtanen, M., Isometsä, E., Aromaa, A., & Lönnqvist, J. (2006). Contribution of burnout to the association between job strain and depression: The Health 2000 study. *Journal of Occupational and Environmental Medicine, 48*, 1023–1030.

Allen, J. G. (1995). *Coping with trauma: A guide to self-understanding*. Washington, DC: American Psychiatric Press.

American Psychiatric Association. (2000). *Diagnostic and statistical manual of mental disorders* (4th ed., Text Revision). Washington, DC: Author.

Arnold, L. E., & Carnahan, J. A. (1990). Child divorce stress. In L. E. Arnold (Ed.), *Childhood stress* (pp. 373–403). New York: Wiley.

Bagdi, A., & Pfister, I. K. (2006). Childhood stressors and coping actions: A comparison of children and parents' perspectives. *Child and Youth Care Forum, 35*, 21–40.

Berthold, S. M. (2000). War traumas and community violence: Psychological, behavioral, and academic outcomes among Khmer. *Journal of Multicultural Social Work, 8*, 15–46.

Bugental, J. F. T. (1981). *The search for authenticity* (Enlarged ed.). New York: Irvington.

Burton, E., Stice, E., & Seeley, J. R. (2004). A prospective test of the stress-buffering model of depression in adolescent girls: No support once again. *Journal of Consulting and Clinical Psychology, 72*, 689–697.

Carlson, E. B., & Dalenberg, C. J. (2000). A conceptual framework for the impact of traumatic experiences. *Trauma, Violence and Abuse, 1*, 4–29.

Carty, J., O'Donnell, M. L., & Creamer, M. (2006). Delayed-onset PTSD: A prospective study of injury survivors. *Journal of Affective Disorders, 90*, 257–261.

Christie, D. J., & Toomey, B. G. (1990). The stress of violence: School, community, and world. In L. E. Arnold (Ed.), *Childhood stress* (pp. 297–323). New York: Wiley.

Coddington, R. D. (1972). The significance of life events as etiological factors in the diseases of children: A study of a normal population. *Journal of Psychosomatic Research, 16*, 205–213.

Committee for Economic Development. (2002). *Preschool for all: Investing in a productive and just society*. New York: Author.

Compas, B. E., & Phares, V. (1991). Stress during childhood and adolescence: Sources of risk and vulnerability. In E. M. Cummings, A. L. Greene, & K. H. Karraker (Eds.), *Life-span developmental psychology: Perspectives on stress and coping* (pp. 111–129). Hillsdale, NJ: Erlbaum.

Compas, B. E., & Wagner, B. M. (1991). Psychosocial stress during adolescence: Intrapersonal and interpersonal processes. In M. E. Colten & S. Gore (Eds.), *Adolescent stress: Causes and consequences* (pp. 67–85). New York: Aldine de Gruyter.

Costello, J. E., Erkanli, A., Fairbank, J. A., & Angold, A. (2002). The prevalence of potentially traumatic events in childhood and adolescence. *Journal of Traumatic Stress, 1*, 99–112.

Creed, F. (1993). Stress and psychosomatic disorders. In L. Goldberger & S. Breznitz (Eds.), *Handbook of stress: Theoretical and clinical aspects* (pp. 496–510). New York: Free Press.

de Vries, M. W. (1996). Trauma in cultural perspective. In B. A. van der Kolk, A. C. McFarlane, & L. Weissaeth (Eds.), *Traumatic stress: The effects of overwhelming experience on mind, body, and society* (pp. 398–413). New York: Guilford Press.

Diamond, L. M., & Lucas, S. (2004). Sexual-minority and heterosexual youths' peer relationships: Experiences, expectations, and implications for well-being. *Journal of Research on Adolescence, 14*, 313–340.

Dinicola, V. F. (1996). Ethnocultural aspects of PTSD and related disorders among children and adolescents. In A. J. Marcella, M. J. Friedman, E. T. Gerrity, & R. M. Scurfield (Eds.), *Ethnocultural aspects of posttraumatic stress disorder* (pp. 389–414). Washington, DC: American Psychological Association.

Dise-Lewis, J. E. (1988). The life events coping inventory: An assessment of stress in children. *Psychosomatic Medicine, 50*, 484–489.

Ebata, A. T., & Moos, R. H. (1991). Coping and adjustment in distressed and healthy adolescents. *Journal of Applied Developmental Psychology, 12*, 33–54.

Elias, M. J. (1989). Schools as a source of stress to children: An analysis of causal and ameliorative influences. *Journal of School Psychology, 27*, 393–407.

Farber, E. D., Kinast, C., McCoard, W. D., & Falkner, D. (1984). Violence in families of adolescent runaways. *Child Abuse and Neglect, 18*, 295–299.

Folkman, S., Chesney, M., McKusick, L., Ironson, D. S., & Coates, T. J. (1991). Translating coping theory into an intervention. In J. Eckenrode (Ed.), *The social context of coping* (pp. 239–260). New York: Plenum Press.

Freedy, J. R., & Donkervoet, J. C. (1995). Traumatic stress: An overview of the field. In J. R. Freedy & S. E. Hobfoll (Eds.), *Traumatic stress: From theory to practice* (pp. 3–28). New York: Plenum.

Friedman, M. J., & Marsella, A. J. (1996). Posttraumatic stress disorder: An overview of the concept. In A. J. Marsella, M. J. Friedman, E. T. Gerrity, & R. M. Scurfield (Eds.), *Ethnocultural aspects of posttraumatic stress disorder: Issues, research, and clinical applications* (pp. 11–32). Washington, DC: American Psychological Association.

Gaffney, D. A. (2006). The aftermath of disaster: Children in crisis. *Journal of Clinical Psychology: In Session, 62*, 1001–1016.

Girdano, D., Everly, G., & Dusek, D. (1990). *Controlling stress and tension: A holistic approach* (3rd ed.). Englewood Cliffs, NJ: Prentice-Hall.

Gonzales, N. A., & Kim, L. S. (1997). Stress and coping in an ethnic minority context: Children's cultural ecologies. In S. A. Wolchik & I. N. Sandler (Eds.), *Handbook of children's coping: Linking theory and intervention* (pp. 481–511). New York: Plenum.

Gore, S., & Colten, M. E. (1991). Adolescent stress, social relationships, and mental health. In M. E. Colten & S. Gore (Eds.), *Adolescent stress: Causes and consequences* (pp. 1–14). New York: Aldine de Gruyter.

Gottlieb, B. H. (1991). Social support in adolescence. In M. E. Colten & S. Gore (Eds.), *Adolescent stress: Causes and consequences* (pp. 281–306). New York: Aldine de Gruyter.

Gottlieb, B. H., & Wagner, F. (1991). Stress and support processes in close relationships. In J. Eckenrode (Ed.), *The social context of coping* (pp. 165–188). New York: Plenum Press.

Gray, M. J. (2004). Psychometric properties of the Life Events Checklist. *Assessment, 11*, 330–341.

Hemphill, S. A., Toumbourou, J. W., Catalano, R. F., & Mathers, M. (2004). Levels and family correlates of positive adolescent development. *Family Matters, 68*, 28–35.

Hendron, R. L. (1990). Stress in adolescence. In L. E. Arnold (Ed.), *Childhood stress* (pp. 247–264). New York: Wiley.

Hobfoll, S. E., Dunahoo, C. A., & Monnier, J. (1995). Conservation of resources and traumatic stress. In J. R. Freedy & S. E. Hobfoll (Eds.), *Traumatic stress: From theory to practice* (pp. 49–72). New York: Plenum.

Holmes, T. H., & Rahe, R. H. (1967). The social readjustment rating scale. *Journal of Psychosomatic Research, 11*, 213–218.

Holt, R. R. (1993). Occupational stress. In L. Goldberger & S. Breznitz (Eds.), *Handbook of stress: Theoretical and clinical aspects* (pp. 342–367). New York: Free Press.

Houston, K. B. (1987). Stress and coping. In C. R. Snyder & C. E. Ford (Eds.), *Coping with negative life events* (pp. 373–399). New York: Plenum Press.

Houseknecht, S. K., & Hango, D. W. (2006). The impact of marital conflict and disruption on children's health. *Youth & Society, 38*, 58–89.

Humphrey, J. H. (1988). *Children and stress.* New York: AMS Press.

Irving, S., & Ferraro, K. F. (2006). Reports of abusive experiences during childhood and adult health ratings. *Journal of Aging and Health, 18*, 458–484.

Ivancevich, J. M., & Matteson, M. T. (1980). *Stress and work: A managerial perspective.* Glenview, IL: Scott, Foresman.

Johnson, C. F., & Cohn, D. S. (1990). The stress of child abuse and other family violence. In L. E. Arnold (Ed.), *Childhood stress* (pp. 267–295). New York: Wiley.

Johnson, J. H. (1986). *Life events as stressors in childhood and adolescence.* Beverly Hills, CA: Sage.

Jones, T. L., & Prinz, R. J. (2005). Potential roles of parental self-efficacy in parent–child adjustment: A review. *Clinical Psychology Review, 25*, 341–363.

Kalter, N. (1987). Long-term effects of divorce on children: A developmental vulnerability model. *American Journal of Orthopsychiatry, 57*, 587–599.

Kessler, R. C. (2006). Katrina spawned mental disorders but not thoughts of suicide. *Bulletin of the World Health Organization.* Retrieved from http://www.psychiatrictimes.com/article/showArticle.jhtml?articleID=192500417

Kilpatrick, K. L., & Williams, L. M. (1998). Potential mediators of posttraumatic stress disorder in child witnesses to domestic violence. *Child Abuse and Neglect, 22*, 310–330.

Kim, K. J., Conger, R. D., Elder, G. H., & Lorenz, F. O. (2003). Reciprocal influences between stressful life events and adolescent internalizing and externalizing problems. *Child Development, 74*, 127–143.

Kimchi, J., & Schaffner, B. (1990). Childhood protective factors and stress risk. In L. E. Arnold (Ed.), *Childhood stress* (pp. 475–500). New York: Wiley.

Klingman, A. (2001). Prevention of anxiety disorders: The case of posttraumatic stress disorder. In W. K. Silverman & P. D. A. Treffers (Eds.). *Anxiety disorders in children and adolescents: Research, assessment and interventions* (pp. 368–391). Cambridge, England: Cambridge University Press.

Kruczek, T., & Salsman, J. (2006). Prevention and treatment of posttraumatic stress disorder in the school setting. *Psychology in the School, 43,* 461–470.

La Greca, A. M., Silverman, W. K., Vernberg, E. M., & Roberts, M. C. (2002). *Helping children cope with disasters and terrorism.* Washington, DC: American Psychological Association.

Lahad, S., Shacham, Y., & Niv, S. (2000). Coping and community resources in children facing disaster. In A. Shalev, R. Yelhuda, & A. C. McFarlane (Eds.), *International handbook of human response to trauma* (pp. 389–395). New York: Plenum.

Larson, R., & Asmussen, L. (1991). Anger, worry, and hurt in early adolescence: An enlarging world of negative emotions. In M. E. Colten & S. Gore (Eds.), *Adolescent stress: Causes and consequences* (pp. 21–41). New York: Aldine de Gruyter.

Lazarus, R. S. (1991). *Emotion and adaptation.* New York: Oxford University Press.

Lazarus, R. S. (1993a). Coping theory and research: Past, present, and future. *Psychosomatic Medicine, 55,* 234–247.

Lazarus, R. S. (1993b). Why we should think of stress as a subset of emotion. In L. Goldberger & S. Breznitz (Eds.), *Handbook of stress: Theoretical and clinical aspects* (pp. 21–39). New York: Free Press.

Lazarus, R. S. (1999). *Stress and emotion: A new synthesis.* New York: Springer.

Lazarus, R. S., & Folkman, S. (1984). *Stress, appraisal, and coping.* New York: Springer.

Low, S. M., & Stocker, C. (2005). Family functioning and children's adjustment: Associations among parents' depressed mood, marital hostility, parent–child hostility, and children's adjustment. *Journal of Family Psychology, 19,* 394–403.

Marsella, A. S., Friedman, M. J., Gerrity, E. T., & Scurfield, R. M. (1996). Ethnocultural aspects of PTSD: Some closing thoughts. In A. J. Marsella, M. J. Friedman, E. T. Gerrity, & R. M. Scurfield (Eds.), *Ethnocultural aspects of posttraumatic stress disorder: Issues, research, and clinical applications* (pp. 529–538). Washington, DC: American Psychological Association.

McFarlane, A. C., & de Girolamo, G. (1996). The nature of traumatic stress and the epidemiology of posttraumatic reactions. In B. A. van der Kolk, A. C. McFarlane, & L. Weissaeth (Eds.), *Traumatic stress: The effects of overwhelming experience on mind, body, and society* (pp. 129–154). New York: Guilford Press.

McMahon, S. D., Grant, K. E., Compas, B. E., Thurm, A. E., & Ey, S. (2003). Stress and psychopathology in children and adolescents: Is there evidence of specificity? *Journal of Child Psychology and Psychiatry, 44,* 107–133.

McWhirter, J. J., McWhirter, B. T., McWhirter, A. M., & McWhirter, E. H. (1994). High- and low-risk characteristics of youth: The five Cs of competency. *Elementary School Guidance & Counseling, 28,* 188–196.

Moos, R. H., & Schaefer, J. A. (1993). Coping resources and processes: Current concepts and measures. In L. Goldberger & S. Breznitz (Eds.), *Handbook of stress: Theoretical and clinical aspects* (pp. 234–257). New York: Free Press.

Nader, K., Dubrow, N., & Stamm, B. H. (Eds.). (1999). *Honoring difference: Cultural issues in the treatment of trauma and loss.* Philadelphia: Brunner/Mazel.

Nair, H., & Murray, A. D. (2005). Predictors of attachment security in preschool children from intact and divorced families. *Journal of Genetic Psychology, 166,* 245–263.

Oaten, M., & Cheng, K. (2006). Improved self-control: The benefits of a regular program of academic study. *Basic & Applied Social Psychology, 28,* 1–16.

Osofsky, J. D., Rovaris, M., Hammer, J. H., Dickson, A., Freeman, N., & Aucoin, K. (2004). Working with police to help children exposed to violence. *Journal of Community Psychology, 32,* 593–606.

Parson, E. R. (1995). Post-traumatic stress and coping in an inner-city child: Traumatogenic witnessing of interparental violence and murder. *Psychoanalytic Study of the Child, 50,* 272–307.

Pearlin, L. I. (1993). The social context of stress. In L. Goldberger & S. Breznitz (Eds.), *Handbook of stress: Theoretical and clinical aspects* (pp. 303–315). New York: Free Press.

Perren-Klinger, G. (2000). The integration of traumatic experiences: Culture and re-sources. In J. M. Violnati & D. Patton, (Eds.), *Posttraumatic stress intervention: challenges, issues, and perspectives* (pp. 43–64). Springfield, IL: Charles C Thomas.

Peterson, A. C., Kennedy, R. E., & Sullivan, P. (1991). Coping with adolescence. In M. E. Colten & S. Gore (Eds.), *Adolescent stress: Causes and consequences* (pp. 93–110). New York: Aldine de Gruyter.

Piaget, J., & Inhelder, B. (1969). *The psychology of the child.* New York: Basic Books.

Pines, A. M. (1993). Burnout. In L. Goldberger & S. Breznitz (Eds.), *Handbook of stress: Theoretical and clinical aspects* (pp. 386–402). New York: Free Press.

Rabkin, J. G. (1993). Stress and psychiatric disorders. In L. Goldberger & S. Breznitz (Eds.), *Handbook of stress: Theoretical and clinical aspects* (pp. 477–495). New York: Free Press.

Raghavan, C., & Kingston, S. (2006). Child sexual abuse and posttraumatic stress dis-order: The role of age at first use of substances and lifetime traumatic events. *Journal of Traumatic Stress, 19,* 269–278.

Romano, J. L. (1997). Stress and coping: A qualitative study of 4th and 5th graders. *Elementary School Guidance and Counseling, 31,* 273–282.

Roosa, M. W., Wolchik, S. A., & Sandler, I. N. (1997). Preventing the negative effects of common stressors: Current status and future directions. In S. A. Wolchik & I. N. Sandler (Eds.), *Handbook of children's coping: Linking theory and intervention* (pp. 515–533). New York: Plenum.

Ryan-Wenger, N. M. (1992). A taxonomy of children's coping strategies: A step to-ward theory development. *American Journal of Orthopsychiatry, 62,* 256–263.

Salmon, K., & Bryant, R. A. (2002). Posttraumatic stress disorder in children: The in-fluence of developmental factors. *Clinical Psychology Review, 22,* 163–188.

Sandler, I .N., Wolchik, S. A., MacKinnon, D., Ayers, T. S., & Roosa, M. W. (1997). Developing linkages between theory and intervention in stress and coping processes. In S. A. Wolchik & I. N. Sandler (Eds.), *Handbook of children's coping: Linking theory and intervention* (pp. 3–40). New York: Plenum.

Savin-Williams, R. C. (1998). Lesbian, gay and bisexual youths' relationships with their parents. In C. Patterson & A. R. D'Augelli (Eds.), *Lesbian, gay and bisexual identities in families: Psychological perspectives* (pp. 75–98). New York: Oxford University Press.

Saylor, C. F., Belter, R., & Stokes, S. J. (1997). In S. A. Wolchik & I. N. Sandler (Eds.), *Handbook of children's coping: Linking theory and intervention* (pp. 361–383). New York: Plenum.

Scheeringa, M. S., Wright, M. J., Hunt, J. P., & Zeanah, C. H. (2006). Factors affect-ing the diagnosis and prediction of PTSD symptomology in children and ado-lescents. *American Journal of Psychiatry, 163,* 644–651.

Sears, S. J., & Milburn, J. (1990). School age stress. In L. E. Arnold (Ed.), *Childhood stress* (pp. 223–246). New York: Wiley.

Selye, H. (1974). *Stress without distress.* New York: Lippincott.

Selye, H. (1993). History of the stress concept. In L. Goldberger & S. Breznitz (Eds.), *Handbook of stress: Theoretical and clinical aspects* (pp. 7–17). New York: Free Press.

Sherr, L., Bergenstrom, A., & McCann, E. (1999). An audit of a school based counselling provision for emotional and behavioural difficulties in primary school children. *Counselling Psychology Quarterly, 12,* 271–285.

Sigelman, C. K., & Rider, E. A. (2003). *Life-span human development* (4th ed.). Belmont, CA: Wadsworth/Thomas Learning.

Skinner, E. A., & Wellborn, J. G. (1997). Children's coping in the academic domain. In S. A. Wolchik & I. N. Sandler (Eds.), *Handbook of children's coping: Linking theory and intervention* (pp. 387–422). New York: Plenum.

Sleek, S. (1994, September). Psychology is finding a home in school-based health clinics. *APA Monitor,* pp. 1, 34.

Smetana, J. G., Yau, J., Restrepo, A., & Braeges, J. L. (1991). Conflict and adaptation in adolescence: Adolescent–parent conflict. In M. E. Colten & S. Gore (Eds.), *Adolescent stress: Causes and consequences* (pp. 43–65). New York: Aldine de Gruyter.

Sorenson, S. B. (2000). Preventing traumatic stress. *Journal of Traumatic Stress, 15,* 3–7.

Steinberg, A. (1998). Understanding the secondary traumatic stress of children. In C. R. Figley (Ed.), *Burnout in families: The systemic costs of caring* (pp. 29–46). New York: CRC Press.

Stern, M., & Newland, L. M. (1994). Working with children. *The Counseling Psychologist, 22,* 402–425.

Stoddard, F. J., Ronfeldt, H., Kagan, J., Drake, J. E., Snidman, N., Murphy, J. M., et al. (2006). Young burned children: The course of acute stress and physiological and behavioral responses. *American Journal of Psychiatry, 163,* 1084–1090.

Taylor, R. J. (2004). Therapeutic intervention of trauma and stress brought on by divorce. *Journal of Divorce and Remarriage, 41,* 129–135.

Terr, L. C. (1991). Childhood traumas: An outline and overview. *American Journal of Psychiatry, 148,* 10–19.

Tolin, D. F., & Foa, E. B. (2006). Sex differences in trauma and posttraumatic stress disorder: A quantitative review of 25 years of research. *Psychological Bulletin, 132,* 959–992.

Tyler, K. A., Cauce, A. M., & Whitbeck, L. (2004). Family risk factors and prevalence of dissociative symptoms among homeless and runaway youth. *Child Abuse and Neglect, 28,* 355–367.

Undergraff, J. A., & Taylor, S. E. (2000). From vulnerability to growth: Positive and negative effects of stressful life events. In J. H. Harvey & E. D. Miller (Eds.), *Loss and trauma: General and close relationship perspectives* (pp. 3–28). Philadelphia: Brunner-Routledge.

Voelker, R. (2005). Katrina's impact on mental health likely to last years. *Journal of the American Medical Association, 294,* 1599–1600.

Wagner, W. G. (1994). Counseling with children. *The Counseling Psychologist, 22,* 381–401.

Wang, J. L. (2006). Perceived work stress, imbalance between work and family/personal lives, mental disorders. *Social Psychiatry and Psychiatric Epidemiology, 41,* 541–548.

Wasserstein, S. B., & La Greca, A. M. (1998). Hurricane Andrew: Parent conflict as a moderator of children's adjustment. *Hispanic Journal of Behavioral Sciences, 20,* 212–224.

Weisler, R. H., Barbee, J. G., IV, & Townsend, M. H. (2006). Mental health and recovery in the gulf coast after hurricane Katrina and Rita. *Journal of the American Medical Association, 296,* 585–588.

Wertlieb, D. (1991). Children and divorce: Stress and coping in developmental perspective. In J. Eckenrode (Ed.), *The social context of coping* (pp. 31–54). New York: Plenum Press.

Widom, C. S. (1991). Childhood victimization: Risk factors for delinquency. In M. E. Colten & S. Gore (Eds.), *Adolescent stress: Causes and consequences* (pp. 201–221). New York: Aldine de Gruyter.

Wilburn, V. R., & Smith, D. E. (2005). Stress, self-esteem, and suicidal ideation in late adolescents. *Adolescence, 40,* 33–45.

Willis, T. A. (1987). Help-seeking as a coping mechanism. In C. R. Snyder & C. E. Ford (Eds.), *Coping with negative life events* (pp. 19–50). New York: Plenum Press.

Youngs, B. (1985). *Stress in children.* New York: Arbor House.

Zunker, V. G. (2002). *Career counseling: Applied concepts of life planning.* Pacific Grove, CA: Brooks/Cole.

PART THREE

■

Working With Youth at Risk: Prevention and Intervention

In the previous two sections, the topic of youth at risk was introduced and the causes were examined. Part Three addresses issues or behaviors most often identified as placing youth at risk. Each of the chapters in this part of the text contains the following subtopics: an introduction, problem identification, a case study, approaches to prevention, intervention strategies, adaptations for diversity, and a summary. Authors discuss both prevention and intervention from individual, family, school, and community perspectives. In this way the reader is able to obtain a comprehensive and comparative overview of the material in each chapter.

Chapter 8, "I'll Cry Tomorrow": Diverse Youth and the Scars That Don't Show, is new in this fifth edition. It emphasizes multiracial youth, racial and ethnic diverse families, and immigrant youth and families. Within these contexts, academic and behavioral problems, self-esteem, education and career goals, language and communication, and parentification are presented in terms of at-riskness in youth. Attention is also given to culturally appropriate intervention and prevention approaches. Biracial and multicultural models are presented together with the case study of Simone.

Chapter 9, The Secret and All-Consuming Obsessions: Eating Disorders, provides excellent introductory material with respect to the impact of the media, gender socialization, and body image on youth at risk for eating disorders. Risk factors such as gender, age, socioeconomic status, family characteristics, and identification with socialized norms are also discussed. Such background information, along with a thorough discussion of definitions, symptoms, and etiology, creates the context for the case study and subsequent presentation of approaches to prevention and intervention. The chapter includes a current and well-done subsection on diversity issues, including those faced by African American, Latina, Native American, Asian, and non-Western women, men, gay and lesbian individuals, transgender and transsexual individuals, and athletes.

The adolescent at risk for suicide has become an increasing concern for schools and communities throughout the United States. Between 1960 and 1988 the adolescent suicide rate rose by 200% compared with an increase in the general population of approximately 17%. According to some experts, one teenager attempts suicide every 90 seconds and one completes the act of suicide every 90 minutes. Chapter 10, "I Don't Want to Live": The Adolescent At Risk for Suicidal Behavior, presents information all professionals and all parents should know if prevention and intervention efforts are to succeed. Discussions of ethnic and gender differences, methods, risk and protective factors, precipitants, myths, and profiles provide the groundwork for the subsequent case study, prevention, intervention, and diversity material. An adolescent who is suicidal is communicating the fact that he or she is experiencing difficulty with problem solving, self-esteem, managing stress, and expressing feelings. It is important for all of us to respond in constructive, safe, informed ways when working with this very vulnerable adolescent population.

Chapter 11, A Future in Jeopardy: Sexuality Issues in Adolescence, is a combination of two former chapters in earlier editions and focuses on prevention, intervention, and current research around important topics of teen sexuality that put teens at risk for negative outcomes such as teen pregnancy, AIDS and other sexually transmitted diseases, rape and date rape, and sexual predation. In each of these four areas, the authors spell out prevention and intervention approaches from an individual, family, school, and community perspective. Individual risk factors are also set forth as these relate to both rape and date rape and sexual predators. The chapter includes the case study of Julia and concludes with adaptations for diversity.

Chapter 12, "I Am Somebody": Gang Membership, examines the youth gang phenomenon, its historical significance, and the development of gang activities. The chapter looks at present-day gang involvement, including major gangs and their distribution, factors for gang involvement, gang characteristics, gang member characteristics, females in gangs, and ethnic gang involvement, including Asian gangs, African American gangs, Hispanic gangs, and White supremacist gangs. The discussion in this chapter includes an examination of views as to why gangs form, risk factors for gang involvement, and statistics that set the stage for understanding gangs and their impact on society. The case of Christopher profiles a young man involved in gangs as a way of understanding the reality of those factors shaping the choices and lives of our youth. From the information about gang organization, risks, and statistics, the focus shifts to an understanding of diversity and gang involvement, prevention approaches, and strategies for intervention.

Chapter 13, Counseling Queer Youth: Preventing Another Matthew Shepard and Gwen Araujo Story, discusses the public's lack of scientific knowledge regarding sexual differentiation and the heterosexual assumptions that do not embrace the pluralistic society that forms the fiber of U.S. culture. This chapter explores the many stressors that queer youth face, such as invisibility, isolation, victimization, suicide potential, substance abuse, and exposure to sexually transmitted diseases because of high-risk behaviors. The author makes the important point that although queer youth must address these stressors, counselors need to shift much of the focus of their efforts to the community at large to transform the cultural context in which queer youth live. The cases of Juan and Paul are used to illustrate the author's points.

Chapter 14, Death in the Classroom: Violence in Schools, addresses the recent escalation of violence in schools. This is a particularly timely chapter given the fact that we are hearing and reading more and more about school violence and its consequences. The author defines the problem and presents aspects of prevention and intervention from individual, family, school, and community perspectives. Several current intervention and prevention programs utilized by schools and communities are presented. The author uses the case of Thurston High School and Kip Kinkle to illustrate significant points within the chapter. The chapter concludes with adaptations for diversity.

Adolescent substance abuse often results in harm to youths, their families, communities, and society as a whole. According to the 2002 U.S. Department of Health and Human Service statistics, drug and alcohol abuse contribute to the death of more than 120,000 Americans and cost taxpayers more than $143 billion every year in preventable health care costs, lost productivity, automobile crashes, law enforcement, and crime. Alcohol use is associated with over half of all murders and rapes in the United States and is a factor in 40% of all violent crimes. As the authors point out in Chapter 15, "I Can't Live Without It": Adolescent Substance Abuse, substance abuse is not a problem limited to adults. Significant percentages of youths and adolescents are experimenting with and becoming regular users of chemical substances, particularly alcohol, nicotine, marijuana, inhalants, methamphetamines, and the nonmedical use of prescription-type pain relievers, tranquilizers, stimulants, and sedatives. This chapter focuses on why teens turn to drugs, the physiological mechanisms of drug use, and the roles that individuals, families, schools, and the community have in both prevention and intervention. The case of Julie is used to illustrate the authors' points. The chapter closes with adaptations for diversity.

Chapter 16, Nowhere to Turn: The Young Face of Homelessness, addresses the topic of homelessness in at-risk youth. Families with small children now represent approximately 40% of the homeless population. The National Center of Family Homelessness reports that up to 1 million children and at least half a million youths in the United States are homeless. From the most recent statistics available, it is clear that the faces of the homeless have changed drastically since the days of the White, male, alcoholic or "skid row bum." Forty percent of the homeless are families and 25% are children. Homeless children's differences in appearance, behavior, and ability demand tolerance and flexibility from teachers and school administrators. This chapter describes the problem of homelessness for two specific groups: children living with their families and youths living alone. The authors define the problem, the characteristics for both groups, and specific contributing factors for homelessness for each group. Strategies for prevention and intervention are presented from individual, family, school, and community perspectives. A family case study is used by the authors to illustrate major points. Adaptations for cultural diversity closes the chapter.

The text concludes with Chapter 17, "This Isn't the Place for Me": School Dropout. The placement of this chapter at the end of the book is fitting because the problem of the school dropout involves many of the personal, family, and social issues discussed in previous chapters. As of October 2000, 3.8 million young people between the ages of 16 and 24 had dropped out of school. The authors define the problem and follow this by discussions on ethnicity, socioeconomic status, and a school, family, and peer perspective. Early warning signs, underlying causes, the case of Mark, clinical and systemic approaches to prevention and intervention, and adaptation for diversity form the basis for this informative and cutting-edge chapter.

CHAPTER 8

■

"I'll Cry Tomorrow": Diverse Youth and the Scars That Don't Show

Laura R. Simpson and Jeannie Falkner

The U.S. population has witnessed considerable social, cultural, and demographic changes. Youth of racial and ethnic minorities, including those of color, immigrant youth, and biracial youth, experience a variety of internal and external challenges. There are numerous unique characteristics, potential problems, and social needs. These challenges are related to a need to define identities in a society that is many times harsh in response to social dimensions outside of the mainstream. Considerable attention must be focused on providing counseling services to racial and ethnic minority youth. Some issues that are pertinent to working with these populations include racial and ethnic identity development, isolation, career dreams, and academic and behavioral concerns (Harris, 2002; Herring, 1992). The professional helper's multicultural knowledge, awareness, and skills in working with people from diverse backgrounds are critical to effective counseling. It is clear from research that racial and ethnic minorities are more vulnerable to social, emotional, and academic problems and that limited support systems are available to racial and ethnic minority youth (Esquivel & Keitel, 1990). This chapter addresses stressors encountered by these minority youth and issues pertinent to counseling. A case study is provided as well as suggestions for prevention and intervention strategies.

WHO IS THE MULTIRACIAL YOUTH?

Although any attempt to explain the dynamics of growing up in a particular racial or ethnic group risks the loss of the uniqueness of the individual, counselors must nevertheless strive to appreciate the complexity of racially and culturally diverse families. Every individual is born into and influenced by his or her cultural context, which includes existing beliefs, values, rules, roles, and family practices (Sue & Sue, 2003).

Racial identity, more specifically, refers to a collective identity based on perceived membership into a group that shares cultural traditions and racial group membership (Phelps, Taylor, & Gerard, 2001). In 2000, 28.7% of all people in the United States were racial and ethnic minority individuals (U.S. Census Bureau, 2000, as cited in Davidson, Yakushka, & Sanford-Martens, 2004). However, a growing segment of the population of the United States claims to be of multiple heritages, which creates unique needs "related to their ambiguous ethnicity and their need to define their identities in a society where race has always been a significant social dimension" (Gibbs, 1990, p. 322).

The National Center for Health Statistics (2006) estimated the number of biracial youths is growing rapidly, to between 2 and 5 million. This is considered by many to be an underestimation, as biracial and multiracial children have often been identified with a parent of color, resulting in people of mixed heritages often being ignored or neglected, or forcing the multiracial youth to choose one heritage to the exclusion of others (Harris, 2002; Phelps et al., 2001; Sue & Sue, 2003).

Biracial and Multiracial Youth in Context: A Sociocultural Perspective

A sociocultural perspective highlights that, to a greater or lesser extent, racial and ethnic minority youth undergo a socialization that includes learning to adapt to the external pressures of the dominant culture. Poverty, unemployment, exposure to crime and violence, discrimination, and inadequate health care are just some of the environmental issues facing minority youth (Orton, 1996). These contextualized factors compound the difficulties for multiracial minority youth as they strive to adapt to their environment.

Social ostracism and racism continue to be direct external stressors to many interracial couples and their children. As late as 1945, over half of the states in the United States had active laws that banned interracial marriages. Only in 1967 did the Supreme Court formally ban states from prohibiting interracial marriages. The stigma attached to the family becomes a silent barrier for the couple and their children as they attempt to establish their place in the American social order.

To add to the difficulty of acceptance within a society whose dominant culture has only relatively recently sanctioned multiracial marriages, the biracial child is often raised in a number of nontraditional family compositions, including single parents, never-married parents, and stepfamilies. While such nontraditional families are increasing, the stigma of not conforming to the traditional family norm mirrors a larger societal belief that nonnuclear families are unstable and represent declining "family values" (Hill, 1999; Orton, 1996).

Racial and ethnic minority youth are faced with constant cultural messages from a monoracial society. When outside prejudices and values are internalized by the minority youth, this negative internalization can lead to problems of identity (Herring, 1995). The lack of multiracial and culturally diverse families in the media and children's books, and the inability to check more than one racial identity on most demographic surveys (which, until 2000, included the U.S. Census Bureau), continue to promote cultural isolation.

Limited research has been focused on multiracial children and youth, mostly on the offspring of African American and European American relationships (Nishimura, 1995). Previous research focused primarily on the negative features of multiracial marriages, which corroborated cultural stereotypes of multiracial and ethnic minorities as experiencing low self-esteem, feelings of inferiority, and being a social or occupational failure (Herring, 1992). Few studies have been conducted that highlight the resilience and strengths of the minority youth and their families.

Community Acceptance of Racial and Ethnic Minorities

The concept of community includes the geographical location of one's residence and the ethnic composition of one's neighborhood. This sense of community extends beyond the geographical restriction and encompasses the rules and roles prescribed for its members. When an individual matches the racial and ethnic roles prescribed by the community, this sense of community provides a structure of support networks that can buffer the individual from the demands of daily life (Swartz-Kulstad & Martin, 1999).

Difficulties can arise when youths move into a neighborhood where social stratification occurs among racial and economic lines. When such divisions and community norms are juxtaposed with those of the individual, psychological distress can distort self-evaluations of personal competence and result in failure to engage in supportive interpersonal relationships (Sandhu, Portes, & McPhee, 1996).

Racially and Ethnically Diverse Families

The role of ethnicity in the life of the multiracial youth is affected by the immediate environment as well as by the historical and sociopolitical context (Herring, 1992). The most immediate influence in the socialization of children is that of the family. The family is considered a major organizing force in an individual's life, and nuclear and extended family members have been found to be the primary source of psychological support for an individual's ethnocultural background (Akutsu, Snowden, & Organista, 1996; Swartz-Kulstad & Martin, 1999).

For the multiracial family, this can prove to be a formidable task, as two or more heritages must be integrated into a composite that reduces dissonance for the children as they assimilate their cultural uniqueness. The greater the difference between spouses or partners in cultural background, the more difficulty the family has been found to have in the transmission of a cultural heritage (Herring, 1992; McGoldrick, 1982). Interracial couples often react to each other as "though the other's behaviors were a personal attack rather than just a difference rooted in ethnicity" (Herring, 1992, p. 123). When the marital stress is unresolved, children may feel they are to blame for their parents' problems. Under such circumstances, the multiracial child may feel quite isolated and find little support from their parents.

It is important for counselors to appreciate the possible existence of antagonism between racial and ethnic groups in the context of the multiracial minority family. A social system that maintains the myth of monoracialism tends to assign the multiracial person the heritage of the least desirable racial status (Root, 1996). Because of an oppressive historical context, African Americans are often considered less desirable than their Asian counterparts (Hill, 1999).

Children from interracial marriages between Asian Americans and European Americans are more likely to be considered multiracial, whereas children who have an African American parent are often considered Black (Root, 1996; Sue & Sue, 2003).

For the children to internalize the positive cultural heritages, the parents must first address the differences and be open to communication about their children's socialization process. As parents face the difficulties of conflict among community, family, social, and intergenerational roles, parents must also attempt to help the child develop healthy adaptations.

Herring (1992) noted, "Interracial parents are inclined to socialize their children in one of three ways. They may promote the minority identity in their children; attempt to socialize their children to have a dual identity; or deny that race or color is an issue, and emphasize being 'simply human' to their children" (p. 124). Any one of these will have an impact on the children's socialization.

Immigrant Youth and Families

In addition to the issues of identity faced by racial and ethnic minority youth, one or more family members may be a recent immigrant into the United States. U.S. immigrants represent a large number of school-age children and youth. Of these, those with Asian and Hispanic backgrounds represent the largest groups of recent immigrants (Constantine, Erickson, Banks, & Timberlake, 1998; Marotta & Garcia, 2003; Olatunji, 2005).

First-generation immigrant families face multiple adjustments to their new culture. Acculturation is a socialization process that involves adapting to a new culture as a result of changes in cultural attitudes, values, and behaviors (T. L. Robinson, 2005). Acculturation requires the immigrant to negotiate this transition to improve his or her life conditions in a manner that is congruous with the new environment. Acculturation is multifaceted and involves cognitive, behavioral, and self-identification that occur through contact over an extended period of time (Kopala, Esquivel, & Baptiste, 1994). Predisposing variables such as age, language proficiency, education, previous contact, family structure, and cultural similarity all influence the acculturation process.

Assimilation describes those people who do not desire to maintain their cultural identities and instead identify and associate with the new environmental culture (T. L. Robinson, 2005). Historically, immigrants of European heritage have assimilated more easily into the mainstream culture than immigrants whose heritages are noticeably different. Current immigration patterns consist primarily of Asian and Latin Americans, who have not been so easily assimilated into a predominantly Eurocentric culture.

Immigrant families and youth experience physical, social, and cultural changes that may result in physical or mental disorders (Kopala et al., 1994). These families may have limited support systems and be reluctant to utilize the professional support systems that may be available. Language barriers and the demands and challenges associated with living in a new country may overwhelm immigrant family members and create additional psychological concerns for the family.

Academic and Behavioral
Problems of Racial and Ethnic Minority Youth

Although many racial and minority youth will adapt with resilience to the multiple challenges faced, some will experience academic and behavioral problems that require intervention. Racial and ethnic identity issues will not generally be the presenting problem in a school setting. Students instead will be referred for reasons that include poor academic achievement, off-task behavior, poor social skills, social isolation, negative attitudes, aggressive behavior toward parents, sadness and depression, interfamilial conflicts, or acting-out behaviors (Herring, 1992, 1995; Orton, 1996).

Because the cultural context of the U.S. school system is primarily Caucasian middle class, behaviors that are adaptive according to a child's culture may appear maladaptive within the school context (Aaroe & Nelson, 2000; Esquivel & Keitel, 1990). The chance for accurate assessment may be at risk as the number of school children from culturally and linguistically diverse backgrounds is increasing while the number of culturally diverse teachers is declining (Aaroe & Nelson, 2000). Any assessment of academic and behavioral concerns must address the problems associated with cross-cultural linguistic equivalences and differential attention to, interpretation of, and tolerance for adolescent behaviors (Lau et al., 2004).

Research shows that whereas parents from different cultural backgrounds find commonality in identifying negative classroom behaviors and interpersonal school survival adaptations, teachers were significantly dissimilar in their responses (Aaroe & Nelson, 2000). Teachers were, in fact, found to exhibit a lower tolerance and more narrowly defined standard for classroom behavior. This may be a factor in the over-representation of minority youth in programs for the emotionally and behaviorally troubled youth.

Nevertheless, the difficulties faced by minority youth in interactions with their environment must be considered, because cultural variables can be a contributing factor in attempts to adapt to their environment (Swartz-Kulstad & Martin, 1999). Regardless of the competent functioning in their culture of origin, culturally diverse youth and their families risk being judged as deficient relative to the educational norms and cultural differences in a new educational setting (Maital, 2000).

Ethnic Identity and Self-Esteem

Erikson's (1968) concept of identity formation has been primary to counselors' understanding of identity and refers to the self in relation to one's relationship with others. The peer group is one venue from which youth view themselves in relation to others. Group self-esteem focuses on one's feeling about being a member of a racial or ethnic group.

Cultures vary in their orientation toward identity. Some cultural groups value independence and emphasize individualism, whereas other cultures place identity clearly within the family constellation. The minority youth who is at odds with dominant cultural values may have difficulty in balancing the need to be seen as an individual against the value to place the family above self.

As minority youths seek a group in which they can find acceptance, the reality of social marginality may be a cogent perspective from which to view this struggle (Nishimura, 1995). The need for acceptance and validation of their ethnic identity becomes paramount, as ethnic identity has been found to be a significant predictor of wellness for minority adolescents (Rayle, 2004). According to Phinney (1989, as cited in Nishimura, 1995), "Adolescents who explore and are clear regarding the meaning of their ethnicity, show higher scores in the areas of self-evaluation, sense of mastery, social and peer interactions, and family relations than adolescents who have not explored their ethnicity" (p. 53).

Failure to do so may lead to loneliness or acting out as a form of protest in being pressured to fit into someone else's vision of who the youth should be (Herring, 1992). Left to themselves, many students resolve the dissonance by removing themselves from the source of conflict, resulting in further social isolation and a loss of possible support systems. For instance, some African American students have been found to adopt behaviors and attitudes that enhance their academic successes but distance them from their culture, often resulting in symptoms of depression, anxiety, and a loss of racial identity (Arroyo & Zigler, 1995).

Sexuality and gender identity are often played out during adolescence. Gender identity development includes a comprehensive assessment of one's self, including feelings of intrinsic worth, competence, sexuality, and self-approval (T. Robinson, 1993). The special needs of multiracial youth must be recognized, as they are often rejected by both majority and minority peer groups because their physical appearance is unusual, their family background is unorthodox, and they feel torn between two competing set of norms and values (Herring, 1992).

Physical beauty and gender roles are often defined within ethnic and cultural values and beliefs. Especially for female minority youths, pressure to emulate White women's norms of beauty can result in these girls viewing their diverse cultural gender identities from a deficit perspective. For the youth from multiracial and multi-ethnic families, gender role conflicts between conflicting parental values and societal norms may be overwhelming. Pressure to conform to community roles and behaviors can create feelings of living a dual life, resulting in psychological pain and distress for the minority youth (Swartz-Kulstad & Martin, 1999).

Finally, socioeconomic class, race, culture, and gender combine to intensify issues of powerlessness and rejection experiences by the multiracial youth (T. Robinson, 1993). Further difficulties can occur when racial and minority youths move into a neighborhood where social stratification occurs along divided racial and socioeconomic lines. Immigrants living in low-income urban areas have been found to experience more loneliness, anxiety, and isolation than their ethnic peers of suburban environments (Esquivel & Keitel, 1990).

Education and Career Goals

One area of concern for the multiracial minority youth can be the discrepancy between the minority child's cultural values and those encouraged in the U.S. school system. Racial bias and stereotyping may affect the educational and career choices of minority youth. For example, some cultures emphasize cooperation rather than competition, which is prominent in the U.S. educational system. Minority youth also experience inordinately high dropout rates from school (Constantine et al., 1998; Olatunji, 2005).

Many minority youths have had few opportunities to develop motivation for careers that require high educational attainment, are high status, and may be financially rewarding (Constantine et al., 1998). Without the opportunity to create a vision for the future in which education is relevant to career path and financial rewards, the minority youth is left to repeat educational and career choices that lead to employment in low-status, low-paying, and racially stereotypical occupations. These factors, including socialization experiences, perceptions of career barriers, and discrimination, contribute to education and career barriers for some minority youths (Constantine et al., 1998).

In contrast, those individuals whose culture emphasizes education and immigrants who immigrated for educational purposes will adapt more rapidly than others whose educational goals are less valued. A family that is supportive of education and achievement and association with an achievement-oriented peer group are factors that enhance academic success (Constantine & Gushue, 2003).

Language and Communication

When minority children and youth experience difficulties in functioning in the academic setting, it is often due to differences in language and communication styles. Miscommunication can lead to disrupted interpersonal relations and can play a key role in difficulties in successful adaptation to the academic environment (Swartz-Kulstad & Martin, 1999). For effective communication, both parties must be able to accurately send and receive verbal and nonverbal messages appropriately and accurately (Sue & Sue, 2003).

Minority youth risk both culturally biased educational and mental health assessments when communication styles and interpersonal behaviors differ from those of the dominant culture (Cayleff, 1986). Some minority students may lack familiarity with the social and educational norms that exist within the U.S. school system. For example, in classes where verbal expressiveness is encouraged and teachers expect their students to ask questions and enter freely into discussions, minority youths whose culture values implicit aspects of communication and deference to authority may be seen as resistant or withdrawn.

Language is a critical component of communication for the child in the education system. The need to consider linguistic differences and language barriers in education and counseling is imperative. For immigrant children and youth, problems may initially stem from fears of needing to speak standard English in a group situation. This is reflected in bilingual immigrant children who exhibit a high incidence of "elective mutism" (Kopala, Esquivel, & Baptiste, 1994).

Even when a child has learned a new language, it may take 3–5 years to learn those aspects of language related to cognitive and academic functioning. Often these children achieve at lower levels compared with their monolingual counterparts, particularly in the area of reading and language arts. This problem is exacerbated for the student who may have limited exposure to formal learning experiences in their native country. Many adolescents who immigrate to the United States lack literacy skills because they never or seldom ever attended school. As a result, they experience higher levels of academic failure and lowered self-esteem.

Parentification

In examining the relationship between youth and parents in the multiracial and multiethnic family, a postmodern constructionist perspective can be useful as a caution against ascribing family dysfunction based on Eurocentric family values. Intergenerational roles must be viewed within the racial and ethnic makeup of the family and its members. Nevertheless, the caretaking of parents by children has been identified as problematic in a variety of family constellations.

Such parent–child role reversals can cause significant behavioral and emotional problems, especially as the child approaches adolescence (Chase, 1999). One variable seen in such families involves a lack of parent involvement combined with the child's "capacity for concern" (Karpel, 1977, as cited in Chase, 1999, p. 78). Similar patterns exist in families of highly successful business executives and work addiction (B. E. Robinson & Post, 1995). The lack of involvement by the working parent combined with dependence on the youth by the available parent can result in increased levels of depression in the child, poor academic performance, and failure to establish successful peer relationships (Chase, Deming, & Wells, 1998).

Adolescents who feel responsible for listening to others' problems and achieving higher educational attainment than previous family members may subjugate their individual needs in favor of the adults for whom they feel responsible. Cultures that emphasize collective identity achievement and family responsibility may be at odds with an academic environment that promotes individual goals and views academic achievement as paramount to success in adulthood.

DEVELOPMENT AND ROLE OF BIRACIAL AND MULTIRACIAL IDENTITY MODELS

The process for successful identity formation is paramount in the understanding of human behavior as individuals achieve integration of physical, social, and cognitive factors into a sense of selfhood, self-worth, and emotional security. Racial and ethnic identity development models provide practitioners with a framework for understanding the psychological development of ethnic minorities as they exist with the majority population (Aldarondo, 2001).

Several models of biracial identity development have been proposed and can provide a framework from which to examine the development of one's racial identity. W. E. Cross's (1995) model for African American racial identity, Kerwin and Ponterotto's (1995) racial identity model, Root's (1996) identity model, and Poston's (1990) biracial identity model all provide a theoretical foundation for case conceptualization and practice with the multiracial youth.

W. E. Cross's original 1971 hierarchical model of racial identity for African Americans has been updated to include a component of the individual's race salience as well as empirically supported stage revisions. Although the subsequent revisions by Cross may cause some confusion if one is comparing earlier models with more recent ones, the model continues to find prominence in multicultural perspectives of identity formation.

Kerwin and Ponterotto's (1995) biracial model contains seven stages and is based on empirical research that builds on previous models of biracial identity development. This nonlinear, nondirectional model provides a dynamic process through which to examine racial identity. Similarly, Root's (1996) model differs from the more prescriptive paradigms in that more flexibility is allowed within the process, identifying four specific paths from which successful multiracial identify formation may proceed.

Poston's (1990) model attests that any model based on integrating only one racial identity is not salient to biracial identity. Poston's model incorporates the uniqueness of biracial identity formation and can be helpful in highlighting the unique experience of the biracial youth.

Continued development of racial identity models will enhance the promotion of counseling that is sensitive to the unique experiences of the multiracial youth. Each model addresses coping mechanisms on a continuum that prepare the minority group member for managing racial oppression in the larger society (Brinson, 1996). The facilitation of positive socialization is the ultimate goal and is considered paramount for the minority youth.

CASE STUDY

Simone is a 14-year-old high school freshman. She presents in the counselor's office and reports being "really stressed out in school." She is not doing well in her classes and is beginning to believe that school just is not for her. Simone is reluctant to come to the counselor's office because her family is intensely private about personal affairs. However, she has decided to give it one try at the encouragement of her best girlfriend, who assures her that counseling is safe because it is confidential.

Simone lives in a dual-parent home with an Asian father, an African American mother, and two siblings. Her father emigrated from China to the United States as a young adult. He adheres to a strict Asian culture and, as such, the family is bilingual. Simone's coloring and facial features clearly suggest she is of mixed heritage. She struggles with identity issues as she appears to be African American; however, her family upholds traditional Asian values within their household. The school she attends is primarily Caucasian, and Simone feels like an outcast socially as well as academically.

Always performing well in school, her recent academic difficulties have come as a surprise to her. She did not expect this struggle and thought it would get easier over the months. She is beginning to question whether she is a good fit for this school or if she is even smart enough to complete high school. Simone's mother dropped out of high school and completed her GED. She has always encouraged Simone in all her activities, but there has never been an emphasis on education. Simone's father owns a small neighborhood grocery store and has recently been able to move the family into a new home. While grateful for the new home, Simone is resentful that the move resulted in her having to attend a new school.

Simone has always been a well-behaved child and has a great deal of responsibility at home. Because of her parents' work schedule, she has often been the primary caretaker for her two younger siblings. Her father is essentially absent physically because of the amount of time he spends at work, although his influence and expectations of Simone's behavior are powerful. He does not involve himself in the emotional issues of the household and is very stoic with regard to his own feelings. Simone's friends, siblings, and mother always come to her with their problems. Simone now finds herself crumbling under the pressure of not being able to handle her own problems. Everyone at home and in her extended family is proud of her previous achievements and now she feels as if she is letting everyone down. She carries the weight of the expectation that she will break the cycle of underachievement in her family. For example, her mother often says that Simone will be the first college graduate in their family, which sounds like a compliment but feels like a challenge. Simone has been crying a lot and feeling nervous all the time. In terms of academic performance, she knows the material before she takes a test but complains that "her mind goes blank." She reports being unable to concentrate on studying.

In addition to the pressure she is feeling academically, she has a limited social network. Simone does not feel comfortable interacting with the people in her school. She has one friend who is African American in her school, but their contact is limited by their schedules. Prior to the move, the elementary and middle schools she attended were primarily attended by African American students. This social system proved to be more accepting of Simone's biracial culture. She does not feel she really connects with the students in her current school. She feels they do not want to know her and she does not want to know them.

A CULTURALLY APPROPRIATE APPROACH

Simone is questioning who she is, what her purpose is in life, who her friends are, and her academic abilities. She is considering dropping out of school because she feels alienated and academically inferior to her peers.

The growing diversity of the U.S. population suggests that an increased understanding of cultural factors is required for counselors to be culturally competent practitioners. Research supports the concept that racial and ethnic minority children have higher degrees of problems associated with racial identity development, social marginality, isolation, sexuality conflicts, career dreams, and academic and behavioral concerns (Harris, 2002). All clients have culture, and one's culture can and does affect an individual's ability to adapt to his or her environment. As Swartz-Kulstad and Martin (1999) noted, "Adaptation difficulties typically produce concerns that further affect the individual's functioning" (p. 281). Counselors must be prepared to incorporate cultural factors into their conceptualization of the concerns and the treatment process.

Cultural Considerations

To provide more effective cross-cultural counseling, counselors need to be aware of their communication style, counseling style, and the expectations of their clients. A large repertoire of verbal and nonverbal behaviors will be beneficial (Schoen, 2005). Language barriers may be mediated by action-oriented and artistic therapies. For example, concrete activities such as sand play could allow Simone to express her worldview and engage in self-discovery of subconscious themes, emotions, or beliefs.

Deliberate selection of counseling styles and approaches must harmonize with appropriate communication style to enhance outcomes. In taking a culturally sensitive approach, counselors need to know and respect the traditional values of the particular ethnic group with whom they are working. For example, because traditional ethnic values of Asian Americans suggest a preference for self-control in counseling sessions, they can experience greater comfort when the focus of the session is on the expression of thoughts rather than feelings (Schoen, 2005). This need is consistent with the value of the counselor maintaining an unassuming manner.

It is also possible that clients may not trust the counselor because of race. Quality counseling is predicated on trust. Mistrust affects the counseling dynamic negatively. If the client is unable to trust the counselor, the working alliance will not be formed and the true benefits of counseling will be unrealized.

Other potential issues that could contribute to cultural miscommunication are the interpersonal differences that the counselor and client bring to the counseling relationship. For example, if the counselor has a distinctly different communication style from the client, this could alienate the client. If the counselor is not culturally aware, it is possible to ignore race or view the client through racial stereotypes. To address such differences, it is important for the counselor to be aware of self, assumptions, and biases.

Finally, the client's strengths could be ignored by a counselor if they do not mirror the dominant culture (Spanierman, 2002). The counseling process will benefit if the counselor attends to the client's strengths, even if they are different from the strengths that are valued by the dominant culture. As Schoen (2005) noted, "Realistically, being culturally responsive does not imply a comprehensive knowledge of each culture; rather it means conveying an interest and respect for other cultures, evidencing an eagerness to learn about other cultures, and appreciating the particular heritage of the client" (p. 4).

Acculturation Considerations

The norms, values, and assumptions of the dominant culture may be affecting Simone in a variety of ways. For example, stereotypes of African Americans and specifically biracial individuals may be negatively affecting how others view her and the expectations they have of her. In addition, these negative stereotypes may become internalized and affect how Simone perceives herself (Kopala et al., 1994). Because there are few role models with whom Simone can identify, Simone may feel that her particular expression of self is not valued. It is likely that this sense of devaluation, in the larger culture, will affect Simone's view of herself and her academic achievement.

In consideration of all of these factors, counseling for this client should be prudently planned. Because Simone expresses an interest in and values educational achievement, an opportunity to discuss nonthreatening issues may be pursued. The influence of parental expectations should be included in these discussions. When trust and comfort are established, more sensitive issues may be gradually introduced.

Contextual and Historical Considerations

On an individual level, the counselor should first focus on and value Simone's unique strengths. Simone is a young woman with a great deal to offer, and the counselor should try and build on her positive qualities to increase her self-esteem. Second, it will be important to explore with Simone the reasons for her feelings of insecurity across all levels. How Simone feels about herself, what messages she is receiving from her family and her peers, and the meaning she derives from these messages are all important areas to cover. Once this exploration is concluded, Simone could benefit from exploring her sense of identity related to racial identity development. This might also include investigating her thoughts, feelings, and desires with regard to her social network and the struggles she is experiencing while attempting to fit in with her peers.

It will be necessary for Simone and the counselor to explore Simone's environment and for the counselor to recommend strategies to help Simone cope with this environment. The counselor must become an ally and an advocate for Simone against racism. In addition, it seems important to examine her various reference group identities (e.g., African American, Chinese) and to understand how these affect her worldview and her academic decisions. At this time, the counselor may want to explore Simone's family (immediate and extended) to obtain a more complete picture of Simone's presenting concerns. It may be helpful for the counselor to understand the family's reaction to Simone's academic success. To do this, the counselor and Simone may construct an academic genogram so that they can obtain a deeper understanding of Simone's academic development in the context of important family variables. This genogram would be particularly useful if Simone focuses on the multicultural aspects to incorporate contextual factors that may be influencing her choices (Schoen, 2005). By understanding the role the family has on Simone's current choices, she may feel better able to accept or reject these choices for herself.

Simone is currently experiencing social isolation. It will be helpful for the counselor to work with Simone to assist her in understanding that her self-perception is related to how she receives and internalizes the messages from her peers (Spanierman, 2002). For example, if she is experiencing discrimination in the classroom and receiving the message that she does not possess superior academic ability, it is likely that she is internalizing this message. This further isolates her from developing personal relationships with her classmates. It is important that the counselor attempt to validate and acknowledge that these feelings are real and warranted. Normalizing Simone's experience will assist in increasing her self-efficacy, which in turn has the potential to result in increased academic confidence and improved performance.

Because many people in Simone's life hold high expectations for her future, Simone is experiencing tremendous pressure. She seems to believe that she must be a high achiever to win approval. Simone's perceptions are being greatly influenced by the prevailing norms and values society holds about achievement (Hook & Ashton, 2002). Simone seems to be operating from the dominant culture's definition of success that is perpetuated by her parents. She is driven by the concept that to be successful, a person must have distinguished, individual achievements in public domains. Thus, accomplishments that are frequently important to women, such as making connections to others, may not be seen as achievements by others.

To add to the difficulty, Simone must deal with the fact that expectations held by individuals for themselves and those held by others for them may not agree with broader social stereotypes. She will struggle with the contradiction between the familial expectation that she will accomplish great things and the societal perceptions of what achievements are appropriate for her. Because these two beliefs are generally contradictory, this struggle is present at a variety of levels (Hook & Ashton, 2002).

APPROACHES TO PREVENTION

When considering the potential symptoms that a racial or ethnic minority youth might be at risk of experiencing, it becomes especially important to examine what could prevent the onset of these struggles. There is opportunity for protective features to be present on an individual, family, school, and community level. "Prevention efforts that support and maximize protective factors while reducing risk factors are more likely to be successful" (J. McWhirter, McWhirter, McWhirter, & McWhirter, 2007, p. 235). The relationship between prevention and treatment interventions is critical, and prevention efforts are implemented as interventions. Additionally, counselors understand that opportunities exist for youths to participate in prevention efforts even if some of the minority youths are already struggling with issues. To be precise, counselors can offer the program to youths who are at risk for symptom development as well as those already experiencing some level of symptoms. The assumption is that the service will be helpful to all of the youths.

Individual

Because every youth is different, each with a unique personality and character traits, counselors must find a way to respond to and support each individual. When considering the risk for racial and ethnic minorities, education on issues such as responsibility and self-discipline, hope, optimism, and communication skills has the potential to be of great benefit for youths facing such risks as poverty, psychosocial and environmental stressors, or dysfunctional family dynamics.

The socialization and developmental processes of racial and ethnic minority youth can be considerably more complicated that those of racial majority children (Herring, 1995). Counselors must develop prevention and intervention efforts that take into to account the developmental level of the youth, language, learning style, cultural considerations, and the appropriateness of the method for the particular problem.

Family

Because of the impact of factors within the home on a child's identity development, prevention efforts focused on involving parents and families are critical (Lane, Gresham, & O'Shaughnessy, 2002). Biological and developmental factors, family factors, and ineffective parenting all have the potential to contribute to a child's academic and social–emotional problems. Current data suggest that factors are intertwined and thus have an impact on the youth collective (Swartz-Kulstad & Martin, 1999).

The earliest prevention efforts could focus on prenatal and health care programs. Beginning in utero, parents are afforded an opportunity to bond with their children, encouraging stability and support. During infancy, efforts that promote interaction, consistency, and communication assist in building a strong foundation of parental bonding. Ultimately, parent training programs counteract the parent and family risk factors by offering parents opportunities to learn effective discipline methods and supportive parenting that promotes self-confidence, problem-solving skills, and academic success. Although problems may exist, programs designed to address specific issues such as abuse or neglect could assist a family in preventing further deterioration of the family dysfunction.

School

A number of factors contribute to a child's potential success in minimizing the impact of the factors that place them at risk. These include a strong support network of primary and extended family, teachers, mentors, counselors, and other competent, committed adults (Hauser, 1999; Rak & Patterson. 1996). School counselors in particular have a unique opportunity to promote success in youth. The access given school counselors places them in a position to be one of these competent adults who can create a committed support network for the youths they serve (Constantine & Gushue, 2003).

School-based programs have the opportunity to address multiple risk factors in youths, families, and schools as well as build links between these three areas (Rayle, 2004). Prevention in school begins with comprehensive preschools, compensatory programs, and before- and after-school programs (J. McWhirter et al., 2007). School-based programs are more accessible to families and can potentially avoid the stigma associated with services offered in traditional mental health settings. School-based programs also remove some of the practical and social barriers to treatment access, such as lack of transportation or financial resources.

Community

Prevention efforts that encompass the community and larger society generally involve family members, school personnel, and communities. A need exists to provide social support and coordinated programs that enable community members to assist young people. Prevention efforts strengthen existing support for families in the school and in community organizations that work with the schools. Empowering young people and helping them to develop plans for social action is a preventive approach on the individual level. At the community level, they serve as a broader approach to treatment. The target here is not individuals or even groups of individuals but the norms, structures, and practices of organizations, communities, society, and the nation.

INTERVENTION STRATEGIES

Individual

Individual counselors must implement strategies for responding to needs of youth at risk. While counselors choose specific techniques based on the problems presented, all interventions should be sensitive and promote growth. One such strategy is the empowerment model of counseling described by E. H. McWhirter (2004). The empowerment model recognizes the impact of issues such as poverty, racism, sexism, heterosexism, and sociopolitical issues. This approach works from a systemic perspective and encourages individuals to become aware of the impact of forces within their life and assists in the development of skills to be proactive in taking control of one's life.

Ideally, empowerment is a process that promotes insight into internal reactions in relation to self, others, community, and society. The process involves reflection and decision making, developing awareness of one's environment, and understanding how one's circumstances are related to forces such as racism. It endorses connectedness with a community and support for the empowerment of others.

While particular techniques for interventions may vary in response to the ages of the youths or the presenting problem, the counselor–client relationship should be vibrant, characterized by a shared definition of the problem and the mutual development of interventions and strategies for change. Competent counselors should be aware that their own place within the larger culture may influence what they perceive as problems and how they respond to them (Cayleff, 1986). What is vitally important is that youths are invited into the counseling process, that their experiences are validated, and that they are presumed to be knowledgeable about what is important to them. Even when youths are unable to articulate or even acknowledge a problem, letting them know that their opinions and feelings are important and that they are expected to influence the direction of their counseling can lay the groundwork for successful change.

Considering the context in which a particular problem exists allows youths an opportunity to understand what has shaped their thoughts, feelings, and behaviors. This context may include racial identity, family dynamics, school dynamics, and community dynamics (Nishimura, 1995). Addressing the intersections of gender, class, race, and culture allows counselors to explore psychosocial identity formation (T. Robinson, 1993). If counselors acknowledge the role of context in a situation, including how the context serves to maintain or exacerbate the problems, youths have an opportunity to examine internalized messages and determine options for change. Vernon (2004) noted, "Counseling for empowerment implies that young people have the capacity to change, grow, act, and shape their environment despite contextual limitations" (p. 326).

Coping skills training allows counselors an opportunity to assist at-risk youth in dealing with situations that cause conflict and tension. All young people feel fear, disappointment, or anger at one time or another. How they cope with these situations is indicative of their adjustment. The greater the difficulty coping with stress, the greater the risk for establishing unhealthy coping patterns. Ultimately, ineffective strategies like withdrawal, acting out, or denial may emerge. Racial and ethnic minority youth then risk developing anxiety or depression, which may lead to learning problems, poor communication, negative self-talk, conduct problems, or academic underachievement (Esquivel & Keitel, 1990). Fortunately, a number of programs have proved to be effective in enhancing children's skills for coping with stress, anxiety, or depression. For example, the FRIENDS program trains children and their parents to handle stress and anxiety while fostering increased peer social support (Shortt, Barrett, & Fox, 2001).

Overall, a culturally competent counselor should be able to relate to racial and ethnic minority youths and have knowledge of cultural and class factors. It is important to recognize that counseling individuals indicate a need for choosing approaches consistent with lifestyle. Finally, it is important to have the counselor look at racial and ethnic differences as they relate to the counselor's approach and values (Sue, 1977). According to Romero (1981), "The goal of counseling minority people has been to enable entry into the mainstream of society" (p. 385).

Family

The nature of the family structure has been forced to shift in response to the ever-changing social and economic conditions. Because of the increases in blended families, immigrant families, and multiracial families, more and more families are called on to deal with stressors related to racial and ethnic issues. Even normal developmental issues can be difficult to deal with, but family distress can emerge when cultural minority issues are added to the mix. J. McWhirter et al. (2007) noted that "working with the entire family is often the optimal approach for dealing with young people at risk for drop out, substance abuse, pregnancy, delinquency, suicide or other problems" (p. 304).

Parent interventions help parents respond effectively to normal behavior and emotional problems so that these problems do not escalate. Parents gain knowledge of how to provide support for their children's cognitive, social, and emotional growth. Parent training programs can also assist parents with interacting successfully with teachers and advocating for their children's social and academic development. Family training may focus on such issues as communication and problem-solving skills. Ideally, the support offered to the parents will not only enhance fundamental parenting skills but also facilitate parent support, decrease the sense of isolation, and provide strategies to cope with stressful life events. It is most effective if parents are trained to recognize and cope with the signs of risk before the youth's behavior becomes completely unmanageable. Training in behavior management, the implementation of rewards and consequences, and help with communication skills can be particularly effective with younger children (Kim & Lyons, 2003). Because expectations regarding child behavior and accepted methods of discipline are frequently defined by culture, cultural appropriateness is critical to the success of parent training programs. The counselor is best served by getting acquainted with the family and understanding the family traditions, ideals, uniqueness, and traditions.

One adjunct to family counseling is family support groups. Not only do these groups offer education for parents, but they also provide an opportunity for parents to build relationships with other parents in similar circumstances or who have handled similar problems. Parent support groups afford parents opportunities to express their concerns and learn what has or has not worked for other parents in similar circumstances. Such support groups are often available through community resources.

School

Without a doubt, emphasis on academic success is critical for school counselors of racial and ethnic minority children. As Dupper and Poertner (1997) observed, "education, which increases a youth's skills and employment opportunities, is an important route" (p. 415) for a youth to take to counteract the potential consequences of the identified risks. School counselors may address the academic, personal, and career needs of the students they serve. The school counselor serves as a "liaison between teachers, parents, support personnel, and community resources to facilitate successful student development" (American School Counselor Association, 1997, p. 12). With an at-risk population such as racial and ethnic minority youth, the school counselor becomes an essential force in providing opportunities that facilitate self-esteem and subsequent academic success.

In an effort to reach the youth, counselors may seek access via the family (Dupper & Poertner, 1997). Such collaboration may be difficult to achieve as parents may fear cultural insensitivity, condescending school personnel, or accusations of being responsible for their children's difficulties. Conversely, teachers may believe that parents will not respect their expertise, will not participate, or will hold their children's teachers responsible for their problems. These reservations all too often materialize, and the common goal of serving the youth is not enough to overcome the barriers. "Rather, multicultural competence, communication, skills, time, resources, empathy and patience are also required" (J. McWhirter et al., 2007, p. 244).

Because poverty is common among racial and ethnic minorities, there may be diminished focus on the day-to-day needs of the present to meet the basic survival needs of housing and nutrition. These families may be less likely to see the relevance in education if it offers no immediate impact on the families' well-being and there is a lack of resources to connect education to long-term consequences and career potential (T. L. Cross & Burney, 2005). If the lack of emphasis on education is present, the role of the school counselor is often to educate families about the role of education in advancing the lives of youth. Families in repressed economic circumstances are not always aware that education can actually mediate negative outcomes such as delinquency and ongoing poverty.

In addition to educating families, the school counselor may be in a position to educate faculty and staff about the role and impact of racial and ethnic identity development on youth. Counselors can work with faculty to assist them in understanding a student's absences or a seemingly lack of ambition in an otherwise academically competent student (T. L. Cross & Burney, 2005). School counselors often have regular opportunities to serve as advocates for youth and their families.

Providing valuable information to the people involved in the lives of racial and ethnic minority youth is one form of such advocacy.

A third focal point for school counselors is the role of education. Racial and ethnic minority youth may not enter the academic realm with the middle-class standards and aspirations espoused by a school system. While school systems may predict students will pursue a secondary education and then enter into a skilled workforce or postsecondary institution, a primary role of the school counselor is college and career preparatory activities (T. L. Cross & Burney, 2005). With racial and ethnic minority youth, this role is even more vital because many of these individuals may lack role models related to completing a high school education, pursuing higher education, or considering associated career opportunities. Often school counselors find themselves serving as the only voice of high expectation related to postsecondary academic opportunities (Gillespie & Starkey, 2006). Continued awareness of the cultural position of education within the household is critical because it may outweigh the norms of the student's peer groups resulting from profound social and familial pressure.

Finally, the school counselor is afforded the opportunity to assist in the development and implementation of wraparound services that include community, family, health, social services, and educational perspectives. This multidisciplinary approach offers comprehensive involvement with the at-risk youth and distributes the weight of management of these students' needs, which would be difficult for the school counselor to accomplish independently (Bryan, 2005). The involvement of committed networks of supportive and influential adults in the lives of racial and ethnic minority youth serves as a significant strength in preventing negative effects and providing children with the greatest potential for success

Community

When considering what makes up a community, it becomes obvious that it could be composed of many groups, such as family, peers, neighborhoods, or church groups. For ethnic and minority youth, a connection with their community is important to foster a sense of belonging. The community also has an opportunity to offer tools for healthy development, such as role modeling, encouragement, and provision of basic needs.

Racial and ethnic minority youth often lack a sense of community with any other groups in their environment or belong to communities that undermine their resources and abilities (Vernon, 2004). Counselors have the opportunity to promote the building of community and aid youths in accessing or nurturing existing communities. Community programs that promote positive social interactions, build communication skills, and foster a shared sense of identity are especially helpful to this end (Sinclair, Hurley, Evelo, Christenson, & Thurlow, 2002). Prevention efforts within the community could focus on improving socioeconomic conditions, expanding opportunities for adequate housing, assisting parents in accessing child care and job opportunities, and assisting families in integrating into community norms (Lane et al., 2002; J. McWhirter et al., 2007; Vernon, 2004).

Promoting a sense of community can be fostered through participation in clubs or organizations with a particular theme, such as a sports team, volunteer groups, scouts, or Boys and Girls Clubs of America. It is critical for counselors to assist children in accessing community resources and building the skills needed for drawing the community's support, as youths who are already experiencing a sense of isolation may not feel comfortable initiating participation in such activities.

ADAPTATIONS FOR DIVERSITY

There is no one model or pattern for conducting counseling with racial and ethnic minority youth. The approach depends on the problems, the conditions surrounding them, and the counselor's theoretical orientation. The following proactive activities enhance multicultural sensitivity and demonstrate commitment to diversity (Brinson, 1996; Herring, 1992; Montague, 1996; Vernon, 2004).

1. Attempt to identify and understand the issues from the worldview of the client. Practice examining how your life might be different if you were a member of a minority culture.
2. Be comfortable acknowledging and exploring the client's cultural differences. Be open to durable and significant relationships with members of minority cultures. Do not wait to be invited; take some initiative.
3. Identify and embrace the existence of strengths for a culturally diverse family and attempt to incorporate these strengths into coping skills.
4. Be aware of how the client identifies him- or herself racially.
5. Promote sensitivity through the use of sensitive, nonjudgmental interventions and techniques that clarify the client's view and culturally determined perceptions about reality.
6. Read text, watch movies, and attend theater with characters and themes from other cultures.
7. Prior to working with a new cultural group, consider the bias, stereotypes, and negative concepts you may hold against the group.
8. Create your own cultural genogram and use it as a source of connection with members of cultures different from your own.
9. Learn a second language and find venues to practice your new language to facilitate its use within your practice.
10. Find a colleague who can serve as a confidant and consultant with expertise in multicultural issues. Consult honestly and often.

SUMMARY

The many societal changes reflected in the demographic growth and diversification of the United States have greatly influenced the counseling profession. Counseling professionals realize that culture cannot be ignored as an influential aspect of the counseling experience. The growth in the number of racial and ethnic minorities has altered the balance with the majority culture. Because of these changes, counselors are best served to explore their own sense of racial and ethnic identity and to increase their level of training with regard to working with cultural minorities.

Sensitivity to acculturation considerations and a foundation of knowledge regarding culturally appropriate interventions help shape culturally competent counselors. Counselors must learn to consider cultural impact within individual, familial, school, and community context. Doing such offers the greatest opportunity for successful counseling with racial and ethnic minority youth.

REFERENCES

Aaroe, L., & Nelson, J. R. (2000). A comparative analysis of teachers', Caucasian parents', and Hispanic parents' views of problematic school survival behaviors. *Education and Treatment of Children, 23*, 314–324.

Akutsu, P. D., Snowden, L. R., & Organista, K. C. (1996). Referral patterns in ethnic-specific and mainstream programs for minorities and Whites. *Journal of Counseling Psychology, 43*, 56–64.

Aldarondo, F. (2001). Racial and ethnic identity models and their application: Counseling biracial individuals. *Journal of Mental Health Counseling, 23*, 238–256.

American School Counselor Association. (1997). *The national standards for school counseling programs.* Alexandria, VA: Author.

Arroyo, C. G., & Zigler, E. (1995). Racial identity, academic achievement, and the psychological well-being of economically disadvantaged adolescents. *Journal of Personality and Social Psychology, 69*, 903–914.

Brinson, J. (1996). Cultural sensitivity for counselors: Our challenge for the twenty-first century. *Journal of Humanistic Education and Development, 34*, 195–207.

Bryan, J. (2005). Fostering educational resilience and achievement in urban schools through school–family–community partnerships. *Professional School Counseling, 8*, 219–227.

Cayleff, S. (1986). Ethical issues in counseling gender, race, and culturally distinct groups. *Journal of Counseling & Development, 64*, 345–347.

Chase, N. D. (1999). Parentification: An overview of theory, research, and societal issues. In N. D. Chase (Ed.), *Burdened children: Theory, research, and treatment of parentification* (pp. 3–33). Thousand Oaks, CA: Sage.

Chase, N. D., Deming, M. P., & Wells, M. C. (1998). Parentification, parental alcoholism, and academic status among young adults. *American Journal of Family Therapy, 26*, 105–114.

Constantine, M. G., Erickson, C. D., Banks, R. W., & Timberlake, T. L. (1998). Challenges to the career development of urban racial and ethnic minority youth: Implications for vocational intervention. *Journal of Multicultural Counseling and Development, 26*, 82–95.

Constantine, M., & Gushue, G. (2003). School counselors' tolerance attitudes and racism attitudes as predictors of their multicultural case conceptualization of an immigrant student. *Journal of Counseling & Development, 81*, 185–191.

Cross, T. L., & Burney, V. H. (2005). High ability, rural, and poor: Lessons from Project Aspire and implications for school counselors. *Journal of Secondary Gifted Education, 16*, 148–156.

Cross, W. E. (1995). The psychology of nigrescence: Revising the Cross model. In J. Ponterotto, M. Casas, L. Suzuki, & C. Alexander (Eds.), *Handbook of multicultural counseling* (pp. 93–122). Thousand Oaks, CA: Sage.

Davidson, M. M., Yakushka, O. F., & Sanford-Martens, T. C. (2004). Racial and ethnic minority clients' utilization of a university counseling center: An archival study. *Journal of Multicultural Counseling and Development, 32*, 259–271.

Dupper, D. R., & Poertner, J. (1997). Public schools and the revitalization of impoverished communities: School-linked, family resource centers. *Social Work, 42*, 415–422.

Erikson, E. H. (1968). *Identity, youth, and crisis.* New York: Norton.

Esquivel, G., & Keitel, M. (1990). Counseling immigrant children in the schools. *Elementary School Guidance and Counseling, 24,* 213–218.

Gibbs, J. T. (1990). Biracial adolescents. In J. T. Gibbs & L. N. Huang (Eds.), *Children of color* (pp. 322–350). San Francisco: Jossey-Bass.

Gillespie, A., & Starkey, D. S. (2006). The role of the rural school counselor in preparing high school students for college. *Delta Education Journal, 3*(2), 24–28.

Harris, H. (2002). School counselor's perceptions of biracial children: A pilot study. *Professional School Counseling, 6,* 120–130.

Hauser, S. T. (1999). Understanding resilient outcomes: Adolescent. *Journal of Research on Adolescence, 9,* 1–24.

Herring, R. (1992). Biracial children: An increasing concern for elementary and middle school counselors. *Elementary School Guidance and Counseling, 27,* 123–131.

Herring, R. (1995). Developing biracial identity: A review of the increasing dilemma. *Journal of Multicultural Counseling and Development, 23,* 29–39.

Hill, S. (1999). *African American children: Socialization and development in families.* Thousand Oaks, CA: Sage.

Hook, M., & Ashton, K. (2002). Transcending a double bind: The case of Jenna. *Career Development Quarterly, 50,* 321–325.

Kerwin, C., & Ponterotto, J. G. (1995). Biracial identity development: Research and practice. In J. Ponterotto, M. Casas, L. Suzuki, & C. Alexander (Eds.), *Handbook of multicultural counseling* (pp. 199–217). Thousand Oaks, CA: Sage.

Kim, B., & Lyons, H. (2003). Experiential activities and multicultural competence training. *Journal of Counseling & Development, 81,* 400–408.

Kopala, M., Esquivel, G., & Baptiste, L. (1994). Counseling approaches for immigrant children: Facilitating the acculturative process. *School Counselor, 41,* 352–360.

Lane, K. L., Gresham, F. M., & O'Shaughnessy, T. E. (2002). *Interventions for children with or at risk for emotional and behavioral disorders.* Boston: Allyn & Bacon.

Lau, A. S., Garland, A. F., Yeh, M., McCabe, K. M., Wood, P. A., & Hough, R. L. (2004). Race/ethnicity and inter-informant agreement in assessing adolescent psychopathology. *Journal of Emotional and Behavioral Disorders, 12,* 145–156.

Maital, S. L. (2000). Reciprocal distancing: A systems model of interpersonal processes in cross-cultural consultation. *School Psychology Review, 29,* 389–401.

Marotta, S., & Garcia, J. (2003). Latinos in the United States in 2000. *Hispanic Journal of Behavioral Sciences, 25,* 13–34.

McGoldrick, M. (1982). Ethnicity and family therapy: An overview. In M. McGoldrick, J. K. Pearce, & J. Giordana (Eds.), *Ethnicity and family therapy* (pp. 3–30). New York: Guilford Press.

McWhirter, E. H. (1994). *Counseling for empowerment.* Alexandria, VA: American Counseling Association.

McWhirter, J., McWhirter, B., McWhirter, E., & McWhirter, R. (2007). *At risk youth: A comprehensive response for counselors, teachers, psychologists, and human service professionals* (4th ed.). Belmont, CA: Thompson Brooks/Cole.

Montague, J. (1996). Counseling families from diverse cultures: A nondeficit approach. *Journal of Multicultural Counseling and Development, 24,* 37–40.

National Center for Health Statistics. (2006). *National vital statistics reports, 2005.* Retrieved January 26, 2007, from, http://www.cdc.gov/nchs/

Nishimura, N. (1995). Addressing the needs of biracial children: An issue for counselors in a multicultural school environment. *School Counselor, 43,* 52–57.

Olatunji, A. N. (2005). Dropping out of high school among Mexican-origin youths: Is early work experience a factor? *Harvard Educational Review, 75,* 286–305.

Orton, G. L. (1996). *Strategies for counseling with children and their parents*. Pacific Grove, CA: Brooks/Cole.

Phelps, R. E., Taylor, J. D., & Gerard, P. A. (2001). Cultural mistrust, ethnic identity, racial identity, and self-esteem among ethnically diverse Black university students. *Journal of Counseling & Development, 79*, 209–217.

Poston, W. S. C. (1990). The biracial identity developmental model: A needed addition. *Journal of Counseling & Development, 69*, 152–155.

Rak, C., & Patterson, L. (1996). Promoting resilience in at-risk children. *Journal of Counseling & Development, 74*, 368–373.

Rayle, A. (2004). Counseling adolescents toward wellness: The roles of ethnic identity, acculturation, and mattering. *Professional School Counseling, 8*, 81–90.

Robinson, B. E., & Post, P. (1995). Work addiction as a function of family origin and its influence on current family function. *Family Journal, 3*, 200–206.

Robinson, T. (1993). The intersections of gender, class, race and culture: On seeing clients whole. *Journal of Multicultural Counseling and Development, 21*, 50–58.

Robinson, T. L. (2005). *The convergence of race, ethnicity, and gender*. Upper Saddle River, NJ: Pearson Education.

Romero, M. (1981, February). Multicultural reality: The pain of growth. *Personnel and Guidance Journal*, 384–386.

Root, M. P. P. (1996). *The multiracial experience*. Thousand Oaks, CA: Sage.

Sandhu, D. S., Portes, P. R., & McPhee, S. A. (1996). Assessing cultural adaptation: Psychometric properties of the Cultural Adaptation Pain Scale. *Journal of Multicultural Counseling and Development, 24*, 15–25.

Schoen, A. (2005). Culturally sensitive counseling for Asian Americans/Pacific Islanders. *Journal of Instructional Psychology, 32*, 253–258.

Shortt, H., Barrett, P., & Fox, T. (2001). Evaluating the FRIENDS program: A cognitive–behavioral group treatment for anxious children and their parents. *Journal of Clinical Psychology, 30*, 525–235.

Sinclair, M., Hurley, C., Evelo, D., Christenson, S., & Thurlow, M. (2002). Making connections that keep students coming to school. In B. Algozzine & P. Kay (Eds.), *Preventing problem behaviors: A handbook of successful prevention strategies* (pp. 162–182). Thousand Oaks, CA: Sage.

Spanierman, L. B. (2002) Academic self-efficacy within a culture of modern racism: The case of Benita. *Career Development Quarterly, 50*, 331–334.

Sue, D. (1977, March). Counseling the culturally different: A conceptual analysis. *Personnel and Guidance Journal*, 422–425.

Sue, D. W., & Sue, D. (2003). *Counseling the culturally diverse* (4th ed.). New York: Wiley.

Swartz-Kulstad, J., & Martin, W. (1999). Impact of culture and context on psychosocial adaptation: The cultural and contextual guide process. *Journal of Counseling & Development, 77*, 281–294.

Vernon, A. (2004). *Counseling children and adolescents* (3rd ed.). Denver, CO: Love Publishing.

CHAPTER 9

■

The Secret and All-Consuming Obsessions: Eating Disorders

Kimberly Wright and Elva E. Blanks

The standard for body size and weight is socially determined. It is a cultural phenomenon that demands that the current ideal physique is slim. Countries that commonly experience the threat of famine have historically had virtually no cases of anorexia or bulimia, and obesity has been considered desirable (Bruch, 1973; Nasser, 1988). In previous eras in the United States, larger bodies were associated with prosperity, in contrast with current mores that associate thinness with affluence. Obesity is now considered a correlate of the lower class. Continuous images indoctrinate the public with the message that to be considered successful, masterful, and acceptable, one must display a thin physique. This image is one that emphasizes self-control and discipline over self-indulgence. For women, this message is especially strong. Since Twiggy reigned as a premier fashion model in the late 1960s, the United States has promoted a thinner and thinner standard for the female ideal (Garner, Garfinkel, Schwartz, & Thompson, 1980; Stice, 2002). It is within this context that the current escalation of eating disorders in the United States is occurring.

The media has long been recognized as one of the most powerful transmitters of social standards. According to Garner et al. (1980), "the potential impact of the media in establishing identifiable role models cannot be overemphasized" (p. 652). Newspapers, television, movies, magazines, and billboards bombard the public with images and messages about appropriate behavior, dress, food, entertainment, appearance, and beliefs. Avoiding the overt and covert messages of society portrayed through the media would be virtually impossible. For men, the standards portrayed include fitness, power, and independence. For women, the standards portrayed include thinness, femininity, and beauty.

The female ideal as defined by the culture fluctuates. The power of these fluctuations is revealed by a classic study (Garner et al., 1980) comparing the weights and measurements of *Playboy* centerfolds and Miss America Pageant contestants from 1959 to 1978. There was a significant decrease in body weight and body measurements for both groups, despite an increase in height. Additionally, the Miss

America Pageant winners were significantly slimmer than the average contestant in the same pageant. This trend occurred while the average woman under age 30 was becoming heavier during the same time period. The ideal female figure has continued to become thinner, despite the increase in the size of the average woman (Wiseman, Gray, Mosimann, & Ahrens, 1992). A similar trend has more recently been identified among men featured in the media. Leit, Pope, and Gray (2001) noted that by 2001, the average *Playgirl* centerfold man had 12 pounds less fat and 27 extra pounds of muscle than 25 years ago, suggesting that the societal standards for men are becoming as unrealistic for men as they have been for women.

The trend toward a slim female ideal is also illustrated by the changes in diet advertisements over a 20-year period. Between 1973 and 1991, the United States witnessed a consistent increase in television commercials featuring diet products (Wiseman, Gunning, & Gray, 1993). Another classic study of media messages compared food and diet advertisements from 48 women's magazines and 48 men's magazines (Silverstein, Perdue, Peterson, & Kelly, 1986). It is interesting to note that 1,179 different food and diet advertisements appeared in the women's magazines, compared with 10 in the men's magazines. Anderson and DiDomenico (1992) also found that women's magazines contain over 10 times the number of diet advertisements and articles as do men's magazines. The inherent double message has been that women need to indulge in various foods and that they need to diet to avoid weight gain. More recently, men's bodies have been increasingly used in product advertising in women's magazines (Pope, Olivardia, Borowiecki, & Cohane, 2001). The proportion of undressed men in magazines skyrocketed from 3% in the 1950s to 35% in the 1990s.

Few would argue that men and women are socialized in different ways. The female and male socialization experiences can be viewed as representative of different cultures. Women are socialized to draw their self-esteem from their physical appearance rather than from what they do (Beattie, 1988). For men, self-esteem has tended to be more frequently related to success. This discrepancy, combined with the ideal standards for female appearance, increases a woman's vulnerability to eating disorders but does not rule out the vulnerability among men, as evidenced by the recent rise in men's concern about appearance and body image.

Body image is the perception of one's own shape and size. Those who compare themselves with models or other "ideals" often distort their own body image negatively (Kalodner, 1997). The body is perceived to be inadequate if it fails to meet ideal criteria. Stice (2002) noted that nearly 25% of the female models in some magazines were found to satisfy the weight criteria for anorexia nervosa. This provides the standard against which many women measure themselves. It is not unusual to hear women, or even young girls state, "I feel so fat," even when their weight is normal. Body dissatisfaction has been found to increase the risk of eating disturbances (Killen et al., 1996; Perez & Joiner, 2003). Research indicates that increased exposure to these ultra-thin ideals increases the risk of developing eating pathology among vulnerable adolescent girls who already have internalized a thin ideal (Stice, Spangler, & Agras, 2001). Multiple studies demonstrate the impact of the media on self-perception and body image. Women who are exposed to "thin-ideal" television programs (that portray primarily thin, attractive actors) have higher rates of eating disorder symptoms (Bissel & Zhou, 2004), and mainstream television viewing has been found to be related to poorer body image (Schooler, Ward, Merriwether, & Caruthers, 2004). Popular magazines routinely feature celebrities who are identified as eating disordered, with magazine covers often highlighting "before" and "after" photographs revealing stars' substantial weight loss. The thin ideal is inescapable.

This dynamic has also been observed among men. A study of 173 college men (Baird & Grieve, 2006) found that men who are exposed to male models in men's magazines reported increased body dissatisfaction. The visual images of the media become the reference point against which both men and women measure themselves, and the greater the discrepancy between the visual image and the reality, the greater the dissatisfaction in one's own appearance.

Among women, it is now the norm to diet. While it may not be healthy, dieting has become commonplace. This trend is highlighted by the concept of "malnutrition of affluence" (Hill, 2002). Malnutrition is no longer the plight of poverty. Dieting among adolescents has increased and is occurring at younger ages. Twenty-five percent of 11-year-old girls report at least one dieting attempt (Stice, 2002). It is estimated that over half of teenage girls and one third of teenage boys use unhealthy methods to control their weight (Neumark-Sztainer, 2005) and that 40%–50% of women are dieting at any point in time. This same trend is also occurring outside of the United States, most notably in Asian countries such as China and Japan where there is already a low rate of obesity and the natural body type is petite (S. Lee & Katzman, 2002)

Body image distortions have historically been more prevalent among women than among men. Nearly 20 years ago in a study of college men, 65% of a sample of 340 reported that they weighed within 5 percentage points of their ideal weight (Franco, Tamburrino, Carroll, & Bernal, 1988), in contrast to the typical body dissatisfaction of college women. Currently, men are identifying more muscular shapes as the ideal and holding the belief that women also prefer more muscular men than they actually endorse (Grieve, Newton, Kelly, Miller, & Kerr, 2005). The cultural body image distortions for men was revealed by a review of the toys produced for boys over the last 30 years. Pope, Olivardia, Gruber, and Borowiecki (1999) found that boys' actions toys (e.g., G.I. Joe, Star Wars action figures) have become more unrealistically muscular in this period than even real-world body builders.

However, women tend to exhibit greater body dissatisfaction and body image distortion than do men (Connor-Greene, 1988), and weight concerns for girls are commonly seen even before puberty (S. H. Thompson, Rafiroiu, & Sargent, 2003). Even the desired ideal weight among men with bulimia has been found to be more realistic than the desired ideal weight of women with bulimia (Schneider & Agras, 1987). Although the current trend indicates that body image distortions among men are on the rise, men still view themselves as thin when they are 105% of their ideal weight. Women, in comparison, do not see themselves as thin unless they are 90% of their ideal weight or below. Men are more likely to be dissatisfied with their shape rather than their weight and to desire a more muscular physique (Anderson, 2002).

PROBLEM DEFINITION

The prevalence of eating disorders has consistently increased in the United States across the last 40 years despite the recent contention that it has decreased in recent years (Keel, Heatherton, Dorer, Joiner, & Zalta, 2005). This discrepancy is likely due to the differential methods used in defining eating disorders in the research. Keel et al. indicated that the primary difference across cohorts at a large midwestern university in 1982, 1992, and 2002 was a reduction in bingeing behavior; there was not a significant decrease in purging behaviors. Therefore, while bulimia may have been diagnosed less frequently, very dangerous eating disorder behaviors were still occurring. In fact, a large study of 81,247 high school students revealed that approximately 30% of males and 55% of females have "disordered eating" (Croll, Neumark-Sztainer, Story, & Ireland, 2002). It is also possible that the sample at this one university was not representative of students across the country. It is clear that many individuals struggle with the painful reality of eating disorder–type symptoms, even when they do not meet the strict criteria of a diagnosable eating disorder.

Increasing emphasis on thinness and physical fitness has altered the standard for appearance for women and men. The "fitness movement" is misleading. Many individuals flock to gyms and fitness classes under the guise of cardiovascular health and physical fitness, seeking instead to achieve the physical ideal of attractiveness. This is further fueled by recent reports of the significant health risks of obesity and the health benefits of strength training, which has become an obsession among some, especially men. The current trends are not in danger of reversing, which leaves the social climate primed for a continuation of eating pathology.

Risk Factors

Gender

Although anorexia, bulimia, and, to a lesser extent, binge eating disorder are typically characterized as female afflictions, they cross gender lines. While anorexia and bulimia do appear more frequently among females, males can develop these disorders. It is likely that many cases of anorexia or bulimia among males go unreported for several reasons: (a) the reluctance of men to admit symptoms of a "female disorder," (b) eating large quantities of food is not considered abnormal by adolescent boys and young men, and (c) clinicians are less likely to explore eating disorder symptoms among males. Even considering the potential underreporting among men, women are at higher risk for developing anorexia or bulimia because of the value placed on their appearance by the culture. (The gender differences will be reflected by the primary use of the female pronoun throughout, unless specifically referring to males.) Binge eating, typically associated with obesity, is less gender specific, but it also occurs more frequently in women than in men (American Psychiatric Association, 2000; Grilo, 2002). It is important to note, however, that binge eating and obesity are not comparable terms, although they are often used interchangeably. Binge eating refers to a behavior, whereas obesity (excessive weight) refers to the likely consequences of the behavior. Only 25% of obese persons are estimated to be binge eaters, as weight is regulated by a variety of biological and behavioral factors.

Age

Adolescence is a high-risk period for the development of eating disorders. The most frequent period for the emergence of anorexia and bulimia is between the ages 14 and 18; however, atypical onset patterns exist. Late adolescence is also the most likely period for the development of binge eating disorder, with 18 being the modal age of onset (Streigel-Moore, 1993). The developmental tasks of adolescence interact with the physical and social demands of maturation to create a vulnerability to developing eating disorders during adolescence or early adulthood. Binge eating disorder may develop in adulthood, and it is not unusual for the disorder to be diagnosed once bulimia is in remission. This common clinical observation has recently been challenged, however, by some evidence that suggests that this is a rare development (Fairburn, Cooper, Doll, Norman, & O'Connor, 2000). Crossover diagnoses or symptoms fluctuations may be more commonly seen between anorexia and bulimia (Tozzi et al., 2005).

Race

Anorexia and bulimia have historically been more frequently associated with upper-middle-class White populations, and the greatest risk for these disorders continues to be in this group. However, there is recent evidence suggesting that the risk and prevalence are increasing for minority groups (Striegel-Moore & Smolak, 2002). In addition, binge eating and obesity are more common among some minority populations such as African American and some Native American groups (Klesges, DeBon, & Meyers, 1996).

Socioeconomic Status Level

Historically, women with anorexia and bulimia have most frequently come from the middle to upper-middle socioeconomic class (Soh, Touyz, & Surgenor, 2006), whereas obesity (and by extension, binge eating) has tended to be associated with lower socioeconomic status. This pattern is not consistent, however, especially among youth with upwardly mobile aspirations, such as first-generation college students and recent U.S. immigrants. Upward social comparison that leaves individuals feeling inadequate has been noted as one dynamic that might promote eating disorders across sociocultural class lines. Increasing socioeconomic status levels also inspire a greater internalization of the thin ideal more common in the dominant culture.

Family Characteristics

The families of those with eating disorders have been described as chaotic and conflicted, in the case of the bulimic (Humphrey, 1994), or overcontrolling and rigid, in the case of the anorexic (Humphrey, 1994). Those with binge eating disorder report being neglected or overlooked as children, as well as having experienced overinvolvement or lack of structure around meals (Pike & Wilfley, 1996). Although these are simplified, stereotypical portrayals and have not been consistent in recent research (Soh et al., 2006), family problems are common among the eating disordered population. In a review of the literature, Soh et al. (2006) concluded that family members' perception that their family is either overcontrolling or cohesive is a function of both the individuals' temperament and cultural expectations. It is also common for another family member to have struggled with weight problems or an eating disorder. Eating disturbances among women have been found to be related to weight concerns expressed by parents (Keel, Heatherton, Harnden, & Hornig, 1997). Previous research and a review of the literature have indicated convergent evidence that the families of eating disordered individuals have a higher rate of affective disorders, alcoholism, and conflictual and controlling family relationships (McGrane & Carr, 2002; Vandereycken, 2002). Women with eating disorders have been found to have had higher rates of childhood separation anxiety and insecure attachment in adulthood (Troisi, Massaroni, & Cuzzolaro, 2005).

A promising area of research suggests that eating disorders have a strong genetic component (Strober, Freeman, Lampert, Diamond, & Kaye, 2000). Family and twin studies have revealed a likelihood that a susceptibility to eating disorders may be inherited. Researchers are currently investigating genes that may be responsible for this vulnerability.

Identification With Socialized Norms

Among a sample of 682 college students, Mintz and Betz (1988) found that disordered eating similar to that found in anorexia and bulimia was strongly related to the endorsement of sociocultural norms that regard female thinness and attractiveness as indications of worth. Women who held beliefs similar to the traditional gender expectations are at greater risk for these eating disorders. One aspect of the social norms for women has been to strive for the ideal of thinness. It has been reported that persistent weight and shape concerns (Killen et al., 1996) and the internalization of the thinness ideal (J. K. Thompson & Stice, 2001) pose a risk for the development of eating pathology among young women. Certainly, this is related to the continuing phenomenon of women's subordinate position in a society in which women's value is significantly determined by appearance.

Although many of the risk factors prominent in eating disorders are featured in other disturbances of youth, such as alcohol and drug abuse or depression, the sociocultural and gender pressures are the distinguishing features of anorexia nervosa and bulimia. Risk factors for binge eating disorder include depression, low self-esteem, and childhood teasing (Grilo & Masheb, 2005). The anticipated risk factors of childhood obesity and parental obesity have been found to be more predictive of bulimia than binge eating disorder (Grilo, 2002).

Definitions, Symptoms, and Etiology

Anorexia Nervosa

The prevalence of anorexia nervosa (typically referred to as anorexia) among the general population is reported to be between 0.5% to 1.0% (American Psychiatric Association, 2000) but is believed to be higher among high school and college populations. Prevalence is, however, difficult to determine. Recent estimates contend a rise in the prevalence of anorexia in girls ages 15–19 over the past 10 years (Hoek & van Hoeken, 2003), and it is estimated that only one third of all individuals with anorexia receive mental health treatment. Approximately 90% of the cases of anorexia nervosa are female. Cases with restrictive eating disturbances that do not meet all of the criteria for anorexia nervosa are more common. The onset is most likely to occur in adolescence and early adulthood, but cases of earlier and later onset have been reported, with a later onset being more common among ethnic minorities.

Anorexia nervosa is a constellation of symptoms in which an extreme drive for thinness, fear of becoming fat, and a restriction of food intake are central (see Table 9-1 for a symptom summary). Anorexia nervosa is actually a misnomer. Literally translated, anorexia nervosa means "nervous lack of appetite." Although there is a denial of hunger, actual hunger loss does not occur until the very advanced stages of the disorder.

The most recent diagnostic criteria presented in the *Diagnostic and Statistical Manual of Mental Disorders* (4th ed., Text Revision [*DSM–IV–TR*]; American Psychiatric Association, 2000) allow for specificity in diagnosis and highlight the similarity of some symptoms common to both anorexia nervosa and bulimia nervosa. The critical elements of anorexia include the following:

Table 9-1
■
Symptoms of Anorexia Nervosa

Psychological

Perfectionism	Denial of problem
Depression	Anxiety
Distorted body image	Thoughts of suicide
Intense fear of food and weight gain	High need for control
	Mood lability
Inflexibility in thought and behavior	Poor self-esteem
	Compliance
Feelings of guilt about eating	

Behavioral

Extreme food restriction	Preoccupation with food and eating
Isolation from friends and family	
Fatigue and irritability	Compulsive exercise
Extreme physical activity	Vomiting meals
Eating alone	Abuse of laxatives, diet pills, or diuretics
Adoption of loose clothing	
High caffeine intake	

Physical

Noticeable weight loss, 15% or more of total body weight	Lanugo—growth of fine facial and body hair
Absent or erratic menses	Exhaustion
Cognitive disturbances	Cardiac disturbances
Electrolyte imbalance	Malnutrition
Distortion of hunger and satiety	Tooth decay/gum disease
	Lowered metabolism
Hypersensitivity to cold	

- Refusal to maintain body weight at or above a minimally normal weight for age and height (e.g., weight loss leading to maintenance of body weight less that 85% of that expected, or failure to make expected weight gain during period of growth, leading to body weight less than 85% of that expected).
- Intense fear of gaining weight or becoming fat, even though underweight.
- Disturbance in the way in which one's body weight or shape is experienced, undue influence of body weight or shape on self-evaluation, or denial of the seriousness of the current low body weight.
- In postmenarcheal females, amenorrhea, that is, the absence of at least three consecutive menstrual cycle. (A woman is considered to have amenorrhea if her periods occur only following hormone, e.g., estrogen, administration.)

Further, the *DSM–IV–TR* specifies two types of anorexia:

- *Restricting type:* During the current episode of anorexia nervosa, the person has not regularly engaged in binge eating or purging behavior (i.e., self-induced vomiting or the misuse of laxatives, diuretics, or enemas).

- *Binge eating/purging type:* During the current episode of anorexia nervosa, the person has regularly engaged in binge eating or purging behavior (i.e., self-induced vomiting or the misuse of laxatives diuretics, or enemas).

One of the first noticeable symptoms of anorexia is a preoccupation with food, particularly a focus on the fat, carbohydrate, and calorie content of food. The woman with anorexia may begin by restricting herself to a "healthy" or even vegetarian diet or may begin exercising more than usual. She may slowly add to her list of "forbidden foods" until the list of foods she will allow herself to consume becomes scant. The most striking feature is the determination she evidences. As the disorder progresses, she may begin removing herself from social dining situations. She may claim to be too busy to eat lunch with friends or will excuse herself from an invitation by claiming to have already eaten. As her weight begins to drop, she may conceal herself with loose-fitting clothes or wear warmer clothing than would be necessary. She may become compulsive with list-making, being sure that no free time exists in her schedule. As her work or activities begin to consume all of her day, she may stay up late at night in an effort to "burn more calories" or to accomplish more in her drive for perfection and success. As others begin to notice the change in her appearance or behavior, she is likely to become defensive and isolate herself further. She will take any comment regarding her weight loss as a compliment and a sign of success. As the disorder progresses, her cognitive functions become less sharp, decision making becomes more difficult, and her obsession with food becomes unrelenting.

Throughout the process, she becomes more and more entrenched in her behavior. She will appear rigid, will react with denial if confronted, and will become more secretive in her eating rituals. Thoughts of food, calories, exercise, and weight will consume her daily, and she will develop rules that dictate her food intake and exercise behavior. She will become more depressed and anxious and will have frequent mood swings. She may develop comorbid obsessive–compulsive symptoms unrelated to her weight and food obsessions, such as ensuring that her room is orderly, frequent checking behavior, compulsive list-making, or repetitive counting. Her sense of self-worth will become intimately linked with her control of food, largely as a mask for her pervasive feeling of ineffectiveness and inadequacy. True emotional intimacy will be difficult for her to bear, yet she will strive to please others in a process that completely ignores her own needs or identity development. She will strive for extreme achievement and perfection in her endeavors and may believe that she does not deserve to eat, as if eating were a right that had to be earned. Her emotional development and social interactions will be less mature than those of her peers, leaving her feeling even more isolated.

A single etiology of anorexia has yet to be determined. It is currently accepted that the disorder is of a multidimensional nature. Although the anorexic female appears to the world to be a "perfect child" who is a high achiever, is compassionate toward others, and is respectful toward authority, it is believed that personality deficits precede the onset of the illness (Steiger & Houle, 1991). She is compliant, socially inhibited, emotionally restrained, and highly perfectionistic (Wonderlich, 2002). The extreme control exhibited in the young woman with anorexia becomes a compensation for poor coping skills and feelings of instability (Beaumont, 2002).

Psychoanalytic theory postulates that anorexia serves as a defense against maturation. Fears about becoming a woman and developing sexually inspire attempts to control her body and prevent the inevitable. The maintenance of a childlike physique is seen as an unconscious strategy to forestall adult relationships and sexuality. Developmentalists view anorexia as an adaptive tool used to combat great anxiety about developmental crises, such as increased expectations and responsibilities associated with maturation. Sociocultural theorists claim that it is the striving for perfection in appearance as a visible hallmark of success that motivates the woman with anorexia. Learning theory is related to this sociocultural explanation in that initial weight loss is met with praise and positive reinforcement. As the anorexic becomes emaciated, the initial positive attention received from others turns to concern that may be positively reinforcing as well. Internal reinforcement operates simultaneously as the anorexic prides herself on her self-control. The control issue escalates as she resists others' attempts to feed her and refuses external intervention. Negative reinforcement maintains the pattern as the fears of food and fat provide the incentive for the avoidance of food. Family theorists hypothesize that the behavior is a means of gaining control and independence from a critical and overcontrolling parent. Food and the body become the areas in which the anorexic can exert control and feel autonomous. Biological theories suggest that some individuals have a biological, genetic predisposition to developing anorexia. This vulnerability can then be triggered by environmental or developmental stressors. It is most reasonable to propose a multietiological perspective that incorporates several theoretical considerations while recognizing that no single etiological course can apply to each case.

Bulimia Nervosa

Prevalence estimates for bulimia nervosa vary from 1%–3% for women and 0.3% for men (American Psychiatric Association, 2000) to 11%–13% in college populations (Coric & Murstein, 1993; Gray & Ford, 1985), but it has been estimated to have tripled since 1988 among girls and women ages 10–39 (Hoek & van Hoeken, 2003). Despite these considerable statistics, a great number of people exhibit bulimic symptoms without meeting the complete diagnostic criteria (see Table 9-2 for symptom summary and Table 9-3 for a comparison with anorexia). As with anorexia, the typical onset of bulimia nervosa is during adolescence and early adulthood.

Bulimia nervosa is commonly known as bulimia. Roughly translated from the ancient Greek, bulimia means ravenous or oxlike hunger (Stunkard, 1993) and is a disorder characterized by cyclical periods of binge eating, typically followed by purging behavior (vomiting, laxative use, diuretic use, or excessive exercising). Many individuals engage in purging behavior without a binge precursor. This behavior would be classified in *DSM–IV–TR* as eating disorder not otherwise specified (ED NOS) and often takes the form of purging small or normal meals or purging a forbidden food eaten in a small quantity. The latest diagnostic criteria (American Psychiatric Association, 2000) specify two types of bulimia, although in practice the occasional overlap of symptoms with those of anorexia makes the distinctions less clear. The diagnostic criteria for bulimia nervosa are as follows:

- Recurrent episodes of binge eating in which an episode is characterized by both of the following:
    —eating, in a discrete period of time (e.g., within any 2-hour period), an amount of food that is definitely larger than most people would eat during a similar period of time and under similar circumstances
    —a sense of lack of control over eating during the episode (e.g., a feeling that one cannot stop eating or control how much one is eating).

Table 9-2

■

Symptoms of Bulimia Nervosa

Psychological

Low self-esteem	Feeling out of control
Depression	Anxiety
Suicidal thoughts/feelings	Feelings of worthlessness
Overconcern with weight and body image	High need for approval

Behavioral

Cyclical bingeing and purging	Preoccupation with food and body image
Bingeing on high-calorie foods (carbohydrates/fats)	Eating in secret
Increasing time spent on bingeing/purging	Hoarding food
	Isolating from friends and family
Abuse of laxatives, diet pills, diuretics, or exercise	Abusing alcohol or drugs
Poor impulse control	Restroom visits after meals

Physical

Normal weight	Occasional burst blood vessel in the eye
Dehydration	
Irritability and fatigue	Tooth decay/gum disease
Chronic sore throat	Chronic illness
Esophageal erosion	Swollen neck glands
Gastrointestinal problems	Cardiac irregularities
Electrolyte imbalance	

- Recurrent inappropriate compensatory behavior to prevent weight gain, such as self-induced vomiting; misuse of laxatives, diuretics, enemas, or other medications; fasting; or excessive exercise.
- The binge eating and inappropriate compensatory behavior both occur, on average, at least twice a week for 3 months.
- Self-evaluation is unduly influenced by body shape and weight.
- The disturbance does not occur exclusively during episodes of anorexia nervosa.

Table 9-3

■

Distinguishing Features Between Anorexia Nervosa and Bulimia Nervosa

Anorexia	*Bulimia*
Great weight loss	Minor weight fluctuations
More introverted	More extroverted
Pride in weight and food control	Shame in bulimic behavior
Less sexually active	More sexually active
Feels in control with food	Feels out of control with food
Emaciation itself is the goal	Happiness (as a result of thinness) is the goal

Further, the *DSM–IV–TR* specifies two types of bulimia nervosa:

- *Purging type:* During the current episode of bulimia nervosa, the person has regularly engaged in self-induced vomiting or the misuse of laxatives, diuretics, or enemas.
- *Nonpurging type:* During the current episode of bulimia nervosa, the person has used other inappropriate compensatory behaviors, such as fasting or excessive exercise, but has not regularly engaged in self-induced vomiting or the misuse of laxatives, diuretics, or enemas.

Perhaps the first identifiable symptom of bulimia is an occasional binge eating episode. The episode may be in response to feeling a need to nurture oneself with food or to indulge oneself following a period of dieting or restricted food intake. The reinforcement of the binge (feeling soothed, reducing anxiety) leads to repeated binges. The fear of weight gain is often the impetus for later purging behavior, but the relief the purge provides can also be an accidental discovery (as when spontaneous vomiting following a large meal affords physical relief). As with other addictive behaviors, the cycle escalates from an occasional episode to a daily habit.

Binges most commonly occur in the late afternoon or late evening, often after a day of food restriction, but they may begin in the early morning. It is not unusual for bingeing to occur on a daily basis and for normal meals during the day to be vomited as well. Binges are frequently planned, and time alone must be negotiated. Social activities become limited as activities are scheduled with bingeing and purging episodes in mind.

The woman with bulimia may withdraw most noticeably from meals where she will be observed and will become very anxious if prevented from purging (either by interruption or situational factors). Mood swings are common. As the disorder progresses, the bulimic's body image becomes more distorted, and her sense of being out of control is less tolerable. As she exerts more effort into "controlling" her food intake, she increases her sense of deprivation and sets the scenario for future binges. She may steal food from roommates or shoplift in grocery stores when the food requirements for the binges are not readily available. Each day presents a new opportunity to "be good," which translates into significant restricting. Her hunger becomes overwhelming throughout the day, setting in motion an evening binge episode. Guilt about bingeing inevitably leads to another purge. Increasingly, the binge/purge cycle becomes a means of managing all painful emotions, and her awareness of her feelings becomes muted. While her weight will likely remain stable, fluctuating within 5 pounds, she will begin to look less physically well. Her face and neck may appear swollen, and she may develop a burst blood vessel in the eye from the force of vomiting. She may find additional means of purging, including laxative abuse, excessive exercise, or diuretics. The woman with bulimia is susceptible to depression and typically has low self-esteem and poor impulse control. She may abuse drugs or alcohol in the way that she abuses food. Her body image is invariably distorted, and she is highly self-critical. She may become sexually impulsive as a result of being unable to set limits, abusing alcohol, or in hopes of seeking male approval. Like the woman with anorexia, she may define herself as a "people pleaser" and be fearful of confrontation, conflict, or anger. Frequently she will identify feeling lonely, despite the fact that her isolation is often self-imposed.

There is no consensus on the etiology of bulimia, and it appears that there may be many avenues to onset. Some women develop bulimic symptoms following a diet. Childhood obesity and parental obsessions with weight have been identified as risk factors for the development of bulimia (Grilo, 2002). A developmental transition or move may trigger bulimic behavior or intensify existing symptoms (as in the transition to high school or a move away to college; Smolak & Levine, 1996). Losses (such as deaths, parental separations) are particularly painful and difficult for the woman with bulimia to manage (Schmidt, 2002).

Increasingly, the etiology of bulimia nervosa is being viewed as multidimensional. A risk factor model has been proposed that posits interactions among biological, family, developmental, personality, and sociocultural factors (Johnson, Tobin, & Steinberg, 1989). Investigations of the biological factors in eating disorders have found that eating disorders tend to be more common among biological relatives, and there is an increased concordance in monozygotic twins than in dizyotic twins (Bulik, 2002). Another biological factor is the correlation between bulimia and affective disorders, particularly depression. The affective instability typically appears prior to the onset of bulimia and suggests a biological vulnerability to bulimic symptoms. Although the disorder may begin with restrictive dieting, the biological urge for food preempts a binge episode. A binge eating episode is followed by guilt and disgust over the binge, which leads to purging. The purging itself serves to reduce tension and guilt (Beaumont, 2002). This cycle is maintained by the physical need for food and the soothing emotional benefits of the binge (Lacey, Coker, & Birtchnell, 1986). Research has supported the position of family theorists that eating disorders are a response or adaptation to coping with a dysfunctional family (Vandereycken, 2002). The family factors that tend to be related to bulimia include a family environment that is chaotic, conflicted, and neglectful, resulting in children who feel insecure, anxious, and disorganized. The inability of the woman with bulimia to identify internal states is seen as a developmental deficit resulting from the parent's inability to respond to the child in a manner that allows the child to internalize her own awareness. Contributing personality factors are low self-esteem, feelings of ineffectiveness, sensitivity to rejection, and compliance with others. These women have persistent shame and guilt about not meeting their idealized goals. Sociocultural factors include the changing gender roles in the dominant culture, the increased pressure for thinness, and the use of the pursuit of thinness as a means of adaptation and social acceptability.

Binge Eating Disorder

Binge eating disorder is a more recently recognized eating disorder that afflicts between 1% and 10% of the general population depending on the source of the data (Grilo, 2002; Hoek & van Hoeken, 2003). Currently, binge eating disorder falls under the diagnostic criteria of eating disorder not otherwise specified (ED NOS) but has been proposed as a disorder of its own (American Psychiatric Association, 2000). Binge eating disorder is characterized by binge eating (eating a large amount of food in a short period of time) without compensatory behavior and feeling out of control during the binge episode. The disorder may develop in the absence of a history with anorexia or bulimia or may result when the purging aspects of bulimia have been discontinued. Recent evidence suggests, however, that binge eating disorder has a separate course and rarely evolves from bulimic behaviors (Fairburn et al., 2000). The disorder is somewhat more common among women (ratio of 3:2) and is equally common among White and African American women. The modal age of onset is 18, but many experience some episodes of overeating behavior at earlier ages.

The diagnostic category of ED NOS also includes other types of eating pathology that do not meet criteria for anorexia and bulimia. The following are examples of ED NOS:

- For females, all of the criteria for anorexia nervosa are met except that the individual has regular menses.
- All of the criteria for anorexia nervosa are met except that, despite significant weight loss, the individual's current weight is in the normal range.
- All of the criteria for bulimia nervosa are met except that the binge eating and inappropriate compensatory mechanisms occur at a frequency of less than twice a week or for a duration of less than 3 months.
- The regular use of inappropriate compensatory behavior by an individual of normal body weight after eating small amounts of food (e.g., self-induced vomiting after the consumption of two cookies).
- Repeatedly chewing and spitting out, but not swallowing, large amounts of food.
- Binge eating disorder: recurrent episodes of binge eating in the absence of the regular use of inappropriate compensatory behaviors characteristic of bulimia nervosa.

The proposed criteria for binge eating disorder (American Psychiatric Association, 2000) include the following:

- Recurrent episodes of binge eating in which an episode is characterized by both of the following:
  —eating, in a discrete period of time (e.g., within any 2-hour period), an amount of food that is definitely larger than most people would eat in a similar period of time under similar circumstances.
  —a sense of lack of control over eating during the episode (e.g., a feeling that one cannot stop eating or control what or how much one is eating)
- The binge eating episodes are associated with three (or more) of the following:
  —eating much more rapidly than usual,
  —eating until feeling uncomfortably full,
  —eating large amounts of food when not feeling physically hungry,
  —eating alone because of being embarrassed by how much one is eating,
  —feeling disgusted with oneself, depressed, or very guilty after overeating.
- Marked distress regarding binge eating is present.
- The binge eating occurs, on average, at least 2 days a week for 6 months.
- The binge eating is not associated with the regular use of inappropriate compensatory behaviors (e.g., purging, fasting, excessive exercise) and does not occur exclusively during the course of anorexia nervosa or bulimia nervosa.

Although there are many consistencies among those with binge eating disorder, a typical progression is difficult to describe because binge eating disorder develops in more varied ways (see Table 9-4 for a symptom summary). It is common, but not invariable, for the seeds of binge eating to be germinating in childhood and the symptoms to develop slowly throughout adolescence and adulthood. Binge eaters may begin as overweight children who develop an overreliance on food for comfort to assuage hurt feelings or to disconnect from painful events of childhood. They may experience a period of "chubbiness" during which they are teased or are

Table 9-4

■

Symptoms of Binge Eating Disorder

Psychological

Low self-esteem	Feeling out of control
Depression	Preoccupation with food
Anxiety	Shame about bingeing and weight

Behavioral

Frequent, recurrent bingeing	Avoidance of emotional or sexual
Eating alone in private	intimacy
Hoarding food	Social isolation

Physical

Higher than normal weight or obesity	Sexual impairment
High blood pressure	Fatigue
Risk of diabetes	Difficulty with physical activity
Joint strain	Lack of hunger or satiety awareness
Edema of the lower extremities	Renal disease
Coronary disease	Osteoarthritis

made to feel self-conscious about weight. Parental concern may take the form of restricting snacks allowed for other children in the family, criticizing or mocking size or weight, or encouraging them to become more physically active to "slim down." During this time, the children may begin to hoard food without the family's awareness and hide it for later consumption in private. They may be sent to special summer camp programs for overweight children and later refer to it as "fat camp." They may seem undisturbed by the remarks about their weight or robust appetite and may even develop a self-deprecating sense of humor. They may begin to isolate to spare themselves from critical remarks or the harsh judgments of peers. As they enter adolescence, they may become less socially engaged and find greater solace in food rather than take the social risks required of adolescent development. As they become more lonely, they rely on the use of food for managing distressing feelings. Bingeing becomes more frequent, and loss of control is more common. A numbness is experienced during the binge episodes that is almost dissociative. This begins a cycle of bingeing in response to negative affective states, which leads to increased weight, which leads to further guilt and isolation, and to increasingly recurrent binges. Feelings of depression may also escalate simultaneously. Their sense of shame (about their inability to control their eating and increasing weight) is pervasive and hinders the development of interpersonal relationships. Once their binge eating produces considerable weight gain, medical complications may arise, such as hypertension and diabetes.

As with anorexia and bulimia, there is disagreement about the etiology of binge eating disorder. There is some similarity in the etiology of binge eating disorder with that of bulimia. Developmentalists note that the passage through adolescence into adulthood stresses coping skills beyond the person's capacity. This is the time when female sex role socialization promotes an excessive emphasis on appearance and the value of thinness (Striegel-Moore, 1993). The mechanisms operating for men during this time have been less defined, but it is reasonable to assume that the sex role expectations of boys during adolescence are similarly challenging. Biological factors are also implicated in the development of binge eating disorder. While 50%–60% of those with binge eating disorder are estimated to also suffer from a depressive disorder, men with binge eating disorder are also especially prone to anxiety and alcohol abuse (Grilo, 2002). A restraint model posits that binge eating develops in response to a period of dieting, but there is sufficient evidence that this is not always the case. A significant number of binge eaters (22% of late onset to 79% of early onset) develop the disorder without a history of dietary intake restriction or body dissatisfaction (Binford, Mussell, Peterson, Crow, & Mitchell, 2004). A family-based model suggests that factors in the home influence adolescent and adult eating patterns. Individuals who as children are subjected to "control food rules" (e.g., you can have ice cream if you finish your homework) were found to engage in more binge eating as adults (Puhl & Schwartz, 2003). Other family risk factors include severe childhood obesity, family overeating, inadequate parenting, family discord, and high parental demands (Striegel-Moore, Fairburn, et al., 2005). A conditioning model, based on learning theory, suggests that the comfort derived from food gradually reinforces a pattern of self-soothing that relies on food. An addictions model contends that the processes for binge eating are similar to those of an alcohol or drug addiction, and some treatment programs and self-help groups (Overeaters Anonymous) have been based on the 12-step model of recovery (Westphal & Smith, 1996).

The high rate of comorbidity of binge eating disorder with depression has led to the proposition that binge eating is a variant of affective disorders and that the binge eating serves to regulate negative emotional states. Some contend, however, that the most promising model of binge eating disorders is a biopsychosocial model that takes into account biological vulnerability as well as the cognitive, behavioral, and social determinants of binge eating (Polivy & Herman, 1996). The difficulty with this type of model is that it does not account for the various factors operating at different stages of the disorder. Polivy and Herman (1996) suggested that identifying the phases of the disorder would lend valuable information to the research and treatment of binge eating disorder.

CASE STUDY

Carrie is a 19-year-old female of White/Latina heritage. She is in the second semester of her freshman year at a large university. She originally sought counseling to deal with her increasing sense of depression. During her first session with the psychologist, she presented as bright and cheerful, in contrast to her reported feelings of sadness and hopelessness. She was immaculately groomed, of normal weight, and casually dressed.

As Carrie described her current situation, her pain was evident even as she smiled through the tears she fought to keep from falling. She just didn't understand why she couldn't control herself. She had been bingeing and purging (via vomiting) since her junior year of high school and was feeling increasing shame and powerlessness. Although there had been periods when she binged and purged less often (such as during the football season when she was busy with cheerleading and had less time alone), the transition to college escalated the pattern from occasionally to daily. She was also now taking laxatives several times a week and would go for an entire day without eating to "pay" for having binged the day before. Her hunger would eventually lead to another late-night binge, which she would vomit, and the cycle would begin again. However, even these efforts in conjunction with 2 hours of daily aerobic exercise did little to conquer her intense fear that she would gain an enormous amount of weight.

Carrie had begun by self-inducing vomiting when she had overeaten or had been drinking alcohol. She had been an unpopular child, and once she had made the cheerleading squad in high school she feared that she would gain weight and lose her newfound social status. She lived in terror that she would be discovered to be as inadequate as she felt.

She stated that her parents were "perfect," that her mother was her "best friend," and that her younger sister was the "baby" of the family. Mom was a perfectionist who was hardworking and demanded the same from her oldest daughter. Dad worked long hours and was not as involved with the family. Carrie did not mention until a later session that her mother was generally quite critical, especially of Carrie's appearance, dieted chronically, and had very high expectations. Dad was later reported to drink frequently on the occasions when he was home with the family and had paid little attention to Carrie since she entered junior high school.

During the first session Carrie described the painful pattern of her daily life:

Carrie: I just can't seem to control anything. It feels like this is never going to end.

Dr. W: That sounds pretty hopeless.

Carrie: It is hopeless. I've been depressed since I first got to college. At first I thought it was just homesickness, but everything seems to be falling apart. I can barely get out bed, except to eat, and I can't have another semester with the grades as bad as last semester. Everything seems dark, like there's no escape.

Dr. W: Can you tell me what feels so overwhelming?

Carrie: Every day feels overwhelming. It starts out with my planning not to eat at all. As long as I don't eat, I feel okay and pretty happy. If I could just control myself I know I could be happy. But once I start eating I know it's all over.

Dr. W: All over?

Carrie: Yeah, I'll start to eat and I won't be able to stop. When I finally realize how much I've eaten it's too late and my stomach is huge and I have to get rid of it.

Dr. W: It sounds like you aren't aware of your behavior when you're in the middle of a binge.

Carrie: I'm not. It's like I just go numb. Then I feel horrible at what I've done and I get sick.

Dr. W: Does that mean that you intentionally vomit?

Carrie: I don't call it that but that's the only way I will truly feel better. If I can get rid of it, then maybe I'm not so bad and maybe I don't have to feel too guilty.

Dr. W: It doesn't feel like you deserve to eat?

Carrie: Not when I can't control myself. And I usually end up eating bad food anyway.

Dr. W: Bad food?

Carrie: You know, crackers and cookies and ice cream and bread and pizza.

Dr. W: And how are those bad?

Carrie: Do you know the calories and carbs in that stuff? I don't allow myself to eat that kind of food. If I can just make it through the day without eating, everything will be okay. But even when I make it through the day, I can never seem to have the willpower at night. That's the most dangerous time.

Dr. W: So, the food you don't feel you deserve is the food you end up craving. Can you tell me what happens right before you binge?

Carrie: Nothing happens. I just start eating and don't stop.

Dr. W: Are you aware of the circumstances or what you are feeling?

Carrie: Just stressed out.

Dr. W: What does "stressed out" mean to you?

Carrie: I've never thought about it, but I guess I'm nervous a lot. And I'm scared and lonely, which I feel all the time, but mostly at night.

Dr. W: And what makes you frightened?

Carrie: I'm afraid I'll get fat.

Dr. W: What else?

Carrie: I'm afraid that I won't make it at college, that I will lose my friends, that I'll never be good enough.

Dr. W: Good enough for what?

Carrie: Good enough to make everyone happy, good enough to succeed.

Dr. W: Tell me about when you get angry?

Carrie: I never get angry, but I cry a lot.

Dr. W: You never get angry? I wonder if maybe you know when you're scared, or sad, or hurt but not when you're angry?

Carrie: No, I just don't get angry.

Dr. W: You don't let yourself get angry?

Carrie: No. Except at myself when I eat a bunch of bad stuff. I get mad when I don't do what I should.

Dr. W: When would that be?

Carrie: Like when I don't study enough, or call my mom enough, or work out enough, or when I eat too much.

Dr. W: Sounds like you're pretty hard on yourself and your expectations are pretty high. I wonder if anyone could expect to live up those expectations? It doesn't seem like you give yourself much room to make mistakes or have any emotions.

Carrie: I'm supposed to be better than that. I shouldn't get angry at anyone and I shouldn't have to make mistakes. I shouldn't have to eat.

APPROACHES TO PREVENTION

Prevention in the area of eating disorders has recently come under greater scrutiny. Primary prevention has been aimed at preventing the development of eating disorders in unafflicted individuals. The goal of secondary prevention has been to detect early warning signs of eating disorders and encourage treatment for those in the early stages of the disorders. The effectiveness of prevention efforts has recently been called into question, however. Although many school and college programs are designed and administered in an attempt to prevent disturbed eating and the associated psychological problems, there is some evidence that such programs are ineffective or detrimental (Stice & Shaw, 2004). Research has suggested that psychoeducational interventions intended to reduce the risk and incidence of eating pathology may in fact increase the likelihood that a participant will develop disturbed eating symptomatology (Carter, Stewart, Dunn, & Fairburn, 1997). It has been further considered that using the same psychoeducational strategy to accomplish both primary and secondary prevention goals may be ill advised. Mann et al. (1997) contended that primary prevention efforts that stress the severity of the disorders and secondary prevention programs that tend to normalize the disorders to encourage those in need to seek help have conflicted goals. Their study of the effects of prevention programs on female college freshmen revealed that the participants had more symptoms of eating disorders at follow-up than did the control group. Prevention interventions may have an unintentional effect of reducing the stigma and normalizing eating disorders, thereby increasing the likelihood that individuals will engage in such behaviors. Mann et al. recommended that prevention programs may be more effective if they do not attempt to address both primary and secondary prevention goals simultaneously. Cohn and Maine (1998) challenged the conclusions drawn in these studies. They suggested that the methodology of these studies in assessing the effectiveness of prevention programs was faulty and that prevention must be viewed as a developmental process rather than a single effort.

Although abandoning prevention programs based on limited data would not be prudent, more investigation of the impact of prevention programs is necessary. Many studies do indicate that prevention programs can be beneficial. One earlier prevention study with 11- and 12-year-old girls concluded that prevention programs will be most effective with high-risk groups rather than the general population (Killen, 1996). A study of self-selected college women reported positive outcomes from an 8-week prevention program (Franko, 1998). Although eating patterns were not altered as a result, body image concerns and the importance of appearance were reduced. Another small study (60 at-risk, college-age women) did find a reduction in eating pathology and increased self-esteem in response to a prevention program emphasizing cognitive restructuring of negative thoughts related to weight and shape (Zabinski, Wilfley, Calfas, Winzelberg, & Taylor, 2004). One extensive prevention program with college students utilized a longer term intervention (28 classes) and combined psychoeducation of anorexia, bulimia, and obesity (Stice, Orjada, & Tristan, 2006). These researchers found a reduction in eating disorder symptoms, dieting, thin-ideal internalization, and body dissatisfaction. Perhaps most striking was that the results were more robust at the 6-month follow-up than immediately following the intervention.

Some authors have recommended ongoing prevention programs that emphasize health promotion along with opportunities for girls and women to develop attributes beyond attractiveness (Huon, 1996) and the introduction of feminist processes to fully validate the female experience (Piran, 1996). Others have suggested that teaching girls and women to be media literate and educated consumers of the media images that permeate our culture will allow them to evaluate the media more critically (Berel & Irving, 1998). This may be especially important for those with some eating disorder symptomatology given the finding that those with disordered eating are more significantly influenced by the body ideals presented in the media (Stice et al., 2001).

Stice and Ragan (2002) investigated a promising model of prevention strategy based on dissonance theory. Dissonance theory contends that attitudes and behaviors change when individuals adopt a position contrary to their current behaviors, creating cognitive dissonance. Attitudes and behaviors change to resolve the internal conflict between these two sets of beliefs. These researchers designed a program in which at-risk female college students were asked to critique the societal standard of the thin ideal and develop a program for helping younger girls avoid internalizing such an ideal. The three-session experiment resulted in reduced thin-ideal internalization, body dissatisfaction, dieting, negative affect, and bulimic symptoms at both termination of the study and at 4-week follow-up. Given that many prevention programs have struggled to demonstrate effectiveness, this line of research is encouraging. The most notable result is the reduction in bulimic symptoms reported by the participants, because this dimension of eating disturbance had not been shown to be affected by other prevention programs. Others have replicated this model and found a reduction of eating disorder risk factors even with an abbreviated program (Roehrig, Thompson, Brannack, & van den Berg, 2006). Given the health risk of eating disorders and their complex etiology, prevention alone cannot extinguish eating disorders. However, innovative programs such as this may improve the effectiveness of eating disorder prevention in the future. It may be that, as Huon (1996) noted, prevention efforts will require ongoing intervention over a longer period of time to achieve lasting change. It is clear that changing the cultural expectations of our youth and arming them with body and media literacy is an ongoing task.

Individual

Approaches to prevention at the individual level are typically identified as educational programming, especially among groups of high-risk individuals, and early detection of symptoms. In the case of Carrie, high-risk factors were prominent. Her low self-esteem was not ameliorated by her acceptance to a popular peer group and her cheerleading status (a high-risk group in itself). In addition, her family situation compounded her low self-esteem and depression. Never feeling adequate by her mother's standards, feeling fearful of disappointing others, and feeling alienated from her father left her feeling no sense of safety or acceptance, making her acceptance within her peer group that much more salient.

Prevention programs aimed at high-risk groups might have helped Carrie to identify her problems earlier. One important task might be to assist young, developing women in maintaining self-esteem through adolescence when their sense of self-esteem is most tenuous. One program aimed at junior high school girls (Friedman, 1998) reported some success in helping girls to cope with the demands of adolescence and maturation, including respecting their bodies' development and challenging the societal pressure for women's appearance. As has been noted by Huon (1996), girls need opportunities to develop and demonstrate their own sense of power and competence. In addition to programming, secondary prevention efforts at the individual level also require that friends and family members take an active role in identifying the warning signs and confronting the behavior of the person in jeopardy.

Family

The role of the family in the prevention of eating disorders is rarely discussed. Although the stereotypical dysfunctional characteristics of the family with an eating disordered member have been identified, intervention at the family level is more common than prevention. The family can, however, be significant in deterring the development of these disorders.

Avoiding the dysfunctional dynamics that contribute to eating pathology would be prudent for family members. Family environments in which eating disorders flourish tend to be overcontrolling, emotionally neglectful, and conflictual, but members typically do not express their feelings. Families should be encouraged to keep communication open, including discussing unpleasant feelings like anger and disappointment. Further, parents should be instructed to nurture developmental maturation and separation, as is appropriate throughout the adolescent years. With each year, the child is learning to take on new levels of independence and responsibility. This task is impeded when the parents are critical, are doubtful, or foster dependence, refusing to allow the child the freedom to grow and individuate. The goal of alleviating the entrenched battles over food within the family allows the family to address the emotional needs of all family members so that healthy functioning is restored.

The family can also model an acceptance of making mistakes. This includes a tolerance of human mistakes made by others, the parents, and the children. Tolerance is also warranted with regard to appearance. Families who place a strong emphasis on appearance (how each member looks) and on appearances (how they are judged by others) tend to imbue these values in their children. It is the lack of tolerance with imperfection that characterizes the unrealistically high self-standards and shame of the eating disordered adolescent. Removing the value of appearance from the family environment would also require a reduced emphasis on food and weight. Girls have demonstrated greater weight concerns when they perceive family and friends to have weight concerns, and the effect is more significant for White girls than African American girls (S. H. Thompson et al., 2003). Even learning to manage such concerns by family activity or exercise would be an improvement over the diet-obsessed family.

Some authors have recommended that parents can play a key role in the prevention of eating disorders (e.g., Graber & Brooks-Gunn, 1996). They recommend that parents be educated about the normal progression of puberty, the importance of staying involved in the meal practices of adolescents, and the negative impact of parental comments about appearance. They emphasize the need to actively address the changing relationship between parent and child throughout adolescence.

Secondary prevention can take the form of early symptom identification. Because pathological eating is so common (Betz & Fitzgerald, 1993) and eating disorders are difficult to understand, many families do not acknowledge the problem until the illness is in the advanced stages. In their study of 14 European exchange students diagnosed with eating disorders while in the United States, Van den Broucke and Vandereycken (1986) noted that most of the students had evidence of disturbed eating or weight preoccupation prior to their departure from home. These disturbances were ignored by the parents and were not identified in the medical examination required before leaving home. These authors recommended becoming aware of the more obvious risk factors and early detection of preliminary symptoms by family members and professionals (doctors, school nurses, and teachers).

Carrie's family would have been most helpful had they identified the dysfunctional family patterns that allowed Carrie's disorder to escalate without acknowledgment. Addressing the family conflicts, critical style, and withdrawal via alcohol would have likely prevented an extended course of her bulimia.

School

High school and junior high personnel are in an important position to assist with the prevention and early detection of eating disorders among adolescents, but it should also be noted that children, particularly girls, are showing evidence of weight preoccupation and disturbed body image at younger ages (S. H. Thompson et al., 2003). It is not unusual to find elementary school age girls demonstrating concern about their weight and dieting. Some prevention programs have targeted this younger audience with some minimal but positive results (Levine, Smolak, & Schermer, 1996), and Thompson et al. emphasized the importance of earlier prevention efforts. It is unknown if the effects of such programs could be enduring enough to buffer the challenges of adolescence.

With regard to secondary prevention, Omizo and Omizo (1992) suggested that a school counselor should be aware of the risk factors and be watchful of those in high-risk groups such as cheerleaders, drill team members, wrestlers, track team members, gymnasts, and those in the performing arts. In addition to the emphasis on weight and appearance, these are highly competitive environments made more stressful by perfectionistic tendencies and the potential for failure. The first responsibility of the school counselor is recognition of the symptoms of anorexia, bulimia, and compulsive overeating. The counselor should be aware that some students will not admit eating problems or acknowledge their behavior as a problem. Much of the therapeutic work with eating disordered clients is developing enough trust in the relationship that the clients' defenses can recede and they can acknowledge their difficulties. Without the student's willingness to participate, treatment is likely to be ineffective.

Although some school counselors may be trained to work with eating disordered clients, a decision to undertake treatment in a high school setting should be made with caution. Despite the ethical consideration of counseling minors, especially those with serious disorders, the treatment is likely to be more involved than an overextended school counselor could manage.

Because of the setting and frequent contact with groups at high risk for eating disorders, school counselors might more effectively aim their energies toward education and prevention programs. Some programs that have incorporated eating disorder education and evaluation into the school curriculum have been successful in prevention and early detection efforts (Moriarty, Shore, & Maxim, 1990). Given the recent research challenging prevention programming, however, the impact of such programs may be most significant among at-risk groups because most adolescents will not develop an eating disorder. Another recommendation is to incorporate prevention efforts in other curricula rather than see prevention as a single-session event. Research has also indicated that eating disorder behaviors may develop in response to a crisis (Troop & Treasure, 1997). The researchers indicate that anorexic symptoms seem to be related to cognitive avoidance following a crisis, whereas bulimic symptoms seem to be related to cognitive rumination about the event or situation. In both groups, women who felt helpless were more likely than others to develop an eating disorder. The authors recommended that primary and relapse prevention of eating disorders focus on facilitating the development of coping skills. Such programs might have helped Carrie more quickly identify her dilemma, improve her coping strategies, and recognize that help was available.

Many schools have taken additional steps to curb the rise of disturbed eating and obesity (Henderson & Brownell, 2004). Some schools have reduced the availability of soft drinks, fast foods, and less healthy snacks. Others have reduced the amount of food advertising in the schools. These strategies have been challenging for the schools involved because of the revenue generated from these products. Other schools have made more healthy meals available and more appealing to student. These authors promote a strong policy to produce healthier environments at the school level.

Community

At present, community prevention has occurred primarily through the media by publicizing famous cases of anorexia. Perhaps because anorexia is considered more glamorous than bulimia or binge eating, less public attention has been given to the latter two. Primarily female actors, fashion models, and athletes who have struggled with anorexia have been highlighted through news programs and magazine articles. Talk shows have aired episodes in which less-famous eating disordered individuals are interviewed. Television movies have portrayed the consequences of the progression of eating disorders. We have yet to see public service announcements that warn of the dangers of extreme dieting. Given the heavy investment in thinness as the social ideal and the enormous profits generated by the diet industry, community service warnings against dieting are not likely to emerge soon.

The most important community intervention would be to address the larger societal issues. The strong influence of the media on the development and maintenance of eating disorders has led most authors to suggest that a change in the societal norms is necessary (Cohn & Maine, 1998; Levine & Harrison, 2004; Ussery & Prentice-Dunn, 1992). Without a reduced emphasis on the value of thinness within the society, prevention efforts will remain primarily early-detection devices. The task of shifting societal standards, although seemingly monumental, is central to the prevention effort at the community level. It is less likely that Carrie would have developed an eating disorder as a means of managing her distress had the emphasis on women's appearance not been so prominent in our culture. One organization in particular, the National Eating Disorder Association, has as its central mission to educate the public about the dangers of dieting and eating disorders and to promote media literacy.

INTERVENTION STRATEGIES

Given the enormity of the challenge in preventing eating disorders, the majority of theorizing and research has been in the area of intervention and treatment of eating disorders.

Individual

Individual interventions vary depending on the theoretical approach used in conceptualization. Psychoanalytic, cognitive–behavioral, developmental, and feminist counselors may approach the treatment of eating disorders in different ways; however, there are some central unifying principles. Regardless of counseling orientation, an initial consideration is the medical stability of the client. Consultation with a physician is essential during the assessment phase. The medical complications arising from anorexia, bulimia, and binge eating are dangerous, thus it is imperative to monitor the client's physical condition.

A medical evaluation of blood pressure, heart rate, and body temperature will help determine the extent of the client's physical danger. Further laboratory tests are necessary to evaluate vulnerable physical conditions, including electrolyte levels, estrogen and cholesterol levels, liver and thyroid functioning, and cardiac functioning. Continued monitoring by a physician is appropriate when the medical condition of the client warrants close observation, but a medical evaluation should be a component of treatment with all eating disordered clients as a precaution.

A second consideration is the need for nutritional restabilization. Without adequate nutrition, counseling will be less effective because of the cognitive and affective disturbances that result from starvation and/or bingeing. For those with anorexia or bulimia, the quality of the nutritional state is highly compromised as a result of the eating pathology. For the anorexic, the nutritional goal is a restoration of body weight. For the bulimic, the goal is a restabilization of the nutritional process. For the binge eater, the goal is regulation of the caloric intake. Consultation with a nutritionist skilled at nutritional restoration among an eating disordered population is a useful adjunct to treatment, but such interventions must be done skillfully, as the client may be fearful of these interventions, possibly resulting in an escalation of eating disordered behavior. Therefore, except in the most severe cases in which weight stabilization is urgent, delaying the introduction of nutritional counseling may improve the client's acceptance of the intervention.

Counseling Approaches

Once a therapeutic relationship is built through support and trust, individual counseling will proceed on the basis of the therapeutic orientation. Cognitive–behavioral treatment protocols and interpersonal therapy have been the most frequently identified effective treatments of eating disorders (Agras et al., 2000; Loeb et al., 2005; Wilson, Fairburn, & Agras, 1997). It is interesting that the extent of adherence to a manualized treatment (often used in research protocols) has not been found to have a significant impact on therapeutic outcome (Loeb et al., 2005), although gains from interpersonal therapy may take longer to achieve (Von Ranson & Robinson, 2006). Unfortunately, some therapeutic approaches are less amenable to research and have not been experimentally tested. An eclectic approach may be most suited to the multidimensional nature of eating disorders. Treatment should address the behavioral, cognitive, affective, and interpersonal disturbances as they apply to each client. Initial steps in counseling may include helping the client manage affect in more appropriate ways and introducing alternative coping mechanisms that can instill hope that change is possible. Learning alternative means of expressing emotions and self-soothing can interrupt the dysfunctional behavioral patterns. By increasing the client's awareness of the distinction between physiological and emotional states, the client becomes more adept at managing denied feelings. Expressing affect, becoming more self-directed and autonomous, and tolerating ambiguity are reasonable goals for counseling. Behavioral strategies can give the client a sense of structure by introducing small behavioral changes gradually. Cognitive interventions are intended to challenge the distorted thought processes that have served to maintain and support the disordered eating. Challenging the irrational beliefs inherent in eating disorder pathology can address issues of body image and self-esteem. Progress in these areas may lead to the exploration of interpersonal and intrapersonal conflicts that plague clients with eating disorders. A necessary treatment goal is "helping individuals develop a more internalized sense of self-worth independent of the eating disorder" (Pike & Wilfley, 1996, p. 381).

When feasible, family counseling can be a powerful component of treatment for the adolescent or young adult client with anorexia or bulimia (Lock & Le Grange, 2005; Pelch, 1999). In addition to addressing the distress created in the family by the eating disorder, family counseling can intervene in any dysfunctional interpersonal relationships. Common issues in these families are enmeshment, overprotection, hostility, and rigidity (Vandereycken, 2002). The goals of family counseling might include expression of feelings, resolution of conflict, and fostering autonomy. Families are discouraged from monitoring the client's weight or food intake, however, and tend to be less involved if the client is an independent adult (Pike & Wilfley, 1996). Longer term family therapy has been indicated for clients who have more severe symptoms of eating disorder, especially for those with significant obsessive–compulsive features (Lock, Agras, Bryson, & Kraemer, 2005).

Family therapy has not been frequently described in the treatment of binge eating disorder, perhaps because binge eating disorder is more frequently treated in adulthood. It is more likely that family counseling will address issues in the client's current relationships, such as marital or parenting issues, in addition to attempting to resolve those in the family of origin (Pike & Wilfley, 1996; Rhodes, Gosbee, Madden, & Brown, 2005).

Group counseling has also been used successfully with eating disordered clients, although it has been less frequently recommended for those with anorexia (N. F. Lee & Rush, 1986). The use of group counseling in conjunction with individual counseling or for individuals at a more advanced stage of recovery allows clients to reduce the isolation and shame of their disorders. Groups can be effective venues for the development of interpersonal skills and challenging dysfunctional thoughts and behaviors (Nevonen & Broberg, 2006). Clients with anorexia should be carefully screened for level of rigidity and weight competitiveness prior to admission in a counseling group (Hall, 1985).

Pharmacological treatment, especially for bulimia, has gained favor in recent years (American Psychiatric Association, 2000; Garfinkel & Walsh, 1997). The use of antidepressant medication may have some merit in treating the related depression and obsessive–compulsive symptoms and in reducing the compulsion to binge. A review of the literature suggests that antidepressant medication is most effective when combined with cognitive–behavioral counseling for bulimia (Garfinkel & Walsh, 1997). In the treatment of anorexia, the issue is more complicated. Although medications may assist the client with co-occurring depression, obsessional thinking, and compulsive behaviors, many of these symptoms remit without medication once weight stabilization has occurred. In addition, those with anorexia often do not respond to the medication when they are at a low weight. Antidepressant medication may also be helpful in the treatment of binge eating disorder, treating co-occurring depression and helping to break the cycle between negative mood and bingeing. Although controversial, treatments using a pharmacological component seem to be a reflection of the current trend toward a biological-based etiology.

Inpatient treatment is warranted in severe cases. Especially for clients with anorexia who have lost 25% of their expected body weight, inpatient treatment is considered necessary. Some clients with bulimia, especially those who refuse or are unable to sustain any meals or who have severe depression associated with their disorder, are also recommended for inpatient treatment. Inpatient treatment is less often discussed for binge eating disorder but would follow a protocol similar to that for bulimia. Individuals with eating disorders may also be referred for inpatient treatment if they have not responded to outpatient treatment. Clients may be admitted by the family if they are under legal age or are in imminent medical danger, but involuntary hospitalization is complicated; it is most therapeutically useful if the client voluntarily agrees to inpatient care. A program specifically designed for eating disorder treatment is more effective than a general psychiatric inpatient center.

The structured environment of an inpatient setting often helps to reduce the anxiety of the client with an eating disorder. The treatment protocol will differ, however, depending on the disorder. The focus for the treatment of anorexia is often weight restoration. For the treatment of bulimia, the focus is on a normalization of the eating process. Both of these strategies are used in combination with individual, group, and family therapy during the inpatient stay. Inpatient programs vary in length depending on the individual needs and financial resources of the client and can range from 1 week to several months. Close follow-up and extensive outpatient treatment are necessary for these clients because of the high rate of relapse.

Bibliotherapy or self-help books are becoming increasingly common and have carved a niche in this field. This medium can provide a useful adjunct to counseling or may be an introduction to the treatment process. Many individuals strive to avoid the stigma of psychological disorders and are reluctant to present for treatment. The shame that arises from eating disorders makes individuals in this population particularly likely candidates for self-help literature. There are books available on a variety of topics, including anorexia, bulimia, binge eating, self-esteem, and body image. Many of these books contain testimonials that sufferers find helpful in alleviating their sense of isolation and fears that they are alone in their distress. Many communities also offer self-help groups. A self-help approach may be less appropriate for more severe cases, however (Fairburn & Carter, 1997).

Internet Resources

The rise of the Internet as a source of information, companionship, and therapy has brought the eating disorder community both questions and answers. There are over 27,000 Internet sites pertaining to eating disorders (Shafran, 2002). Many of these provide helpful information to individuals who might otherwise be too ashamed to seek help. However, the information on the Internet can vary in accuracy, and some sites actively promote unhealthy behavior (e.g., pro-anorexia sites). Ensuring the validity of the information is impossible; however, a national association or governmental mental health sites are more likely to provide current and accurate information or referrals.

Treatment information is also available on the Internet, where many treatment programs and therapists now advertise. Therapy is now also conducted on the Internet, although this is a risky endeavor for all involved. The client is less able to validate the therapist's credentials, and the therapist is less able to fully evaluate a client with whom there has been no face-to-face contact.

One of the potentially beneficial aspects of the Internet is the ability for those with eating disorders to gain social support through chat rooms and self-help meetings online. For those unwilling to attend a live support group, these contacts can provide understanding and comfort. Some sites monitor the communications to ensure that unhealthy material is not exchanged, but other sites are less proactive and should be used with caution.

Prognosis

Prognosis of eating disorders has been related to type of disorder and body weight. Bulimia has a more positive prognosis than anorexia, and anorexic clients with lower body weights have the poorest prognosis (Herzog et al., 1993). Clinical observation also indicates that anorexia is the more intractable disorder and requires longer term counseling. Research on binge eating disorder treatment indicates that while the relapse rate is high, approximately one third of those in short-term treatment will remain abstinent at follow-up (Agras, 1996).

Family

Family therapy is considered by some to be among the most effective treatments for eating disorders, especially with adolescents, and at the very least, it should be considered as an adjunct to other treatment modalities (Lock et al., 2005; Pelch, 1999). The families of anorexic clients have been described as overcontrolling and rigid, whereas the families of bulimic clients have been described as conflicted and chaotic. Despite these differences, some universal principles in family counseling for clients with eating disorders have been prescribed.

Common issues to be addressed in family counseling often include strengthening boundaries between parents and children, dealing with family and parental conflict in more healthy ways, and openly dealing with other disorders such as depression or alcoholism of another family member (Schwartz, Barrett, & Saba, 1985). Reducing the family's focus on food, weight, and appearance is often an immediate goal of the process. The family members need to learn healthy expression of emotions to move beyond the past issues (Pelch, 1999). Teaching the family to allow appropriate development of adolescents (which includes allowing less reliance on the parents) is also necessary. Particularly for younger clients, family counseling is considered an important piece of the treatment process.

School

Although few school counselors are trained in the treatment of eating disorders, it may be the school personnel who first identify disturbed eating patterns. School personnel should be aware of the eating disorder symptomatology and be prepared to encourage youths suspected of such disturbances to seek counseling. Resources and referrals that are available to the students seeking treatment should be current.

Some school settings offer support groups for eating disorders, and this is reasonable if the counselor is skilled in group counseling with eating disordered clients and treatment consent can be obtained from parents. An assessment of the extent of the student's disorder is prudent prior to beginning any type of intervention at the school level.

Athletic coaches should be especially vigilant in identifying disturbed eating patterns among students. Given the central role that coaches play in the lives of athletes, coaches must avoid encouraging, even tacitly, unhealthy eating practices. For example, R. A. Thompson and Sherman (1998) admonished those coaches who are aware of and allow dangerous weight-cutting practices by competitive wrestlers. This is emphasized in light of the deaths of three competitive wrestlers who died as a direct result of the common practice of trying to "make weight," which entails efforts to drop their weight rapidly to compete in a lighter weight class (R. A. Thompson & Sherman, 1998).

Community

Community interventions are as yet minimal. Perhaps because of the perceived rarity of these disorders, wide-scale community interventions are not practiced. Another possibility for the lack of community-level intervention is the inherent challenge of the societal standards of beauty and appearance should such interventions be proposed. Changes at the community level would require a concerted effort toward abolishing the value placed on thinness and appearance. J. K. Thompson and Heinberg (1999) called for greater social activism and media responsibility in deglamorizing eating disorders and in challenging the thin ideal. The fervor does not appear to exist to orchestrate such a rebellion, but organizations such as the National Eating Disorder Association have gained momentum in recent years and are having a positive impact on the social conscience of the media.

ADAPTATIONS FOR DIVERSITY

Ethnicity

The cultural norms of the United States have historically been dominated by the values of the White middle class. Although the stereotypical picture of the client with an eating disorder is a young White American adolescent female, the increase over the years of anorexia and bulimia among non-White women must be explored. In addition, binge eating disorder and obesity have been commonly identified among people of color (K. H. Gordon, Parez, & Joiner 2002; Mack et al., 2004; O'Neill, 2003; White & Grilo, 2005).

One important consideration, given the impact of the media on eating disorders, is to what extent White-oriented media affects people of color. This is of particular concern because few non-White women are featured in the media, and those depicted often have physical characteristics that are similar to the White standard of beauty (Osvold & Sodowsky, 1993). Findings from recent research in this area seem to vary on the basis of the ethnic group under investigation. Schooler et al. (2004), for example, found that the viewing of mainstream television had a significant effect on the body image of White women but no effect on the body image of African American women. Schooler et al. pointed to social comparison theory as an explanation for this, stating that African American women may be less likely to compare themselves with White women portrayed by mainstream media because they are so different from them. According to Pinhey and Okinaka (2004), however, viewing of Western media did differentially predict the purging behaviors of a non-Western sample of adolescents from Guam. In this study, the number of hours of Western television watched by participants was significantly related to purging, with males purging more and females purging less with increased viewing. Therefore, for these teens, White-oriented media did seem to be influential, despite the physical differences in the appearance of television characters.

Another important consideration when addressing the eating behaviors of women of color is the impact of changes in socioeconomic status. Because eating disorders have been related to socioeconomic status, the increasing status of non-White populations in the United States may serve to increase their vulnerability to eating disorders (Soh et al., 2006). As discussed by Hsu (1987), as African Americans become more upwardly mobile, they may be more likely to adopt more traditional White middle-class values and the related disorders as well. For example, as African Americans more commonly live biculturally, an internalized devaluing of their own race can occur. This can result in greater acceptance of White standards. This may have been evident in a study of British adolescents, which revealed that Black teens who dressed in non-English ways had lower scores on assessments of bulimia than those who dressed in English ways (Bhugra & Bhui, 2003).

The assumption that eating disorders are culture-bound syndromes has been challenged (R. A. Gordon, 2001). It has been suggested that eating disorders do not develop in response to the introduction of Western values but in response to industrialization and consumerism that change the social and economic structure of a culture. In such an environment, there are increased gender role confusion, emphasis on achievement, and increasingly fragmented family structures, all of which contribute to developmental challenges of adolescents. This change in social struc-ture can be especially challenging for women, whose role tends to endure sweep-ing changes as a society shifts from a traditional economic structure to a consumerism structure.

Although eating disorder behaviors may be increasing among people of color, the typical help-seeking patterns and underutilization of mental health services by people of color may continue to obscure the prevalence of the disorders among these groups (Cachelin & Striegel-Moore, 2006; Striegel-Moore & Smolak, 1996). Such rates may be further obscured by the tendency of clinicians to inadequately assess and refer people of color for eating disorder concerns (Becker, Franko, Speck, & Herzog, 2003; Walcott, Pratt, & Patel, 2003). Although Dolan (1991) had warned against using broad statements about racial groups, cultural considerations here will attempt to highlight the similarities and differences between cultures with respect to eating disorders. Multiple studies have identified strong similarities between ethnic groups with regard to eating behaviors. One study compared eating and psychological pathology between White and minority women and found that there were no differences in eating disorder symptomatology between the two groups (Le Grange, Telch, & Agras, 1997). Unfortunately, little can be gleaned from these find-ings given the considerable within-group differences among the minority group (Striegel-Moore & Smolak, 1996). Findings from one ethnic sample cannot neces-sarily be generalized to another, and non-Whites cannot be adequately investigated as if they were a single group.

Still, other better-defined studies have also found strong similarities between eth-nic groups. Shaw, Ramirez, Trost, Randall, and Stice (2004) found that in a sample of 785 Latino, Asian, African American, and Caucasian participants, there were no differences between ethnic groups among measures of eating disorder behaviors, bulimic modeling, restrained eating, emotionality, or self-esteem. The only differ-ence found was that Caucasians and Asians had significantly smaller thin ideals compared with Latinos or African Americans. Similarly, in a study of 427 African Americans, Latinas, and Caucasians, White and Grilo (2005) found no differences in the binge eating behaviors of these participants. Differences were only found with regard to body image dissatisfaction and dietary restraint. Specifically, Caucasians demonstrated more body image dissatisfaction and dietary restraint than other ethnicities.

O'Neill's (2003) meta-analysis of 18 studies considering differences in preva-lence of eating disorder behavior among African American and Caucasian females also found only minimal differences between these groups. In this study, Caucasian women were found to have slightly higher rates of eating disorders in general, but with only a small effect size. No differences in prevalence of bulimia or binge eat-ing were found. Additionally, a large survey of female subscribers (9,971 women) to *Consumer Reports* found that there were no differences among the White, African American, Hispanic, Native American, and Asian American women with respect to reported binge eating behavior (Le Grange, Stone, & Brownell, 1998). Black women were reported to purge more than the other groups, and Asian American women more frequently endorsed exercise as weight control. This sample was identified as being above the median U.S. income level, which likely skewed the results, but may suggest that socioeconomic status level remains an important variable.

Other studies indicate greater differences in the eating pathology of groups of ethnically diverse participants. A study by Bisaga et al. (2005) of 1,445 high school girls found that Hispanic and non-Hispanic White girls had significantly higher levels of eating disorder symptoms than African American and Caribbean girls. Correlates were also found between early dieting and eating disorder symptoms among Caucasian, Caribbean, and mixed-decent girls. In addition, a second study of African American and White female college athletes found that White female athletes had more disturbed eating behaviors, lower self-esteem, higher drives for thinness, and more body dissatisfaction than African American female athletes.

A clear difficulty in interpreting the eating disorder research with ethnic minorities is that the variety of measures and samples make drawing firm conclusions a challenge. However, there has been some consistency with regard to body image and thin ideals. Multiple studies have indicated that White and Asian women have higher body dissatisfaction and smaller thin ideals compared with African American or Latino women (Aruguete, DeBord, Yates, & Edman, 2005; Gluck & Geliebter, 2002; Mack et al., 2004; Shaw et al., 2004; White & Grilo, 2005). A large study of 36,320 boys and girls Grades 7–12 found results both consistent and inconsistent with other literature (Story, French, Resnick, & Blum, 1995). For both boys and girls, higher socioeconomic status was related to greater weight satisfaction and fewer unhealthy weight control practices, which defies other findings. Self-reports indicated that compared with White girls, African American girls vomited more often, Hispanic girls used diuretics more frequently, and Asian American girls reported more binge eating. Among this sample, Black and Native American girls had greater body satisfaction.

Another investigation of White, Hispanic, and Asian American sixth- and seventh-grade schoolgirls identified rates of body dissatisfaction among the Asian American group that were higher than those of the White group but not as high as the Hispanic group (Robinson et al., 1996). The authors contended that body dissatisfaction may be more common among the Asian population than has been recognized. Similar results were obtained by Sanders and Heiss (1998), who found that female Asian immigrant college students reported eating attitudes and body dissatisfaction similar to their Caucasian counterparts but reported a greater fear of fat. It is not clear whether this translates to a higher prevalence of eating disorders as well, because other studies have found less body image dissatisfaction among Asian American men and women than in Whites or Hispanics in a sample of 315 college students (e.g., Altabe, 1998). Contradictory evidence may be related to sampling differences. It cannot be assumed that acculturated Asian Americans will be similar to recent Asian immigrants with respect to eating disorder behaviors, and this distinction tends to be overlooked. As argued by Soh et al. (2006), in a recent review of the literature on eating disturbances across cultures, "conclusions on ethnic differences are difficult to make because studies often neglect to consider the role of both acculturation and 'culture clash' on ethnic minorities" (p. 58). It may be that those who struggle with the clash between traditional and adopted cultures are particularly susceptible to eating disturbances because of a struggle to fit in with the dominant culture. In fact, a study by Perez, Voelz, Pettit, and Joiner (2002) found that self-reported bulimic symptoms were positively correlated with acculturative stress and that among women high in acculturative stress, the higher the body dissatisfaction, the more bulimic symptoms.

Another study with a large ethnically diverse sample (17,159 White, Black, Asian American, Native American, and Hispanic adolescent females) found that among all ethnic groups, body dissatisfaction and perceptions of being overweight were correlated with restricting, purging, and binge eating (French et al., 1997). The researchers concluded that overall, the non-White groups have lower prevalence of dieting and weight concerns, but the "ethnic subculture does not appear to protect against the broader sociocultural factors that foster body dissatisfaction among adolescent females" (p. 315). It may be, as these authors suggested, that the discrepancies between studies are due to the within-group cultural differences of the ethnic groups. Such inconsistencies make it challenging to draw conclusions about eating disorders within non-White groups. Pumariega (1997) warned that the protective factors of the native culture of people of color are eroding as adolescents, hungry for acceptance by the mainstream culture, abandon their native values. He recommended continued investigations to address the cultural values, beliefs, and level of acculturation.

Women

African American Women

Historically, African American women have not been at risk for developing anorexia or bulimia because of several protective factors. First, they have typically not identified with White standards of thinness portrayed in the media, instead endorsing a larger body size (Altabe, 1998; Aruguete et al., 2005; Mack et al., 2004; White & Grilo, 2005). Second, they have displayed greater acceptance of their body sizes and less body dissatisfaction (Aruguete et al., 2005; Shaw et al., 2004; Vander Wal, 2004; White & Grilo, 2005).

In considering the disordered eating behaviors and thoughts of African Americans, newer research highlights some important points:

- African American females may no longer be at less risk of developing an eating disorder than Caucasian American females. Some studies indicate lower prevalence rates of eating disorders among African Americans (Croll et al., 2002; Sischo, Taylor, & Yancey Martin, 2006), whereas others find little difference, particularly with binge eating and bulimia (O'Neill, 2003; Shaw et al., 2004; White & Grilo, 2005).
- Better body esteem for African American women may have more to do with a heightened sense of "body ethics" than cultural ideals of beauty, thereby demonstrating greater self-acceptance and rejecting mainstream cultural pressures (Rubin, Fitts, & Becker, 2003).
- African American women may in fact have pressures to attain their own ethnic group's thin ideal, although this ideal is different from the thin ideal of the dominant White culture. This pressure increases the risk of bulimic symptoms and body image dissatisfaction regardless of race.
- Presentation of bulimic behaviors may differ between African American and White women, with African American women demonstrating predominantly bingeing characteristics and White women demonstrating predominantly purging characteristics (Striegel-Moore, Franko, et al., 2005). It should not be assumed that African Americans do not suffer from eating disorders simply because their presentation is somewhat different.

Counselors and researchers are urged to be conscious of the later age occurrence of anorexia and bulimia among African American women. Additionally, as acculturation to the dominant White culture increases, a higher incidence of eating disorder symptoms among African American women is likely.

A greater understanding of the factors believed to be protective against anorexia and bulimia might lend needed information to the prevention efforts for all groups. If messages sent to children in the Black community help these children guard against unrealistic appearance goals, these messages should be incorporated into the rearing of all children. It is unclear, however, if these messages place African American women at greater risk for binge eating disorder.

Latina Women

Although studies of eating disorders among Latina women in the United States are more limited, those available seem to indicate that disordered eating practices are prevalent in this population (Bisaga et al., 2005; Sischo et al., 2006; White & Grilo, 2005). As with Caucasian females, one strong risk factor that seems to predict both bulimic and anorexic symptoms among Latinas is body dissatisfaction (Joiner & Kashubeck, 1996; Perez et al., 2002).

Recent research indicates several specific areas of concern for Latina Americans that need further investigation:

- A relationship between acculturative stress, body dissatisfaction, and bulimic symptoms may exist. Perez et al. (2002) reported that there were more bulimic symptoms among minority women high in acculturative stress and body dissatisfaction. In minority women low in acculturative stress, however, the association between body dissatisfaction is not significant.
- Even among African American and Latina girls in the fourth and fifth grades, body dissatisfaction is observed, with Latina girls having lower body esteems than African Americans (Vander Wal, 2004). This highlights the importance of early intervention with this group.
- Binge eating, in particular, may be a significant problem for Latina females. In a study of 81,247 adolescents, Latina females had the highest rates of binge eating of all ethnic groupings including American Indian, Caucasian, Asian, and African Americans (Croll et al., 2002).
- Latina women may be less likely to seek out and receive appropriate treatment for eating disorders than Caucasian women (Cachelin & Striegel-Moore, 2006). If treatment is sought, Latina women appear to be less likely to receive appropriate assessments and referrals for treatment of eating disorders than Caucasian women (Becker et al., 2003).

Native American Women

Few data are available on the prevalence of eating disorders among Native American women, who are among the least researched ethnic group in the eating disorders literature. The data available, however, suggest a very high risk for eating pathology among this group, indicating need for additional focus in this area (Croll et al., 2002; Snow & Harris, 2002). Initial studies highlight some important concerns for Native Americans:

- An investigation of 81,247 high school students indicated that Hispanic and American Indian youth have more disordered eating behaviors than other racial/ethnic groups and that American Indian females most commonly used fasting, skipping meals, smoking, diet pills, vomiting, and laxatives to control weight (Croll et al., 2002)

- Appearance concerns and alcohol use may be important risk factors for Native American girls, whereas family connectiveness may be a protective factor (Croll et al., 2002).
- Prevalence rates of eating disorders among Native American women may be underestimated and negatively affect Native Americans' ability to get appropriate treatment. At least one study has found that Native Americans are less likely to be appropriately assessed and to receive appropriate referrals for treatment of eating disorders than their Caucasian counterparts (Becker et al., 2003).

It is clear that Native American populations are at high risk for eating disturbances. Further exploration is needed before more concrete conclusions can be drawn about eating disorders among Native Americans.

Asian American Women

Although anorexia is well known in Japan (including a specially named binge episode related to anorexia), few studies of eating disorders among Asian American women have been reported in the literature. Available research offers mixed results. Some indicate no difference in prevalence rates of eating disorder behaviors between Asian Americans and Caucasian Americans (Shaw et al., 2004; Walcott et al., 2003), whereas others indicate higher rates for Asian American (Croll et al., 2002; Story et al., 1995). Bulimia, in particular, may be underreported in this population. When trying to make conclusions about the eating behaviors and thoughts of Asian Americans, some important points should be considered:

- Conflicts in findings of eating pathology among Asian Americans may relate to issues of research methodology. In Gluck and Geliebter's (2002) study of Caucasian, African American, and Asian American females, Asian Americans were found to have significantly lower body mass indices than the other groups. Controlling for body mass index highlighted the eating pathology that had been obscured in Asian American populations (Gluck & Geliebter, 2002).
- Asian Americans may be less likely to exhibit or report eating disorder symptoms and may go to medical doctors rather than mental health professionals for treatment. If symptoms are acknowledged, they are likely to be somatic in nature (e.g., headaches, nausea, loss of appetite), thereby preventing accurate diagnosis (Kempa & Thomas, 2000; Sue & Sue, 1990)
- Within-group differences may also complicate the research findings. Significant differences in acculturation level, ethnic and cultural identity, and body dissatisfaction are likely among Japanese Americans, Chinese Americans, Korean Americans, and other Asian groups. These differences may affect research findings because Asian Americans are often categorized as a single group.
- As a group, Asian Americans tend to have a strong internalization of a thin ideal and tend to be smaller than Caucasian, African American, Native American, and Hispanic Americans (Shaw et al., 2004).
- A large study of disordered eating behaviors of high school students (81,247 students in total) indicated some potential protective and risk factors for eating disorders for Asian American females. A two-parent household and higher self-esteem and emotional well-being were found to be protective factors for Asian American females, and appearance concerns and cigarette use were found to be risk factors (Croll et al., 2002)

Non-Western Women

An increase in anorexia and bulimia has been reported in many countries outside the United States and Western societies, most notably in the Asian countries of Japan, Hong Kong, Taiwan, Singapore, China, and the Philippines. The literature has begun to accumulate evidence suggesting that the risk for eating disorders among non-Western women increases with the level of exposure to White standards.

- The negative impact of the media on bulimic and anorexic behaviors of adolescents from both Korea and Guam has also been demonstrated, suggesting that the media is a strong and rapid transmitter of societal norms (Pinhey & Okinaka, 2004; Roh Ryu & Lyle, 2003).
- A sample of women with anorexia on the island of Curacao revealed that no diagnosed cases were from the majority Black population, but instead all cases were of mixed race, from a higher socioeconomic status, from a higher education sector, and the majority had spent time abroad (Katzman, Hermans, Van Hoeken, & Hoek, 2004).
- *DSM–IV–TR* criteria may not accurately describe eating disorders in non-Western women. Many Asian women with apparent anorexia do not report "fear of fat" among their symptoms. Instead, they attribute their food refusal to stomach bloating or loss of appetite. This phenomenon may be due to (a) denial of their weight concerns, (b) the disorder being instead a form of somaticized depression, or (c) their genetic thinness making them less vulnerable to weight gain concerns. The Asian culture may not support fat phobia as a valid concern, whereas physical symptoms such as stomach bloating may be more culturally accepted (S. Lee & Katzman, 2002).

Recommendations for counseling women of color or nondominant cultures in the United States include having an awareness of the cultural aspect of the disorders. Especially with anorexia, the criteria and interpretation of the disorder may vary with culture. Feminists have charged that viewing eating disorders as an appearance disorder is belittling and minimizes food refusal as a universal means of proclaiming self-control, which may be more apparent in Asian societies.

Males

Although females have been the most affected by eating disorders, the prevalence among males may be underestimated (Anderson, 2002). A recent review of the literature suggests that 10% of individuals with anorexia or bulimia are men and that they account for as much as 25% of those with binge eating disorder (Weltzin et al., 2005). Similar factors that make women vulnerable to anorexia and bulimia operate to make men vulnerable as well:

- Risk factors for men include athletic involvement (especially in sports with a physical appearance orientation such as wrestling or body building), history of obesity, and homosexuality (Russel & Keel, 2002; Weltzin et al., 2005).
- White men tend to report less "drive for thinness" and are more likely to endorse a "drive for fitness" or muscle dysmorphia, which includes preoccupation with appearance, anxiety about body image, hiding one's own body, and compulsive preoccupation with food and exercise (Anderson, 2002; Aruguete et al., 2005; Kashubeck-West, Mintz, & Weigold, 2005; Maida & Armstrong, 2005; Schneider & Agras, 1987; Sischo et al., 2006). A recent review

of the literature suggests a worldwide prevalence of up to 100,000 males suffering from muscle dysmorphia (Leone, Sedory, & Gray, 2005).

- In a large study of the disordered eating patterns of 81,247 adolescents, 55% of females and 30% of males acknowledged symptoms of disordered eating (Croll et al., 2002).
- Like females, males with eating disorders develop hormone irregularities as their testosterone levels drop, and they typically report less sexual interest. These men are at even greater risk than women for osteopenia and osteoporosis and, when compared with women, have lower bone density levels (Anderson, Watson, & Schlechte, 2000).
- Men are less likely to develop anorexia, but those who do tend to have a similar course of the disorder. A recent study by Crisp et al. (2006) indicated that men were significantly more likely to be vegetarian and abuse alcohol and to have family backgrounds involving more frequent severe psychopathology, more parental overprotectiveness, and enmeshment.
- Differences in associations between anger and bulimia also appear in men and women. Bulimic attitudes have been associated with immediate feelings of anger in men but anger suppression in women (Meyer et al., 2005).
- Of all the eating disorders, men are most likely to develop binge eating disorders (American Psychiatric Association, 2000). As much as 25% of those with binge eating disorders are males (Weltzin et al., 2005). Eating disorders among men often go unreported and undiagnosed.

Gay, Lesbian, Bisexual, and Transgender Individuals

Recent research has begun to challenge prior findings that anorexia and bulimia were more common among gay men but less likely among lesbian women. Feminist values and greater appreciation for the female form have been considered to be protective factors for lesbian women, whereas the emphasis on appearance in the gay male subculture has been considered a risk factor. However, the distinctions may be blurring as more lesbian women and heterosexual men express dissatisfaction with their bodies.

- Lesbian women were found to have lower drives for thinness and more focus on weight control when exercising compared with heterosexual women (Moore & Keel, 2003). No differences were found, however, between heterosexual and lesbian women in bulimia, body dissatisfaction, or weight concern.
- As with previous studies, heterosexual girls have been found to be more preoccupied with looking like female media portrayals, more likely to diet, and more likely to be dissatisfied with their bodies than lesbian/bisexual girls. Gay bisexual boys were more likely to binge and were more preoccupied with looking like male media portrayals than heterosexual boys (Austin et al., 2004).
- Gay men have been reported to have eating disorder symptomatology (primarily anorexia and bulimia) at higher rates than are found among heterosexual men (Russel & Keel, 2002; Wichstrom, 2006; Yelland & Tiggeman, 2003).
- Gay men have been found to diet more, be more fearful of becoming fat, be more dissatisfied with their muscularity and bodies, and have more distorted cognitions about the need for ideal body figures compared with straight men (Kaminski, Chapman, Haynes, & Own, 2005). As a group, gay men feel the same pressure that heterosexual women feel to be attractive to males and may

be more conscious of the competition for partners. This explanation is supported by the long tradition among men in general to seek attractive partners.

Affectional Orientation

Very few studies have examined the possible relationships among gender identity disorder, transgender/transsexualism, and eating disorders. Investigations have relied on case studies of one or two individuals, and the data here are preliminary. The emotional distress and body dissatisfaction inherent in gender identity disorder would seem to leave this group more vulnerable to eating disorder behaviors.

- For those with gender identity disorder, anorexia and bulimia may serve as a means of suppressing secondary sex characteristics and sexual identity (Hepp, Milos, & Braun-Scharm, 2004; Winston, Acharya, Chaudhuri, & Fellowes, 2004).
- For male-to-female transsexuals, eating disorders may suppress their libido and allow for more correspondence with female ideals of attractiveness. For female-to-male transsexuals, eating disorders, particularly anorexia, may suppress secondary sexual characteristics such as breasts and menstruation (Hepp & Milos, 2002).

Athletes

Despite anecdotal data, evidence suggests that athletes are not, as a group, at greater risk for developing eating disorders, particularly anorexia and bulimia (Kirk, Singh, & Getz, 2001). In fact, studies have found more eating disorder symptoms in female nonathletes than in female collegiate athletes (Gutgesell, Moreau, & Thompson, 2003; Reinking & Alexander, 2005). Certain sport groups may, however, produce an increased vulnerability for developing eating disorder symptoms:

- Among females, lean sport athletes (e.g., swimming, cross-country) had higher scores on body dissatisfaction than nonlean sport athletes (e.g., basketball, volleyball, field hockey, softball; Reinking & Alexander, 2005).
- Different sports have been found to be more vulnerable to different types of eating pathology. Higher drive for thinness scores were found among participants in swimming, basketball, and gymnastics. Gymnasts and wrestlers had significantly higher purging scores and were more likely to restrict their intake. Cross-country runners had significantly higher bingeing scores than other athletes.
- Leone et al. (2005) warned that men involved in strength-related sports such as football, wrestling, and body building may also be at higher risk for developing muscle dysmorphia because of these sports' strong focus on the body and on obtaining muscle mass.
- White female athletes were found to have lower self-esteem, higher drive for thinness, more body dissatisfaction, and more disturbed eating patterns than African American female athletes, African American male athletes, or White male athletes (Engel et al., 2003).
- Eating disorders in the athletic community can be obscured. The personality traits associated with eating disordered individuals (perfectionism, competitiveness, emphasis on achievement) are common in athletics (Byrne, 2002;

Waldrop, 2005) but less likely to be identified as problematic. Fostered by the athletic culture, these traits can be precursors to eating pathology that goes unrecognized because athletes seem to have a purpose for their efforts (exercise as purging goes unnoticed) and tend to present with higher levels of self-esteem.

- Prevention efforts in athletics have included recommendations that preparticipation physicals screen for the female athletic triad (disturbed eating, amenorrhea, and osteoporosis) as well as symptoms of eating disorders and that athletes, coaches, trainers, and parents be educated about these symptoms in an effort to prevent the onset of eating disorders (Waldrop, 2005). Unfortunately, appearance and performance values are so embedded in the athletic culture that disturbed eating practices are customary.

SUMMARY

A clear conclusion is that eating disorders reflect an interaction of social, interpersonal, intrapersonal, and physical variables. The societal ideal for people, especially women, to be thin and attractive promotes greater pressure for young girls and women with regard to appearance and places them at greater risk for developing anorexia and bulimia. It is during adolescence or young adulthood that these disorders manifest, usually as a means of coping with problems or life transitions. Other risk factors include higher socioeconomic status, participation in some types of athletics, disturbed family dynamics, and low self-esteem. Binge eating disorder is a more recently acknowledged syndrome that threatens to affect more individuals and often results in obesity and the associated health and social risks. Although a small proportion of the population may develop a clinical eating disorder, great numbers of individuals suffer with subclinical symptoms of disturbed eating and dieting patterns.

Treatment may include individual, group, and/or family counseling. A medical evaluation and nutritional counseling are also recommended. In severe cases, inpatient or pharmacological treatment may be warranted. Treating the eating disordered client requires patience and an understanding of the psychological depth of the disorder. Recovery from an eating disorder is often a slow process and the relapse rate is high.

Prevention efforts at the individual, family, school, and community levels should be considered by those involved with adolescents or young adults, especially those youths in high-risk groups. Special attention should be paid to atypical groups such as people of color and men. These groups are least likely to be identified as at risk for an eating disorder and may be neglected in treatment and research of eating disorders.

It is recommended that the power of society and the media not be overlooked. Each individual has the responsibility to challenge the damaging and demeaning messages of our culture. It is equally important to teach our youth to challenge those same messages, whether the messages stem from the media, their peers, their families, or from their own internalized belief systems.

REFERENCES

Agras, W. S. (1996). Short-term psychological treatments for binge eating. In C. G. Fairburn & G. T. Wilson (Eds.), *Binge eating* (pp. 270–286). New York: Guilford Press.

Agras, W. S., Walsh, B. T., Fairburn, C. G., Wilson, G. T., & Kraemer, H. C. (2000). A multicenter comparison of cognitive–behavioral therapy and interpersonal psychotherapy for bulimia nervosa. *Archives of General Psychiatry, 57*, 459–466.

Altabe, M. (1998). Ethnicity and body image: Quantitative and qualitative analysis. *International Journal of Eating Disorders, 23*, 153–159.

American Psychiatric Association. (2000). *Diagnostic and statistical manual of mental disorders* (4th. ed., Text Revision). Washington, DC: Author.

Anderson, A. E. (2002). Eating disorders in males. In C. G. Fairburn & K. D. Brownell (Eds.), *Eating disorders and obesity* (pp. 188–192). New York: Guilford Press.

Anderson, A. E., & DiDomenico, L. (1992). Diet vs. shape content of popular male and female magazines: A dose–response relationship to the incidence of eating disorders? *International Journal of Eating Disorders, 11*, 283–287.

Anderson, A. E., Watson, T., & Schlechte, J. (2000). Osteoporosis and osteopenia in men with eating disorders. *Lancet, 355*, 1967–1968.

Aruguete, M. S., DeBord, K. A., Yates, A., & Edman, J. (2005). Ethnic and gender differences in eating attitudes among Black and White college students. *Eating Behaviors, 6*, 328–336.

Austin, S. B., Ziyadeh, N., Kahn, J. A., Camargo, C. A., Colditz, G., & Field, A. E. (2004). Sexual orientation, weight concerns, and eating disordered behaviors in adolescent girls and boys. *Journal of the American Academy of Child and Adolescent Psychiatry, 43*, 1115–1123.

Baird, A., & Grieve, F. (2006). Exposure of male models in advertisements leads to a decrease in men's body satisfaction. *North American Journal of Psychology, 8*, 115–122.

Beattie, H. J. (1988). Eating disorders and the mother–daughter relationship. *International Journal of Eating Disorders, 7*, 453–460.

Beaumont, P. J. V. (2002). Clinical presentation of anorexia nervosa and bulimia nervosa. In C. G. Fairburn & K. D. Brownell (Eds.), *Eating disorders and obesity* (pp. 162–170). New York: Guilford Press.

Becker, A. E., Franko, D. L., Speck, A., & Herzog, D.B. (2003). Ethnicity and differential access to care for eating disorder symptoms. *International Journal of Eating Disorders, 33*, 205–212.

Berel, S., & Irving, L. M. (1998). Media and disturbed eating: An analysis of media influence and implications for prevention. *Journal of Primary Prevention, 18*, 415–430.

Betz, N. E., & Fitzgerald, L. F. (1993). Individuality and diversity: Theory and research in counseling psychology. *Annual Review of Psychology, 44*, 343–381.

Bhugra, D., & Bhui, K. (2003). Eating disorders in teenagers in East London: A survey. *European Eating Disorder Review, 11*, 46–57.

Binford, R. B., Mussell, M. P., Peterson, C. B., Crow, S. J., & Mitchell, J. E. (2004). Relation of binge eating age of onset to functional aspects of binge eating in binge eating disorder. *International Journal of Eating Disorders, 35*, 286–292.

Bisaga, K., Whitaker, A., Davies, M., Chuang, S., Feldman, J., & Walsh, B. T. (2005). Eating disorder and depressive symptoms in urban high school girls from different ethnic backgrounds. *Journal of Development and Behavioral Pediatrics, 26*, 257–266.

Bissel, K. L., & Zhou, P. (2004). Must see TV or ESPN: Entertainment and sports media exposure and body-image distortion in college women. *Journal of Communication, 54*, 5–21.

Bruch, H. (1973). *Eating disorders.* New York: Basic Books.

Bulik, D. (2002). Eating disorders in adolescents and young adults. *Child and Adolescent Psychiatric Clinics of North America, 11,* 201–218.

Byrne, S. (2002). Sport, occupation, and eating disorders. In C. G. Fairburn & K. D. Brownell (Eds.), *Eating disorders and obesity* (pp. 256–259). New York: Guilford Press.

Cachelin, F. M., & Striegel-Moore, R. H. (2006). Help seeking and barriers to treatment in a community sample of Mexican American and European American women with eating disorders. *International Journal of Eating Disorders, 39,* 154–161.

Carter, J. C., Stewart, A., Dunn, V. J., & Fairburn, C. G. (1997). Primary prevention of eating disorders: Might it do more harm than good? *International Journal of Eating Disorders, 22,* 167–172.

Cohn, L., & Maine, M. (1998). More harm than good. *Eating Disorders, 6,* 93–95.

Connor-Greene, P. A. (1988) Gender differences in body weight perception and weight-loss strategies of college students. *Women and Health, 14,* 27–42.

Coric, C., & Murstein, B. I. (1993). Bulimia nervosa: Prevalence and psychological correlates in a college community. *Eating Disorders, 1,* 39–51.

Crisp, A., Simon, G., Joughin, N., McClelland, L., Rooney, B., Nielson, S., et al. (2006). Anorexia nervosa in males: Similarities and differences to anorexia nervosa in females. *European Eating Disorder Review, 14,* 163–167.

Croll, J., Neumark-Sztainer, D., Story, M., & Ireland, M. (2002). Prevalence and risk and protective factors related to disordered eating behaviors among adolescents: Relationship to gender and ethnicity. *Journal of Adolescent Health, 31,* 166–175.

Dolan, B. (1991). Cross-cultural aspects of anorexia nervosa and bulimia: A review. *International Journal of Eating Disorders, 10,* 67–78.

Engel, S. G., Johnson, C., Powers, P., Crosby, R. D., Wonderlich, S. A., Wittrock, D. A., & Mitchell, J. E. (2003). Predictors of disordered eating in a sample of elite Division I college athletes. *Eating Behaviors, 4,* 333–343.

Fairburn, C. G., & Carter, J. C. (1997). Self-help and guided self-help for binge-eating problems. In D. M. Garner & P. E. Garfinkel (Eds.), *Handbook of treatment for eating disorders* (2nd ed., pp. 494–499). New York: Guilford Press.

Fairburn, C. G., Cooper, Z., Doll, H. A., Norman, P., & O'Connor, M. (2000). The natural course of bulimia nervosa and binge eating disorder in young women. *Archives of General Psychiatry, 57,* 659–665.

Franco, K. S. N., Tamburrino, M. B., Carroll, B. T., & Bernal, G. A. A. (1988). Eating attitudes in college males. *International Journal of Eating Disorders, 7,* 285–288.

Franko, D. L. (1998). Secondary prevention of eating disorders in college women at risk. *Eating Disorders, 6,* 29–40.

French, S. A., Story, M., Neumark-Sztainer, D., Downes, B., Resnick, M., & Blum, R. (1997). Ethnic differences in psychosocial and health behavior correlates of dieting, purging, and binge eating in a population-based sample of adolescent females. *International Journal of Eating Disorders, 22,* 315–322.

Friedman, S. S. (1998). Girls in the 90s: A gender-based model for eating disorder prevention. *Patient Education and Counseling, 33,* 217–224.

Garfinkel, P. E., & Walsh. B. T. (1997). Drug therapies. In D. M. Garner & P. E. Garfinkel (Eds.), *Handbook of treatment for eating disorders* (2nd ed., pp. 372–380). New York: Guilford Press.

Garner, D. M., Garfinkel, P. E., Schwartz, D., & Thompson, M. (1980). Cultural expectations of thinness in women. *Psychological Reports, 47,* 647–656.

Gluck, M. E., & Geliebter, A. (2002). Racial/ethnic differences in body image and eating behaviors. *Eating Behaviors, 2,* 143–151.

Gordon, K. H., Perez, M., & Joiner, T. E. (2002). The impact of racial stereotypes on eating disorder recognition. *International Journal of Eating Disorders, 32*, 219–224.

Gordon, R. A. (2001). Eating disorders East and West: A culture bound syndrome unbound. In M. Nasser, M. A. Katzman, & A. Gordon (Eds.), *Eating disorders and cultures in transition* (pp. 1–16). New York: Taylor & Francis.

Graber, J. A., & Brooks-Gunn, J. (1996). Prevention of eating problems and disorders: Including parents. *Eating Disorders, 4*, 348–363.

Gray, J. J., & Ford, K. (1985). The incidence of bulimia in a college sample. *International Journal of Eating Disorders, 4*, 201–211.

Grieve, F., Newton, C., Kelly, L., Miller, R. C., & Kerr, N. (2005). The preferred male body shapes of college men and women *Individual Differences Research, 3*, 188–192.

Grilo, C. M. (2002). Binge eating disorder. In C. G. Fairburn & K. D. Brownell (Eds.), *Eating disorders and obesity* (pp. 178–182). New York: Guilford Press.

Grilo, C., & Masheb, R. (2005). Correlates of body image dissatisfaction in treatment seeking men and women with binge eating disorders. *International Journal of Eating Disorders, 38*, 162–166.

Gutgesell, M. E., Moreau, K. L., & Thompson, D. (2003). Weight concerns, problem eating behaviors and problem drinking behaviors in female collegiate athletes. *Journal of Athletic Training, 38*, 62–66.

Hall, A. (1985). Group psychotherapy for anorexia nervosa. In D. M. Garner & P. E. Garfinkel (Eds.), *Handbook of psychotherapy for anorexia nervosa and bulimia* (pp. 462–475). New York: Guilford Press.

Henderson, K. E., & Brownell, K. D. (2004). The toxic environment and obesity: Contributions and cure. In J. K. Thompson (Ed.), *Handbook of eating disorders and obesity* (pp. 339–348). New York: Wiley.

Hepp, U., & Milos, G. (2002). Gender identity disorder and eating disorders. *International Journal of Eating Disorders, 32*, 473–478.

Hepp, U., Milos, G., & Braun-Scharm, H. (2004). Gender identity disorder and anorexia nervosa in male monozygotic twins. *International Journal of Eating Disorders, 35*, 239–243.

Herzog, D. B., Sacks, N. R., Keller, M. B., Lavori, P. W., von Ranson, K. B., & Gray, H. M. (1993). Patterns and predictors of recovery in anorexia nervosa and bulimia nervosa. *Journal of the American Academy of Child and Adolescent Psychiatry, 32*, 835–842.

Hill, A. J. (2002). Prevalence and demographics of dieting. In C. G. Fairburn & K. D. Brownell (Eds.), *Eating disorders and obesity* (pp. 80–83). New York: Guilford Press.

Hoek, H., & van Hoeken, D. (2003). Review of the prevalence and incidence of eating disorders. *International Journal of Eating Disorders, 34*, 382–396.

Hsu, L. K. G. (1987). Are eating disorders becoming more common in Blacks? *International Journal of Eating Disorders, 6*, 113–125.

Humphrey, L. L. (1994). Family relationships. In K. A. Halmi (Ed.), *Psychobiology and treatment of anorexia nervosa and bulimia nervosa* (pp. 263–282). Washington DC: American Psychiatric Press.

Huon, G. F. (1996). Health promotion and the prevention of dieting-induced disorders. *Eating Disorders, 4*, 27–32.

Johnson, C. L., Tobin, D. L., & Steinberg, S. L. (1989). Etiological, developmental and treatment considerations for bulimia. In L. C. Whitaker & W. N. Davis (Eds.), *The bulimic college student* (pp. 57–73). New York: Haworth Press.

Joiner, G. W., & Kashubeck, S. (1996). Acculturation, body image, self-esteem, and eating-disorder symptomatology in adolescent Mexican-American women. *Psychology of Women Quarterly, 20*, 419–435

Kalodner, C. R. (1997). Media influences on male and female non-eating disordered college students: A significant issue. *Eating Disorders, 5,* 47–57.

Kaminski, P., Chapman, B., Haynes, S., & Own, L.(2005). Body image, eating behaviors and attitudes towards exercise among gay and straight men. *Eating Behaviors, 6,* 179–187.

Kashubeck-West, S., Mintz, L. B., & Weigold, I. (2005). Separating the effects of gender and weight loss desire on body satisfaction and disordered eating behaviors. *Sex Roles, 53,* 505–518.

Katzman, M. A., Hermans, K. M. E., Van Hoeken, D., & Hoek, H. W. (2004). Not your "typical island women": Anorexia nervosa is reported only in subcultures of Curacao. *Culture, Medicine, and Psychiatry, 28,* 463–492.

Keel, P. K., Heatherton, T. F., Dorer, D. J., Joiner, T. E., & Zalta, A. K. (2005). Point prevalence of bulimia nervosa in 1982, 1992, and 2002. *Psychological Medicine, 25,* 1–9.

Keel, P. K., Heatherton, T. F., Harnden, J. L., & Hornig, C. D. (1997). Mothers, fathers, and daughters: Dieting and disordered eating. *Eating Disorders, 5,* 216–228.

Kempa, M., & Thomas, A. (2002). Culturally sensitive assessment and treatment of eating disorders. *Eating Disorders: The Journal of Treatment and Prevention, 8,* 17–30.

Killen, J. D. (1996). The development and evaluation of a school-based eating disorder symptoms prevention program. In L. Smolak, M. Levine, & R. Striegel-Moore (Eds.), *The developmental psychopathology of eating disorders* (pp. 313–339). Mahwah, NJ: Erlbaum.

Killen, J. D., Taylor, C. B., Hayward, C., Haydel, K. F., Wilson, D. M., Hammer, L., et al. (1996). Weight concerns influence the development of eating disorders: A 4-year prospective study. *Journal of Consulting and Clinical Psychology, 64,* 936–940.

Kirk, G., Singh, K., & Getz, H. (2001). Risk of eating disorders among female college athletes and nonathletes. *Journal of College Counseling, 4,* 122–132.

Klesges, R. C., DeBon, M., & Meyers, A. (1996). Obesity in African American women: Epidemiology, determinants, and treatment issues. In J. K. Thompson (Ed.), *Body image, eating disorders, and obesity* (pp. 461–478). Washington, DC: American Psychological Association.

Lacey, J. H., Coker, S., & Birtchnell, S. A. (1986). Bulimia: Factors associated with its etiology and maintenance. *International Journal of Eating Disorders, 5,* 475–487.

Lee, N. F., & Rush, A. J. (1986). Cognitive–behavioral group therapy for bulimia. *International Journal of Eating Disorders, 5,* 599–615.

Lee, S., & Katzman, M. A. (2002). Cross cultural perspectives on eating disorders. In C. G. Fairburn & K. D. Brownell (Eds.), *Eating disorders and obesity* (pp. 260–264). New York: Guilford Press.

Le Grange, D., Stone, A. A., & Brownell, K. D. (1998). Eating disturbances in White and minority female dieters. *International Journal of Eating Disorders, 24,* 395–403.

Le Grange, D., Telch, C. F., & Agras, W. S. (1997). Eating and general psychopathology in a sample of Caucasian and ethnic minority subjects. *International Journal of Eating Disorders, 21,* 285–293.

Leit, R., Pope, H. G., & Gray, J. J. (2001). Cultural expectations of muscularity in men: The evolution of *Playgirl* centerfolds. *International Journal of Eating Disorders, 29,* 90–93.

Leone, J. E., Sedory, E. J., & Gray, K. A. (2005). Recognition and treatment of muscle dysmorphia and related body image disorders. *Journal of Athletic Training, 40,* 352–359.

Levine, M., Smolak, L., & Schermer, F. (1996). Media analysis and resistance by elementary school children in the primary prevention of eating problems. *Eating Disorders, 4,* 310–322.

Levine, M. P., & Harrison, K. (2004). Media's role in the perpetuation and prevention of negative body image and disordered eating. In J. K. Thompson (Ed.), *Handbook of eating disorders and obesity* (pp. 695–717). New York: Wiley.

Lock, J., Agras, W. S., Bryson, S., & Kraemer, H. (2005). A comparison of short term and long term family therapy for adolescent anorexia nervosa. *Journal of American Academy of Child and Adolescent Psychiatry, 44,* 632–639.

Lock, J., & Le Grange, D. (2005). Family based treatment of eating disorders. *International Journal of Eating Disorders, 37,* 564–567.

Loeb, K. L., Pratt, E. M., Walsh, B. T., Wilson, G. T., Labouvie, E., Hayaki, J., et al. (2005). Therapeutic alliance and treatment adherence in two interventions for bulimia nervosa: A study of process and outcome. *Journal of Counseling and Clinical Psychology, 73,* 1097–1107.

Mack, K. A., Anderson, L., Galuska, D., Zablotski, D., Holtzman, D., & Ahluwalia, I. (2004). Health and sociodemographic factors associated with body weight and weight objectives for women: 2000 Behavioral Risk Factor Surveillance System. *Journal of Women's Health, 13,* 1019–1032.

Maida, D. M., & Armstrong, S. L. (2005). The classification of muscle dysmorphia. *International Journal of Men's Health, 4,* 73–91.

Mann, T., Nolen-Hoeksema, S., Huang, K., Burgard, D., Wright, A., & Hanson, K. (1997). Are two interventions worse than none? Joint primary and secondary prevention of eating disorders in college females. *Health Psychology, 16,* 215–225.

McGrane, D., & Carr, A. (2002). Young women at risk for eating disorders: Perceived family dysfunction and parental psychological problems. *Contemporary Family Therapy, 24,* 385–398.

Meyer, C., Leung, N., Waller, G., Perkins, S., Paice, N., & Mitchell, J. (2005). Anger and bulimic psychopathology: Gender differences in a nonclinical group. *International Journal of Eating Disorders, 37,* 69–71.

Mintz, L. B., & Betz, N. E. (1988). Prevalence and correlates of eating disordered behavior among college women. *Journal of Counseling Psychology, 35,* 463–471.

Moore, F., & Keel, P. (2003). Influence of sexual orientation and age on disordered eating attitudes and behaviors in women. *International Journal of Eating Disorders, 34,* 370–374.

Moriarty, D., Shore, R., & Maxim, N. (1990). Evaluation of an eating disorder curriculum. *Evaluation and Program Planning, 13,* 407–413.

Nasser, M. (1988). Culture and weight consciousness. *Journal of Psychosomatic Research, 32,* 573–577.

Neumark-Sztainer, D. (2005). Can we simultaneously work towards prevention of obesity and eating disorders in children and adolescents? *International Journal of Eating Disorder, 38,* 220–227.

Nevonen, L., & Broberg, A. G. (2006). A comparison of sequenced individual and group psychotherapy for patients with bulimia nervosa. *International Journal of Eating Disorders, 39,* 117–127.

Omizo, S. A., & Omizo, M. M. (1992). Eating disorders: The school counselor's role. *The School Counselor, 39,* 217–224.

O'Neill, S. K. (2003). African American women and eating disturbances: A meta analysis. *Journal of Black Psychology, 29,* 3–16.

Osvold, L. L., & Sodowsky, G. R. (1993). Eating disorders of White American, racial and ethnic minority American, and international women. *Journal of Multicultural Counseling and Development, 21,* 143–154.

Pelch, B. L. (1999). Eating-disordered families: Issues between generations. In R. Lemberg (Ed.), *Eating disorders: A reference sourcebook* (pp. 121–123). Phoenix, AZ: Oryx Press.

Perez, M., & Joiner, T. (2003). Body image dissatisfaction and disordered eating in Black and White women. *International Journal of Eating Disorders, 33,* 342–350.

Perez, M., Voelz, Z., Pettit, J. W., & Joiner, T. E. (2002). The role of acculturative stress and body dissatisfaction in predicting bulimic symptomatology across ethnic groups. *International Journal of Eating Disorders, 31,* 442–454.

Pike, K. M., & Wilfley, D. E. (1996). The changing context of treatment. In L. Smolak, M. Levine, & R. Striegel-Moore (Eds.), *The developmental psychopathology of eating disorders* (pp. 365–397). Mahwah, NJ: Erlbaum.

Pinhey, T. K., & Okinaka, A. M. (2004). Exploring the purging behaviors of Asian pacific adolescents in Guam: Does heavy television viewing make a difference? *Deviant Behavior, 25,* 27–41.

Piran, N. (1996). The reduction of preoccupation body weight and shape in schools: A feminist approach. *Eating Disorders, 4,* 323–333.

Polivy, J., & Herman, C. P. (1996). Etiology of binge eating: Psychological mechanisms. In C. G. Fairburn & G. T. Wilson (Eds.), *Binge eating: Nature, assessment, and treatment* (pp. 173–205). New York: Guilford Press.

Pope, H. G., Olivardia, R., Borowiecki, J., & Cohane, G. (2001). The growing commercial value of the male body: A longitudinal survey of advertising in women's magazines. *Psychotherapy and Psychosomatics, 70,* 172–189.

Pope, H. G., Olivardia, R., Gruber, A., & Borowiecki, J. (1999). Evolving ideals of male body image as seen through action toys. *International Journal of Eating Disorders, 26,* 65–72.

Puhl, R. M., & Schwartz, M. B. (2003). If you are good you can have a cookie: How memories or childhood food rules link to adult eating behaviors. *Eating Behaviors, 4,* 283–293.

Pumariega, A. J. (1997). Body dissatisfaction among Hispanic and Asian-American girls. *Journal of Adolescent Health, 21,* 1.

Reinking, M. F., & Alexander, L. E. (2005). Prevalence of disordered eating behaviors in undergraduate female collegiate athletes and nonathletes. *Journal of Athletic Training, 40,* 47–51.

Rhodes, P., Gosbee, M., Madden, S., & Brown, J. (2005). Communities of concern in the family-based treatment of anorexia nervosa: Towards a consensus in the Maudsley model. *European Eating Disorder Review, 13,* 392–398.

Robinson, T. N., Killen, J. D., Litt, I. F., Hammer, L. D., Wilson, D. M., Haydel, K. F., et al. (1996). Ethnicity and body dissatisfaction: Are Hispanic and Asian girls at increased risk for eating disorders? *Journal of Adolescent Health, 19,* 384–393.

Roehrig, M., Thompson, J. K., Brannack, M., & van den Berg, P. (2006). Dissonance based eating disorder prevention program: A preliminary dismantling investigation. *International Journal of Eating Disorders, 39,* 1–10.

Roh Rue, H., & Lyle, R. M. (2003). Factors associated with weight concerns and unhealthy eating patterns among young Korean females. *Eating Disorders, 11,* 129–141.

Rubin, L. R., Fitts, M. L., & Becker, A. E. (2003). Whatever feels good in my soul: Body ethics and aesthetics among African American and Latina women. *Culture, Medicine, and Psychiatry, 27,* 49–75.

Russel, C., & Keel, P. (2002). Homosexuality as a specific risk fact for eating disorders in men. *International Journal of Eating Disorders, 31*, 300–306.

Sanders, N. M., & Heiss, C. J. (1998). Eating attitudes and body image of Asian and Caucasian college women. *Eating Disorders, 6*, 15–28.

Schmidt, U. (2002). Risk factors for eating disorders. In C. G. Fairburn & K. D. Brownell (Eds.), *Eating disorders and obesity* (pp. 247–250). New York: Guilford Press.

Schneider, J. A., & Agras, W. S. (1987). Bulimia in males: A matched comparison on with females. *International Journal of Eating Disorders, 6*, 235–242.

Schooler, D., Ward, L. M., Merriwether, A., & Caruthers, A. (2004). Who's that girl: Television's role in the body image development of young White and Black women. *Psychology of Women Quarterly, 28*, 38–47.

Schwartz, R. C., Barrett, M. J., & Saba, G. (1985). Family therapy for bulimia. In D. M. Garner & P. E. Garfinkel (Eds.), *Handbook of psychotherapy for anorexia nervosa and bulimia* (pp. 280–307). New York: Guilford Press.

Shafran, R. (2002). Eating disorders and the Internet. In C. G. Fairburn & K. D. Brownell (Eds.), *Eating disorders and obesity* (pp. 362–366). New York: Guilford Press.

Shaw, H., Ramirez, S., Trost, A., Randall, P., & Stice, E. (2004). Body image and eating disturbances across ethnic groups: More similarities than differences. *Psychology of Addictive Behaviors, 18*, 12–18.

Silverstein, B., Perdue, L., Peterson, B., & Kelly, E. (1986). The role of the mass media in promoting a thin standard of bodily attractiveness for women. *Sex Roles, 14*, 519–532.

Sischo, L. ,Taylor, J., & Yancey Martin, P. (2006). Carrying the weight of self-derogation? Disordered eating practices as social deviance in young adults. *Deviant Behavior, 27*, 1–30.

Smolak, L., & Levine, M. P. (1996). Adolescent transitions and the development of eating disorders. In L. Smolak, M. P. Levine, & R. Striegel-Moore (Eds.), *The developmental psychopathology of eating disorders* (pp. 207–234). Mahwah, NJ: Erlbaum.

Snow, J. T., & Harris, M. B. (1989). Disordered eating in southwestern Pueblo Indians and Hispanics. *Journal of Adolescence, 12*, 329–336.

Soh, N. L., Touyz, S. W., & Surgenor, L. J. (2006). Eating and body image disturbances across cultures: A review. *European Eating Disorders Review, 14*, 56–65.

Steiger, H., & Houle, L. (1991). Defense styles and object-relations disturbances among university women displaying varying degrees of "symptomatic" eating. *International Journal of Eating Disorders, 10*, 145–153.

Stice, E. (2002). Sociocultural influences on body image and eating disturbance. In C. G. Fairburn & K. D. Brownell (Eds.), *Eating disorders and obesity* (pp. 103–107). New York: Guilford Press.

Stice, E., Orjada, K., & Tristan, J. (2006). Trial of a psychoeducational eating disturbance intervention for college women: A replication and extension. *International Journal of Eating Disorders, 93*, 233–239.

Stice, E., & Ragan, J. (2002). A preliminary controlled evaluation of an eating disturbance psychoeducational intervention for college students. *International Journal of Eating Disorders, 31*, 159–171.

Stice, E., & Shaw, H. (2004). Eating disorder prevention programs: A meta-analytic review. *Psychological Bulletin, 130*, 206–227.

Stice, E., Spangler, D., & Agras, W. S. (2001). Exposure to media-portrayed thin-ideal images adversely affects vulnerable girls: A longitudinal experiment. *Journal of Social and Clinical Psychology, 20*, 270–288.

Story, M., French, S. A., Resnick, M. D., & Blum, R. W. (1995). Ethnic/racial and socioeconomic differences in dieting behaviors and body image perceptions in adolescents. *International Journal of Eating Disorders, 18*, 173–179.

Striegel-Moore, R. (1993). Etiology of binge eating: A developmental perspective. In C. G. Fairburnn & G. T. Wilson (Eds.), *Binge eating: Nature, assessment and treatment* (pp. 144–172). New York: Guilford Press.

Striegel-Moore, R. H., Fairburn, C. G., Wilfley, D. E., Pike, K. M., Dohm, F. A., & Kraemer, H. C. (2005). Toward an understanding of risk factors for binge eating disorder in Black and White women: A community-based case-control study. *Psychological Medicine, 35*, 907–917.

Striegel-Moore, R. H., Franko, D. L., Thompson, D., Barton, B., Schreiber, G. B., & Daniels, S. R. (2005). An empirical study of the typology of bulimia nervosa and its spectrum variants. *Psychological Medicine, 35*, 1563–1573.

Striegel-Moore, R., & Smolak, L. (1996). The role of race in the development of eating disorders. In L. Smolak, M. P. Levine, & R. Striegel-Moore (Eds.), *The developmental psychopathology of eating disorders* (pp. 259–284). Mahwah, NJ: Erlbaum.

Striegel-Moore, R., & Smolak, L. (2002). Gender, ethnicity, and eating disorders. In C. G. Fairburn & K. D. Brownell (Eds.), *Eating disorders and obesity* (pp. 251–255). New York: Guilford Press.

Strober, M., Freeman, R., Lampert, C., Diamond, J., & Kaye, W. (2000). Controlled family study of anorexia nervosa and bulimia nervosa: Evidence of shared liability and transmission of partial syndromes. *American Journal of Psychiatry, 157*, 393–401.

Stunkard, A. J. (1993). A history of binge eating. In C. G. Fairburn & G. T. Wilson (Eds.), *Binge eating: Nature, assessment and treatment* (pp. 15–34). New York: Guilford Press:

Sue, D., & Sue, D. (1990). *Counseling the culturally different* (2nd ed.). New York: Wiley.

Thompson, J. K. (Ed.). (2004). *Handbook of eating disorders and obesity*. Hoboken, NJ: Wiley.

Thompson, J. K., & Heinberg, L. J. (1999). The media's influence on body image disturbance and eating disorders: We've reviled them, now can we rehabilitate them? *Journal of Social Issue, 55*, 339–353.

Thompson, J. K., & Stice, E. (2001). Thin-ideal internalization: Mounting evidence for a new risk factor for body-image disturbance and eating pathology. *Current Directions in Psychological Science, 10*, 181–183.

Thompson, R. A., & Sherman, R. T. (2005). Athletes, eating disorders, and the four minute mile. *Eating Disorders, 13*, 321–324.

Thompson, S. H., Rafiroiu, A. C., & Sargent, R. G. (2003). Examining gender, racial, and age differences in weight concern among third, fifth, eighth, and eleventh graders. *Eating Behaviors, 3*, 307–323

Tozzi, R., Thornton, L. M., Klump, K. L., Fichter, M. M., Halmi, K. A., Kaplan, A. S., et al. (2005). Symptom fluctuation in eating disorders: Correlates of diagnostic crossover. *American Journal of Psychiatry, 162*, 732–740.

Troisi, A., Massaroni, P., & Cuzzolaro, M. (2005). Early separation anxiety and adult attachment style in women with eating disorders. *British Journal of Clinical Psychology, 44*, 89–97.

Troop, N. A., & Treasure, J. L. (1997). Psychosocial factors in the onset of eating disorders: Responses to life-events and difficulties. *British Journal of Medical Psychology, 70*, 373–385.

Ussery, L. W., & Prentice-Dunn, S. (1992). Personality predictors of bulimic behavior and attitudes in males. *Journal of Clinical Psychology, 48,* 722–729.

Van den Broucke, S., & Vandereycken, W. (1986). Risk factors for the development of eating disorders in adolescent exchange students: An exploratory survey. *Journal of Adolescence, 9,* 145–150.

Vander Wal, J. S. (2004). Eating and body image concerns among average-weight and obese African American and Hispanic girls. *Eating Behaviors, 5,* 181–187.

Vandereycken, W. (2002). Families of patients with eating disorders. In C. G. Fairburn & K. D. Brownell (Eds.), *Eating disorders and obesity* (pp. 215–220). New York: Guilford Press.

Von Ranson, K. M., & Robinson, K. E. (2006). Who is providing what type of psychotherapy to eating disorder clients? A survey. *International Journal of Eating Disorders, 39,* 27–34.

Walcott, D. D., Pratt, H. D., & Patel, D. (2003). Adolescents and eating disorders: Gender, racial, ethnic, sociocultural and socioeconomic issues. *Journal of Adolescent Research, 18,* 223–243.

Waldrop, J. (2005). Early identification and intervention for female athlete triad. *Journal of Pediatric Health Care, 19,* 213–220.

Weltzin, T. E., Weisensel, N., Franczyk, D., Burnett, K., Klitz, C., & Bean, P. (2005). Eating disorders in men: Update. *Journal of Men's Health and Gender, 2,* 186–193.

Westphal, V. K., & Smith, J. E. (1996). Overeaters Anonymous: Who goes and who succeeds? *Eating Disorders, 4,* 160–170.

White, M. A., & Grilo, C. M. (2005). Ethnic differences in the prediction of eating and body image disturbances among female adolescent psychiatric inpatients. *International Journal of Eating Disorders, 38,* 78–84.

Wichstrom, L. (2006). Sexual orientation as a risk factor for bulimic symptoms. *International Journal of Eating Disorders, 39,* 448–453.

Wilson, G. T., Fairburn, C. G., & Agras, W. S. (1997). Cognitive–behavioral therapy for bulimia nervosa. In D. M. Garner & P. E. Garfinkel (Eds.), *Handbook of treatment for eating disorders* (pp. 67–93). New York: Guilford Press.

Winston, A. P., Acharya, S., Chaudhuri, S., & Fellowes, L.(2004). Anorexia nervosa and gender identity disorder in biological males: A report of two cases. *International Journal of Eating Disorders, 36,* 109–113.

Wiseman, C. V., Gray, J. J., Mosimann, J. E., & Ahrens, A. H. (1992). Cultural expectations of thinness in women: An update. *International Journal of Eating Disorders, 11,* 85–89.

Wiseman, C. V., Gunning, F. M., & Gray, J. J. (1993). Increasing pressure to be thin: 19 years of diet products in television commercials. *Eating Disorders, 1,* 52–64.

Wonderlich, S. A. (2002). Personality and eating disorders. In C. G. Fairburn & K. D. Brownell (Eds.), *Eating disorders and obesity* (pp. 204–209). New York: Guilford Press.

Yelland. C., & Tiggemann, M. (2003). Muscularity and the gay ideal: Body dissatisfaction and disordered eating in homosexual men. *Eating Behaviors, 4,* 107–116.

Zabinski, M. F., Wilfley, D. E., Calfas, K. J., Winzelberg, A. J., & Taylor, C. B. (2004). An interactive psychoeducational intervention for women at risk of developing an eating disorder. *Journal of Consulting and Clinical Psychology, 72,* 914–919.

CHAPTER 10

■

"I Don't Want to Live": The Adolescent at Risk for Suicidal Behavior

David Capuzzi and Douglas R. Gross

The adolescent at risk for suicidal preoccupation and behavior has become an increasing concern for schools and communities throughout the United States. Between 1960 and 1988, the suicide rate among adolescents increased much more dramatically than it did in the general population (King, 2001a). The adolescent suicide rate rose by 200% compared with an increase in the general population of approximately 17% (Garland & Zigler, 1993). Much of the current literature (Coy, 1995; Zenere & Lazarus, 1997) ranks suicide, following accidents, as the second leading cause of death for youth in the United States.

The topic of adolescent suicide has been a major focus for newspaper features, television specials, and legislative initiatives as the problem of adolescent suicide has reached epidemic proportions (Hafen & Frandsen, 1986). In 1999, Surgeon General David Satcher made urgent recommendations to the public regarding suicide, stating that "the country is facing an average of 85 suicides and 2,000 attempts per day" (p. 1). In 2000, there were nearly 4,000 adolescent suicides recorded, accounting for 15% of deaths for young people between the ages of 15 and 24 (National Center for Health Statistics, 2002). Such data provide the basis for ranking suicide as the third leading cause of death among the 11–24 age group (American Academy of Pediatrics, 2004; National Institute of Mental Health, 2002). According to the Centers for Disease Control and Prevention's (2000) surveillance data from 1999, 19.3% of high school students had seriously considered attempting suicide, 14.5% had made plans to attempt suicide, and 8.3% had made more than one suicide attempt during the 12-month period prior to the survey. Because teachers in typical U.S. high school classrooms can expect to have at least one young man and two young women who attempt suicide in the last year (King, 2000), counselors, teachers, and parents are becoming more and more concerned about their responsibilities (Maples et al., 2005). Many states are requiring that schools include guidelines for suicide prevention, crisis management, and postvention in their written tragedy response plans.

PROBLEM DEFINITION

Ethnic and Gender Differences

The suicide rate is higher among adolescent males than among females (although adolescent females attempt three to four times as often as adolescent males). Caucasian and Native American adolescent males complete suicide more often than any other ethnic group (Canetto & Sakinofsky, 1998; Judge & Billick, 2004; Metha, Weber, & Webb, 1998; Price, Dake, & Kucharewski, 2001). A number of explanations to explain the differences in rates between genders and races have been proposed, but no clear answers have been found. As early as 1954, Henry and Short provided an explanation based on a reciprocal model of suicide and homicide, which suggested that some groups were seen as more likely to express frustration and aggression inwardly, whereas others were more likely to express it outwardly. Empirical data, however, do not support this reciprocal relationship. Some models used to explain racial differences in suicide have suggested that the extreme stress and discrimination that confront African Americans in the United States help to create protective factors, such as extended networks of social support, that lower the risk and keep the suicide rates for African American adolescents lower than those of Caucasian adolescents (Borowsky, Ireland, & Resnick, 2001; Bush, 1976; Gibbs, 1988). It is important to note, however, that despite the overall pattern suggested by the data, during the period between 1980 and 1994, the suicide rates for African American adolescent males showed a 320% increase in the 10–14 age group and a 196% increase in the 15–19 age group (Lyon et al., 2000; Metha et al., 1998; Rutter & Behrendt, 2004).

Native Americans have the highest adolescent suicide rates of any ethnic group in the United States (Committee on Adolescence, 2000; Shaughnessy, Doshi, & Jones, 2004). There is considerable variability across tribes; the Navajos, for example, have suicide rates close to the national average of 11 to 13 per 100,000 of the population; some Apache groups have rates as high as 43 per 100,000 (Berlin, 1987). The high suicide rates in the Native American population have been associated with factors such as alcoholism and substance abuse, unemployment, availability of firearms, and child abuse and neglect (Berman & Jobes, 1991). In general, less traditional tribes have higher rates of suicide than do more traditional tribes (Wyche, Obolensky, & Glood, 1990). Suicide rates for both Asian American and Hispanic American adolescents continue to be lower than those for African and Native American youth even though the 1980–1994 time period bore witness to much higher rates than previously recorded (Hallfors et al., 2006; Metha et al., 1998).

Methods

The use of firearms outranks all other methods of completed suicides; firearms are now being used by both genders. Studies in the United States show that availability of guns increases the risk of adolescent suicide (Brent et al., 1993; Committee on Adolescence, 2000). The second most common method is hanging, and the third most common is gassing. Males use firearms and hanging more often than do females, but females use gassing and ingestion more often than do males for completed suicides (Berman & Jobes, 1991). The most common method used by suicide attempters is ingestion or overdose.

Risk Factors

As noted by Garland and Zigler (1993) and Shaffer and Craft (1999), the search for the etiology of suicide spans many areas of study (Orbach, 2001). Risk factors that have been studied include neurotransmitter imbalances and genetic predictors, psychiatric disorders, poor self-efficacy and problem-solving skills, sexual or physical abuse, concerns over sexual identity or orientation, availability of firearms, substance abuse, violent rock music, divorce in families, unemployment and labor strikes, loss, disability, giftedness, and phases of the moon. It is important to note that almost all adolescent suicide victims have experienced some form of psychiatric illness (Beautrais, 2005). The most prevalent psychiatric disorders among completed adolescent suicides seem to be affective disorders, conduct disorder or antisocial personality disorder, and substance abuse (Shaffer, 1988; Shaffer & Craft, 1999). Among affective disorders, particular attention should be paid to bipolar illness and depressive disorder (see this volume, Chapter 6) with comorbidity such as attention deficit disorder, conduct disorder, or substance abuse (Rohde, Lewinsohn, & Seeley, 1991).

The suicide of a family member or a close friend of the family can also be a risk factor for adolescent suicide; prior attempts also escalate risk (Judge & Billick, 2004). An adolescent experiencing a physical illness that is chronic or terminal can also be at higher risk (Capuzzi, 1994). Many researchers have studied cognitive and coping style factors, such as generalized feelings of hopelessness and poor interpersonal problem-solving skills (Beautrais, 2005), as risk factors for adolescent suicide (Garland & Zigler, 1993). High neuroticism and low extraversion, high impulsiveness, low self-esteem, and an external locus of control have also been studied and can be used to predict risk (Beautrais, Joyce, & Mulder, 1999). Alcohol and drug abuse, the breakup of a relationship, school difficulties or failure, social isolation, a friend who committed suicide, chronic levels of community violence, and availability of lethal methods have also been studied and identified as risk factors (Hallfors et al., 2006; Price et al., 2001).

The best single predictor of death by suicide seems to be a previous suicide attempt (Hallfors et al., 2006; King, 2000; Shaffer, Garland, Gould, Fisher, & Trautman, 1988). Some studies indicate that as many as 40% of attempters will make additional suicide attempts and as many as 10%–14% of these individuals will complete suicide (Diekstra, 1989).

Protective Factors

Although there is a plethora of research on risk factors for suicide, there is not so much on protective factors. One might assume that in conjunction with any of the risk factors discussed above, not having that factor would be considered protective. This is probably true in many cases, and that may be why there is not as much research for this aspect of suicidality. One important fact that has come out of the research within the last 10 years is that it may be more effective to increase the protective factors in a suicidal client's life than it is to try to reduce the number of risk factors (Haley, 2004). Whereas a client may have several risk factors, having some protective factors may reduce the risk of a suicide attempt. Increasing protective factors has been effective even in cases where one cannot eliminate the risk or where the risk is ill defined (Haley, 2004). In a well-done overview of the literature (Haley, 2004), the following protective factors were found to be essential and important.

Social network/external support. Having a strong network of social support can minimize conditions of suicidality. Having people to turn to, to discuss problems with, and to get feedback regarding the reality of a situation can be immensely helpful. Having a social network is seen as protective for adolescents and youth; those adolescents who are connected to their families and have a good network of friends are less likely to make a suicide attempt. The implications for counselors are that it is important to assess for a client's connectedness with others. Just as social isolation is a risk factor, social connectedness is a protective factor. One intervention in a suicidal client's life might be to encourage him or her to become more connected with others. Counselors should also understand that the therapeutic relationship becomes even more important as a means of social connectedness when a client is suicidal.

Reasons for living. This protective factor seems obvious. If one has no sense of purpose or feels there is no future, one is much more likely to make a suicide attempt. Most research conducted on this subject has dealt with the population of adolescents and young adults.

Self-efficacy/self-esteem. What minimal studies have been done looking at self-efficacy as a protective factor have showed that having a sense of personal control over the events of one's life is seen as an important protective factor. Self-efficacy can be defined as a perceived ability in coping with problems and influencing positive outcomes. So, rather than feeling hopeless, an individual has a sense of empowerment that things will work out. The individual has confidence he or she can resolve problems, can make things happen for himself or herself, can learn to adjust or cope with difficult situations, and can know that things will get better eventually. This fundamental attitude, in contrast with the hopelessness described by many depressed and suicidal individuals, minimizes that individual's risk that he or she may eventually attempt a suicide.

Emotional well-being. Emotional well-being is another protective factor that seems obvious; however, not much research has been done in this area either. For the research that has been conducted, strong associations have been found between emotional well-being and protection from suicide. As suicide is highly correlated with loneliness, depression, and anger, not having these aversive emotions serves as a protective factor.

Problem-solving skills. The ability to effectively solve life's problems may serve as a protective factor. This sense of being "able" may also tie in with issues of self-esteem and self-efficacy.

Gender. As noted in the earlier discussion on risk factors, there are gender differences when it comes to suicide. Current research shows that more females attempt suicide but more males complete it. There are many postulations as to why this may be so. However, in general, it appears there are different risk factors for males and females, or risk factors and protective factors affect both genders in different ways. Generally, being female is more protective than being male, at least statistically.

Ethnicity. Not being White can also be seen as an element of protection. Non-White ethnic minority adults have approximately half the rate of completed suicide rate as White individuals.

Religiosity. Several authors have mentioned the role of religion as a protective factor against suicide. It could be that a person's religious faith precludes him or her from engaging in activities that could be considered risk factors for suicide. Another prospective reason is that people who attend church or other places of worship usually have a greater amount of fellowship with a support network. They are less isolated because presumably they attend church at least once per week, if not attending other church activities throughout the week. Generally, too, people with faith have a belief that God will take care of their problems.

Precipitants

Often, completed suicide is precipitated by what, to the adolescent, is interpreted as a shameful or humiliating experience (e.g., failure at school or work, interpersonal conflict with a romantic partner or parent). There is mounting evidence indicating that adolescents who do not cope well with major and minor life events and who do not have family and peer support are more likely to have suicidal ideation (Hallfors et al., 2006; Mazza & Reynolds, 1998; Stanard, 2000). The humiliation and frustration experienced by some adolescents struggling with conflicts connected with their sexual orientation may precipitate suicidal behavior (Harry, 1989; Kitts, 2005), although being gay or lesbian, in and of itself, may not be a risk factor for suicide (Blumenthal, 1991; Russell & Joyner, 2001). Hoberman and Garfinkel (1988) found the most common precipitant of suicide in a sample of 229 youth suicides to be an argument with a boyfriend, a girlfriend, or a parent (19%) followed by school problems (14%). Other humiliating experiences such as corporal punishment and abuse also serve as precipitants; the experience of sexual or physical assault seems to be a particularly significant risk factor for adolescent women (Hoberman & Garfinkel, 1988).

Understanding the Myths

The biggest problem connected with the topic of adolescents at risk for suicide is the fact that parents, teachers, mental health professionals, and the adolescents themselves are not made aware of a variety of myths and misconceptions as well as the signs and symptoms associated with adolescent suicide (Moskos, Achilles, & Gray, 2004). Because subsequent case study, prevention, and intervention information in this chapter are based on prior awareness of these two areas, the following information about myths and the suicidal profile is pertinent.

It is important to disqualify myths and misconceptions surrounding the topic of adolescent suicide at the beginning of any initiative to provide prevention, crisis management, and postvention services. The following are some of the most commonly cited misconceptions (Capuzzi, 1988, 1994; Capuzzi & Gross, 2004; King, 1999).

Adolescents who talk about suicide never attempt suicide. This is probably one of the most widely believed myths. Suicidal adolescents make attempts (either verbally or nonverbally) to let a friend, parent, or teacher know that life seems to be too difficult to bear. Because a suicide attempt is a cry for help to identify options, other than death, to decrease the pain of living, always take verbal or nonverbal threats seriously. Never assume such threats are only for the purpose of attracting attention or manipulating others. It is better to respond and enlist the aid of a professional than it is to risk the loss of a life.

Suicide happens with no warning. Suicidal adolescents leave numerous hints and warnings about their suicidal ideations and intentions. Clues can be verbal or in the form of suicidal gestures such as taking a few sleeping pills, becoming accident

254 ■ Working With Youth at Risk: Prevention and Intervention

prone, reading stories focused on death and violence, and so on. Quite often, the social support network of the suicidal adolescent is small. As stress escalates and options, other than suicide, seem few, suicidal adolescents may withdraw from an already small circle of friends, making it more difficult for others to notice warning signs.

Most adolescents who attempt suicide fully intend to die. Most suicidal adolescents do not want to end their lives. They feel desperate and ambivalent about whether it would be better to end their lives and, thus, their emotional pain or try to continue living. This confusion is usually communicated through both behavior and verbal communication (both of which are discussed in a subsequent subsection of this chapter).

Adolescents from affluent families attempt or complete suicide more often than adolescents from poor families. This, too, is a myth. Suicide is evenly divided among socioeconomic groups.

Once an adolescent is suicidal, he or she is suicidal forever. Most suicidal adolescents are suicidal for a limited period of time. In our experience, the 24–72-hour period around the peak of the crisis is the most dangerous. If counselors and other mental health professionals can monitor such a crisis period and transition the adolescent into long-term counseling/therapy, there is a strong possibility there will never be another suicidal crisis. The more effort that is made to help an adolescent identify stressors and develop problem-solving skills during this postsuicidal crisis period and the more time that passes, the better the prognosis.

If an adolescent attempts suicide and survives, he or she will never make an additional attempt. There is a difference between an adolescent who experiences a suicidal crisis but does not attempt suicide and an adolescent who actually makes an attempt. An adolescent who carries through with an attempt had identified a plan, had access to the means, and maintained a high enough energy level to follow through. He or she may believe that a second or third attempt may be possible. If counseling/therapy has not taken place or has not been successful during the period following an attempt, additional attempts may be made. Most likely, each follow-up attempt will become more lethal.

Adolescents who attempt or complete suicide always leave notes. Only a small percentage of suicidal adolescents leave notes. This is a common myth and one of the reasons why many deaths are classified and reported as accidents by friends, family members, physicians, and investigating officers when suicide has actually taken place.

Most adolescent suicides happen late at night or during the predawn hours. This myth is not true for the simple reason that most suicidal adolescents actually want help. Mid to late morning and mid to late afternoon are the time periods when most attempts are made because a family member or friend is more likely to be around to intervene than would be the case late at night or very early in the morning.

Never use the word suicide *when talking to adolescents because using the word gives some adolescents the idea.* This is simply not true; you cannot put the idea of suicide into the mind of an adolescent who is not suicidal. If an adolescent is suicidal and you use the word, it can help an adolescent verbalize feelings of despair and assist with establishing rapport and trust. If a suicidal adolescent thinks you know he or she is suicidal and realizes you are afraid to approach the subject, it can bring the adolescent closer to the point of making an attempt by contributing to feelings of despair and helplessness.

The most common method for adolescent suicide completion involves drug overdose. Guns are the most frequently used method for completing suicide among adolescents, followed by hanging. The presence of a gun or guns in the home escalates the risk of adolescent suicide approximately five times even if such firearms are kept locked in a cabinet or drawer. Restricting the presence of and access to guns significantly decreases the suicide rates among adolescents.

All adolescents who engage in suicidal behavior are mentally ill. Many adolescents have entertained the thought of suicide, but this does not indicate mental illness. Adolescents who attempt or complete suicide are usually not suffering from a mental disorder but are having a great deal of difficulty coping with life circumstances.

Every adolescent who attempts suicide is depressed. Depression is a common component of the profile of a suicidal adolescent, but depression is not always a component. Many adolescents simply want to escape their present set of circumstances and do not have the problem-solving skills to cope more effectively, lower stress, and work toward a more promising future.

Suicide is hereditary. Although suicide tends to run in families, just as physical and sexual abuse do and has led to the development of this myth, suicide is not genetically inherited. Members of families do, however, share the same emotional climate because parents model coping and stress management skills as well as high or low levels of self-esteem. The suicide of one family member tends to increase the risk among other family members that suicide will be viewed as an appropriate way to solve a problem or set of problems. In conjunction with this myth, it should be noted that some adolescents are predisposed, because of genetic factors, to depression as a response to life circumstances. Because of the connection between depression and suicide, many have mistakenly come to the belief that suicide can be genetically inherited.

If an adolescent is intent on attempting suicide, there is nothing anyone can do to prevent its occurrence. Two of the most important things a counselor, teacher, or parent can do are to know the risk factors and warning signs connected with adolescent suicide and to know how to respond. It is important for counselors to be prepared to provide preventive and crisis management services and for teachers and parents to know how to facilitate a referral to a qualified professional. Suicide can be prevented in most cases.

Recognizing the Profile

A number of experts believe that about 90% of the adolescents who complete suicide (and lethal first attempts can result in completions) give cues to those around them in advance (Beautrais, 2005; Beautrais et al.,1999; Capuzzi, 1994; Capuzzi & Golden, 1988; Cavaiola & Lavender, 1999; Cohen, 2000; Curran, 1987; Davis, 1983; Fernquist, 2000; Hafen & Frandsen, 1986; Hallfors et al., 2006; Hussain & Vandiver, 1984; Johnson & Maile, 1987; Judge & Billick, 2004; Maples et al., 2005; Mazza & Reynolds, 1998; Rutter & Behrendt, 2004). Whether these cues or hints are limited or numerous will depend on the adolescent, because each adolescent has a unique familial and social history. It is important for adults (and young people as well) to recognize the signs and symptoms to facilitate intervention. A comment such as "I talked with her a few days ago and she was fine—I am so shocked to learn of her death" may mean that no one was aware of the warning signs. One of the essential components of any staff development effort is teaching the profile of the suicidal or potentially suicidal adolescent so that referral and intervention can take place. Behavioral cues, verbal cues, thinking patterns and motivations, and personality traits are the four areas that we describe below.

Behavioral Cues

The following are some behavioral cues that can be possible warning signs of adolescents who are suicidal.

Lack of concern about personal welfare. Some adolescents who are suicidal may not be able to talk about their problems or give verbal hints that they are at risk for attempting suicide. Sometimes such adolescents become unconcerned with their personal safety in the hopes that someone will take notice. Experimenting with medication, accepting dares from friends, reckless driving, carving initials into the skin of forearms, and other behaviors may all be ways of gesturing or letting others know that the adolescent is in pain and does not know how to continue with life if nothing changes.

Changes in social patterns. Relatively unusual or sudden changes in an adolescent's social behavior can provide strong cues that such a young person is feeling desperate. A cooperative teenager may suddenly start breaking the house rules that parents have never had to worry about enforcing. An involved adolescent may begin to withdraw from activities at school or end long-term friendships with school and community-related peers. A stable, easygoing teenager may start arguing with teachers, employers, or other significant adults with whom prior conflict was never experienced. One should note such pattern changes and talk about them with the adolescent who does not seem to be behaving as he or she usually has in the past.

A decline in school achievement. Many times, adolescents who are becoming more and more depressed and preoccupied with suicidal thoughts are unable to devote the time required to complete homework assignments and maintain grades. If such an adolescent has a history of interest in the school experience and has maintained a certain grade point average, loss of interest in academic pursuits can be a strong indication that something is wrong. The key to assessing such a situation is the length of time the decline lasts.

Concentration and clear thinking difficulties. Suicidal adolescents usually experience marked changes in thinking and logic. As stress and discomfort escalate, logical problem solving and option generation become more difficult. It becomes easier and easier to stay focused on suicide as the only solution as reasoning and thinking become more confused and convoluted. Capuzzi (1988) noted, "It may become more and more obvious that the adolescent's attention span is shorter and that verbal comments bear little relationship to the topic of a conversation" (p. 6).

Altered patterns of eating and sleeping. Sudden increases or decreases in appetite and weight, difficulty with sleeping, or wanting to sleep all the time or all day can all be indicative of increasing preoccupation with suicidal thoughts. These altered patterns can offer strong evidence that something is wrong and that assistance is required.

Attempts to put personal affairs in order or to make amends. Often, once a suicide plan and decision have been reached, adolescents will make last-minute efforts to put their personal affairs in order. These efforts may take a variety of directions: attempts to make amends for a troubled relationship, final touches on a project, reinstatement of an old or neglected friendship, or the giving away of prized possessions (skis, jewelry, CDs, collections, etc.).

Use or abuse of alcohol or drugs. Sometimes troubled adolescents use or abuse alcohol or other drugs to lessen their feelings of despair or discontent. Initially, they may feel that the drug enhances their ability to cope and to increase feelings of self-esteem. Unfortunately, the abuse of drugs decreases ability to communicate accurately and problem solve rationally. Thinking patterns become more skewed, impulse control lessens, and option identification decreases. Rapid onset of involvement with illicit or over-the-counter drugs is indicative of difficulty with relationships, problem solving, and ability to share feelings and communicate them to others.

Unusual interest in how others are feeling. Suicidal adolescents often express considerable interest in how others are feeling. Because they are in pain but may be unable to express their feelings and ask for help, they may reach out to peers (or adults) who seem to need help with the stresses of daily living. Such responsiveness may become a full-time pastime and serves to lessen preoccupation with self and to become a vehicle for communicating, "I wish you would ask me about my pain" or "Can't you see that I need help too?"

Preoccupation with death and violence themes. Reading books or poetry in which death, violence, or suicide is the predominating theme may be the major interest of an adolescent who is becoming increasingly preoccupied with the possibility of suicide. Such adolescents may be undecided about the possibility of choosing death over life and may be working through aspects of such a decision with such reading. Other examples of such preoccupation can include listening to music that is violent; playing violent video games; writing short stories focused on death, dying, and loss; drawing or sketching that emphasizes destruction; or watching movies or videos that emphasize destruction to self and others.

Sudden improvement after a period of depression. Suicidal adolescents often fool parents, teachers, and friends by appearing to be dramatically improved, after a period of prolonged depression, in a very short period of time. This improvement can sometimes take place overnight or during a 24-hour period and encourages friends and family to interpret such a change as a positive sign. It is not unusual for a change, such as the one described here, to be the result of a suicide decision and the formulation of a concrete suicide plan on the part of the adolescent at risk. It may mean that the suicide attempt (and the potential of completion) is imminent and that the danger and crisis are peaking. The important point for family and friends to remember is that it is not really logical for a depression to lessen that rapidly. It takes time, effort, and, at times, medical assistance to improve coping skills and lessen feelings of depression, just as it took time (months or years) to develop nonadaptive responses to people and circumstances and feelings of hopelessness.

Sudden or increased promiscuity. It is not unusual for an adolescent to experiment with sex during periods of suicidal preoccupation in an attempt to refocus attention or lessen feelings of isolation. Unfortunately, doing so sometimes complicates circumstances because of an unplanned pregnancy or an escalation of feelings of guilt.

Verbal Cues

As noted by Schneidman, Farbverow, and Litman (1976), verbal statements can provide cues to self-destructive intentions. Such statements should be assessed and considered in relation to behavioral signs and changes in thinking patterns, motivations, and personality traits. There is no universal language or style for communicating suicidal intention. Some adolescents will openly and directly say something like "I'm going to commit suicide" or "I'm thinking of taking my life." Others will be far less direct and make statements such as "I'm going home," "I wonder what death is like," "I'm tired," "She'll be sorry for how she has treated me," or "Someday I'll show everyone just how serious I am about some of the things I've said."

The important thing for counselors, parents, teachers, and friends to remember is that when someone says something that could be interpreted in a number of ways, it is always best to ask for clarification. It is not a good idea to make assumptions about what a statement means or to minimize the importance of what is being communicated. Suicidal adolescents often have a long-term history of difficulty with communicating feelings and asking for support. Indirect statements may be made in the hopes that someone will respond with support and interest and provide or facilitate a referral for professional assistance (Capuzzi & Gross, 2004).

Thinking Patterns and Motivations

In addition to the areas previously described, thinking patterns (Gust-Brey & Cross, 1999) and motivations of suicidal adolescents can also be assessed and evaluated. For such an assessment to occur, it is necessary to encourage self-disclosure to learn about changes in an adolescent's cognitive set and distortions of logic and problem-solving ability. As noted by Velkoff and Huberty (1988), the motivations of suicidal adolescents can be understood more readily when suicide is viewed as fulfilling one of three primary functions: (a) an avoidance function that protects the individual from the pain perceived to be associated with a relationship or set of circumstances; (b) a control function that enables an adolescent to believe he or she has gained control of someone or something thought to be out of control, hopeless, or disastrous; and (c) a communication function that lets others know that something is wrong or that too much pain or too many injuries have been accumulated.

Often suicidal adolescents distort their thinking patterns in conjunction with the three functions of avoidance, control, and communication so that suicide becomes the best or only problem-solving option. Such distortions can take a number of directions. All-or-nothing thinking, for example, can enable an adolescent to view a situation in such a polarized way that the only two options seem to be continuing to be miserable and depressed or carrying out a suicide plan; no problem-solving options to cope with or overcome problems may seem possible (Capuzzi, 1988; Capuzzi & Gross, 2004). Identification of a single event that is then applied to all events is another cognitive distortion, that of overgeneralization. Being left out of a party or a trip to the mountains with friends may be used as evidence for being someone no one likes, a loser, or someone who will always be forgotten or left out. "I can't seem to learn the material for this class very easily" becomes "I'm never going to make it through school" or "I'll probably have the same difficulties when I start working full time." Adolescents who are experiencing stress and pain and who are becoming preoccupied with suicidal thoughts often experience more and more cognitive distortions. Such distortions result in self-talk that becomes more and more negative and more and more supportive of one of the following motivations for carrying through with a suicide plan:

- wanting to escape from a situation that seems (or is) intolerable (e.g., sexual abuse, conflict with peers or teachers, pregnancy, etc.),
- wanting to join someone who has died,

- wanting to attract the attention of family or friends,
- wanting to manipulate someone else,
- wanting to avoid punishment,
- wanting to be punished,
- wanting to control when or how death will occur (an adolescent with a chronic or terminal illness may be motivated in this way),
- wanting to end a conflict that seems unresolvable,
- wanting to punish the survivors, and
- wanting revenge.

Personality Traits

As noted by Capuzzi (1988), it would be ideal if the research on the profile of the suicidal adolescent provided practitioners with such a succinct profile of personality traits that teenagers at risk for suicide could be identified far in advance of any suicidal risk. Adolescents who fit the profile could then be assisted through individual and group counseling and other means. Although no consensus has yet been reached on the usual, typical, or average constellation of personality traits of the suicidal adolescent, researchers have agreed on a number of characteristics that seem to be common to many suicidal adolescents (Orbach, 2001).

Low self-esteem. Several studies have connected low self-esteem with suicide probability (Beautrais et al., 1999; Cull & Gill, 1982; Faigel, 1966; Freese, 1979; King, 1999; Price et al., 2001; Stein & Davis, 1982; Stillion, McDowell, & Shamblin, 1984). Our counseling experience as well as the experience of other practitioners seems to substantiate the relationship between low self-esteem and suicide probability (see this volume, Chapter 5). Almost all such clients have issues focused on feelings of low self-worth, and almost all such adolescents have experienced these self-doubts for an extended time period.

Hopelessness/helplessness. Most suicidal adolescents report feeling hopeless and helpless in relation to their circumstances as well as their ability to cope with these circumstances. The research support for verification of what clinicians report is growing (Beautrais et al., 1999; Cull & Gill, 1982; Kovacs, Beck, & Weissman, 1975; Jacobs, 1971; Maples et al., 2005; Peck, 1983; Rutter & Behrendt, 2004; Stanard, 2000). Most practitioners can expect to address this issue with suicidal clients and to identify a long-term history of feeling hopeless and helpless on the part of most clients.

Isolation. Many, if not most, suicidal adolescents tend to develop a small network of social support. They may find it uncomfortable to make new friends and rely on a small number of friends for support and companionship. (This may be the reason why so often those around a suicide victim state they did not notice anything unusual; the suicidal adolescent may not be in the habit of getting close enough to others so that changes in behavior, outlook, and so on can be noted.) A number of authorities support this observation (Gust-Brey & Cross, 1999; Hafen, 1972; Kiev, 1977; Peck, 1983; Sommes, 1984; Stein & Davis, 1982).

High stress. High stress coupled with poor stress management skills seem to be characteristic of the suicidal adolescent. A number of studies have addressed this trait in terms of low frustration tolerance (Cantor, 1976; Kiev, 1977; Stanard, 2000). Chapter 7 of this text provides a comprehensive overview of stress as a causal factor relating to suicidal and other at-risk behaviors.

Need to act out. Behaviors such as truancy, running away, refusal to cooperate at home or at school, use or abuse of alcohol or other drugs, and experimentation with sex are frequently part of the pattern present in the life of a suicidal adolescent. Such behaviors may be manifestations of depression. Often, adults remain so focused on the troublesome behavior connected with an adolescent's need to act out that underlying depressive episodes may be overlooked.

Need to achieve. Sometimes, adolescents who are suicidal exhibit a pattern of high achievement. This achievement may be focused on getting high grades, being the class clown, accepting the most dares, wearing the best clothes, or any one of numerous other possibilities. In our counseling experience, this emphasis on achievement often is a compensation for feelings of low self-esteem. Readers should be cautioned, however, about jumping to the conclusion that every adolescent who achieves at a high level is suicidal. This trait, along with all of the other traits and characteristics connected with the profile of the suicidal adolescent, must be assessed in the context of other observations.

Poor communication skills. Suicidal adolescents often have a history of experiencing difficulty with expression of thoughts and feelings. Such adolescents may have trouble with identifying and labeling what they are feeling; self-expression seems awkward if not stressful. It is not unusual to discover that adolescents who have become preoccupied with suicidal thoughts have experienced a series of losses or disappointments that they have never been able to discuss and, understandably, integrate or resolve.

Other-directedness. Most suicidal adolescents are "other-directed" rather than "inner- directed." They are what others have told them they are instead of what they want to be; they value what others have said they should be instead of what they deem to be of personal value and worth. This trait may also be linked to low self-esteem and may lead to feelings of helplessness or inability to control interactions or circumstances around them.

Guilt. Usually connected with feelings of low self-esteem and a need to be other-directed, the guilt experienced by many suicidal adolescents is bothersome and sometimes linked to their wanting to be punished as a motivation for suicide. Some statements common to the guilt-ridden suicidal adolescent might include "Nothing I do seems to be good enough," "I feel so bad because I disappointed them," or "I should not have made that decision and should have known better."

Depression. Depression is a major element in the total profile of the suicidal adolescent (Beautrais, 2005; Judge & Billick, 2004; Kitts, 2005; Maples et al., 2005; Mazza & Reynolds, 1998). Hafen and Frandsen (1986) pointed out that there are sometimes differences between depression in an adult and depression in an adolescent. Adults are often despondent, tearful, sad, or incapable of functioning as usual. Although adolescents sometimes exhibit these characteristics, they may also respond with anger, rebelliousness, truancy, running away, using and abusing drugs, and so on. Those adults and peers who associate depression only with feelings of sadness and despondency may not recognize depression in adolescents, who mask the depression with behavior that creates discomfort in family and school environments.

As noted by Capuzzi (1988),

> Given the complexity of being an adolescent in the late 1980's, coupled with the normal ups and downs of the developmental stage of adolescence, it is normal for every adolescent to experience short periods of depression. But when depressive periods become more and more frequent, longer and longer, and of such intensity that the adolescent has difficulty functioning at school and at home, they could be a strong warning sign of suicide

potential, especially if other aspects of behavior, verbalization, motivations and cognitive distortions have been observed. (p. 10)

It is extremely important for counselors and other professionals who may be working with suicidal adolescents to complete additional course work or training to learn about the different types of depression. Although familiarity with resources and guidelines such as those provided by McWhirter and Kigin (1988) and the *Diagnostic and Statistical Manual of Mental Disorders* (4th ed., Text Revision [*DSM–IV–TR*]; American Psychiatric Association, 2000) are readily available to mental health practitioners, case supervision and consultation may be needed to accurately determine the nature of a depressive episode. Frequently, well-meaning practitioners fail to discriminate between depression created by a constellation of factors (negative self-talk, poor problem-solving skills, high stress, etc.) and depression that is a result of the body chemistry an adolescent inherited at birth. Treatment or counseling plans are different based on the kind of depression being experienced. Counselors, therapists, and core or crisis team members need to liaison with nurse practitioners and psychiatrists when medical assessment and subsequent medication are appropriate for depression.

In conjunction with the topic of depression as it relates to suicidal ideation, attempts, and completions, it should be noted that pharmacotherapy is often used in conjunction with counseling. Selective serotonin reuptake inhibitors (SSRIs) have been shown to be effective in treating adolescents with depression (Gould, Greenberg, Velting, & Shaffer, 2003). In the last decade, however, there has been controversy over whether SSRIs can induce suicidal behavior. It is thought that, in some instances, symptoms such as anxiety, panic attacks, hostility, hypomania, and self-harming behaviors have developed in response to taking SSRIs (Judge & Billick, 2004). Parents should be cautioned to watch for such symptoms if they begin to develop and immediately notify their child's counselor and prescribing physician, psychiatrist, or nurse practitioner.

Poor problem-solving skills. Most parents notice differences in the problem-solving ability of their children. Some children are more resourceful than others in identification of problem resolution options. Suicidal adolescents seem, in our experience, to have less ability to develop solutions to troublesome situations or uncomfortable relationships. This may be a reason why suicidal preoccupation can progress from a cognitive focus to an applied plan with little dissonance created by the formulation and consideration of other problem-solving options and decisions.

CASE STUDY

Jim was a 17-year-old high school junior and the son of affluent, well-educated parents. Jim's dad was a successful attorney, and his mom was an assistant superintendent for the local school district. Jim's 15-year-old sister, Janell, was well liked, a cheerleader, and involved in a variety of school and community-related activities. Janell had a beautiful singing voice and frequently accepted prominent roles in school, church, and community musical productions.

Although Jim had a few close friends, he preferred to spend most of his time reading and studying and was a straight A student. He accepted an opportunity to spend most of his junior year traveling and studying in Europe and thought such an experience would provide an excellent educational option as well as time away from his parents. Jim resented the high expectations his parents placed on both him and Janell and felt that his father did not approve of his earlier decision not to participate in varsity sports. Both parents, Jim felt, pressured him to be involved in school and community civic and social organizations; Jim preferred more solitary and intellectual pursuits. Jim felt somewhat self-conscious and awkward in social situations and never felt that he could present himself as well as his sister could, or in a way acceptable to his parents. He felt directed and criticized by both parents and resented the fact that his parents always seemed too busy to listen to him talk about things of importance to him. He really resented his father's lack of approval and felt that no one in his family seemed to understand his point of view.

Jim had experienced periodic episodes of depression, and because he had decided that it was best not to talk with family members about his feelings, he usually tried to keep his sister and his parents from knowing when he felt really down. Jim noticed that his depression was the worst when he was under a lot of stress with respect to completing class assignments and during times that his parents pressured him into social situations. Bob, Jim's best friend, became so concerned about Jim toward the end of the exam period in the spring of their sophomore year that he told Jim's parents. Jim's parents took him to a psychiatrist who prescribed an antidepressant and recommended weekly therapy. Jim's parents were angry with him, resented the additional expense, and demanded that Jim get better as soon as possible. Janell hoped her friends would not find out because she was in the midst of being nominated for Queen of the Rose Festival and had already been selected as a Rose Festival Princess. Jim did not like the psychiatrist and felt as criticized by him as he did by his parents. He disliked the side effects of the medication, often skipped his weekly therapy session, and could hardly wait to leave home in late August to attend the orientation session at Cambridge prior to initiation of his travel/study itinerary.

Shortly after Thanksgiving, Jim's parents received a call from Switzerland; Jim had nearly died after an overdose of his medication and was recovering in a hospital in Zurich. Jim was sent home during the first part of December.

APPROACHES TO PREVENTION

Individual

Individually focused preventive counseling with Jim could have been focused in several ways. Jim could have benefited from a therapeutic relationship that included self-esteem enhancement as part of the treatment plan. If counseling/therapy had been initiated during elementary school years, Jim might not have responded with depression and, to a great extent, isolation and withdrawal from all but a few friends who provided a limited network of social support. Jim might also have been encouraged to share feelings and communicate with his parents. He also would have benefited from assertiveness training to assist him with sending needed messages to his parents at times when his parents were more preoccupied with career-related responsibilities and interests. Jim's counselor/therapist would probably have worked with him to become more aware of stressors and more adept at managing stress or removing stressors from his environment. Possibly, the combination of efforts made by his parents in couples counseling and by Jim in the context of his individual work would have resulted in outcomes very different from those described in the previous case description.

Family

Most suicidal adolescents have developed their at-risk profiles over time beginning during early childhood. In families in which there is more than one child, it is often easy for parents to identify differences in self-esteem, communication skills, stress management, problem solving, and so on. By the time a child is in elementary school, there may be visible indicators or traits that, if no intervention takes place, will result in the child's involvement in one or several at-risk behaviors. It is our opinion that such a child, by the time the middle school or junior high transition occurs, will be vulnerable to becoming pregnant, contracting AIDS, abusing drugs, developing an eating disorder, dropping out of school, or attempting or completing suicide.

Jim's family could have noted his low self-esteem, discomfort with respect to sharing feelings, depression, response to stress, poor stress-management skills, and resentment toward them. They might have been able to detect changes in his thinking patterns or fluctuations in day-to-day behaviors had they developed a relationship with him that included more open lines of communication. Jim's parents did not realize that their son experienced even higher levels of stress in conjunction with the European study program and felt compelled to succeed at all costs. Jim also did not anticipate the amount of interchange and collaboration required by the group-living situations he found himself in as he and his peers and teachers traveled from one community to another and had begun to feel less self-assured than ever. Ideally, Jim's parents should have sought counseling assistance for themselves and their son when Jim was in elementary school. A counselor might have done an assessment of possible risk factors connected with Jim's family of origin and the families of his grandparents so that counseling could have compensated for predisposing factors and included an educational component for Jim's parents.

School and Community

There are a number of steps that can be taken to involve both the school and the community in prevention efforts (King, 2001b). In general, it is easier to initiate efforts in the school setting than it is in the context of a mental health center, because schools can easily access young people, reach and prepare school faculty and staff, involve parents, and collaborate with mental health professionals from the surrounding community.

A number of steps must be taken to facilitate a successful school–community prevention effort. These include collaboration with administrators, faculty/staff in-service, preparation of crisis teams, individual and group counseling options, parent education, and classroom presentations. We describe each of these steps in the following subsections.

Collaboration With Administrators

There is a compelling need for prevention, crisis management, and postvention programs for the adolescent suicide problem to be put in place in elementary, middle, and high schools throughout the United States (Metha et al., 1998; Speaker & Petersen, 2000; Zenere & Lazarus, 1997). On the basis of our experience in the process of working with school districts all over the country, one of the biggest mistakes made by counselors, educators, and coordinators of counseling/student services is to initiate programs and services in this area without first obtaining commitment and support of administrators and others in supervisory positions (Reddy & Richardson, 2006). Too often efforts are initiated and then canceled because little or no negotiation with those in decision-making positions has taken place (Adelman & Taylor, 2000). Building principals and superintendents must be supportive, otherwise all efforts are destined for failure. Developing understanding of the parameters connected with suicide prevention and intervention must start with the building principal and extend to all faculty and staff in a given building (Adelman & Taylor, 2000; King, 2001b) so that advance understanding of why quick action must take place is developed. During a crisis, schedules must be rearranged, and faculty and staff may be called on to teach an extra class or assist with an initial assessment. Everyone connected with a given building must have advance preparation.

In addition to the groundwork that must be done on the building level, it is also important to effect advance communication and planning on the district level. The superintendent, assistant superintendent, curriculum director, staff development director, student services coordinator, research and program evaluation specialist, among others, must all commit their support to intervention efforts. When administrators have the opportunity to listen to an overview of proposed efforts and ask questions, a higher level of commitment can be established and efforts can be more easily expedited. The probability of extending proposed programming to all schools in a given district is also increased.

Faculty/Staff In-Service

Because teachers and other faculty and staff usually learn of a student's suicidal preoccupation prior to the situation being brought to the attention of the school counselor or another member of the core or crisis team (assuming such a team exists), *all* faculty and staff must be included in building- or district-level in-service on the topic of adolescent suicide. Teachers, aides, secretaries, administrators, custodians, bus drivers, food service personnel, librarians, and school social workers all come in contact with adolescents at risk for suicide. It is imperative that all such adults be educated about both adolescent suicide and building and district policies and programs for prevention, crisis management, and postvention. There are a growing number of publications that provide excellent guidelines for elements of prevention programming focused on school faculty and staff (Beautrais, 2005; Davidson & Range, 1999; Kirchner, Yoder, Kramer, Lindsey, & Thrush, 2000; Maples et al., 2005; Metha et al., 1998; Reddy & Richardson, 2006; Speaker & Petersen, 2000; Zenere & Lazarus, 1997). When a young person reaches out to a trusted adult, that adult must have a clear understanding and a considerable amount of self-confidence so he or she knows exactly what to say and do as well as what not to say and do.

Many schools and school districts have actually precipitated suicide attempts by not providing for faculty/staff in-service on the topic prior to introducing discussion among student groups. When middle and high school students participate in educational programs on the topic of adolescent suicide, they begin to realize that they, as well as some of their friends, are at risk and they may approach admired adults for assistance. Adults in the school who have no knowledge of what to do and who have not had the opportunity to have their questions answered and their apprehension lowered may be threatened by what a student is sharing and fail to make appropriate comments and decisions. Highly stressed, depressed, suicidal adolescents do not have the perspective to realize that such responses are connected with discomfort on the part of the adult and have little to do with what could be interpreted as disapproval and lack of acceptance. For these adolescents, awkward and minimal responses to suicidal self-disclosure on the part of a trusted adult can be interpreted as the loss of the last link to society and provide additional reinforcement for finalizing a suicide plan.

It is unethical not to prepare school faculty and staff in advance of the presentation of information on suicide to the students in a school. It could also become the basis for legal action by parents and family members. Much of the content in this chapter can become the basis for necessary in-service efforts.

Preparation of Crisis Teams

Many schools have crisis or core teams composed of faculty, staff, and parents connected with a particular building. These teams often exist in conjunction with a program for the prevention and intervention efforts necessary to cope with the drug problem among the young people in today's schools. Such teams usually consist of some combination of teachers, counselors, parents, social workers, school psychologists, school nurses, and school administrators. Usually these teams have been educated about traits that place adolescents at risk for substance use and abuse and have had supervision and instruction on the use of appropriate communication, diagnostic, and intervention skills necessary to begin the long-term process of recovery from alcoholism and other addictions. With education beyond that which is provided during the faculty/staff in-service discussed previously, as well as additional supervision and evaluation of clinical skills, a core or crisis team can be taught how to facilitate prevention efforts in a school and how to respond to a student already experiencing a suicidal crisis or in need of postvention efforts. In addition, such a team can be expected to write a policy statement that covers all parameters connected with prevention, crisis management, and postvention efforts. Such a policy could be adopted in other schools; in reality, except for specifics connected with a given building, the same policy statement should be adopted and followed throughout a school district. It is important to realize that everyone who is called on to assist a suicidal adolescent must know what to do. Confusion or lack of certainty about a chain of command or procedures about notification of parents can result in delays and interfere with efforts to save a young person's life.

Individual and Group Counseling Options

Prior to providing students with any information about suicide and suicide prevention efforts in a school, arrangements must be made for the individual and group counseling services that will be needed by those students who seek assistance for themselves or their friends. Unless such counseling options are available, any effort at prevention, crisis management, or postvention will be doomed to failure. This may present a problem to school personnel, particularly on the secondary level, unless there is a commitment on the part of administrators to free counselors from scheduling, hall monitoring, and other duties not related to the emerging role of the counselor of the 21st century. Working with suicidal adolescents requires a long-term commitment on the part of those interested in intervening. No counselor, psychologist, or social worker can undo the life experiences and self-perceptions of a lifetime without providing consistent, intensive opportunities for counseling.

If the school district cannot make a commitment to providing counseling, then arrangements for referral to community agencies and private practitioners must be made. It is important to provide adolescents and their families with a variety of referral possibilities along with information on fee schedules. There may be some question about whether the school district will be liable for the cost of such counseling if the referral is made by the school. (This issue should be explored by whatever legal counsel is retained by the district.) The dilemma, of course, is that unless counseling takes place when a suicidal adolescent has been identified, the probability is high that an attempt or a completion will take place. If the school is aware of a teenager's suicidal preoccupation and does not act in the best interests of such a teenager, families may later bring suit against the district. Counselors in the school and members of the mental health network in the community must preplan to work in concert for the benefit and safety of adolescents at risk for suicide.

Parent Education

Parents of students in a school in which a suicide prevention program is to be initiated should be involved in the school's efforts to educate, identify, and assist young people in this respect. Parents have a right to understand why the school is taking such steps and what the components of a schoolwide effort will be (Maples et al., 2005; Reddy & Richardson, 2006). Evening or late-afternoon parent education efforts can be constructive and engender additional support for a school or school district. Parents have the same information needs as faculty and staff with respect to the topic of adolescent suicide. They will be more likely to refer themselves and their children to the school for assistance if they know of the school's interest in adolescent suicide prevention, have had an opportunity to ask questions about their adolescent sons' and daughters' behavior, and have been reassured about the quality and safety of the school's efforts.

Classroom Presentations

There is continuing debate surrounding the safety of adolescent suicide prevention programs that contain an educational component that is presented to adolescents. This debate is similar to the one that emerged years ago when schools initiated staff development and classroom presentations on the topic of physical and sexual abuse. There are a number of advocates of education and discussion efforts that are focused on students in conjunction with a schoolwide suicide prevention effort (Capuzzi, 1988, 1994; Capuzzi & Golden, 1988; Curran, 1987; Ross, 1980; Sudak, Ford, & Rushforth, 1984; Zenere & Lazarus, 1997). Providing adolescents with an appropriate forum in which they can receive accurate information, ask questions, and learn about how to obtain help for themselves and their friends does not precipitate suicidal preoccupation or attempts (Capuzzi, 1988, 1994; Capuzzi & Gross, 2004). Because newspaper and television reports of individual and cluster suicides do not usually include adequate education on the topic, and because many films have unrealistically presented or romanticized the act of suicide, it is important for schools to address the problem in a way that provides information and encourages young people to reach out for help before they reach the point of despair.

A carefully prepared and well-presented classroom presentation made by a member of the school's core team (or another presenter who has expertise on the topic) is essential. Such a presentation should include information on causes, myths, and symptoms as well as information about how to obtain help through the school. Under no circumstances should media be used in which adolescents are shown a suicide plan. In addition, on the elementary level, school faculty should not present programs on the topic of suicide prevention; their efforts are better focused on developmental counseling and classroom presentations directed at helping children overcome traits (such as low self-esteem or poor communication skills) that may put them at risk for suicidal behavior at a later time. Although these efforts should be continued through secondary education, middle and high school students are better served through presentations that address adolescent suicide directly. (Middle and high school students almost always have direct or indirect experience with suicide and appreciate the opportunity to obtain information and ask questions.)

Legal Considerations

Prior to discussing intervention strategies in the next section of this chapter, it seems appropriate to comment about some legal aspects of suicide prevention and intervention efforts in schools. In an excellent review of the results of school violence litigation against schools, Hermann and Remley (2000) noted that even though those who are employed by school districts are expected to exert reasonable care to prevent harm to students, the courts have been reluctant to find educators liable for injuries related to violence or self-harm. State law claims usually fail because much of today's school violence (and suicide attempts and completions are components of school violence) results from what can be termed spontaneous acts of violence. This fact should not, however, lull school personnel into a false sense of security or complacency. A growing number of legal opinions have indicated that an unanticipated act of violence can be predictable and, thus, actionable under state law. Therefore, counselors, teachers, administrators, and other members of school staffs can protect themselves, as well as the youths they serve, by writing and implementing suicide prevention, crisis management, and postvention policy and procedures. These policy and procedures documents should mandate staff development for all school personnel so that all adults in the school setting recognize risk factors; possible behavioral, verbal, cognitive, and personality indicators; as well as role responsibilities and limitations. What we view as best practices are more likely to be followed if schools take a proactive rather than a reactive stance to this growing epidemic in our country's youth.

INTERVENTION STRATEGIES

Individual and Family

There are times when adolescents at risk for suicide are not identified until a crisis state has been reached. In such circumstances, it is important for all concerned to initiate action for the purpose of assessing lethality and determining appropriate follow-up. Because many professionals who are not counselors lack experience with adolescents who are in the midst of a personal crisis, the following guidelines may prove helpful. Note that these guidelines can be read in the context of working with Jim. The assumption that one would have to make, however, is that all the adults traveling with Jim and his peers would have participated in staff development efforts and would include a counselor or other professional who could assess suicidal risk. An additional assumption is that families would be supportive of the use of these guidelines, either because they realized that the situation had escalated beyond their capacity to handle the situation or because they had participated in a school-sponsored presentation to the community on the topic of adolescent suicide prevention and intervention.

1. *Remember the meaning of the term crisis management.* When thinking of crisis management, it is important to understand the meaning of the word *crisis* as well as the word *management*. The word *crisis* means that the situation is not usual,

normal, or average; circumstances are such that a suicidal adolescent is highly stressed and in considerable emotional discomfort. Adolescents in crisis usually feel vulnerable, hopeless, angry, low in self-esteem, and at a loss for how to cope. The word *management* means that the professional involved must be prepared to apply skills that are different from those required for preventive or postvention counseling. An adolescent in crisis must be assessed, directed, monitored, and guided for the purpose of preventing an act of self-destruction. Because adolescents who are experiencing a suicidal crisis may be quite volatile and impulsive, the need for decisive, rapid decision making on the part of the intervener is extremely important.

2. *Be calm and supportive.* A calm, supportive manner on the part of the intervener conveys respect for the perceptions and internal pain of an adolescent preoccupied with suicidal thoughts. Remember that such an adolescent usually feels hopeless and highly stressed. The demeanor and attitude of the helping person are pivotal in the process of offering assistance.

3. *Be nonjudgmental.* Statements such as "You can't be thinking of suicide, it is against the teachings of your church" or "I had a similar problem when I was your age and I didn't consider suicide" are totally inappropriate during a crisis situation. An adolescent's perception of a situation is, at least temporarily, reality and that reality must be respected. The same caution can be applied to the necessity of respecting a suicidal adolescent's expression of feelings whether these feelings are those of depression, frustration, fear, or helplessness. Judgmental, unaccepting responses and comments only serve to further damage an already impaired sense of self-esteem and decrease willingness to communicate. Adolescents could sink further into depression or increase their resolve to carry through with a suicide plan if others are critical and unwilling to acknowledge what appear, to the adolescent, to be insurmountable obstacles.

4. *Encourage self-disclosure.* The very act of talking about painful emotions and difficult circumstances is the first step in what can become a long-term healing process. A professional helper may be the first person with whom such a suicidal adolescent has shared and trusted in months or even years, and this may be difficult to do simply because of lack of experience with communicating thoughts and feelings. It is important to support and encourage self-disclosure so that an assessment of lethality can be made early in the intervention process.

5. *Acknowledge the reality of suicide as a choice but do not normalize suicide as a choice.* It is important for practitioners to let adolescents know that they are not alone and isolated with respect to suicidal preoccupation. It is also important to communicate the idea that suicide is a choice, a problem-solving option, and there are other choices and options. This may be difficult to do in a way that does not make such an adolescent feel judged or put down. An example of what could be said to an adolescent in crisis is, "It is not unusual for adolescents to be so upset with relationships or circumstances that thoughts of suicide occur more and more frequently; this does not mean that you are weird or a freak. I am really glad you have chosen to talk to me about how you're feeling and what you are thinking. You have made a good choice since, now, you can begin exploring other ways to solve the problems you described."

6. *Listen actively and reinforce positively.* It is important, during the initial stages of the crisis management process, to let the adolescent at risk for suicide know you are listening carefully and really understanding how difficult life has been. Not only will such careful listening and communicating on the part of the professional make it easier for the adolescent to share, but it also it will provide the basis for a

growing sense of self-respect. Being listened to, heard, and respected are powerful and empowering experiences for anyone who is feeling at a loss for how to cope.

7. *Do not attempt in-depth counseling.* Although it is very important for a suicidal adolescent to begin to overcome feelings of despair and to develop a sense of control as soon as possible, the emotional turmoil and stress experienced during a crisis usually makes in-depth counseling impossible. Developing a plan to begin lessening the sense of crisis an adolescent may be experiencing is extremely important, however, and should be accomplished as soon as possible. Crisis management necessitates the development of a plan to lessen the crisis; this plan should be shared with the adolescent so that it is clear that circumstances will improve. Counseling/therapy cannot really take place during the height of a suicidal crisis.

8. *Contact another professional.* It is a good idea to enlist the assistance of another professional, trained in crisis management, when an adolescent thought to be at risk for suicide is brought to your attention. School and mental health counselors should ask a colleague to come into the office and assist with assessment. It is always a good idea to have the support of a colleague who understands the dynamics of a suicidal crisis; in addition, the observations made by two professionals are likely to be more comprehensive. Because suicidal adolescents may present a situation that, if misjudged or mismanaged, could result in a subsequent attempt or completion, it is in the best interest of both the professional and the client for professionals to work collaboratively whenever possible. It should also be noted that liability questions are less likely to become issues and professional judgment is less likely to be questioned if assessment of the severity of a suicidal crisis and associated recommendations for crisis management have been made on a collaborative basis. No matter what the circumstances, document all that is done on behalf of the youth through keeping careful case notes.

9. *Ask questions to assess lethality.* A number of dimensions must be explored to assess lethality. This assessment can be accomplished through an interview format (a crisis situation is not conducive to the administration of a written appraisal instrument). The following questions help determine the degree of risk in a suicidal crisis; all of them do not need to be asked if the interview results in the spontaneous disclosure of the information.

- *"What has happened to make life so difficult?"* The more an adolescent describes the circumstances that have contributed to feelings of despair and hopelessness, the better the opportunity for effective crisis management. The process of describing stress-producing interpersonal situations and circumstances may begin to lower feelings of stress and reduce risk. It is not unusual for an adolescent in the midst of a suicidal crisis to describe a multifaceted set of problems with family, peers, school, and drugs, for example. The more problems an adolescent describes as stress-producing and the more complicated the scenario, the higher the lethality or risk.
- *"Are you thinking of suicide?"* Although this may not be the second question asked during an assessment of risk (ask it when you think the timing is right), it is listed here because it is the second most important question to ask. Adolescents who have been preoccupied with suicidal thoughts may experience a sense of relief to know there is someone who is able to discuss suicide in a straightforward manner. Using the word *suicide* will convey that the helping professional is listening and is willing to be involved; using the word will not put the idea of suicide in the mind of a nonsuicidal adolescent. This

particular question need not be asked until such time the assessor has developed the rapport and trust of the adolescent; timing is important in this regard so that relief rather than resistance is experienced on the part of the adolescent.

- *"How long have you been thinking about suicide?"* Adolescents who have been preoccupied with suicide for a period of several weeks are more lethal than those who have only fleeting thoughts. One way to explore several components of this question is to remember the acronym FID: When asking about suicidal thoughts, ask about *frequency* or how often they occur, *intensity* or how dysfunctional the preoccupation is making the adolescent ("Can you go on with your daily routine as usual?"), and *duration* or how long the periods of preoccupation last. An adolescent who reports frequent periods of preoccupation so intense that it is difficult or impossible to go to school, to work, or to see friends, and for increasingly longer periods of time so that periods of preoccupation and dysfunction are merging, is more lethal than an adolescent who describes a different set of circumstances.

- *"Do you have a suicide plan?"* When an adolescent is able to be specific about the method, the time, the place, and who will or will not be nearby, the risk is higher. (If the use of a gun, knife, medication, or other means is described, ask if that item is in a pocket or purse and request that the item be left with you. Never, however, enter into a struggle with an adolescent to remove a firearm. Call the police or local suicide or crisis center.) Most adolescents will cooperate with you by telling you about the plan and allowing you to separate them from the means. Remember, most suicidal adolescents are other-directed; such a trait should be taken advantage of during a crisis management situation. Later, when the crisis has subsided and counseling is initiated, the adolescent's internal locus of control can be strengthened.

- *"Do you know someone who has committed suicide?"* If the answer is yes, the adolescent may be at higher risk, especially if this incident occurred within the family or a close network of friends. Such an adolescent may have come to believe that suicide is a legitimate problem-solving option.

- *"How much do you want to live?"* An adolescent who can provide only a few reasons for wishing to continue with life is at higher risk than an adolescent who can enumerate a number of reasons for continuing to live.

- *"How much do you want to die?"* The response to this question provides the opposite view of the one above. An adolescent who gives a variety of reasons for wishing to die is more lethal than an adolescent who cannot provide justification for ending life. It may be unnecessary to ask this question if the previous question provided adequate data.

- *"What do you think death is like?"* This question can be an excellent tool for assessment purposes. Adolescents who do not seem to realize that death is permanent, that there is no reversal possible, and that they cannot physically return are at higher risk for an actual attempt. Also, adolescents who have the idea that death will be romantic, nurturing, or the solution to current problems are at high risk.

- *"Have you attempted suicide in the past?"* If the answer to this question is yes, then the adolescent is more lethal. Another suicide attempt may occur that could be successful because a previous attempter has the memory of prior efforts and the fact that he or she conceptualized and carried through with a suicide plan. An additional attempt may correct deficits in the original plan and result in death.

- *"How long ago was this previous attempt?"* This question should be asked of any adolescent who answers yes to the previous question. The more recent the previous attempt, the more lethal the adolescent and the more critical the crisis management process.
- *"Have you been feeling depressed?"* Because a high percentage of adolescents who attempt or complete suicide are depressed, this is an important question. Using the acronym FID to remember to ask about frequency, intensity, and duration is also helpful in the context of exploring an adolescent's response to this question. As previously discussed, a determination needs to be made about the existence of clinical depression if such a condition is suspected. Adolescents who report frequent, intense, and lengthy periods of depression resulting in dysfunctional episodes that are becoming closer and closer together or are continuously experienced are at high risk.
- *"Is there anyone to stop you?"* This is an extremely important question. If an adolescent has a difficult time identifying a friend, family member, or significant adult who is worth living for, the probability of a suicide attempt is high. Whoever the adolescent can identify should be specifically named; addresses, phone numbers, and the relationship to the adolescent should also be obtained. (If the adolescent cannot remember phone numbers and addresses, look up the information, together, in a phone book.) In the event it is decided that a suicide watch should be initiated, the people in the network of the adolescent can be contacted and asked to participate.
- *"On a scale of 1 to 10, with 1 being low and 10 being high, what is the number that depicts the probability that you will attempt suicide?"* The higher the number, the higher the lethality.
- *"Do you use alcohol or other drugs?"* If the answer to this question is yes, the lethality is higher because use of a substance further distorts cognition and weakens impulse control. An affirmative response should also be followed by an exploration of the degree of drug involvement and identification of specific drugs.
- *"Have you experienced significant losses during the past year or earlier losses you've never discussed?"* Adolescents who have lost friends because of moving, vitality because of illness, their family of origin because of a divorce, or other losses are vulnerable to stress and confusion and are usually at higher risk for attempting or completing suicide if they have been preoccupied with such thoughts.
- *"Have you been concerned, in any way, with your sexuality?"* This may be a difficult question to explore, even briefly, during a peaking suicidal crisis. Generally, adolescents who are, or think they may be, gay or lesbian are at higher risk for suicide. It is quite difficult for adolescents to deal with the issue of sexual orientation because of fear of being ridiculed or rejected. They may have experienced related guilt and stress for a number of years never daring to discuss their feelings with anyone.
- *"When you think about yourself and the future, what do you visualize?"* A high-risk adolescent will probably have difficulty visualizing a future scenario and will describe feeling too hopeless and depressed to even imagine a future life.

As noted at the beginning of this discussion, it is not necessary to ask all of these questions if the answers to them are shared during the course of the discussion. Also, it is appropriate to ask additional questions after a response to any of the above when it seems to be constructive to do so. It should be noted that the interviewing team must make judgments about the truthfulness of a specific response by considering the response in the total context of the interview.

10. *Make crisis management decisions.* If, as a result of an assessment made by at least two professionals, the adolescent is at risk for suicide, a number of crisis management interventions can be considered. They may be used singularly or in combination; the actual combination will depend on the lethality determination, resources and people available, and professional judgment. It is the responsibility of the professionals involved, however, to develop a crisis management plan to be followed until the crisis subsides and long-term counseling or therapy can be initiated.

- *Notify parent/legal guardians.* Parents of minors must be notified and asked for assistance when an adolescent is determined to be at risk for a suicide attempt. Often, adolescents may attempt to elicit a promise of confidentiality from a school or mental health counselor who learns about suicidal intent. Such confidentiality is not possible; the welfare of the adolescent is the most important consideration, and parents should be contacted as soon as possible.

  Sometimes parents do not believe that their child is suicidal and refuse to leave home or work and meet with their son or daughter and members of the assessment team. At times, parents may be adamant in their demands that the school or mental health professional withdraw their involvement. Although such attitudes are not conducive to the management of a suicidal crisis, they are understandable because parents may respond to such information with denial or anger to mask true emotions and cope with apprehensions that perhaps their child's situation reflects their personal inadequacies as people and parents. Because an adolescent at risk for a suicide attempt cannot be left unmonitored, this provides a dilemma for a school or a mental health agency. Conforming to the wishes of uncooperative parents places the adolescent at even greater risk, thus steps must be taken despite parental protests. Although some professionals worry about liability issues in such circumstances, liability is higher if such an adolescent is allowed to leave unmonitored and with no provision for follow-up assistance. It may be necessary to refer the youth to protective services for children and families when parents or guardians refuse to cooperate. Schools and mental health centers should confer with legal counsel to understand liability issues and to make sure that the best practices are followed in such circumstances.

- *Consider hospitalization.* Hospitalization can be the option of choice during a suicidal crisis (even if the parents are cooperating) when the risk is high. An adolescent who has not been sleeping or eating, for example, may be totally exhausted or highly agitated. The care and safety that can be offered in a psychiatric unit of a hospital is often needed until the adolescent can experience a lowered level of stress, obtain food and rest, and realize that others consider the circumstances painful and worthy of attention. In many hospital settings, multidisciplinary teams (physicians, psychiatrists, counselors, social workers, nurses, nurse practitioners, teachers) work to individualize a treatment plan and provide for outpatient help as soon as the need for assistance on an inpatient basis subsides.

- *Write contracts.* At times, professionals may decide that developing a contract with the adolescent may be enough to support the adolescent through a period of crisis and into a more positive frame of mind after which the adolescent would be more receptive to long-term counseling or therapy. Such a contract should be written out and signed and dated by the adolescent and the counselor. The contract can also be witnessed and signed by other professionals, friends, or family members.

   Contracts should require the adolescent to:

   a. Agree to stay safe.
   b. Obtain enough food and sleep.
   c. Discard items that could be used in a suicide attempt (guns, weapons, medications, etc.).
   d. Specify the time span of the contract.
   e. Call a counselor, crisis center, and so on if there is a temptation to break the contract or attempt suicide.
   f. Write down the phone numbers of people to contact if the feeling of crisis escalates.
   g. Specify ways time will be structured (walks, talks, movies, etc.).

- *Organize suicide watches.* If hospital psychiatric services on an inpatient basis are not available in a given community and those doing the assessment believe the suicide risk is high, a suicide watch should be organized by contacting the individuals that the adolescent has identified in response to the question, "Is there anyone to stop you?" After receiving instruction and orientation from the professional, family members and friends should take turns staying with the adolescent until the crisis has subsided and long-term counseling or therapy has begun. In our opinion, it is never a good idea to depend on a family member alone to carry out a suicide watch; it is usually too difficult for family members to retain perspective. Friends should be contacted and included in a suicide watch even though confidentiality, as discussed earlier, cannot be maintained.

- *Refuse to allow the youth to return to school without an assessment by a mental health counselor, psychologist, psychiatrist, or other qualified professional.* An increasing number of school districts are adopting this policy. Although it could be argued that preventing a suicidal youth from returning to school might exacerbate suicidal ideation and intent, this policy increases the probability that the youth will receive mental health counseling and provides the school with support in the process of preventing the youth from engaging in self-harm.

School and Community

When an adolescent has attempted or completed a suicide, it is imperative, particularly in a school setting, to be aware of the impact of such an event on the entire system. Usually, within just a few hours, the fact that an adolescent has attempted or completed suicide has been chronicled through the peer group. This could present a problem to the faculty and staff in a given school building, because not answering questions raised by students can engender the sharing of misinformation or rumors and encouraging open discussion could embarrass an attempter on his or her return.

The following guidelines should prove helpful. Had Jim been in the regular school program when he made his attempt, these guidelines would have been put into effect immediately.

1. The principal of the building in which a student has attempted or completed suicide (even though such an incident most likely occurred off the school campus) should organize a telephone network to notify all faculty and staff that a mandatory meeting will take place before school the next morning. (Prior to the meeting, the principal should confirm the death through the coroner's office or through the student's family.) The principal should share information and answer questions about what happened during such a meeting. In the case of a suicide completion, it is recommended that the principal provide all faculty and staff with an announcement that can be read, in each class rather than over a public address system, so that everyone in the school receives the same information. The announcement should confirm the loss and emphasize the services the school and community will be providing during the day and subsequent days. Details about the circumstances or the family of the deceased should not be given so that confidentiality is maintained in that regard.

2. Faculty and staff should be instructed to answer student questions that spontaneously arise but should be told not to initiate a discussion of suicide in general.

3. Faculty and staff should be told to excuse students from class if they are upset and need to spend time in the office of the building counselor or another member of a core or crisis team.

4. Parents who are upset by the suicidal incident should be directed to a designated individual to have questions answered. Parents should also be provided with options for counseling, whether this counseling is provided by school personnel or referred to members of the mental health community.

5. At times, newspaper and television journalists contact the school for information about both the attempt or the completion and the school's response to the aftermath. Again, it is important to direct all such inquiries to a designated individual to avoid the problems created by inconsistency or sharing inaccurate information.

6. If a suicidal attempt occurs prior to the initiation of prevention and crisis management efforts in a given building, it is not a good idea to immediately initiate classroom mental health education even if faculty, staff, and core teams have been prepared and a written policy has been developed. Allow sufficient time to pass to prevent embarrassment to the returning student and his or her family.

7. Be alert to delayed or enhanced grief responses on the part of students prior to the anniversary of a suicide completion. Often students will need opportunity to participate in a support group with peers or individual counseling prior to and, perhaps, beyond the anniversary date.

8. Do not conduct a memorial service on the school campus after a suicide because doing so may provide reinforcement to other students preoccupied with suicidal ideation. This means that it is unwise to conduct an on-campus memorial service after a death for any reason—it is difficult to explain why a student who has committed suicide is not being remembered when another student, faculty, or staff has been memorialized previously. Students who wish to attend the off-campus memorial or funeral should be excused. Do the same thing after deaths for other reasons.

9. Early in the sequence of events, as listed above, one or two individuals from the school should contact the family and ask if there is any support they might need that the school can provide. It is a good idea to offer such assistance periodi-

cally, as time passes, because so many families are left alone with their grief once the memorial or funeral has taken place.

ADAPTATIONS FOR DIVERSITY

It is important to note that the information contained in the introductory section of this chapter suggests a number of adaptations for diversity particularly with respect to prevention efforts. Because data suggest that Caucasian adolescent males are the highest risk group for suicide, extra efforts should be made to involve those young men who may be vulnerable in early prevention efforts. Individual and group counseling focused on some of the personality traits described earlier could and should be initiated in the elementary school years. Such early prevention efforts are preferable to waiting until suicidal preoccupation develops and observations about behavior can be observed. Because Native Americans have the highest adolescent suicide rates of any ethnic group in the United States, teachers, counselors, and parents should be alerted to early signs so that efforts can be made to avert the development of at-risk behaviors.

The etiology of suicide is something that all adults should be made aware of so that young people experiencing psychiatric illness, abuse, confusion about sexual identity, chronic or terminal physical illness, and other problems discussed earlier in the chapter can be monitored, supported, and referred for counseling/therapy when needed. Staffing sessions should be routinely conducted in elementary, middle, and high school settings so that young people who may be at risk for suicide attempts or completions could be routinely monitored and assisted. Because we know that adolescents who experience what they interpret as shameful or humiliating experiences with peers and with family members may, at times, be at high risk, these young people should also be the focus of observation and action should the need for prevention or intervention efforts be identified. In general, the more adults can be made aware of both risk factors and the suicidal profile, the earlier and more effective the prevention or intervention efforts.

SUMMARY

We believe that individuals who are interested in working with suicidal youths must obtain more extensive information than that provided in this chapter. In addition, such individuals should obtain supervision from professionals qualified to provide such supervision after observing actual assessment interview and counseling/therapy sessions. Generally, neither assessment nor preventive or postvention sessions should be attempted by anyone who has graduated from a graduate program with *less than* a 2-year course work and practicum/internship requirement. (In the case of counselors, such a graduate program should follow the standard set by the Council for the Accreditation of Counseling and Related Educational Programs.) In addition, membership in the American Association of Suicidology, participation in workshops and conferences focused on the topic of adolescent suicide, and consistent reading of the journal *Suicide and Life-Threatening Behavior* and other books and journals are imperative.

Readers should also be cautioned not to use the material in this chapter as the sole basis for mental health education on the topic of adolescent suicide prevention or faculty/staff development in schools. This chapter provides an overview and an starting point for professionals. Those without expertise on the topic or graduate preparation as a counselor, social worker, psychologist, psychiatric nurse, or other helping professional will not be able to answer questions of clients, families, and other professionals from reading a single chapter on this topic. Finally, anyone reading this chapter should be cautioned against initiating an adolescent suicide prevention, crisis management, and postvention program without writing a description of the various components so it can be checked by other professionals (including attorneys) and followed by all those involved in such an initiative.

An adolescent who becomes suicidal is communicating the fact that he or she is experiencing difficulty with problem solving, managing stress, expressing feelings, and so on. It is important for us to respond in constructive, safe, informed ways because the future of our communities (whether local, national, or international) depends on individuals who are positive, functional, and able to cope with the complex demands of life. As research and clinical experience provide additional and more sophisticated information about adolescent suicide, it will be necessary to incorporate this information into prevention, crisis management, and postvention efforts. To abdicate our responsibility to do so would communicate a lack of interest in the youth of today and a lack of concern about the future of society.

REFERENCES

Adelman, H. S., & Taylor, L. (2000). Moving prevention from the fringes into the fabric of school improvement. *Journal of Educational and Psychological Consultation, 11,* 7–36.

American Academy of Pediatrics. (2004). Policy statement: School-based mental health services. *Pediatrics, 113,* 1839–1845.

American Psychiatric Association. (2000). *Diagnostic and statistical manual of mental disorders* (4th ed., Text Revision). Washington, DC: Author.

Beautrais, A. L. (2005). National strategies for the reduction and prevention of suicide. *Crisis, 26,* 1–3.

Beautrais, A. L., Joyce, P. R., & Mulder, R. T. (1999). Personality traits and cognitive styles as risk factors for serious suicide attempts among young people. *Suicide and Life-Threatening Behavior, 29,* 37–47.

Berlin, I. N. (1987). Suicide among American Indian adolescents: An overview. *Suicide and Life-Threatening Behavior, 17,* 218–232.

Berman, A. L., & Jobes, D. A. (1991). *Adolescent suicide: Assessment and intervention.* Washington DC: American Psychological Association.

Blumenthal, S. J. (1991). Letter to the editor. *Journal of the American Medical Association, 265,* 2806–2807.

Borowsky, I. W., Ireland, M., & Resnick, M. D. (2001). Adolescent suicide attempts: Risks and protectors. *Pediatrics, 107,* 485–493.

Brent, D. A., Perper, J. A., Moritz, G., Baugher, M., Schweers, J., & Roth, C. (1993). Firearms and adolescent suicide: A community case-control study. *American Journal of Diseases in Children, 147,* 1066–1071.

Bush, J. A. (1976). Suicide and Blacks. *Suicide and Life-Threatening Behavior, 6,* 216–222.

Canetto, S. S., & Sakinofsky, I. (1998). The gender paradox in suicide. *Suicide and Life-Threatening Behavior, 28,* 1–23.

Cantor, P. (1976). Personality characteristics found among youthful female suicide attempters. *Journal of Abnormal Psychology, 85,* 324–329.

Capuzzi, D. (1988). *Counseling and intervention strategies for adolescent suicide prevention* (Contract No. 400-86-0014). Ann Arbor, MI: ERIC Counseling and Personnel Services Clearinghouse.

Capuzzi, D. (1994). *Suicide prevention in the schools: Guidelines for middle and high school settings.* Alexandria, VA: American Counseling Association.

Capuzzi, D., & Golden, L. (Eds.). (1988). *Preventing adolescent suicide.* Muncie, IN: Accelerated Development.

Capuzzi, D., & Gross, D. R. (2004). "I don't want to live": The adolescent at risk for suicidal behavior. In D. Capuzzi & D. R. Gross (Eds.), *Youth at risk: A prevention resource for counselors, teachers, and parents* (4th ed., pp. 275–302). Alexandria, VA: American Counseling Association.

Cavaiola, A. A., & Lavender, N. (1999). Suicidal behavior in chemically dependent adolescents. *Adolescence, 34,* 735–744.

Centers for Disease Control and Prevention. (2000). CDC surveillance summaries. *MMWR, 49*(No. SS-5), 10.

Cohen, E. M. (2000). Suicidal ideation among adolescents in relation to recalled exposure to violence. *Current Psychology, 19,* 46–56.

Committee on Adolescence. (2000). Suicide and suicide attempts in adolescence. *Pediatrics, 105,* 871–874.

Coy, D. R. (1995). The need for a school suicide prevention policy. *National Association of Student Services Professionals Bulletin, 79,* 1–9.

Cull, J., & Gill, W. (1982). *Suicide probability scale manual.* Los Angeles: Western Psychological Services.

Curran, D. F. (1987). *Adolescent suicidal behavior.* Washington, DC: Hemisphere.

Davidson, M. W., & Range, L. M. (1999). Are teachers of children and young adolescents responsive to suicide prevention training modules? Yes. *Death Studies, 23,* 61–71.

Davis, P. A. (1983). *Suicidal adolescents.* Springfield, IL: Charles C Thomas.

Diekstra, R. F. (1989). Suicidal behavior in adolescents and young adults: The international picture. *Crisis, 10,* 16–35.

Faigel, H. (1966). Suicide among young persons: A review of its incidence and causes, and methods for its prevention. *Clinical Pediatrics, 5,* 187–190.

Fernquist, R. M. (2000). Problem drinking in the family and youth suicide. *Adolescent Psychology, 35,* 551–558.

Freese, A. (1979). *Adolescent suicide: Mental health challenge.* New York: Public Affairs Committee.

Garland, A. F., & Zigler, E. (1993). Adolescent suicide prevention: Current research and social policy implications. *American Psychologist, 43,* 169–182.

Gibbs, J. T. (1988). Conceptual, methodological, and sociocultural issues in Black youth suicide: Implications for assessment and early intervention. *Suicide and Life-Threatening Behavior, 18,* 73–79.

Gould, M. S., Greenberg, T., Velting, D. M., & Shaffer, D. (2003). Youth suicide risk and preventative interventions: A review of the past 10 years. *Journal of the American Academy of Child and Adolescent Psychiatry, 42,* 386–405.

Gust-Brey, K., & Cross, T. (1999). An examination of the literature base on the suicidal behaviors of gifted students. *Roeper Review, 22,* 28–35.

Hafen, B. Q. (Ed.). (1972). *Self-destructive behavior.* Minneapolis, MN: Burgess.

Hafen, B. Q., & Frandsen, K. J. (1986). *Youth suicide: Depression and loneliness.* Provo, UT: Behavioral Health Associates.

Haley, M. (2004). Risk and protective factors. In D. Capuzzi (Ed.), *Suicide across the life span: Implications for counselors* (pp. 95–138). Alexandria, VA: American Counseling Association.

Hallfors, D., Brodish, P. H., Khatapoush, S., Sanchez, V., Cho, H., & Steckler, A. (2006). Feasibility of screening adolescents for suicide risk in "real world" high school settings. *American Journal of Public Health, 96*, 282–287

Harry, J. (1989). *Sexual identity issues—Report of the Secretary's Task Force on Youth Suicide: Vol. 2. Risk factors for youth suicide* (DHHS Publication No. ADM 89-1622). Washington, DC: U.S. Government Printing Office.

Henry, A. F., & Short, J. F. (1954). *Suicide and homicide.* Glencoe, IL: Free Press.

Hermann, M. A., & Remley, T. P., Jr. (2000). Guns, violence, and schools: The results of school violence litigation against educators and students shedding more constitutional rights at the school house gate. *Loyola Law Review, 46*, 389–439.

Hoberman, H. M., & Garfinkel, B. D. (1988). Completed suicide in children and adolescents. *Journal of the American Academy of Child and Adolescent Psychiatry, 27,* 688–695.

Hussain, S. A., & Vandiver, K. T. (1984). *Suicide in children and adolescents.* New York: SP Medical and Scientific Books.

Jacobs, J. (1971). *Adolescent suicide.* New York: Wiley-Interscience.

Johnson, S. W., & Maile, L. J. (1987). *Suicide and the schools: A handbook for prevention, intervention, and rehabilitation.* Springfield, IL: Charles C Thomas.

Judge, B., & Billick, S. B. (2004). Suicidality in adolescence: Review and legal considerations. *Behavioral Sciences and the Law, 22,* 681–695.

Kiev, A. (1977). *The suicidal patient.* Chicago: Nelson-Hall.

King, K. A. (1999). Fifteen prevalent myths concerning adolescent suicide. *Journal of School Health, 69,* 159–161.

King, K. A. (2000). Preventing adolescent suicide: Do high school counselors know the risk factors? *Professional School Counseling, 3,* 255–263.

King, K. A. (2001a). Developing a comprehensive school suicide prevention program. *Journal of School Health, 71,* 132–137.

King, K. A. (2001b). Tri-level suicide prevention covers it all. *Education Digest, 67,* 55–61.

Kirchner, J. E., Yoder, M. C., Kramer, T. L., Lindsey, M. S., & Thrush, C. (2000). Development of an educational program to increase school personnel's awareness about child and adolescent depression. *Education, 121,* 235–246.

Kitts, R. L. (2005). Gay adolescents and suicide: Understanding the association. *Adolescence, 40,* 621–628.

Kovacs, M., Beck, A., & Weissman, A. (1975). The use of suicidal motives in the psychotherapy of attempted suicides. *American Journal of Psychotherapy, 29,* 363–368.

Lyon, M. E., Benoit, M., O'Donnell, R. M., Getson, P. R., Silber, T., & Walsh, T. (2000). Assessing African American adolescents' risk for suicide attempts. *Adolescence, 35,* 121–134.

Maples, M. F., Packman, J., Abney, P., Daugherty, R. F., Casey, J. A., & Pirtle, L. (2005). Suicide by teenagers in middle school: A postvention team approach. *Journal of Counseling & Development, 83,* 397–405.

Mazza, J. J., & Reynolds, W. M. (1998). A longitudinal investigation of depression, hopelessness, social support, and major and minor life events and their relation to suicidal ideation in adolescents. *Suicide and Life-Threatening Behavior, 28,* 358–374.

McWhirter, J. J., & Kigin, T. J. (1988). Depression. In D. Capuzzi & L. Golden (Eds.), *Preventing adolescent suicide* (pp. 149–186). Muncie, IN: Accelerated Development.

Metha, A., Weber, B., & Webb, L. D. (1998). Youth suicide prevention: A survey and analysis of policies and efforts in the 50 states. *Suicide and Life-Threatening Behavior, 28,* 150–164.

Moskos, M. A., Achilles, J., & Gray, D. (2004). Adolescent suicide myths in the United States. *Crisis, 25,* 176–182.

National Center for Health Statistics. (2002). Deaths: Leading causes for 2000. *National Vital Statistics Reports, 50*(16).

National Institute of Mental Health. (2002). *Suicide facts.* Retrieved December 21, 2002, from http://www.nimh.nih.gov/research/suifact.htm

Orbach, I. (2001). Therapeutic empathy with the suicidal wish: Principles of therapy with suicidal individuals. *American Journal of Psychotherapy, 55,* 166–184.

Peck, D. (1983). The last moments of life: Learning to cope. *Deviant Behavior, 4,* 313–342.

Price, J. H., Dake, J. A., & Kucharewski, R. (2001). Assets as predictors of suicide attempts in African American inner-city youths. *American Journal of Health Behavior, 25,* 367–375.

Reddy, L. A., & Richardson, L. (2006). School-based prevention and intervention programs for children with emotional disturbance. *Education and Treatment of Children, 29,* 379–404.

Rohde, P., Lewinsohn, P., & Seeley, J. R. (1991). Comorbidity of unipolar depression: Comorbidity with other mental disorders in adolescents and adults. *Journal of Abnormal Psychology, 100,* 214–222.

Ross, C. (1980). Mobilizing schools for suicide prevention. *Suicide and Life-Threatening Behavior, 10,* 239–243.

Russell, S. T., & Joyner, K. (2001). Adolescent sexual orientation and suicide risk: Evidence from a natural study. *American Journal of Public Health, 91,* 1276–1281.

Rutter, P. A., & Behrendt, A. E. (2004). Adolescent suicide risk: Four psychosocial factors. *Adolescence, 39,* 295–302.

Satcher, D. (1999). *Remarks at the release of the Surgeon General's call to action to prevent suicide.* Retrieved November 21, 2002, from http://www.surgeongeneral.gov/library/calltoaction/remarks.htm

Schneidman, E., Farbverow, N., & Litman, R. (1976). *The psychology of suicide.* New York: Jason Aronson.

Shaffer, D. (1988). The epidemiology of teen suicide: An examination of risk factors. *Journal of Clinical Psychiatry, 49,* 36–41.

Shaffer, D., & Craft, L. (1999). Methods of adolescent suicide prevention. *Journal of Clinical Psychiatry, 60,* 70–74.

Shaffer, D., Garland, A., Gould, M., Fisher, P., & Trautman, P. (1988). Preventing teenage suicide: A critical review. *Journal of the American Academy of Child and Adolescent Psychiatry, 27,* 675–687.

Shaughnessy, L., Doshi, S. R., & Jones, S. E. (2004). Attempted suicide and associated health risk behaviors among Native American high school students. *Journal of School Health, 74,* 177–182.

Sommes, B. (1984). The troubled teen: Suicide, drug use, and running away. *Women and Health, 9,* 117–141.

Speaker, K. M., & Petersen, G. J. (2000). School violence and adolescent suicide: Strategies for effective intervention. *Educational Review, 52,* 65–73.

Stanard, R. P. (2000). Assessment and treatment of adolescent suicidality. *Journal of Mental Health Counseling, 22,* 204–217.

Stein, M., & Davis, J. (1982). *Therapies for adolescents.* San Francisco: Jossey-Bass.

Stillion, J., McDowell, E., & Shamblin, J. (1984). The suicide attitude vignette experience: A method for measuring adolescent attitudes toward suicide. *Death Education, 8,* 65–81.

Sudak, H., Ford, A., & Rushforth, N. (1984). Adolescent suicide: An overview. *American Journal of Psychotherapy, 38,* 350–369.

Velkoff, P., & Huberty, T. J. (1988). Thinking patterns and motivation. In D. Capuzzi & L. Golden (Eds.), *Preventing adolescent suicide* (pp. 111–147). Muncie, IN: Accelerated Development.

Wyche, K., Obolensky, N., & Glood, E. (1990). American Indian, Black American, and Hispanic American youth. In M. J. Rotheram-Borus, J. Bradley, & N. Obolensky (Eds.), *Planning to live: Evaluating and treating suicidal teens in community settings* (pp. 355–389). Tulsa: University of Oklahoma Press.

Zenere, F. J., III, & Lazarus, P. J. (1997). The decline of youth suicidal behavior in an urban, multicultural public school system following the introduction of a suicide prevention and intervention program. *Suicide and Life-Threatening Behavior, 27,* 387–403.

CHAPTER 11

■

A Future in Jeopardy: Sexuality Issues in Adolescence

Melinda Haley and Jason Vasquez

Erik Erikson theorized in his model for psychosocial development that adolescents between the ages of 12 and 18 need to achieve a sense of identity in many areas, such as occupation, sex roles, politics, and religion ("Erik Erikson's Eight Stages," 2006). Therefore, adolescence can be a busy time. It can be a time of exploration, identity formation, and social activity. This is a period when an adolescent is attempting to figure out who he or she is as an entity separate from parents, family, and friends. Adolescents are active in exploring what their values are, what they believe in, and who they want to be as adults.

G. Stanley Hall (1904) once deemed adolescence as a period of "storm and stress," and since then, many have viewed adolescence as a period during which an individual goes through many developmental changes. As a part of this exploration, identity formation, and developmental change, many adolescents will face issues pertaining to teen pregnancy and parenthood, drug and alcohol use, rape and date rape, contraction or prevention of sexually transmitted diseases (STDs), career or college decisions, sexual orientation exploration, as well as many other exciting and daunting tasks associated with growing into adulthood. It can be a confusing time for teens and a time in which they are faced with many choices, especially in the area of sexuality.

This time of adolescent exploration and identity formation may also then include sexual awakening and exploration. Along with this burgeoning awareness of sexuality comes risk and responsibility. This chapter focuses on youth at risk for the areas of teen pregnancy, STDs (including HIV/AIDS), rape and date rape, and teens as targets for sexual predators. The following case study might be considered typical of a youth at risk. We ask that you keep the case of Julia in mind as you read through this chapter. As you read about these topics in terms of risk factors, prevention, and intervention strategies, consider how Julia might be helped, or what might need to change in Julia's life, to help her minimize her risk for potential negative outcomes.

CASE STUDY

Julia is a 16-year-old, White, heterosexual female. She is a junior at a large south-western high school and is not doing well academically. Julia's mother and father are divorced, and Julia has not seen her father since she was 11 years old. Julia's parents' relationship has been fraught with domestic violence, and Julia is not allowed to see her father. Despite her father's actions toward her mother, Julia really misses her father and wishes he were still around. Julia feels that if her parents really loved her they would work things out. Julia often feels bad about herself and doesn't feel she is really loved by anyone.

Julia became sexually active at age 14 when she lost her virginity to her biggest crush. Soon after the big event, Julia's crush dumped her. Julia was devastated and felt ugly and stupid. These feelings further fueled Julia's beliefs that she is not worthy. She began to date other boys to prove that she was attractive and to find the love she so desperately wanted from someone. She gained a reputation in school as "easy" and now feels isolated from other girls because she gets teased a lot and gets called derogatory names.

About 2 months ago Julia began to indulge in alcohol and marijuana with some of her recent boyfriends and male friends. Her recent drug use has further deteriorated her relationship with her mother, who found pot in Julia's room. Julia does not feel close to her mother and blames her for the loss of her father.

Julia uses condoms most of the time when she has sex, but not always. She tries to be prepared, but sometimes her preparations fall through. Julia feels loved, wanted, and special while having sex but feels used and disgusted with herself afterward. Yet, she cannot seem to say no when a boy she likes wants to have sex with her. Even when she says no, she often doesn't mean it; it is like a game to her. When a boy pursues her, she feels wanted. It will be useful to keep Julia in mind as you read the following sections related to issues facing youth at risk: teen pregnancy, STDs, rape and date rape, and sexual predators.

TEEN PREGNANCY

Adolescent pregnancy has been, and continues to be, a significant social problem in the United States. For over 30 years, from 1960 to 1992, the birthrate among women ages 15–19 years quadrupled (Hogan, Sun, & Cornwell, 2000). In 1986, 107 pregnancies occurred per 1,000 adolescent girls ages 15–19 years, and by 1990 that number rose by 11% to 117 per 1,000 (Darroch & Singh, 1999). However, by 1996 the rate fell to 97 pregnancies per 1,000 girls ages 15–19 years (National Campaign to Prevent Teen Pregnancy [NCPTP], 2004).

Current estimates suggest there appears to have been an overall decline in childbirths for women ages 15–19 from 1990 to 2000 (Darroch & Singh, 1999). In 2002, the overall teen pregnancy rate declined from 111 per 1,000 in 1980 to 83.6 per 1,000 for women ages 15–19 years old (Centers for Disease Control and Prevention, 2002). Yet almost 1 million teenagers continue to become pregnant each year, and 2,700 teens become pregnant each day in this country (Darroch & Singh, 1999; Monahan, 2002).

Overall, the United States continues to have one of the highest teen pregnancy rates among the developed countries (Kirby, 2002a; NCPTP, 2006). In 1999, the U.S. pregnancy rate for adolescents between the ages of 15 and 19 was estimated at 87 per 1,000 females; by comparison the rate in France was 10 per 1,000, in Canada it was 25 per 1,000, and in Britain it was 28 per 1,000 (Moss, 2004). The data suggest that teenagers in the United States remain at a greater risk for conception than their peers from other industrialized nations.

Findings from epidemiological studies suggest that despite the nationwide decline in teen birth rates, major disparities continue to exist across racial and ethnic subgroups. For example, since 1990, birth rates among Hispanic youth continue to be among the highest in the United States, and currently Hispanic adolescent females between the ages of 15 and 19 have one of the highest birth rates in the country (Moss, 2004). In a study by Darroch and Singh (1999), 24% of Hispanic teenagers had a first birth before the age of 20 compared with 8% of non-Hispanic Whites. In essence, these findings suggest that for some racial/ethnic groups, teen pregnancy continues to be a major problem.

Teen pregnancy and childbirth continue to be associated with a number of negative effects for young women and their children (Stevens-Simon, Sheeder, Beach, & Harter, 2005; Yampolska, Brown, & Vargo, 2004). Babies born to teen mothers are more likely to be preterm, of low birth weight, at greater risk for serious illness or developmental delays, and of greater risk for dying within the first year compared with babies born to older mothers. Many of these children are also more likely to experience child abuse and neglect (As-Sanie, Gantt, & Rosenthal, 2004). As a result, children born to teen parents have a greater risk of doing poorly in school, engaging in early sexual activity and teen pregnancy, and getting into trouble with the law (NCPTP, 2003).

Although teen mothers only represent a small proportion of those who are on welfare, the societal costs of medical care, food and housing, and employment training for teen mothers are estimated at $7 billion per year (NCPTP, 2004). Compared with their peers, teen mothers have a higher risk of reporting low self-esteem and depression (As-Sanie et al., 2004), and less than one third of teen mothers ever finish their high school education (NCPTP, 2004). Consequently, teen mothers are more likely to experience mental health problems, be unprepared for the job market, and be at a greater risk of raising their children in poverty (J. Cohen, 2006).

Risk Factors

Previous research on the risk factors correlated with teen pregnancy had focused on rate of teen sexual activity, quality of parental supervision, effects of poverty, and childhood trauma (Monahan, 2002). There are numerous factors associated with the current trend in teen pregnancy and childbirth, such as parental relationships, pregnancy intentions, pubertal development, and alcohol and drug use (Brook et al., 2004; Davies et al., 2004; B. C. Miller, 2002; Periera, Canavarro, Cardosa, & Mendonca, 2005; Rosengard, Phillips, Adler, & Ellen, 2004; 2005; Talashek, Peragallo, Noor, & Dancy, 2004). However, given that there is not enough space to fully address this topic, the following is an overview of recent research on teen pregnancy risk factors.

Some studies support the view that adolescent girls who are raised by single parents with low educational attainment and low income are at a high risk of becoming teen mothers (B. C. Miller, 2002; Periera et al., 2005). These studies suggest that the stress and conflict associated with poverty influence adolescent sexual behavior and risk taking. Yet, other studies suggest that regardless of the socioeconomic factors, the quality of the parental relationship is an important determinant associated with teen pregnancy. In summarizing the research in this area, the National Campaign to Prevent Teen Pregnancy (2004) indicated that teens who are not close to their parents are more likely to engage in early sexual activity, have multiple sexual partners, and are less likely to use contraception on a consistent basis.

Pregnancy intentions have also been found to predict pregnancy outcomes among teens. For instance, Rosengard et al. (2004) found that among adolescent girls who indicated clear pregnancy intentions (planning and likely) and inconsistent pregnancy intentions (not planning and likely) were more apt to report suspected pregnancies or positive test results compared with those who revealed no intention of getting pregnant (not planning and not likely). Similarly, in their study on the pregnancy intentions of teenage boys, Rosengard et al. (2005) reported that a majority of those surveyed had no plans of getting someone pregnant. However, some revealed that they were likely to get their female partner pregnant in the near future.

Another factor related to risky sexual behavior and teen pregnancy is early onset pubertal development. Girls who mature early are less likely to be prepared for the transition and others' expectations of maturation. These girls are at a higher risk of attracting attention from older males, which in turn increases their risk for engaging in high-risk behaviors (Davies et al., 2004). Deardorff, Gonzales, Christopher, Roosa, and Millsap (2005) found that adolescent girls who matured earlier (before the age of 12) were more likely to engage in early onset alcohol use and sexual activity.

The association between early alcohol and drug use to risky sexual behaviors has been well documented in the literature. For example, results from Brook et al.'s (2004) study of Puerto Rican and African American youth showed that early illicit drug use predicted future sexually risky behaviors. Findings from that study indicated that early onset alcohol and drug use predicted inconsistent contraceptive use, multiple sex partners, and adolescent pregnancy.

On the basis of findings from previous studies, teen pregnancy continues to represent a serious risk to the overall life success of youth. For example, teens who become pregnant are less likely to complete their education, less prepared for the job market, at a greater risk of developing mental health problems, and more likely to live in poverty. In addition, children of teen mothers are at a greater risk for developmental delays, child abuse or neglect, early alcohol or drug use, and problems with the law (As-Sanie et al., 2004; J. Cohen, 2006; Stevens-Simon et al., 2005; Yampolska et al., 2004). As a result, researchers and government officials continue to develop programs aimed at reducing the risk of pregnancy among teenagers. Therefore, the next section of this chapter provides an overview of the current trends in teen pregnancy prevention.

Approaches to Prevention

Nearly 7 years ago the estimated teen pregnancy rate was 87 pregnancies per 1,000 women ages 15–19 years. However, since that time the pregnancy rate has declined. Yet, over 900,000 adolescent girls continue to become pregnant each year in the United States, and, as mentioned, the U.S. adolescent pregnancy rate remains among the highest in the industrialized world (Moss, 2004). Thus, prevention efforts are vital to continuing the overall decline in teen pregnancy.

During the past 30 years, research on the efficacy of pregnancy prevention programs has become increasingly more advanced. In a review of past research on prevention programs, Kirby (1999) found five different areas in which the field has improved: (a) Research has become increasingly sophisticated, (b) sample sizes and calculations of statistical power have increased, (c) researchers have increased the use of experimental designs with random assignment, (d) researchers have increased use of longitudinal designs, and (e) researchers have increased the use of more sophisticated statistical techniques. The following subsections discuss the most recent teen pregnancy prevention strategies targeted at the individual, family, school, and community level.

Individual

In the past, prevention strategies for individuals were geared toward reducing adolescent pregnancies and childbirth through education focused on delaying the initiation of sexual activity (Darroch & Singh, 1999). These abstinence-only programs suggest that the only effective means of avoiding teen pregnancy is by delaying sexual activity until marriage. Abstinence-only programs typically do not discuss contraception and contraceptive failure. One advantage to these types of programs is that they are diverse. For example, some are religious based whereas others are curriculum oriented, and some last as few as 1 session whereas others can be 20 sessions in length. To date, few studies have examined the effectiveness of abstinence-only programs.

In one of the few studies to review the efficacy of different types of pregnancy prevention programs, Kirby (2002a) found that abstinence-only programs have failed to delay the initiation of sexual activity. Similarly, As-Sanie et al. (2004) reported that abstinence-only programs did not significantly alter self-reported rates of intercourse and pregnancy. However, both Kirby (2002a) and As-Sanie et al. (2004) cautioned that the data concerning the effectiveness of abstinence-only programs are largely inconclusive because of methodological limitations (e.g., small sample sizes, no comparison group, lack of random assignment, participant attrition, and lack of follow-up) and diversity of abstinence programs (e.g., religious, curriculum, etc.).

Other current prevention strategies geared toward individuals include the following: sex and contraceptive counseling with male adolescents (As-Sanie et al., 2004), sex education focused on gender roles (Rose, 2005), and culturally sensitive service providers (e.g., openness and knowledge of the unique aspects of the clients' language, cultural values, community institutions, and experiences of discrimination; Wilkinson-Lee, Russell, Lee, & The Latina/o Teen Pregnancy Prevention Workgroup, 2006).

Family

Parents play a critical role in adolescents' ability to avoid sexual risk-taking behaviors through critical factors, such as degree of family involvement, family structure, parental monitoring, and parent–child communication (Lederman & Mian, 2003). Past efforts in the area of family prevention include enhancement of parenting skills and facilitation of parent–child relationships through the improved communication (Flores, Montgomery, & Lee, 2005). Intervention strategies that have been shown to have a positive impact on facilitating parent–child communication about sex and enhancing parental skills include (a) giving honest answers about sexual issues, (b) knowing what your values are about sexual issues, (c) replacing street slang with correct words, (d) answering questions age-appropriately, (e) trying not to be judgmental, and (f) practicing answering questions with another adult (Juarez, 2005).

School

Pregnancy prevention efforts have long been established in U.S. schools. In a recent review of school-based pregnancy prevention programs in the United States, Bennett and Assefi (2005) found that a majority of the programs were abstinence-only programs. However, findings from that study revealed that these types of programs only showed a modest impact in delaying the initiation of sexual activity among youths. Similarly, sexual education programs in schools tend to produce a relatively modest impact on delaying teen sex (Lederman & Mian, 2003). The following are suggestions for school-based prevention programs: increase awareness of the importance of school and education, encourage high school graduation and exploration of career interests, learn risks associated with sex and negative consequences of early sexual activity, and promote wellness and healthy life choices among students (Yampolskaya et al., 2004). Others suggestions include targeting specific goals focused on reducing one or more sexual behaviors that lead to teen pregnancy, building social skills through role-playing and interviewing, and using culturally relevant messages about sexual behavior (Lederman & Mian, 2003).

Community

Although the rate of unintended pregnancy and child bearing in the United States has declined over the past 20 years, some of our nation's poorest communities continue to have alarmingly high rates. Youths who live in neighborhoods marked by poverty, high crime, single-parent families, and lower levels of education among its residents are more likely to engage in sexual risk-taking behaviors. In addition, there continues to be a dearth of research on the efficacy of community prevention efforts, and there seems to be a lack of uniformity among community prevention programs.

To address this critical need, As-Sanie et al. (2004) and Kirby (1999) suggested the following guidelines for community pregnancy prevention program curricula: (a) Focus on more than one of the sexual antecedents that lead to unintended teen pregnancy (e.g., sexual beliefs, sexual attitudes, norms, intentions, and self-efficacy); (b) ground curriculum on a theoretical orientation that has been demonstrated to explain and reduce sexually risky behavior; (c) specify both the risk and protective factors to be modified by curriculum activities; (d) provide both basic and current information about the risks of unprotected sex and contraceptive methods; (e) include activities that address peer pressure; (f) provide modeling and demonstrative effective communication skills (e.g., negotiation and refusal skills); (g) use a variety of teaching methods designed to reach different learning styles; (h) use behavioral goals, teaching methods, and materials appropriate for participants' age, sexual experience, and cultural background; and (i) ensure that sessions last long enough to complete important activities.

Intervention Strategies

The following subsections explore current intervention strategies aimed at reducing harm and disadvantageous outcomes for children and teen parents and preventing future unwanted pregnancies.

Individual

Teen pregnancy and childbirth are associated with numerous detrimental outcomes. In an effort to reduce harm and prevent future unwanted pregnancies, intervention efforts at the individual level should include regular obstetric health screenings during pregnancy. Other recent trends in interventions efforts with pregnant teens include nutrition counseling, sex and contraceptive counseling, and brief counseling interventions with teen mothers (As-Sanie et al., 2004; Handmaker & Wilbourne, 2001; Lake & Drake, 1995).

Brief counseling, especially during the onset of pregnancy, may help clarify the teen mother's pregnancy and postpregnancy options. A recommended brief counseling approach to use with pregnant teens is a *motivational interviewing* approach (Handmaker & Wilbourne, 2001). Motivational interviewing is a directive and client-centered approach to counseling that focuses on helping clients explore and resolve ambivalence regarding behavior change (W. R. Miller & Rollnick, 2002). The assumptions behind motivational interviewing are that clients have existing motivation to change and counselors can enhance but not create motivation.

For some teen mothers, the decision to keep the baby, give it up for adoption, or have an abortion is a difficult one. The potential value of motivational interviewing is that it may help pregnant teens explore this conflict in an atmosphere characterized by warmth, compassion, and positive regard. Motivational interviewing has been found to reduce the risk of drinking during pregnancy (Handmaker & Wilbourne, 2001). It has also been found to be useful in contraceptive counseling (Peterson et al., 2004). Motivational interviewing also may be especially helpful for helping clarify teen mothers' postpregnancy options.

Family

Family support has long been understood as an essential component to positive long-term outcomes among teen mothers and their children. One recent trend in family interventions is to help assist parents of pregnant teens to improve their relationships with their children by fostering communication (Todd, 2000). For example, the Parent–Adolescent Relationship Education program was designed to help enhance communication between teen mothers and their parents (Lederman & Mian, 2003). This psychoeducational program focuses on strengthening family communication by providing parents with strategies about discussing sexual issues and behavior. Other family interventions include group psychotherapy, solution-focused therapy with parents of pregnant teens, and strategies to increase fathers' involvement and knowledge of parenting skills (Cervera, 1989; Doherty, Erickson, & LaRossa, 2006; Todd, 2000).

School

Some suggest that being in school helps reduce the deleterious factors, such as poverty, associated with teen parenthood (Kirby, 2002b). Simply put, teen parents who finish high school have more options than those who do not. School-based pregnancy intervention programs differ in their focus, content, length, and methodology. Because of these differences, researchers have found it difficult to systematically evaluate the effectiveness of pregnancy interventions in schools. One of the most common school-based intervention programs is called the Teen-Age Parenting Program (Rodriguez & Moore, 1995). The primary purpose of this program is to provide an academic environment with medical and social services for teen parents and their children. Although a review of all the different kinds of intervention strategies is beyond the scope of this chapter, some of the recent trends in school-based pregnancy interventions include condom availability programs, service learning programs focused on increasing the pregnant teens' bond with the school, and peer mentoring programs (Bowman & Palley, 2003; Kirby, 2002b; Rubenstein, Panzarine, & Lanning, 1990).

The following are suggestions for working with pregnant teens in a school context: (a) Encourage parental support and communication; (b) encourage communication about the teen mother's expectations regarding the baby's father, pregnancy outcomes, and postpregnancy plans; (c) encourage focus on the mental and physical health of the pregnant teen; (d) adopt a family systems approach; (e) promote resiliency and strengths; and (f) link the teen with community resources (Benson, 2004; Bowman & Palley, 2003).

Community

Despite declines in the overall rate of unintended pregnancies among women ages 15–19, the rate in the United States continues to rank in the top 10 among developed countries. As a result, unintended pregnancy and childbirths pose a significant public health concern for policymakers and researchers.

At the macro level, U.S. policymakers have responded to this concern by passing a number of acts targeting teen pregnancy prevention and intervention. The following are some recent bills aimed a reducing teen pregnancy: the Personal Responsibility, Work, and Family Promotion Act of 2003, Compassion and Personal Responsibility Act, Strengthening of Families Act of 2003, and Building on Welfare Success Act of 2003.

On the micro level, both state and federal governments provide funding for family planning services and supplies. These clinics are designed to meet the needs of individuals from low-income backgrounds and link them with public health and social services. Title X program provides the largest source of funding for such programs (Sonfield, 2003). In addition to more public funding for prevention programs and resources, some have suggested that better child support enforcement may help curb unintended teen pregnancy and risky sexual behavior (Huang, 2005; Plotnick, Garfinkel, McLanahan, & Ku, 2004).

Can you identify the risk factors discussed in this chapter that apply to our youth at risk, Julia? What might you suggest for Julia in terms of prevention efforts and intervention strategies? Take a moment to reflect what you would do if you were Julia's counselor. Continue to think about Julia as we turn our discussion to the next section on sexually transmitted diseases. Is Julia at risk in this domain also?

AIDS AND OTHER SEXUALLY TRANSMITTED DISEASES

Recent estimates suggest that the United States has the highest incidence of STD acquisition in the developed world (Van Devanter, 1999). The acquisition of STDs is associated with numerous negative outcomes and numerous health problems. For example, some estimates suggest that chlamydia and gonorrhea are the leading causes of major health problems, such as pelvic inflammatory disease, ectopic pregnancy, infertility, and chronic pelvic pain (Koumans et al., 2005).

Despite increased efforts to reduce the incidence and mortality of STDs in the United States, each year more than 12 million people contract an STD (K. E. Miller, Ruiz, & Graves, 2003). As suggested in the previous section of this chapter, at-risk youth tend to engage in risky sexual behavior, and one possible consequence of risky sexual behavior is the acquisition of STDs such as HIV, chlamydia, and gonorrhea.

Risk Factors

The incidence of sexually risky behavior among adolescents in the United States is high. A teenager gets an STD every 13 seconds (Rural Center for AIDS/STD Prevention, 1994). At least 25% of sexually active teenagers have contracted an STD during their lifetime (Centers for Disease Control and Prevention, 2002). Some estimates suggest that between 112,000 and 250,000 adolescents are currently HIV positive (Goodenow, Netherland, & Szalacha, 2002). Compared with older adults, persons under the age of 25 are at a higher risk for acquiring STDs (American Academy of Pediatrics, 2001), and teens who initiate sex at an earlier age are more likely to have multiple partners and less likely to practice safe sex (Bachanas et al., 2002).

A report by the Centers for Disease Control and Prevention (2002) revealed that sexually active teenagers have the highest rate of chlamydia infection in the United States. Findings from that report showed that women between the ages of 15 and 24 years had the highest rates of gonorrhea compared with women of all ages in the United States. In general, adolescent girls are more vulnerable to STD infection, and those who have an STD are at a higher risk for developing cancer; becoming infertile; having an ectopic pregnancy, spontaneous abortion, or stillbirth; and having babies with a low birthrate (Van Devanter, 1999).

Research suggests that the following risk factors have been associated with HIV/STD acquisition in adolescence: gender, ethnicity, socioeconomic status, inconsistent condom use, illicit drug use, and unprotected anal intercourse (Brook et al., 2004; Goodenow et al., 2002; Gurman & Borzekowski, 2004). According to the Rural Center for AIDS/STD Prevention (1994), other factors associated with HIV/STD risk in adolescence include drug and substance abuse, problem behaviors, attitudes, social/cultural conditions, institutions, and high-risk situations. Taken together, this information suggests that STDs constitute a significant health problem for U.S. youth. In addition, the economic cost of STDs is shocking. Recent estimates suggest that the direct and indirect cost of prevention and treatment is around $10 billion (D. A. Cohen, Nsuami, Martin, & Farley, 1999). The next section provides a brief overview of the current trends in STD prevention.

Approaches to Prevention

Despite continuing efforts to reduce HIV and other STD transmission, the rate of acquisition among U.S. teens is alarmingly high. Currently, the primary focus of HIV and other STD prevention programs is on diagnosis, treatment, partner notification services, and surveillance of disease patterns (Van Devanter, 1999). Because teens are at greater risk for HIV/STD infection than adults, prevention efforts are especially vital to reducing the incidence of STD transmission in the country. The following subsections provide an overview of the HIV/STD prevention efforts geared toward teens.

Individual

Current STD prevention programs geared toward teens include programs focused on teens' abstaining from oral, anal, and vaginal intercourse and programs aimed at teaching teens to consistently use a male latex condom during heterosexual and homosexual intercourse (Christ, Razska, & Dillon, 1998; K. E. Miller et al., 2003). However, research findings from numerous studies suggest that condom use among adolescent males continues to be inconsistent, and females report less condom use than their male counterparts despite the prevalence of sexual education programs (Committee on Adolescence, 2001). To make these programs more effective, some have suggested that cultural factors surrounding the discussion of sex and contraception should be integrated into sexual education prevention curriculum (Ibanez, Van Oss Martin, Villareal, & Gomez, 2005). Others have argued that sexual education programs should also include an overview of how teens can negotiate having safe sex with their partners (Lewis, Melton, Succop, & Rosenthal, 2000).

Finally, in terms of individual prevention counseling, a number of different counseling approaches have been utilized with clients in terms of educating about specific strategies that can reduce the risk of HIV/STD transmission. For example, client-centered HIV/STD counseling has been shown to be beneficial in terms of risk reduction and empowering clients to make choices about their sexual health (Centers for Disease Control and Prevention, 2006).

Family

One of the most critical elements of family prevention of STD transmission among teens is parent–child communication. Parents are quite simply the agents of primary prevention. The messages that they communicate about sex are critical factors in shaping adolescents' beliefs about sex roles and sexual behaviors. According to the Centers for Disease Control and Prevention (2006), the following are guidelines on how parents can approach the topic of safe sex with their teens: (a) Talk calmly about sex; (b) practice talking about sex with another adult; (c) listen to your teen and answer his or her questions as openly and honestly as possible; and (d) discuss the issues of STDs and prevention, peer pressure, birth control, different forms of sexuality, and date rape with your teen.

In terms of family prevention programming, program evaluators and researchers may want to consider incorporating cultural beliefs and practices into their curriculum. For instance, when working with Latino adolescents and their families, prevention programs may want to address the influence of *machismo* and *marianismo* on sexual roles and behavior. The concept of *marianismo* refers to characteristics of the Virgin Mary and helps lead to the socialization of Latinas as selfless, virtuous, good daughters, and respectful and obedient to men. In contrast, *machismo* refers to the potency, virility, and strength of the Latino male as the head of the family. *Machismo* leads to greater acceptance and expectation of Latino adolescent males' premarital sexual behavior. These cultural beliefs may put Latino adolescents at an elevated risk for engaging in early sexual activity without contraception (Talashek et al., 2004).

School

Schools have become a critical ally in the effort to increase the likelihood that prevention messages regarding safe sex and the consequences of STDs are received by teens. For the last three decades, schools have implemented numerous HIV and other STD prevention programs. Yet, despite the prevalence of such programs, adolescents continue to engage in risky sexual behavior and contract HIV and other STDs. In a review of school prevention programs, Kirby (2002b) found that although these programs helped increase students' knowledge about sex, few had made a significant impact on teens' risky sexual behavior. One of the main criticisms of school prevention programs is that they focus almost exclusively on the individual and do not address the various environments, such as school and family, that help contribute to risky sexual behavior among adolescents (Coyle et al., 1999).

Lederman, Chan, and Roberts-Gray (2004) suggested the following guidelines for STD prevention efforts in schools: (a) Target sixth, seventh, and eighth graders and start prevention efforts earlier; (b) provide psychoeducational programs focused on the risks and protective measures for HIV/AIDS and unplanned pregnancy; (c) focus on fostering positive family interactions; (d) provide opportunities to engage teens and their parents in small group settings; and (e) provide booster sessions to reinforce prevention messages to teens. Researchers have also suggested that making contraceptives more available in school health clinics may increase teen use of contraceptives and help curb risky sexual behavior and ultimately decrease STD transmission (Kirby, 1999).

Community

U.S. teens have one the highest rate of STD transmission in the developed world (Huberman, 2001). Consequently, focusing on HIV/STD acquisition is considered one of the major priorities in public health legislation and prevention programming today. The following recommendations are for community prevention programs: (a) Develop and modify health services to help teens make healthy and safe choices about sex, (b) implement policies that help facilitate the process for teens to receive both basic and reproductive health care, (c) provide oral contraceptives and other kinds of contraceptives to women under the age of 20 without requiring them to take a pap smear or pelvic exam, (d) provide more youth-friendly services (including hours of operation, waiting room space, less invasive paperwork, and services at a nominal cost), (e) improve access to condoms and other contraceptives to all sexually active individuals, and (f) increase knowledge and access to emergency contraception (Huberman, 2001).

Other prevention suggestions are that teens need to get more involved in community prevention programs. The Centers for Disease Control and Prevention (2006) offered the following guidelines for getting more youth participation in community prevention agencies: (a) Take teen involvement seriously, (b) involve teens in the planning and activities of the program's goals, (c) use teens' input when developing messages and marketing campaigns targeting teens, (d) provide teens with the appropriate training and make them an integral part of prevention programming efforts, (e) work with teens to make risky sexual behavior taboo in teen culture, (f) take your program message to places where teens congregate, (g) encourage teens to be your media and community ambassadors, (h) help give teens a voice with policymakers and other community leaders, and (i) offer incentives for teens to work for your organization (e.g., scholarships, stipends, grants).

Intervention Strategies

This section explores recent literature and research findings on individual, family, school, and community interventions for adolescents who have contracted an STD.

Individual

In a summary of individual-level interventions for HIV and other STD transmission, D. A. Cohen and Scribner (2000) found that most of these levels of interventions focused on counseling, screening, and treatment. In terms of individual interventions, one of the most vital components of treatment is medication adherence. For some at-risk youths, the task of adhering to a strict treatment regimen may be exceptionally difficult. One intervention that has been shown to affect adherence among other at-risk populations is motivational interviewing. Adamian, Golin, Shain, and DeVellis (2004) reported that a single motivational interviewing session with HIV-positive patients was able to help them facilitate the process of developing strategies for maintaining their antiviral medication regimen and their relationships with their doctors.

Although abstinence is the surest way of preventing STD infection, the following strategies are recommended by the Centers for Disease Control and Prevention (2006) for adolescents to protect themselves from contracting an STD: (a) Have a mutually monogamous sexual relationship with an uninfected partner, (b) consistently and correctly use male latex condoms, (c) use sterile needles if injecting intravenous drugs, (d) delay having sexual relationships as long as possible, (e) have regular checkups for STDS, (f) learn the symptoms of STDS, (g) avoid having sexual intercourse during menstruation, (h) avoid anal intercourse, and (i) avoid douching.

Family

The importance of family during an adolescent's treatment for HIV or other STDs cannot be understated. Parents and other family members can be a tremendous source of support for teens who have just found out that they have an STD or for those who are undergoing treatment. Consequently, family intervention strategies usually involve a family systems approach, in which the parents, the affected teen, and any siblings are all part of the treatment process. However, one recent trend in family intervention involves couples counseling. Relationship-based counseling has been found to be useful in promoting HIV counseling, testing, and condom use. Relationship-based counseling can be administered with either both partners in session or individually.

Perhaps the most important benefit to couples counseling is that it provides both partners with a safe place to disclose highly personal information that they may not have otherwise shared with each other. Because issues surrounding trust and commitment often influence condom and other contraceptive use in long-term relationships, individuals in these types of relationships are often vulnerable to acquiring STDs. The following recommendations are for couples counseling: (a) Programs need to teach effective communication skills; (b) interventions need to provide accurate information about HIV and other STDs, as well as the risk factors associated with each; and (c) interventions need to also look at participants' nonverbal strategies for maintaining safe sex, such as putting a condom on themselves or their partner (Bird, Harvey, Beckman, Johnson, & The Partners Project, 2001; El-Bassel et al., 2003).

School

In general, STDs have disproportionately affected teens in the United States. Consequently, because most teens are enrolled in school long before the initiation of sexual behavior, schools may potentially be effective in reducing teen sexual risk-taking behavior. In one study, D. A. Cohen et al. (1999) found that school-based screening and treatment programs for STDs were effective for reducing the prevalence of gonorrhea and chlamydia among a cohort of at-risk adolescent boys.

In addition to screening and treatment programs, case management services in schools may be helpful in reducing premature morbidity and mortality among teens who are infected with STDs. For instance, case management services may play a critical role in assessing the needs, identifying resources, and coordinating services for HIV-infected youth (Remafedi, 2001).

Lastly, a reality group therapy approach may be effective in modifying behaviors and attitudes related to school dropout in at-risk youth. Comisky (1993) found that reality therapy group work was effective in improving at-risk teens' self-esteem, locus of control, academic achievement, school attitude, attendance, and classroom behavior. Because of its focus on the present, on need fulfillment, and on unique problem-solving approaches, reality therapy may also be effective in working with teens who have contracted HIV or any other STD.

Community

Little research has been published on the efficacy of community interventions on the prevalence and treatment of HIV and other STDs (Van Devanter, 1999). In one of the few studies that have examined the efficacy of community interventions, the Centers for Disease Control and Prevention AIDS Community Demonstration Projects Research Group (1999) reported the results of a five-city community intervention project aimed at effecting behavioral changes among at-risk populations. The community intervention consisted of three main components: (a) mobilization of community members to be advocates of prevention messages and to distribute prevention materials, (b) creation of small media materials that consisted of stages-of-change theory-based prevention messages (see Prochaska & Velicer, 1997, for a full description of the transtheortical model of health behavior change), and (c) increased availability of bleach kits and other contraceptives. Results from that study showed significant increases in condom carrying and stages-of-change scores for bleach use among at-risk populations. In discussing the significance of these findings, the Centers for Disease Control and Prevention AIDS Community Demonstration Projects Research Group (1999) noted that the use of stages-of-change model as a foundation for the intervention was vital to the success of the community intervention. This model may be helpful for developing community programs aimed at teens who engage in risky sexual behavior.

In returning to Julia, our youth at risk, what behaviors is Julia engaging in that will make it more likely she will contract an STD? If you were the counselor working with Julia, what type of prevention effort or intervention strategy would you want to use? Keep Julia in mind as we turn to another topic for youth at risk, rape and date rape.

RAPE AND DATE RAPE

Rape and date rape are increasing statistics in the U.S. population. Some say rape is the fastest growing crime in the United States (R. Hall, 2004). Estimates are that one woman is raped every 6 minutes (Shultz, Scherman, & Marshall, 2000). Although heterosexuals, homosexuals, males, or females can commit rape, sexual assault, and dating violence, it is more common for heterosexual males to be the abuser and heterosexual females to be the victim (Committee on Adolescence, 2001; Foubert & Newberry, 2006; Freedner, Freed, Yang, & Austin, 2002; Hensley, 2002; Lefkowitz, Paharia, Prout, Debiak, & Bleiberg, 2005; Rickert, Vaughan, & Wiemann, 2002). Because of space limitations, the chapter focuses on heterosexual women as the victim of heterosexual sexual violence.

Rape and date rape is an issue concerning all men and women, but one that especially affects adolescents. It is estimated that over 300,000 children and adolescents are sexually abused each year in the United States (Webster, 2001). The peak age of victimization for women in the United States is between 16 to 19 years old; the second highest age range for victimization is 20 to 24 years old (Bureau of Justice Statistics, 2004; Committee on Adolescence, 2001). Women of the 16- to 19-year-old age range are four times more likely to be victims of sexual violence than any other age group (Rickert et al., 2002; Rickert, Wiemann, & Vaughn, 2005).

Date rape is the most common form of rape in this age group; data suggest that date or acquaintance rape accounts for 80%–90% of all sexual assaults, whereas stranger rape occurs only 10%–20% of the time, and date-related violence and sexual assault may be as high as 39% within the adolescent population (Ackard & Neumark-Sztainer, 2002; Rickert et al., 2002; Smith, White, & Holland, 2003; Yeater, Miltenberger, Laden, Ellis, & O'Donohue, 2001). It is estimated that during their teen years, 1 in 10 girls and 1 in 20 boys will be victims of dating violence, and 85% of all sexual assaults are perpetrated by someone the victim knows ("Teen Dating Violence," 2006).

Rape has been defined as "any form of penetration in any part of the body without consent or intercourse without consent," *acquaintance rape* is defined as "any instance of sexual assault (including rape) in which the victim and the perpetrator were previously known to each other," and *date rape* is a type of acquaintance rape and is not consensual sex between dating partners. *Sexual assault* is "any form of sexual contact without consent (kissing, touching, and so forth) including rape" (Craig, 1994, p. 84).

Risk Factors for Women

As with any complex behavior, the factors associated with date rape are also complex. Estimates are that between 15% and 40% of all adolescents have become violent toward their dating partners (Rickert et al., 2002). Research has indicated there are many associated factors that place adolescent women at increased risk for sexual victimization from a dating partner. Among these are use of alcohol and/or drugs, heavy cigarette use, high levels of consensual sexual activity or many sexual partners, early age of first date, losing virginity at a young age, history of sexual abuse, being socially isolated or having poor peer relationships, problems adjusting to school, poor interpersonal control, low self-esteem, depression, having considered or attempted suicide, emotionality, coming from an abusive home, parental aggression, attitudes and beliefs condoning dating violence, beliefs in rape stereotypes, incidence rate of community and school violence, level of satisfaction in the relationship, seriousness and length of the dating relationship, relationship conflict, and being isolated from others in a dating situation (Abbey, Buck, Zawacki, & Saenz, 2003; "Coercive Sexual Experiences," 2005; Feiring, Deblinger, Hoch-Espada, & Haworth, 2002; Holcomb, Savage, Seehafer, & Waalkes, 2002; Howard & Wang, 2005; Maxwell, Robinson, & Post, 2003; Rickert et al., 2002; Yeater et al., 2001).

Approaches to Prevention

The literature is bountiful in terms of current prevention efforts to combat adolescent date rape and sexual victimization statistics. Holcomb et al. (2002) claimed there are "1,140 possible strategies designed to prevent rape" (p. 169). Most outreach programs and prevention strategies developed to address the problem of sexual assault and date rape have traditionally focused on changing the behavior of women rather than the behavior of men (Holcomb et al., 2002). However, in recent years this trend has changed and men are becoming a focus (Foubert & La Voy, 2000). The following subsections highlight some of the prevention strategies that are currently being used.

Individual

Determining empirically supported prevention strategies has been difficult because of lack of published research of prevention programs, lack of comparability between programs, ineffective outcome and program evaluation research, lack of a systematic evaluation of one program over time, and lack of theory in prevention programming. In addition, outcome measures have traditionally focused on attitudes and not on how change in attitudes can change behaviors ("Coercive Sexual Experiences," 2005; Gidycz et al., 2001; Lanier, Elliott, Martin, & Kapadia, 1998; Shultz et al., 2000; Yeater et al., 2001).

However, some of the current prevention strategies discussed in the professional literature for individuals include the following: (a) raising the consciousness of individuals regarding the sexual rights of women and the prevalence of date rape; (b) social skills and assertiveness training for women; (c) increasing women's self-efficacy to negotiate for safer sex; (d) shifting men's and women's attitudes concerning traditional sex and gender roles, adversarial sexual beliefs, and rape stereotypes and myths; (e) establishing empathy with rape survivors to increase men's awareness and sensitivity to rape; (f) focusing on attitudes and beliefs that create a culture whereby dating violence is accepted; (g) increasing the focus on how drugs and alcohol affect dating violence; (h) teaching women self-defense, response, and risk perception strategies; (i) educating individuals on rape myth acceptance; (j) educating to change rape-supportive beliefs; and (k) increasing awareness about date rape drugs (Committee on Adolescence, 2001; Foubert & La Voy, 2000; Foubert & Newberry, 2006; Hensley, 2002; Holcomb et al., 2002; Rickert et al., 2002; Shultz et al., 2000; Yeater et al., 2001).

While mixed-gender rape prevention programs have been shown to be effective (Holcomb et al., 2002), recent trends have used single-gender groups with success and minimized retraumatization for women who have been abused (Foubert & La Voy, 2000; Foubert & Newberry, 2006; Stark, 2003). Strategies that seemed to be most effective with men included (a) using nonconfrontational information with a focus on identifying when consent to have sex is given or not given; (b) building victim empathy; (c) teaching participants how to help women recover from a rape experience; (d) using peer education formats; (e) facilitating a balanced discussion of date rape issues; (f) using multiple sources of persuasion in a presentation (e.g., videos, multiple presenters, readings); (g) conveying presenters as expert, reliable, trustworthy, and credible; (h) adopting programs that are nonconfrontational and that do not focus on all men as being potential rapists; and (i) using the elaboration likelihood model, which posits that lasting attitude and behavior change comes when participants are motivated to hear the message, understand the message, and perceive the message as being relevant to them personally (Foubert & La Voy, 2000; Foubert & Newberry, 2006; Holcomb et al., 2002; Woods & Bower, 2001).

Also in terms of individual prevention efforts, there are many suggestions women can take to protect themselves and reduce their risk for rape and date rape. These include the following: use the "buddy system" and look out for each other, monitor your and your friends' alcohol consumption, do not become intoxicated, keep control over your own drink, drink only from sealed bottles rather than open containers such a punch bowls, and discard any drink that does not look or taste right ("Date Rape Drugs," 2001; DePresca, 2003; Romeo, 2004).

Family

Parents are often a teen's greatest protective factor. Building a strong, supportive family whereby each member is valued and heard is one of the best ways of prevention. Parents can help their children prevent being a victim of rape or date rape by talking to their kids about sexual violence and teaching them to say no, modeling what healthy relationships look like, modeling healthy beliefs and behaviors and setting clear standards, keeping the line of communication open and creating a safe place for a teen to come to talk, looking for behavioral cues that a teen may be a victim (e.g., withdrawal and isolation from friends, repeated absences and tardiness at school, visible signs of injuries, and feeling depressed, anxious, or sad), and discussing what sexual harassment is and what a teen should do about it. More information can be found in the Web sites of Committee For Children (http://www.cfchildren.org/) and Safe To Live (http://www.safetolive.org/).

School

Prevention efforts have been well established on college campuses and have been apparent on high school campuses within the last 10 years (Foshee et al., 1998; Himelein, 1999). Many prevention efforts have targeted women and have been focused on challenging rape-supportive attitudes. Some suggestions for school prevention efforts are (a) providing psychoeducational material that helps women recognize the warning signs of male aggression and teen dating violence; (b) infusing curriculum about rape and assault; (c) challenging societal gender role expectations; and (d) providing information and education about date rape drugs, including composition, effects of abuse, effects of involuntary ingestion and sexual assault, risk of consuming beverages at clubs, and legal issues associated with use and abuse ("Early Warning Signs," 2006; Hensley, 2002; Stark, 2003).

There is research evidence indicating that rape education and prevention programs are successful on high school and college campuses and help change the mind-set and attitudes about rape. These types of programs generally are administered in a single session lasting from 30 minute to 2 hours (Lonsway & Kothari, 2000). However, these large, single-session, educational prevention efforts have not been shown to be effective in helping women who have already been victimized or those who have the highest risk for being raped. Smaller, single-sexed groups generate more empirical support (Foubert & La Voy, 2000; Himelein, 1999).

Strategies that have increasing empirical support include (a) rape prevention programs that focus on the dynamics of gender socialization and on how society supports a power differential between men and women; (b) educational programs such as "Safe Dates" that discuss dating violence, warning signs, and how to protect oneself; (c) peer-led psychoeducational programs focusing on topics of sexual assault risk reduction, rape culture, how to help a victim, and male responsibility in preventing sexual assault; and (d) same-sex programs rather than mixed-gender groups (Feltey, Ainslie, & Geib, 1991; Foshee et al., 1998; Foubert & McEwen, 1998; Smith & Welchans, 2000).

Community

Community prevention strategies have included better lighting in parking structures and parking lots on and off high school and college campuses, trimming shrubbery to improve visibility, developing statutory rape laws, and challenging social norms regarding rape. Community preventions that address the broader context in which sexual violence against females occur is emerging but is not yet well developed ("Coercive Sexual Experiences," 2005; Leitenberg & Saltzman, 2003; Stark, 2003).

Other community prevention efforts include a federal mandate that directs every university receiving federal funds to have some kind of rape and sexual assault prevention program on campus; the American Bar Association's National Teen Dating Violence Prevention Initiative that was created to help develop awareness of teen date rape and its causal factors; and the Violence Against Women Act, which was amended in 2002 by the U.S. Congress to include legal assistance for victims of dating violence (Gidycz et al., 2001; "Teen Dating Violence," 2006).

Intervention Strategies

Interventions can take place on a variety of levels. Some are aimed at the perpetrators to reduce the number of offenses, and some are aimed at the victims of sexual assault and rape. Most would agree that early intervention in either case is more effective. For example, it has been found that interventions aimed to prevent sexual assault by male perpetrators are more effective when they begin early in the teen years, before females are at greatest risk of sexual violation and before males have developed patterns of sexual aggression. Toward this end, interventions that challenge teen attitudes, knowledge, and norms are essential in intervention efforts (Lonsway & Kothari, 2000; Rickert et al., 2002).

Many victims of rape or sexual assault never report the crime to authorities or seek help; the number of victims nonreporting may be as high as 50% (Finkelhor & Berliner, 2001; Millar, Stermac, & Addison, 2002). This means that many victims never receive the help they need either medically or psychologically. Interventions for teens who have been victimized by rape or date rape are important for many reasons. Research findings indicate that many victims of rape do not receive health care and subsequently suffer from a host of physical and psychological issues and can suffer from posttraumatic stress disorder and rape trauma syndrome. Psychological issues are considered to be the most important medical problem for victims of sexual assault (J. L. Jones & Whitworth, 2002).

Survivors of rape and date rape may suffer from feelings of self-blame, anger, and powerlessness; have nightmares, issues with trust, lowered self-esteem, suicidal thoughts, self-injurious behaviors, and conduct problems; develop eating disorders; have difficulty having sex with a wanted partner; have dissociative episodes and impaired memory, derealization, depersonalization, social adjustment problems, academic problems, increased somatic complaints, and changes in sleep patterns; increase use of substances; and have constant fear for their own safety (Ackard & Neumark-Sztainer, 2002; Committee on Adolescence, 2001; Cook-Cottone, 2004; Foubert & Newberry, 2006; Hensley, 2002; Hodak, 2004; Resnick, Acierno, Holmes, Dammeyer, & Kilpatick, 2000; Rickert et al., 2002; Romeo, 2004; Webster, 2001). This section explores possible interventions for individuals, families, schools, and communities.

Individual

Interventions at the individual level should include crisis care, psychological care, care of physical injuries, treatment of STDs, and treatment for unwanted pregnancy

(Azikiwe, Wright, Cheng, & D'Angelo, 2005; J. A. Cohen, Berliner, & Mannarino, 2003). A baseline urine pregnancy test can be conducted to help the adolescent determine whether pregnancy occurred as a result of the rape or prior to it, and counseling can help a teen decide if she wants to keep her baby (Committee on Adolescence, 2001).

Psychological therapy, both individual and group, is imperative to help someone overcome sexual trauma. A literature review suggests the following modalities are particularly effective in working with adolescents who have been raped or victims of sexual predators: cognitive processing therapy, cognitive–behavioral therapy, art therapy, constructivistic bibliotherapy, prolonged exposure therapy, animal-assisted exposure therapy, relaxation therapy, eye movement desensitizing and reprocessing (EMDR), or Foa's treatment for trauma victims. In addition, a treatment focus on anxiety and stress management, development of coping skills, thought stopping, positive imagery, psychoeducation, sexual education, and normalizing have been found effective (Arellano, Deblinger, Cohen, Danielson, & Mannarino, 2005; "Coercive Sexual Experiences," 2005; Cook-Cottone, 2004; Lefkowitz et al., 2005; Nishith, Nixon, & Resick, 2005; Nixon, Nishith, & Resick, 2004; Rothbaum, 1997; Rubenzahl & Gilbert, 2002; Webster, 2001; Yeater et al., 2001).

The following are other interventions at the individual level: (a) conducting health provider screenings that ask women about intimate partner violence; (b) providing a safe environment for women and adolescents to talk about victimization; and (c) crisis counseling services in high schools and colleges that include psychoeducation about rape and trauma to normalize reactions, assist the rape survivor in addressing guilt feelings, and help the survivor to vocalize feelings about the rape ("Coercive Sexual Experiences," 2005; Hensley, 2002; Nishith et al., 2005; Rickert et al., 2005; Rothbaum, 1997; Webster, 2001; Yeater et al., 2001). Victims of rape and date rape can also use crisis lines such as 1-888-99-VOICE or Teen Link Crisis Line 1-866-TeenLink ("Teen Dating Violence," 2006).

Family

For children and adolescents suffering from trauma reactions from sexual assault and rape, behaviorally based interventions are thought to be the best treatment option, as well as including parents and families in the treatment (Arellano et al., 2005; J. A. Cohen et al., 2003). Arellano et al. (2005) asserted that parent training is essential for the treatment of these children. Parents have a lot of control over their children's environment, behaviors, and feelings of security. By engaging parents and other family members, children and adolescents are getting consistent care between home and therapeutic environments. For the same reasons, it can also be helpful to include the child or adolescent's teacher(s) in this healing process and ensure that parents or teachers are not reinforcing trauma-related behavior problems. Parents and teachers can be taught to reinforce desirable behaviors with positive social reinforcement and token economies (Arellano et al., 2005).

Nelson-Gardell (2001) conducted a focus group with survivors of sexual abuse to learn what helped them survive their sexual abuse. Survivors had this to say: (a) Believe and support them when they say they have been abused, (b) allow them to talk about what happened to them, (c) allow them to talk about their feelings regarding what happened to them, and (d) engage them in group counseling. Many survivors stated therapy in a group was helpful, presumably because of the universal factors associated with groups (e.g., universality, instillation of hope, imparting information, altruism) and normalizing the trauma reaction.

School

Cook-Cottone (2004) asserted that school interventions can be effective under the following conditions: (a) A complete comprehensive assessment has been conducted to ascertain the needs of the adolescent; (b) it is determined that school-based support is the appropriate, least restrictive level of intervention; (c) the adolescent's parents have given informed consent of all treatment options; (d) the child is experiencing adequate adjustment and academic success with intervention; and (e) consultation, supervision, and referral are readily utilized by the school psychologist. As noted above, it can be effective to have teachers be a part of the treatment team in terms of providing correct reinforcement of desired behaviors, assisting the student with symptom management, and providing a safe environment as well as helping with the coordination of communication among school personnel, family members, and the treatment team (Arellano et al., 2005; Cook-Cottone, 2004). Research suggests that trauma-focused, cognitive–behavioral therapy is the most efficacious and has the most empirical support when working with traumatized adolescents (see individual interventions above for specific cognitive–behavioral therapy interventions; J. A. Cohen et al., 2003; Cook-Cottone, 2004).

Community

Interventions for community efforts include (a) providing rape kits for hospitals and emergency rooms; (b) developing specialized medical/examiner programs that train nurses and doctors in the treatment and care of rape victims; (c) passing a federal law that designates funds to have more rape kits analyzed; (d) developing better testing methods to test for the presence of date rape drugs such as flunitrazepam (Rohypnol), gamma hydroxy butyrate (GHB), and ketamine; (e) increasing the statute of limitations for prosecuting rapes; (f) developing new colposcopic procedures that allows for better examination of genital trauma; and (g) providing advocates who go to the hospital and advocate and provide support for the victim (Baumgardner, 2001; "Coercive Sexual Experiences," 2005; Committee on Adolescence, 2001; DePresca, 2003; Hensley, 2002; Jansen & Theron, 2006; Nicola, 2002; Resnick, Kilpatrick, & Holmes, 2005).

However, community efforts in these areas are seriously lacking in effectiveness and comprehensiveness. Baumgardner (2001) stated that many emergency room and hospital personnel are untrained in using rape kits, and there are only 600 out of 5,000 hospitals nationwide that have trained staff on board. For those who are trained, the rape kits themselves are woefully inadequate. Other problems with community interventions include (a) too many items in the rape kit for professionals to navigate and many steps of evidence collection often get overlooked, which hinders prosecution efforts; (b) not enough analysts to look at evidence, and rape kits are being stacked up all over the country waiting to be examined; (c) the cost of the rape kit is often a victim's burden to pay; (d) date rape tests are often ineffective or inconclusive; and (e) many health professionals simply do not have time or do not want to provide assessments for rape and assault (Baumgardner, 2001; Nicola, 2002; Resnick et al., 2000).

As a counselor working with Julia, what do you see as potential factors in Julia's life that might put her at risk for sexual abuse from a partner or as a victim of rape or date rape? How might you try to intervene in Julia's life to try to minimize these risk factors or increase her protective factors? Which of the discussed prevention efforts or intervention strategies do you think most efficacious in helping Julia at this point in her development? Are there any other warning flags present in the case of

Julia that might make her a target of a sexual predator? The next section of this chapter discusses teens at risk for sexual predation and teens at risk of becoming sexually abusive or predatory in their behaviors.

SEXUAL PREDATORS

Sexual predators come in all shapes, sizes, colors, and life circumstances. A sexual predator can be a family member, a friend of the family, a neighbor, a classmate, a teacher, a coach, a priest or clergy member, or an online friend. Sexual predators do not have to be older than the victim. In the United States, it is estimated that 20% of reported rapes and 30%–50% of child molestations are committed by children under the age of 18, and adolescent sex offenders, as compared with adult offenders, use more threats of harm to victims and use more pornography in their attempt to draw another child into a sexual relationship (Becker & Reilly, 1999; Dombrowski, LeMasney, Ahia, & Shannon, 2004; Driedger, 2003; Edwards, 1999; Roberts, 2003).

Sexual offenses toward children do not have to be perpetrated by one individual. It is estimated that 100,000 to 300,000 children in the United States are exploited as prostitutes each year (Imber, 2003). Sexual predators who target children are twice as likely to have multiple victims as a sex offender who targets adults (Daley, 1997; "How to Protect Your Children," 2002).

Teachers and educators may also be likely predators. One survey of high school graduates found that 17.7% of males and 82.2% of females had been sexually harassed by faculty or staff, and 13.5% of teens had engaged in sexual intercourse with a teacher (Berson, Berson, Karges-Bone, & Parker, 1999). The sexual predation of children and adolescents is insidious. One study conducted by the National Institute of Mental Health that examined the behavior of 453 pedophiles found that each pedophile molested an average of 52 girls or 150 boys and that most sexual predators have offended an average of 30 times before being caught by law enforcement (Imber, 2003).

Risk Factors

There are several risk factors associated with sexually aggressive male adolescent offenders. Some of these factors include male acceptance of traditional gender roles and date rape myths, male initiation and dominance in dating relationships, disparity of power in relationships, miscommunication regarding sex, heavy alcohol or drug use, anger, sexual frustration, male hostility toward women, disinhibition, sexual experience, situational factors, interpersonal violence, and adversarial attitudes about relationships (Earle, 1996; Lanier & Elliott, 1997; Shultz et al., 2000).

Some of the risk factors associated with sexual predators (e.g., serial rapists, pedophiles) are growing up in poverty, having a dysfunctional childhood, having a history of sexual or physical abuse as a child, having a history of alcohol and drug abuse, being arrogant and hostile, using manipulation and force with women, being highly sensitive to rejection by women, using sex to achieve dominance, lacking empathy, having impersonal sex with one partner after another, being highly impulsive, being emotionally callous, and being consumed by sexual thoughts and fantasies (Bower, 2002; Daley, 1997).

Being a physically attractive youth with low self-esteem and living in a dysfunctional or impoverished family are among the risk factors that make youths more susceptible to be a victim of a sexual predator. Children who are friendly, open, and persuadable; adolescents with behavioral or emotional problems; and adolescents with a history of peer rejection and/or problems at school are also vulnerable as victims (Dombrowski et al., 2004).

Perhaps the most frightening scenario for parents is the Internet sexual predator. These predators strike up Internet chat relationships with adolescents, posing as a same-sex or at least a same-age peer (Rawe et al., 2006). These predators have mastered the Internet shorthand and lingo and prey on children and adolescents. It is estimated that one out of every five adolescents have received unwanted sexual propositions online (Garfield, 2004; "Kids With A Clue," 2003), and the Federal Bureau of Investigation (FBI) states that arrests of online predators have tripled since 2001 (Dombrowski et al., 2004; Garfield, 2004; "On Sexual Predation," 2004; Rawe et al., 2006). A parent might be in the same room and witness his or her child being subjected to a sexual predator and not even know it.

Approaches to Prevention

This section discusses individual, school, family, and community preventions for keeping adolescents safe from sexual predators.

Individual

Some suggestions that adolescents can follow to keep from presenting themselves as a target for a sexual predator include the following: (a) Adolescents should always stay in groups, never walk alone, and avoid remote places; (b) adolescents should not use personal information of any kind, no matter how innocent it may seem, when talking online to individuals they do not know; (c) adolescents should never go alone when meeting someone they met online; (d) adolescents should tell if another person keeps accidentally touching them, brushing up against them, or making sexual suggestions; (e) adolescents should not accept rides from anyone without parental permission, even if it is from a friend's parent (if the parent is in the car alone); and (f) adolescents should be aware that single-parent families are targets for pedophiles (Becker & Reilly, 1999; "Kids With A Clue," 2003).

Family

Family prevention efforts are often directed toward increasing knowledge for both parents and children/adolescents on how to stay safe from sexual predators. Recommendations that apply to educating and protecting adolescents include the following: (a) Parents should talk to their teens about situations or behaviors that could lead to sexual exploitation; parents should not talk about looking for certain types of individuals (e.g., appearance) because there is no one "type," but there are many scenarios or situations that are similar; (b) parents can conduct role-plays with their adolescents to help them learn methods of defense should they be targeted by a sexual predator; (c) parents can monitor their adolescent's computer use and should educate them about giving out personal information; (d) parents can keep computers in a central location within the home for easy monitoring of teen activities; (e) parents can consider installing spyware on their adolescent's computer to track what sites their teen is accessing and who he or she is talking to; (f) parents can monitor and get to know their teen's online friends just as he or she would an "in-person" friend; (g) parents can monitor their teen's online screen name and eliminate any potentially sexually provocative ones; (h) parents can go to www.google.com and enter their adolescent's name in a search to see if he or she has personal information on a Web site; and (i) parents can teach their adolescents to walk in groups to and from activities and to take different routes each day to common destinations, for example, school, work, or a friend's house (Becker & Reilly, 1999; Dombrowski et al., 2004; "How to Protect Your Children," 2002; "Kids With A Clue," 2003).

School

Many schools are becoming more proactive in protecting students from danger by establishing school lockdown procedures and installing telephones, intercoms, and Internet access in each classroom to notify teachers quickly of emergencies (e.g., principals can alert teachers by sending e-mails with "mark urgent" capabilities so that a chime rings when the teacher receives the e-mail). Schools can use pagers, 900-MHz portable phones, cellular phones, or two-way radios to contact those classes and teachers out of the main building (e.g., classes in portables, physical education classes held outside). In addition, schools can install closed-circuit TV so that administrators can notify all students at one time, in each classroom, of crucial events. Schools can send "stranger alert" newsletters home to warn parents when a sexual predator was spotted in the neighborhood and can use a "Parent Link" system, which is an elaborate, computer-based telephone, voicemail, and messaging system, to notify all parents in case of emergency (Van Horn, 1998).

Schools are also recognizing teachers as sexual abusers and are becoming more proactive in their screening methods. For example, standards were developed by the Interstate New Teacher Assessment and Support Consortium to screen potential teaching candidates. These standards include dispositional dimensions that allow teacher educators to assess character elements in preservice teachers. If a potential teaching candidate has a predisposition toward exploitation of children, the person can be screened out of educator programs before he or she has an opportunity to harm a child or adolescent. These along with background checks are helping to make students safer from faculty and staff predators (Berson et al., 1999).

Community

Communities are fighting back against sexual predators by advocating and passing more stringent laws such as community notification (Megan's law); requiring sex offender registration and stringent rules about how close a sexual predator can be in vicinity to children; using indeterminate sentencing, longer sentencing, and civil commitment (*Kansas v. Hendricks*, 1997); and requiring chemical castration for sexual offenders (Daley, 1997; Imber, 2003; Roberts, 2003; L. A. Wilson, 1998). Police officers are also going online and are having some success posing as young children and adolescents, luring sexual predators out into the open, and then arresting them (FBI's Operation Innocent Images; Fields-Meyer, 2002; "Kids With A Clue," 2003). *MSNBC Dateline*, which is a primetime TV program, has created exposure to the significant issue of the online sexual predation of children in their show "To Catch a Predator." There is also an online tip line (www.cybertipline.com) established in 1998 by the National Center for Missing and Exploited Children where people can report any form of sexual exploitation of a child or adolescent (Dombrowski et al., 2004; Garfield, 2004). Reports may be made 24 hours per day, 7 days per week online or by calling 1-800-843-5678.

Other cyber tools include an Internet computer game kids can play that teaches them Internet safety in a fun way and in a manner in which kids can relate (e.g., the

Missing Kit; www.livewwwires.com), Web sites that have information to help parents understand how to keep their kids safe online (e.g., www.missingkids.com), and online reporting when a teen receives an unwanted sexual advance online (e.g., www.cybertipline.com; McDonald, 2001). In addition, some states are attempting to pass laws that raise the legal age one can participate in online social networking sites, such as Myspace, Facebook, Xanga, and Bebo, to 18 years of age. Some states are looking into requiring a mandatory 24-hour waiting period before one can view changes made to someone's profile, and some states are checking into technology that could help screen online content for red flags (Rawe et al., 2006).

Intervention Strategies

It is estimated that 70%–80% of sex offenders were themselves childhood victims of sexual abuse (Adams, 2003). One of the best ways to intervene in the development of a sexual predator is to prevent that abuser's own childhood abuse. This is not to imply that all sexual offenders were sexually molested themselves, but the statistic is high enough that this section is warranted. Because the statistic for adolescent sex offenders is so high, this section describes the current research literature of treatment and intervention for sexual predators.

Individual

Becker and Reilly (1999) suggested there are three levels of prevention and intervention with regard to sexual offenders: (a) primary, to identify and stop inappropriate sexual conduct before it begins; (b) secondary, to identify those individuals most at risk of offending; and (c) tertiary, to target individuals who have a history of sexually inappropriate gestures. Therefore, at the primary level it is essential to prevent an adolescent from becoming a victim to reduce the possibility that he or she will become a sexual predator. One suggestion for an intervention at this level is sex education and psychoeducation that discusses victimization, such as how to recognize sexual abuse, what to do about it, who to tell, how to get support, what is inappropriate touching, and how to defend oneself against it. Of these strategies, knowledge of sex abuse concepts, self-defense instruction, and programs that considered the developmental level of the child had the most empirical support for preventing sexual attacks (Becker & Reilly, 1999).

Secondary efforts are aimed at holding the potential sexual offender responsible for his or her actions. Interventions at this stage include education of potential perpetrators in terms of increasing empathy for sexual assault victims; programs such as STOP IT NOW (www.stopitnow.com/) and Victim Awareness Program (VAP), which advocate that the sexual offender can control his or her behavior and offers education and support to help offenders stop offending; and programs that attack the social norming of adolescent drinking, as drinking has been found to be highly associated with sexual assault (Becker & Reilly, 1999). Of these interventions, empirical support has been found for the STOP IT NOW program and education about alcohol (Becker & Reilly, 1999).

Tertiary interventions are aimed at adolescents who are engaged in norm-violating sexual behavior. Interventions at this stage would include treatment, management, and supervision of offenders and relapse prevention (Becker & Reilly, 1999). In terms of treatment, cognitive–behavioral therapy (e.g., cognitive restructuring, anger management, assertiveness training, social skills training, sexual education, stress reduction and relaxation management, autobiographical awareness, covert sensitization, assisted covert sensitization, imaginal desensitization, olfactory conditioning, satiation techniques, and sexual arousal reconditioning) and hormonal treatment have received the most empirical support (Becker & Reilly, 1999; "Practice Parameters," 1999). Risk assessment for sexual offender recidivism should also be conducted in terms of intervening in sexual perpetration, and some advocate that steps should be taken to prevent reoffending up to, and including, incarceration and civil commitment, use of polygraph tests, and use of a plethysmograph, a device which is attached to the offender's penis and measures the appropriateness of his physical responses to inappropriate sexual images (e.g., child pornography; Proeve, Day, Mohr, & Hawkins, 2006; Teir & Coy, 1997; Tharp, 1997).

Family

Families of adolescent offenders are frequently involved in treatment (Bischof, Stith, & Whitney, 1995). Bischof et al. (1995) conducted a literature review that looked at how family home environment affected juvenile sex offenders and found research that suggests the family environment is highly influential. Teen sexual offenders were more likely to come from families characterized as rigid in response to change and emotionally disengaged. Bischof et al. also found that degree of violence was related to the type of family systems (e.g., the more rigid and disengaged the family system, the more violent the offense). Therefore, key interventions may need to target families and well as offenders. Family therapy can help facilitate communication, build a support network, and help the offender regulate his or her behavior. Counseling for the family is also recommended in terms of psychoeducational interventions to help educate regarding sexually abusive behavior, risk and protective factors, treatment strategies, and family interactions that can contribute to family dysfunction ("Practice Parameters," 1999).

School

In terms of preventing sexual assault at high schools and college campuses, the following interventions are associated as effective for enhancing positive change: a lecture discussing cultural rape mythologies, interactive participation, multimedia presentations, integration of the idea that rape is about power and control, avoidance of confrontational techniques that alienate individuals, repeat exposure to the information in a variety of contexts, psychoeducational material aimed at men to develop skills and behaviors likely to reduce incidences of sexual assault, challenges to male socialization practices, teaching men to have empathy for victims, and decreasing rape myth (Lonsway & Kothari, 2000; Stark, 2003). These types of interventions are designed to combat other research findings that suggest those individuals who are more tolerant of rape and are more likely to engage in these types of behaviors or be tolerant of them include individuals who adhere to traditional sex role attitudes, maintain adversarial attitudes toward females, and have an accepting attitude regarding violence toward women (Holcomb et al., 2002).

Community

When offenses have occurred, one way of tracking offenders to make sure they do not reoffend is through a community-based sexual offender management protocol, which combines parole supervision and relapse prevention treatment (R. J. Wilson, Stewart, Stripe, Barrett, & Cripps, 2000). This has been an effective method for the management of sexual recidivism in the community where it has been researched in Canada. There are four general principles that underlie this method: (a) assessing the level of the offender's risk to the community, (b) targeting for intervention those factors specifically related to criminal behavior, (c) appropriate monitoring of activities in the community, and (d) appropriate sharing of information among those engaged in treatment and supervision of the offender.

Another community intervention, also conducted in Canada, is the circle of support and accountability (CoSA; Evans, 2004). The circle of trust is designed for an offender who is identified while still in prison as a high-risk sexual offender who is about to be released into the public; the offender has a high level of need with little or no support from a social network (e.g., family, friends); and the offender is being released on the expiration of his or her prison sentence and therefore will not be under the requirement of probation or parole supervision.

The way CoSa works is that the offender becomes the center of attention and is a core member of the group. The offender meets regularly with a team of volunteers at least weekly for 1–3 hours per week. There is a daily check-in in which two to three members of this group are always available to the offender if he or she needs support. The offender agrees to follow his or her release plan, ground rules are established for conduct and behavior, and the circle support team confronts any behavior that indicates the offender is not sticking to the plan. CoSa has been seen as an effective way the community can assist with the reintegration of high-risk offenders and to encourage the offender to take personal responsibility for his or he actions (Evans, 2004).

Matson (2002) stated, "The most effective approaches to managing sex offenders in the community share several common characteristics, including a collaborative approach among those responsible for, or involved in, specialized supervision and treatment, intensive supervision using individually tailored case management plans, and a victim-centered philosophy" (p. 114). This appears to echo the Canadian studies referenced above.

In the case of Julia, what behaviors does she engage in that might put her at greater risk for being the victim of a sexual predator or a sexually aggressive teenage male? As her counselor, how might you approach Julia in educating her as to how her behaviors might be detrimental to her well-being and positive growth? Which of the prevention approaches might be more applicable given Julia's situation? Keep Julia in mind as we turn to the next section, adaptations for diversity. What are Julia's diversity variables, and how might this affect the work you do with her? How does her ethnicity, sex, age, family status, or socioeconomic status help protect her or place her at greater risk?

ADAPTATIONS FOR DIVERSITY

When reading the literature about the issues discussed in this chapter, it is clear there is a focus on how people differ from one another on a variety of variables connected to these topics. For example, the literature suggests that people of color have higher rates of infectious diseases than do Caucasians. Statistics imply that Blacks have higher rates of bacterially based sexual infections such as chlamydia and gonorrhea, and minority women in general and Hispanics specifically have disproportionate rates of HIV/AIDS infections (Apoola, Mantella, Wotton, & Radcliff, 2005; Gurman & Borzekowski, 2004; D. L. Jones et al., 2001).

Brindis, Park, Paul, and Burg (2002) stated that there are significant health disparities among adolescents in terms of ethnicity and gender in the areas of unintentional injury, violence, mental health, substance abuse, sexual behavior, and disease prevention. They also noted that Black and Hispanic adolescents are more likely to have engaged in sex than a Caucasian adolescent (see also Arellano, Kuhn, & Chavez, 1997; Bazargan & West, 2006).

Research also suggests there may be ethnic differences in symptom manifestation among sexually traumatized youth, with Hispanic and Black children developing more severe and longer lasting emotional and behavioral problems compared with Caucasian children. There may also be ethnic differences in the way we view and label individuals who commit sexual offenses on these youths based on ethnicity (J. A. Cohen et al., 2003). For example, West and Templer (1994) asserted that male sexual offenders were categorized differently on the basis of ethnic differences. White men were more often categorized as "child molesters," whereas Black men were more often labeled as "child rapists." Both of these terms are value and emotionally laden; the term *molester* has different images and associations than *rapist*. These stereotypes and labels may also carry over into the mental health profession, influencing the way we work with adolescents who are culturally different from ourselves (Brindis et al., 2002).

There may be a variety of reasons for these disparities noted above, such as limited or poor research representing women and minorities, diminished access or barriers to health care, diminished resources, and skewed research based on stereotyping and labeling (D. L. Jones et al., 2001). Regardless, mental and medical health care providers need to be aware of how ethnic, social, and other contextual factors may be affecting an adolescent's health care. It is also important for us to examine our own biases and stereotypes, as well as how we may be treating an adolescent differently based on our own assumptions, socialization, and myths.

Some programs are recognizing the need to tailor intervention and prevention programs to address specific groups (Lonsway & Kothari, 2000). All intervention and prevention efforts should include diversity variables such as age, ethnicity, sexual orientation, religious affiliation, ableness, cultural worldview, gender, and stage of emotional, physical, and cognitive development of the individual receiving services (Arellano et al., 2005; Cook-Cottone, 2004). Attention to multicultural issues will increase the likelihood that culturally different individuals will benefit from therapy and not drop out (J. A. Cohen et al., 2003).

Practitioners should also be aware of differences in perception regarding mental health treatment. Not all cultures view counseling and psychotherapy alike. For example, there may be ethnic differences in treatment-seeking behaviors, and there is evidence that treatment may be more accepted among ethnic minority members if recommended by the family pediatrician (J. A. Cohen et al., 2003).

SUMMARY

This chapter has focused on prevention, intervention, and current research around important topics of teen sexuality that put teens at risk for negative outcomes such as teen pregnancy, STDs, rape and date rape, and sexual predation. The field of counseling and psychotherapy is advancing in its knowledge of risk and protective factors pertaining to youth in many developmental areas including teen sexuality. Many gains have also been made in the field in terms of using more sophisticated techniques to study outcome effectiveness, such as Kirby's (1999) observations of increased sample sizes, statistical power, use of experimental designs, random assignment, and so forth.

However, the literature review for this chapter also indicated that more work needs to be done in the areas of program comparability, outcome and program evaluation research, increased need for a systematic evaluation of one program over time, and increased need for use of theory in prevention programming. One important trend in the literature is the increased recognition of ethnic and diversity issues in working with teen populations at risk. Different risk factors exist for different diverse populations, and in turn different intervention and prevention strategies are needed to address specific variables and trends within these populations.

The limitation of this chapter is its restricted availability to pursue each current prevention, intervention, and risk factor analysis study because of space constraints. Therefore, we attempted to give an overview of some of the most current or empirically validated interventions and preventions while trying to personalize the material through the case study of Julia. We also attempted to highlight areas that needed further attention based on our extensive review of the literature.

There are many young people like Julia in our communities who are at risk for negative outcomes. The case study of Julia just puts one face on the epidemic that is facing our youth today in terms of consequences for their sexual choices (e.g., STDs, pregnancy). As this chapter also pointed out, many of our youth are at risk, not because of their choices but because of the choices of others (e.g., sexual predators, sexual assault). This chapter barely scratched the surface of these issues, and we recommend that parents, educators, and counselors working with youth use this chapter as a starting place, not an ending point, in finding more effective ways to help the youth of this nation.

REFERENCES

Abbey, A., Buck, P. O., Zawacki, T., & Saenz, C. (2003). Alcohol's effects on perceptions of a potential date rape. *Journal of Studies on Alcohol, 64,* 669–677.

Ackard, D. M., & Neumark-Sztainer, D. (2002). Date violence and date rape among adolescents: Associations with disordered eating behaviors and psychological health. *Child Abuse and Neglect, 26,* 455–473.

Adams, M. J. (2003). Victim issues key to effective sex offender treatment. *Sexual Addiction and Compulsivity, 10*(1), 1–5.

Adamian, M. S., Golin, C. E., Shain, L. S., & DeVellis, B. (2004). Brief motivational interviewing to improve adherence to antiretroviral therapy: Development and qualitative pilot assessment of an intervention. *AIDS & Patient Care, 18,* 229–238.

American Academy of Pediatrics, Committee on Adolescence. (2001). Condom use by adolescents. *Pediatrics, 107,* 1463–1469.

Apoola, A., Mantella, I., Wotton, M., & Radcliff, K. (2005). Treatment and partner notification outcomes for gonorrhea: Effect of ethnicity and gender. *International Journal of STD and AIDS, 16,* 287–289.

Arellano, A. E., Deblinger, E., Cohen, J. A., Danielson, C. K., & Mannarino, A. R. (2005). Community outreach program for child victims of traumatic events: A community-based project for underserved populations. *Behavior Modification, 29,* 130–155.

Arellano, C. M., Kuhn, J. A., & Chavez, E. L. (1997). Psychosocial correlates of sexual assault among Mexican American and White non-Hispanic adolescent females. *Hispanic Journal of Behavioral Sciences, 19,* 446–460.

As-Sanie, S., Gantt, A., & Rosenthal, M. S. (2004). Pregnancy prevention in adolescents. *American Family Physician, 70,* 1517–1524.

Azikiwe, N., Wright, J., Cheng, T., & D'Angelo, L. J. (2005). Management of rape victims: Do academic emergency departments practice what they preach? *Journal of Adolescent Health, 36,* 446–448.

Bachanas, P. J., Morris, M. K., Lewis-Gess, J. K., Sarett-Cuasay, E. J., Sirl, K., Ries, J. K., & Sawyer, M. K. (2002). Predictors of risky sexual behavior in African American adolescent girls: Implications for prevention interventions. *Journal of Pediatric Psychology, 27,* 519–530.

Bazargan, M., & West, K. (2006). Correlates of the intention to remain sexually inactive among underserved Hispanic and African American high school students (control of teen pregnancy). *Journal of School Health, 76,* 25–33.

Baumgardner, J. (2001). Burden of proof. *Harpers, 303,* 72–73.

Becker, J. V., & Reilly, D. W. (1999). Preventing sexual abuse and assault. *Sexual Abuse: A Journal of Research and Treatment, 11,* 267–278.

Bennett, S. E., & Assefi, N. P. (2005). School-based teen pregnancy prevention programs: A systematic review of randomized controlled trials. *Journal of Adolescent Health, 36,* 72–85.

Benson, M. J. (2004). After the adolescent pregnancy: Parents, teens, and their families. *Child and Adolescent Social Work Journal, 21,* 435–455.

Berson, I. R., Berson, M. J., Karges-Bone, L., & Parker, J. K. (1999). Screening teacher education candidates for sexual predators. *The Educational Forum, 63,* 150–155.

Bird, S. T., Harvey, S. M., Beckman, L. J., Johnson, C. H., & The Partners Project. (2001). Getting your partner to use condoms: Interviews with men and women at risk of HIV/STDs. *Journal of Sex Research, 38,* 233–240.

Bischof, G. P., Stith, S. M., & Whitney, M. L. (1995). Family environments of adolescent sex offenders and other juvenile delinquents. *Adolescence, 30,* 157–171.

Bower, B. (2002). Men of prey. *Science News, 162*(4), 59–60.

Bowman, E. K., & Palley, H. A. (2003). Improving adolescent pregnancy outcomes and maternal health: A case study of comprehensive case managed services. *Journal of Health and Social Policy, 18,* 15–42.

Brindis, C., Park, M. J., Paul, T., & Burg, S. (2002). A profile of adolescent health: The role of race, ethnicity and gender. *Journal of Ethnic and Cultural Diversity in Social Work, 11,* 1–32.

Brook, J. S., Adams, R. E., Balka, E. B., Whiteman, M., Zhang, C., & Sugarman, R. (2004). Illicit drug use and risky sexual behavior among African American and Puerto Rican urban adolescents: The longitudinal links. *Journal of Genetic Psychology, 165,* 203–220.

Bureau of Justice Statistics. (2004). *Victimization rates for persons age 12 and over, by type of crime and age of victims.* Retrieved July 23, 2006, from http://www.ojp.usdoj.gov/bjs/pub/pdf/cvus/current/cv0403.pdf

Centers for Disease Control and Prevention. (2002). STDs in adolescents and young adults. In *STD surveillance, 2002: Special focus profiles.* Washington DC: Author.

Centers for Disease Control and Prevention. (2006, April). Sexual transmitted diseases: Treatment guidelines, 2006. *Morbidity and Morality Weekly Report, 55*(RR-11), 1–100.

Centers for Disease Control and Prevention, AIDS Community Demonstration Projects Research Group. (1999). Community level intervention in 5 cities: Final outcome data from the CDC AIDS Community Demonstration Projects. *American Journal of Public Health, 89*, 336–345.

Cervera, N. (1989). Groupwork with parents of unwed pregnant teens: Transition to unexpected grandparenthood [Special issue: Social work with multi-family groups]. *Social Work With Groups, 12*, 71–93.

Christ, M. J., Razska, W. V., & Dillon, C. A. (1998). Prioritizing education about condom use among sexually active adolescents females. *Adolescence, 33*, 735–744.

Coercive sexual experiences during adolescence and young adulthood: A public health problem. [Editorial]. (2005). *Journal of Adolescent Health, 36*, 359–361.

Cohen, D. A., Nsuami, M., Martin, D. H., & Farley, T. A. (1999). Repeated school based screening for sexually transmitted diseases: A feasible strategy for reaching adolescents. *Pediatrics, 104*, 1281–1299.

Cohen, D. A., & Scribner, R. (2000). An STD/HIV prevention/intervention framework. *AIDS Patient Care and STDs, 14*, 37–45.

Cohen, J. (2006). Teenage sex at the margins. *Young Consumers, 1*, 44–55.

Cohen, J. A., Berliner, L., & Mannarino, A. P. (2003). Psychosocial and pharmacological interventions for child crime victims. *Journal of Traumatic Stress, 16*, 173–186.

Comisky, P. (1993). Using reality therapy group training with at-risk high school freshmen. *Journal of Reality Therapy, 12*(2), 59–64.

Committee on Adolescence. (2001). Care of the adolescent sexual assault victim. *Pediatrics, 107*, 1476–1479.

Cook-Cottone, C. P. (2004). Childhood posttraumatic stress disorder: Diagnosis, treatment, and school reintegration. *School Psychology Review, 33*, 127–139.

Coyle, K., Basen-Engquist, K., Kirby, D., Parcel, G., Banspach, S., Harrist, R., et al. (1999). Short-term impact of Safer Choices: A multicomponent, school-based HIV, other STD, and pregnancy prevention program. *Journal of School Health, 69*, 181–188.

Craig, J. (1994). Acquaintance rape prevention workshop outline for facilitators. In *Men and rape: New directions for student services* (Vol. 65, pp. 83–85) San Francisco: Jossey-Bass.

Daley, M. J. (1997). Do sexually violent predators deserve constitutional protections?: An analysis in light of the Supreme Court's ruling in Kansas vs. Hendricks. *Southern Illinois University Law Journal, 23*, 715–734.

Darroch, J. E., & Singh, S. (1999). *Why is teenage pregnancy declining? The roles of abstinence, sexual activity, and contraceptive use* (Occasional Report No. 1). New York: Allan Guttmacher Institute.

Date rape drugs: What parents should know. (2001). *Cleveland Clinic Journal of Medicine, 68*, 551–552.

Davies, S. L., DiClemente, R. J., Wingood, G. M., Person, S. D., Crosby, R. A., Harrington, K. F., & Dix, E. S. (2004). Relationship characteristics and sexual practices of African American adolescent girls who desire pregnancy. *Health and Education Behavior, 31*, 85S–96S.

Deardorff, J., Gonzales, N. A., Christopher, F. S., Roosa, M. W., & Millsap, R. E. (2005). Early puberty and adolescent pregnancy: The influence of alcohol use. *Pediatrics, 116*, 1451–1456.

DePresca, J. (2003). Date rape drugs. *Law and Order, 51*, 210–213. Retrieved August 12, 2006, from www.Lawandordermag.com

Doherty, W. J., Erickson, M. F., & LaRossa, R. (2006). An intervention to increase father involvement and skills with infants during the transition to parenthood. *Journal of Family Psychology, 20,* 438–447.

Dombrowski, S. C., LeMasney, J. W., Ahia, C. E. D., & Shannon, A. (2004). Protecting children from online sexual predators: Technological, psychoeducational, and legal considerations. *Professional Psychology: Research and Practice, 35,* 65–73.

Driedger, S. D. (2003). The teacher's lesson. *Maclean's, 116,* 56–65.

Earle, J. P. (1996). Acquaintance rape workshops: Their effectiveness in changing the attitudes of first year college men. *NASPA Journal, 34,* 2–18.

Early warning signs of teen dating violence. (2006). Retrieved August 15, 2006, from http://www.tri-countycouncil.org/sa/teen-warningsigns.cfm

Edwards, T. M. (1999, January 25). Playground predators? *Time, 35.*

El-Bassel, N., Witte, S. S., Gilbert, L., Wu, E., Chang, M., Hill, J., & Steinglass, P. (2003). The efficacy of a relationship based HIV/STD prevention program for heterosexual couples. *American Journal of Public Health, 93,* 963–969.

Erik Erikson's Eight Stages of Psychosocial Development. (2006). Retrieved September 30, 2006, from http://web.cortland.edu/andersmd/ERIK/sum.HTML

Evans, D. G. (2004). Faith community celebrates 10 years of circles of support. *Corrections Today, 66,* 132–136.

Feiring, C., Deblinger, E., Hoch-Espada, A., & Haworth, T. (2002). Romantic relationship aggression and attitudes in high school students: The role of gender, grade, and attachment and emotional styles. *Journal of Youth and Adolescence, 31,* 373–385.

Feltey, K. M., Ainslie, J. J., & Geib, A. (1991). Sexual coercion attitudes among high school students: The influence of gender and rape education. *Youth and Society, 23,* 229–250.

Fields-Meyer, T. (2002, September 16). Not the girl he seems. *People Weekly, 79.*

Finkelhor, D., & Berliner, L. (2001). Police reporting and professional help seeking for child crime victims: A review. *Child Maltreatment, 6,* 17–30.

Flores, J. E., Montgomery, S., & Lee, J. W. (2005). Organization and staffing barriers to parent involvement in teen pregnancy prevention programs: Challenges for community partnerships. *Journal of Adolescent Health, 37,* 108–114.

Foshee, V., Bauman, K. E., Arriaga, X. B., Helms R. W., Koch, G. G., & Linder, G. F. (1998). An evaluation of Safe Dates, an adolescent dating violence prevention program. *American Journal of Public Health, 88,* 45–50.

Foubert, J. D., & La Voy, S. A. (2000). A qualitative assessment of "The Men's Program": The impact of a rape prevention program on fraternity men. *NASPA Journal, 38,* 18–30.

Foubert, J. D., & McEwen, M. K. (1998). An all-male rape prevention peer education program: Decreasing fraternity men's behavioral intent to rape. *Journal of College and Student Development, 39,* 548–555.

Foubert, J. D., & Newberry, J. T. (2006). Effects of two versions of an empathy-based rape prevention program on fraternity men's survivor empathy, attitudes, and behavioral intent to commit rape or sexual assault. *Journal of College Student Development, 47,* 133–148.

Freedner, N., Freed, L. H., Yang, W., & Austin, S. B. (2002). Dating violence among gay, lesbian, and bisexual adolescents: Results from a community survey. *Journal of Adolescent Health, 31,* 469–474.

Garfield, B. (2004, June). Garfield's AdReview. *Advertising Age, 75,* 7.

Gidycz, C. A., Layman, M. J., Rich, C. L., Crothers, M., Gylys, J., Matorin, A., & Jacobs, C. D. (2001). An evaluation of an acquaintance rape prevention program: Impact on attitudes, sexual aggression, and sexual victimization. *Journal of Interpersonal Violence, 16,* 1120–1138.

Goodenow, C., Netherland, J., & Szalacha, L. (2002). AIDS related risk among adolescent males who have sex with females, males or both: Evidence from a statewide survey. *American Journal of Public Health, 92,* 203–210.

Gurman, T., & Borzekowski, D. L. G. (2004). Condom use among Latino college students. *Journal of American College Health, 52,* 169–178.

Hall, G. S. (1904). *Adolescence.* New York: Appleton.

Hall, R. (2004). It can happen to you: Rape prevention in the age of risk management. *Hypatia, 19*(3), 1–19.

Handmaker, N., & Wilbourne, P. (2001). Motivational interventions in prenatal clinics. *Alcohol Research and Health, 25,* 219–229.

Hensley, L. G. (2002). Drug-facilitated sexual assault on campus: Challenges and interventions. *Journal of College Counseling, 5,* 175–181.

Himelein, M. J. (1999). Acquaintance rape prevention with high-risk women: Identification and inoculation. *Journal of College Student Development, 40,* 93–96.

Hodak, K. M. (2004). Court sanctioned mediation in cases of acquaintance rape: A beneficial alternative to traditional prosecution. *Ohio State Journal on Dispute Resolution, 19,* 1089–1118.

Hogan, D. P., Sun, R., & Cornwell, G.T. (2000). Sexual and fertility behaviors of American females aged 15–19 years: 1985, 1990, and 1995. *American Journal of Public Health, 90,* 1421–1425.

Holcomb, D. R., Savage, M. P., Seehafer, R., & Waalkes, D. M. (2002). A mixed-gender date rape prevention intervention targeting freshman college athletes. *College Student Journal, 36,* 165–179.

How to protect your children from sexual predators and other dangers. (2002). *Ebony, 57,* 116–120.

Howard, D. E., & Wang, M. Q. (2005). Psychosocial correlates of U.S. adolescents who report a history of forced sexual intercourse. *Journal of Adolescent Health, 36,* 372–379.

Huang, C. C. (2005). Pregnancy intention from men's perspectives: Does child support enforcement matter? *Perspectives on Sexual and Reproductive Health, 37,* 119–124.

Huberman, B. (2001). Lessons from abroad: European approaches to adolescent sexuality. *Independent School, 60*(2), 24–33.

Ibanez, G. E., Van Oss Martin, B., Villareal, C., & Gomez, C. A. (2005). Condom use at last sex among unmarried Latino men: An event analysis. *AIDS and Behavior, 9,* 433–441.

Imber, S. (2003). Sexual offenses: Prohibit sexual predators from residing with proximity of schools or areas where minors congregate. *Georgia State University Law Review, 100,* 20–30.

Jansen, K. L. R., & Theron, L. (2006). Ecstasy (MDMA), methamphetamine, and date rape (drug-facilitated sexual assault): A consideration of the issues. *Journal of Psychoactive Drugs, 38*(1), 1–12.

Jones, D. L., Weiss, S. M., Malow, R., Ishii, M., Devieux, J., Stanley, H., et al. (2001). A brief sexual barrier intervention for women living with AIDS: Acceptability, use and ethnicity. *Journal of Urban Health, 70,* 593–604.

Jones, J. L., & Whitworth, J. M. (2002). Emergency evaluation and treatment of the sexual assault victim. *Topics in Emergency Medicine, 24*(4), 47–63.

Juarez, V. (2005, November 21). Talking to teenagers about. *Newsweek,* p. 45.

Kansas v. Hendricks, 521 U.S. 346 (1997).

Kids with a clue. (2003). *People Weekly, 60*(11), 60–63.

Kirby, D. (1999). Reflections on two decades of teen sexual behavior and pregnancy. *Journal of School Health, 69*(3), 89–94.

Kirby, D. (2002a). Effective approaches to reducing adolescent unprotected sex, pregnancy, and childbearing. *Journal of Sex Research, 39,* 51–57.

Kirby, D. (2002b). The impact of schools and school programs upon adolescent sexual behavior. *Journal of Sex Research, 39,* 27–33.

Koumans, E. H., Sternberg, M. R., Motamed, C., Kohl, K., Schillinger, J. A., & Markowitz, L. E. (2005). Sexually transmitted diseases services at U.S. colleges and universities. *Journal of American College Health, 53,* 211–217.

Lake, R. S., & Drake, L. M. (1995). Nutrition intervention for pregnant girls. *Public Health Reports, 110,* 208.

Lanier, C. A., & Elliott, M. N. (1997). A new instrument for the evaluation of a date rape prevention program. *Journal of College Student Development, 38*(6), 673–676.

Lanier, C. A., Elliott, M. N., Martin, D. W., & Kapadia, A. (1998). Evaluation of an intervention to change attitudes toward date rape. *College Teaching, 46*(2), 76–78.

Lederman, R. P., & Mian, T. S. (2003). The Parent–Adolescent Relationship Education (PARE) program: A curriculum for prevention of STDs and pregnancy in middle school youth. *Behavioral Medicine, 29,* 33–41.

Lederman, R. P., Chan, W., & Roberts-Gray, C. (2004). Sexual attitudes and intentions of youth aged 12–14 years: A comparison of parent–teen prevention and control groups. *Behavioral Medicine, 29,* 155–163.

Lefkowitz, C., Paharia, I., Prout, M., Debiak, D., & Bleiberg, J. (2005). Animal-assisted prolonged exposure: A treatment for survivors of sexual assault suffering post-traumatic stress disorder. *Society and Animals, 13,* 275–295.

Leitenberg, H., & Saltzman, H. (2003). College women who had sexual intercourse when they were underage minors (13–15): Age of their male partners, relation to current adjustment, and statutory rape implications. *Sexual Abuse: A Journal of Research & Treatment, 15,* 135–147.

Lewis, L. M., Melton, R. S., Succop, P. A., & Rosenthal, S. L. (2000). Factors influencing condom use and STD acquisition among African American college women. *Journal of American College Health, 49,* 19–23.

Lonsway, K. A., & Kothari, C. (2000). First year campus acquaintance rape education: Evaluating the impact of a mandatory intervention. *Psychology of Women, 24,* 220–232.

Matson, S. (2002). Sex offender treatment: A critical management tool. *Corrections Today, 64*(6), 114–119.

Maxwell, C. D., Robinson, A. L., & Post, L. A. (2003). The nature and predictors of sexual victimization and offending among adolescents. *Journal of Youth and Adolescence, 32,* 465–477.

McDonald, M. (2001, February 5). 'New kids' video game spotlights Web predators. *U.S. News and World Report,* p. 57.

Millar, G., Stermac, L., & Addison, M. (2002). Immediate and delayed treatment seeking among adult sexual assault victims. *Women and Health, 35*(1), 53–64.

Miller, B. C. (2002). Family influences on adolescent sexual and contraceptive behavior. *Journal of Sex Research, 39,* 22–26.

Miller, K. E., Ruiz, D. E., & Graves, J. C. (2003). Update on the prevention and treatment of sexually transmitted diseases. *American Family Physician, 67,* 1915–1922.

Miller, W. R., & Rollnick, S. (2002). *Motivational interviewing: Preparing people for change* (2nd ed.). New York: Guilford Press.

Monahan, D. (2002). Teen pregnancy prevention outcomes: Implications for social work practice. *Families in Society: The Journal of Contemporary Human Services, 83,* 431–439.

Moss, T. (2004). *Adolescent pregnancy and childbearing in the United States.* Washington, DC: Advocates for Youth.

National Campaign to Prevent Teen Pregnancy. (2003). *Fact sheet: A look at the real costs of teen pregnancy.* Washington, DC: Author.

National Campaign to Prevent Teen Pregnancy. (2004). *Fact sheet: Why the education community cares about teen pregnancy.* Washington DC: Author.

National Campaign to Prevent Teen Pregnancy. (2006). *Fact sheet: Teen sexual activity, teen pregnancy, and childbearing among Latinos in the United States.* Washington, DC: Author.

Nelson-Gardell, D. (2001). The voices of victims: Surviving child sexual abuse. *Child and Adolescent Social Work Journal, 16,* 401–416.

Nicola, J. (2002, October 19). Doubts cast over rape drug detectors. *New Scientist,* 9–10.

Nishith, P., Nixon, R. D. V., & Resick, P. A. (2005). Resolution of trauma-related guild following treatment of PTSD in female rape victims: A result of cognitive processing therapy targeting comorbid depression? *Journal of Affective Disorders, 86,* 259–265.

Nixon, R. D., Nishith, P., & Resick, P. A. (2004). The accumulative effect of trauma exposure on short-term and delayed verbal memory in a treatment-seeking sample of female rape victims. *Journal of Traumatic Stress, 17,* 31–35.

On sexual predation. (2004). *Issues in Science and Technology, 20*(2), 46.

Periera, A. J., Canavarro, M. C., Cardosa, M. F., & Mendonca, D. (2005). Relational factors of vulnerability and protection for adolescent pregnancy: A cross-sectional comparative study of Portuguese pregnant and nonpregnant adolescents of low socioeconomic status. *Adolescence, 40,* 655–671.

Peterson, R., Payne, P., Albright, J., Holland, H., Cabral, R., & Curtis, K. M. (2004). Applying motivational interviewing to contraceptive counseling: ESP for clinicians. *Contraception, 69,* 213–217.

Plotnick, R. D., Garfinkel, I., McLanahan, S. S., & Ku, I. (2004). Better child support enforcement: Can it reduce teenage premarital childbearing? *Journal of Family Issues, 25,* 634–657.

Practice parameters for the assessment and treatment of children and adolescents who are sexually abusive of others. (1999). *Journal of the American Academy of Child and Adolescent Psychiatry, 38,* 55–128.

Prochaska, J., & Velicer, W. (1997). The transtheoretical model of health behavior change. *American Journal of Health Promotion, 12,* 38–48.

Proeve, M., Day, A., Mohr, P., & Hawkins, K. (2006). Specific risk assessment based on victim type in child sexual offenders. *Psychiatry, Psychology, and Law, 13,* 28–42.

Rawe, J., August, M., Bennett, B., Schmidt, T., Hylton, H., & Ressner, J. (2006, July 3). How safe is my space? *Time,* 34–36.

Remafedi, G. (2001). Linking HIV-seropositive youth with health care: Evaluation of an intervention. *AIDS Patient Care and STDs, 15,* 147–151.

Resnick, H., Acierno, R., Holmes, M., Dammeyer, M., & Kilpatick, D. (2000). Emergency evaluation and intervention with female victims of rape and other violence. *Journal of Clinical Psychology, 56,* 1317–1333.

Resnick, H., Kilpatrick, D. G., & Holmes, M. (2005). Description of an early intervention to prevent substance abuse and psychopathology in recent rape victims. *Behavior Modification, 29,* 156–188.

Rickert, V. I., Vaughan, R. D., & Wiemann, C. M. (2002). Adolescent dating violence and date rape. *Current Opinion in Obstetrics and Gynecology, 14,* 495–500.

Rickert, V. I., Wiemann, C. M., & Vaughn, R. D. (2005). Disclosure of date/acquaintance rape: Who reports and when. *Journal of Pediatric Adolescence Gynecology, 18,* 17–24.

Roberts, Y. (2003, August 19). Can we detect young sexual predators? *Community Care,* 21–27.

Rodriguez, C., & Moore, N.B. (1995). Perspectives of pregnant/parenting teens: Reframing issues for an integrated approach to pregnancy problems. *Adolescence, 30,* 685–706.

Romeo, F. F. (2004). Acquaintance rape on college and university campuses. *College Student Journal, 38,* 61–65.

Rose, S. (2005). Going too far? Sex, sin, and social policy. *Social Forces, 84,* 1207–1232.

Rosengard, C., Phillips, M. G., Adler, N. E., & Ellen, J. M. (2004). Adolescent pregnancy intentions and pregnancy outcomes: A longitudinal examination. *Journal of Adolescent Health, 35,* 453–461.

Rosengard, C., Phillips, M. G., Adler, N. E., & Ellen, J. M. (2005). Psychosocial correlates of adolescent males' pregnancy intention. *Pediatrics, 116,* 414–419.

Rothbaum, B. O. (1997). A controlled study of eye movement desensitization and reprocessing in the treatment of posttraumatic stress disordered sexual assault victims. *Bulletin of the Menninger Clinic, 61,* 317–334.

Rubenstein, E., Panzarine, S., & Lanning, P. (1990). Peer counseling with adolescent mothers: A pilot program. *Families in Society: The Journal of Contemporary Human Services,* 136–141.

Rubenzahl, S. A., & Gilbert, B. O. (2002). Providing sexual education to victims of child sexual abuse: What is a clinician to do? *Journal of Child Sexual Abuse, 11,* 1–20.

Rural Center for AIDS/STD Prevention. (1994). *Fact sheet: Preventing HIV/STD among adolescents.* Bloomington, IN: A Joint Project of Indiana University, University of Colorado, & University of Kentucky.

Shultz, S. K., Scherman, A., & Marshall, L. J. (2000). Evaluation of a university-based date rape prevention program: Effect on attitudes and behavior related to rape. *Journal of College Student Development, 41,* 193–201.

Smith, P., & Welchans, S. (2000). Peer education: Does focusing on male responsibility change sexual assault attitudes? *Violence Against Women, 6,* 1255–1268.

Smith, P., White, J., & Holland, J. (2003). A longitudinal perspective on dating violence among adolescent and college age women. *American Journal of Public Health, 93,* 1104–1109.

Sonfield, A. (2003, December). Preventing unintended pregnancy: The need and the means. *The Guttmacher Report on Public Policy,* 7–10.

Stark, C. (2003). Engaging men as social justice allies in ending violence against women: Evidence for a social norms approach. *Journal of American College Health, 52,* 105–112.

Stevens-Simon, C., Sheeder, J., Beach, R., & Harter, S. (2005). Adolescent pregnancy: Do expectations affect intentions? *Journal of Adolescent Health, 37*, 243.

Talashek, M. L., Peragallo, N., Noor, K., & Dancy, B. L. (2004). The context of risky sexual behavior for Latino youth. *Journal of Transcultural Nursing, 15*, 131–138.

Teen Dating Violence Fact Sheet. (2006). Chicago: American Bar Association. Retrieved September 2, 2006, from http://www.kcsarc.org/publications/Teen_Dating_Violence_Fact_Sheet.pdf

Teir, R., & Coy, K. (1997, Summer). The treatment of sex offenders: Approaches to sexual predators. *New England Journal on Criminal and Civil Confinement*, 405–428.

Tharp, M. (1997, July 7). Tracking sexual impulses. *U.S. News & World Report, 123*, 34–39.

Todd, T. (2000). Solution focused strategic parenting of challenging teens: A class for parents. *Family Relations, 49*, 165–168.

Van Devanter, N. (1999). Prevention of sexually transmitted diseases: The need for social and behavioral science expertise in public health departments. *American Journal of Public Health, 89*, 815–818.

Van Horn, R. (1998). Keeping children safe. *Phi Delta Kappan, 79*, 633–634.

Webster, R. E. (2001). Symptoms and long-term outcomes for children who have been sexually assaulted. *Psychology in the Schools, 38*, 533–547.

West, J., & Templer, D. I. (1994). Child molestation, rape, and ethnicity. *Psychological Reports, 75*, 1326.

Wilkinson-Lee, A. M., Russell, S. T., Lee, F. C. H., & The Latina/o Teen Pregnancy Prevention Workgroup. (2006). Practitioners' perspectives on cultural sensitivity in Latina/o teen pregnancy prevention. *Family Relations, 55*, 376–389.

Wilson, L. A. (1998, Spring). No longer free to offend: Involuntary civil commitment statutes for sexual predators create the basis for a uniform act. *Northern Illinois University Law Review, 18*, 351–386.

Wilson, R. J., Stewart, L., Stirpe, T., Barrett, M., & Cripps, J. E. (2000). Community-based sex offender management: Combining parole supervision and treatment to reduce recidivism. *Canadian Journal of Criminology, 42*, 177–190.

Woods, S., & Bower, D. J. (2001). College students' attitudes toward date rape and date rape backlash: Implications for prevention programs. *American Journal of Health Education, 32*, 194–198.

Yampolskaya, S., Brown, E., & Vargo, A. C. (2004). Assessment of teen pregnancy interventions among middle school youth. *Child and Adolescent Social Work Journal, 21*, 69–83.

Yeater, E. A., Miltenberger, P., Laden, R. M., Ellis, S., & O'Donohue, W. (2001). Collaborating with academic affairs: The development of a sexual assault prevention and counseling program within an academic department. *NASPA Journal, 38*, 438–450.

CHAPTER 12

■

"I Am Somebody":
Gang Membership

Lisa Langfuss Aasheim and Sonja C. Burnham

Youth gangs have been present in history for centuries. Jackson and McBride (1987) defined gangs as "a group of people that form an allegiance for the common purpose, and engage in unlawful or criminal activity" (p. 20). Spergel (1990) added that "the principal criterion currently used to define a *gang* may be the group's participation in illegal activity" (p. 179). Gangs are bonded not only by common behaviors but also by identifying symbols (such as colors, clothing, and territory) and common needs (protection, power, solidarity; Fleisher, 2005). Even a short stint as a gang member correlates to a significantly greater likelihood of delinquency (Thornberry, Krohn, Lizotte, Smith, & Tobin, 2003). Gang involvement also correlates strongly to involvement in drug selling, use, and abuse (Gordon et al., 2004).

To fully understand the phenomena of youth gang membership, it is necessary to examine the history of youth gangs, the appeal of such organizations, the positive and negative consequences of involvement, and the relationship between cultural identification and gang involvement. To prevent gang membership, one needs to become familiar with prevention programs, familial and social system supports as related to prevention, and community involvement in prevention efforts. The solutions to the gang problems in the United States are neither quick nor simple (Wyrick & Howell, 2004), so a thorough understanding of both prevention and intervention strategies is necessary to reduce the individual and societal effects of gang involvement.

Gangs have an enormous impact on society in all parts of the United States. No geographical area, racial or cultural group, or school district is immune to problems that may be traced to some aspect of gang activity. Because the gang problem has become so extensive, approaches to prevention of increased gang activity and intervention of existing gang activity need to be undertaken simultaneously. Approaches to prevention of gang involvement involve both the gang members and their larger systems, including (but not limited to) families, schools, communities, and law enforcement agencies. A recent review of nearly 60 gang-reduction programs reveals that few of these programs have been studied and evaluated for effectiveness and feasibility (Klein & Maxson, 2006). Although President Bush pledged $150 million to help troubled youth avoid "apathy, gangs, or jail" in his State of the Union Address in 2005, it has long been understood that the youth gang problem will not be easily resolved.

This chapter first examines the historical significance and development of gang and gang activities. Next, the chapter looks at present-day gang involvement, including characteristics of gangs, male and female gang members, and ethnic gangs. A case study profiles the life of Christopher, a young man involved in a gang. The chapter considers approaches to prevention and intervention strategies at individual, family, school, and community levels and concludes with a discussion of adaptations for diversity.

PROBLEM DEFINITION

Youth gangs have been present in the United States for centuries. Their membership levels and violent activities correspond to peak levels of immigration and population shifts, most notably in the early 1800s, 1920s, 1960s, and late 1990s (Johnson & Mulhausen, 2005). During the 1920s cities were becoming industrialized and grew rapidly. Cities such as New York, Boston, and Chicago became urbanized with ever-increasing populations. Large numbers of immigrants from varying cultures flocked to these cities seeking a better life for themselves and their children. They were not accepted into the mainstream culture, which was White, Anglo-Saxon, and Protestant. The immigrant parents typically worked at low-paying jobs that barely allowed them to earn a living while trying to assimilate into the culture; the youth banded together for socialization and protection as they experienced adolescence in an unfamiliar country that was frustrating and alien to them. Dozens of gangs made up of members from similar racial, ethnic, and cultural backgrounds emerged. These gangs provided outlets for marginalized youths to socialize, release aggression, and control territory (Johnson & Mulhausen, 2005). These gangs became destructive and often were well known by their gang names and unique clothing (Sachs, 1997).

Thrasher (1926), an early investigator of gang activity during the late 1920s, viewed youth gangs as means to socialize young delinquents to organized crime and to turn the youths into "gangsters" as they became adults. The large urban areas were the birthplace of many of the notorious Mafia gangs, and gang wars ensued over territorialism, bookmaking, extortion, gunrunning, and liquor sales. Because southern cities experienced less rapid growth and immigrants did not migrate to the South in as large numbers, economic growth as well as gang growth moved in that region at a slower pace.

During the 1930s and 1940s a change occurred within the overall racial and cultural makeup of gangs. African American, Puerto Rican, and Mexican American gangs began to outnumber the previously predominant White gangs. Areas such as Los Angeles, California, saw a significant increase in the number of African American gang members as African Americans attempted to buy houses outside of the designated Black settlement area (Alonso, 2004). Gang wars escalated with the use of handguns, knives, chains, and other self-made implements. Drug use as well as drug trafficking among gang members increased. Gang conflicts continued through the 1950s and saw a slight decrease during the 1960s, perhaps because of the Vietnam war.

Estimates of gang activity today vary. The U.S. Department of Justice estimated that more than 16,000 different gangs, with more than 500,000 gang members, are active (Huff, 1998); estimates in the *American Bar Association Journal* have put the figures nearer to 23,338 different gangs and a membership of 665,000 (Gibeaut, 1998). The National Youth Gang Survey found that there are nearly 22,000 gangs in the United States with nearly a million members (Johnson & Mulhausen, 2005). Figure 12-1 shows the major gangs found in the United States and their major locations (Los Angeles and Chicago) as well as the various types of gangs throughout the country. As the figure indicates, the Crips and the Bloods, which were the two most powerful Black gangs during the first half of the 20th century, continue in a dominant position in Los Angeles. In Los Angeles, gang-related murder decreased in the mid 1990s but had a resurgence of 143% between 1999 and 2000 (T. McCarthy, 2001).

Factors for Gang Involvement

Researchers remain interested in the individual, familial, and societal factors that contribute to youth gang involvement. In examining individual factors, some theorists view gangs as a subculture that is the result of lower-class male youth being unable to attain wealth and success through traditional and acceptable means (Cloward & Ohlin, 1960; Cohen, 1955). Because working-class youths often are not

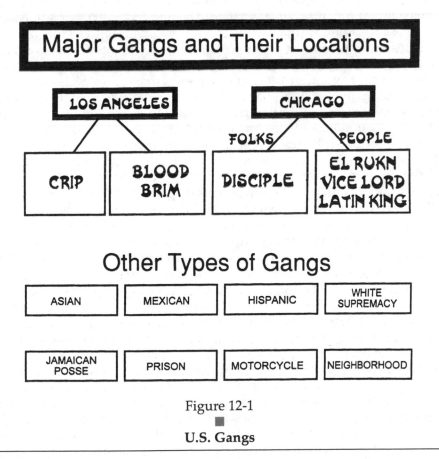

Figure 12-1
■
U.S. Gangs

Various gangs and/or sects may join forces with other factions.

adequately trained to meet the requirements of middle-class society, gangs are the means of reacting to and making adjustments in their lives to find their own social status and acceptance. Further, gangs have an organizational structure that spells out rules concerning expected levels of aggressive behavior as well as the status and prestige earned as a result of adhering to these rules (Bernard, 1990). Matza (1964) disagreed with the subculture theory, instead viewing adolescents as being suspended between childhood and adulthood and seeing this time as a period of risk for males who are discovering their identities and trying to become aligned with a peer group. Because these youths fear losing status by not being accepted, they are easy targets for gangs that specify a rigid structure of behavior in those who want to become members. More recently, researchers have questioned whether gangs are attractive to youth who are already engaging in delinquent behavior or if the criminal behavior occurs following gang involvement (Bendixen, Endresen, & Olweus, 2006). Individual factors indicating a propensity toward gang involvement may also include low autonomic arousal, early antisocial behaviors, deviant values, and association with peers who engage in deviancy (Hill, Lui, & Hawkins, 2001).

Morales (1992) viewed the family as a crucial factor for putting youths at risk for gang involvement and stated that those families whose structure and functioning have disintegrated and broken down through poverty, alcoholism, drug addiction, chronic illnesses, and incarcerated family members put youths at great risk. Thus, according to Morales, adolescents who are involved with overwhelming family problems seek gang membership as a way to belong and gain recognition and protection. These ideas are further delineated in research by Eitle, Gunkel, and Van Gundy (2004), who stated that differences in exposure to stressful life events are associated with adolescent crime and delinquency, thus stressful life experiences is a likely contributor to gang involvement. Stressful family life events that are contributors to gang involvement may include traumatic events (either repeated or single episode), criminality in the family, addiction in the family, financial difficulty, family disruption, and attachment issues (Eitle et al., 2004).

Other factors linked by researchers to gang involvement include delinquency (Bendixen et al., 2006; Curry & Spergel, 1992), lower socioeconomic status (Hirschi, 1969), ethnic minority status and identity (Gray-Ray & Ray, 1990; Hagadorn, 1991; Vigil, 1988), and lack of influence by parents (Fagan, 1989; Fagan, Piper, & Moore, 1986). In one research study, data were collected using structured family interviews (Black, 2002). The researcher was looking for connections among familial criminality, drug use and gang membership, and youth involvement in these activities when they occur in a youth's family of origin. Data analysis revealed that parental criminality and drug use are significant factors related to the increased risk of gang membership, drug use, and delinquency. Tsunokai (2005) described conditions of *multiple marginality* as a predictor of gang involvement; that is, youths who are dealing with several factors that keep a youth in the minority, such as (but not limited to) low socioeconomic status, dual-culture conflict, governmental neglect, racism, and discrimination.

The psychosocial control theory, which concerns the factor of delinquency and its relation to gang involvement, has been both influential and supported by research. Internal control was emphasized by Hirschi (1969) as the mechanism for explaining conformity and delinquency, with such factors as poor family relations and failure in school being indicators of increased potential for delinquency. A newer version of the theory (Gottfredson & Hirschi, 1990) presented six factors of adolescents who have high self-control that are thus factors inversely related to delinquency and, consequently, gang membership: (a) ability to defer gratification, (b) stamina to persist in a course of action, (c) ability to be cognitive and verbal, (d) ability to engage in long-term pursuits, (e) ability to perceive the value of cognitive and academic skills, and (f) possession of sensitivity and feelings of altruism toward others.

Many factors for gang involvement already described were supported in a study by Dukes and Martinez (1994) that examined the precursors and consequences associated with gang membership in the United States. These researchers found that the youths in the study who were active gang members shared similar characteristics: They came from poor backgrounds, were living away from their parents, and had low self-esteem and poor psychosocial health. In addition, they were members of ethnic minority groups and also had less resistance to peer pressures.

Gang Characteristics

In the last decade, as researchers have worked with specific gangs in specific areas of the United States to identify factors that can be ameliorated, they have observed gang structures and characteristics. Spergel (1995), for example, defined three major types of delinquent youth culture or gang activity that can be characterized by (a) racket activities, (b) violent conflict, and (c) theft. He further stated that without appropriate analysis of the particular community's gang activity, the intervention into and prevention of these activities will be extremely difficult. Further, Bendixen et al. (2006) found that gang members had marked increase in the amount of violent activity they engaged in upon joining a gang, followed by a significant decrease in violent behavior upon leaving the gang.

Klein, Maxon, and Miller (1995) studied Chicanos and Black gangs in Los Angeles for several decades and concluded that the leadership of these gangs is of paramount importance. However, this leadership is not a position, but more a collection of functions with the gang leader's duties varying with each function, such as fighting, athletics, or girls. Skolnick (1995), in another example, concluded that there are two types of gangs: entrepreneurial and cultural. He proposed that the more a gang is involved in the drug trade, the less it becomes a cultural phenomenon and the more it becomes a business enterprise, which presents great difficulty when intervention strategies are sought to decrease gang activity. A related finding, by Knox, Laske, and Tromanhouser (1992), who researched gangs over the last decade, is that there is a direct correlation between the presence of gangs in and around schools and increases in school violence.

Yablonsky (1997), after a review of the research available on gangs, reached the following conclusion about gang characteristics:

1. Gangs are fiercely involved with their territory, their hood, or barrio and will fight ferociously to protect their turf.
2. There are different levels of participation in gangs, in part due to age, and these can be characterized by core or marginal participants.
3. Diverse patterns of leadership exist in gangs.
4. Many gangs are totally and intensely involved in the commerce of drugs.
5. Gangs, in part, are generated by their cultural milieu in response to a society that blocks opportunity to achieve the success goals of the larger society. (p. 184)

Gang Member Characteristics

A typical gang member is usually male, a poor student, or a school dropout. He is unemployed and is often unemployable because he has a police record. Gang

membership has been repeatedly described as a strong predictor of antisocial behavior (Bendixen et al., 2006). Because the gang provides identity, status, and a
surrogate family, members develop complete loyalty. Some family members support their children's involvement in gangs to support their own drug habits. In
general, gang members are from a lower economic background and are prevalent
in African American and Hispanic populations. However, Caucasians join gangs
such as skinheads, Hell's Angels, and satanic groups. Gang members tend to stay
on their turf and commit crimes against those who are unable to defend themselves. Their violent work has the advantage of being done during the nighttime
hours, from speeding cars to overpowering victims by their numbers to shooting
from rooftops and other familiar vantage points (C. McCarthy, 1998).

To characterize gang members fully, however, we need to define the term *gang
member*. According to Yablonsky (1997), the word *member* as defined in the dictionary—
"one of the individuals composing a group; a constituent part of a whole" (*Merriam-
Webster's*, 1995, p. 724)—does not necessarily fit most gang members because gangs
are neither distinct nor clearly delineated groups. In his research Yablonsky instead
observed three general but distinct statuses of gang membership:

1. *Wannabes (Wbs):* These are youths from about age 9 to age 13 who aggressively seek roles and status in a gang.
2. *Gangbangers (Gs):* These youths are ages 13 to 25 and already accepted as gang
   members. This group is considered the core—or soldiers—of a gang and comprises about 80% of members in the contemporary multipurpose violent gang.
3. *Older (or original) gangsters (Ogs):* These youths are usually founders of the
   gang and have achieved permanent status in their gang. Many Ogs are retired
   or semiretired but continue to maintain the permanent status of Og. Note
   that *gangster* is a term often used in place of *gang member*.

Wannabes in general seldom attend school and often come from stressful family situations in which substance use and emotional, physical, and/or sexual abuse
are commonplace. Wannabes work for older gangsters, often as mules for drugs,
with the ultimate goal of becoming a gangbanger. As wannabes work for gangbangers and older gangsters and commit violent acts to prove their worthiness to
be a gangbanger, they are often promoted into the full status of a gangbanger.
Generally, wannabes continue a life of crime and violence and serve time in prison.

The general public carries a misconception that all individuals involved with
gangs participate to a similar degree. Some gang members are only involved in
gang activities in a limited way, whereas others—primarily gangbangers and old
gangsters—have daily involvement in gangs. The gangbangers and old gangsters
not only are fully committed to their gang but also often live near each other.
Generally, the gang serves all their social needs. Marginal gang members are often
designated as more active participants if they are seen with other core gang members, dress in a similar manner to those gang members, and are caught in activities
associated with certain gangs. Police and other authorities will label such individuals as gang members, sometimes even after the gang affiliation has terminated
(Yablonsky, 1997). For these individuals, shedding the gangster label is almost impossible because law enforcement agencies are slow to believe that a gang member
at any level has disaffiliated with the gang. (About half of all active gang members
in the United States today have tried to quit gang life, according to the National
Gang Crime Research Center, 1998.) Core gang members are totally involved with

the activities of the gang and become vehemently encouraging and supportive of violent behavior. Many gangbangers are swept into a delusionary state of being persecuted by police, other gangs, or anyone who gets in their way. These gang members believe that self-esteem, status in the world, and pleasurable activities are all tied to the gang. They may be easier to recognize because they have 24-hour participation and involvement and live out the paranoid gangster code of ethics and lifestyle. No matter what the level of involvement may be, gang members share the beliefs and values that allow them to behave in ways that will gain them prestige, acceptance, and status in the gang world. Gang members often use graffiti to advertise what gangs control certain regions. These are often elaborate and symbolize various gang codes, slogans, or affiliations, as shown in Figure 12-2.

Because of their dysfunctional backgrounds, gang members are almost always in some way emotionally on the edge. The sociopathic personality that some gang members exhibit contributes to the total involvement and commitment that they have to their gang. The attitudes these gang members have set them up for violence in all their interactions.

Male gang members often look at females as sex objects to be treated in any way they choose for their own pleasure. These attitudes can be clearly heard in much "gangsta" rap. Their attitude toward females in general is one of disdain, with gang members delineating their women as either whores or saints. The whores are only there to be used in any manner gang members choose, whereas the saints are there to mother their children and be idolized.

Many young girls are first introduced to gangs through rap music. As young females become drawn to rap and its forbidding lyrics, which repeat over and over racial epithets, violent acts, various forms of sexual abuse, and death, their attitudes may be affected by the ideas presented in progang music. Girls often turn to

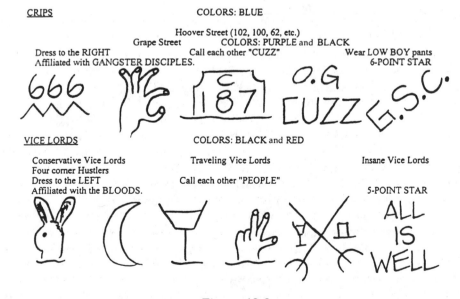

Figure 12-2
▪
**Examples of Gang Graffiti in Memphis, Tennessee:
Colors and Speech and Dress Codes**

gangs and gang members as a way of self-protection from violence, family problems, and mistreatment from other people in their lives (Joe & Chesney-Lind, 1995). Ironically, such gang involvement typically results in an increase of mistreatment and various forms of victimization (Miller, 1998). Girls with interest in gangs and gang members often are brought into the gang for sexual use, prostitution, or violence at the command of gang leaders (Palango, 1997).

Often gang members are overtly homophobic and will present themselves with a macho image to dismiss the insecurities they may have about their own masculinity (Yablonsky, 1997). In prisons, aggressions toward homosexuals, or perceived homosexuals, can be brutal beatings, often leading to death.

While acting out irrational violent behavior, core sociopathic gang members tend to show little social conscience or real concern for others. Sympathy for others is not a primary concern for gangsters. Their only concern is for their own emotional and material comfort. In short, these individuals exhibit the following characteristics: "(a) limited feeling of guilt, (b) few feelings of compassion or empathy for others, (c) behavior which is dominated by egocentrism and satisfying their own goals, and (d) manipulation of others for immediate self gratification" (Yablonsky, 1997, p. 113).

It is the norm for gang members to have low self-esteem. Their violent behavior serves to allow them some means to stroke their egos. Violence often allows them to become enmeshed in a state of euphoria. They get their highs from the violent, brutal acts that they perpetrate to gain these feelings. Their ability to rationalize away this behavior is a function of gang involvement.

It is no wonder that gangs offer a seductive alternative to impoverished, unadventurous, or humdrum lives. Youths who see gang members wearing cool clothes and jewelry and buying sought-after material goods of the moment are lured into aspiring to be one of them. Joining a gang also gives members protection from other gangs, because protecting their own "home boys" is paramount for gang members.

Females in Gangs

Traditionally, the literature on gang activities and membership has focused on males. Females were typically defined in terms of their primary role, to provide sexual services to male gang members (Yablonsky, 1997).

However, female gang members have become more independent and liberated in the past few decades and have taken on roles more comparable with those of male gang members (LeBinh, 1997). Serious crime by females has steadily increased over the past two decades (Campbell, 1987, 1992; Spergel, 1992; Taylor, 1993). Research suggests that female gang members now comprise up to 38% of gang membership (Esbensen, 1996). Fishman (1992) noted that females in gangs have become more violent and more oriented to male crime since the 1980s, and Taylor (1993) stated that "female gang members are hard core and deadly" (p. 45). Females in gangs have committed serious crimes such as drive-by shootings, armed robberies, muggings, and automobile thefts as well as drug dealing (Covey, Menard, & Franzese, 1992; Molidor, 1996). The increased level of violence is often attributed to the availability of guns and other sophisticated weapons.

In one of the few studies of female gang members, Molidor (1996) conducted interviews to learn about criminal behavior as well as the physical, sexual, and psychological abuses the females experienced as gang members. Factors for female gang involvement were found to be similar to those of male gang members (Molidor, 1996), with lack of education and severely dysfunctional family life as major factors (Covey et al., 1992). Many young females came from homes and neighborhoods in which alcohol and drug use and distribution were prevalent. Female initiations into gangs were also often severely painful and humiliating. However, once the females were part of a gang, they too felt they belonged to a family and acquired a sense of power.

In a comparative study of females involved in gangs and other adolescent females, Shulmire (1996) collected data focused on family demographics and family relationships, school functioning, psychosocial functioning, and level of contacts with gangs. Among findings were that (a) mothers of gang-involved females had lower educational levels than mothers of the other females, (b) gang-involved females reported feeling mistreated at home more often than other females, (c) gang-involved females revealed problematic relationships with their fathers, and (d) the friendship patterns and social-structural considerations of gang-involved females were connected to gang membership.

Research has indicated that female gang members tend to engage in less dangerous criminal activity than male gang members, yet are still involved in considerably more criminal activities than nongang members (Fagan, 1990). Being a female in a gang means being deemed either "off-limits" (meaning safe from within-gang crime) or an easy target for criminal acts and victimization (Miller, 1998).

Female gang members are more likely to engage in risky sexual behavior and drug abuse (Kivisto, 2001). A study by Hunt, Joe-Laidler, and MacKenzie (2005) examined the experience of motherhood for teenagers who had been involved in gangs. This study found that these female gang members decreased the amount of time spent with their gang friends and reduced risky behaviors, including the time they spent on the streets, alcohol and drug consumption, and overall criminality.

Gang membership for females appears to be tied to personal self-esteem, relationships to members of their families of origin, and their environment, school, and neighborhood. If they are to choose an alternative lifestyle, these female gang members will need to have their needs met in these areas. In addition, even though current research into female gang members has revealed that their factors for gang involvement are similar to many of those observed for male gang members, prevention and intervention for females in gangs may need to be developed separately from those for males involved in gangs.

Ethnic Gangs

Earlier in this chapter, the concept of multiple marginality was introduced to describe some factors that can make gang involvement appealing. These factors include dual-culture conflict, governmental neglect, racism, and discrimination, among others (Tsunokai, 2005). These factors are often experienced by youths who are not part of the majority culture in the United States. Because gangs are useful in fulfilling the needs that may not be met in the home or by the family, it stands to reason that youths who are disenfranchised on multiple levels would seek involvement with other similar individuals, often those of the same ethnic and cultural identification.

Gang membership tends to reflect the local ethnic population and varies geographically. For example, Asian gangs are found in the Northwest and other locations with significant Asian populations. In Los Angeles, where Hispanics make up the largest minority group, Hispanic gang membership is significant. Any organized response to gang activity must include knowledge of the culture and its influence on members of the gang. The brief descriptions of Asian, African American, Hispanic, and White supremacist gangs that follow illustrate the commonalities and ethnic influences.

Asian Gangs

Most Asian gang members arrived in the United States as minors or young adults. These adolescents and young adults, with little or no support system and often without knowledge of the majority language, are at high risk to associate with gang members of the same race who speak the same language. This bond increases their alienation from the mainstream culture. Because of experiences in their homelands, many Asians do not trust the police and rely on gangs for protection and problem solving. Unemployment and lack of marketable skills make Asian gang members look to extortion, physical assaults, residential robbery, and burglary as means to get money.

Palmer (1992) described three levels of the Asian gangs. A *casual gang* is a group of friends who operate together in committing crime by consensus with no leadership; these members participate in the most violent of crimes. The *informal gang* is headed by a charismatic leader, but gang membership fluctuates and is transient in nature. The *formal gang* has an even more defined administrative structure with a defined chain of command.

Extortion is acknowledged to be the most prevalent form of crime committed by Chinese gang members and their primary source of income. Through extortion, the gangs exert their control on the Chinese community. Police estimate that more than 90% of Chinese business owners regularly pay one or more gangs. When retail businesses refuse to pay, their shops may be vandalized, burglarized, or set on fire. Asian gangs were once thought of as being exclusively ethnic Chinese. However, with the migration of Southeast Asians into the United States, gang membership presently includes Cambodian and Vietnamese youth. Organized crime is the thrust of much of the literature on Asian gangs (Palmer, 1992).

Tsunokai's (2005) study of Asian gang members in Southern California reveals perhaps surprising results: Unlike the typical gang member, a significant number of Asian gang members attend college and come from families who earn over $60,000 annually. However, similar to most gang members, these study participants feel that they are, in general, not treated in a just and fair manner in society and that society as a whole is against them.

African American Gangs

African American gangs often exist in neighborhoods where household heads are single females and gang affiliations regularly occur. Gangs tend to form in sets based on a locality. Gang names include surnames, such as Crips or Bloods, with the full name being, for example, the Rolling 70s Crips or the Insane Gangsta Bloods. Black gangs exist in the same territory as other ethnic gangs but typically do not fight across ethnic boundaries. Little formal administrative structure exists (unlike the Asian gangs). Gang members frequently sell crack cocaine and heroin, but it is unusual for gang members to use these drugs. Most Black gang members drink beer and smoke marijuana. Gang members are totally opposed to authority. Teenage parents teach their children gang signs and dress them in gang colors. Gang members frequently recruit their siblings. Dress and color are important symbols of some types of African American gangs, and gang members may adopt certain items of clothing that are worn in designated colors or in specific ways. For example, members of the Los Angeles-based African American gang, the Crips, wear blue clothing to display their loyalty. Their rival gang, the Bloods, wear red clothing. Although the colors differ, the articles of clothing that identify an individual as a gang member are often the same. Examples include bandannas, colored shoelaces, or a particular style of trousers. These gangs have their own brand of violence and revenge. Drive-by shootings can result from disagreement over turf. Other activities include robberies and assaults, prostitution, and sale of sophisticated weapons (Jackson & McBride, 1987).

African American youth may be at an increased risk for gang involvement because they have been found more likely than White, Hispanic, or Asian youth to initiate physical fighting and weapon-related violence and are more likely to suffer fatal and nonfatal injuries from physical assaults (Centers for Disease Control and Prevention, 2004; Wright & Fitzpatrick, 2006). Additionally, increased exposure to violence positively correlates to an increased frequency of violent behavior as a child (Fitzpatrick, 1997). The intergenerational connectedness inherent to African American culture can be a considerable strength in preventing gang affiliation, yet can also be a considerable factor in promoting it when youths are exposed to the violence and lifestyle.

Hispanic Gangs

Hispanic gangs were recorded in Southern California in the early 1890s and grew in strength after the Zoot Suit Riots of 1943. These riots involved off-duty military and Hispanic males who were not involved in World War II because of their immigrant status. The discrimination and prejudice of this incident caused Latinos to band together. Soon the Hispanic criminal element took the opportunity to engage in more unlawful pursuits (Allender, 2001). Hispanic immigrants from various sections of Mexico formed gangs to defend their newly acquired territory. Then, as now, Hispanic gangs form alliances for purposes of strength. Their belief that the gang is more important that the individual reflects a value in their culture (Morales, 1982).

Hispanic gangs are generational and primarily male. Young males are known as PeeWees or Lil Winos. An individual gang member who lives to age 22 becomes a *veterano*. Veteranos act as advisors to younger gang members, and they also hide members, dispose of weapons, and arrange meeting places. Gangs are usually named after the street, housing project, or barrio from which the gang originates. Members identify closely with their neighborhood (or hood), and it is this name they tattoo on themselves and write on walls throughout the city. Gangs are composed of divisions roughly based on age cohort. In a sense, the gang is similar to an army, with the divisions operating with some autonomy while still loyal to the hood. These gangs ostensibly operate to protect the hood but actually are operating to promote prized violent behaviors. The size of the gang roughly correlates to the size of the barrio in which the gang lives. Gangs range in size from 30 members to 300 members. Gang boundaries are dynamic, changing as members move in and out, often in response to a specific situation. For core members, the gang becomes a total institution, much like a commune or a military unit, completely absorbing the individual into the subculture. Core members of the gang interact with one another according to established patterns that are binding to them as gang members and that are clearly identifiable, both by other gang members and by others not involved in the gang. Interaction within the gang is specific and ritualistic in form, with sanctions applied whenever someone does not adapt to the patterned form of behavior. Members from rival gangs challenge each other to test group fidelity and to establish membership. The challenge is one of the rituals that clearly identifies gang membership and intensifies the sense of belongingness to the group (Morales, 1992).

White Supremacist Groups

White supremacists are often referred to as skinheads because of their closely cropped hair or shaved heads. The movement began in England in 1968 and moved formally into the United States in 1984. In 1986, the Skinheads of America formed an alliance with the Aryan Nation, an existing White supremacist organization. This group believes that the White race is superior to all others. They do not believe in mixing the races. Skinheads promote racial hatred and violence by distributing literature targeting people of color, gays, lesbians, and Jews. They seek to intimidate and harass individuals through physical attacks and through racial slurs. Disenfranchised adolescents who are experiencing academic problems or drug and alcohol abuse or who have been physically or sexually abused are especially at risk for involvement in these groups. At-risk youth are recruited through school activities, through literature, and on the Internet. The goal of the gang is to gain superiority and power through intimidation. Gang members dress in military-style clothes, steel-toed boots, and T-shirts with White Pride logos. Symbols used by skinheads include the circled swastika, an upside-down two-sided ax, a circled A, and a rifle sight (Palmer, 1992). A 1988 nationwide survey of neo-Nazi skinheads indicated continued membership growth and persistent propensity for engaging in violence—mainly against racial and religious minorities. The gangs are composed overwhelmingly of teenagers, many as young as 13 and 14 years of age. It is alarming to note that the skinheads provide a recruitment pool for other White supremacy groups, such as the Order, the Nationalist Socialist Vanguard, and the White Aryan Resistance. White supremacy groups draw from skinhead gangs in the effort to recruit "soldiers dedicated to the cause" (Palmer, 1992).

CASE STUDY

Christopher, a 13-year-old New York youth, lives in Brooklyn's dangerous, gang-infested Bedford Stuyvesant section, one of the oldest Black ghettos in the United States. Christopher lives on the fourth floor of a crumbling tenement with his aunt and cousins, with whom he shares a mattress. His mother, a 31-year-old with a crack cocaine addiction, is in and out of jail and lost custody of Christopher several years ago. His father, with whom he has had little contact except when he was being beaten by him, is also an addict and is in prison for a drug deal "gone bad." Christopher knows his dangerous surroundings and carries a .25 automatic for protection like most of his home boys. He seldom attends school and is unable to read or write well. He smokes marijuana to relax and drinks heavily. He wears designer jeans, a T-shirt, and a $60 pair of Pumas with starched shoelaces.

By the time Christopher was around 9 or 10 years old, he was exhibiting pregang behaviors in elementary school. He was usually found during recess playing "gangs" with others who were from similar backgrounds. As Christopher became older, he began to volunteer to do simple errands for local gang members who showed him attention and brief admiration. He often ran money or drugs between members, or helped provide distraction while gang members committed theft and property crimes.

Christopher continued his move toward full gang affiliation through his willingness to do any errand or activity that brought him closer to actual gang members. He isolated himself from any friends who were not interested in gangs and was soon considered a loner. He quit attending school entirely as he saw no use in attending.

As he moved into adolescence, Christopher began to wear the colors of his chosen gang and became involved in wannabe gang behaviors that broke the law and involved violence. The police labeled him as a gang member even though he was still only an apprentice. Christopher was on his way to becoming a full gang member and was invested in reaping the benefits that gang involvement would eventually provide. He was willing to do anything to gain the respect and admiration he believed the full gang members had earned.

APPROACHES TO PREVENTION

The emergence and spread of gang activity has no geographical boundaries. Although largely considered an urban problem, even rural areas are feeling the impact of some gang activity. Often ganglike activities are perpetrated by gang wannabes instead of hard-core gangsters. The presence of individuals willing to strive for the gang lifestyle in any location sends a message to all. Those who are concerned with trying to reclaim these individuals from gangs and redirect them into socially acceptable lifestyles know that a variety of interventions must be used. It is also clear that even with some successful interventions, the social system that promotes and tolerates injustice and encourages gang activity must be changed. Disintegrated families, drugs, lack of economic opportunities, unacceptable ways to gain social status, and poor social support structures such as schools and community agencies are all areas that need to be addressed. Because the problem is large and spreading, it requires strategies that are undertaken concurrently to make any successful impact. Programs that offer the best hope for success are those that lead these youths back from lives of crime and violence to a society that can offer them an attainable social status, as well as social programs that help them to realize the need for change while offering a clear path to follow.

Individual

Consider the case of Christopher. What difference would a few invested adults have made if they had taken a personal interest in his life and living conditions, especially early on in his tragic youth?

Individual prevention efforts can begin early through various early childhood prevention programs. The Montreal Preventive Treatment Program uses a multiple-component prevention strategy that addresses several early childhood risk factors for gang involvement (Tremblay, Masse, Pagani, & Vitaro, 1996). One of the key aims of this program is to address and reduce antisocial behavior in boys of low socioeconomic status who demonstrate problematic rule-breaking behavior in kindergarten (Office of Juvenile Justice and Delinquency Prevention, 2000). The boys in the program receive social skills training, and the boys' parents receive an average of 17 training sessions that help them increase prosocial behavior in their children.

The following list of critical ages and activities describes life span development of gang members and illustrates how early these young gang wannabes begin to develop and how young boys and girls may begin their journey to violence and often death.

Average Age	Activity
8.9 years	First heard anything about gangs
9.2 years	First bullied by someone in a gang
9.2 years	First met someone in a gang
10.4 years	First bullied someone else in school
11.3 years	First fired a pistol or revolver
11.3 years	First saw trauma (killing or injury) from gang violence
12.0 years	First joined the gang
12.0 years	First arrested for a criminal offense
12.3 years	First got his or her own gun
13.0 years	First got a permanent tattoo
16.5 years	Age of typical current gang member
24.1 years	Age they expect to get married
26.1 years	Age they expect to quit the gang
59.5 years	Age they expect to die

Children can make better choices about their behavior when they have adequate information and are given skills to control their behavior. The following points may help youths to know what to do when it concerns gangs:

1. Know how gang members recruit others. Wanting to belong may make children accept intimidation by gang members.
2. Know how to respond to gang member invitations to join their gang.
3. Take fears seriously about being around gang members and talk with trusted adults about these fears.
4. Know what your goals are and don't let joining a gang deter you from what it is that you really want out of life.
5. Surround yourself with positive individuals.
6. Use common sense. If being around gang members is uncomfortable, make plans that will keep you safely involved in other activities (Ezarik, 2002).

Note that even though gang members think they will leave their gang and live until at least 60, the grim reality is that many die very young (Knox, 1998). Imagine the lifestyle Christopher is leading. Given the dangerousness of his surroundings, the availability of guns, and the criminal and drug involvement, it is quite unlikely that he can expect to live beyond a few decades old.

Adults who work with youths like Christopher must find ways to help them meet their needs through ways that are both nonviolent and acceptable to the youth being helped. If family or adult mentors are not available, other youths often are ready to assist at-risk youths. Peer helping programs have been developed across the United States, and because these programs involve peer group interaction, they often have more chance of success. Peer pressure, which can negatively affect the choices youths make, can also be a powerful positive prevention tool.

One-to-one mentoring programs have also been developed based on positive role modeling. Youths who are at risk for gang involvement are particularly receptive to the positive effects of being mentored by a successful role model, and research has demonstrated that at-risk minority youths paired with successful role model minorities benefit greatly (Landre, Miller, & Porter, 1997). One such program is Big Brother/Big Sister, a well-recognized, long-established program that pairs a child with an adult for the purpose of guidance and friendship. Other programs, sponsored by local agencies, community groups, and business and industry, are additionally available in most communities. The G.R.E.A.T. Program (Gang Resistance Education and Training) is a program sponsored by the Bureau of Alcohol, Tobacco, and Firearms and has shown positive preliminary results in reducing levels of gang affiliation and delinquency (Esbensen & Osgood, 1999). When at-risk youths experience one-to-one mentoring and interact with a positive mentor similar to themselves, they often become able to look toward a gang-free future.

Family

According to many surveys and task forces, a primary tool for fighting gang involvement is parental involvement. Strong families are a major asset. In one study of 300 participants from a high school in Miami, Florida, researchers discovered the vital importance of the family as an antigang prevention mechanism (Black, 2002). The majority of the participants were from single-parent families. Over half of the students were Latino, about 25% were African American, and the rest were White or other. The researcher was looking for a parenting style that seemed to have some effect on behavior; however, when individual ethnic group results were extracted from the data, the African American participants resulted in better behavior over time. Another interesting finding was that the level of gang involvement decreased over the course of the first year of high school, which might indicate that being in a gang was perhaps a temporary behavior for many students that would wane after the first year of high school. In other words, parenting does matter, and the ethnic group one belongs to may have a big impact on which children become gang members and stay with it through to adulthood. Again considering the life of Christopher, imagine how his circumstance might have been different if he had the benefit of positive, supportive familial involvement.

The U.S. Department of Justice indicated that young gang members are less likely to reoffend when their parents and family members are involved in prevention and intervention efforts (Office of Juvenile Justice and Delinquency Prevention, 2000). In cases like Christopher's, the parents were unavailable to provide such support. However, other adults in a youth's life can take on the job of parenting and can gain the respect and trust of that youth, even though they are not the true parent that the child often longs for.

Further, a study of 300 ninth-grade students examined the moderating effects of parental style on adolescent problem behavior and gang involvement (Walker-Barnes & Mason, 2004). The researchers found that higher levels of gang involvement are found in youths whose parent(s) use a coercive, guilt-based form of control along with lower levels of parental behavioral control. In other words, the more active a parent is in moderating the child's behavior, the greater the impact that control will have on reducing gang affiliation and antisocial behavior.

Many antigang programs are in operation across the nation. Those that are successful (a) provide more leisure-time activities with youngsters; (b) support a tougher law enforcement against gang activities in the community; (c) increase efforts to dry up sources of gang revenue, such as drugs and narcotics; and (d) increase parental supervision of children, including their activities and their friends (Moore, 1998).

Parents can also fight gangs by becoming better parents, that is, by improving their skills and taking more serious responsibility for their children. According to C. McCarthy (1998), parents who become effective gang fighters (a) monitor the company their children keep; (b) monitor their children's whereabouts; (c) keep their children busy with positive activities at school, at church, or in organized recreational activities; (d) model good behavior for their children and let them know how they are valued as individuals; (e) spend time with their children and include them in family activities often; and (f) watch for signs of pregang behavior, and at the first sign, intervene quickly and seek help from school, community groups, and law enforcement. Police officials are willing to help deter youth from gang involvement (C. McCarthy, 1998).

School

In recent years, youths have become anxious about their safety because of increased violence in the schools, and research has clearly illustrated that increased violence in communities and school comes with gang involvement. Although not all school violence is gang related, there is enough gang-related violence to cause many schools to adopt a dress code with zero tolerance for gang paraphernalia, such as gold chains, baggy pants, and bandanas (see Figure 12-2). Special drug and gang prevention officers often are seen patrolling the halls of many urban schools. Metal detectors are commonplace, and a sense of being under siege often pervades the school setting. Strong schools, however, are a major asset in blocking gang activity. School is an ideal place to identify and work closely with troubled students such as gang wannabes. Schools can also help make sure that parents are involved with their children at school every step of the way, even if it means trying unconventional things such as having parents' night on a Saturday morning when parents can attend and providing day care for younger children in the family. School counselors, teachers, and administrators must all take an active role in finding more appropriate ways of dealing with all the issues underlying drug activity. They must work closely with law enforcement and with social service agencies that can provide services that may shore up a disintegrating family (Lieutenant W. Hissong, Southaven, Mississippi, police force gang specialist, personal communication, March 22, 1999). For example, creative scheduling of school instruction and atypical school hours might serve to meet the needs of students who come from homes where the older children become parents to younger siblings. Many law enforcement personnel state that in schools "teachers are naturally the first line of defense." Partnering with school personnel police can make significant progress in preventing violence in the schools. Police are providing training in the schools so teachers can recognize gang signs, language, dress, and other gang paraphernalia. Many teachers are flabbergasted with the kinds of weapons that gang members use as well as their level of commitment to violent behavior. A significant impact is made when jailed gang members agree to come to talk at school about their lives of crime. Because of the increasing number of gangs throughout the United States, "gang training" needs to be an ongoing activity (Steindorf, 2002).

Gang members are often bright and resourceful. They belong to organizations that have elaborate social and organizational structures that must be known and remembered. The systems of codes and symbols of typical gangs attest to the fact that many gang members possess exceptional cognitive abilities. For example, gangs use alphabets that are individualized for their own gang (see Figure 12-3

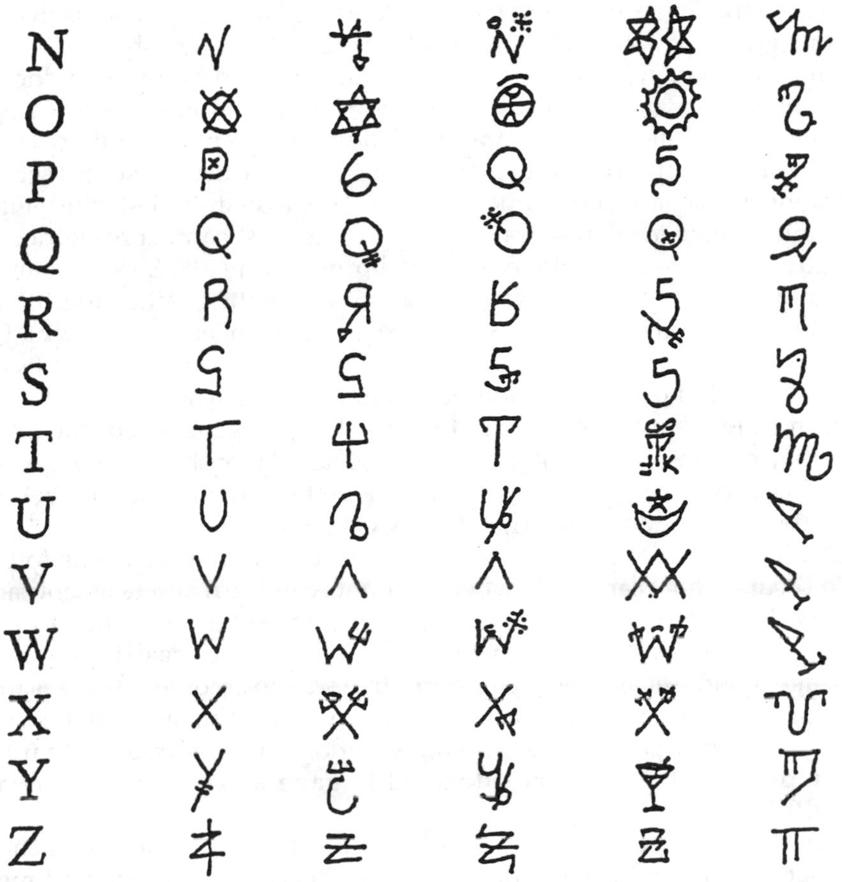

N
O
P
Q
R
S
T
U
V
W
X
Y
Z

Figure 12-3

■

Gang Alphabets

for partial alphabets), and they communicate using these alphabets so other gangs or law enforcement will not detect their plans. Gangs are dynamic groups that change over time and are influenced by their environment. For example, some gangs that previously used symbols such as bandanas, hats, or baggy clothes to identify themselves have now gone to more public symbols, such as apparel from the NFL and NBA.

Schools are recognizing and changing their approach to academic accountability. With academic competence also comes a measure of social prestige. This can go a long way in keeping marginal gang wannabes in the mainstream of the school culture (Dunston, 1993; Meeks, Heit, & Page, 1995).

Gang prevention programs must emphasize increasing the self-esteem of at-risk youth. Interventions to build self-esteem rest on the assumption that if a person likes himself or herself, he or she will be less likely to engage in activities that are harmful to self or others (Wilson-Brewer & Jacklin, 1990). Self-esteem enhancement is a long-term process. It must begin with healthy parenting practices, be nourished by the community, and be consistently enhanced by schools through activities that give adolescents a feeling of belonging and accomplishment. Alternative community support systems that enhance self-esteem development should, for example, focus on manhood development with emphasis on rites-of-passage programs to assist male teens in the move from adolescence into adulthood.

Among effective approaches to prevention that can be used in school settings are two techniques that have been demonstrated to be successful: conflict resolution education and dispute mediation training. One of the first conflict resolution curricula for adolescents was developed by Prothrow-Smith (1987). Participants learn how to communicate in such a way as to not escalate the conflict, to utilize problem-solving skills, and to maintain self-control through anger management. Conflict resolution education focuses on the use of peers as dispute mediators. Selected students are trained in communication, leadership, problem solving, and assertiveness. In middle schools, peer mediators resolve playground conflicts. In high schools, they may resolve disputes in interpersonal relationships. Teachers, security personnel, and others may receive dispute mediation training so they can help to resolve problems that are inherent in their work.

The ultimate goal of gang awareness and prevention activities is to provide safe and secure school campuses where students can learn and teachers can teach effectively (Elder, Fisher, & Forthman, 1994). If successful prevention of gang involvement is the goal, students must be involved in school-based programs from an early age (Landre et al., 1997). One definitive way to accomplish this is to invest as much money in hiring elementary school counselors as school systems do in hiring high school counselors (Peep, 1996). Additionally, all school staff, including auxiliary personnel, need to be educated in gang awareness and prevention (Trump, 1993).

Children who are economically deprived need to be provided with choices at school that will make dropping out less likely. Teaching methods and materials need to be evaluated for appropriateness to real-life situations. Youth grow up today in an MTV fast-paced world. Much of what happens at school is not relevant or presented in a palatable way. Instructional methods such as cooperative learning, cross-age tutoring, and team building can all help increase students' involvement and interaction with teachers (Bodinger-deUriate, 1993). Changes in the power structure in school also help drive children away. Children need to be respected no matter what their socioeconomic status or cultural background may be (Lal, Lal, & Achilles, 1993). School needs to be a caring and nurturing environment that encourages students to be involved and connected with their peers and teachers.

School programs with the best chance for preventing gang involvement offer gang prevention topics such as (a) consequences of gang membership, (b) gang resistance skills and assertiveness training skills (Elder et al., 1994; Meeks et al., 1995), (c) coping and stress management skills, (d) decision-making skills, (e) conflict prevention and peer mediation, (f) character development and responsibility, and (g) drug and substance abuse prevention (Meeks et al., 1995; Miars, 1996; Trump, 1993). One program that presents a number of these gang prevention skills is Gang Resistance and Education Training (G.R.E.A.T), which has been presented to eighth graders. Preliminary results have suggested that students who complete this program report more prosocial behavior than their peers who do not complete the program or who do not participate in the program (Esbensen & Osgood, 1997).

Another program that offers students training in coping skills is the Improving Social Awareness—Social Problem-Solving (ISA) Project. This program includes instruction in critical thinking skills and problem solving at the elementary level and targets topics such as substance abuse of gang resistance at the secondary level.

Other school (and community) programs that provide students with alternatives in learning and playing that have great promise include using sports and field trips, which provide students opportunities they might never have otherwise because of their financial and family circumstances, and incorporating opportunities for vocational training and job placement into the curriculum (Bodinger-deUriet, 1993). Research has suggested that youths who are in gangs will select reputable employment over crime if given that option. Job placement and job tryouts need to be funded for at-risk youth so that they will aspire toward long-term employment once they finish school (Taylor, 1990). The School-to-Work Opportunities Act, signed into law in 1994, provides for funding to support a comprehensive high-quality, school-to-careers transition system to enable all students to successfully enter the workplace. A major component of this initiative is to ensure that all students, even those with academic deficiencies or disabilities, are provided adequate training that will lead to jobs offering livable wages and advancement (Moore, 1998).

Return once again to the case of Christopher, our case study wannabe. A school counselor or teacher who had been able to identify the risk factors present in Christopher's home environment, coupled with his need for protection (by carrying a .25 pistol) as well as his feelings of being misplaced in school, may have been able to bring in additional resources to help Christopher get his needs met in other ways. A school counselor or social worker could work with Christopher around his home and family situation and resulting feelings, and a mentor could help Christopher create more safety in his surroundings. A tutor could have helped Christopher in his academic life early on so that he did not feel so inept at classroom activities. An athletic mentor or coach could help Christopher find a recreational activity or sport that allows him the same feelings of belonging, accomplishment, respect, and admiration that he longs for via gang activity. Christopher's strengths could have been capitalized on in a positive way, rather than being directed to his life of drugs, crime, and danger.

Community

Taylor (1990) suggested that what is necessary for the control or reduction of gangs is the availability of jobs and the larger world of business and industry. Gang members often get involved in gangs via involvement in drug trafficking. All youths want to have a certain level of material goods. We see this in advertisements that play to the wants and peer pressures of our youth. When youths get involved in gangs, even in a minor way, they make a lot more money than can be made at a fast food restaurant or car wash. Many more jobs must be developed for youth that pay more than minimum wage. Communities must make a concerted effort to contribute to this concept through local business and industry.

Many communities have struggled with youth violence and gang development. A number of programs have been developed and implemented at local levels, and some have produced positive results. No one program, no set of strategies, can be considered the answer to the multifaceted and complex problem of gang involvement, however. As the 21st century unfolds, Americans need to be ready to take back the youth of our society from gangs. To do this, there must be dramatic changes in families, schools, communities, and in this nation. No one group is able to do the work alone.

INTERVENTION STRATEGIES

Individual

Two strategies for dealing with individual gang members, especially those still on the fringes, are counseling and the use of psychodrama. Both of these intervention strategies have an effective therapeutic component and can be easily incorporated with other programs in schools, through community agencies, or in prisons. Counseling is most effective with marginal gang members or wannabes because it teaches new behavioral alternatives that allow these youths to become involved in constructive activities. Group counseling can provide opportunities for members to help each other gain insights and see their faulty thinking and behavior patterns. Group counseling is like a gang interaction. Members are more comfortable and able to participate fully in the activity. Positive changes often occur through working in this type of group because all the members are working from a similar family and community background (Yablonsky, 1997).

Psychodrama differs from counseling because the primary activity is for the individual to work through his or her personal, home, and community problems by acting them out using an alter ego. The success of this intervention is rooted in the fact that if gang members are able to take a minute and work through some of their reactionary behavior in reality, chances are greater that the negative behavior can be thwarted. If, for example, a male gang member has reacted to a minor threat from one of his own gang by vowing to kill him, he can instead role-play through the drama in his head, work through some of the anger, and particularly work on what consequences await him if he goes through with this threat. Often, after psychodrama occurs, underlying causes may surface that have triggered an inappropriate reaction to a relatively minor problem. Counseling and psychodrama have great value when working with gangsters. They provide direct training to those involved, allow opportunities for individuals to vent their anger and rage in a controlled environment, and slow down events so that gangsters can take time to see and understand what is actually taking place.

Gangsters live in the moment and react to whatever stimuli are affecting them. They need a mechanism by which they are given a chance to think through their behavior or make changes in their initial behavioral reaction to the stimuli. Psychodrama and group counseling allow gangsters to learn from each other in an open environment that what causes their violent impulses is often based on the emotional, physical, or sexual abuse they may have received as young children in a dysfunctional family system (Yablonsky, 1997).

Family

Today, many families are headed by a single parent, usually the mother, who is the only wage earner and, therefore, is unable to monitor the children. For these families, after-school and weekend programs often provide a safe haven for latchkey youngsters as well as give parents peace of mind while they are at work. For example, the Family Network Partnership is a program jointly sponsored by a university and community agency to help support families by providing recreation, tutoring, and peer helping (Moore, 1998).

Schools

Schools are also beginning to be more of a clearinghouse for family resources by sending home information to parents via school newsletters and other community publications. The intervention most needed in schools usually is during the hours of 3:00 p.m. until 7:00 p.m., which is often referred to by law enforcement as the prime time for crime. With good after-school programs, youths can be kept busy and will not have to spend time engaged in unproductive or unlawful activities (Moore, 1998). Many parent–teacher groups are beginning to see this need, and parent volunteers are investing their time with groups of youths after school by providing them with interesting and enjoyable activities.

Many schools are also used in the summer for remedial and recreational activities. Youths whose parents are unable to afford camps and sports activities need alternatives that provide safe and constructive programming for their children.

Community

One of the earliest interventions was begun by the New York City Youth Board in 1946. It was known as the detached worker project. This project had the following goals: (a) reduce antisocial behavior, particularly street fighting; (b) increase friendly interactions with other street gangs; (c) increase democratic participation within the gangs; (d) broaden social horizons; (e) increase responsibility for self-direction; (f) improve personal and social adjustment of the individual; and (g) improve community relations. In this model a professional, such as a social worker or police officer, works directly with a gang on its own turf. Each professional is assigned to a particular gang. Even though this approach had some success, the project worker often cannot provide the proper interventions commensurate with the level of gang involvement. Marginal gang members can often be helped by getting them to counseling groups, providing recreation to fill some of their time and connect them with more wholesome male role models, and providing job opportunities for them. Core gang members require a more intense level of intervention. Problems occur when project workers make incorrect diagnoses of gang structure and makeup. These programs also require that an effective police presence is available in the community (Yablonsky, 1997).

Another early program that emerged in cities like New York, Chicago, and Boston during the 1930s was known as the Adult Youth Association (AYA) approach. Settlement houses or community recreation centers were developed to deal with youth in these areas, where boredom, low economic status, and cultural differences were all contributing to the alienation of young men.

The AYA approach is primarily based on the premise that male youths, in particular, need good role models to learn basic acceptable socialization skills and that the role models can be provided by community volunteers working with at-risk youth in recreational endeavors and other social activities. It is also based on the knowledge that even in ghetto areas it is not unusual to see known gang members involved in a pickup game of basketball. The success of this approach is based on the fact that community volunteers can better know and serve the needs of the community's youth because they are members of the same community (Yablonsky, 1997). This type of program often draws on its own success stories for future volunteers. Those at-risk individuals who were able to turn their lives around often return to their own neighborhoods to become the youth leaders and role models for the next generation.

Because the AYA is well integrated into each community, and the workers are members or returning members of that community, the chance of successful outcomes is raised. The fact that AYAs uses recreation as a focus often leads to teams and leagues developing in one or more sports. Those at-risk youths who belong to these leagues often replace the idea of being in a gang with the idea of joining an athletic league and derive the positive aspects of this organization. Marginal gang members, who may disengage more easily because of their low level of gang involvement, may replace the benefits of gangs with those of a sports league. The most important aspect of any AYA is to allow the recreational and social activities to evolve naturally through the interaction of the local community volunteers and the youth. If communities bring already developed programs to neighborhoods without allowing for local youth to participate in the planning, the chance for success is diminished.

Throughout the 1990s and early 2000s, gangs have continued to grow in numbers, strength, and violence. Many communities have attempted to fight back against gang proliferation and expansion by enacting more serious consequences to gang activity and involvement. On a federal level, HR 1279, known as the Gang Deterrence and Community Protection Act of 2005, was pushed through the House of Representatives as a measure that federalizes gang crimes and allows for 16- and 17-year-old gang members to be tried as adults (Bennefield, 2005). Further, this measure states that the death sentence will be given to any person whose gang crime resulted in the death of another human. This act and its companion S.2358 increased federal funding to $100 million over the span of 5 years to support antigang efforts and to share intelligence among law enforcement agencies so that joint prosecution of gang members can occur. A National Gang Intelligence Center would also be developed at the FBI, again to help create a network to more effectively fight gang activity (http://gangresearch.net).

In addition, several local governments have created programs to address the gang problems. Boston's Operation Ceasefire (Braga, Kennedy, Waring, & Piehl, 2001) is a highly regarded and often replicated strategy of gang intervention that intends to reduce serious juvenile and gang violence in Boston (http://ojjdp. ncjrs.org/pubs/gun_violence/profile21.html). Many cities are replicating similar tactics, which include an emphasis on communicating to gang members that there will be swift, certain, and severe punishments for violent activities, coupled with a focus on catching and prosecuting offenders (Chermak & McGarrell, 2004; McGloin, 2005).

Austin, Texas, long plagued with gangs, experienced several acutely violent and savage murders in 1990 that alerted the entire city to the need for action. All elected officials made controlling gang activity their number one priority. A task force of elected officials, schools, social services, and citizens worked from a multidisciplinary approach to find ways to control gang activity. City officials felt the Austin police force should have a special unit devoted to gangs. The criminal intelligence unit started publishing bulletins about gang activities. Police were given special training on how to recognize and report gang activity, and local prosecutors were committed to making gang-related crime the top prosecution priority. In addition, a public service media campaign was developed, and gang unit efforts were complemented by beefed-up budgets to social service, health, and child-care agencies. As a result, Austin now has several programs that work toward controlling and eliminating the level of gang crime that was apparent in 1990.

A study completed in 1996 by the Police Executive Research Forum (PERF) examined the history and nature of gangs as well as the responses of public agencies to gangs from 1991 to 1996 in five major cities: Austin, Chicago, Kansas City (Kansas), Metro-Dade (Florida), and San Francisco (Painter & Weisel, 1997). The study also reviewed how individual police responded to particular local gang problems. Each city worked to find solutions that fit its particular needs because no one antigang program works for all cities, given the diversity of region, race, and culture. For example, the study suggested that all gang activity is not necessarily tied to heavy drug activity and that the city's geographical location may influence the amount of drug activity. From the PERF study's highlights of what each of the five cities has done to respond to gangs and their affiliated activities, it seems clear that each community will have to find its own most appropriate ways to respond to local gang activity. This will require a collaborative community approach, carried out by a well-informed, trained police force and supported by governmental leadership.

Taylor (1990) suggested strategies that should be incorporated in any community team effort. One is that the community needs to put up a strong fight against the negative effects of drugs, and this fight needs to start at home at an early age. Another is to get parents talking with their children. Being a good role model is paramount, but parents must be explicit in their zero tolerance for any drug activity. Yet another is to encourage strong homes. Whether they are in a Chicago ghetto or in a more rural area of Colorado, such homes form the foundation for antidrug, gang-free communities. Even poor families or single-parent homes can be strong against the issues that support gang activity.

In Milwaukee, Wisconsin, where a high level of gang activity exists, including violent crime, a former Jesuit priest who has had previous experience in the business sector developed what he called the Homeboyz Interactive. It is a nonprofit training business that takes gang-involved and drug-addicted youths off the streets, puts them through a treatment program, supports them through high school until they graduate, and guides them to full-time employment. About one fourth of these individuals choose to become computer programmers while the rest are given technical training and move to a variety of jobs. Of the 150 participants who completed this program, none has ever been fired (Grennan, Schlumpf, & Schorn, 2002).

With the advent of easily accessible technology via the Internet, gangs have found an avenue to get their messages out locally, nationally, and internationally. One such Web site, known as Glock3, was established in January 1996 in Detroit and was used by local gangs to seek out other gangs for the purpose of creating national alliances. When the Internet provider discovered the nature of this site, it deleted it from its service; however, it was picked up by an Internet provider in New Zealand. This site has a great deal of instructional information, which it shares with other gangs throughout cyberspace. Subjects include how to obtain better weapons, the best way to traffic drugs, and in particular how to hook gang wannabees into a gang. Another Web site, www.Gangsta.com, brags that it is the best site for reaching an estimated 700,000 gang members in 700 cities in the United States. Many of these Web sites are in English and Spanish so it is easy for many ethnic groups to communicate. Many gang members use these and other sites to brag about their activities and justify what they do (Smith, 1997). There are a variety of Web sites that parents, teachers, and law enforcement may find helpful when learning about gangs. Appendix 12-1 lists other Web sites related to youth and gangs.

To be successful in preventing gang activity in communities, programs need a strong theoretical framework. However, this is an area that is extremely complex and not easily researched (Miller, 1990). The lack of systematic evaluation plans to determine long-term effectiveness of prevention and intervention strategies is one major cause of promising programs being scrapped before they are fully implemented. The only data collected and used to judge success or failure are often increases or decreases in crime statistics during new program implementation. Community programs also need a two-pronged program so as to include prevention as well as intervention (Regini, 1998).

The American gang policy, developed by the National Gang Crime Research Center in Chicago, adopted a zero tolerance to gangs and gang activity in the 1980s. Its slogan was "Say no to gangs." There was funding to fight the drug aspect of gangs, but not enough. For the 21st century, the center's gang policy is adopting a negative tolerance toward gangs. This policy's slogan is "Say goodbye to gangs." This policy states that the cost is high for doing gang business. Money will be available to use civil, administrative, and criminal sanctions to prevent new recruits and target hardcore gang members for stiff sentences. All economic incentives must be removed from gang involvement. New and smarter laws will need to be passed to deal with gangs. The message must be sent to gangs in a strong and consistent way that gang terror is over (National Gang Crime Research Center, 1998).

ADAPTATIONS FOR DIVERSITY

Prevention and intervention strategies will be of little value to those who work to block gang involvement if there is not a basic understanding of the ethnic and cultural factors that influence individuals. People have always clustered together in groups for social interaction, protection, self-development, and simply because of their proximity to each other. Basic social expressions such as language, norms, sanctions, and values reveal valuable information (Axelson, 1999). This information is critical when developing the best approaches to diverse gangs.

All individuals come from their own particular ethnic and cultural group. Ethnic characteristics can be traced back to national origins or geographic regions. Culture is learned from experiences in the environment. Because the United States is a pluralistic society in terms of culture, there are a variety of ethnic groups to address. There are also subcultures that are racial, ethnic, regional, economic, or social communities that are distinctly different from other dominant groups in society. Gangs can be considered a subculture unto their own (Baruth & Manning, 1991).

Knowing that gangs represent diverse ethnic and cultural groups is of great importance when choosing approaches to block their influence and spread, as the earlier discussion of ethnic gangs has suggested. In the case of Christopher, whose ethnic roots are African American, his cultural roots or learned experiences are steeped in the drug-infested and extreme poverty of his ghetto and place him at extremely high risk of joining a gang. It is easy to recognize that Christopher views the gang as a way of meeting his need to be part of a culture that offers him friends for social interaction, a unique language, a set of values, and codes to live and work by, even though the work is crime related.

For helping professionals who work with gangs, it is imperative that the ethnic and cultural backgrounds of specific gangs are reviewed as prevention programs are planned or interventions are undertaken. Uninformed assumptions about how gangs view the world or what norms or values they adhere to will not lead to successful outcomes. Providing opportunities that offer gang members a chance to reclaim ethnic pride or learn to function in an acceptable cultural milieu will enhance the likelihood of a successful outcome.

SUMMARY

Gangs and gang members have had serious and tragic consequences on society as a whole for decades. The financial and individual losses to communities and families can be seen in towns, large and small. Gang members are a diverse group, but they all seek to have their individual social and emotional needs met through gang involvement. Being part of a gang organization allows them to feel protected and affirmed by those who matter to them and to have a sense of belonging in an environment that alienates them from mainstream culture. Many factors in families, schools, and communities influence gang wannabes to become gang members. Thus it is important to intervene very early with potential gang members with interventions developed to combat the causes that are individual to each community while providing ongoing prevention activities. Effective laws and law enforcement are also needed. Diversity issues in gangs need to be addressed to find ways to solve the problems specific to a geographical region, large city, or small town in America. It is only when communities work collaboratively with all the resources they have toward strong prevention programs and effective intervention activities that progress will be achieved.

REFERENCES

Allender, D. (2001, December). Gangs in middle America. *Law Enforcement Bulletin, 70*(12).

Alonso, A. (2004). Racialized identities and the formation of Black gangs in Los Angeles. *Urban Geography, 25,* 658–674.

Axelson, J. (1999). *Counseling and development in a multicultural society* (3rd ed.). New York: Brooks/Cole.

Baruth, L. G., & Manning, M. L. (1991). *Multicultural counseling and psychotherapy: A life-span perspective.* New York: Macmillan.

Bendixen, M., Endresen, I. M., & Olweus, D. (2006). Joining and leaving gangs: Selection and facilitation effects on self-reported antisocial behavior in early adolescence. *European Journal of Criminology, 3,* 85–114.

Bennefield, R. M. (2005, July/August). Experts fear new gang legislation will unfairly target minority youth. *The Crisis,* 7–8.

Bernard, T. J. (1990). Angry aggression among the truly disadvantaged. *Criminology, 28,* 73–75.

Bodinger-deUriate, C. (1993). *Membership in violent gangs fed by suspicions.* Los Alamitos, CA: Southwest Regional Laboratory. (ERIC Document Reproduction Service No. ED358 399)

Braga, A. A., Kennedy, D. M., Waring, E. J., & Piehl, A. M. (2001). Problem-oriented policing, deterrence, and youth violence: An evaluation of Boston's Operation Ceasefire. *Journal of Research in Crime and Delinquency, 38,* 195–225.

Campbell, A. (1987). Self-definition by rejection: The case of gang girls. *Social Problems, 34,* 451–456.

Campbell, A. (1992). *The girls in the gang.* Malden, MA: Blackwell.

Centers for Disease Control and Prevention. (2004). Youth Risk Behavior Surveillance Survey, 2003. *Morbidity and Mortality Weekly Report, 53*(SS02), 1–96.

Chermak, S., & McGarrell, E. (2004). Problem-solving approaches to homicide: An evaluation of the Indianapolis Violence Reduction Partnership. *Criminal Justice Police Review, 15,* 161–192.

Cloward, R. A., & Ohlin, L. E. (1960). *Delinquency and opportunity: A theory of delinquent gangs.* New York: Free Press.

Cohen, A. K. (1955). *Delinquent boys: The culture of the gang.* New York: Free Press.

Covey, H. C., Menard, S., & Franzese, R. J. (1992). *Juvenile gangs.* Springfield, IL: Charles C Thomas.

Curry, G. D., & Spergel, I. A. (1992). Gang involvement and delinquency among Hispanic and African American adolescent males. *Journal of Research in Crime and Delinquency, 29,* 273–291.

Dukes, R. I., & Martinez, R. (1994). The impact of ethgender on self-esteem among adolescents. *Adolescence, 29,* 105–115.

Dunston, M. S. (1993, March/April). Signs of the times: Gangs and their symbols. *Police Marksman,* 16–38.

Eitle, D., Gunkel, S., & Van Gundy, K. (2004). Cumulative exposure to stressful life events and male gang membership. *Journal of Criminal Justice, 32,* 95–111.

Elder, R., Fisher, C., & Forthman, J. A. (1994). *On alert! Gang prevention school inservice guidelines.* Sacramento: California Department of Education. (ERIC Document Reproduction Service No. ED 370 170)

Esbensen, F. A. (1996, June). Comments presented at the National Institute of Justice/Office of Juvenile Justice and Delinquency Prevention Cluster meetings, Dallas, TX.

Esbensen, F. A., & Osgood, D. W. (1997, November). *National evaluation of G.R.E.A.T.* (National Institute of Justice research in brief). Washington, DC: U.S. Department of Justice, Office of Justice Programs.

Esbensen, F. A., & Osgood, D. W. (1999). Gang resistance education and training (G.R.E.A.T): Results from the national evaluation. *Journal of Research in Crime and Delinquency, 36,* 194–225.

Ezarik, M. (2002, March). How to avoid gangs. *Current Health, 28*(7), 20.

Fagan, J. A. (1989). The social organization of drug use and drug dealing among urban gangs. *Criminology, 27,* 633–669.

Fagan, J. A. (1990). Social processes of delinquency and drug use among urban gangs. In C. R. Huff (Ed.), *Gangs and America* (pp. 183–219). Newbury Park, CA: Sage.

Fagan, J. A., Piper, E. S., & Moore, M. (1986). Violent delinquents and urban youth. *Criminology, 23,* 439–466.

Fishman, L. T. (1992, March). *The Vice Queens: An ethnographic study of Black female gang behavior.* Paper presented at the annual meeting of the American Society of Criminology, Chicago, IL.

Fitzpatrick, K. M. (1997). Fighting among America's youth: A risk and protective factors approach. *Journal of Health and Social Behavior, 38,* 131–148.

Fleisher, M. S. (2005). Fieldwork research and social network analysis. *Journal of Contemporary Criminal Justice, 21,* 120–134.

Gibeaut, J. (1998). Gang busters. *American Bar Association Journal, 84,* 64–69.

Gordon, R. A., Lahey, B. B., Kawai, E. Loeber, R., Stouthamer-Loeber, M., & Farrington, D. P. (2004). Antisocial behavior and youth gang membership: Selection and socialization. *Criminology, 42,* 55–87.

Gottfredson, M., & Hirschi, T. (1990). *A general theory of crime*. Stanford, CA: Stanford University Press.

Gray-Ray, P., & Ray, M. C. (1990). Juvenile delinquency in the Black community. *Youth and Society, 22*, 67–84.

Grennan, H., Schlumpf, H., & Schorn, J., (2002, March). Good news. *U.S. Catholic, 67*(3), 11.

Hagadorn, J. M. (1991). Gangs, neighborhoods, and public policy. *Social Problems, 38*, 529–541.

Hill, K. G., Lui, C., & Hawkins, J. (2001). *Early precursors of gang membership: A study of Seattle youth* (Juvenile Justice Bulletin). Washington, DC: Office of Juvenile Justice and Delinquency Prevention.

Hirschi, T. (1969). *Causes of delinquency*. Berkeley: University of California Press.

Huff, C. R. (1998, March). *Criminal behavior of gang members and at-risk youths* (National Institute of Justice research review). Washington, DC: U.S. Department of Justice, Office of Justice Programs.

Hunt, G., Joe-Laidler, K., & MacKenzie, K. (2005). Moving into motherhood: Gang girls and controlled risk. *Youth and Society, 36*, 333–373.

Jackson, R., & McBride, D. (1987). *Understanding street gangs*. Sacramento, CA: Custom.

Joe, K. A., & Chesney-Lind, M. (1995). Just every mother's angel: An analysis of gender and ethnic variations in youth gang membership. *Gender and Society, 9*, 408–430.

Johnson, S., & Mulhausen, D. B. (2005). North American transnational youth gangs: Breaking the chain of violence. *Trends in Organized Crime, 9*(1), 38–54.

Kivisto, P. (2001). Teenagers, pregnancy and childbearing in a risk society. *Journal of Family Issues, 22*, 1044–1065.

Klein, M., & Maxon, C. (2006). *Street gang patterns and policies*. London: Oxford University Press.

Klein, M., Maxon, C., & Miller, J. (Eds.). (1995). *The modern gang reader*. Los Angeles: Roxbury.

Knox, G. (1998). What do we know about the gang problem in American today? *Official Proceedings of the 1998 Second International Gang Specialist Training Conference, 1*, 419.

Knox, G., Laske, D., & Tromanhauser, E. (1992). *Schools under siege*. Dubuque, IA: Kendall/Hunt.

Lal, S. R., Lal, D., & Achilles, C. M. (1993). *Handbook on gangs in schools: Strategies to reduce gang-related activities*. Newbury Park, CA: Corwin Press.

Landre, R., Miller, M., & Porter, D. (1997). *Gangs: A handbook for community awareness*. New York: Facts on File.

LeBinh, P. (1997). *Girl-only gangs: A bibliography*. (ERIC Document Reproduction Service No. ED 413 275)

Matza, D. (1964). *Delinquency and drift*. New York: Wiley.

McCarthy, C. (1998). What are gang characteristics? *Official Proceedings of the 1998 Second International Gang Specialist Training Conference, 1*, 443.

McCarthy, T. (2001, September 3). L.A. gangs are back. *Time*, 46.

McGloin, J. M. (2005). Policy and intervention considerations of a network analysis of street gangs. *Criminology and Public Policy, 4*, 607–636.

Meeks, L., Heit, P., & Page, R. (1995). *Violence prevention: Totally awesome teaching strategies for safe and drug free schools*. Blacklick, OH: Meeks Heit.

Merriam Webster's collegiate dictionary (10th ed.). (1995). Springfield, MA: Merriam-Webster.

Miars, R. D. (1996). Stress and coping in today's society. In D. Capuzzi & D. R. Gross (Eds.), *Youth at risk: A prevention for counselors, teachers, and parents* (2nd ed., pp. 129–147). Alexandria, VA: American Counseling Association.

Miller, W. (1998). Lower class culture as a generating milieu of gang delinquency. *Journal of Social Issues, 14,* 5–19.

Miller, W. B. (1990). Why the United States has failed to solve its youth gang problem. In C. R. Huff (Ed.), *Gangs in America* (pp. 263–287). Newbury Park, CA: Sage.

Molidor, C. E. (1996). *Female gang members: A profile of aggression and victimization.* (ERIC Document Reproduction Service No. EJ 530 433)

Moore, M. (1998). Investing in our children: Report on youth violence and school safety. *Official Proceedings of the 1998 Second International Gang Specialist Training Conference, 1.*

Morales, A. (1982). The Mexican American gang member: Evaluation and treatment. In R. M. Becerra, M. Karno, & J. Escobar (Eds.), *Mental health and Hispanic Americans: Clinical perspectives.* New York: Grune & Stratton.

Morales, A. (1992). A clinical model for the prevention of gang violence and homicide. In R. C. Cervantes (Ed.), *Substance abuse and gang violence* (pp. 105–120). Newbury Park, CA: Sage.

National Gang Crime Research Center. (1998). A message from the National Gang Crime Research Center: Understanding the "negative tolerance" policy on and about gangs. *Journal of Gang Research, 5*(3), 76.

Office of Juvenile Justice and Delinquency Prevention. (2000). *Comprehensive responses to youth at risk: Interim findings from the Safe Futures Initiative.* Washington, DC: Author.

Painter, E., & Weisel, D. (1997). Crafting local response to gang problems: Case studies from five cities. *Public Management, 79*(7), 75.

Palango, P. (1997, December 8). Danger signs. *Maclean's, 110*(49).

Palmer, M. (1992). *Gang profiles.* Portland, OR: Northeast Coalition of Neighborhoods.

Peep, B. B. (1996). Lessons from the gang: What gang members think about their schools suggests new direction for classroom reform. *Social Administrator, 53,* 26–31.

Prothrow-Smith, D. (1987). *Violence prevention curriculum for adolescents.* Newton, MA: Education Development Center.

Regini, L. A. (1998). Combating gangs. *FBI Law Enforcement Bulletin, 67,* 1–5.

Sachs, S. L. (1997). *Street gangs awareness: A resource guide for parents and professionals.* Minneapolis, MN: Fairview Press.

Shulmire, S. R. (1996). *A comparative study of gang-involved and other adolescent women.* (ERIC Document Reproduction Service No. ED 412 477)

Skolnick, J. (1995). Gangs and crime as old as time: But drugs change gang culture. In M. Klein, C. Maxon, & J. Miller (Eds.), *The modern gang reader* (pp. 222–227). Los Angeles: Roxbury.

Smith, G. (1997, March). Cyber thugs. *Popular Science, 250,* 32.

Spergel, I. A. (1990). Youth gangs: Continuity and change. In M. Tonry & N. Morros (Eds.), *Crime and justice: A review of research* (pp. 171–275). Chicago: University of Chicago Press.

Spergel, I. A. (1992). Youth gangs: An essay review. *Social Service Review, 6,* 121–140.

Spergel, I. A. (1995). *The youth problem.* New York: Oxford University Press.

Steindorf, S. (2002, June 25). Police give teachers a primer on gangs. *Christian Science Monitor*, p. 14.

Taylor, C. S. (1990). *Dangerous society*. East Lansing: Michigan State University Press.

Taylor, C. S. (1993). Female gangs: A historical perspective. In C. S. Taylor (Ed.), *Girls, gangs, women, and drugs* (pp. 13–47). East Lansing: Michigan State University Press.

Thornberry, T. P., Krohn, M. D., Lizotte, A. J., Smith, C. A., & Tobin, K. (2003). *Gangs and delinquency in developmental perspective*. New York: Cambridge University Press.

Thrasher, T. (1926). *The gang: Study of 1,313 gangs*. Chicago: University of Chicago Press.

Tremblay, R. E., Masse, L., Pagani, L., & Vitaro, F. (1996). From childhood physical aggression to adolescent maladjustment: The Montreal Prevention Experiment. In R. D. Peters & R. J. McMahon (Eds.), *Preventing childhood disorders, substance abuse, and delinquency* (pp. 268–298). Thousand Oaks, CA: Sage.

Trump, K. S. (1993). Tell teen gangs: School's out. *American School Board Journal*, *180*, 39–42.

Tsunokai, G. T. (2005). A descriptive portrait of Asian gang members. *Journal of Gang Research, 12*(4), 37–57.

Vigil, D. (1998). *Barrio gangs: Street life and identity in southern California*. Austin: University of Texas Press.

Walker-Barnes, C. J., & Mason, C. A. (2004). Delinquency and substance use among gang-involved youth: The moderating role of parenting practices. *American Journal of Community Psychology, 34*, 235–250.

Wilson-Brewer, R., & Jacklin, B. (1990, December). *Violence prevention strategies targeted at the general population of minority youth*. Paper presented at the Forum on Youth Violence in Minority Communities: Setting the Agenda for Prevention, Atlanta, GA.

Wright, D. R., & Fitzpatrick, K. M. (2006). Violence and minority youth: The effects of risk and asset factors on fighting among African American children and adolescents. *Adolescence, 41*, 251–262.

Wyrick, P., & Howell, J. C. (2004). Strategic risk-based response to youth gangs. *Juvenile Justice, 9*(1), 20–29.

Yablonsky, L. (1997). *Gangsters: Fifty years of madness, drugs, and death on the streets of America*. New York: New York University Press.

APPENDIX 12-1

Web Sites

Administration for Native Americans
http://www.acf.hhs.gov/programs/ana/

Academy for Educational Development
http://www.aed.org/

Building Blocks for Youth
http://buildingblocksforyouth.org

Center on Juvenile and Criminal Justice
  http://cjcj.org

Gang Prevention, Incorporated
  http://gangpreventioninc.com/

Gangs OR Us
  http://www.gangsorus.com/

Juvenile Justice Evaluation Center: Disproportionate Minority Contact
  http://www.jrsa.org/jjec/programs/dmc/index.html

Kids Count
  http://www.aecf.org/MajorInitiatives/KIDSCOUNT.aspx

National Crime Justice Reference Service
  http://ncjrs.gov/app/topics/topic.aspx?topicid=122

National Gang Crime Research Center
  http://ngcrc.com

CHAPTER 13

Counseling Queer* Youth: Preventing Another Matthew Shepard and Gwen Araujo Story

Fernando J. Gutierrez

Russell Henderson and Darren McKinney saw Matthew sitting at a bar. McKinney stated that Matthew "looked like a queer." They approached Matthew pretending they were gay and Matthew bought them a drink. They had targeted Matthew to take him home and burglarize his apartment. Matthew followed the two young men to their truck. While in the truck, one of the men said to Matthew, "We're not fags. You've just been jacked" (A&E Network, 2001). The men took Matthew to the countryside. Henderson tied Matthew to the fence and McKinney beat Matthew with the butt of his gun. On October 7, 1998, Matthew Shepard was found tied up and unconscious, his face covered with blood except for two tracks on his face where tears had wiped the blood clean; his skull was crushed in several places and his brain stem was smashed (A&E Network, 2001).

Gwen Araujo was born Eddie Araujo. At the age of 14, she had been living as a young woman. At the age of 17, Gwen was beaten and strangled by a group of young men after they discovered she was biologically a male (St. John, 2004). On June 24, 2004, the California Superior Court granted the posthumous name change petition for the slain Bay Area transgender teen.

---

*The term *queer* is used in this chapter as an acceptable term within the sexual minority communities who have reowned the label that society has placed on these minorities. Reowning the label is a coping mechanism to remove the sting from the attempted insult by society. The term includes lesbians, gays, bisexuals, transgender, and questioning persons. Transgender persons also refer to themselves or are referred to as *gender-queer* (Roman, 2005), *transsexual, gender-variant* (Carroll, Gilroy, & Ryan, 2002), and *gender-atypical* (Haldeman, 2000). Other terms included are *questioning, intersexed,* and *pansexual* (Reck, 2005).

Queer adolescents are the least visible of the adolescent minority groups. This invisibility is a significant problem for them because they have to live hidden lives, and clinicians have difficulty identifying struggles these youths may be having as a result of their sexual orientation (O'Connor, 1992). The focus in working with queer adolescents has generally been on assisting the adolescents to cope with and adjust to their sexual orientation, which makes the adolescent the "identified client." However, to continue addressing only the psychological maladjustment is like treating the symptom rather than the cause. Many of the issues troubling queer youth are the result of living in a society that stigmatizes and marginalizes them (Hershberger & D'Augelli, 2000). Hershberger and D'Augelli (2000) attributed the source of this stigmatization and marginalization to a motive by some members of society to force queer youth to internalize this disdain so as to force them to rid themselves of their queer feelings and identity and replace them with socially acceptable heterosexuality. Hershberger and D'Augelli concluded that, in counseling queer youth, it is not the queer identity that needs to be repaired but the hostility expressed against it.

The purpose of this chapter is to discuss the prevention needs of queer youths and the interventions that counselors can make at the individual, organizational, and societal levels to change these youths' cultural context to prevent more deaths of innocent persons, such as Matthew Shepard and Gwen Araujo, who are victimized because of ignorance just for being who they are.

Queer teenagers face several problems: deterioration of academic performance, homelessness, substance abuse, arrests for criminal activity, sexual victimization, sexually transmitted diseases, and attempted suicides (Cochran, Stewart, Ginzler, & Cauce, 2002; Herr, 1997; Remafedi, 1987). As counselors we need to treat these adolescents; however, the problems these adolescents face do not stem from an intrapsychic psychopathology but from adjustment reactions and responses to victimization by society (Hershberger & D'Augelli, 1995; Savin-Williams, 1994).

Other stressors for queer youths are the assumptions of others, such as society, family, and friends, that queer youths are defective; these assumptions result in stigmatization because of perceived deviance (Herdt, 1989). A study of queer youths in a sample from 14 metropolitan communities in the United States found that 80% of queer youths had been victims of verbal insults, 44% had received threats of attack, 23% had property damaged, 33% had objects thrown at them, 30% had been chased and followed, 22% had been sexually assaulted, 17% had been physically assaulted, 13% had been spat on, and 10% had been assaulted with a deadly weapon (Hershberger & D'Augelli, 1995). Queer youths are also vulnerable to forced or encouraged sexual conduct prior to age 19 (Doll et al., 1992). Another study in Massachusetts showed that one third of gay teens had been threatened with a weapon at school within the past month, compared with 7% of heterosexual students (Woodiel, Angermeier-Howard, & Hobson, 2003).

In a sample of 1,925 lesbians, 24% had been beaten or physically abused as they were growing up, 19% were survivors of incest, and 21% were victims of rape or sexual molestation during childhood (Bradford, Ryan, & Rothblum, 1994). In a study of gay and bisexual male youth, almost 60% of the youths interviewed were abusing substances at the time of the interview, and their substance abuse pattern met the clinical criteria for substance abuse. Of these participants, 17% had participated in a chemical dependency treatment program.

According to Bethard (2004), in a study by the Sexuality Information and Education Council of the United States, it was found that 41.7% of queer youths did not feel safe in their school, and 69% had experienced some form of harassment. Homophobic remarks from faculty and staff, while in school, were overheard by one third of queer students. As a result, 28% of queer youths drop out of school, which is over three times the national average.

Heterosexual adolescents have other visible heterosexual adolescents from whom to learn and emulate, whereas queer youths often feel that they must remain invisible and, therefore, have become very isolated in navigating the complex adolescent stage of development (Tobias-Neely, 2005). Dating for a queer adolescent can be fraught with impediments, according to Savin-Williams (2005). First the adolescent has to find a suitable partner, but most queer adolescents are not out to themselves, let alone someone else. Then when they find a mate, they are exposed to verbal and physical harassment by peers, according to Savin-Williams, who pointed out the lack of "celebration" of positive queer relationships. For queer youth, relationships are something to be condemned, ridiculed, or ignored, according to Savin-Williams.

Plummer (1989) pointed to the heterosexist and homophobic peer adolescent culture as a contributor to the development of the negative self among queer youth. Coleman and Remafedi (1989) suggested that in addition to positive affirmations of these adolescents' sexual orientation, the counselor must address the following psychological problems resulting from stigmatization: psychological maladjustment, impaired psychosocial development, family alienation, inadequate interpersonal relationships, alcohol and drug abuse, depression and suicidal ideation, and concerns about HIV infection and other sexually transmitted diseases (see also Coleman, 1988).

For transgender youth, a diagnosis of gender dysphoria occurs as a result of the lack of knowledge within society about the issue and the unwillingness of society to acknowledge transsexuals as a legitimate sexual identity. Take the example of "Pat." "Pat" is a 5-year-old biological male child who strongly believes she is female. "Pat" began school in the fall in Broward County, Florida (Santiago, 2006). The school district at first refused to allow "Pat" to attend school as a female. Mental health professionals diagnosed "Pat" with gender dysphoria, as opposed to transgender. This implies that "Pat" has a clinical diagnosis, as opposed to an "orientation" similar to being gay, lesbian, or bisexual. After 2 years of examining "Pat," these mental health professionals have determined that she is not simply effeminate or going through a phase, according to Santiago. The case of "Pat" is not unique to Broward and Miami-Dade counties. Both schools have policies in place on how to address these students' "condition" (this word is used to describe how the counties view these students).

"Pat" looks quite feminine and likes playing with dolls. She hates her penis and refuses to wear boys' clothing. "Pat" lives in a middle-class neighborhood, the child of an attorney father and a mother who has a master's degree in counseling (Santiago, 2006, p. 2A). "Pat" is the youngest of four children. She has two sisters and a brother. According to Santiago, after long consultations with pediatric endocrinologists and psychotherapists and school officials, the parents made a decision that it was in "Pat's" best interest to live as a girl.

"Pat's" attorney conceded: "The school officials have agreed to continue working with the family and medical professionals to help create an environment that will maximize the child's ability to learn and grow within the school system" (Santiago, 2006, p. 2A). However, when one examines the school's position, the school is not acting in the child's best interest, but in its interest to deny the existence of a transgender identity. The school system's stance is more concerned about protecting its perception by the community. Santiago (2006) stated: "At the school, teachers and the principal are prepared. The child will use unisex bathroom facilities, will be addressed by a unisex name—not Pat—and has been asked to dress in gender-neutral clothing, such as shorts or pants and shirt" (p. 2A). Somehow the school feels that raising "Pat" as unisex will be in "Pat's" best interest. They do not realize how damaging this will be to "Pat." What will happen when "Pat" gets older and students begin to ask questions, or when "Pat" decides to stop living a lie as "unisex" and owns who she really is? Leah Kelly, executive director of student support services and exceptional student education, states: "[T]he Broward school system has admitted transgendered children before, and that is a private matter between the parents, school administrators, and the child" (Santiago, 2006, p. 2A). This is an attempt by the school district to keep the "problem" in the closet by making it a "private" matter. How private is one's external appearance and identity?

What will happen when "Pat" becomes a teenager and begins to show characteristics of her birth gender as a male? Will the school be as accommodating when "Pat" begins to have hormone treatments that will give her the female characteristics of her acknowledged gender? These are the unique struggles identified by Roman (2005).

Treatment issues should no longer focus on assisting gender-dysphoric individuals in adjusting to their new gender but to affirm a new transgender identity (Carroll et al., 2002). Carroll et al. suggested that a shift needs to occur from a focus on transforming transgendered clients to one focusing on transforming the cultural context in which these clients live. Other counselors have made similar suggestions regarding queer individuals.

Burke (1996) suggested that some researchers in the area of transgender identity believe that it is easier to change individuals than it is to change society. However, Haldeman (2000, p. 196) warned that

> [T]treatments aimed at gender conformity never assess the potential harm that may result to the individual's sense of well-being. If such treatments indirectly communicate to children that they are somehow "broken," then it is reasonable to consider that negative effects on self-esteem from social rejection could be exacerbated by the treatment itself. For even if it is possible to redirect the child's interests and affections without causing internal damage, should not the families, peers, and institutions in the child's life take responsibility for becoming more welcoming, safe places for a diverse range of behaviors? School psychologists, counselors, and teachers can, through their own behavior and their specific recommendations, make an impact on the school's climate for tolerance.

Dworkin and Gutierrez (1992) advocated a shift in priorities toward a community counseling approach to addressing queer issues. Dworkin and Gutierrez recommended delivering services to the community and not just responding to the onset of pathology. They identified counselor activities recommended by the Boston Conference on the Education of Psychologists for Community Mental Health Committee in 1966, including active participation in community affairs, preventive intervention at the community level, collaboration with responsible laypeople to reduce community tensions, promotion of research that supports sexual minority status as a difference rather than a pathology, collaboration with lawmakers to develop public policy, and education of the public about erroneous queer stereotypes.

PROBLEM DEFINITION

An Underinformed Public

The public at large holds a heterosexual bias based on myths and stereotypes of queer youth. Dworkin and Gutierrez (1989) stated that "because we do not know the process by which sexual orientation develops, we cope by using methods that are familiar though not always relevant. In the past, when we didn't understand something, we labeled it as a sin or illness" (p. 6). As an example, Dworkin and Gutierrez noted that it used to be considered heresy to claim that the world was round. Royce (1981) pointed out that in the 1950s the immoral stigma of alcoholism was removed by the World Health Organization after scientists began to learn more about alcoholism as a disease. Likewise, queer orientation is going through a similar transformation from immoral to disease to condition to orientation. Dworkin and Gutierrez traced the historical background of this transformation. In the mid-1800s, for example, Karl Heinrich Uhlrichs believed that homosexuals were a third sex and that their sexual orientation was inborn. Karoly Benkert, a physician who first coined the term *homosexual*, argued for an end to discrimination against gay people, according to Dworkin and Gutierrez. They added that the repression of the 1930s put an end to this movement toward more positive attitudes. Dworkin and Gutierrez pointed out that this stigmatization is institutionalized in our laws, religious institutions, and helping professions.

The cases of Matthew Shepard, Gwen Araujo, and "Pat" illustrate societal attempts to keep queer people hidden so that society does not have to deal with their presence. Matthew Shepard and Gwen Araujo were made examples of what would happen if people come out. "Pat" must live in hiding for her own good, instead of society being educated about queer orientation and teaching acceptance.

Money (1987) addressed heterosexual bias when he stated that *sexual preference* is a moral and political term rather than a scientific term, one which implies a voluntary choice. Money pointed out the danger of this heterosexual bias because holding this view gives biased individuals justification to impose heterosexuality on others. If it is a preference, then queer folk could be legally forced to choose heterosexuality or experience punishment. However, there is legal precedent that such pressure is unconstitutional. In *Skinner v. Oklahoma* (1942), a case in which the state wanted to sterilize habitual criminals, Justice Jackson stated: "There are limits to the extent which a legislatively represented majority may conduct biological experiments at the expense of the dignity and personality and natural powers of a minority—even those who have been guilty of what the majority defines as crimes" (p. 541).

Gutierrez (1994, p. 245) stated: "To force a gay, or lesbian, to behave heterosexually is such an abhorrent experiment conducted by the current legislatively represented majority, which is conducting this experiment at the expense and the dignity and personality of gays and lesbians." Imagine the psychological damage if the reverse were to happen: that heterosexuals be forced to live gay and lesbian lives because a group in power decides that it is the law of the land for everyone to behave homosexually (Hally, 1993).

Why Do We Feel This Way?

Female blue crabs "paint their fingernails" (Fahrenthold, 2005), that is, the tips of their claws turn bright red during the process of aging. Underneath the shell, there should be a shape of the U.S. Capitol. Male crabs are distinguished as male because of their blue claw tips. Underneath, their shell is the shape of the Washington Monument. Fahrenthold reported that, on May 21, 2005, a crab was trapped by a fisherman near Gwynns Island, Virginia. This was no ordinary crab. The right claw was red but the left claw was blue. When the fisherman turned it over, he saw a wavy arrow, which seemed to be a combination of both genders. Farenthold reported that this creature is called a *bilateral gynandromorphy* because it is a split between two genders. Confused as to whether to put this crab among the male or female crabs, the fishermen dropped the half-and-half crab into a tank with a female crab that was ready to mate. The fishermen observed that the half-and-half crab cradled the female under its legs, as a male crab would do in preparation for mating; however, the half-and-half crab lost interest and let the female crab go. The next day, the fishermen found that the female crab had been half eaten. A wild female crab will normally eat other competing female crabs after the female crabs have shed their shells and become vulnerable (Farenthold, 2005). The half-and-half crab was exhibiting biological and behavioral characteristics of both male and female crabs. A scientist at the Virginia Institute of Marine Science in Gloucester Pointe, Virginia, explained that the crab's makeup is the result of a chromosomal change in which, as the cells began to divide, one sex chromosome may have been lost or changed, so the two halves developed according to different genetic blueprints.

Because there are restrictions on experimental hormone manipulation in humans, it is difficult to show hormonal influences on sexual orientation in humans (Collaer & Hines, 1995, p. 60). Extrapolations must then be made from cases of naturally occurring hormonal differences to determine the role of these differences in humans, according to Collaer and Hines.

Inquiry on the formation of sexual orientation in humans has focused on three main areas: genetics, brain structure, and hormonal influences (Bohan, 1996). Bohan pointed out that the most popular theory on the formation of sexual orientation is the neuroendocrinological theory (p. 75). The reason neuroendocrionological theory is the most popular hypothesis is that research has shown that prenatal hormones have an impact not only on the differentiation of the genitalia but also on the sexually differentiated organization of the brain (Bohan, 1996). Neuroendocrinological theory addresses the role of hormones in the influence of sexual behavior in animals. The theory shows vividly how organ structures can be affected by hormonal influences. This area is the most fascinating approach to the explanation of sexual orientation.

Bohan (1996) pointed out that theorists hypothesize that homosexuality manifests itself through cross-identity, an attraction to the same sex as a result of cross-sex brain organization. She identified three main assumptions to this theory: (a) Prenatal exposure and sensitivity to sex hormones shape sexually differentiated brain organization; (b) brain organization creates sex-typical behaviors; and (c) lesbian, gay, and bisexual identities reflect cross-sex brain organization in their cross-sex behavior, such that lesbians exhibit brains that are similar to heterosexual males, and gay men have brains that exhibit heterosexual female organization. To these, I would add that bisexual persons exhibit brain organizations that have characteristics of both heterosexual men and women. There is evidence within animal research and human research that sexual orientation and gender variation are biological processes; therefore, to answer the question, we need to understand the biological process of sexual differentiation.

Genetic Studies

Genetic studies describe a genetic association that suggests genetic influences. Bailey and Pillard (1991) studied the sexual orientation of siblings of 110 gay men. There was an orientation concordance rate of 52% for identical or monozygotic twins, 22% for fraternal or dizygotic twins, 9% for nontwin brothers, and 11% for adopted brothers. In a similar lesbian study, Bailey, Pillard, Neale, and Agyei (1993) studied lesbians and bisexual women and found an orientation concordance rate of 48% for identical twins, 16% for sororal twins, 14% for nontwin sisters, and 6% for adoptive sisters. Hamer, Magnuson, Hu, and Pattatucci (1993) discovered the presence of a particular segment of the xq28 chromosome shared by a sample of gay men, giving more credence to the possibility of a biological basis for sexual orientation formation.

Neuroendocrinological Theories

Neuroendocrinological studies and theories dramatically show the influence of hormones on the formation of male and female genitalia (Lips, 1978; Money, 1987). To answer the question as to the origins of sexual orientation formation, we need to understand the biological process. Sexual differentiation proceeds as a result of the influence of the following subsystems: "chromosomal sex, H-Y antigenic sex, gonadal sex, prenatal hormonal sex, internal genital sex, external genital sex, pubertal hormonal sex and rearing, and gender identity/role formation" (Money, 1987, p. 389). These subsystems create sexual differentiation in three major biological systems of the human body: the reproductive tract, the external genitalia, and the brain and central nervous system (Money, 1987).

Migeon and Wisniewski (1998) explained that sex refers to the biological qualities such as chromosomal, morphological (internal and external), gonadal, and hormonal characteristics. Genetic sex is the first step in sex differentiation, according to Migeon and Wisniewski. The egg has 23 X chromosomes and the sperm can carry either 23 X or 23 Y chromosomes. The fusion of the 23 X chromosomes of the egg with the 23 X chromosomes of the sperm creates a genetic female, whereas the fusion of the 23 X chromosomes of the egg and the 23 Y chromosomes of the sperm creates a genetic male. During the first weeks of development of the embryo, according to Migeon and Wisniewski, the internal ducts and external genitalia are bipotential in both male and female embryos. This means that the biological wiring in both embryos have the potential of becoming male or female. It is like the hard drive of a computer that is wired to be able to accept various programs, such as Word, WordPerfect, Lotus 123, and so on. The wiring must be able to handle the differentiations in the programs (hormonalization).

Migeon and Wisniewski (1998) noted,

> During the first six weeks of embryonic development the gonadal ridge, germ cells, internal ducts, and external genitalia are bipotential in both 46, XX and 46, XY embryos. Under circumstances of sex differentiation: Z(1) the bipotential gonadal ridges differentiate into either ovaries or testes; (2) germ cells develop into either oocytes or

spermatocytes; (3) one of the two sets of internal ducts develop while the other regresses, and (4) bipotential external genitalia either masculinize or remain feminine. In contrast, individuals with conditions of intersex show varying degrees of discordance between the sex of their gonads, internal ducts and external genitalia. (p. 246)

According to Collaer and Hines (1995), "manipulations of steroids during critical periods of prenatal and neonatal development can produce an animal [or human] with the chromosomal makeup of one sex but the behavior and neural features of the other" (p. 56). The role of placental hormones seems to be equally important as the role of intrafetal hormones (Collaer & Hines, 1995). Androgens (or masculinizing hormones) are produced mainly by the testes and, to a lesser degree, by the adrenal gland, whereas estrogens and progestins (or feminizing hormones) are produced mainly by the ovary and the placenta (Collaer & Hines, 1995). Collaer and Hines explained that females escape the masculinizing effects of natural ovarian estrogens by estradiol exposure through protective mechanisms that occur in the placenta.

Reproductive Tract

Money (1987) stated that the human embryo during the first 8 weeks after conception is actually female. The embryo continues to develop as female unless masculinizing hormones are introduced as a result of the messages sent from the X-Y (male) chromosome. The reproductive tract is formed by the differentiation of the gonads into either testes or ovaries. One set of ducts develops while the other set regresses. The male hormones prevent the mullerian ducts from developing into the uterus, fallopian tubes, and posterior portion of the vagina, according to Money (1987) and Migeon and Wisniewski (1998). Testosterone then allows the wolffian ducts to develop into the prostate gland, epididymis, vas deferens, and seminal vesicles. The wolffian ducts appear in the 4th week of gestation while the mullarian ducts appear later, during the 6th week of gestation, if the embryo will be female (Migeon & Wisniewski, 1998, p. 246). Sometimes, a male embryo will experience an undescended testicle, for example. This seems to occur because of the interference in the message sent to the gonads to differentiate into either a testicle or an ovary.

External Genitalia

The external genitalia in the fetus forms the labia minora in the female and the clitoris and hood. If the fetus is to be a male, according to Money (1987), the tissues that are the labia minora in the female fuse along the midline and forms the scrotum in the male (Money, 1987). Sometimes a mutation occurs in the fusing of the tissue of the penis, creating differences in penile formation. For example, in some fetuses that differentiate to male, the opening of the urethra, instead of being at the end and center of the head of the penis, will be underneath the head of the penis along the shaft. The clitoris in the female elongates to form the penis in the male.

Brain and Central Nervous System

Collaer and Hines (1995) explained that hormones can influence behavior in adulthood by influencing brain organization at earlier stages of development; at later stages, hormones activate existing neural systems. The organizing effects of gonadal hormones influence masculinization and/or feminization, according to Collaer and Hines. They explained that organizational effects are more permanent, whereas activational effects are more transient.

According to Collaer and Hines (1990), masculinization and feminization have slightly critical periods. The direction or effect of masculinization or feminization can depend on the magnitude of exposure (or levels of hormone) and timing of exposure. The result in these critical periods can produce an animal that demonstrates female-typical and male-typical behaviors, such as the blue crab, by providing testosterone during the critical period for masculinization and withholding it during the period of feminization.

Berenbaum and Snyder (1995) stated,

> Hormonal effects on sexual orientation (or any behavior) probably reflect not just simple changes in levels at a circumscribed point in development, but rather a process reflecting such factors as timing, duration, dose, type of hormone exposure, variation in hormone receptor sensitivity, and different sensitive periods for different aspects of behavior. (p. 32)

Money (1987) explained that hormonalization of the brain is ambitypic, meaning that there are two processes going on. If the brain differentiates into a male, the hormones are masculinizing the brain. According to Money, testosterone is the primary masculinizing hormone. The converse is not feminization, but demasculinization. At the same time, another process is going on in which the brain is differentiating as male and is being defeminized. The converse of this process, according to Money, is feminization of the brain. Money explained that this ambitypic differentiation allows for the coexistence of both feminine and masculine "nuclei and pathways, and the behavior they govern, in some, if not all parts of the brain" (p. 387). Money further explained,

> There are alternative ways in which one side [of the brain] could be rendered masculine and the other feminine to a sufficient degree to constitute bisexuality. Likewise, there are alternative ways in which the brain may be masculinized when the genitals are feminized, or vice versa, so as to constitute homosexuality. (p. 388)

Money (1987) stated that it is possible for masculinization to occur without defeminization and for feminization to occur without demasculinization. This explains the potential for the existence of bisexuality and same-sex sexual orientation. In the process of masculinization and feminization, it is possible for the brain to differentiate in such a way that the brain organization can move to a different direction than the internal and external genitalia of the fetus. Brain differentiation, according to Money, occurs later than that of genitalia and extends into the first few days or weeks of postnatal life. The ambitypic differentiation of the brain allows for the coexistence of both masculine and feminine nuclei and pathways and the behaviors they govern.

According to Money (1987), disparities can form on the basis of the amount of hormone needed and the amount available to each hemisphere of the brain, the availability and timing of each side, the synchrony or disynchrony of the programming of the hormones on each side, and the continuity of the hormonal supply to each side (p. 388). Because of this differentiation, Money suggested that one side could be rendered masculine and the other side feminine such as to constitute bisexuality.

Sexual differentiation generally proceeds in the same direction at every stage; that is, a person develops internal genitalia of the same sex as the external genitalia and the same sex as the brain/central nervous system (Lips, 1978). Lips explained variations in the differentiation process that allow for a person to differentiate as male in one stage and as female in the other stages. A person can have internal and external genitalia of one sex and the brain formation of another or both sexes. Thus, a gay man can be clear as to his gender, male, but perceive the world from a more feminine perspective and be sexually attracted to other males because of the specific development of the brain/central nervous system toward this direction.

Cognitive Differences

Berenbaum and Snyder (1995) reported that cognitive differences have been found between heterosexuals and gays and lesbians. For example, heterosexual men have been found to have higher spatial ability and lower verbal facility than gay men and heterosexual women. Gay men and lesbian women have a higher rate of left-handedness than their heterosexual counterparts. Berenbaum and Snyder summarized studies that indicate that homosexual males are more likely to participate in girls' games than their heterosexual counterparts, more likely to experiment with cosmetics and jewelry, and less likely to participate in sports. Lesbians, on the other hand, are more likely to participate in sports and less likely to experiment with cosmetics and jewelry and to wear dresses than their heterosexual counterparts. Lesbians were also more likely to play with opposite-sex playmates in childhood than heterosexual females. Berenbaum and Snyder suggested that early hormones are responsible for the influence in both sex-typed behavior and same-sex orientation.

Collaer and Hines (1995) reported that "prenatal exposure of girls to androgen-based progesterone has been associated with increases in some male typical characteristics: higher levels of tomboyism, preferences for male-typical toys and male playmates, and elevated tendencies toward physical aggression" (p. 87).

Money (1987) concluded that

> [T]he only scholarly position is to allow that prenatal and postnatal determinants are not mutually exclusive. . . . When nature and nurture interact at critical developmental periods, the residual products may persist immutably. . . .The postnatal determinants that enter the brain through the senses by way of social communication and learning also are biological, for there is biology of learning and remembering. (p. 398)

We have just seen the many steps and complexity of events that create sexual differentiation. In any of these steps, variations can occur to explain differentiations in sexual orientation and gender variations.

Heterosexist Assumptions

Because heterosexuals are a majority in society, there is a tendency to view the world strictly from a heterosexual perspective. The United States is a pluralistic society. A characteristic of a pluralistic society is that it respects the rights and differences of the minority groups in the society and does not impose a "majority view." Levine and Padilla (1980, p. 3) defined pluralistic counseling as "therapy that recognizes the client's culturally based beliefs, values, and behaviors that is concerned with the client's adaptation to his or her particular cultural milieu . . . [and] considers all facets of the client's personal history, family history, and social and cultural orientation." Sexual orientation and gender variation should be added to this definition.

Levine and Padilla (1980) suggested that a pluralistic counselor will be knowledgeable about majority and minority cultures, the points of impact between cultures, and the processes by which cultural elements influence individuals. Counselors can be effective only if their own attitudes toward homosexuality are positive and congruous with the current scientific knowledge about sexual orientation and transgender issues, that is, that these are variations of sexual expression (Coleman & Remafedi, 1989).

For example, Erikson (1968) developed a psychosocial/psychosexual stage of identity development. During the adolescent period, according to Erikson, adolescents must deal with the nuclear conflict between identity and identity confusion. Erikson identified further "part" conflicts related to this stage, which he defined as the conflict between sexual polarization and bisexual confusion. Erikson made a heterosexual assumption when he described this psychosocial/sexual stage. A queer-affirmative interpretation of this stage would view the resolution of the conflict as sexual identity versus sexual identity confusion, without creating a heterosexual bias and assumption that heterosexuality is the preferred mode of resolving the conflict or that bisexuality is a confused state. Erikson's theory, however, acknowledges different potentialities for sexual orientation. His mistake was in assuming that heterosexuality is the ultimate outcome in the resolution of this conflict.

CASE STUDY

Juan is an 18-year-old college freshman dealing with coming out to himself. Juan is a first-generation Hispanic male who immigrated with his parents when he was 11 years old. Juan was born with an undescended testicle, and when he was 8 years old, he received shots to assist the descent of the testicle. At the age of 6, he began to become aware of sexual feelings. Juan would play doctor with a female classmate of his at school. He also learned to masturbate by placing his penis between his legs and squeezing.

When Juan came to the United States, his parents became friends with other people from their country of origin. One of these friends was a body builder who had a picture of himself in a brief-bikini type bathing suit sitting on his nightstand in the bedroom. One day Juan had to go into the bedroom to get something for his family friend and saw the picture and became very aroused upon seeing the picture.

The next year, Juan entered the sixth grade. He had a male teacher who was an attractive, tall, black-haired, sensitive Italian man. Juan developed a secret crush on his sixth-grade teacher. Juan had all these feelings that confused him. He remembered that the school counselor had visited his class, inviting students to speak to him if they needed to talk about anything. Juan also remembered the admonition that his father had given him at the age of 7. His dad had commented in front of Juan that he hoped he would never have a gay son. Having a gay son in the Hispanic culture would mean shame on the family. Juan did not go see the school counselor and continued carrying the confusing feelings with him as he was growing up.

At age 15, Juan had a friend living nearby, Julio, from his same country and of the same age. This friend was more sexually sophisticated than Juan and had access to his father's heterosexual X-rated magazines. Julio invited Juan to view the X-rated magazines in Julio's bedroom. They both unzipped their pants and began masturbating themselves while looking at the photos. Juan and Julio did not view this as a homosexual experience, despite the fact that, after a while, the sexual play changed focus from looking at the photos of naked women to watching each other masturbate. Julio's sister came home shortly after Julio and Juan were finished masturbating. Juan felt a lot of guilt and shame, and when Julio invited him to do it on another occasion, Juan declined. Juan gave the excuse that his religious beliefs did not allow him to focus on sex, especially since he was an altar boy at this age.

Juan attended a college preparatory high school for boys. When Juan was in high school, two of his classmates in his homeroom who appeared quite effeminate befriended him. One day they made a surprise visit to Juan's house and Juan's mother greeted them. These friends did not know exactly where Juan lived so they had stopped at the neighbor's house to ask where Juan's house was. Juan's mother was embarrassed that the neighbor saw these effeminate boys looking for Juan and that somehow the family would be shamed by the association. Juan himself was not effeminate. When the classmates left, Juan's mother confronted Juan angrily about these friends and forbade Juan to see these friends again or to have them come to the house again.

Juan went through high school having secret crushes on male teachers and classmates. He felt lonely because he could not talk about his feelings with anyone. He thought about talking to a priest during confession, but he felt attracted to the priest to whom he would confess his "sins." Also, giving a voice to these feelings would mean that Juan would have to own these homosexual feelings, and he wasn't ready to do that. During his high school years, Juan would deny his gay feelings. He felt much pressure to like girls, so he would fantasize about them in the hopes that he would "straighten out."

Juan did not have much contact with girls during this period since he went to an all boys' school. He had to study a lot so he did not have much time for dating anyway. This was a good excuse for Juan to avoid the issue of dating during high school. He did go to the high school prom with the daughter of the family at whose house his two effeminate friends had stopped to ask for directions a couple of years back. Juan felt good that he was somehow covering up that incident by showing interest in their daughter.

Juan continued to feel lonely and isolated during high school. Note that these years are the years for an adolescent to resolve the developmental nuclear conflict of intimacy versus isolation (Erikson, 1968). Juan would cry himself to sleep on many occasions because of the pain he felt about hurting his parents and family if they found out about his gay feelings.

After graduating from high school, Juan went away to college. His decision to go away to school was an unconscious desire to create some psychological distance between him and his family so he could explore his identity without their intrusion. Juan did very well during his first semester in college; however, during his second semester, his grades began to slip. He became depressed and lost interest in extracurricular activities. He decided to go to the counseling center for help. During the counseling sessions, Juan talked about several issues. The counselor noticed that Juan avoided issues of dating and intimacy. The counselor suggested to Juan that Juan might want to talk about his social life for the next session.

When Juan came to his next session, instead of coming into the office through the front door, Juan decided to enter the office from the back door that day. The counselor opened the session by reminding Juan that they had agreed to discuss Juan's social life. Juan made attempts to talk about prior heterosexual dates. Juan sensed that his counselor knew that he was not being honest. Juan's defense mechanism of denial was no longer working for him. Juan told the counselor: "I know you know. Now somebody else knows." Juan's fear that the counselor would reject him overwhelmed him and he ran out the door. The counselor followed Juan and saw him go into the campus chapel. The counselor called Juan at home later to ensure he was going to be alright.

Juan wrote the counselor the following letter:

> Your words have not left my mind since you called. You're right—it is very painful for me (and always has been). But you're wrong. I'm not "O.K."; I am in essence a *freak!* (God, how I wish to be normal . . .why doesn't *He* help me?) I found out in your office the truth—it was then that someone else knew too!! I don't want it known!—ever!! Ever since, my life has collapsed. I'm gripped with the constant fear of my family finding out. (I'm sick.) *Never*, never have I entered a church for help; never have I felt so vacant, so cheap, so hollow, so VULGAR!; and help never came—well *screw you* GOD!
>
> My greatest wish (and has been) to love and be loved, and to love as nature *meant* it to be; all I feel is bitter, apathetic . . . nothing matters any more (school nor music nor myself).
>
> Thank you for caring.
>
> I hurt.
>
> I wish to be alone . . . forever.
>
> J.
>
> P.S. I need time to think.

Bracciale, Sanabria, and Updyke (2003) pointed out that it is important for counselors not to hurry their clients in examining and owning their sexual orientation. In Juan's case, Juan felt overwhelmed even at the thought of talking about his social life. Perhaps a better approach by the counselor would have been to ask Juan if he wanted to talk about it as opposed to reminding Juan that they had agreed to talk about it. Reminding Juan that they had made that agreement did not give him a choice as to whether to pursue the exploration, and it created a crisis for him that caused him to flee the anxiety-producing situation. Bracciale et al. emphasized the need for the client to set his or her own pace in figuring out his or her sexual orientation. Sometimes the counselor, in his or her eagerness to help the client get there, can push a little too soon.

APPROACHES TO INTERVENTION

Individual

The case of Juan illustrates the loneliness and isolation that many queer youths feel. According to Uribe and Harbeck (1992), members of minority groups receive support and acculturation by and from other family members and community resources regarding their status as a member of that minority group. However, the queer teenager is often alone and isolated while dealing with the awareness of his or her newly acquired minority status as queer. "While many minority groups are the target of prejudice (beliefs) and discrimination (actions) in our society, few persons face this hostility without the support and acceptance of their family as do many gay, lesbian, and bisexual youth" (Uribe & Harbeck, 1992, p. 13).

Because a support group did not exist in Juan's high school campus, Juan had to put his developmental growth on hold until he reached college, where there was a program that could assist him in his exploration. Juan had to put on hold the resolution of his part conflict of sexual identity versus sexual identity confusion, which, in turn, affected his ability to move to the next nuclear conflict of intimacy versus isolation. Heterosexual students, however, get to experiment with dating and sexual attraction and behavior in high school, building their psychosocial/sexual skills necessary to move to the next stage of development.

Family

Another approach to prevention for the benefit of queer youth is educating the parents. In general, parental reactions consist of two facets: (a) The parents apply their negative perceptions of homosexual identity to their child and reject the child as a stranger, and (b) the parents feel guilt and failure for fear that somehow they caused their child to become homosexual (Strommen, 1989).

For the parent, and members of society at large, a subjective perception is developed that the homosexual is a "member of another species, someone whose essential wants are unrecognizable and different" (Weinberg, 1972, p. 97). This subjective perception turns into prejudice. Sometimes, this prejudice can in turn create hatred, such as the hatred that allowed individuals to terrorize, torture, and take the life of Matthew Shepard and Gwen Araujo. Haldeman (2000, p. 198) asked, "Is the child's behavior unacceptable to the family's norms? If so, it may be important to work with the entire family, or at least, with the parents." Any approach to prevention with the queer community needs to involve the dissemination of state-of-the-art scientific information regarding this population.

School

Woodiel et al. (2003) stated that school districts have an obligation "backed by a legal liability" to change a school's culture and climate that ignores or promotes homophobia. The American Civil Liberties Union (ACLU, 2005) reported that the 1996 case of *Nabozny v. Podlesny* established the precedent that schools can be held liable for deliberately ignoring antigay harassment. The court awarded the plaintiff punitive damages of almost $1 million after his school in rural Wisconsin ignored harassment of Nabozny by a group of students who engaged in a mock rape of Nabozny. According to the ACLU, there have been 11 other cases awarding punitive damages ranging from $41,000 to $450,000. Most recently, in *Donovan and Ramelli v. Poway Unified School District* (2005), the San Diego County Superior Court awarded the plaintiffs $300,000 for repeated subjections to harassment, discrimination, and intimidation by students, staff, and faculty on the basis of actual or perceived sexual orientation (see California Bar Journal, 2006, p. 4).

Several programs have been designed to create safe environments for students in schools: Project 10 (Uribe & Harbeck, 1992); Coordinated School Health Program, or CSHP (Woodiel et al. 2003); Youth, Inc. (1997); and Gutierrez's (1987) campus ecology model for Catholic college campuses.

Uribe and Harbeck (1992) described the formation of Project 10, an in-school counseling program at Fairfax High School in Los Angeles, California, with two purposes: (a) to provide emotional support, information, resources, and referrals to queer youths or individuals who wanted accurate information on the subject of sexual orientation; and (b) to heighten the school community's acceptance and sensitivity to queer issues. This project, the first of its kind, has grown in impact to the national level as a forum for the expression of the needs of queer teenagers.

In forming Project 10, Uribe and Harbeck (1992) identified three steps that needed to be taken to create a receptive environment to the project:

1. Break through the wall of silence surrounding the topic of homosexuality to reach the target group.
2. Provide a safe and supportive atmosphere so youths could discuss their sexuality in a nonthreatening way.
3. Develop a nonjudgmental posture to serve as a guideline in dealing with queer youth.

Project 10 provided not only counseling support groups for queer students but also education and educational materials, school safety measures, faculty and staff training, human rights advocacy, dropout prevention strategies, and use of community resources.

The Coordinated School Health Program (CSHP) focused on eight different dimensions on health and education of students and adults in a school system: (a) healthy school environment, (b) health education, (c) physical education, (d) nutrition services, (e) health services, (f) health promotion for staff, (g) counseling and psychological services, and (h) family and community services (Woodiel et al., 2003).

Youth, Inc. (1997) created a resource guide for school staff with suggestions on creating safe schools for lesbian and gay students. The guide included 10 suggestions for reducing homophobia in the school environment, addressing name-calling in the classroom, starting a Gay/Straight Alliance in the schools, and creating safe zones for queer youths within the school itself.

At the college level, Gutierrez (1987) discussed the formation of a campus program at a Catholic college based on a campus ecology model. A campus ecology model shifts the focus away from the individual and toward the creation of an environment that facilitates the personal growth and development of queer students. To do so, the academic institution must examine its implicit and explicit attitudes, rules and regulations, and factors that affect queer youth on campus (Gutierrez, 1987). The focus is on the individual growth of the queer student, as well as the growth of heterosexual students, faculty, staff, administrators, and the community at large so that they can reach acceptance, not just tolerance, of sexual orientation and gender variational differences.

This college campus program, like Project 10, encouraged counselors, faculty, and staff to deal with their own internalized homophobia because of fear of being seen as homosexual or being discovered as a homosexual. Uribe and Harbeck (1992) pointed out that most minorities cannot hide their status as a member of that minority group. Queer individuals, however, can often hide their homosexuality, giving rise to a socialization process that requires learning to hide (Uribe & Harbeck, 1992). One cannot fight the fight while remaining in the closet.

Community

Approaches to prevention must target different levels of audiences. One must target the affected group (i.e., the queer youth), but one must also target the environment and community that impact on this group.

Addressing the needs of queer youth within the schools can be a very political process. For programs to be effective, school districts must work with the community to involve them in the process so that the school districts can obtain the backing of the community. Education must begin with the parents and community leaders to make them aware of the need for the intervention strategies within the school systems.

Other approaches to prevention involve participation in professional organizations that provide the leadership to mold the agenda of the profession to address the needs of queer youth (Dworkin & Gutierrez, 1992). Research funding to generate studies on issues affecting queer youths are essential, according to Dworkin and Gutierrez, who stated, "The best weapon to counteract the oppression by specific interest groups is research" (p. 337). Dworkin and Gutierrez also encouraged counselors to stand up and take action to inform lawmakers and government officials involved in setting public policy regarding the reality of the queer population to avoid decisions from being made on the basis of fears and erroneous stereotypes.

PREVENTION STRATEGIES

Rappaport (1977, as cited in Banning, 1980, p. 214) identified four intervention strategies from an ecological perspective: individual strategies, group strategies, associational strategies, and institutional strategies. Individual strategies include advising, counseling, or psychotherapy. Group strategies focus on particular groups, such as couples counseling and sensitivity groups. Associational strategies focus on the aspects of an organization that do not adapt to the needs of its members or whose structure impedes the developmental growth of members within the organization. The focus is on organizational dynamics or the operational system of the organization; these include consultation, organizational development, or social organization consultation. Institutional strategies include working to effect change in the attitudes of the organizational administration, faculty, and staff toward the students, as well as the organization's value orientation, policies, and other factors that contribute to a poor ecology for student growth and development (Gutierrez, 1987).

Individual

Individual strategies, according to Gutierrez (1987), focus on the coming-out process of queer youth. Recognition of same-sex sexual attraction often occurs around age 10 (McClintock & Herdt,1996). For Juan, his awareness to same-sex sexual attraction came even earlier, at age 6. Self-labeling as queer typically occurs at about age 15 (Hershberger & D'Augelli, 1995). This self-labeling can be quite traumatic to individuals. Once a person self-labels as queer, he or she is at the point of no return; the person owns the label and cannot take it back. This awareness can be very frightening to an individual and is the cause of many suicide attempts by queer youths. It is estimated that approximately 30% of suicides among young adults are related to sexual orientation issues (National Center for Health Statistics, 1986).

For Juan, his admission to the counselor that he felt same-sex sexual attraction was the point of no return. Sharing this information with others is even more frightening than admitting it to oneself, because to admit it to oneself can be changed by defense mechanisms such as intellectualization, rationalization, denial, and reaction formation, but admitting to another is harder to deny or take back. Many times, the client will beat around the bush with the counselor. The client will say things like "I'm really afraid to say this to you," "I don't know how you will take it," or " I think you will be shocked." A response to these statements can be: "Did you kill somebody?" This response often works to alleviate the anxiety the client feels because the client knows that what he or she is about to reveal is not as serious as murder-ing somebody and it reduces his or her anxiety level to a more manageable level.

Troiden (1989) described the coming-out process as consisting of four stages:

1. *Sensitization*, in which the youth develops an awareness of being different from others;
2. *Identity confusion*, in which the youth begins to recognize behaviors and feel-ings that could be labeled queer;
3. *Identity assumption*, in which the youth begins to own this queer identity; and
4. *Commitment*, in which queer becomes a way of being as opposed to a way of behaving.

Juan felt this identity confusion. He needed support in sorting out his feelings and seeing how the queer label fit him. For a client to go through these stages, he or she needs an affirming counselor who can reframe all the negative messages that the client has received about queer orientations. Once these messages have been neutralized and the client receives positive messages, the client can learn to accept who he or she is. For queer youths, it is not a matter of "choosing the lifestyle" but of accepting who they are without societal value judgments about who they are. When they met again, Juan's counselor talked to Juan about his letter. The counselor pointed out to Juan that, perhaps, God put the counselor in Juan's path, thereby gently challenging Juan's perception of abandonment by God. The counselor assured Juan that he did not perceive Juan as a freak. The counselor pointed out to Juan that his yearning to love and be loved as nature meant it to be can be different for different people. In Juan's case, nature meant him to love and be loved by another man.

For Juan, this acceptance by the counselor was a reenactment of the nuclear conflict of trust versus mistrust (Erikson, 1968). During this nuclear conflict, the child learns to trust himself and his world and his sense of self in relationship to his parents and significant others. To incorporate this new information into his self-identity, Juan needed to revisit this nuclear conflict and resolve it so that he could learn to trust himself and his world again as a queer person.

After coming out to oneself, the next step in the coming-out process is to share this new discovery with a significant other. D'Augelli, Hershberger, and Pilkington (1998) conducted a study with queer youths and found that three quarters of these youths chose a close friend to share this first disclosure. Only 9% chose a parent as the first person to whom to disclose this new identity, and all of these were to their mothers.

Once clients accept their own same-sex attraction, they are now ready to face other people like themselves. Juan asked to meet other students on campus who were going through the same process. Because there was no queer student organ-ization on campus, the counselor arranged to introduce him to another student on campus, Paul. It was safe for Juan to meet with just another student rather than to join a group. Dealing with individual differences of another student is not as over-whelming. It does not involve the peer pressure of being like the other members of the group. This way Juan could compare his situation with that of the other student and could evaluate similarities and differences without the pressure of having to be "politically correct" in his identity.

This stage for Juan was similar to Erikson's (1968) nuclear conflict of autonomy versus shame and doubt. In this stage, children learn that they are separate from their parents and begin to explore their world and assert their own individuality. Juan and Paul could further evaluate the norms and values of the queer world without having to commit to it and accept everything about this world. As in any other culture, there are variations within the queer culture (Gutierrez, 1994), and Juan and Paul needed to figure out where they fit in relationship to these variations. As Juan and Paul developed their queer identity, eventually they were ready to join a support group of other students who were dealing with their issues.

The Logo cable television channel offers a program called "Coming Out Stories" that features queer people coming out to their families and professionally. Cable shows such as this provide a safe and private haven for individuals or family members to observe how other queer people and families cope with the coming out process.

Family

Individual strategies can also assist the parents of these youths. On learning of their son's or daughter's queer status, parents often go through similar feelings of shock and isolation (Boxer, Cook, & Herdt, 1995). They go through stages of loss similar to those of someone who experiences a death in the family: denial, anger, bargaining, depression, and acceptance (Kubler-Ross, 1969). Parents may feel that their son or daughter is just "going through a phase." They may be angry at whomever "exposed" their son or daughter to this lifestyle. They may become angry at themselves and blame themselves for "causing" their son's or daughter's "queerness." They may even become angry at God, like Juan did in his letter to the counselor.

Queer youths and their parents may go through the bargaining stage, where they bargain with God that if God changes the youth back to "normal" they promise to do x, y, or z. When they see that bargaining is not working for them, they become depressed. Eventually, as they receive more information about the situation, they gradually learn to accept what is going on within themselves or their children and are able to accept themselves as parents of a queer son or daughter, and their children as queer.

Robinson, Walters, and Skeen (1989) identified three factors that contribute to a sense of grief of the parents on finding out that their child is queer: (a) an assumption that the child is part of the accepted heterosexual majority and the loss of the "dreams" of a traditional marriage for the child and the child's continuing the family lineage by generating grandchildren, (b) the realization that the child is part of a minority group, and (c) the fact that the minority group to which their child belongs has a long history of persecution.

D'Augelli et al. (1998) found that 51% of mothers were accepting of their children's revelations of their queer status, 30% were tolerant, 9% were intolerant, and 10% were rejecting. D'Augelli et al. also found that 27% of fathers were accepting of their children's revelations of queer status, 32% were tolerant, 16% were intolerant, and 29% were rejecting. This same study found that 57% of siblings were accepting of their siblings' revelations of queer status, 19% were tolerant, 9% were intolerant, and 15% were rejecting.

Although the above figures are encouraging for most queer youths, too many other youths who disclose their queer status to family members risk doing so. D'Augelli et al. (1998) found that mothers verbally abused 38% of daughters and 24% of sons after they revealed their status; 10% of mothers of lesbian daughters and 3% of mothers of gay sons physically attacked their children when they revealed their status. In contrast, 19% of fathers abused their revealing daughters and sons; 10% of fathers physically threatened their revealing daughters while 2% of fathers physically threatened their revealing sons; and 5% of fathers actually physically attacked their revealing daughters while 2% of fathers actually attacked their revealing sons. These figures suggest that lesbian youths are more likely to be rejected by both parents and to be victimized by them.

D'Augelli et al. (1998) found that, among revealing lesbians, 19% of brothers and 10% of sisters verbally abused them, 5% of brothers and 14% of sisters physically threatened them, and 0% of brothers and 7% of sisters physically attacked their lesbian sisters. Among revealing gay youths, 22% of brothers and 13% of sisters verbally abused their gay brother; 14% of brothers and 0% of sisters physically threatened them; and 7% of brothers and 2% of sisters physically attacked the gay youths after the revelation of their queer status. These figures indicate that lesbian and gay youths receive rejection and are victimized by same-sex siblings more than by opposite-sex siblings.

The grief process for heterosexual parents and family members appears to take 2 years to work through and fully accept the child's sexual orientation (Borhek, 1983), which seems to be the same amount of time associated with the resolution of grief of a divorce or death of a loved one (Robinson et al., 1989).

While in the majority of the cases the families of queer youths were either accepting or tolerant, the incidents of abuse, even if verbal, were sufficiently high as to make the queer youths question the risk of revealing their queer status to their families. In Juan's case, the counselor suggested to Juan that he might want to first test the family's reactions to homosexuality in general. Juan might want to have a discussion with his family about Rosie O'Donnell's or Lance Bass of N'Sync's coming out, for example, to see how receptive or supportive his parents are to learning that someone with whom they are familiar is queer.

Because Juan is away at college and does not get home very often, the counselor recommended to Juan to wait until the summer break before bringing the subject up with his family. Holidays, which tend to be emotionally charged times of the year when all kinds of issues for families arise, may not be the best time to bring up the subject. Waiting until the summer also gave Juan enough time to continue exploring his sexual orientation in a group and to learn from other members of the group who had already come out to their parents how they approached it, what worked for them, and what did not.

Another intervention for Juan's parents included the referral of Juan's parents to their local priest. The counselor identified a priest in Juan's family's Catholic parish who was supportive of sexual orientation issues. He then referred Juan's parents to speak to this priest so the priest could provide pastoral guidance around sexual orientation issues. Many religions support pastoral programs that affirm a person's sexual orientation (Gutierrez, 1987).

School

Group Strategies

Group strategies can consist of counselor-led support groups for queer youths or for their parents. Groups can also be self-help, such as those led by Parents and Friends of Lesbians and Gays (PFLAG). Given the above statistics of family responses to queer youths' disclosures of their queer status, it is imperative that schools, queer youth community centers, and community mental health centers establish programs for family members to explore their reactions to their queer family members' revelations and to educate these family members about the biological as well as psychosocial aspects of their queer status. Youth, Inc. (1997) suggested guidelines for the formation of a Gay/Straight Alliance on campus.

Counselors need to be aware of the culture of the group with whom they are working. In Juan's case, the counselor must be aware of not only the gay culture but also the Hispanic culture (the ethnic issues are addressed below, in the Adaptation for Diversity section). Juan's counselor could refer Juan to the local lesbian/gay community center and to social groups in which Juan could meet others like himself, such as the local gay/lesbian chorus, bicycle club, runner's group, and so on. In San Jose, California, for example, there is a group called Pro Latino, for gay Hispanics. A good resource for obtaining information regarding queer Hispanics is a national organization called *llegó*, which stands for the Latino Lesbian and Gay Organization (the word *llegó* translated from Spanish means "s/he arrived").

Meeting other queer youths in these contexts can give youths a different picture of who they are as queer youth and what life can be like for them. This process is similar to Erikson's (1968) nuclear conflict of identity versus identity confusion. Of course, certain oppressive elements of society would like queer youths to think that their lives are doomed if they continue to live this lifestyle. Other school group strategies can include lesson plans in the school's health education class on topics such as bullying, violence prevention, anger management, name-calling, and so on (Woodiel et al. 2003; Youth, Inc., 1997).

With individual and group counseling support, Juan was able to understand the biological basis for his feelings. His parents were able to stop blaming Juan for being who he is and also stopped blaming themselves for causing Juan's queerness. They learned that they had no control over Juan's status and were able to stop feeling guilty about themselves as parents. For many queer youths, however, there is a sense of a foreshortened future. Feeling that their lives are doomed, they turn to the immediate pleasures of life because they do not know what tomorrow will bring. The perspective for adolescents is very short term. Because adolescents are forced to go underground for their social network, they have very few positive role models and adult supervision. This situation creates an environment in which substance abuse and high-risk behaviors can flourish. Because the adolescents do not see a future for themselves, why sacrifice and delay gratification?

Paul was able to develop his queer identity; however, unlike Juan, he chose a different path. He did not have the same support from his family that Juan was able to receive from his family. Paul was a strikingly handsome Scandinavian-looking blond young man. He became unsure of his identity, so he sought validation from other gay men by becoming promiscuous. Paul's parents were extremely religious and rejected him after he came out to them. They went as far as throwing him out of the house and cutting off his tuition assistance. Erikson (1968) stated that the counterpart of distancing is distantiation, or the readiness to repudiate those forces or people whose essence seems dangerous to one's own. Paul's reaction to his parents' religiosity and rejection of him was to reject those forces whose essence was dangerous to his own, his gayness. Erikson warned that youths who are not sure of their identity shy away from interpersonal intimacy and throw themselves into acts that are promiscuous or with self-abandon. These youths develop what Erikson called the negative identity. While parents of queer youths are not responsible for their child's queer status, they do influence the child's ability to develop a healthy sense of identity.

Paul would go to the local gay bar, and because he was not yet of age to enter the bar, he would hang out in the bar's parking lot, offering free oral sex indiscriminately to patrons entering the bar. Paul felt validated for being popular with the bar patrons. Even though he was in college, Paul had no sense of a positive future for himself, so he behaved in a manner that exposed him to sexually transmitted diseases. Paul chose to become a porn movie actor in same-sex pornographic movies. Because of his high-risk behaviors, Paul contracted AIDS and died from it. Because queer youths are vulnerable to substance abuse and high-risk sexual behaviors as a coping mechanism for stressors as a result of their queer status, it is imperative that these youths receive information and support regarding these issues to prevent deaths such as Paul's from happening.

Associational Strategies

As mentioned earlier, associational strategies focus on the aspects of an organization that do not adapt to the needs of its members or whose structure impedes the developmental growth of members within the organization. The focus is on organizational dynamics or the operational system of the organization. These strategies include consultation, organizational development, or social organization consultation around the organization's maladaptive environment.

Hershberger and D'Augelli (1995) cited a study by Gross, Aurand, and Adessa (1988) that showed that in a sample of gay men, 50% of them reported victimization in junior high school and 59% reported victimization in high school; lesbians in the sample reported that 12% of them were victimized in junior high school and 21% in high school. Savin-Williams (1994) cited studies by Remafedi (1987) that show that over two thirds of gay and bisexual youths have school-related problems; nearly 40% were truant, and 28% dropped out of school. These statistics indicate that schools are not safe places for queer youth. Vowels (2005) reported on a survey conducted by the Gay, Lesbian, Straight Education Network in 2003 that indicated that 84% of queer students reported being verbally harassed because of their sexual orientation and, shockingly, 82.9% of students reported that faculty rarely or never intervened when they observed the incidents.

Schindel (2005) stated that

> creating a climate of safety for [queer] youth entails both an exposure of the violence and harassment that many [queer] youth face in their schools, and also promoting a sense of safety that is less concerned with violence and more attuned to creating spaces that represent, validate, and support queer youth. (p. v)

Schindel noted that creating a safe environment "entails a tension between, and balance of, protection *from* violence and oppression and generation *of* a visible, self-reliant, and active queer youth community" (p. 4).

Only eight states have passed school laws forbidding discrimination based on sexual orientation: California, Connecticut, Massachusetts, Minnesota, New Jersey, Vermont, Wisconsin, and Washington. Of these, only three include protections based also on gender identity (Mollison, 2004). Seven states prohibit the positive portrayal of homosexuality in schools: Alabama, Arizona, Mississippi, Oklahoma, South Carolina, Texas, and Utah (Mollison, 2004).

To counteract maladaptive elements that interfere with the safety of queer youth in the schools, Uribe and Harbeck (1992) discussed various associational strategies that they implemented at the beginning of Project 10 at Fairfax High School, such as developing an informational brochure that was distributed throughout the community regarding the project and training a core group of teachers, administrators, and counselors. Uribe and Harbeck's feedback to the high school was that, as an organization, the high school was not meeting the needs of gay and lesbian students. The structure of the services in place did not address the needs of these students because the faculty and staff did not have the proper knowledge and training to address these issues.

There was a lack of awareness that this was even a problem in the organization. The brochure that was designed and circulated provided a context for the program and educated the high school, the Board of Education, and the community at large as to the problem and the need for the Project 10 program. A training program for staff and faculty bridged the gap of services that were being provided to heterosexual students by training the faculty and staff on the issues facing queer youth and providing these faculty and staff with the skills they required to address not only the needs of the queer youth but also the heterosexual students' needs in adjusting to the reality of sharing a campus with queer youth. The initial reaction to the program was very positive, according to Uribe and Harbeck. Only 10 negative phone calls were recorded initially.

The CHSP program (Woodiel et al., 2003) recommended staff development workshops to address queer issues, including legal obligations and responsibilities, education of correct terminology, and exploration of faculty and staff values and beliefs and how they contribute to the maladaptive environment of the high school.

Gutierrez (1987) implemented several associational strategies at the college level. He began the consultation by meeting with his director to obtain approval of the outreach to queer youth on campus. Prior to this point, the counseling center had not made any affirmative efforts to communicate to queer youth that they were welcome in the counseling center and that the staff of the counseling center was knowledgeable, able, and willing to serve the specific needs of queer youth on campus.

Gutierrez expanded his consultation to the campus ministry office, and both the counseling center and campus ministry offices began to explicitly list sexual orientation issues among the issues addressed by the centers, thereby giving sexual orientation visibility as an issue to be addressed on campus. This was done in a queer-affirmative way to prevent the wrong impression that these offices were there to "cure" students of their queerness.

The counselor then created a collaboration among the counseling center, the campus ministry office, and the women's center to expand the consultation base of the university. These offices cosponsored the showing of the movie *Word Is Out* (Epstein, 1978) on campus, followed by a discussion afterward. Eighty students attended this showing. The average attendance for workshops sponsored by the counseling center had usually been 5–8 students. This response was indicative of the yearning for these services by students on campus, queer and heterosexual alike, who were searching for information and support around these issues. This event was followed by the showing of the documentary film *Pink Triangles* (Blumenfeld et al., 1982) at a later date. The counselor expanded the consultation by enlisting the assistance of a professor from the master's program in marriage and family counseling to facilitate the discussion, with the intent of involving the academic program as a support for the institutional change that the counselor was about to embark on.

A training workshop was also conducted for resident assistants and hall directors on how to conduct conflict resolution when problems arose in the residence halls regarding sexual orientation. Issues addressed in these trainings could include how to counsel a resident who finds out that his or her roommate is queer; how to counsel a queer resident who is feeling attracted to his or her roommate who does not reciprocate the feelings; how to diffuse animosity on the floor regarding the presence of a queer student in the residential community; how to conduct educational programming for residents around queer issues; and how to lead discussions of safe sex that include queer issues.

The university, a Catholic school, received only two negative phone calls from parents who had found out about the university's new approach. These phone calls were fielded to the counselor, who was able to educate the parents regarding the importance of a university education in creating awareness about diversity in our society, which includes queer individuals. The parents were satisfied with the counselor's response, and there were no further complaints.

Woodiel et al. (2003) and Youth, Inc. (1997) also encouraged the formation of gay/straight alliances. Youth, Inc. described 10 easy steps on how to go about it.

Institutional Strategies

Any change in an institution must have the involvement of the policy and decision makers within the institution if effective change is to take place. A study at Oberlin College by Norris (1992) regarding the institutional culture of the college revealed that, although the college has a progressive tradition and was one of the first institutions of higher learning to adopt a nondiscrimination clause based on sexual orientation in 1973, the implementation of the clause has been lacking. Norris suggested that the paradox results from two competing sets of values, one focused on equal rights and the other on heterosexual orthodoxy. Norris concluded that the inability of the institution to have a legitimate discussion of sexuality and the concerns of queers on its campus prevents an open airing of issues and concerns.

Gutierrez (1987) described how the president of Santa Clara University, a Catholic Jesuit institution in California, obtained the backing of the Board of Trustees before the issue of sexual orientation was addressed on the campus. The president legitimized the discussion of the issue of sexual orientation by making the issue part of a universitywide Institute On the Family, which was open to the public.

For Project 10, Uribe and Harbeck (1992) obtained the backing of the school board members, administrators, teachers, and the students, both queer and heterosexual, as well as members of the community. For example, the City of West Hollywood became involved in providing the funding for library materials, a hotline, incidental costs of publicity, awards, and scholarships sponsored by Project 10. Having such a united front prevents scapegoating of the staff attempting to implement the program and creates a shared pride in the success of the program. It also insulates the institution from attacks from opposing groups, because opposing groups can see how much support from the community there is for the program.

The institution must also ground its rationale and actions in research and scholarly works. At Santa Clara University, for example, the success of the program was the result of solid grounding in theological and pastoral context that was congruous with and not adverse to the religious values of the institution. When mainstream institutions fail to meet the needs of queer youth, institutions must be formed to meet these needs. Such was the case of the Harvey Milk School in New York City. Most of the students attending this school had dropped out of other New York City public schools primarily because of peer harassment (Martin & Hetrick, 1988). However, this type of institutional strategy should be utilized sparingly, lest we create a world of separate but equal institutions.

The separate but equal method was tried with African Americans in the 1950s, and the U.S. Supreme Court in *Brown v. Board of Education* (1954) held that this type of arrangement was unconstitutional. Another precedent that discourages the separation of individuals who are different from the mainstream is seen in the Individuals With Disabilities Education Improvement Act (2004). This act prohibits the separation of students with disabilities and requires school districts to mainstream these students and provide a least restrictive environment and a free and appropriate education. So too, queer youths are entitled to a free and appropriate public education free of harassment and free of a hostile environment because of their unique characteristics.

Other institutional strategies identified by the CHSP (Woodiel et al., 2003) included the following: establishing classroom guidelines to stop name-calling and developing respect for different points of view; including positive visuals and images in the classroom; including queer books and resources in class and in the school library; recognizing all family structures when discussing family constellations; providing lists of community resources for students, staff, and faculty; facilitating an online discussion or question/answer session; and training peer counselors for sensitivity to queer youth issues. Youth, Inc. (1997) included guidelines for a workshop on preventing name-calling in the classroom.

Some other institutional strategies in high schools include the discussion of the contribution of queers in all subject areas, from kindergarten to Grade 12, and the consideration of alternative restrooms and locker room accommodations for transgender youth (Haynes, 2001). Also, the creation of safe zones on campus has been suggested (Youth, Inc., 1997). A safe zone is created by using stickers that have a rainbow flag or pink and black triangles with the words "Safe Zone" to identify to students supportive adults in the school system who they can approach to discuss their sexuality and sense of safety in the school.

A great movie to show at the high school level to encourage family dialogue is the movie *Get Real* (Shore, 1998), about two young teenage boys coming to terms with their sexual orientation. One student is the high school jock and the other a writer for the school newspaper. The movie addresses bullying issues, coming out, family acceptance, and how the school deals with an article published by the writer anonymously in a school magazine.

On a national scale, the National Association of School Psychologists incorporated principles applied to the needs of sexual minority youth into their Code of Ethical Principles, under the categories of Professional Relationships and Responsibilities, Professional Competency, and Professional Practices (Bahr, Brish, & Croteau, 2000), requiring sensitivity to individual differences, affirmation of diversity based on sexual orientation, and prohibition of discriminatory practices based on sexual orientation. They also require competence in knowledge regarding sexual orientation issues, monitoring of personal values and beliefs so as not to interfere with the professional responsibility to provide effective services to sexual minority youth and their families, and keeping current on professional practices based on sexual minority needs. Practitioners must also advocate for sexual minority student rights and welfare and ensure that assessment and treatment procedures selected for sexual minority youth respect their dignity and address their individual differences.

ADAPTATIONS FOR DIVERSITY

Individual Strategies

In working with ethnic minority queer youths, the counselor must be aware that these students are not only dealing with their queer identity but also their ethnic identity as well as their personal identity. These identities must be integrated. Therefore, the counselor must become aware of not only the theories of queer identity (Cass, 1979; Troiden, 1989) but also models of minority identity development (Atkinson, Morten, & Sue, 1979; Gutierrez, 1985; Loiacano, 1989; Parham, 1989).

Chan (1992) identified several factors to look at in the family background of ethnic minority individuals. These include the following: (a) Is the client an immigrant or American born? (b) What is the client's ethnic group? (c) What are the specific values of the ethnic group, the client's family, and the client's? (d) How closely does the client follow traditional ethnic customs? (e) What is the client's socioeconomic status? and (f) What is the client's level of bilingualism?

Latinos and Latinas represent a variety of nations and races and cultures, therefore, they belong to no one group (Morales, 1992). Generally, however, Latinos/ Latinas hold the cultural values of *familismo, machismo, simpatía, personalismo,* and *respeto*, according to Morales. These values need to be explored as to how they are affected by the superimposed queer context. Ethnic minority groups such as African Americans experience the same racism in the queer culture that they experience in mainstream heterosexual White society, so they are forced to go back to their African American community for support, yet here, they encounter the homophobia that also exists in the White heterosexual mainstream society (Gutierrez & Dworkin, 1992).

Juan was very transculturated; he is bilingual and bicultural. Juan's ethnic identity was really not an issue for him, but his sexual identity was. Juan held all the internalized homophobic perceptions of seeing himself as a freak and that in order to love as nature meant it to be, he had to love heterosexually. These homophobic values are further magnified in his Hispanic culture, in which machismo and Catholicism are so strong. Juan needs to explore how machismo, familismo, respeto, and Catholicism fit into his life as a gay individual.

Juan needs the validation of other Hispanic gays. In many major cities there are gay and lesbian Hispanic organizations that provide emotional and social support within a cultural context. These queer ethnic minority organizations are crucial in preventing the split identified by Gutierrez and Dworkin (1992) between the racist queer community and the homophobic ethnic minority community. Counselors need to become familiar with these organizations to be able to provide the information to their clients.

With the newly formed Logo television channel, there are television programs that can be very educational to ethnic minority youth. For example, the program *The Two Cubas* tells the story of two young gay Cuban men as their friendship unfolds. Another program called *Noah's Ark* follows the lives of African American friends living their gay lives.

Family Strategies

Juan's parents are predominantly Spanish speaking, so they needed referrals to support services that are bilingual and bicultural. For example, earlier, I mentioned that Juan's parents could be referred to a priest who is gay affirming. It would be important for the counselor to prescreen a referral for the family to ensure that the priest who ministers to the Hispanic community is affirming of sexual minorities. Juan could be helpful to the counselor in identifying this priest.

Another resource for families can be the Metropolitan Community Churches. These churches exist in most major cities in the United States and around the world. The services in these churches are quite similar to a Catholic Mass, except that women are allowed to participate at the altar table as celebrants. At these churches, queer people often bring family members so that the family can experience the love shared for queer people by these churches.

Many communities now have PFLAG chapters offering assistance and support in Spanish. Otherwise, PFLAG can assist the counselor in finding an appropriate support network for the family, depending on the family's ethnic or racial background. A support group such as PFLAG can be invaluable in providing families with guidance and role modeling from other parents and family members of the family's ethnic/racial background. It is important to send out the message to all racial/ethnic groups that queer youth exist in all cultures and races.

As family members grow in their acceptance of their children and the issues that their children's sexual orientation raised for the family, eventually they could be encouraged to take a leadership role in PFLAG or in the school system or community to advocate for the needs of queer youths and their families, especially those families who are members of the same ethnic/racial background.

School Strategies

Unless schools hold the value of diversity to begin with, it will be difficult for institutional strategies to be implemented. This is why the involvement of individuals identified under the Community Strategies subsection below is crucial. When school organizers have the group backing of key individuals in the various organizations that make up the community, the task becomes simpler. The more groups the program organizers have behind them, the easier it will be to convince the less supportive members of the community to participate in the project. These leaders can then approach the decision makers of the school to bring them on board to back the programs and to give their blessings to strategies to change the institutional attitudes and values.

Ethnic communities have become accustomed to the White majority making the decisions and excluding ethnic group voices. In fact, in her doctoral dissertation, Reck (2005) pointed out that, even in the Castro district of San Francisco, queer youth may not feel welcomed. She identified issues of classism and racism that demand that queer people assimilate to a homonormative White, middle-class, gay identity in order "to become cultural and political 'Castro citizens'" (p. 6). Therefore, ethnic minorities have become accustomed to the exclusion, and they stay away from the decision-making process. Ethnic minority leaders must be identified and empowered to initiate the dialogue with their communities. Some school strategies that have been identified by CHSP (Woodiel et al., 2003) include creating and posting antislur policies and evaluating school forms to ensure inclusivity of and sensitivity to diverse families.

Community Strategies

Uribe and Harbeck (1992) pointed out that the implementation of Project 10 was not successful in predominantly African American and Hispanic schools, suggesting that particular strategies need to be developed to address these populations. What is essential in working with specific groups is that the program designer involve the members of the population one is attempting to reach in the planning of the program. To make Project 10 work in the African American and Hispanic communities, for example, the program organizers need to meet with the leaders of each community individually.

The organizers can involve queer leaders of the ethnic minority community as bridges to the leaders of the ethnic minority heterosexual communities. In one recent example, a gay Hispanic leader was invited by the campaign committee of a gay White political candidate who was courting the support of Hispanic politicians. The gay Hispanic leader was not asked by the campaign committee to contact the Hispanic politicians, many whom he knew. When the gay Hispanic leader got to the home where the meeting was to be held, he was told that the meeting had been canceled because of lack of response by the Hispanic politicians. The organizers had not called him to let him know the meeting had been canceled. The mistake by the White gay/lesbian campaign committee was not to utilize the gay Hispanic leader as a bridge between the two communities. This occurred because of the lack of diversity awareness from the political organizers and the White gay/lesbian leaders on how to approach ethnic minority communities. It is important that the organizers identify the following leaders from the various groups: the leaders in the ethnic minority churches (both lay and clergy), the leaders of the ethnic minority PTA groups, the political leaders, the ethnic minority members of the school board, the ethnic minority student leaders from the heterosexual community, the queer student leaders, and the queer ethnic minority student leaders.

Additionally, because machismo tends to be more highly held in the ethnic minority communities, perhaps involvement of athletes who can be seen as leaders and role models can legitimize the discussion of queerness within ethnic minority schools. For example, Kanye West, an African American straight rapper, recently spoke out against antigay lyrics in the hip hop world because he had gay friends and he realized the damage that the hip hop world is doing to sexual minorities by institutionalizing oppression through their music industry (Associated Press, 2005). Once these group leaders have been identified, they must be trained and sensitized to the issues of queer youth, so that, in turn, they can join the struggle of institutionalizing sexual minority affirmative programs.

A while back, I was invited by *The Cristina Show*, the Hispanic equivalent of *The Oprah Winfrey Show*, to be the professional guest on a show about gay, lesbian, and transgender youth coming out to their parents. This show is seen by millions of Spanish-speaking television viewers around the world. It was my opportunity to educate millions of Hispanic viewers about sexual orientation. The studio audience was filled with teenagers from various schools who had been bused to be in the audience. When we left the television studio, the audience was waiting for us outside. We were not pelted with stones or insults. Instead, we were treated as one would treat a movie star leaving the entertainment venue. We knew we had done our job of educating these students.

Another powerful community strategy occurred at the Miss America Pageant for 2002. Teresa Benitez, Miss Nevada, offered a declamation as her talent portion of the competition. Her declamation was from the words of Matthew Shepard's mother, spoken during the sentencing phase in the trial of Matthew's assailants. It was a significant contribution toward the education of millions of television viewers about people who are "different," which was the context of Miss Nevada's declamation. The Miss America Pageant is a conservative organization, and there were many messages and references to Christianity and "my Savior Jesus Christ" among the contestants. Miss Nevada's message rang loud and clear within these messages. Ms. Benitez came in as third runner-up in the Miss America competition. She intends to become a U.S. senator someday. As a Hispanic gay person, I was moved by her courage. This is the type of community education that needs to happen.

SUMMARY

According to Uribe and Harbeck (1992),

> Cultural taboos, fear of controversy, and deeply rooted, pervasive homophobia have kept the educational system in the United States blind-folded and mute on the subject of childhood and adolescent homosexuality. The paucity of literature and understanding in this area is a national disgrace. Young men and women struggling with their sexual orientation during a time of intense physical, social, and developmental change are failed by physicians, educators, mental health professionals, and clergy who breach their ethical and professional obligations by being uninformed and unresponsive to the special problems and need of these youth. (p. 11)

In this chapter, I have defined the problem as the public's lack of scientific knowledge regarding sexual differentiation and the heterosexual assumptions that do not embrace the pluralistic society that forms the fiber of American culture. I have explored the many stressors that queer youth face, such as invisibility, isolation, victimization, suicide potential, substance abuse, and exposure to sexually transmitted diseases because of high-risk behaviors. These unique stressors call for affirmative counseling interventions by culturally sensitive and queer-affirming counselors.

The point was made that while queer youth need to address these stressors, counselors need to shift the focus of treatment to the true client, the community at large, to transform the cultural context in which queer youth live. To create this transformation, an ecological approach needs to be undertaken that would include individual, group, associational, and institutional strategies to effect the social changes.

We experienced slices of the lives of Juan and Paul with differing outcomes. Both had an affirming counselor who was able to move these individuals toward acceptance of their sexual identity. However, queer youths do not live in a vacuum. They need the love and support of significant others, especially family. Ironically, Paul's family was the more "religious" of the two families. However, being religious does not necessarily translate to the values that many religions profess—to love one's neighbor as one loves oneself. The case of Juan shows how a loving family can go a long way toward a person's self-acceptance and successful resolution of an identity crisis. The case of Paul was tragic and could have been averted by the loving guidance of parents who could accept their son as nature made him.

In the last edition of *Youth At Risk*, I asked the question: How many more Matthew Shepards must die before society replaces hatred toward queers with understanding and acceptance? Sadly, I am adding Gwen Araujo's name to the title of this chapter as evidence that the struggle continues, despite the advances that we have made since the last edition of this chapter.

Chandler Burr (1995), a science journalist, conducted an interview for an article in *The Advocate*, a magazine that focuses on sexual orientation issues, with two noted human geneticists, Dr. Richard Pillard and Dr. Michael Bailey, and the noted neuroanatomist, Dr. Laura Allen. These individuals have done extensive research on the biological differentiations of sexual orientation. Dr. Pillard and Dr. Bailey conducted studies on gay and lesbian twins, and Dr. Allen conducted studies on differences between the brains of gay and heterosexual men.

When asked to comment about the importance of research on sexual orientation differentiation, Dr. Pillard suggested that the discovery of the gay gene could link neuroanatomical findings resulting in the explanation of the wiring of the brain (see Burr, 1995, p. 38). Dr. Allen suggested that further discoveries in the biological formation of sexual orientation could provide us with the mechanism of evolution. Dr. Bailey believed that the most important reason for answering the inquiry as to what forms sexual orientation is to address the political hate-mongers who profess that gays and lesbians recruit others to homosexuality (see Burr, 1995). Finally, Freud (1905/1962) suggested that the importance of the study of variation in sexual orientation can facilitate our understanding of heterosexual development.

In 1972, the year before the American Psychiatric Association and American Psychological Association removed homosexuality as an illness from the *Diagnostic and Statistical Manual of Mental Disorders*, Dr. Pillard was the psychiatrist who was instrumental in assisting me in leaving the Air Force. In the fall of my senior year in college, I began to own my sexual orientation more and more and was very anxious about having to accept a commission as an Air Force officer and attempt to survive 4 years in the Air Force in the closet. I was not asked, but I told the Air Force that I was gay.

At my request, Dr. Pillard, then a psychiatry professor at Boston University, wrote a psychiatric report to the Air Force documenting my anxiety about serving in the military because of my evolving sexual orientation. Because I had not acted on my sexual orientation at that time, the Surgeon General of the Air Force could not give me a "diagnosis" of homosexuality, since the diagnosis of homosexuality required an acting out of the homosexual behavior, so he ruled me fit for duty. I was honorably discharged anyway for "the good of the Air Force" despite the fact that I had been "Outstanding Commander" twice during corps training competitions and had ranked in the top 10%–15% of my Air Force class academically and in the top 10% in corps training performance. In fact, I was in line to receive the Outstanding Cadet Award, the highest honor given to a cadet at each university.

According to Byne (2005), "Perhaps the answers to the most salient questions in this debate reside not in the biology of human brains, but within the cultures those brains have created" (p. 248). Baumrind (1995) stated, "Society's acceptance should be forthcoming not on the basis of renunciation of choice, but rather on the basis of respect for people's right to behave as they choose in their private lives, for their social contributions nonheterosexual people have made, and on appreciation of diversity in culture and lifestyle" (p. 135).

The half-and-half crab that is both blue and red is not concerned with morality, nor is it concerned as to whether the blue and red represent the color of the voting leanings of the states in the last presidential election. The crab simply is both male and female. It behaves according to its nature, as it was created to be, in its natural state, as its genes and hormones defined it. It is a great scientific question to learn its origin of sexual differentiation simply because of its curious nature. It is another question when the curiosity leads to an attempt to "cure" or manipulate its chemistry to change its nature This would be unnatural, immoral, and unethical. Uribe and Harbeck (1992, p. 27) said it best: "The pain and hardship suffered by adolescent, gay, lesbian, and bisexual [and transgender] youth is no longer invisible, and our lack of action is no longer professionally or ethically acceptable."

I would like to leave you with the words of a poem "Does it Matter?" written by an anonymous gay youth (as cited in Witt, Thomas, & Marcus, 1997):

■

Does It Matter?

My father asked me if I am gay
I asked Does it matter?
He said No not really
I said yes.
He said get out of my life
I guess it mattered.

My boss asked if I am gay
I asked Does it matter?
He said No not really
I told him yes.
He said you're fired faggot
I guess it mattered.

My friend asked if I am gay
I said Does it matter?
He said No not really
I told him yes.
He said Don't call me your friend
I guess it mattered.

My lover asked Do you love me?
I asked Does it matter?
He said yes.
I told him I love you
He said Let me hold you in my arms
For the first time in my life something matters.

My God asked me Do you love yourself?
I said Does it matter?
He said YES.
I said How can I love myself? I am gay
He said That is the way I made you
Nothing will ever matter again.

REFERENCES

A&E Network. (2001). *The Matthew Shepard story*. New York: Towers Productions.

American Civil Liberties Union. (2005, June 20). *Summary of school harassment lawsuits*. Retrieved http://www.aclu.org/lgbt/youth/11898res2005620.html

Associated Press. (2005, August 18). *Kayne West calls for an end to gay bashing*. Retrieved from http://www.usatoday.com/life/people/2005-08-18-kayne-west_x.htm?csp=34

Atkinson, D., Morten, G., & Sue, D. (1979). *Counseling American minorities*. Dubuque, IA: Brown.

Bahr, M., Brish, B., & Croteau, J. (2000). Addressing sexual orientation and professional ethics in the training of school psychologists in school and university settings. *School Psychology Review, 29*, 217–230.

Bailey, J., & Pillard, R. (1991). A genetic study of male sexual orientation. *Archives of General Psychiatry, 48*, 1089–1096.

Bailey, J., Pillard, R., Neale, M., & Agyei, Y. (1993). Heritable factors influence sexual orientation in women. *Archives of General Psychiatry, 50*, 217–223.

Banning, J. (1980). The campus ecology manager role. In U. Elsworth & G. Hanson (Eds.), *Student services: A handbook for the profession* (pp. 209–227). San Francisco: Jossey-Bass.

Baumrind, D. (1995). Commentary on sexual orientation: Research and social policy implications. *Developmental Psychology, 31*, 130–136.

Berenbaum, S., & Snyder, E. (1995). Early hormonal influences in childhood sex-typed activity and playmate preferences: Implications for the development of sexual orientation. *Developmental Psychology, 31*, 130–136.

Bethard, R. (2004). New York's Harvey Milk School. *Journal of Law and Education, 33*, 417–423.

Blumenfeld, W., Friedman, A., Greeley, R., Heumann, M., Hoffman, C., Lazarus, M., et al. (1982). *Pink triangles* [Film]. Cambridge, MA: Cambridge Documentary Films.

Bohan, J. (1996). *Psychology and sexual orientation: Coming to terms*. New York: Routledge.

Borhek, M. (1983). *Coming out to parents: A two-way survival guide for lesbians and gay men and their parents*. New York: Praeger.

Boxer, A., Cook, J., & Herdt, G. (1995). Double jeopardy: Identity transitions and parent child relations among gay and lesbian youth. In A. D'Augelli & C. Patterson (Eds.), *Lesbian, gay and bisexual identities over the lifespan* (p. 170). New York: Oxford University Press.

Bracciale, M., Sanabria, S., & Updyke, J. (2003, March). *Assisting parents of gay and lesbian youth*. Workshop presented at the annual convention of the American Counseling Association, Anaheim, CA.

Bradford, J., Ryan, C., & Rothblum, E. (1994). National lesbian health care survey: Implications for mental health care. *Journal of Consulting and Clinical Psychology, 62*, 228–242.

Brown v. Board of Education of Topeka, 347 U.S. 483 (1954).

Burke, P. (1996). *Gender shock*. New York: Doubleday.

Burr, C. (1995). The destiny of you. *The Advocate, 697*, 36–42.

Byne, W. (2005). Why we cannot conclude sexual orientation is a biological phenomenon. In J. Davidson & N. Moore (Eds.), *Speaking of sexuality* (pp. 245–248). Los Angeles: Roxbury.

California Bar Journal. (2006, June). Sexual orientation, verdict: $300,000. *Trials Digest*, p. 4.

Carroll, L., Gilroy, P., & Ryan, J. (2002). Counseling transgendered, transsexual, and gender-variant clients. *Journal of Counseling & Development, 80,* 131–139.

Cass, V. (1979). Homosexuality identity formation: A theoretical model. *Journal of Homosexuality, 4,* 219–235.

Chan, C. (1992). Cultural considerations in counseling Asian American lesbians and gay men. In S. Dworkin & F. Gutierrez (Eds.), *Counseling gay men and lesbians: Journey to the end of the rainbow* (pp. 115–124). Alexandria, VA: American Counseling Association.

Cochran, B., Stewart, A., Ginzler, J., & Cauce, A. (2002). Challenges faced by homeless sexual minorities: Comparison of gay, lesbian, bisexual, and transgender homeless adolescents with their heterosexual counterparts. *American Journal of Public Health, 92,* 773–776.

Coleman, E. (Ed.). (1988). *Psychotherapy with homosexual men and women.* New York: Haworth.

Coleman, E., & Remafedi, G. (1989). Gay, lesbian, and bisexual adolescents: A critical challenge to counselors. *Journal of Counseling & Development, 68,* 36–40.

Collaer, M., & Hines, M. (1995). Human behavioral sex differences: A role of gonadal hormones during early development? *Psychological Bulletin, 118,* 55–107.

D'Augelli, A., Hershberger, S., & Pilkington, N. (1998). Lesbian, gay, and bisexual youth and their families: Disclosure of sexual orientation and its consequences. *American Journal of Orthopsychiatry, 68,* 361–371.

Doll, L., Joy, D., Bartholow, B., Harrison, J., Bolan, G., Douglas, J., et al. (1992). Self-reported childhood and adolescent sexual abuse among adult homosexual and bisexual men. *Child Abuse and Neglect, 16,* 855–864.

Dworkin, S., & Gutierrez, F. (1989). Counselors be aware: Clients come in every size, shape, color, and sexual orientation. *Journal of Counseling & Development, 68,* 6–15.

Dworkin, S., & Gutierrez, F. (1992). Epilogue: Where do we go from here? In S. Dworkin & F. Gutierrez (Eds.), *Counseling gay men and lesbians: Journey to the end of the rainbow* (pp. 335–339). Alexandria, VA: American Counseling Association.

Epstein, R. (Director). (1978). *Word is out* [Film]. New York: New Yorker Films.

Erikson, E. (1968). *Identity youth and crisis.* New York: Norton.

Farenthold, D. (2005, June 17). Watermen net rare half-male, half-female crab: Scientists plan to decode its odd genetics. *The Washington Post,* p. 2A.

Freud, S. (1962). *Three essays of the theory of sexuality.* New York: Avon Books. (Original work published 1905)

Gross, L., Aurand, S., & Adessa, R. (1988). *Violence and discrimination against lesbian and gay people in Philadelphia and the Commonwealth of Pennsylvania.* Unpublished report, Philadelphia Gay and Lesbian Task Force.

Gutierrez, F. (1985). Bicultural personality development: A process model. In E. Garcia & R. Padilla (Eds.), *Advances in bilingual education research* (pp. 96–124). Tucson: University of Arizona Press.

Gutierrez, F. (1987). *Managing the campus ecology of gay and lesbian students in Catholic college campuses.* (ERIC Document Reproduction Service No. ED324612)

Gutierrez, F. (1994). Gay and lesbian: An ethnic identity deserving equal protection. *Law and Sexuality: A Review of Lesbian and Gay Legal Issues, 4,* 195–247.

Gutierrez, F., & Dworkin, S. (1992). Gay, lesbian, and African-American: Managing the integration of identities. In S. Dworkin & F. Gutierrez (Eds.), *Counseling gay men and lesbians: Journey to the end of the rainbow* (pp. 141–156). Alexandria, VA: American Counseling Association.

Haldeman, D. (2000). Gender atypical youth: Clinical and social issues. *School Psychology Review, 29,* 192–200.

Hally, J. E. (1993). *The construction of heterosexuality, fear of a queer planet: Queer politics and social theory.* Minneapolis: University of Minnesota Press.

Hamer, D., Hu, S., Magnuson, V., Hu, N., & Pattatucci, A. (1993, July 16). A linkage between DNA markers on the X chromosome and male sexual orientation. *Science, 261,* 321–327.

Haynes, V. (2001, July 26). California trying to make schools less hostile for gays plan spurs debate on free speech, religious rights. *Chicago Tribune,* p. 10.

Herdt, G. (1989). Gay and lesbian youth: Emergent identities and cultural scenes at home and abroad. *Journal of Homosexuality, 17,* 1–42.

Herr, K. (1997). Learning lessons from school: Homophobia, heterosexism and the construction of failure. *Journal of Gay and Lesbian Social Services, 7*(4), 51–64.

Herzshberger, S., & D'Augelli, A. (1995). The impact of victimization on the mental health and suicidality of lesbian, gay, and bisexual youths. *Developmental Psychology, 31,* 65–74.

Hershberger, S., & D'Augelli, A. (2000). Issues in counseling lesbian, gay, and bisexual adolescents. In R. M. Perez, K. De Bord, & K. Bieschke (Eds.), *Handbook of counseling and psychotherapy with lesbian, gay, and bisexual clients* (pp. 225–248). Washington, DC: American Psychological Association.

Individuals With Disabilities Education Improvement Act of 2004, 20 U.S.C. § 1400.

Kubler-Ross, E. (1969). *On death and dying.* New York: McMillan.

Levine, E., & Padilla, A. (1980). *Crossing cultures in therapy: Pluralistic counseling for the Hispanic.* Monterey, CA: Brooks/Cole.

Lips, H. (1978). Sexual differentiation and gender identity. In H. Lips & N. Colwill (Eds.), *The psychology of sex differences* (pp. 52–79). Englewood Cliffs, NJ: Prentice-Hall.

Loiacano, D. (1989). Gay identity issues among Black Americans: Racism, homophobia, and the need for validation. *Journal of Counseling & Development, 68,* 21–25.

Martin, A., & Hetrick, E. (1988). The stigmatization of the gay and lesbian adolescent. *Journal of Homosexuality, 15,* 163–183.

McClintock, M., & Herdt, G. (1996). Rethinking puberty: The development of sexual attraction. *Current Directions in Psychological Science, 5,* 178–183.

Migeon, C., & Wisniewski, A. (1998). Sexual differentiation: From genes to gender. *Hormone Research, 50,* 245–251.

Mollison, A. (2004, July 3). Bias against gays lingers in schools: Teachers eye ways to help staff, youths. *The Atlanta Journal-Constitution,* p. A.11.

Money, J. (1987). Sin, sickness, or status? Homosexual and gender identity and psycho-neuroendocrinology. *American Psychologist, 42,* 384–399.

Morales, E. (1992). Counseling Latino gays and Latina lesbians. In S. Dworkin & F. Gutierrez (Eds.), *Counseling gay men and lesbians: Journey to the end of the rainbow* (pp. 125–139). Alexandria, VA: American Counseling Association.

National Center for Health Statistics. (1986). *Vital statistics of the United States: Vol. 2. Mortality, Part A.* Hyattsville, MD: Author.

Nabozny v. Podlesny, 92 F.3d 446, 458–59 (7th Cir. 1996).

Norris, W. (1992). Liberal attitudes and homophobic acts: The paradoxes of homosexual experience in a liberal institution. In K. Harbeck (Ed.), *Coming out of the classroom closet: Gay and lesbian students, teachers, and curricula* (pp. 81–120). New York: Harrington Park Press.

O'Connor, M. (1992). Psychotherapy with gay and lesbian adolescents. In S. Dworkin & F. Gutierrez (Eds.), *Counseling gay men and lesbians: Journey to the end of the rainbow* (pp. 3–21). Alexandria, VA: American Counseling Association.

Parham, T. (1989). Cycles of psychological nigrescence. *The Counseling Psychologist, 17,* 187–226.

Plummer, K. (1989). Lesbian and gay youth in England. *Journal of Homosexuality, 17,* 195–223.

Reck, J. (2005). *Be queer . . . but not here! Queer and transgender youth, the Castro 'MECCA,' and spatial gay politics.* Unpublished doctoral dissertation, University of California, Santa Cruz.

Remafedi, G. (1987). Adolescent homosexuality: Medical and psychological implications. *Pediatrics, 79,* 331–337.

Robinson, B., Walters, L., & Skeen, P. (1989). Response of parents to learning that their child is homosexual and concern over AIDS: A national study. *Journal of Homosexuality, 18,* 59–80.

Roman, M. (2005, May 21). Initiative helps transgendered with unique struggles. *Telegram & Gazette,* p. A2.

Royce, J. (1981). *Alcohol problems and alcoholism.* New York: Free Press.

Santiago, R. (2006, July 10). 5-year-old 'girl' starting school is really a boy. *The Miami Herald,* pp. 1A–2A.

Savin-Williams, R. (1994). Verbal and physical abuse as stressors in the lives of lesbian, gay male, and bisexual youths: Associations with school problems, running away, substance abuse, prostitution, and suicide. *Journal of Consulting and Clinical Psychology, 62,* 261–269.

Savin-Williams, R. (2005). Dating and romantic relationships among gay, lesbian, and bisexual youths. In J. Davidson & N. Moore (Eds.), *Speaking of sexuality* (pp. 306–315). Los Angeles: Roxbury.

Schindel, J. (2005). *Challenging sexual prejudice, creating safe spaces, promoting sexual diversity: A case study of LGBTQ youth activism in the San Francisco Bay Area.* Unpublished doctoral dissertation, Stanford University.

Shore, S. (Director). (1998). *Get real* [Film]. Los Angeles: Paramount

Skinner v. Oklahoma, 316 U.S. 535 (1942).

St. John, K. (2004, May 26). Posthumous request for a name change: Slain transgender teen's mom wants 'Gwen' to be official. *San Francisco Chronicle,* p. B-1.

Strommen, E. (1989). You're a what?: Family member reaction to the disclosure of homosexuality. *Journal of Homosexuality, 18,* 37–57.

Tobias-Neely, J. (2005, June 12). Surviving in a straight world: When it comes to relationships, many young gay people face a world of obstacles without much support. *Spokesman Review,* p. D1.

Troiden, R. (1989). The formation of homosexual identities. *Journal of Homosexuality, 17*(1/2), 43–73.

Uribe, V., & Harbeck, K. (1992). Addressing the needs of lesbian, gay, and bisexual youth: The origins of Project 10 and school-based intervention. In K. Harbeck (Ed.), *Coming out of the classroom closet: Gay and lesbian students, teachers, and curricula* (pp. 9–28). New York: Harrington Park Press.

Vowels, K. (2005). *Assessing principals' perceptions of heterosexism and homophobia in a large urban public school district.* Unpublished doctoral dissertation, Texas A&M University–Commerce.

Weinberg, G. (1972). *Society and the healthy homosexual.* New York: St. Martin's Press.

Witt, L., Thomas, S., & Marcus, E. (Eds.). (1997). *Out in all directions: A treasury of gay and lesbian America*. New York: Warner Books.

Woodiel, K., Angermeier-Howard, L., & Hobson, S. (2003). School safety for all: Using the coordinated school health program to increase safety for LGBTQ students. *American Journal of Health Studies, 18,* 98–103.

Youth, Inc. (1997). *Creating safe schools for lesbian and gay students: A resource guide for school staff*. Retrieved from http://members.tripod.com/~+wood/guide.html

CHAPTER 14

■

Death in the Classroom: Violence in Schools

Abbé Finn

Before the school shootings in the last half of the 1990s, there was little research conducted on the issue of school violence prevention (Furlong, Morrison, Skiba, & Cornell, 2004). After the Columbine massacre in 1999, school safety concerns were catapulted onto the front pages and into the minds of most Americans. For example, before 1992 there were only 21 references in PsycINFO under the search topic "school violence," compared with 513 from 1999 to 2006. The outbreak of school shootings shined the light on the problem of youth violence. In the 10 years from 1992 to 2002, 234 children were killed in and around American schools (Centers for Disease Control and Prevention, 2006). Many intervention programs were rushed into place in an effort to "do something" about the problem (Furlong et al., 2004). Years later, the evaluative process was instituted to measure which programs were most helpful and which were ineffective.

Fortunately, the violence rate has been steadily decreasing and the rate of students carrying weapons to school has declined from 12% in 1992 to 6% in 2002 (9% for males and 3% for females). During the academic years from 1992–1993 to 1998–1999, there were approximately 30 murders on campus each academic year. After the Columbine shootings, there was a decline in the murder rate to approximately 14 per year (DeVoe, Peter, Noonan, Snyder, & Baum, 2005). Clearly, this is still an unacceptable rate of violence in a place that should be a sanctuary from crime. However, it does show a trend toward improvement. This may show the impact of national policy developed to address the causes of school violence. Many intervention programs have been implemented, and some have been shown to be effective and others have not (U.S. Department of Health and Human Services [USDHHS], 2001a). Many were implemented without scientific investigation or any demonstration of efficacy (Elliott, 1998; Skiba & Knesting, 2002) and, contrary to logic, some have been shown to increase the rate of violence (Derzon, 2006; Mendel, 2000).

Issues contributing to the problem of youth violence are multidimensional and caused by many factors working together (Herrenkohl et al., 2000; USDHHS, 2001a). Some of these factors are explored in this chapter. Violence is defined as any action or threat of action that would result in intimidation, coercion, physical harm, personal injury, or death. The topic is examined from the perspective of the various types of prevention and intervention programs, with special attention paid to describe programs that have been evaluated and that demonstrate effectiveness.

The alarming rate of violence has raised national awareness and concern resulting in great public demand for the development and implementation of prevention and intervention programs to reduce the bloodshed (Furlong et al., 2004). Remedies include increased school security, zero tolerance policies, psychosocial profiling, school climate reform, social skills training, peer mediation programs, and parent training. To be effective, the prevention and intervention programs need to be based on the theoretical causes of youth violent behavior.

PROBLEM DEFINITION

The decade from 1983 to 1993 marked a period described as a "violence epidemic" (Cook & Laub, 1998). No social class, neighborhood, or community in the United States was immune from the widespread consequences. Lasting physical and emotional scars were left on individuals, families, schools, and communities. Many children were killed or maimed during this time period (USDHHS, 2001a). Twenty-five percent of inner-city youths have been victims or witnesses to extreme forms of violence. Community hostilities and violence often bleed into the school environment (Mulvey & Cauffman, 2001). This is why many prevention and intervention programs coordinate their efforts across the school and community domains.

During this same period, the rate of violent crime committed by children rose by 1,000%. It has been estimated that violence costs the United States $508 billion a year: $90 billion is spent on the criminal justice system, $65 billion on security, $5 billion on the treatment of victims, $170 billion on lost productivity, with $178 billion in expenses to the victims (Illinois Center for Violence Prevention, 1998). It is estimated that children under the age of 20 committed one third of the murders in the United States. Among African American adolescent males, murder was the second leading cause of death (Center to Prevent Handgun Violence, 1990; James & Gilliland, 2000). Between 1985 and 1994 the rate of incarceration and arrest increased by 67% for young males and by 125% for young females (Dahlberg, 1998). Suicide, another extreme form of violence, was the third leading cause of death (Flannery, Singer, & Wester, 2001). Adolescent suicide and murder are highly correlated. Vossekuil, Reddy, Fein, Borum, and Modzeleski (2000) studied the student assailants in 37 school shootings and found that approximately 75% of the perpetrators had threatened or attempted suicide prior to committing the school shootings. Most school shooters plan to die on a battlefield of their own creation. Some have begged others to shoot them.

Schools, usually perceived as safe havens from violence, became part of the battleground. Ninety-two percent of secondary and 87% of middle schools reported at least one incidence of violence each year. The violent incidents are unequally distributed, with 16% of the schools reporting 75% of the crime. Twenty percent of schools reported at least one serious violent incident. These incidents included rape, sexual assault, physical attack with and without a weapon, murder, and suicide. There were 60,719 incidents reported in the 2000 School Survey on Crime and

Safety (National Center for Education Statistics, 2003). During the 1986–1987 academic year, the school crime report from the School Safety Council (1989) indicated that 3 million faculty, staff, students, and visitors were victims of crime in U.S. schools. From 1986 to 1990, 71 people were killed at U.S. schools; of these, 65 were students and 6 were employees. An additional 242 were held hostage at gunpoint and 201 were seriously wounded (Center to Prevent Handgun Violence, 1990). For every hour school was in session in the United States, 900 teachers were threatened, and approximately 40 teachers and more than 2,000 students were physically assaulted (Futrell, 1996; Shafii & Shafii, 2001). In a 1996 survey, 47% of teens responded that they thought violence was increasing in schools, with 10% reporting that they feared a classmate would shoot them. From February 1997 to April 1999, there were eight incidents of mass school shootings with at least 32 deaths (Chandras, 1999; Gibbs & Roche, 1999; King & Murr, 1998). More recently, from between July 1, 2001 and June 1, 2002, there were 17 homicides and 5 suicides. During this same period, 11% of teachers in city schools were threatened by students or attacked by students. In addition, 2.2% of educators in secondary schools and 0.9% of elementary school teachers were victims of theft or violent crime (DeVoe et al., 2005). According to the 1999–2000 School Survey on Crime and Safety, 71% of elementary and secondary school in the United States experiences some type of violent event equaling 1.5 million occurrences in 59,000 schools. A smaller portion (20%) experienced severe violence, including murder, rape, other forms of sexual assault, assaults with weapons, threats of assault using a weapon, and robbery. Twenty-five percent of these attacks went unreported to the authorities. Other crimes committed at schools included possession of alcohol or other illegal drugs (27%), sale and distribution of drugs (12%), possession of a knife (43%), and possession of a firearm or explosive device (6%; U.S. Department of Education, 2004).

Most of the violence occurring in schools was not as extreme as school shootings. The majority of school violence occurs in undersupervised areas (Astor, Mayer, & Behre, 1999). Fearing victimization, 5% of the surveyed students reported that they were too intimidated to use the school restrooms and avoided particular hallways, locker rooms, and stairwells as well as school activities (DeVoe et al., 2005). This is a decrease from 9% in 1998 (Elliott, Hamburg, & Williams, 1998).

Fortunately, there has been a slight but steady decline in violent crime among adolescents since this violence epidemic. However, the Report of the Surgeon General (USDHHS, 2001b) cautioned against complaisance. Although the rate of arrests of youthful offenders has declined, confidential self-reports indicate that the rate of potentially lethal acts of violence has remained unchanged. Despite the decline in violence, the rates of arrests are still 70% higher than they were before 1983 (USDHHS, 2001b), and the number of mass murders or suicide paired with homicide at schools has increased, averaging 5 per year from 1994 to 1999 (USDHHS, 2001a). According to the National Center for Educational Statistics and the Bureau of Justice Statistics, students reporting that they were victims of crime at school decreased from 10% to 8% between 1995 and 1999 (Kaufman et al., 2001). In addition, fewer students are carrying weapons to school. Approximately 6.5% of high school students carried a weapon to school in 2005 in the previous 30 days (DeVoe et al, 2005) compared with 12% in 1993 (Kann et al., 1995). However, if the data are sorted by gender, 10% of males self-reported that they had carried a weapon in school during the previous 30 days. Although this is an improvement, it continues to cause concern for schools and communities because these statistics mean that in a school of 2,000 students, 130 students (on one or more occasions) carried weapons to school during each month (Centers for Disease Control and Prevention, 2006). Therefore, on any given day there could be several students at school carrying weapons (Hermann & Finn, 2002).

Students, educational professionals, parents, and community leaders are very concerned with school safety and greatly distressed with the outbreak of youth violence. Most prevention programs follow the public health prevention model of primary, secondary, or tertiary prevention. Primary prevention programs identify characteristics that increase the risk of the public health problem and intervene with large heterogeneous groups through education or behavioral change. For example, with underage alcohol abuse, teens are encouraged through public service announcements not to drink and drive. Secondary prevention programs identify individuals or groups of people at risk for the specific problem and target them for intervention. As an example of secondary prevention, teens who use drugs were targeted to receive counseling. Tertiary prevention programs attempt to limit the reoccurrence of a problem or further deterioration of people exhibiting symptoms of a public health problem (Lawler, 2000). A methadone clinic is an example of a tertiary or harm reduction program.

CASE STUDY

The day began at Thurston High in a deceptively normal way. Some students were arriving in a rush fearing they would be late, others were early and eating their breakfast while finishing their homework. Only the shooter had a premonition of the disaster that was about to strike. At 7:50 a.m. on May 21, 1998, 15-year-old Kip Kinkle arrived at school armed with a .22-caliber semiautomatic rifle concealed in the folds of his trench coat, two pistols, and a hunting knife tucked into the waistband of his pants. On his way down the hall, he encountered a student who had teased him for public display of affection at school. Without breaking stride Kip shot him in the head. Seconds later Kip passed another student, one he didn't even know, and shot him in the face. Moments before the first period bell rang, Kip strode into the cafeteria filled with approximately 400 students. Striding from the doorway he opened fire, emptying the rifle's 50-round clip. He shot into the crowd but sometimes fired point blank at specific students. When the chamber was empty, four boys tackled Kip to the ground in an attempt to halt the carnage. Kip continued to struggle and was able to reach one of his concealed handguns and shot several of the children who were restraining him. One of the boys was shot in the chest and had a collapsed lung. While on the ground, Kip begged the other students to shoot him. Later, the students, who had moments before been his targeted victims, said that shooting Kip had never crossed their minds even though they were holding Kip's guns. By the end of the day Kip had killed 4 people and injured 20.

After his arrest, Kip was handcuffed and placed in an interrogation room. While in the cell he wriggled out of the handcuffs, removed a knife he'd taped to his leg and attacked a police officer. The officer escaped injury by subduing him with pepper spray. During the attack, Kip begged the officer to shoot him.

The killing spree had actually begun the afternoon before when Kip killed his father and then waited to ambush and kill his mother. Earlier that day, Kip had been arrested for buying a stolen gun and suspended from school for storing it in his locker. He was detained by police and released to his father's custody.

In the aftermath of these horrible events, people wondered how this could happen in a sleepy, all-American small town like Springfield, Oregon. However, upon closer examination, Kip gave many signals that he was in serious trouble.

Physically, Kip was small, standing 5 feet 5 inches, weighing 125 pounds with red hair and freckles. He was emotionally immature, socially isolated, targeted for teasing by the bigger boys, and scholastically challenged. Both of his parents were very respected educators, and his older sister was an excellent student. In contrast, Kip struggled in school. Even though his parents were loving and caring, there was not a good fit between Kip and his family. They were intellectual and athletic, whereas he was a poor student who was awkward and clumsy. Kip was diagnosed with learning disabilities and was also suffering from depression. For a short time, he was treated by a psychologist and had been prescribed antidepressants, which he stopped taking. Adding to his depression, Kip had recently endured the breakup of a romantic relationship. After the shootings, Kip disclosed that he was hearing voices. Unfortunately, he failed to report to his psychologist that he was having auditory hallucinations. He had developed a fascination with the suicide pact in *Romeo and Juliet.* When the police arrived at his home to investigate his confessed murder of his parents, the soundtrack was blasting from Kip's stereo.

After the fact, students came forward with other information foreshadowing Kip's future violence. For example, Kip had reportedly bragged about skinning a live cat and also about making bombs. He made bombs and exploded them in an abandoned stone quarry. After the killings, police discovered 20 live bombs set to go off in his home. Some were large enough to cause collateral damage to the neighborhood, and their discovery resulted in the evacuation of 15 nearby houses. Kip nurtured a deep fascination with weapons and explosives. He had persuaded his parents to buy him several guns. Over the years he acquired an arsenal, which he kept hidden in the attic over his bedroom. On May 20th, Kip's father brought him home from jail and told him that he was confiscating all of his guns. Kip later reported to the police that he felt compelled to kill his parents to spare them the shame he brought to the family (Dowling & Johnson, 1998; Kesey, 1998; Sullivan, 1998).

APPROACHES TO PREVENTION

Effective violence prevention programs share several common characteristics. Nine elements have been identified as necessary for programs to work: (a) clear policies; (b) skills training; (c) comprehensive multimodal approaches; (d) coordination among programs within and outside of the school; (e) changes to the physical plant; (f) at least 10 to 20 sessions; (g) training for the entire school staff, parents, and community; (h) multiple teaching methods; and (i) a sensitivity to the school and community culture (Henry, Farrell, & The Multisite Violence Prevention Project, 2004; Lawler, 2000). These elements are endorsed by Nation et al. (2003) with the addition of theory-driven approaches and outcome evaluation.

The first necessary component of an effective prevention or intervention program is a clear and consistent school policy. Schools should promote peaceful resolution to problems and discourage violence. The teachers, coaches, administrators, parents, and community members should be in agreement on the value of peaceful resolutions to problems. The second necessary components for the program are skills training for students, faculty, and parents. The skills training curriculum should include anger management, conflict resolution, taking the social perspective of others, problem solving, peer negotiations, and active listening skills. Part of the peer negotiations training includes ways to resist peer pressure and techniques for making new friends. The third characteristic of successful programs is that they are comprehensive, integrated, and multimodal. They involve the community leaders, law enforcement, school personnel, and members of the press. A consistent message of peaceful resolution and antiviolence is encouraged and is infused into all forms of communication.

The fourth element is the coordination of all of the prevention programs. For example, the drug abuse prevention program is coordinated with the violence prevention program that is in concordance with the suicide prevention program and the teen pregnancy program. All share common elements of decision-making skills, peer refusal skills, social competency, and self-esteem. These skills are infused into the curriculum for subjects such as social sciences, health, physical science, and English composition. When learning is reinforced across the curriculum, more of the information is retained, and it is more likely to become part of students' daily lives. The fifth element concerns the physical design and administrative policies of the school. In effect, an assessment is made regarding security risks that are present in the school and these are remedied. For example, fences might be built surrounding the school to control the access to school grounds, and outdoor lighting might be installed to improve the security for people attending school functions after dark. Administrative policy decisions are made to reduce congestion and increase adult supervision. Another example of administrative policy is the decision to require school uniforms to reduce the showing of gang colors, thereby reducing the influence of gangs at school. The sixth characteristic of programs that work is the amount of exposure that students have to the training program. Students need to have between 10 to 20 sessions the first year followed by repeated exposures (5 to 10 sessions) in the following years (Lawler, 2000). The more severe the problems and the greater the students' deficits, the more exposure they will require (Nation et al., 2003). Schools that have a high rate of new admissions to the school should include all new students in the prevention program in their first year.

The seventh characteristic involves training for the teachers, students, parents, and community. The program should begin with teacher and administrative in-service training before school starts in the early fall to set the stage for the entire year. Key student leaders should be identified and trained in the summer, with the rest of the student population exposed to the program as soon as school begins. The program should be integrated into the curriculum across all grades. The normative education should begin in kindergarten and continue throughout the entire school career.

The eighth characteristic of an effective program concerns multimodal approach to learning. The students are exposed to the curriculum through a variety of teaching approaches, including role-plays, literature, quizzes, discussions, group projects, and current events. The final element necessary for an effective program is related to the cultural sensitivity of the program and intervention procedures to the needs of the community. All methods and principles of the program must be consistent with the ethnic and cultural makeup of the school and community (Lawler, 2000). Including input of community and school members during the design phase of the program can ensure cultural sensitivity.

Many of the effective youth violence prevention programs are shown to be cost beneficial. They can save taxpayers from the expenses of the criminal justice system, medical care of crime victims, social service costs for children supported while the parents are incarcerated, and increased work productivity of people who would otherwise spent their lives in jail (USDHHS, 2001b). The youth violence prevention programs that targeted specific populations of youthful offenders were most cost effective. These are secondary prevention programs because they target the people most likely to offend again and come under the supervision of the legal system

(Washington State Institute of Public Policy, 1999). Some of the prevention programs reduce violence through indirect means by preventing some of the conditions such as child abuse known to give rise to violence later on. The discussion of prevention programs is organized by their emphasis: the individual, family, school, and community levels.

Individual

Psychosocial profiling is the most controversial individual youth violence prevention strategy. This is because although most youthful violent perpetrators fit some of the profile, many more will fit the profile but never become violent (Mulvey & Cauffman, 2001). Relying on the psychosocial profiles alone would result in many young people being falsely labeled as violent who would never commit a violent act (Vossekuil, Reddy, & Fein, 2001). Even the report by the Federal Bureau of Investigation recommending the use of "threat assessment teams" through psychosocial profiles states that there are no reliable profiles or distinguishing characteristics that reliably discriminate between people who commit violence and those who do not (O'Toole & The Critical Incident Response Group, 2000; USDHHS, 2001a). Consequently, in the worst case scenario, overreliance on a checklist of characteristics can overlook some violent youths if the checklist is too accurate, or falsely identify some youth as dangerous who are not if the checklist is too sensitive (Baily, 2001; Finn & Remley, 2002).

On the side of the debate favoring profiling, violent youth and school shooters share some common characteristics. To overlook psychosocial profiling as one of many tools to prevent violence may increase risk of harm by ignoring what is known about violent students. Many educators fear that ignoring warning signs outlined by the psychosocial profile increases the school's liability (Lumsden, 2000). Theoretically, the greater the number of severe characteristics the youth presents, the higher the likelihood for violence (Finn & Remley, 2002; USDHHS, 2001b). The best use of psychosocial profiling is in the identification of students in need of counseling or some other form of supportive intervention (Baily, 2001; Finn & Remley, 2002; Herman & Finn, 2002). It is hoped that if students get the appropriate intervention in a timely fashion, violence can be averted. Dwyer, Osher, and Warger (1998) identified early warning signs.

The following characteristics describe the perpetrators of the multiple school shootings. Almost all of the shooters were European American males. The students who perpetrate the most severe acts of violence at schools planned them at least 2 weeks in advance. They had multiple reasons for their attacks and believed that they were justified in their actions. Seventy-five percent of the attackers held grievances against students, teachers, or administrators. They could not keep their violent plans to themselves and told others. Among the school shooters, 75% told friends or classmates. One school-shooting perpetrator told a total of 24 acquaintances (Vossekuil et al., 2001). Certainly, the majority of people making threats never carry them out; however, most people who harm others have made threatening remarks. Some make clearly threatening statements listing time, place, targeted victims, and choice of weapons. For example, the shooters at Columbine presented a video in their media arts class describing their plan of attack. They also threatened and indeed shot another student they had specifically named on their Internet Web site (Gibbs & Roche, 1999). In other cases, the students make obscure statements. On the other hand, youth may only make obscure threats through poetry, artwork, or journal writing (Dwyer et al., 1998).

Students who commit the most violent crimes show a fascination with weapons and ultraviolent films, video games, and music (Dwyer et al., 1998). Sometimes they mimic the dress, posture, and behavior of main characters from the films. The school shooters at Moses Lake, Oregon, and Littleton, Colorado wore trench coats modeling their clothing after antagonists in their favorite movies.

Violent youths are socially withdrawn or belong to the socially rejected, antisocial group (Borduin & Schaeffer, 1998; Kashani, Jones, Bumby, & Thomas, 1999; USDHHS, 2001a). Many also show symptoms of severe psychiatric disorders (Dwyer et al., 1998), with some hearing voices commanding them to commit the violent crimes. For example, the school shooters from Pearl, Mississippi, and Springfield, Oregon had hallucinations. Both began their killing spree by shooting their parent(s). Many violent young people did not receive the appropriate level of psychiatric treatment or stopped taking their medication on purpose to increase their level of violence (James & Gilliland, 2000). Many engaged in angry outbursts at school and other public places or assaulted others with little provocation (Vossekuil et al., 2001) with the level of violence escalating rapidly.

Revenge was a common motive for the school shootings (Vossekuil et al., 2001). The perpetrators express a belief that their actions are justified because of previous histories of having been bullied by other students (Ross, 1996) or having had a failed romance. The shooters in Jonesboro, Arkansas; Pearl, Mississippi; and Springfield, Oregon specifically targeted the girls they believed had wronged them.

There are several ways to classify the factors associated with youth violence. The Surgeon General Report categorized the youth violence risk factors according to the size of the effect on the statistical outcome (USDHHS, 2001a). Their research showed that a history of criminal offenses, substance abuse, weak social connections, antisocial delinquent peers, and belonging to a gang had the largest statistical impact on the outcome (USDHHS, 2001a). The factors associated with youth violence were further subcategorized by domain. Late-onset individual characteristics include all of the above plus risk-taking behaviors, commission of crimes, and violent acts toward others. However, the report also identified protective factors. These include tolerance toward social differences, having a high IQ, having prosocial values, and believing that there are negative consequences for antisocial actions (USDHHS, 2001a).

Early-onset violence risk factors in the family domain include living in poverty, parents who demonstrate antisocial behaviors, having a poor parent–child relationship, poor parental supervision and discipline, living in a single-parent home, and having abusive or neglectful parents. Late-onset factors include low parental involvement and family conflict. Protective factors in the family domain include having warm, supportive, and involved parents who like the child's friends (USDHHS, 2001a).

Early-onset factors in the school domain include having poor school performance and having a poor attitude toward school and learning. In addition to the previous factors, late-onset factors contributing to violence include grade failure and retention. Factors that protect children from violence in the school domain include the student's involvement in school activities, having a commitment to school, and getting recognition at school for success.

Factors in the peer group domain correlated with an early onset of violence are having a weak connection with friends and having friends who behave in an antisocial manner. Late-onset factors also include gang membership. The mitigating factor in the peer group domain is having friends with conventional values. In the community domain, only late-onset factors were identified. These included living in drug-infested, high-crime neighborhoods that are poorly organized and fail to meet the needs of the community (USDHHS, 2001a). Characteristics in the individual domain with early onset that increase the likelihood of violence include legal offenses, substance use, being male, acting out aggressively, hyperactivity, having a psychological disorder, exposure to violence in the media, expression of antisocial behavior (individual, family, school, peer group, or community), and age of onset (USDHHS, 2001a).

Family

Lasting changes with children can only be made if changes are also made in the family system. The earlier interventions are made, the better the outcome is for the child. Early intervention can improve prenatal care, reduce maternal drug use, and protect the developing fetus from the many negative consequences of these behaviors. One of the programs demonstrated to be effective is the Home Visitation by Nurses Program. It begins before the child is born and continues through the child's 2nd birthday. The purpose of this program is to improve the health outcomes by supporting and guiding young, often single women through the prenatal and postnatal period to the toddler years. In this program, the same nurse visits the young woman and her family twice monthly during the pregnancy and weekly following childbirth. The nurse gets to know the family and is able to train the mother in parenting skills. By taking this program to the mother's home, the nurses circumvent the problems young mothers have with transportation and other difficulties keeping appointments. Depending on the needs of the family, the nurse may visit once monthly after the child is 6 weeks old. The nurse advises the mother, monitors her health during the pregnancy, and monitors the child's health and development following delivery. The visits usually last between 1 and 1.5 hours. With low-income women, the program has demonstrated effectiveness through a 15-year follow-up. The women's behavior was healthier during pregnancy because of the intervention. This was especially true for the cessation of smoking and drinking while pregnant. There were fewer complications such as hypertension and kidney infections. There were significantly fewer cases of child abuse, neglect, and injuries to the children. The women participants also took more responsibility for their lives, including planning future pregnancies, reduction in welfare dependence, and reduction in substance abuse and illegal behavior. In a 16-year follow-up, the children whose mothers participated in this program had significantly fewer arrests, convictions, and lower alcohol consumption. This program has been shown to be cost beneficial at a rate of at least 4:1. The cost of the program is recovered by the time the child reaches age 4. The future benefits extend to other children born to these mothers in later years (Lawler, 2000; Olds, Hill, Mihalic, & O'Brien, 1998; USDHHS, 2001a).

School

Derzon (2006) conducted a meta-analysis of 74 different school-based prevention programs. He found that most of the programs were implemented in the classroom, with the teacher delivering the curriculum once or twice a week, during the regular classroom period. The teachers underwent an extensive amount of training, and most included all of the students in the class. Derzon concluded that most of the reviewed prevention programs were effective in reducing violence and antisocial behavior by 5% (with many much more); however, a few programs indicated an increase in violent, antisocial, and problem behaviors over the comparison groups.

The earliest attempts to prevent school violence focused on improving school security. These security precautions include mandated use of school uniforms, controlled access to schools, increased presence of uniformed security guards or police, the removal of hall lockers, and the installation of metal detectors. Some students and parents have questioned the right of administrators to search students and their belongings, but courts have consistently found that schools have this right in order to keep schools safe. They are granted this prerogative through the concept that teachers and administrators act in the role of the students' parents (*in loco parentis*). School personnel have an obligation to protect the children from others and themselves. The duty to protect students takes precedence over the students' right to privacy (Yell & Rozalski, 2000).

Many school districts have spent a great deal of their resources on the installation of metal detectors to halt the influx of weapons onto school campuses. For example, in 1 year, New York City spent over $28 million dollars for this purpose (Kemper, 1993). At least 25% of the largest urban school districts use metal detectors (National School Safety Center, 1990). The cost of security and detection devices goes way beyond the initial investment in equipment. There is a continuous need for training, manpower, and maintenance of the detection devices. Trump (1997) warned that the school must react at a level consistent with the security threat in their school and community. He also stated that the security force must be trained in working with adolescents, deescalation, and conflict resolution. If not, a poorly trained security force can decrease rather than increase safety.

With so many resources devoted to security, it is important to ask whether these measures are effective in reducing violence at schools. The Centers for Disease Control and Prevention (1991) found that these devices were effective in reducing the number of students carrying weapons at school but had no effect on the number of students carrying weapons outside of school. Because the majority of the most serious violence and injury occur outside of school property, these measures do not have an appreciable impact on the overall safety of children. Mercy and Rosenberg (1998) concluded that they could not find any studies investigating whether these measures decrease the incidence of gun violence at schools. However, it is reasonable to conclude that having fewer weapons in schools equals safer schools. Some communities have adopted community-policing policies to increase the safety of students walking to school. "Safe School Routes" are designated and community volunteers are on duty observing the children as they pass twice daily. This program has been shown to increase the children's perception of safety with a minimal cost to the community (Mercy & Rosenberg, 1998).

The Bullying Prevention Program (BPP) specifically addresses the most common form of violence occurring in schools (Batsche & Knoff, 1994). Bullying can include coercive verbal comments, physical intimidation, or a combination of the two. It is sometimes more similar to chronic, systematic terrorism carried out by one or more people targeting a specific person (Furlong, Sharma, & Rhee, 2000). As a result, the child becomes a social outcast with a drastic reduction in self-esteem.

Victims of bullying tend to share certain physical characteristics, such as being overweight or underweight, being small in stature, or projecting general weakness. They also share certain personality characteristics, such as shyness, passivity, or (for males) effeminacy (Furlong et al., 2000; Olweus, 1997; Olweus, Limber, Mihalic,

1999). In general, the bully has much more power than the victim. Olweus (1997) described two types of victims: passive or provocative. The passive types of victims are more anxious, insecure, introverted, shy, and quiet; demonstrate low self-esteem; and feel lonely and abandoned at school. Provocative victims show many characteristics of attention-deficit hyperactivity disorder. In contrast to the passive victims, the provocative victims aggravate and annoy their attackers, leading to the harassment. This in no way justifies the bullying that later takes place.

There are gender differences between the ways boys and girls bully. When boys bully they tend to use physical intimidation, abuse, and humiliating pranks. The pattern of behavior for girls is not so obvious but just as emotionally damaging. Girls tend to tease and exclude girls who are targeted for bullying. In the United States, 23% of middle school children reported that they had been the targets of bullies on several occasions in the past 3 months (Olweus et al., 1999). The negative consequences of bullying are not limited to childhood. Many adults report lasting effects from their childhood bullying (Olweus, 1994). The bully also suffers negative consequences. Bullies, especially males, are more likely to break rules, act in other antisocial ways, use and abuse drugs, and commit crimes. Permitting bullies to act out also has a negative impact on the general classroom and school climate. Tolerance of bullying behavior creates a more hostile atmosphere (Olweus et al., 1999). In order for bullies to operate, there must be support by other classmates with tacit approval by teachers and administrators.

The Bullying Prevention Program confronts these behaviors by addressing the issues at the school, classroom, and individual levels. Intervention at the school level begins with an anonymous survey of the students regarding the nature, severity, and prevalence of bullying at the school. The school then holds a daylong meeting to discuss the results and plan their schoolwide intervention. The schoolwide plan targets areas on the school grounds requiring higher supervision. At the classroom level, rules are established that discourage bullying and intimidation. Classroom meetings are held with open discussions defining bullying behavior and describing the negative outcomes from bullying. Students are given an opportunity to discuss alternatives to bullying behavior. At the individual intervention level, children identified as bullies are given individual and group counseling to learn other more appropriate behavior. Children identified as victims are also given an opportunity for counseling. All of the parents of children receiving counseling are invited to participate in family counseling at the school. The counselors also act as consultants to the teachers who have students identified as bullies or victims of the bullies. The outcomes of the program showed a large and statistically significant reduction in the number of students reporting victimization by bullies. Other antisocial behaviors such as vandalism, violence, theft, and truancy were also significantly reduced. Students and teachers reported a significant improvement in school climate. There were significantly fewer discipline problems, improved attitude toward scholastic activities, and improvement in the social relationships among students (Lawler, 2000; Olweus et al., 1999; USDHHS, 2001a). Other violence prevention programs target the members of the community.

Community

The Midwestern Prevention Project (MPP) is a primary prevention program and is an example of a broad-based community intervention program. It incorporates the mass media, educational systems, families, community, health care providers, and peer groups. The goal is to interrupt the pattern of addiction starting with tobacco use and progressing to alcohol use and abuse of other illegal substances. This prevention approach is multimodal, targeting students, parents, and community leaders in various domains. The drug abuse prevention message is transmitted in print and electronic media at least 31 times per year. The mass media campaign ranges from 15-second public service announcements to hour-long talk shows and continues for 5 years. Educational programs are offered to parents throughout the life of the program.

The program relies on support from the community to maintain the goal of drug use abstinence by youth. Communities support the ideals by refusing to sell drugs and alcohol to minors and offering activities that compete with the drug culture. The community also takes a lead in supporting community mental health centers for the treatment of drug abuse to decrease the demand for drugs. Law enforcement contributes to the program by controlling the supply side of the problem, diligently prosecuting merchants selling alcohol to underage children and drug dealers. Judges can mandate offenders to diversionary programs where they get treatment, maintain abstinence, or go to jail.

When Willie Sutton was asked why he robbed banks, he answered, "because that's where the money is." Schools are the appropriate location for drug prevention programs because that's where the children are. The school portion of the MPP begins in the sixth or seventh grade. Teachers, counselors, and peer mediators are trained and take leadership roles in the program. The students participate in 10 to 13 class sessions in the first year, with at least 5 booster sessions the following year. The sessions focus on peer pressure and drug refusal and decision-making skills. At school, the message is supported by taking every opportunity across the curriculum to educate students about the risks of drug abuse.

Families support the program by modeling responsible behavior and refusing to serve alcohol to minors on any occasion. Parents also learn to recognize the early warning signs of drug use among their children and ways to confront their children when they begin experimentation. The parents refuse to tolerate any substance use. They are encouraged to model responsible alcohol use. To learn these skills, parents participate in parenting classes twice a year focusing on discipline and communication skills.

The MPP was an effective prevention program for children and also had an impact on the behavior of the parents. It resulted in a 40% drop in daily cigarette smoking among the student participants and a similar reduction in parental drug use. This resulted in more positive parent–child communications and relations. The program also resulted in a reduction in the demand for drug treatment because fewer people in the community initiated drug use to begin with (Lawler, 2001; Pentz, Mihalic, & Grotpeter, 1998; USDHHS, 2001a). The MPP had an impact on individuals and the entire community.

INTERVENTION PROGRAMS

Intervention programs are synonymous with secondary prevention programs from the public health model previously discussed in the chapter. They are intended to interrupt behaviors that have already begun. They usually target particular groups of people who are either exhibiting the behavior or at risk for this dangerous behavior. There is a price paid by individuals participating in intervention rather than prevention programs because they are already in trouble. Some damage may already have been done. On the other hand, because intervention programs target specific individuals, families, students in school, and community members, they are more cost effective. Only the people in need of care participate in the program.

Individual

Some programs focus on the school environment, others on family functioning, others on internal and interpersonal processes. The Promoting Alternative Thinking Strategies (PATHS) program is an example of the last. This program is designed for implementation in schools for children in kindergarten to fifth grades. The goal of the PATHS program is to reduce violence and high-risk behaviors while increasing prosocial behaviors and improving peer relationships. The curriculum contains developmentally appropriate activities promoting emotional competency and increasing understanding of self and others.

The teacher gets support from the project staff and coordinator in teaching the PATHS curriculum in regular and special education classrooms. It is integrated into the daily assignments. The materials consisting of an instructor's manual and six volumes of lessons in three major units are shared with the parents in parent meetings. The first unit teaches self-control covered in 12 lessons. The second unit focuses on feelings and interpersonal relationships taught in 56 lessons. The third unit concentrates on teaching the 11 steps to problem solving in 33 lessons. A supplementary unit reviews the principles of the program in 30 additional lessons. There are five themes in the PATHS program: self-control, emotional understanding, positive self-esteem, interpersonal relationships, and problem-solving skills. One hundred thirty-one lessons are introduced over 5 years. Each lesson can last for up to five class meetings. The curriculum is based on a multimodal approach using direct instruction, pictures, role-plays, supplemental reading, and classroom discussions. Parents are notified about their child's progress through the mail. Homework assignments are designed to keep the parents involved with the curriculum and program goals. As a result of the program, participants significantly increased their ability to recognize and understand emotions and were better able to solve social problems and develop solutions. They also decreased aggressive or violent behavior. Teachers reported increased frustration tolerance and successful conflict resolution. In a 1-year follow-up study, the teachers reported that participants showed decreased sadness, increased self-esteem, decreased angry outbursts, decreased violence, and fewer conduct problems. The average cost of implementation of the program over a 3-year period was $15 to $45 per year per student (Greenberg, Kusché, & Mihalic, 1998; Lawler, 2000; USDHHS, 2001a).

Family

The Functional Family Therapy (FFT) program targets young people who have demonstrated delinquent, substance-abusing, or violent behavior. Other participants have been diagnosed with oppositional defiant disorder, conduct disorder, or other disruptive behaviors. The program aspires to change the participant's behavior by increasing protective factors and reducing risk factors. One or two therapists (counselors, nurses, social workers, or physicians) are assigned to the youths and their families. They deliver counseling and other services to the youths and their families in their homes, schools, and clinics. There are five phases to the FFT program: engagement, motivation, assessment, behavior change, and generalization.

In the engagement phase, the therapists establish a relationship with the youths and their families and are on the lookout for signs of premature termination. During the motivation phase, the therapists design interventions targeting maladaptive behaviors, emotions, and beliefs. They work to build a strong therapeutic alliance, trust, hope, and the change agenda. In the assessment phase, the therapists observe the family interactions and analyze the strengths and weaknesses in the family system. During the behavior change phase, the therapists focus on communication training, basic parenting skills, contracting for behavior change, and recognition of behavior costs and consequences. The final phase is the generalization phase, in which newly acquired skills are implemented into other domains of the participants' lives. The therapeutic team individualizes the program to meet the needs of each family and maintains the goal to make long-term positive gains.

The FFT program has been shown to make positive changes with children diagnosed with conduct, oppositional defiant, disruptive, and other behavior disorders. There was a significant reduction of substance abuse and violent delinquent behavior by the termination of the program. The participants were much less likely to commit crimes and to need further contact with social service organizations. Younger children in the family also benefited from the counseling services, with significant reduction of delinquent and substance abuse behaviors. The program costs approximately $1,350 to $3,750 for an average of 12 home visits. The costs are quickly offset when compared with the expense once a person enters the criminal justice system with the loss of future income. The FFT model has been used for over 28 years with thousands of families (Alexander et al., 1998; Lawler, 2000; USDHHS, 2001a).

School

The theoretical basis for school violence prevention programs assumes that violence occurs in a cultural context. Therefore, to decrease violence in schools, there must be changes in the school environment. It is presumed that there are characteristics of the culture that promote the use of violence to meet the wants and needs of students. These can include an attitude that is permissive and encouraging of the use of force to achieve goals. Just think for a moment of the cheers heard at football games. Words such as *fight*, *beat*, and *hit* predominate. This attitude does not exist only at schools. Many children are instructed by their parents to hit back if someone hits them first. Because of the rise in concern over school violence, schools have adopted a zero tolerance for violence. The driving force of zero tolerance is the belief that school violence occurs because the schools and communities have ignored warning signs that violence is imminent. There is a great deal of evidence demonstrating this; for example, the student perpetrators gave many clues regarding their intention to cause grievous harm but the signs were overlooked in Littleton, Colorado; Pearl, Mississippi; Paducah, Kentucky; and Springfield, Oregon.

Zero tolerance is a concept that became popular during "the war on drugs." This get-tough policy implies that strict rules will be applied without any excuses for major as well as minor infractions. Overapplication of the policy with resulting negative consequences to individuals is considered an acceptable price to pay for safety (Skiba & Knesting, 2002). Under this policy, students are suspended or expelled for any weapons violation, threat to others, or use or sale of drugs at school. The Gun-Free Schools Act of 1994 made zero tolerance a national policy. It has been applied in districts to include any object that may be used as a weapon. Students and their parents are informed of the consequences of violating school policy. Many parents believe that this policy is carried to an extreme. For example, as a result of this policy, a 5-year-old child was expelled for wearing a toy axe as part of a fireman's costume at a Halloween party at school (Skiba & Knesting, 2002).

States have also enacted laws making it a crime to bring weapons to school, resulting in suspension, expulsion, and arrest of offending students. Following the carnage of the 1980s and 1990s, this policy makes sense. Schools are caught in the dilemma of preventing violence through hypervigilance or repeating mistakes of the past by ignoring student threats. The courts have consistently upheld administrators' decisions to expel and discipline students bringing weapons to school, dealing or using drugs, or threatening other people (Skiba & Knesting, 2002; Yell & Rozalski, 2000). The controversy arises when administrators expel and suspend students for trivial offenses. An important research question is: Does zero tolerance reduce the risk of violence? Skiba and Knesting (2002) concluded that it does not. They believe that it might exacerbate student misbehavior and reduce student morale. This is supported by evidence in the case of Kip Kinkle, the school shooter near Springfield, Oregon. The day before he killed his parents and shot 24 people at school, Kip Kinkle was suspended and arrested for bringing a gun to school.

In many schools, the administrators ignore a certain amount of bullying and teasing because they perceive it as normal and harmless. In reality, experiencing bullying can have lasting negative effects on children. The person who is bullied may in turn become a bully, or the bullying may have lasting impact on his or her self-confidence and self-esteem (Ross, 1996). The Secret Service National Threat Assessment Center identified school shooting perpetrators as students who had a past history of having been the victim of bullying, persecution, threats, and injury from peers. They associated a past history of bullying with 66% of the school shooting incidents (Vossekuil et al., 2001). In addition, schools that promote antisocial behavior over prosocial behavior increase the risk of violence and other antisocial activities. In contrast, recognizing and rewarding prosocial actions increases the occurrence of this behavior and decreases antisocial activities (Mattaini & Lowery, 2000). Behaviorists have long been encouraging parents and teachers to catch children in the act of doing something right. However, children are often admonished, corrected, and punished as the main means of behavior control. Consequently, children can recite a litany of things that they are not supposed to do but are challenged to come up with things that they are *encouraged* to do. By changing the focus from punishment to praise, the focus changes from the negative to the positive. Mayer, Butterworth, Nafpaktitis, and Sulzer-Azaroff (1983) recommended written praise over spoken praise. They suggested that written notes praising students and parents are far more effective than spoken recognition. They used praise boards to recognize students' accomplishments on a daily or weekly basis. They found that merchants were willing to contribute to the program by issuing gift certificates as rewards for the students' accomplishments. This further builds a bridge from the school to the community. Community involvement has consistently been associated with effective school violence prevention and intervention programs (Lawler, 2000).

The Quantum Opportunities Program (QOP) is another example of a school-based violence intervention program. The QOP addresses the problem of violence intervention by increasing economic and educational opportunities for participants. This program targets specific groups of students. The goal of the QOP is to provide educational, social, and vocational opportunities to disadvantaged youth from the 9th through the 12th grades. The QOP provides an opportunity for 750 hours of education (computer instruction, tutoring for basic academic skills), service (community service, volunteering with agencies), and personal development activities (exposure to cultural activities, training in life skills, college planning, job preparation, and assistance with applications for scholarships). Approximately 20 students meet in each group with one adult throughout the year; the adult functions as a mentor, teacher, counselor, disciplinarian, and problem solver. Financial incentives are offered to the children for participating in the program. Results showed that there were substantial benefits for QOP participants. For example, they were more likely than the control group to graduate from high school (63% vs. 42%), more likely to attend college (42% vs. 16%), less likely to have children while in their teens (24% vs. 38%), and somewhat less likely to have been arrested (19% vs. 23%). The program costs $10,600 per participant over the 4 years and is considered cost beneficial because of reduced expenses for the criminal justice system and increased lifetime earnings by the participants because of their increased rate of high school graduation and secondary education (Lattimore, Mihalic, Grotpeter, & Taggart, 1998; Lawler, 2000; USDHHS, 2001a).

Community

The Multisystemic Therapy (MST) program is a community intervention program that has demonstrated effectiveness. It focuses on families, schools, and the community and targets violent, substance-abusing juvenile offenders from the ages of 12 to 17 years. The causes of the problems are viewed as stemming from the individual, family, and school factors, therefore the interventions encompass all of these domains. The strengths that naturally occur within these areas are assessed and supported to encourage positive change. The MST program addresses the issues faced by families raising adolescents and empowers the participating youths to deal with problems in the schools, families, and community. The purpose is to improve parental disciplinary practices, improve family communication and family relationships, and decrease the power of deviant peer relationships while improving the participants' social skills and social relationships. Another goal is to improve the participants' school and vocational performance. The program mobilizes the support networks within the extended family, neighbors, and friends to back up the goals of the family. The MST program is another home-based program. The therapists focus on skill building for parenting, family therapy, and cognitive–behavioral approaches. Special attention is paid to the social networks that contribute to delinquency and drug abuse. The therapists work to remove the barriers to support services each family receives every week. The program usually includes 60 hours of therapeutic contact over 4 months. The length of involvement is determined by the needs of the family and client.

The MST program has been shown to be effective with serious juvenile offenders and where many other interventions have failed. The program has shown long-term results, including 25% to 70% reduction in rearrests, improvement in family functioning, and decreased problems associated with mental health disorders. The average cost of the intervention per participant was $4,500. This program was determined to be the most cost-effective intervention for juvenile offenders (Henggler, Mihalic, Rone, Thomas, & Timmons-Mitchell, 1998).

ADAPTATIONS FOR DIVERSITY

Children living in large, inner-city, ethnically heterogeneous neighborhoods characterized by high-density, high-poverty homes that are dilapidated and generally run down are more likely to live surrounded by crime (Smith & Jarjoura, 1988). This describes most children attending large, inner-city schools. Ethnic heterogeneity is believed to cause an increase in crime because residents of diverse backgrounds are less likely to get to know each other and, therefore, are less likely to watch out for each other and their property (Taylor & Gottfredson, 1986). Children living in high-crime neighborhoods are at increased risk for victimization and for observation of crimes. Over 60% of inner-city youths have directly witnessed a shooting, and 50% have observed stabbings, with 60% of these resulting in deaths (Jenkins & Bell, 1994). The violent criminal activity in childhood is increased when children grow up in communities where the gangsters are the only ones with money and crime seems to pay. Children attending schools where they represent the ethnic minority are at much risk for violent victimization (U.S. Department of Justice, 1991). Therefore, school leaders should be sensitive to the need to protect children from each other. Administrators and teachers should be knowledgeable about diverse cultures and be sensitive to the needs of these children and their families. Schools must represent a safe haven for children from violence. Teachers and administrators must welcome students representing diverse backgrounds into the schools.

Each of the prevention and intervention programs described in this chapter was developed with the diverse ethnic, socioeconomic, and cultural makeup of the participants in mind. They were designed to include the input from the students, their families, faculty, administrators, and community members. Many began with a needs assessment. This is an important element because school violence has occurred at schools representing every type of community. Contrary to public expectations, the worst mass shootings have occurred at schools where there seemed to be few individual, family, or community indications of violence. Littleton, Pearl, Jonesboro, and Springfield are suburban, middle-class communities. The perpetrators were apparently affluent, White, male students. Because school violence perpetrators defy stereotypes, each violence prevention or intervention program must be designed with the diverse population of the school and community in mind.

SUMMARY

From 1983 until 1993, the United States was rocked by youth violence. The murder and suicide rates increased dramatically. In the years that followed, the unthinkable happened: Young men terrorized and murdered their classmates and teachers at school. Some of them began their killing sprees by murdering their parents. This explosion of violence caused students to fear for their lives while at school. These concerns have brought about many changes in the ways that schools operate.

Several programs have been initiated to prevent violence in the communities, homes, and schools. Schools have taken new security measures in an effort to help students feel safe. Administrators have also initiated zero tolerance policies to discourage students from making threats in and outside of school and have a plan to intervene when they do.

Experts on violence prevention have studied young violent offenders and have compiled lists of characteristics shared by the most violent. However, overreliance on these lists can result in false positives. Many prevention and intervention programs have been designed to address maladaptive behaviors. These programs address school climate, community environment, family issues, interpersonal relationships, and career and educational opportunities. All of the reviewed prevention and intervention programs demonstrated their effectiveness and were cost beneficial.

Youth violence is a complicated problem. Although there are no easy solutions to youth violence, there are prevention and intervention programs that work. Effective programs are comprehensive, coordinating individual, family, school, and community services. The programs are designed to last for an extended period of time. The implementation of these programs requires commitment from youth, families, schools, and communities. Online resources are available in Appendix 14-1.

To help students with their myriad of problems, schools should have full service counseling centers. Here, students in need of intervention can be assessed, treated, and when necessary, referred to other mental health professionals for the appropriate level of care. Parents and teachers should see themselves as partners, with similar goals to help every child achieve his or her full potential. Americans should never again mourn the loss of children to school violence.

REFERENCES

Alexander, J., Barton, C., Gordon, D., Grotpeter, J., Hansson, K., Harrison, R., et al. (1998). *Blueprints for violence prevention: Book 3. Functional Family Therapy.* Boulder, CO: Center for the Study and Prevention of Violence.

Astor, R., Mayer, H., & Behre, W. (1999). Unowned places and times: Maps and interviews about violence in high schools. *American Educational Research Journal, 36,* 3–42.

Baily, K. (2001). Legal implications of profiling students for violence. *Psychology in the Schools, 38,* 141–155

Batsche, G. M., & Knoff, H. M. (1994). Bullies and their victims: Understanding a pervasive problem in the schools. *School Psychology Review, 23,* 165–174.

Borduin, C. M., & Schaeffer, C. M. (1998). Violent offending in adolescence: Epidemiology, correlates, outcomes, and treatment. In T. P. Guillotta, G. R. Adams, & R. Montemayor (Eds.), *Delinquent violent youth: Theory and interventions* (pp. 144–174). Newbury Park, CA: Sage.

Centers for Disease Control and Prevention. (1991). *Attempted suicide among high school students, United States 1990.* Atlanta, GA: U.S. Department of Health and Human Services.

Centers for Disease Control and Prevention. (2006, June 9). Surveillance summaries. *Morbidity and Mortality Weekly Report, 55*(No. SS-5).

Center to Prevent Handgun Violence. (1990). *Caught in the crossfire: A report on gun violence in our nations schools.* Washington, DC: Author.

Chandras, K. (1999). Coping with adolescent school violence: Implications for counselors. *College Student Journal, 33,* 302–311.

Cook, P., & Laub, J. H. (1998). The unprecedented epidemic in youth violence. In M. Yonry & M. H. Moore (Eds.), *Youth violence, crime and justice: A review of research* (Vol. 24, pp. 27–64). Chicago: University of Chicago Press.

Dahlberg, L. L. (1998). Youth violence in the United States: Major trends, risk factors, and prevention approaches. *American Journal of Preventive Medicine, 14,* 259–272.

Derzon, J. (2006). How effective are school-based violence prevention programs in preventing and reducing violence and other antisocial behaviors? A meta-analysis. In S. Jimerson & M. Furlong (Eds.), *The handbook of school violence and school safety* (pp. 429–441). Mahwah, NJ: Erlbaum.

DeVoe, J. F., Peter, K., Noonan, M., Snyder, T. D., & Baum, K. (2005). *Indicators of school crime and safety, 2005* (NCES 2006-001/NCJ 210697). Washington, DC: U.S. Government Printing Office.

Dowling, C., & Johnson, L. (1998, July). High school heroes. *Life, 21*(8), 52–62.

Dwyer K., Osher, D., & Warger, C. (1998). *Early warning, timely response: A guide to safe schools.* Washington, DC: U.S. Department of Education.

Elliott, D. S. (1998). Editor's introduction. In D. S. Elliott (Ed.), *Blueprints for violence prevention: Book 8. Multisensorial treatment foster care.* Boulder, CO: Center for the Study and Prevention of Violence

Elliott, D., Hamburg, B., & Williams, K. (1998). *Violence in American schools.* Cambridge, England: Cambridge University Press.

Finn, A., & Remley, T. P. (2002). Prevention of school violence: A school and community response. In D. Rea & J. Bergin (Eds.), *Safeguarding our youth: Successful school and community programs* (pp. 19–27). New York: McGraw-Hill.

Flannery, D., Singer, M., & Wester, K. (2001). Violence exposure, psychological trauma, and suicide risk in a community sample of dangerously violent adolescents. *Journal of the American Academy of Child and Adolescent Psychiatry, 40,* 435–442.

Furlong, M., Morrison, G., Skiba, R., & Cornell, D. (2004). Methodological and measurement issues in school violence research: Moving beyond the social problem era. In M. Furlong, G. Morrison, R. Skiba, & D. Cornell (Eds.), *Issues in school violence research* (pp. 5–12). Binghampton, NY: Haworth Press.

Furlong, M., Sharma, B., & Rhee, S. (2000). Defining school violence victim subtypes: A step toward adapting prevention and intervention programs to match student needs. In D. Sandhu & C. Aspy (Eds.), *Violence in American schools: A practical guide for counselors* (pp. 67–87). Alexandria, VA: American Counseling Association.

Futrell, M. (1996). Violence in the classroom: A teacher's perspective. In A. Hoffman (Ed.), *Schools, violence, and society* (pp. 3–19). Westport, CT: Praeger.

Gibbs, N., & Roche, T. (1999, December 20). The Columbine tapes. *Time,* 40–60.

Greenberg, M. T., Kusché, C., & Mihalic, S. F. (1998). *Blueprints for violence prevention: Book 10. Promoting Alternative Thinking Strategies (PATHS).* Boulder, CO: Center for the Study and Prevention of Violence.

Henggler, S. W., Mihalic, S. F., Rone, L., Thomas, C., & Timmons-Mitchell, J. (1998). *Blueprints for violence prevention: Book 6. Multisystemic Therapy.* Boulder, CO: Center for the Study and Prevention of Violence.

Henry, D., Farrell, A., & The Multisite Violence Prevention Project. (2004). Design of the Multisite Violence Prevention Project. *American Journal of Preventive Medicine, 26,* 12–19.

Hermann, M., & Finn, A. (2002). An ethical and legal perspective on the role of school counselors in preventing violence in schools. *Professional School Counseling, 6,* 46–54.

Herrenkohl, T., Maguin, E., Hill, K., Hawkins, D., Abbott, R., & Catalono, R. (2000). Developmental risk factors for youth violence. *Journal of Adolescent Health, 26,* 176–186.

Illinois Center for Violence Prevention. (1998). *Fact sheets: Cost of violence.* Chicago: Author

James, R., & Gilliland, B. (2000). *Crisis intervention strategies* (4th ed.). Belmont, CA: Brooks/Cole.

Jenkins, E. J., & Bell, C. C. (1994). Violence among inner city high school students and post-traumatic stress disorder. In S. Freidman (Ed.), *Anxiety disorders in African Americans* (pp. 76–78). New York: Springer.

Kann, L., Warren, C. W., Harris, W. A., Collins, J. L., Douglas, K. A., Collins, M. E., et al. (1995). Youth Risk Behavior Surveillance—United States, 1993. *Morbidity and Mortality Weekly Report, 44,* 1–56.

Kashani, J., Jones, M., Bumby, K., & Thomas, L. (1999). Youth violence: Psychosocial risk factors, treatment, prevention, and recommendations. *Journal of Emotional and Behavioral Disorders, 7,* 200–211.

Kaufman, P., Chen, X., Choy, S. P., Peter, K., Ruddy, S. A., Miller, A. K., et al. (2001). *Indicators of school crime and safety, 2001* (NCES 2002-113/NCJ-190075). Washington, DC: U.S. Departments of Education and Justice.

Kemper, P. (1993, Fall). Disarming youth. *California School Boards Journal,* 25–33.

Kesey, K. (1998, July 9). Land of the free, home of the bullets. *Rolling Stone,* 51–55.

King, P., & Murr, A. (1998, June 1). A son who spun out of control. *Newsweek,* 32–33.

Lattimore, C. B., Mihalic, S. F., Grotpeter, J. K., & Taggart, R. (1998). *Blueprints for violence prevention: Book 4. The Quantum Opportunities Program.* Boulder, CO: Center for the Study and Prevention of Violence.

Lawler, M. (2000). School-based violence prevention programs: What works? In D. Sandhu & C. Aspy (Eds.), *Violence in American schools: A practical guide for counselors* (pp. 247–266). Alexandria, VA: American Counseling Association.

Lumsden, L. (2000). Profiling students for violence. *ERIC Digest, 139.* (ERIC Document Reproduction Service No. ED446344)

Mattaini, M., & Lowery, C. (2000). Constructing cultures of peace and nonviolence: The PEACE POWER! Toolkit. In D. Sandhu & C. Aspy (Eds.), *Violence in American schools: A practical guide for counselors* (pp. 123–138). Alexandria, VA: American Counseling Association.

Mayer, G. R., Butterworth, T., Nafpaktitis, M., & Sulzer-Azaroff, B. (1983). Preventing school vandalism and improving school discipline: A three year study. *Journal of Applied Behavior Analysis, 16,* 135–146.

Mendel, R. A. (2000). *Less hype, more help: Reducing juvenile crime; what works—and what doesn't.* Washington, DC: American Youth Policy Forum.

Mercy, J., & Rosenberg, M. (1998). Preventing firearm violence in and around schools. In D. Elliott, B. Hamburg, & K. Williams (Eds.), *Violence in American schools* (pp. 159–187). Cambridge, England: Cambridge University Press.

Mulvey, E., & Cauffman, E. (2001). The inherent limits of predicting school violence. *American Psychologist, 56,* 797–802.

Nation, M., Crusto, C., Wandersman, A., Kumpfer, K., Seybolt, D., Morrissey-Kane, E., & Davino, K. (2003). What works in prevention. *American Psychologist, 58,* 449–456.

National Center for Education Statistics. (2003). *Violence in US public schools: 2000 school survey on crime and safety* (Statistical analysis report, NCE-2004-314). Washington, DC: Author.

National School Safety Center. (1990). *Weapons in schools* (NSSC resource paper). Malibu, CA: Author.

Olds, D., Hill, P., Mihalic, S., & O'Brien, R. (1998). *Blueprints for violence prevention: Book 7: Prenatal and home visitation by nurses.* Boulder, CO: Center for Study and Prevention of Violence.

Olweus, D. (1994). Bullying at school: Long term outcomes for the victims and an effective school based intervention program. In H. Rowell (Ed.), *Aggressive behavior: Current behavior* (pp. 97–130). New York: Plenum Press.

Olweus, D. (1997). Tackling peer victimization. In D. P. Fry & K. Bjoerkqvist (Eds.), *Cultural variation in conflict resolution: Alternatives to violence* (pp. 215–231). Mahwah, NJ: Erlbaum.

Olweus, D., Limber, S., & Mihalic, S. F. (1999). *Blueprints for violence prevention: Book 9. Bullying Prevention Program.* Boulder, CO: Center for the Study and Prevention of Violence.

O'Toole, M. E., & The Critical Incident Response Group. (2000). *The school shooter: A threat assessment prospective.* Quantico, VA: Federal Bureau of Investigation.

Pentz, M. A., Mihalic, S. F., & Grotpeter, J. K. (1998). *Blueprints for violence prevention: Book 1: The Midwestern Prevention Project.* Boulder, CO: Center for the Study and Prevention of Violence.

Ross, D. (1996). *Childhood bullying and teasing: What school personnel, other professionals, and parents can do.* Alexandria, VA: American Counseling Association.

School Safety Council. (1989). *Weapons in schools.* Washington, DC: U.S. Department of Justice.

Shafii, M., & Shafii, S. L. (2001). *School violence: Assessment, management, and prevention.* Washington, DC: American Psychiatric Association.

Skiba, R., & Knesting, K. (2002). Zero tolerance, zero evidence: An analysis of school disciplinary practice. In R. Skiba & G. Noam (Eds.), *Zero tolerance: Can suspension and expulsion keep schools safe?* (pp. 17–43). San Francisco: Jossey-Bass.

Smith, D., & Jarjoura, G. R. (1988). Social structure and criminal victimization. *Journal of Research in Crime and Delinquency, 25,* 27–52.

Sullivan, R. (1998, October 1). A boy's life. *Rolling Stone,* 46–54.

Taylor, R., & Gottfredson, J. (1986). Environmental design, crime, and prevention: An examination of community dynamics. In A. J. Reiss Jr. & M. Tony (Eds.), *Communities and crime* (pp. 244–262). Chicago: University of Chicago Press.

Trump, K. (1997). Security policy, personnel, and operations. In A. Goldstein & J. Close (Eds.), *School violence intervention: A practical handbook* (pp. 265–289). New York: Guilford Press.

U.S. Department of Education. (2004). *Crime and safety in America's public schools: Selected findings from the School Survey on Crime and Safety.* Washington, DC: Author.

U.S. Department of Health and Human Services. (2001a). *Youth violence: A report of the Surgeon General.* Rockville, MD: U.S. Department of Health and Human Services, Centers for Disease Control and Prevention, National Center for Injury Prevention and Control; Substance Abuse and Mental Health Services Administration, Center for Mental Health Services; and National Institutes of Health, National Institute of Mental Health.

U.S. Department of Health and Human Services. (2001b). Youth violence: A report of the Surgeon General: Executive summary. *American Journal of Health Education, 32,* 169–174.

U.S. Department of Justice, Bureau of Justice Statistics. (1991). *School crime: A national victimization survey report.* Washington, DC: U.S. Government Printing Office.

Vossekuil, B., Reddy, M., & Fein, R. (2001). The Secret Service safe school initiative. *Education Digest, 66*(6), 4–11.

Vossekuil, B., Reddy, M., Fein, R., Borum, R., & Modzeleski, W. (2000). *U.S.S.S. safe school initiative: An interim report on the prevention of targeted violence in schools.* Washington, DC: U.S. Secret Service, National Threat Assessment Center.

Washington State Institute for Public Policy. (1999). *The comparative costs and benefits of programs to reduce crime.* Olympia, WA: Author

Yell, M., & Rozalski, M. (2000). Searching for safe schools: Legal issues in the prevention of school violence. *Journal of Emotional and Behavioral Disorders, 8,* 187–197.

APPENDIX 14-1

Online Resources

American School Counseling Association School Shooting Resource Page
http://www.schoolcounselor.org/content.asp?contentid=496

Center for the Prevention of School Violence
http://www.ncdjjdp.org/cpsv/

Early Warning, Timely Response: A Guide to Safe Schools
http://www.ed.gov/about/offices/list/osers/osep/gtss.html

Facing Fear: Helping Young People Deal With Terrorism and Tragic Events
http://www.redcross.org/article/0,1072,0_332_1005,00.html

Kid Peace—School Shooting Prevention Tips
http://www.kidspeace.org/SchoolShootingPreventionTips.htm

Knowledge Path: Adolescent Violence Prevention
http://www.ed.gov/about/offices/list/osers/osep/gtss.html

National Alliance for Safe Schools
http://mentalhealth.samhsa.gov/_scripts/redirect.asp?ID=587

National Association of School Psychologists—Crisis Response
http://www.nasponline.org/NEAT/crisismain.html#general

National Education Association Safe Schools Now
http://www.nea.org/schoolsafety/index.html

National Youth Violence Prevention Campaign
http://www.violencepreventionweek.org/

Safe and Healthy Schools: Practical Prevention Strategies
http://www.schoolcounselor.org/store_product.asp?prodid=177

Safe Schools Healthy Students
  http://www.Sschs.samsha.gov

University of Minnesota Extension—Talk to Children About Shootings
  http://www.extension.umn.edu/extensionnews/1999/JP1084.html

CHAPTER 15

■

"I Can't Live Without It": Adolescent Substance Abuse

Camea J. Gagliardi-Blea, Dana J. Weber,
Crystal Rofkahr, and Sharon E. Robinson Kurpius

Adolescents use substances for a variety of reasons, including excitement or thrill-seeking, consolation or escape, fitting in, and rebellion. Indeed, use of psychoactive substances is common for adolescents. In 2005, an estimated 19.7 million Americans 12 years or older were current (past-month) illicit drug users. This estimate represents 8.1% of the population ages 12 or older (Substance Abuse and Mental Health Services Administration, 2006). The broad spectrum of negative consequences that adolescents experience related to substance use includes increased risk of serious drug use later in life, school failure, poor judgment (which puts adolescents at increased risk for traffic accidents), violence, unsafe sex, pregnancy, and suicide. The substance use problem among adolescents remains unsolved. The increases in prevalence of tobacco use, hazardous alcohol use, and most illicit drug use seen throughout much of the 1990s have remained steady and high throughout the early 2000s (Johnston, O'Malley, & Bachman, 2006). Interventions are not uniformly effective, although interventions focusing on the adolescents' social environment hold considerable promise (Fisher, Stafford, Maynard-Reid, & Parkerson, 2005), and family-based interventions with a developmental orientation are widely recognized as the most effective approaches for adolescent substance abuse (National Institute on Drug Abuse [NIDA], 2002; Rowe & Liddle, 2003; Williams & Chang, 2000).

Current evidence suggests that self-report measures of substance use by adolescents are typically reliable and stable, with lifetime use being highest among alcohol users and lowest for cigarette and marijuana users (Shillington & Clapp, 2000). The NIDA has supported the Monitoring the Future (2005) national school-based survey that provides data on drug use among 8th, 10th, and 12th graders, as well as three attitudinal indicators related to drug use. The MTF survey reported the following trends: High rates of drug use continued at all grade levels, and illicit drug use among 8th, 10th, and 12th graders remained stable or decreased in some cases across a 4-year period. Although marijuana use remained stable, there were small reductions in cigarette smoking at all three grades, and the increased ecstasy use reported in 2000 significantly decreased among 12th graders. According to the 2005 MTF study, 3.1% of 8th graders, 4.1% of 10th graders, and 4.5% of 12th graders reported lifetime use of methamphetamine (Office of National Drug Control Policy, 2006).

Adolescent substance abuse often results in harm to youth, their families, communities, and society as a whole. According to the U.S. Department of Health and Human Services (2002) statistics, drug abuse and alcohol abuse contribute to the death of more than 120,000 Americans and cost taxpayers more than $143 billion every year in preventable health care costs, lost productivity, automobile crashes, law enforcement, and crime. More specifically, alcohol use is associated with over half of all murders and rapes in the United States and is a factor in 40% of all violent crimes as about 20,000 crimes involved alcohol or other drugs (Inaba & Cohen, 2000). Although the yearly estimated costs of health care, lost productivity, and legal and social support systems are extreme, monetary amounts do not describe the emotional, social, and psychological costs to families and communities.

PROBLEM DEFINITION

In addressing the issue of adolescent substance use, several questions are raised. First, what drugs are currently being used and abused? Second, what psychosocial factors influence adolescent substance use and abuse? Third, what types of prevention and intervention strategies can be implemented for adolescents and their families? Fourth, what adaptations need to be made for cultural differences in the prevention and intervention of adolescent substance abuse?

The first step in understanding substance use and abuse issues is to contextualize the discussion of these concerns. As such, we provide a description of the physiological mechanisms of drug use, followed by a summary of drugs commonly used by adolescents. Next, we present a discussion of the psychosocial risk and protective factors related to adolescent substance use. Finally, prevention and intervention strategies for educators, counselors, parents, and families are highlighted within the systemic contexts of schools, families, and communities.

Two assumptions need to be made explicit in the discussion on drug use. Specifically, drugs are not inherently good or bad. Instead, it is the attributes of who is taking drugs, for what purposes, when and where the drugs are taken, and how much and how frequently drugs are taken that influence value judgments regarding certain chemical substances (Gagliardi & Lambert, 2005). For example, an adult having a glass of wine or a beer after work might be considered relatively benign, whereas an adolescent having a glass of wine or a beer after school might be viewed as at-risk behavior for substance abuse. Despite a plethora of literature differentiating use and abuse, such a distinction may be disputable given that *any* use by adolescents is considered illegal given age restrictions on tobacco and alcohol use. As such, it may be considered as a form of abuse. It is the premise of this chapter that psychosocial, cultural, and contextual differences are helpful to understanding adolescent drug use and abuse.

PSYCHOPHYSIOLOGY OF DRUGS

Drug Phases

The psychophysiology of different drugs varies from drug to drug and from individual to individual; however, *all* drugs go through a series of phases:

Phase 1: *Absorption of the drug into the body* (see Table 15-1).

Phase 2: *Transport of the drug.* The drug is transported via the bloodstream to the part of the body where it will exert its effect.

Phase 3: *Action of the drug.* An effect or action of the drug depends on the type, potency, and purity of the drug, the contaminant or ingredient (e.g., baby powder) used to cut the drug, the personality and physiology of the user, and the social environment in which the drug is taken.

Phase 4: *Excretion of the drug.* When the body metabolizes the drug, its action is stopped and the drug is excreted from the body.

The Nervous System

The nervous system is made up of the central nervous system (CNS) and the peripheral nervous system (PNS; Figure 15-1). Comprising the brain and the spinal cord, the CNS is responsible for interpreting and acting on body sensations. The PNS comprises various nerve processes that connect the CNS with receptors, muscles, and glands. The PNS is often subdivided into the somatic nervous system and the autonomic nervous system.

The somatic nervous system interfaces with the CNS to control voluntary muscular actions such as arm and leg movements. In contrast, the autonomic nervous system controls involuntary body actions such as heart rate, digestion, and breathing. The autonomic nervous system, comprising the sympathetic and parasympathetic nervous systems, stimulates or inhibits an organ's activities.

Drugs influence specific structures of the brain that are responsible for particular thoughts and behaviors (see Figure 15-2). For instance, the cerebral cortex controls reasoning, language, and sensory discrimination. The hypothalamus is involved in eating, drinking, temperature, and sex drive, whereas the limbic system is involved in emotions, physical activity, and memory. Further, the medial forebrain bundle is known as the pleasure center, the brainstem controls respiration and vomiting, and the medulla oblongata is involved in aggression (Carlson, 2001).

Chemical messengers that carry information throughout the nervous system can be classified as either hormones or neurotransmitters. Although drugs can

Table 15-1

■

Absorption of the Drug Into the Body (Phase 1)

Method of Drug Ingestion	Entry Into the Blood Steam	Examples of Drugs
Swallowed or taken orally (the most common method)	Absorbed through the intestinal walls	Alcohol, tranquilizers, and stimulants
Smoked or inhaled	Absorbed through the lungs	Marijuana, nicotine, and inhalants
Snorted	Absorbed through the mucous membranes	Cocaine and crank
Injected into a vein (mainlining) or under the skin (skin-popping)	Shot directly into the blood stream	Heroin

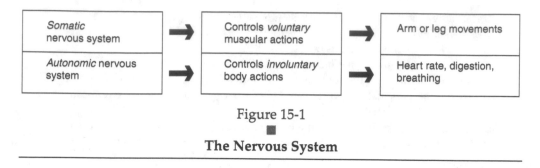

Figure 15-1
■
The Nervous System

influence the release of hormones by a gland into the blood, their major impact is on neurotransmitters, chemicals released by nerve cells throughout the CNS. Neurotransmitters influence the transmission of nerve impulses from one nerve cell to another. The major neurotransmitters that interact with psychoactive substances are acetylcholine, dopamine, norepinephrine, serotonin, gamma-aminobutryic acid (GABA), and endorphins. The influence of different drugs on neurotransmitters varies, and the exact process of influence continues to be explored (Carlson, 2001).

Behaviors are influenced when drugs excite, inhibit, or block the actions of neurotransmitters. For instance, cocaine is believed to block a nerve cell's reuptake of norepinephrine and dopamine in areas such as the medial forebrain bundle, resulting in a feeling of euphoria for an extended time (Figure 15-3). In contrast, tranquilizers block the reuptake of dopamine in the basal ganglia, resulting in muscle relaxation. Tranquilizer abuse, however, can result in muscle rigidity. Influencing

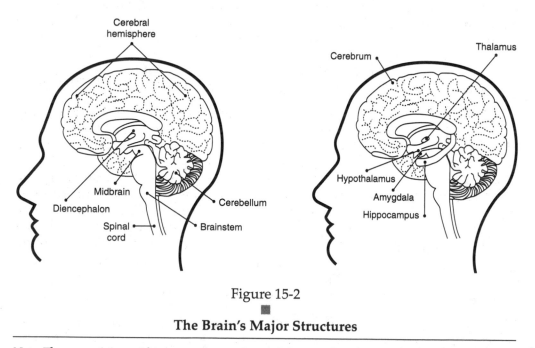

Figure 15-2
■
The Brain's Major Structures

Note: The amygdala and hippocampus are located deep within the brain and are shown in approximate areas in which they are located. From *Mind Over Matter: The Brain's Response to Drugs,* by the National Institute on Drug Abuse, 2000. In the public domain.

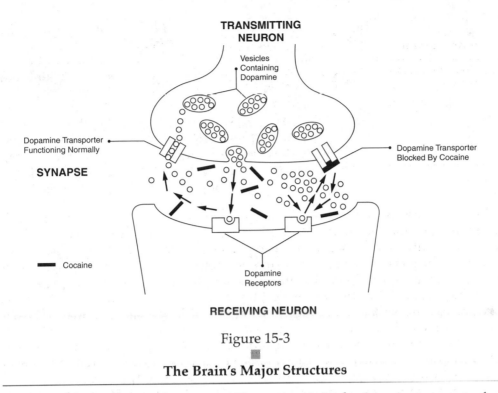

TRANSMITTING
NEURON

Figure 15-3

■

The Brain's Major Structures

Note: A picture of cocaine in the synapses. The cocaine blocks the dopamine transporter from pumping dopamine back into the transmitting neuron. The synapse is flooded with dopamine, which intensifies and prolongs the stimulation of receiving neurons in the brain's pleasure circuits, resulting in a cocaine "high." From *Mind Over Matter: The Brain's Response to Drugs,* by the National Institute on Drug Abuse, 2000. In the public domain.

the neurotransmitters in the medulla oblongata, PCP or angel dust can result in violent and bizarre aggressive behaviors.

Although research on the interaction of neurotransmitters, drugs, and behavior is just beginning to uncover these complex relationships, it is clear that psychoactive drugs affect the body's chemical pathways. When drugs are abused, overused, or combined, the effects can be dangerous or even deadly. For example, combining alcohol with sedatives, barbiturates, or tranquilizers may result in respiratory failure. Drugs interfere with the normal functioning of the nervous system and other body organs. The decision to use drugs should thus be considered with caution and information. All drug users, particularly adolescents, must be aware that research has not yet fully discovered the many physiological or psychological side effects of drug use.

UNDERSTANDING DRUGS AND THEIR EFFECTS

The best predictor of drug abuse in adolescents is early age of onset of experimental use. Adolescents who used substances before sixth grade were found to have poorer decision-making skills, more susceptibility to peer pressure, more negative perceptions of school, and less confidence in their skills than adolescents who did not use by the end of sixth grade (Sobeck, Abbey, Agius, Clinton, & Harrison, 2000).

Adolescents report use of many illicit drugs, including amphetamines (e.g., black beauties and white bennies), methamphetamines (i.e., meth, chalk, speed, crank, crystal, ice, fire, and glass), cocaine (i.e., coke, snow, nose candy, flake, blow, big C, lady, white, and snowbirds), heroin (i.e., smack, horse, brown sugar, junk, big H, and dope), phencyclidine (i.e., PCP, ozone, wack, rocket fuel, and angel dust), lysergic acid diethylamide (i.e., LSD, dots, zen, loony toons, battery acid, and superman), and ecstasy (i.e., X, E, XTC, eccy, and love drug). Although not illegal, adolescents can also easily access chemicals such as diet pills, over-the-counter stimulants (e.g., NoDoz), coffee, or buzz beans (i.e., chocolate-covered coffee beans). For purposes of this review, however, only alcohol, nicotine, marijuana, inhalants, methamphetamine, and the nonmedical use of prescription-type pain relievers, tranquilizers, stimulants, and sedatives are reviewed in depth.

Alcohol

In the United States, the most commonly used drugs are beer and wine. In 2005, slightly more than half (51.8%, or 126 million people) of Americans ages 12 or older reported being current drinkers of alcohol (Substance Abuse and Mental Health Services Administration, 2006). Nearly 7.2 million respondents (18.8%) were binge drinkers and 2.3 million (6.0%) were heavy drinkers (Substance Abuse and Mental Health Services Administration, 2005). Compared with females, males ages 12 to 20 reported more current alcohol use (27.5% vs. 28.9%, respectively), binge drinking (16.1% vs. 21.3%), and heavy drinking (4.3% vs. 7.6%; Substance Abuse and Mental Health Services Administration, 2006). According to NIDA (2000), more than 70% of 8th graders perceive alcoholic beverages as "fairly easy" or "very easy" to get, and 30% of 12th graders, 26.2% of 10th graders, and 14.1% of 8th graders reported binge drinking (5+ drinks in a row) in the 2 weeks prior to the survey.

Found in all alcoholic beverages, ethanol acts as a depressant on the CNS. When an individual's blood alcohol level (BAL) is .04% (usually after one or two alcoholic beverages), the cerebral cortex becomes less efficient such that he or she will have decreased alertness, relaxed inhibition, impaired judgment, increased heart rate, and a general sense of feeling good. As a person's BAL increases, judgment ability declines, reaction time is slowed, and both sensory and motor capabilities are impaired. Most states define drunkenness at a BAL of .10. The vomiting reflex (controlled by the brainstem) can be activated at .12% BAL. Intoxication is officially reached at .20 BAL, a stupor at .30 BAL, and .35 BAL is the minimal level that can result in respiratory failure and death. Alcohol causes lower levels of blood flowing to the brain, thus decreasing oxygen levels as well as nutrient and waste removal.

Alcohol-related changes in cortical functions can also result in behavioral changes. The more rapid the intake of alcohol, the greater the behavioral changes as one becomes less inhibited. Withdrawal symptoms for adolescents who have been heavy alcohol users can include tremors, perspiring, agitation, disorientation, and brief seizures. With prolonged abuse, gastritis with hemorrhaging and inflammation of the pancreas can result. Bleeding, severe vomiting, and changes in the blood necessitate hospitalization. Chronic heavy drinking can increase one's risk for certain cancers including liver, throat, esophagus, and larynx. Additionally, over an extended period, excessive alcohol consumption can cause liver cirrhosis, immune system complications, brain damage, and harm to the fetus during pregnancy (National Institute on Alcohol Abuse and Alcoholism, 2001). Lifetime prevalence of alcohol use is 79.7% for high school seniors, 70.1% for 10th graders, and 50.5% for 8th graders (NIDA, 2000).

Nicotine

Nicotine, the primary active ingredient in tobacco, is ingested through cigarettes, cigars, pipes, and smokeless tobacco (i.e., chew). The most popular method of ingesting nicotine is by smoking. Adolescent girls are more frequent users of cigarettes, whereas adolescent boys are more likely to use smokeless tobacco.

The pharmacological and behavioral processes that determine physiological tobacco addiction are complex because nicotine acts as both a stimulant and sedative to the CNS. Specifically, nicotine results in a rapid and evenly absorbed distribution or "kick" because of the sudden release of epinephrine, which stimulates the CNS to release glucose for energy. After the glucose is used by the body, a period of low energy leads the user to use more nicotine (NIDA, 2006a). When nicotine is absorbed, it is carried on droplets of tar (Inaba & Cohen, 2000), which can vary from 7 mg for a low-tar cigarette to 15 mg for a regular cigarette. The half-life of nicotine is 2 hours; however, regular smoking results in an accumulation of nicotine in the body. Thus, daily smokers are exposed to the effects of nicotine 24 hours a day (NIDA, 2006a).

Smokers have increased heart rates because the carbon monoxide in cigarette smoke causes them to lose 15% of the oxygen-carrying capacity of their blood. Furthermore, decreased blood flow (and oxygen) to the skin results in smokers appearing older than nonsmokers. Smoking also makes artery walls less flexible, increasing the risk and severity of hardening of the arteries. Smokers have a higher expectancy rate of lung cancer, emphysema, and bronchial disorders (NIDA, 2006a). The negative health effect of second-hand or sidestream smoke is also a concern, particularly for nonsmokers. Nonsmoking spouses have a higher rate of lung cancer than do spouses of nonsmokers, and young children and infants exposed to second-hand smoke have more respiratory and asthma problems (Inaba & Cohen, 2000).

Use of cigarettes by teenagers in the United States has decreased since 1996, paralleling an attitudinal shift against smoking (NIDA, 2000), a trend that continued in 2005. Nevertheless, the prevalence rate of adolescents who smoke remains high, and adolescents who smoke have higher rates of alcohol use and other drug use, particularly marijuana use.

Marijuana

The most widely used illegal drug in the United States, marijuana is generally the first illegal drug that adolescents use. From 1999 through 2004, marijuana use remained stable for 10th and 12th graders, although 8th graders made a significant decrease in use. NIDA (2006c) reported past-year marijuana use as 32.2% for 10th graders and 15.6% for 8th graders.

Consisting of dried, shredded flowers and leaves of the hemp plant, the mind-altering psychoactive effect of marijuana is achieved from the chemical delta-9-tetrahydrocannabinol (THC). Currently, there are over 200 slang terms for marijuana (i.e., pot, weed, reefer, herb, grass, dope, ganja, maryjane, and hash). Marijuana is generally smoked as a cigarette (i.e., joint or nail) or in a pipe or bong. Blunts or cigars that have been emptied of tobacco and filled with marijuana are also used. There are various grades or types of marijuana, including sensimilla, containing as much as 8% THC, and hashish, containing up to 50% THC. Marijuana sold on the street is estimated to contain between 2% and 5% THC.

When marijuana is smoked, THC is rapidly absorbed into the blood. Although marijuana creates a sedative, dreamy high, it alters the metabolization of serotonin and dopamine. Further, the long half-life of marijuana means that daily smokers may be continually high as it is never out of the body's system. Heavy marijuana smoking has also been linked to the amotivational syndrome of lethargy and decreased motivation in adolescents. In particular, adolescents who use marijuana before or during the school day impair their desire and ability to learn. According to the National Household Survey on Drug Abuse (Substance Abuse and Mental Health Services Administration, 2002), adolescents with an average grade of D or below were more than four times as likely to have used marijuana in the past year than were adolescents who reported an average grade of A. Many of the effects of smoking marijuana are similar to those of drinking alcohol, including lowered secretions of sex hormones; impaired motor coordination, reaction time, and sensory perception; and decreased ability to follow moving objects. With poorer motor coordination and distorted time/distance perceptions, those who drive under the influence of marijuana have the same safety risks as those who drive under the influence of alcohol.

There is an increasing belief that marijuana smoke affects the lungs in a manner similar to tobacco smoke. Chronic smoking of marijuana impairs airflow in the lungs and is more likely to produce daily coughs, symptoms of bronchitis, and more frequent chest colds (NIDA, 2006c). As users inhale more deeply to hold marijuana smoke in their lungs, the amounts of tar and carbon monoxide are three to five times greater than for tobacco smokers (NIDA, 2006c). Only long-term research will be able to verify the relationship between marijuana smoking and cancer.

Inhalants

Inhalants are ordinary household products that are inhaled or sniffed by children to get high. Inhalants include solvents, gases, and nitrites. Solvents are household substances such as paint thinner, degreasers, gasoline, glue, and office supply substances such as correction fluids or felt-tip markers. Gases include butane lighters, whip cream dispensers (i.e., whippets), spray paint, hair spray, and medical anesthetic gases (e.g., ether, chloroform, and nitrous oxide). In 2004, according to the National Survey on Drug Use and Health (Substance Abuse and Mental Health Services Administration, 2005), 1.2% of minors ages 12 to 17 were using inhalants (NIDA, 2006b). Moreover, according to the 2005 MTF survey, 17.1% of 8th graders, 13.1% of 10th graders, and 11.4% of 12th graders reported lifetime (i.e., at least once in their lives) use of inhalants. From 2002 to 2005, based on survey responses, there was a significant increase in 8th graders' annual abuse of inhalants from 7.7% to 9.5%.

Inhalants contain volatile hydrocarbons that cause a strong short-lived, euphoric high. Inhaled through the nose or mouth (i.e., huffing), inhalants can cause intoxicating effects that last only a few minutes or several hours when ingested repeatedly (NIDA, 2006b). Symptoms of inhalant use are similar to those of alcohol use, including lack of coordination, restlessness, confusion, disorientation, difficulty walking, and delirium. One-time use of inhalants can cause death by acute intoxication as oxygen is displaced in the lungs, which is a particular concern in light of the fact that one in five eighth-grade students reported using inhalants at least once in their lives (NIDA, 2006b). Further, sudden sniffing death can occur when excessive exercise and stress immediately follow inhalant abuse. Although adolescents may enjoy the giddy high associated with sniffing, chronic use of inhalants can result in hearing loss (from paint sprays and glues), limb spasms (from glues, gasoline, and whipping cream dispensers), brain damage (from paint sprays and glues), and bone marrow damage (from gasoline; NIDA, 2006b).

Methamphetamines

Methamphetamine is a psychologically addictive stimulant drug. Although chemically similar to amphetamine, methamphetamine has longer lasting and more toxic effects on the CNS (NIDA, 2006d). The drug releases high levels of the neurotransmitter dopamine, which stimulates brain cells, often resulting in euphoria, wakefulness, increased libido, and inhibited pain. Other side effects of the drug include irritability, aggressiveness, tremors, convulsions, anxiety, paranoia, repetitive behaviors, jaw clenching, tooth decay ("meth mouth"), hyperthermia, increased heart rate and blood pressure, and increased metabolism (NIDA, 2006d). Chronic, long-term use of methamphetamine can lead to psychotic behavior (e.g., auditory hallucinations, mood disturbances, and delusions), anhedonia, kidney damage, liver damage, anorexia, insomnia, and strokes (NIDA, 2006d). Methamphetamine also damages brain cells that contain the neurotransmitters dopamine and serotonin. Although "dopamine- and serotonin-containing neurons do not die after methamphetamine use, their nerve endings are cut back and re-growth is limited" (NIDA, 2006d). The damage to the brain caused by methamphetamine use reflects the damage caused by Alzheimer's disease, stroke, and epilepsy (NIDA, 2006d).

Illicit methamphetamine comes in a variety of forms and can be ingested in several ways. Although the drug is most commonly sold as a white powder, it also comes in clear chunky crystals ("crystal meth" or "ice") and small, brightly colored tablets known as "yaba" (Thai for "crazy medicine"; see "Methamphetamine," n.d.). Methamphetamine can be taken through intravenous injection, smoking, and orally or intranasally (NIDA, 2006d). Methamphetamine users experience a short (few minutes), yet intensely pleasurable sensation (called a rush or flash) immediately after intravenous injection or smoking. Oral or intranasal use produces euphoria (a high with no rush). Regardless of consumption style, methamphetamine users usually become addicted quickly, using higher doses with increasing frequency (NIDA, 2006d).

According to the 2004 National Survey on Drug Use and Health (see Substance Abuse and Mental Health Services Administration, 2005), approximately 11.7 million Americans ages 12 and older reported trying methamphetamine at least once during their lifetimes, representing 4.9% of that population age group (NIDA, 2006d). Approximately 1.4 million (0.6%) reported past-year methamphetamine use and 583,000 (0.2%) reported past-month use (NIDA, 2006d). Among students surveyed as part of the 2005 MTF study, 3.1% of 8th graders, 4.1% of 10th graders, and 4.5% of 12th graders reported lifetime use of methamphetamine (NIDA, 2006d). According to NIDA, some cocaine and MDMA (ecstasy) users are switching to methamphetamine, ignorant of its severe toxicity ("Methamphetamine," n.d.).

Prescription Drugs

Drugs prescribed by a physician can be beneficial if used according to the doctor's specifications and if used only by the prescribed person. Nonmedical use of prescription drugs has become a recent concern, however, with the relative ease with which individuals can order prescription drugs from foreign countries via the Internet without a prescription. Some teens engage in what they call *pharming*, a slang term for grabbing a handful of prescription drugs and swallowing some or all of them. Three main types of drugs popular among adolescents include opioids, CNS depressants, and stimulants.

Opioids are pain relievers and work by attaching to specific protein receptors found in the brain, the gastrointestinal track, and the spinal cord. Once attached, opioids then affect specific regions of the brain to change perceptions of pleasure. They can cause shortness of breath, drowsiness, and constipation. If used in excessive amounts or combined with other drugs, they can cause death by respiratory malfunction (NIDA, 2006e). The two most common opioids abused for nonmedical purposes are oxycodone (OxyContin) and hydrocodone (Vicodin). NIDA reported that OxyContin annual use by 12th graders has risen from 4.0% in 2002 to 5.5%. Tenth graders (3.2%) and 8th graders (1.8%) reported a lower but stable annual use of OxyCotin. Vicodin use, on the other hand, was higher for all grades: 9.5% among 12th graders, 5.9% among 10th graders, and 2.6% among 8th graders (NIDA, 2006e).

CNS depressants such as valium and xanax are most commonly prescribed for anxiety, sleep disorders, and mood disorders. They work by slowing brain activity, thus making the person drowsy. Possible side effects are seizures, decreased heart rate, and respiratory depression (NIDA, 2006e). Stimulants are used for treating attention-deficit hyperactivity disorder, narcolepsy, and asthma, to name a few. Stimulants increase alertness, heart rate, blood pressure, and energy. Stimulants most typically abused by adolescents are Adderall, Concerta, and Ritalin. Stimulants enhance brain activity because they are similar to specific neurotransmitters located in the brain. This type of medication blocks reuptake and, therefore, increases the amount of neurotransmitters in the synaptic gap. Stimulants may cause high body temperatures, irregular heart rates, and seizures. If misused, stimulants can be addictive (NIDA, 2006e). According to the 2004 National Survey on Drug Use and Health (see Substance Abuse and Mental Health Services Administration, 2005), 2.5% of the population 12 years and older had used prescription medication for nonmedical purposes.

PSYCHOSOCIAL INFLUENCES OF SUBSTANCE USE

In addition to the physiological influences of drug use, researchers have identified psychosocial influences of adolescent substance use and abuse. A current model of substance use is first provided, followed by a brief review of the risk and protective factors related to adolescent substance abuse and cultural and ethnic differences in adolescent substance abuse.

Continuum of Drug Use: A Psychosocial Perspective

Muisener (1994) created a drug use and experience continuum for adolescents, identified as the adolescent chemical use experience (ACUE) continuum (see Table 15-2). Likened to other psychosocial frameworks of drug use, the ACUE continuum considers social and environmental factors that influence drug use. Although the stages of Muisener's model overlap and cutoff points are arbitrary, it provides a framework from which to distinguish different substance use experiences.

Table 15-2
■
Drug Use Continuum

	Stage 1	Stage 2	Stage 3	Stage 4
Type of use	Experimental	Social use with peers	Operational; also known as compensatory users (Nowinski, 1990)	Dependent
Reason for use	Bored, curious, seeking fun, responding to peer pressure	Seeks a mood swing of drugs with friends (Macdonald & Newton, 1981)	Preoccupation with the mood swing of drugs (Macdonald & Newton, 1981)	Use chemicals in order to feel normal
Characteristics of drug use	Aware of differences between having fun and getting into danger	Considered fairly adaptive and normative for many adolescents	Actively engage in the drug effects. Two types of operational users: 1. Pleasure pursuant: those who seek the effects of the drug to feel good 2. Pain avoidant: those who use drugs to avoid dealing with painful feelings or to cope with life events and concerns	Adolescents devote a great deal of time and energy to getting high. Become experts or connoisseurs of street drugs. Drugs are an escape or a means to avoid discomfort rather than experience pleasure (Avis, 1990). Sense of self and identity is often interwoven with drug use
Outcome of drug use	Adolescents typically do not develop serious drug problems	Adolescents who misuse or overindulge in substances are at risk for continued drug use	Adolescents at higher risk for drug abuse if they establish an unhealthy coping mechanism of using drugs to deal with issues	Adolescents at high risk for health concerns

All adolescents will differ in their experiences across the ACUE continuum (Muisener, 1994). Of those adolescents who are experimental or social drug users, only a fraction will progress to dependency. When considered at a national level, however, this represents a staggering 1 million teenagers. Similarly, approximately

4% to 5% of teens between the ages of 15 and 19 use illicit drugs regularly. Muisener noted, however, that those who abuse substances can regress to less problematic stages of use at a later time.

Risk and Protective Factors

Research on the psychosocial risk and protective factors for adolescent drug use and abuse has focused on the interrelationships among factors in multiple psychosocial domains, including childhood and adolescent personality characteristics, parental characteristics, previous drug use, parental marital relationship, adolescent relationships with family members, peer relationships, and community characteristics. While a detailed discussion of the complex interactions between the different psychosocial domains is beyond the scope of this chapter, several key findings are particularly relevant to the current emphasis in the field on the developmental context of adolescent substance abuse and treatment. Although relationships with drug-using peers have been found to be the most critical factor in the initiation and maintenance of adolescent drug use across ethnic groups (Donovan, 1996; Swaim, Bates, & Chavez, 1998), this is not true for drug abuse. Peer drug use does not seem to lead directly to drug abuse as much as other factors, such as biological vulnerabilities, self-drug use, parental drug use, and conflicted parent–child relationships (Brook, Brook, & Pahl, 2006).

Among the most critical findings in the developmental literature has been the centrality of the mutually affectionate, nonconflicted parent–child relationship in preventing the development of risk factors for drug abuse. Parents of adolescents who abstain from drug use reported greater warmth and less conflict in their relationships with their children compared with parents of adolescents who abused drugs (Brook, Whiteman, Finch, & Cohen, 1998; Brook, Brook, de la Rosa, Whiteman, & Montoya, 1999). Also, Brook, Rosen, and Zhang's study (cited in Brook, Brook, de la Rosa, Whiteman, & Montoya, 2006) showed that low family bonding (e.g., low marital harmony, parent–adolescent conflict, and less maternal satisfaction with adolescent) predicted early substance use disorders in young adults. Adaptive family functioning seems to be critical in offsetting multiple risk factors for adolescent drug abuse.

Ethnic/Cultural Differences in Substance Use

According to the National Survey on Drug Use and Health (2006), White youth tend to use alcohol and most other drugs at higher rates than do Asian, Black, or Hispanic youth. American Indian students have the highest alcohol use rate, whereas Black students have the highest abstention rate from alcohol. Black and Hispanic youth begin marijuana use at a later age and are less likely to become heavy users than are their White counterparts. As racial/ethnic minority adolescents are highly influenced by their families and extended families (Carr, Moore, & Robinson Kurpius, 2005; Hart & Robinson Kurpius, 2005), effecting change using the support of families is essential (Trainer Haas & Robinson Kurpius, 2005). For this reason, prevention and intervention programs need to utilize the family systems to change drug use patterns.

Ultimately, there is no typical profile of an adolescent drug abuser. Factors that influence adolescent substance use vary and require comprehensive and multidimensional prevention and intervention approaches that are culturally congruent at the individual, familial, and community levels through the integration of psychological, social, and cultural contexts.

CASE STUDY

Julie is a White 15-year-old high school sophomore who lives with her family in a large urban city in the Midwest. Having lived in the city all her life, her father's company is in the process of downsizing, and there is an expected financial need for the family to move to a smaller and more affordable place of residence. Julie is the youngest of three children. Marlene, age 17, is a high school senior, and Camille, age 21, is a junior at a college 2 hours away from home. Julie has few major responsibilities at home; however, one includes helping Marlene cook dinner and wash dishes. Julie is interested in joining an academically related club, but she has opted not to join the French and German language clubs like she did last year because it requires her mother to pick her up in the early evening.

In Julie's family, her father is the primary source of income as her mother has had an inconsistent work history. Although Julie's mother has a college degree in accounting, she has had difficulty maintaining employment given her alcohol use over the last 10 years and more recent marijuana use. With the possibility of moving, Julie's mother's drinking has escalated to the point of her passing out in the family room on a daily basis. When this occurs, Julie's father and older sister typically refer to her mother as "feeling sick" and "needing time to rest," although Julie has noticed a marked increase in verbal abuse between her parents when her mother drinks.

Julie has a tendency to lack self-confidence, has difficulty with unstructured settings, attempts to serve as caretaker for others (particularly her mother), and yearns for social recognition and attention. At school, she often goes along with others in order to be accepted. A B+ student, Julie's grades have dropped as she has consistently failed to turn in her homework assignments. Noting that she seems tired and easily distracted in class, several of her teachers have referred her to the school counselor, Ms. Latrice.

After becoming comfortable with Ms. Latrice, Julie admits that for the last 5 months she has been drinking alcohol before school as she "wants to know what my mom feels like during the day." Also, she has found and smoked several of her mother's marijuana cigarettes after dinner when her father retreats to his home office to contend with financial issues and her mother has passed out from drinking. Julie claims to have made a new set of "cool" friends at school since she brought one of her mother's marijuana cigarettes to school.

APPROACHES TO PREVENTION

The primary question that frequently arises when dealing with adolescent drug use is, What can parents, educators, and counselors do to prevent or deter adolescents from using drugs? The NIDA published a research-based guide titled *Preventing Drug Use Among Children and Adolescents* (Sloboda & David, 2001). This guide posits that the most crucial risk factors for drug abuse related to the family include the following: chaotic home environments, particularly when parents abuse substances or suffer from mental illnesses; ineffective parenting, especially with children with difficult temperaments and conduct disorders; and lack of mutual attachments and nurturing. Other risk factors relate to children interacting with others outside of the family, specifically the school, peers, and the community. These include inappropriate, shy, and aggressive behavior in the classroom; failure in school performance; poor social coping skills; affiliations with peers who exhibit deviant behaviors; and perceptions of approval of drug-using behaviors in the school, peer, and community environments.

The NIDA guide also identifies certain protective factors, the most salient of which include strong bonds with family; experience of parental monitoring with clear rules of conduct within the family unit and involvement of parents in the lives of their children; success in school performance; strong bonds with prosocial institutions, such as the family, school, and religious organizations; and adoption of conventional norms about drug use.

Prevention factors can enhance protective factors and move toward reversing or reducing risk factors. The NIDA research-based guide also describes 10 prevention programs that have been tested in a family, school, or community setting with positive results: Project STAR, the Life Skills Training Program, Adolescent Alcohol Prevention Trial, Seattle Social Development Project, Adolescents Training and Learning to Avoid Steroids: The ATLAS, Project Family, Strengthening Families Program, Focus on Families, Reconnection Youth Program, and Adolescent Transitions Program. Prevention and education regarding substance abuse among children and adolescents are often targeted toward families and schools.

Family

Many of the psychosocial models explaining adolescent drug involvement support a complex etiology of substance use with multiple determining factors. Among these factors are biological factors, environmental factors, and societal and cultural influences (Swadi, 1999). Much of this research posits environment as a moderator of risk factors, stressing the importance for children to bond with peers, parents, and others with drug-resistant attitudes (Hart & Robinson Kurpius, 2005; Sobeck et al., 2000). Research has demonstrated the importance of a mutually affectionate, non-conflicted parent–child relationship, in particular, as a moderator of risk factors for adolescent substance abuse (Brooks et al., 1998, 1999).

As families are the most essential socialization system for children, they must be an integral component of broad-based prevention methods. Abusive, alcoholic, single-parent, and blended families, families with latchkey children, families with inconsistent limit setting and rules for behavior, and families with low bonding have been related to adolescent drug use. Girls are more likely to engage in chemical use and risky sexual behavior when they lack attachment to their fathers and when they have older siblings who engage in risky behavior (Hart & Robinson Kurpius, 2005). Regardless of family difficulties, the role of the family in preventing adolescent substance use can be significant (Carr et al., 2005).

Although parents may be knowledgeable about alcohol and drug use, they may be unaware or deny that their children have been exposed to or have used alcohol/drugs. Furthermore, it is often difficult for parents and families to acknowledge substance abuse, and their attitudes often deter them from acting against drug use (e.g., talking with their children about the dangers of drug use). Recognizing and requesting help with the problem may trigger intense feelings of anger, hurt, betrayal, or failure for parents. Additional barriers to parents addressing substance use with their children include a lack of time, a misperception of their child's world, difficulty in communicating with their children regarding sensitive issues, not wanting to appear as if they mistrust their children, and lacking current information.

Family-based prevention for Julie. NIDA (Sloboda & David, 2001) offers five research-based prevention principles for family-based programs. First, family-based programs should reach families of children at each stage of development. Research has shown that the highest risk periods for drug use among adolescents are during developmental transitions and during difficult life changes. Julie has already experienced many transitions from infancy to young adulthood, including leaving home to go to school for the first time, transitioning from elementary school to middle school, and experiencing the social and academic pressures associated with high school. Second, prevention programs should train parents in behavioral skills to reduce conduct problems in children, improve parent–child relations, provide consistent discipline and rulemaking, and monitor adolescents' activities. Third, an educational component should provide parents with drug information for themselves and their children. Fourth, programs should be directed to families whose children are in kindergarten through 12th grade to enhance protective factors at all stages of development. Finally, programs should provide access to counseling services for families at risk. A comprehensive family-based prevention program for Julie would need to involve her parents in skills-based training and drug use education and provide intervention for her alcoholic mother and possibly group counseling for her family.

School

Peer drug use has been identified as the single factor most likely to predict current drug use (Chassin, Curran, Hussong, & Colder, 1996; Iannotti, Bush, & Weinfurt, 1996). Hart and Robinson Kurpius (2005) found that girls' risk behavior levels, in particular, were positively correlated with their perceptions of their peers' risk behavior levels for substance use, risky sexual behavior, and suicidality. Oetting's (Dinges & Oetting, 1993) peer cluster theory helps to explain the strong relationship between drug use and the drug involvement of peers. The basic premise is that adolescent drug use is a group activity that takes place in the social context of peer clusters who establish group norms for drug use. According to the theory, strong connections between family members provide a solid foundation for doing well in school and building friendships with other young people who share positive norms and ideals. When there are weak bonds with the family and/or school, when the family is dysfunctional, or when antisocial or prodrug norms are communicated, young people are more likely to be attracted to and associate with other problem youth. For example, Chassin et al. (1996) found that parental alcoholism encouraged adolescent substance use through impairment of parental monitoring and increased stress. According to peer cluster theory, this increases the likelihood that adolescents will associate with peers who support substance use. Experiences with family, school, religion, or other social factors all interact to determine an adolescent's likelihood of joining a drug-using friendship group (Dinges & Oetting, 1993).

School-based prevention for Julie. NIDA (Sloboda & David, 2001) offers eight research-based prevention principles for school-based programs. First, the school-based programs should reach children from kindergarten though high school, or at the very least during the critical middle school or junior high years. Second, the programs should contain multiple years of intervention. Third, they should use well-tested, standardized interventions with detailed lesson plans and student materials, facilitated by age-appropriate interactive teaching methods (i.e., modeling, role-playing, discussion, reinforcement). Fourth, they should foster prosocial bonding to the school and community. Fifth, school-based programs need to teach communication, self-efficacy, and assertiveness, as well as drug resistance skills that are culturally and developmentally appropriate. Sixth, they should promote positive peer influence and antidrug social norms and emphasize skills-training teaching methods. Seventh, they should include 10–15 sessions in the first year and 10–15 follow-up sessions. These sessions should adhere to the effective intervention core elements of structure, content, and delivery, and they should be periodically evaluated for effectiveness. A comprehensive school-based intervention would pay particular attention to Julie's need for prosocial bonding to her school and community and training in self-efficacy and assertiveness, given her need to be accepted and her tendency to lack self-confidence. Finally, attention needs to be paid to helping Julie become more successful in school behavior and performance to increase the likelihood that she will form prosocial bonds with her peers and the school.

Community

According to NIDA, "Prevention programs work at the community level with civic, religious, law enforcement, and governmental organizations to enhance anti-drug norms and prosocial behavior through changes in policy or regulation, mass media efforts, and community-wide awareness programs" (Sloboda & David, 2001, p. 5). Johnston, O'Malley, and Bachman (2002) noted that there has been a steady decline in inhalant use since 1995, as perceived risk has grown due, in part, to the active efforts of the Partnership for a Drug-Free America and other community organizations. Community-based prevention programs might include new laws and enforcement, advertising restrictions, and drug-free school zones.

Community-based prevention for Julie. Community-based prevention for Julie would provide the broader context of a cleaner, safer, more drug-free environment in which individually targeted family and school programs can function effectively. NIDA (Sloboda & David, 2001) offers six research-based prevention principles for community-based programs. First, a comprehensive community prevention program would have components for the individual, the family, the school, the media, community organizations, and health providers that are integrated in theme and content. Second, it would use the media and community education strategies to increase public awareness, attract support, and reinforce family and school-based programs. Third, ideally, the program components would be coordinated with other community efforts to reinforce prevention messages. Fourth, the prevention curriculums should be carefully designed to reach different populations at risk and be of sufficient duration to have an impact. Fifth, the program should include a needs assessment for that community, planning, implementation, and review for refinement, with feedback to and from the community at each stage. Finally, the community program's objectives and activities should be specific, time-limited, feasible, and integrated so that they can work together across program components and can be used to evaluate program progress and outcomes.

INTERVENTION STRATEGIES

If intervention rather than prevention is warranted for adolescent substance abuse, it often occurs in more structured settings, such as treatment programs targeted for individuals. Treatment programs vary by type, services, and setting. For example, settings include short-term inpatient crisis care, inpatient programs, day-care programs, residential treatment, halfway houses, and outpatient treatment programs. Although all programs make extensive use of group and individual therapy, they also require some parental or familial involvement and attempt to provide family counseling to focus on underlying problems in the family milieu. Indeed, it is now widely recognized that family-based interventions with a developmental orientation are the most effective approaches for adolescent substance abuse (NIDA, 2002; Rowe & Liddle, 2003; Williams & Chang, 2000). Further, research has also suggested that treatment intensity and participation in after-care programs are significant for predicting recovery (Brown, D'Amico, McCarthy, & Tapert, 2001).

Adolescent Substance Abuse: The Emergence of a Science-Based Discipline

Through the late 1990s and early 2000s, adolescent-focused substance abuse treatment has distinguished itself from both adult drug abuse treatment and substance abuse prevention (Liddle, 2004). Indeed, large-scale evaluation studies have revealed that standard, community-based intervention programs available in the 1990s, models largely borrowed from adult addiction programs, were inappropriate for teenagers (Dennis, Dawud-Noursi, Muck, & McDermeit, 2003; Etheridge, Smith, Rounds-Bryant, & Hubbard, 2001). For example, the Services Research Outcomes Study of the Substance Abuse and Mental Health Services Administration found that whereas adult patients improved in drug abuse programs, adolescent patients actually increased their alcohol and drug use in the years following treatments (Rowe & Liddle, 2006). It has become clear that efficacious treatments for adolescent substance abusers need to take into account the unique developmental needs and risk factors of adolescents.

Two empirically validated individual interventions for adolescent substance abuse—across individual, family, school, and community modalities—include behavioral management approaches (e.g., contingency management) and cognitive–behavioral therapy (CBT). The basic goal of behavioral management approaches is to replace maladaptive substance use behaviors with healthy adaptive behaviors. For instance, behaviors that adolescents are more likely to engage in (e.g., participating in after-school activities, going out with friends, talking on the phone) can reinforce those behaviors that they are less likely to engage in (e.g., cleaning their room, making curfew, completing chores). The first step of a behavioral intervention is to determine what the adolescent considers to be positive reinforcements. Behavioral management approaches may be particularly useful for adolescents, who have less freedom than adults to alter their environments. Roll (cited in Roll & Watson, 2006) applied contingency management strategies in the treatment of adolescent cigarette smokers and found that adolescent smokers receiving contingency management were approximately three times as likely to remain abstinent for the duration of the intervention compared with adolescent smokers in the comparison group. Although caution should be used in generalizing these results to other types of adolescent substance abuse disorders and to making inferences about the durability of treatment effects, the results are encouraging and provide occasion for more research in this area with adolescent substance abuse populations.

The recent emergence of treatment protocols for adolescent substance abuse disorders and CBT has resulted in strong empirical support for CBT in this population, with initial level of change emerging as the best predictor of long-term outcomes (e.g., Dennis et al., 2004). Most CBT intervention approaches implement multiple components derived from classical conditioning, operant conditioning, and social learning perspectives, including such strategies as self-monitoring, avoidance of stimulus cues, modeling, coping-skills training, assertiveness training (e.g., drug and alcohol refusal skills), communication skills, anger management, and relapse prevention.

Individual

Individual counseling for adolescent substance abuse can be obtained from community mental health agencies, hospitals, health maintenance organizations (HMOs), and private practice therapists. Some HMOs provide both inpatient and outpatient drug and alcohol counseling, although the number of sessions is often limited.

Exploring the adolescent's perceptions of home, school, and peers can help to identify the motives, beliefs, and behaviors that contribute to his or her substance use. Counseling should also address self-esteem, self-efficacy, anger, hopelessness, and the need to belong. Motivation is also critical for stopping alcohol and drug abuse. More successful youths recognize that they have a problem and want to change. Those who are less likely to be successful are referred by the criminal justice system, have used drugs for a longer time, are more immersed in the drug culture, come from families where the adults are substance abusers, and have histories of violence and gang involvement. Regardless of the history of the abuser, self-motivation and family involvement are paramount for change to occur.

Individual interventions for Julie. Julie has been experimenting with alcohol and marijuana over the last several months. Therapeutic interventions would foster discussion of what is happening at home and at school and how this relates to her substance use. The counselor can discuss how Julie's self-perceptions (e.g., low self-esteem and low self-efficacy) and her desire for peer recognition could be related to her at-risk behaviors. Involving Julie in group counseling with similar at-risk youths could foster her coping skills and her sense of self-worth while providing her with accurate information about potential consequences of her drug use. She would probably benefit from being in a group that included other adolescents, particularly girls, thus reinforcing her gender identity and increasing her overall sense of self-worth.

Family

Parents and family play a critical role in adolescent substance abuse interventions because they are the single most important contributors to an adolescent's environment and are instrumental in bringing the family to counseling. Specifically, parents transmit cultural values and beliefs and provide support, encouragement, and acceptance within the family. If parents suspect that their child is using drugs, they are encouraged to talk with their child about their concerns and why drugs are harmful. Parents need to communicate that they are opposed to any drug use and that they intend to enforce that position. Parents are encouraged to be understanding ("I realize you're under a lot of pressure from friends to use drugs"), firm ("As your parent, I cannot allow you to engage in harmful activities"), and self-examining ("Are my own alcohol and drug habits exerting a bad influence on my child?"). Sarcasm, accusations, sympathy-seeking, or self-blaming behaviors will only make a child defensive and inattentive to parents. Acknowledging that one's child is using drugs and that one needs assistance does not imply parental failure but instead reflects caring and parental support.

A confrontation with a child regarding drugs can be charged with many emotions; however, parents need to remain calm, open, loving, and firm. Children respect fair limits that take into consideration their age and maturity level. Consistency in setting limits helps a child understand acceptable parameters for behavior. Although adolescence is a time for seeking independence, autonomy, and self-identity (Erikson,

1964), most adolescents need and want some parental direction. A balance between adolescent autonomy and family is needed, particularly as low family attachment and involvement are associated with increased risk of substance abuse (Wang, Bahr, & Marcos, 1995). This balance is particularly relevant for adolescents and families who value familialism and interdependence (Gloria & Peregoy, 1996).

Parents can look for changes in mood, attitude, grades, peer group, extracurricular activities, and interpersonal interactions as indicators of possible substance use. When parental discipline designed to change substance use behaviors is not effective, a family systems approach is warranted. Within a family systems framework, counselors focus on both the adaptive and maladaptive exchanges among family members and between the adolescent and his or her environment. Emphasis is on improving the transactions that occur within the family, using the family as a natural support system, and applying the experiences of the family system.

A second recommended intervention focuses on communication dynamics within the parent–adolescent relationship. Adolescents often feel that parents criticize, make demands, control, rarely listen, and do not understand their pressures, concerns, or feelings. Effective communication is important in light of findings that weak family relations, low bonding, perceived lack of support, and a high number of family conflicts are related to a higher frequency and severity of substance use (Carr et al., 2005). Although the content of what is being said is important, parents also need to listen for the feelings that accompany the message. Hearing the underlying emotional message may be difficult or painful, and thus parents may find a third party, such as a counselor, helpful in facilitating, teaching, and modeling communication with their adolescents.

A good parent–child relationship serves as a buffer between the environment and the child (Carr et al., 2005; Hart & Robinson Kurpius, 2005). Additional family factors that promote a positive outcome for adolescents include rewarding them for independence with moderate risk taking, encouraging them to assume responsibility, and modeling examples of helpfulness and caring. Further, as some cultures value interdependence of family members, counselors can create a balance of adolescent–parent involvement. Such a balance allows for culturally relevant and meaningful interventions (Thurman, Swaim, & Plested, 1995).

In addition to behavioral management approaches, another behavioral intervention for adolescent substance abuse is applying logical consequences for adolescent behaviors. This approach challenges adolescents to take responsibility for their behaviors. As parents apply logical consequences firmly and consistently, these behaviors must be accompanied by discussion and respect. As with positive reinforcements, logical consequences will differ for each adolescent. Being grounded for a weekend may seem drastic and earth shattering for one adolescent but endurable or irrelevant for another. To prevent challenging of parental authority, inappropriate and unacceptable behaviors must be clearly defined and specific at the start of the behavioral intervention.

Behavioral contracting between parents and adolescents allows for the specific determination of rules and consequences while providing a catalyst for clear communication. Defining acceptable and unacceptable behaviors and identifying logical and feasible consequences (e.g., grounded for the weekend vs. forever) can help to ensure success of such interventions. A possible contract might include no drinking at parties, no ditching classes, and no mouthing off to teachers. Privileges such as telephone use, peer interactions, and dating need to be linked to specific acceptable behaviors such as consistent school attendance and honoring curfews. As adolescents fulfill requirements, terms of the contract can be renegotiated, thereby increasing their self-efficacy and sense of responsibility.

Family interventions for Julie. Julie would benefit from her family being more aware of the impact family dynamics can have on her self-worth and behaviors. Unfortunately, Julie's mother is modeling maladaptive coping with life's problems by drinking alcohol and smoking marijuana. Family counseling would not only address Julie's behaviors but also help her mother develop more effective strategies for dealing with her problems. In addition, more open and effective communication between Julie and her parents could be facilitated. The counselor can also explore how Julie's older sister could help relieve some of the stresses resulting in Julie's drinking and smoking marijuana. Further, because Julie has relatively few responsibilities at home, perhaps a contract can be developed between Julie and her parents that would encourage her to join the French and German language clubs if she meets specific goals with respect to her school work and her alcohol and marijuana use behaviors.

School

Although the school system is the primary arena for substance abuse recognition, prevention/education, and intervention, estimates suggest that only 10% of adolescents with a substance use problem receive treatment in school (Dennis & White, 2002). A major disadvantage of school-based treatments is that they do not necessarily reach high school dropouts or school truants, students who are at a particularly high risk for drug abuse (McCluskey, Krohn, Lizotte, & Rodriguez, 2002). Nevertheless, trusted relationships with teachers and counselors can create a refuge from the home environment, allowing for disclosure of family, peer, or school difficulties, as well as drug use, in nurturing learning environments.

School intervention approaches can be both informal and formal. For instance, the Just Say No approach of telling adolescents to refuse drugs is an example of an informal, unidimensional, simplistic approach to a multidimensional, complex problem. Students are told to respond behaviorally without addressing the cognitions or feelings involved in making such a decision. More important, rather than integrating sociocultural considerations into the program's premise, such programming is based on the premise that the inability to say no is due to one's deviance. Specifically, substance use is often a coping response to factors beyond an individual's control, such as ignorance, poverty, racism, prejudice, sexual/physical abuse as a child, dysfunctional family life, and/or mental incompetence (Warheit & Gil, 1998).

Other informal approaches involve developing a working partnership with the parents to prevent drug use. Depending on parental cooperation and school counselor availability, workshops can occur after normal school hours for students and their parents. Information and skill-based training, such as assertiveness training and decision-making skills, can help students make informed decisions about substance use (McWhirter, McWhirter, McWhirter, & McWhirter, 2007). These workshops can help students identify situations and circumstances that promote and maintain their substance use. School counselors can apply innovative strategies in their workshops, such as talks by recovered abusers, movies, group outings, and drug-free parties. In addition to workshops, school counselors can serve as liaisons to parents regarding adolescents' behavior and academic performance. For changes to occur, students must perceive the counselor's role as an advocate, not as a narcotic agent or another adult who does not understand.

Another informal school-based intervention targets naturally occurring peer groups. As most students trust and relate to their peers, peer support and education groups are effective ways of relaying information to adolescents (Robinson Kurpius, 2000). Peer discussion groups allow students to discuss their experiences and difficulties with peer pressure and acceptance. Students can find validation in knowing they are not alone in their experiences and feelings. Similarly, finding out that not everyone is using drugs can help to dispel adolescent drug myths. Most important, the group can help foster healthy peer relationships that promote self-growth. Students Against Drunk Driving (SADD) is an example of this type of intervention. Involvement in extracurricular activities such as sports, clubs, or music programs can also serve as an informal source of adolescent support.

There are a multitude of formal, structured programs for the prevention and intervention of adolescent substance use. Multicomponent programs are more effective than unidimensional approaches (Gonet, 1998). The most commonly used multidimensional school-based treatment approach for adolescent substance abusers is the Student Assistant Program (SAP), a program modeled after employee assistance programs. The SAP involves procedures for identifying substance-abusing students, motivating them to enter the program, intake and assessment, intervention or referral for treatment, and follow-up. These programs tend to be highly variable in their assessment framework, conceptualization of dysfunction, and intervention targets, but they are consistent in targeting substance abuse, academic performance, and school conduct. As described by Wagner and Macgowan (2006), most SAPs fall into either the "core team model," in which the program depends on trained school personnel to assess and identify students and then refer to the community for treatment, or the "Westchester County, New York, model," which relies on SAP specialty counselors who assess and treat the students at the school.

Another school-based program is the Talented At-Risk Girls: Encouragement and Training for Sophomores (TARGETS; Robinson Kurpius, Kerr, & Harkins, 2005). This project, funded by the National Science Foundation, focuses on the career aspirations and at-risk behaviors of teenage girls. Through activities such as future-day fantasies, individual career counseling sessions, and group discussions of at-risk behaviors such as alcohol and drug use, sexuality, and suicide, adolescent girls are provided with self-care knowledge and encouragement to pursue their career dreams. Three to 4-month follow-up with over 500 girls revealed that the TARGETS program enhanced career aspirations, job and future self-efficacy, and self-esteem while decreasing at-risk behaviors.

Regardless of whether the school-based program is formal or informal, it should address the primary factors involved in the etiology of substance abuse. These factors include peer use of illicit substances and peer pressure (Hart & Robinson Kurpius, 2005), familial relations (Carr et al., 2005), cultural influences (Gloria & Peregoy, 1996; Thurman et al., 1995), and media influences (Vega & Gil, 1998b). Also, incorporating behavioral, cognitive, and affective strategies is important in all treatment efforts.

School-based interventions for Julie. Perhaps the most appropriate school-based intervention for Julie is the TARGETS program. By participating in this research-based program, Julie would be exposed to both group and individual counseling that would support increased efforts at school and decreased substance use. The program also addresses self-esteem and self-efficacy issues. These are particularly relevant for Julie given her need to be liked, to use substances to escape, and to allow her peers to influence her behaviors. In addition to the TARGETS program, it would be helpful if Julie were involved in an ongoing school-based support group of peers who are struggling with similar problems. Given Julie's high need for approval and peer acceptance, she might do well in a peer-led group.

Community

McWhirter et al. (2007) identified five community-based programs presently available for adolescents with the drug abuse problems: drug-free programs, residential treatment facilities, day-care programs, aftercare programs, and therapeutic communities. Drug-free programs are usually outpatient programs within a residential treatment program. Activities range from individual and group counseling to challenging experiential programs. Residential treatment facilities are inpatient and focus on long-term recovery. Requiring the adolescent to live on-site, these programs focus on resocializing youth by teaching new life skills. Learning and applying bicultural skills to manage different cultures is especially necessary for adolescents from racial/ethnic minority backgrounds. Day-care programs, on the other hand, typically are less structured than residential programs. Their services usually include academic learning and counseling as well as supervised social activities. Aftercare programs target the adolescent who has been discharged from treatment. The premise of these programs is that treatment is a life-long process.

Although therapeutic communities (TCs) vary widely in terms of their size (20–200), their location (rural, urban, or suburban), and their duration of treatment (6 months to more than 1 year), all TCs posit substance abuse as a disorder of the whole person and focus on mutual help as the primary agent of change. This perspective of the problem supports a multicomponent rehabilitative treatment approach that occurs in a 24-hour setting. As described by Jainchill (2006), the basic components of TCs include community separateness; an environment that focuses on community rather than personal use of space; community activities; peers who are community members as well as role models; staff who are rational authorities, role models, facilitators, and guides; a structured day; a phased therapeutic process; job functions; and peer groups. Focusing on extinguishing substance use, TCs rely on peer influence and group action to change attitudes and destructive behaviors. Few studies have evaluated the effectiveness of TCs, and none to date have included control or comparison groups with random assignment of youths to different treatment conditions (Jainchill, 2006).

Other community-based interventions often involve law enforcement systems that collaborate with the community. Police often talk with the parents of the adolescent arrested for a substance use offense. Police, parents, schools, and community task forces can work together effectively to design communitywide prevention and intervention programs to combat adolescent substance use. For instance, Boys and Girls Clubs and community YMCAs provide alternative activities for youth. Adult volunteers and recovered users often staff these programs, providing healthy, productive, and positive role models. Such organizations bring individuals, schools, and communities together to share responsibility for preventing and intervening in adolescent substance use and abuse.

Community-based interventions for Julie. Getting Julie involved with the school and local French and German language clubs would be beneficial. These interventions could foster a sense of belonging as well as pride in who she is as an emergent linguistic and female. She needs more positive experiences in her life, and these community interventions can provide her with the positive individual and group-member recognition she needs and wants.

ADAPTATIONS FOR DIVERSITY

Despite data citing high rates of substance use and abuse among American Indian and Hispanic communities, little empirical research has been done on these vulnerable populations (Boyd-Ball & Dishion, 2006; Santisteban, Mena, & Suarez-Morales, 2006). It should not be assumed that an empirically supported treatment will necessarily be effective for a minority group that has not been tested. Because many adolescent prevention and intervention programs do not include cultural or contextual issues, Wallack and Corbett (1990) called for a combination of approaches affecting the political, social, and cultural environment, in addition to the individual. Specifically, the environmental issues of discrimination and racism are of particular concern. Labouvie (1986) found that a sense of powerlessness or helplessness was related to heavy substance abuse because substance use helped adolescents achieve a sense of emotional self-regulation. Because approximately 10% of adolescents are lesbian, gay, or bisexual, same-sex interests often result in familial and internal conflict (Darcy, 2005). Accordingly, these youths are vulnerable to alcohol and drug use as they often feel rejected by the self and the heterocentic values of the United States. Individual, peer, and family developmental processes associated with substance use and abuse should be considered in relation to the cultural and historical contexts of various cultural groups.

Underscoring the importance of integrating contextual and cultural considerations into prevention and intervention programming, Lotta and Benally (2005) identified ineffective strategies for working with American Indian adolescents. Programs with good ideas but identified as ineffective focused on improving self-esteem; viewed alcohol as a substitute for social acceptance; perceived depressed, anxious, or emotionally disturbed youth as alcohol users; and did not actively or completely exclude alcohol use. Although these preventive activities may be ineffective for one specific cultural group, the same activities may be effective with adolescents from other cultural backgrounds. Just as prevention and intervention research on adolescent substance use and abuse takes into account the unique developmental needs and risk factors of adolescents, so should essential culture-related processes be considered in future research in this emerging field. Adolescent substance abuse is a serious issue; therefore, researchers, parents, school systems, and counselors cannot afford to administer a one-size-fits-all prevention or intervention program.

There are several alternatives to access information about substance use prevention and intervention. First, the public library is an excellent source for information about state laws related to drugs. Learning about state laws and the legal rights of minors can be helpful in providing straight talk and accurate information about drugs. Second, if parents or adolescents are concerned about openly seeking information, a variety of free publications, pamphlets, posters, and other drug education information can be ordered by phone. For instance, the first research-based drug prevention guide for children and adolescents, *Preventing Drug Use Among Children and Adolescents*, is available through the National Clearinghouse for Alcohol and Drug Information (NCADI; toll-free telephone: 1-800-729-6686). Similarly, the publication *Keeping Youth Drug Free* is also available from NCADI. It is estimated that NCADI receives over 250,000 inquiries and distributes over 20 million information products each year.

The Internet is another rich source of information regarding substance use and abuse prevention. A variety of government and private agency Web sites are available and user-friendly. For families interested in obtaining information about drugs, a few Internet addresses to visit include the following:

7

- www.samhsa.gov to access the Substance Abuse and Mental Health Services Administration
- www.nida.nih.gov to access the National Institute on Drug Abuse
- www.niaaa.nih.gov to access the National Institute on Alcohol Abuse and Alcoholism
- www.whitehousedrugpolicy.gov to access the Office of National Drug Control Policy

Within most sites, links and programs specifically target adolescents and different racial and ethnic minority groups. Most information is easy to read and presented in a fun and attention-getting fashion. Most sites also provide additional links (i.e., other sites of potential interest) and referral information. Addresses and phone numbers for different prevention and treatment organizations are also generally provided. The majority of information on Web sites can be downloaded for parents or adolescents to use in later discussions. Finally, the NIDA InfoFacts provides a 24-hour toll-free phone line from which drug information can be ordered via fax or mail. Audio information on topics such as the health effects of drugs, drug use and AIDS, and drug treatment and prevention can also be listened to in English or Spanish. The phone numbers are 1-888-644-6432 and 1-888-889-6432 (hearing-impaired); it can also be accessed on the Web at http://www.nida.nih.gov/Infofacts/Infofaxindex.html.

SUMMARY

The most recent data from NIDA indicate that the substance use problem among adolescents remains unsolved. Adolescents, parents, teachers, counselors, and other community members must share responsibility in the prevention and intervention of adolescent drug use. Both prevention and intervention programs need to educate adolescents about the negative effects of drugs and provide opportunities for them to bond with peers, parents, and others who have drug-resistant attitudes (Sobeck et al., 2000). The programs should focus on adolescents' behaviors, feelings, and thoughts within a culturally and socially congruent environment (Amick-Lofton & Robinson Kurpius, 2005; Gloria & Peregoy, 1996). The focus and manner in which programs focus on adolescents, however, must be informed by cultural values and beliefs specific to group and subgroup norms (Thurman et al., 1995; Vega & Gil, 1998a). That is, prevention and intervention programs must be designed to be congruent with the values and worldview of the culture within which they are implemented. Although we may never totally stop substance use or abuse, one of our most important tasks is to prepare our youth to be wise decision makers and to draw on their cultural, social, and familial strengths and supports.

REFERENCES

Amick-Lofton, L., & Robinson Kurpius, S. E. (2005). Are racial/ethnic minority girls more at risk? In S. Kurpius, B. Kerr, & A. Harkins (Eds.), *Handbook for counseling girls and women* (pp. 33–66). Mesa, AZ: Nueva Science.
Avis, H. (1990). *Drugs and life*. Dubuque, IA: William C. Brown.
Boyd-Ball, A. J., & Dishion, T. (2006). Family-centered treatment for American Indian adolescent substance abuse: Toward a culturally and historically informed strat-

egy. In H. A. Liddle & C. L. Rowe (Eds.), *Adolescent substance abuse: Research and clinical advances* (pp. 423–448). Cambridge, England: Cambridge University Press.

Brook, J. S., Brook, D. W., de la Rosa, M., Whiteman, M., & Montoya, I. D. (1999). The role of parents in protecting Colombian adolescents from delinquency and marijuana use. *Archives of Pediatrics and Adolescent Medicine, 153*, 457–464.

Brook, J. S., Brook, D. W., & Pahl, K. (2006). The developmental context for adolescent substance abuse intervention. In H. A. Liddle & C. L. Rowe (Eds.), *Adolescent substance abuse: Research and clinical advances* (pp. 25–51). Cambridge, England: Cambridge University Press.

Brook, J. S., Whiteman, M., Finch, S., & Cohen, P. (1998). Mutual attachment, personality, and drug use: Pathways from childhood to young adulthood. *Genetic, Social, and General Psychology Monographs, 124*, 492–510.

Brown, S. A., D'Amico, E. J., McCarthy, D. M., & Tapert, S. F. (2001). Four-year outcomes from adolescent alcohol and drug treatment. *Journal of Studies on Alcohol, 62*, 381–388.

Carlson, N. R. (2001). *Physiology of behavior*. Needham Heights, MA: Allyn & Bacon.

Carr, E. M., Moore, E. G. J., & Robinson Kurpius, S. E. (2005, April). *The role of fathers in adolescent girls' at-risk behaviors*. Paper presented at the American Educational Research Association annual meeting, San Francisco, CA.

Chassin, L., Curran, P. J., Hussong, A. M., & Colder, C. R. (1996). The relation of parent alcoholism to adolescent substance use: A longitudinal follow-up study. *Journal of Abnormal Psychology, 105*, 70–80.

Darcy, M. (2005). Adolescent women's sexuality: A negotiated terrain. In S. Kurpius, B. Kerr, & A. Harkins (Eds.), *Handbook for counseling girls and women* (pp. 227–257). Mesa, AZ: Nueva Science.

Dennis, M. L., Dawud-Noursi, S., Muck, R. D., & McDermeit, M. (2003). The need for developing and evaluating adolescent treatment models. In S. J. Stevens & A. R. Morral (Eds.), *Adolescent substance abuse treatment in the United States: Exemplary models from a national evaluation study* (pp. 3–34). New York: Haworth Press.

Dennis, M. L., Godley, S. H., Diamond, G., Tims, F. M., Babor, T., Donaldson, J., et al. (2004). The Cannabis Youth Treatment (CYT) study: Main findings from two randomized trials. *Journal of Substance Abuse Treatment, 27*, 197–213.

Dennis, M. L., & White, M. K. (2002). *The effectiveness of adolescent substance abuse treatment: A brief summary of studies through 2001*. Bloomington, IL: Chestnut Health Systems.

Dinges, M. M., & Oetting, E. R. (1993). Similarity in drug use patterns between adolescents and their friends. *Adolescence, 28, 110*, 253–267.

Donovan, J. E. (1996). Problem-behavior theory and the explanation of adolescent marijuana use. *Journal of Drug Issues, 26*, 379–404.

Erikson, E. H. (1964). *Childhood and society*. New York: Norton.

Etheridge, R. M., Smith, J. C., Rounds-Bryant, J. L., & Hubbard, R. L. (2001). Drug abuse treatment and comprehensive services for adolescents. *Journal of Adolescent Research, 16*, 563–589.

Fisher, T. A., Stafford, M. E., Maynard-Reid, N., & Parkerson, A. (2005). Protective factors for talented and resilient girls. In S. E. Kurpius, B. Kerr, & A. Harkins (Eds.), *Handbook for counseling girls and women* (pp. 347–379). Mesa, AZ: Nueva Science.

Gagliardi, C., & Lambert, C. D. (2005). Ripped, blitzed, smashed potential: Substance use and talented at-risk girls. In S. E. Kurpius, B. Kerr, & A. Harkins (Eds.), *Handbook for counseling girls and women* (pp. 273–303). Mesa, AZ: Nueva Science.

Gloria, A. M., & Peregoy, J. J. (1996). Counseling Latino alcohol and other substance users/abusers: Cultural considerations for counselors. *Journal of Substance Abuse Treatment, 13,* 119–126.

Gonet, A. M. (1998). Groups for drug and alcohol abuse. In K. C. Stoiber & T. R. Kratochwill (Eds.), *Handbook of group intervention for children and families* (pp. 172–192). Needham Heights, MA: Allyn & Bacon.

Hart, S., & Robinson Kurpius, S. E. (2005). Relationship of personality, parent and peer attachment to adolescent girls sexual behavior. In S. Kurpius, B. Kerr, & A. Harkins (Eds.), *Handbook for counseling girls and women* (pp. 257–273). Mesa, AZ: Nueva Science.

Iannotti, R. J., Bush, P. J., & Weinfurt, K. P. (1996). Perceptions of friends' use of alcohol, cigarettes, and marijuana among urban schoolchildren: A longitudinal analysis. *Addictive Behaviors, 21,* 615–632.

Inaba, D. S., & Cohen, W. (2000). *Uppers, downers, and all arounders: Physical and mental effects of psychoactive drugs.* Ashland, OR: CNS Publications.

Jainchill, N. (2006). Adolescent therapeutic communities: Future directions for practice and research. In H. A. Liddle & C. L. Rowe (Eds.), *Adolescent substance abuse: Research and clinical advances* (pp. 313–332). Cambridge, England: Cambridge University Press.

Johnston, L. D., O'Malley, P. M., & Bachman, J. G. (2002). *Monitoring the Future national results on adolescent drug use: Overview of key findings, 2001.* Bethesda, MD: National Institute on Drug Abuse.

Johnston, L. D., O'Malley, P. M., & Bachman, J. G. (2006). *Monitoring the Future national results on adolescent drug use: Overview of key findings, 2005.* Bethesda, MD: National Institute on Drug Abuse.

Labouvie, E. W. (1986). Alcohol and marijuana use in relation to adolescent stress. *International Journal of Addictions, 21,* 333–345.

Liddle, H. A. (2004). Family-based therapies for adolescent alcohol and drug abuse: Research contributions and future research needs. *Addiction, 99*(Suppl. 2), 76–92.

Lotta, C. C., & Benally, N. (2005). Talented, at risk Native American girls. In S. Kurpius, B. Kerr, & A. Harkins (Eds.), *Handbook for counseling girls and women* (pp. 67–90). Mesa, AZ: Nueva Science.

MacDonald, D. I., & Newton, M. (1981). The clinical syndrome of adolescent drug abuse. *Advances in Pediatrics, 28,* 1–15.

McCluskey, C. P., Krohn, M. D., Lizotte, A. J., & Rodriquez, M. L. (2002). Early substance use and school achievement: An examination of Latino, White, and African-American youth. *Journal of Drug Issues, 32,* 921–943.

McWhirter, J. J., McWhirter, B. T., McWhirter, E. H., & McWhirter, R. J. (2007). *At risk youth: A comprehensive response* (4th ed.). Pacific Grove, CA: Brooks/Cole.

Methamphetamine. (n.d.). Washington, DC: U.S. Drug Enforcement Administration. Retrieved from http://www.usdoj.gov/dea/concern/meth_factsheet.html

Monitoring the Future. (2005). Bethesda, MD: National Institute on Drug Abuse. Retrieved from http://www.monitoringthefuture.org/

Muisener, P. P. (1994). *Understanding and treating adolescent substance abuse.* Thousand Oaks, CA: Sage.

National Institute on Alcohol Abuse and Alcoholism. (2001). *Alcoholism: Getting the facts.* Retrieved from http://pubs.niaaa.nih.gov/publications/GettheFacts_HTML/facts.htm.

National Institute on Drug Abuse. (2000). *Mind over matter: The brain's response to drugs.* Retrieved from http://www.drugabuse.gov/MOM/MOMIndex.html

National Institute on Drug Abuse. (2002). *Improving behavioral health services and treatment for adolescent drug abuse* (Report RFA-DA-03-003). Bethesda, MD: National Institutes of Health.

National Institute on Drug Abuse. (2006a). *NIDA InfoFacts: Cigarettes and other nicotine products.* Retrieved from http://www.nida.nih.gov/Infofacts/tocacco.html

National Institute on Drug Abuse. (2006b). *NIDA InfoFacts: Inhalants.* Retrieved from http://www.nida.nih.gov/Infofacts/inhalants.html

National Institute on Drug Abuse. (2006c). *NIDA InfoFacts: Marijuana.* Retrieved from http://www.nida.nih.gov/Infofacts/marijuana.html

National Institute on Drug Abuse. (2006d). *NIDA InfoFacts: Methamphetamine.* Retrieved from http://www.nida.nih.gov/Infofacts/methamphetamine.html

National Institute on Drug Abuse. (2006e). *NIDA InfoFacts: Prescription drugs.* Retrieved from http://www.nida.nih.gov/Infofacts/prescriptiondrugs.html

National Survey on Drug Use and Health. (2006). *2005 national survey on drug use and health.* Retrieved from http://oas.samhsa.gov/NSDUH/2k5NSDUH/2k5results.htm

Nowinski, J. (1990). *Substance abuse in adolescents and young adults: A guide to treatment.* New York: Norton.

Office of National Drug Control Policy. (2006). *Drug facts: Methamphetamine.* Retrieved from http://www.whitehousedrugpolicy.gov/drugfact/methamphetamine/index.html

Robinson Kurpius, S. E. (2000). Peer counseling. In A. E. Kazdin (Ed.), *Encyclopedia of psychology.* Washington, DC: American Psychological Association and Oxford University Press.

Robinson Kurpius, S. E., Kerr, B., & Harkins, A. (Eds.). (2005). *Handbook for counseling girls and women.* Mesa, AZ: Nueva Science.

Roll, J. M., & Watson, D. (2006). Behavioral management approaches for adolescent substance abuse. In H. A. Liddle & C. L. Rowe (Eds.), *Adolescent substance abuse: Research and clinical advances* (pp. 375–395). Cambridge, England: Cambridge University Press.

Rowe, C. L., & Liddle, H. A. (2003). Substance abuse. *Journal of Marital and Family Therapy, 29,* 97–120.

Rowe, C. L., & Liddle, H. A. (2006). Treating adolescent substance abuse: State of the science. In H. A. Lidle & C. L. Rowe (Eds.), *Adolescent substance abuse: Research and clinical advances* (pp. 1–21). Cambridge, England: Cambridge University Press.

Santisteban, D. A., Mena, M. P., & Suarez-Morales, L. (2006). Using treatment development methods to enhance the family-based treatment of Hispanic adolescents. In H. A. Liddle & C. L. Rowe (Eds.), *Adolescent substance abuse: Research and clinical advances* (pp. 449–470). Cambridge, England: Cambridge University Press.

Shillington, A. M., & Clapp, J. D. (2000). Self-report stability of adolescent substance use: Are there differences for gender, ethnicity and age? *Drug and Alcohol Dependence, 60,* 19–27.

Sloboda, Z., & David, S. L. (2001). *Preventing drug use among children and adolescents: A research-based guide* (NIH Publication No. 02-4212). Bethesda, MD: National Institute on Drug Abuse.

Sobeck, J., Abbey, A., Agius, E., Clinton, M., & Harrison, K. (2000). Predicting early adolescent substance use: Do risk factors differ depending on age of onset? *Journal of Substance Abuse, 11,* 89–102.

Substance Abuse and Mental Health Services Administration. (2002). *National household survey on drug abuse—The NHSDA report: Marijuana use among youths.* Retrieved from http://www.health.org/govstudy/shortreports/MJ&dependence/

Substance Abuse and Mental Health Services Administration. (2005). *Overview of findings from the 2004 National Survey on Drug Use and Health* (Office of Applied Studies, NSDUH Series H-27, DHHS Publication No. SMA 05-4061). Bethesda, MD: Author.

Substance Abuse and Mental Health Services Administration. (2006). *Results from the 2005 National Survey on Drug Use and Health: National findings* (Office of Applied Studies, NSDUH Series H-30, DHHS Publication No. SMA 06-4194). Bethesda, MD: Author.

Swadi, H. (1999). Individual risk factors for adolescent substance use. *Drug and Alcohol Dependence, 55*, 209–224.

Swaim, R. C., Bates, S. C., & Chavez, E. L. (1998). Structural equation socialization model of substance use among Mexican-American and White non-Hispanic school drop-outs. *Journal of Adolescent Health, 23*, 128–138.

Thurman, P. J., Swaim, R., & Plested, B. (1995). Intervention and treatment of ethnic minority substance abusers. In J. F. Aponte, R. Y. Rivers, & J. Wohl (Eds.), *Psychological interventions and cultural diversity* (pp. 215–233). Boston: Allyn & Bacon.

Trainer Haas, C., & Robinson Kurpius, S. E. (2005). Mothers, fathers, and adolescent girls. In S. Kurpius, B. Kerr, & A. Harkins (Eds.), *Handbook for counseling girls and women* (pp. 379–394). Mesa, AZ: Nueva Science.

U.S. Department of Health and Human Services. (2002). *Fact sheet: Substance abuse— A national challenge: Prevention, treatment and research at HHS*. Retrieved from http://www.hhs.gov/news/press/2002pres/subabuse.html

Vega, W. A., & Gil, A. G. (Eds.). (1998a). *Drug use and ethnicity in early adolescence*. New York: Plenum.

Vega, W. A., & Gil, A. G. (1998b). Prevention implications and conclusions. In W. A. Vega & A. G. Gil (Eds.), *Drug use and ethnicity in early adolescence* (pp. 177–196). New York: Plenum.

Wagner, E. R., & Macgowan, M. J. (2006). School-based group treatment for adolescent substance abuse. In H. A. Liddle & C. L. Rowe (Eds.), *Adolescent substance abuse: Research and clinical advances* (pp. 333–356). Cambridge, England: Cambridge University Press.

Wallack, L., & Corbett, K. (1990). *Illicit drug, tobacco, and alcohol use among youth: Trends and promising approaches in prevention* (Office for Substance Abuse Prevention, Monograph No. 6). Washington, DC: U.S. Department of Health and Human Services.

Wang, G. T., Bahr, S. J., & Marcos, A. C. (1995). Family bonds and adolescent substance use: An ethnic group comparison. In C. K. Jacobson (Ed.), *American families: Issues in race and ethnicity* (pp. 463–492). New York: Garland.

Warheit, G. J., & Gil, A. G. (1998). Substance use and other social deviance. In W. A. Vega & A. G. Gil (Eds.), *Drug use and ethnicity in early adolescence* (pp. 37–70). New York: Plenum.

Williams, R. J., & Chang, S. Y. (2000). A comprehensive and comparative review of adolescent substance abuse treatment outcome. *Clinical Psychology: Science and Practice, 7*, 138–166.

CHAPTER 16

■

Nowhere to Turn:
The Young Face of Homelessness

Melissa A. Stormont and Rebecca B. McCathren

The face of the homeless person has changed over the past several decades. Often now, the face is that of a child or teenager, on the streets with no place to call home. Families with small children now represent approximately 40% of the homeless population (Children's Defense Fund, 2005; National Center on Family Homelessness, 1999; U.S. Conference of Mayors, 2005). The National Center on Family Homelessness (1999) reported that up to 1 million children are homeless in the United States. More recent reports have indicated that well over 1 million children are homeless (Institute for Children and Poverty, 2004). Conservative estimates indicate that at least 500,000 youths are homeless in the United States (Haber & Toro, 2004).

Given these prevalence estimates, every educational professional needs to be aware of the characteristics of children and youth who are homeless and the resources available to address their needs. Children who are homeless are at great risk for academic, social, emotional, and behavioral problems in school (Children's Defense Fund, 2005; Davey, 2004; National Center on Family Homelessness, 1999). Many homeless youths do not attend school at all and are very likely to be the victims of abuse and to engage in destructive behaviors (Haber & Toro, 2004). For young people who are homeless, it is evident that their educational needs will only be met through collaborative outreach efforts and interventions from teachers, counselors, administrators, and communities.

Accordingly, this chapter first describes the problem of homelessness for two specific groups: children living with their families and youths living alone. To define the problem of homelessness, the characteristics of both groups are presented first, followed by specific contributing factors for homelessness for each group. Next, the chapter describes the strategies for prevention and intervention with young people who are homeless from individual, family, school, and community perspectives. Adaptations for diversity are addressed in the final section and include additional considerations for working with single mothers and increasing knowledge of different cultures to enhance cultural sensitivity.

PROBLEM DEFINITION

Homelessness means having a primary residence that is a public or private shelter, emergency housing, hotel or motel, or any other public space including public parks, cars, abandoned buildings, or aqueducts (Institute for Children in Poverty, 2001; National Coalition for the Homeless, 2006). Other definitions of homelessness also include those individuals who have to double up in housing with friends and family members or live in overcrowded housing conditions (National Coalition for the Homeless, 1998b). The latter definition includes those individuals who are homeless and living in rural areas where there are more limited shelter facilities (National Coalition for the Homeless, 1999c). Regardless of how homelessness is defined, being homeless means more than not having a fixed place to sleep. People who are homeless have nowhere to put the things they cherish, things that connect them to their past. Youths who are homeless have often lost contact with their family and friends, and families who are homeless may have to uproot their children from school. More specific characteristics and contributing factors to homelessness for children and youth are presented next.

CHILDREN AND FAMILIES WHO ARE HOMELESS

Characteristics

According to research that has been conducted on increases in shelter capacity, homelessness has increased two to three times over the past two decades (National Coalition for the Homeless, 1999b). From the most recent statistics available, it is clear that the faces of the homeless have changed drastically since the days of the White, male, alcoholic or "skid row bum." Families are the fastest growing group of homeless and now account for approximately 40% of the homeless population (National Center on Family Homelessness, 2004). The number of homeless families living in shelters is about 500,000, and the number of children living in shelters is about 1.35 million (Institute for Children and Poverty, 2004). The average age of the children is 6 years old (Institute for Children and Poverty, 2004; National Coalition for the Homeless, 1998a).

Demographically, children who are homeless are from all geographical areas and ethnic backgrounds. Although many assume that homelessness is an urban problem, the rate of homelessness may be more than twice as high in small towns or rural areas (Fisher, 2005). In rural areas, people who are homeless were more apt to be female, married, and working (Fisher, 2005). In addition, the population is less intractable, with a higher percentage being homeless for the first time and homeless for a shorter length of time than for those in urban areas (Fisher, 2005). Children who are homeless also represent different ethnicities. However, a disproportionate number of minorities, especially African Americans and Latinos, are represented in the homeless population (Haber & Toro, 2004), with some research reporting that more than half of the homeless population are from African American backgrounds (Institute for Children and Poverty & Homes for the Homeless, 2005; National Coalition for the Homeless, 1998b). Children's needs may vary according to their different cultural backgrounds, which will need to be addressed in a culturally sensitive way. These adaptations for diversity are presented later in the chapter.

Children who are homeless are at risk for moving, some many times (Institute for Children and Poverty & Homes for the Homeless, 2005; National Coalition for the Homeless, 2006). Each time children move, instructional time is lost and children fall further behind their same-age peers. Every year, 40% of children who are homeless change schools once and 28% change schools twice. At least 20% of children who are homeless are retained once (Institute for Children and Poverty & Homes for the Homeless, 2005), and 20% of children who are homeless do not attend school at all (National Center on Family Homelessness, 2004; National Coalition for the Homeless, 2006). Multiple barriers are present that discourage children from attending school. For example, children who are homeless may not have school records, immunization records, a permanent address, transportation, school supplies, gym shoes, or appropriate clothing (National Center on Homelessness, 2004). Removing barriers and increasing school attendance are critical parts of prevention and intervention efforts and are addressed later in this chapter.

The lack of appropriate health care is another serious concern for children living in conditions that will increase their vulnerability for getting sick (National Center on Family Homelessness, 2004). One study found that 61% of children living in New York homeless shelters were deficient in immunizations (National Coalition for the Homeless, 1999a). According to the National Center on Family Homelessness (2004), homeless children are in poor health four times as often as children from middle-class families. They also have much higher rates of illness and experience stomach ailments five times as often, ear infections twice as often, and asthma four times more often than other children (National Center on Family Homelessness, 2004). Children who are homeless are also at high risk for social, emotional, and behavioral problems, with over two thirds having significant or clinical problems in these areas (Davey, 2004). The emotional problems faced by children who are homeless begin as early as preschool (National Center on Family Homelessness, 2004). Unfortunately, mental health treatment services are also lacking for this population (National Center on Family Homelessness, 2004).

Children living in homeless conditions are also at risk for experiencing stressors that further contribute to risk for serious emotional and behavioral problems. Children are at risk for having been exposed to domestic violence (National Center on Family Homelessness, 2004). They are three times more likely than children who are not homeless to have been the victim of sexual abuse and twice as likely to have been the victim of physical abuse (National Center on Family Homelessness, 2004). They are also at risk for being placed in foster care.

Overall, to place children's lives in context, consider Maslow's (1968) hierarchy of needs, whereby shelter, security, and food must be obtained before one reaches higher order needs such as psychological and self-actualization needs. While homeless children are not getting their most basic needs fulfilled, their psychological health is also at stake. Children who are homeless worry about where they will sleep and live and that something bad will happen to their families (National Center on Family Homelessness, 2004). The case study presented below illustrates the potential impact of homelessness on young children.

CASE STUDY

It was 3:00 a.m. At a local gas station, a man was trying to bum $5 worth of gas off the attendant as his family waited, shivering, in their junky car. The attendant obliged the family and called a local homeless shelter asking if they would let the family stay even though their doors were closed for the night. The children arrived at the shelter, hungry and cold. Their parents tucked them in and stayed up for a while chatting with the volunteers. They were homeless because their father lost his job as a result of an illness, and they couldn't pay their bills or rent. He tried to find another full-time job but there weren't any available. He had a series of part-time jobs, but they just didn't pay enough to cover rent, electricity, and their other expenses. They tried to survive in their trailer without heat, lights, or hot water, but they all just kept getting sick and that cost even more money. For the children, seeing how sad their dad was and how scared their mom was made everything even worse. They tried to be good, but it was hard when all they wanted to do was go home.

The children woke up and ate breakfast. Their clothes were wrinkled. They were dirty and extremely tired. They went to school after less than 3 hours of sleep with a lot more on their minds than reading and math. What will their teachers think when they fall asleep in class? How will they get food for lunch? What will their peers think? Will the other kids notice they didn't change clothes? Will someone say something mean about needing a bath? In addition to worrying about how they look, they are also concerned about how to make friends and talk with others in their class. They have had to grow up too fast. Their worries are not the same as those of other children. They are worried about their next meal and where they will seek shelter. They are worried about their parents and if they'll be okay. They are worried about what else might happen. Even though they have adult worries, their needs are the same as other children. They need a home and all of the securities that come with it. They also need an education.

Factors That Contribute to Family Homelessness

How do families become homeless? As illustrated in the case study above, many families teeter on the brink of homelessness by living paycheck to paycheck, and when one bill cannot be paid they may become homeless. Many factors contribute to and perpetuate homelessness, including poverty, low wages, lack of affordable housing, and inadequate physical and mental health care. These factors are briefly described.

Since 1970, there has been a substantial increase in the number of people living in poverty, and there has been an increase in the number of Americans living in extreme poverty, with 40% of people who are poor living on incomes that are well below the poverty level (National Coalition for the Homeless, 1998a). Two contributing factors to poverty are low wages and lack of affordable housing (Institute for Children and Poverty, 2001; National Coalition for the Homeless, 1998c). When the task of trying to obtain affordable housing interacts with the low wages that people who are impoverished receive, finding housing becomes almost impossible (National Center on Family Homelessness, 2004; National Coalition for the Homeless, 2006). The National Coalition for the Homeless (1998c) reported that "in the median state a minimum-wage worker would have to work 83 hours each week to afford a two-bedroom apartment at 30% of his or her income, which is the federal definition of affordable housing" (p. 2). Furthermore, according to the Institute for Children and Poverty (2001), "in 2000, a full-time worker making the minimum wage could not afford the fair market rent for a two-bedroom apartment anywhere in the US" (p. 2). Many working-class people are struggling to escape homelessness by trying to pay their rent and meet the other needs of their families. Wages have not kept up with the rising costs of housing and living.

The prospects of additional low-income housing in the future are dubious. In 1970, this was not a problem; there were housing options available to people with low incomes (Institute for Children and Poverty, 2001). Between 1970 and 1995, 4.4

million families needed low-income housing that was not available. Further, the housing units from the 1970s are in poor conditions, and over 60,000 will be demolished (Institute for Children and Poverty, 2001). Thus, the gap will widen. The extent of the problem of the lack of low-income housing is shocking. When states (e.g., New York) attempt to address the issue, the magnitude becomes very clear. For example, a little over 5 years ago, New York allocated $1.2 billion to new low-income housing units, which will result in approximately 10,000 units. The number of people in New York on a waiting list at that time was 380,000.

As many states have faced severe fiscal distress, and with welfare reform, they also have made drastic cuts in programs that assist the poor. State programs such as Aid to Families With Dependent Children (AFDC), general assistance benefits, and Supplemental Security Income for elderly poor and people with disabilities have been cut. Overall, over a 24-year period (1970–1994), AFDC benefits for families of three fell 47% (National Coalition for the Homeless, 1998c). A new program titled Temporary Assistance to Needy Families (TANF) was designed to replace AFDC; however, TANF typically only provides assistance to people who are well below the level of poverty. These cutbacks have left holes in the safety net. Without these benefits to fall back on, many people were and are destined for economic hardship and homelessness (Institute for Children and Poverty, 2001).

The health care system in the United States is also severely lacking. Poor physical health is often cited as a contributing factor to becoming homeless. According to the U.S. Bureau of the Census, in 1997 approximately 33% of people living in poverty indicated that they had absolutely no health insurance (National Coalition for the Homeless, 1999a). This is particularly troublesome given the high rates of chronic and acute health problems in this population. For example, people who are homeless are more likely than people with housing to have tuberculosis, diabetes, hypertension, upper respiratory infections, frostbite, and addictive disorders (National Coalition for the Homeless, 1999a). Furthermore, for homeless people with addictions, the traditional substance abuse treatment methods are inadequate (National Coalition for the Homeless, 1999a). Issues of poverty, physical and mental illness, and remediating skill deficits are rarely included as a part of treatment but are blatant barriers to a potential life of stability and self-sufficiency. The programs that do exist are often unable to meet the service demands.

Another important contributing factor for homelessness is being raised in homeless conditions. That is, many youths who are homeless and living in shelters or on the street were raised in families who experienced homelessness (Haber & Toro, 2004). Many of these youths then have children and recreate the cycle of homelessness for another generation. In a study of homeless adolescent females from New York City and Denver, Colorado, researchers found that almost 50% either were pregnant or had been pregnant (Kral, Molnar, Booth, & Watters, 1997). Research has not documented what happens to young homeless youths who become pregnant. However, because the majority of homeless mothers are in their 20s (Burt, Aron, Lee, & Valente, 2001), it is likely that there is considerable overlap between homeless youth and homeless families (Haber & Toro, 2004). Most research on homeless families has excluded families headed by teen mothers, and most studies of homeless youth have not specifically looked at those who are mothers (Haber & Toro, 2004). Thus, the characteristics and contributing factors for these groups (children, families, and youth) need to be understood for prevention purposes. Characteristics and additional contributing factors for youth who are homeless are presented next.

YOUTH WHO ARE HOMELESS

Characteristics

The Center for Law and Social Policy (2003) estimated the number of homeless youths is between 500,000 to 1.3 million. The range is quite large because the number of adolescents who are homeless is difficult to calculate (Harber & Toro, 2004). Some adolescents may run away from home and stay with friends for a few nights before returning to their families. Others may leave for the night after a fight with parents but go home the next morning. Should they be included in the count? Youths who are homeless also tend to move around quite frequently and may stay in different shelters or different places. Overall, youths who are homeless fit into two broad categories: those who live in shelters or other makeshift arrangements and those who have spent time on the streets (Haber & Toro, 2004). However, living arrangements for homeless youth are fluid, and most youths who have lived on the street have also had other living arrangements in shelters, with other relatives, or with friends (Haber & Toro, 2004; Unger et al., 1998). Therefore, time spent on the street could be considered an indication of the severity of homelessness.

Homeless youth in shelters are often experiencing homelessness for the first time and usually have not been homeless for long (Haber & Toro, 2003). When researchers specifically studied demographic characteristics of youth living in shelters, the numbers of males or females were either the same or more were female (Heinze, Toro, & Urberg, 2004). In contrast, adolescents who were living on the street were more likely to be male (Cauce et al., 2000). Unlike the demographic characteristics of homeless families, 57% of homeless youth are Caucasian, 17% are African American, 15% are Hispanic, and 11% are from other ethnic groups (Hammer, Finkelhor, & Sedlak, 2002).

Although being homeless is laden with risks regardless of age, young adolescents (12–15 years old) may have characteristics and risks that differ from older adolescents. Unger et al. (1998) compared the demographic characteristics of younger adolescents with those of older adolescents and found that there was a higher percentage of females and a higher percentage of Latinos than in the sample of older adolescents. They are also more likely to be involved with a gang than older adolescents and more likely to rely on other people for shelter. Another particularly important difference between the two groups is that about 66% of younger adolescents had attended school in the past month compared with only 27% of older adolescents (Unger et al., 1998).

In terms of more specific behavioral characteristics, youths who are homeless have been found to have rates of oppositional defiance disorder at extremely high rates (40% to 51%; Cauce et al., 2000; McCaskill, Toro, & Wolfe, 1998; Toro & Goldstein, 2000). Although researchers removed "running away from home" as one of the criterion for the diagnosis, many homeless youths engaged in other behaviors associated with the diagnosis. For example, in one study 23% of the homeless youth reported stealing, 14% reported breaking into homes, 20% sold drugs, and 2% reported selling sex for money (Whitbeck, Hoyt, & Ackley 1997). It is sad to note that many of the youths stated they engaged in these behaviors to pay for housing or food (Haber & Toro, 2004).

Drug and alcohol use and abuse is also more common in homeless youth and may appear at younger ages than for housed youth (Boesky, Toro, & Bukowski, 1997). Greenblatt and Robertson (1993) found that rates of drug and alcohol abuse were five to eight times higher in adolescents who were homeless. Toro and Goldstein (2000) found that homeless youths had significantly higher rates of both alcohol and drug use. In addition to drug and alcohol use, homeless youths engage in high-risk sexual behavior, including unprotected sex (Lombardo & Toro, 2004; Whitbeck & Hoyt, 1999), and unprotected sex with intravenous drug users (Rotheram-Borus, Parra, Cantwell, Gwadz, & Murphy, 1996). The repercussions for such high-risk behaviors include contracting sexually transmitted diseases such as AIDS (Lombardo & Toro, 2004; Sweeney, Lindegen, Buehler, Onorato, & Janssen, 1995). Youths who are homeless may be engaging in "survival sex" whereby partners provide drugs, shelter, or money in exchange for sex (Anderson et al., 1996). In a multisite study, Anderson and colleagues found that up to 41% of the homeless youths interviewed had participated in this type of sexual activity. Overall, as illuminated in the following case study, youths who are homeless are typically in situations in which they feel that they have nowhere to turn.

CASE STUDY

Latisha entered the shelter that her high school counselor had told her about. She was tired, scared, confused, and a little dizzy. How did she get here? Although she knew the answer to the question, it still felt so desperate to not have anyone to turn to and nowhere to go besides a homeless shelter. She is 15, and she is pregnant. She left home because she couldn't handle the physical abuse of her stepfather anymore, especially after she found out she was pregnant. She also figured she would get quite the beating when her parents found out about her pregnancy. Latisha is still going to school, and she confides in her counselor.

The days living in the shelter become weeks. Latisha can stay at the shelter for 1 month, and then she hopes she will have a placement in a house for pregnant teens. Her counselor is working with community agencies to help Latisha and meets with her daily to see how she is doing. One of her counselor's major concerns is that Latisha has allowed the father of her child, a much older and married man, to reestablish communications with her. He is a known drug dealer and, although Latisha denies it, her counselor believes that he is abusive.

Factors That Contribute to Homelessness in Youth

In an effort to prevent homelessness in youth, it is important to understand life conditions that are also associated with the onset and sustainment of homelessness. As illustrated in the case of Latisha, many homeless youths become homeless because of chronic negative experiences at home, including physical or sexual abuse, neglect, or parental drug addiction (National Coalition for the Homeless, 2006; Robertson & Toro, 1999; Whitbeck & Hoyt, 1999). Maltreatment and neglect are substantially higher in youths who become homeless than in the broader group of adolescents (Haber & Toro, 2004). One study found that half of homeless youths reported being asked to leave their homes by their parents, and almost half (47%) reported being sexually abused (Rew, Taylor-Seehafer, Thomas, & Yockey, 2001). Other research with a large sample of homeless youths found that 50% of youths reported being sexually abused at some point in their life (Rew, Fouladi, & Yockey, 2002). In addition to being the victims of maltreatment, youths who became homeless also reported higher rates of being verbally or physically abusive toward their parents (Haber & Toro, 2003).

Other research has investigated more specific family factors that may contribute to alcohol abuse and homelessness in teenage youth (McMorris, Tyler, Whitbeck, & Hoyt, 2002). The approach used to frame the relationships among family and youth characteristics was a risk amplification model (McMorris et al., 2002). Youths who were homeless and abused alcohol had a history of parental alcohol abuse, parental rejection, and physical and sexual abuse. The youths who reported higher rates of alcohol use had spent more time on the streets, more time with deviant peers, and engaged in antisocial or self-deprecating acts to survive on the street. Research has also investigated characteristics that were associated with resilience in youth (Rew et al., 2001). Youths who were more likely to believe in their own competence and were more accepting of themselves (i.e., high ratings of resilience) were less likely to report feeling lonely and hopeless and engaging in risky behaviors.

Another subgroup of adolescents who are at increased risk for becoming homeless are those who are in foster care. In fact, the National Center on Family Homelessness (2004) identified being in foster care as one of only two risk factors in childhood to predict homelessness in adulthood. According to their estimates, 20% of all homeless mothers had been in foster care during their childhoods. A final group of youths who are at risk for becoming homeless are those who have serious psychiatric problems. Researchers followed adolescents who had been treated in a residential program for 5 years postdischarge; a large percentage (33%) had experienced homelessness at least once after being discharged, with half of these youths having this experience within a year after being discharged (Embry, Stoep, Evens, Ryan, & Pollock, 2000). In addition to early psychiatric disorders, youths who were more likely to experience homelessness had a history of physical and drug and alcohol abuse.

APPROACHES TO PREVENTION

Because of the negative effects of homelessness described in the previous sections, it is crucial to focus efforts on prevention for young children and youths who are homeless. It is clear that homelessness is a complicated social issue that will require a multilevel and multisystem approach. Providing permanent affordable housing is only part of the solution. Ending homelessness is a matter of providing people with opportunities for housing, decent wages, health insurance, treatment for health problems, and an education. Strategies for ending homelessness include prevention and intervention, which are closely related. Many strategies can be deemed prevention when they target people who are currently housed but at risk for becoming homeless and can be deemed intervention when they target the homeless (Haber & Toro, 2004). The following sections address specific preventative strategies that can be utilized for individuals (youths) and families who are homeless. These prevention efforts can be utilized by schools and community agencies.

Individual

Youths who are homeless are often hard to reach if they are not currently in school. However, when youths are in school, community and school efforts can be focused on targeting youths who are having problems in school or problems with their families and providing appropriate services. In fact, many adolescents who run away report they had recent school stresses, including failing a grade, being expelled, or having particular problems with teachers (Rotheram-Borus et al., 1996). It is also critical to support follow-up outreach and intervention efforts for youths who are included in treatment programs. If youths are in treatment programs and have a history of family maltreatment, then it is even more critical to provide outreach and support for these individuals. If youths have a history of physical abuse in their families, they may be less likely to seek or to receive support from their families upon release and may continue a destructive pattern of substance abuse.

Another group of youths to target for prevention are those in foster care. Research has found that a substantial number of youths and adults who are homeless lived in foster care when they were children. Given the lack of strong family connections for many in foster care, it appears that when youths age out of the system they have no place to go (Haber & Toro, 2004; National Center on Family Homelessness, 2004). Prevention strategies for these youths could include connecting them with resources in the community to support their transition to adult life. The resources that are critical for youths who are at risk for sudden displacement include those that help them establish housing and employment and those that teach life skills.

After youths become homeless, it appears that younger adolescents may be in a better position for professionals to assist them and help get them off the streets (Milburn et al., 2005). They rely more on other people and are more at risk for gang affiliations possibly because they have difficulty making it alone on the streets (Unger et al., 1998). Early intervention is very important with adolescents who are living on the streets because the health risks are substantially higher for adolescents who have been on the street for more than 1 year (Unger, Kipke, Simon, Montgomery, & Johnson, 1997).

Family

Although it seems obvious, the best way to prevent homelessness for families is to identify families at risk for homelessness and provide support services. It is more cost effective to spend money preventing homelessness by preventing evictions (e.g., providing vouchers to landlords for past payments, legal assistance, cash assistance programs), keeping families in shared housing situations, and assisting families who are living in condemned buildings by providing them with transition help than it is to support families in shelters once they become homeless (Lindholm, 1996). Another prevention strategy is to create "alternative families" to prevent homelessness (Haber & Toro, 2004). For example, a family might live with an elderly woman, who is less apt to be homeless than younger women with children, and provide caretaking tasks in exchange for rent. Such arrangements may be feasible as an alternative to becoming homeless or may be an intervention for a family who is homeless. More important than cost effectiveness is the fact that once families are homeless, the road to reestablishing self-sufficiency is much more difficult, and the effects of homelessness on children may be traumatizing not solely because of the lack of permanent housing but also because of the other risks that may accompany homelessness.

Another strategy for preventing homelessness for families includes providing comprehensive prevention services to low-income families and their children, particularly those who have additional risk factors. Many early childhood programs that target children living in poverty function as prevention programs for many later risks, including homelessness (Haber & Toro, 2004). These programs support children when they provide high-quality child care that prepares young children to succeed in school. These programs also make it more likely that parents will be able to work because child care is affordable (Haber & Toro, 2004). When programs focus directly on parents, they may also help prevent homelessness. Finally, when schools participate fully in the broader community and provide education and supports to families, it is more likely that families will be able to avoid homelessness and that children and youth will remain housed. Schools can also prevent homelessness by providing a wide variety of supervised after-school programs for children and adolescents so that parents can work and not worry about their children's supervision (Chen et al., 2004).

INTERVENTION STRATEGIES

Given a problem of this magnitude, prevention efforts currently are not affecting a large percentage of the homeless population. Accordingly, it is critical that professionals also understand interventions that can be applied to individual youths who are homeless and families. Specific interventions that can be applied in school settings for children and youth are also discussed, followed by efforts to intervene at the community level.

Individual

To work effectively with homeless adolescents, it is important to understand the barriers to providing services to this population and the needs of this population. The immediate needs of adolescents include their physical needs for shelter, clothing, and food and their medical needs, including education on behaviors that will place them at risk for HIV infection and other sexually transmitted diseases. When educators and service providers attempt to reach out to street youth, it is important to understand the day-to-day lifestyle of adolescents who are living on the streets. In addition, many adolescents may distrust adults and, therefore, will not access services. So the question is, How can professionals work with this population of homeless youth?

The first goal of intervention, whenever possible, is to involve both the adolescent and his or her parents or a significant family member in setting goals and developing interventions (Haber & Toro, 2004). This strategy may be particularly effective for youths who are newly homeless (Milburn et al., 2005). Auerswald and Eyre (2002) found that homeless youths are most receptive to intervention when they are newly homeless or when they are in crisis. Other research has also underscored the need to support family bonds and relationships and to attempt to reestablish family connections quickly after youths become homeless (Milburn et al., 2005). A program in Australia, called Reconnect, has provided family intervention to 23,000 youths and their families, and 70% of the participants had a positive change as a result of the intervention (Regan, 2003).

Because of the high rates of HIV, pregnancy, and sexually transmitted diseases in homeless youth, a number of intervention programs have focused on health care. One recommendation is to have programs that are specifically designed for youth (e.g., substance abuse, counseling, medical care) streamlined and accessible in one place (Nyamathi et al., 2005). There have been successful programs documented in the literature, including storefront services for youths to drop in and pick up information about AIDS (Lloyd & Kuszelewicz, 1995). Focus groups that are led by adults who have similar demographic characteristics, and who have possibly been homeless themselves, is another intervention option. One study (Rotheram-Borus,

Koopman, Haignere, & Davies, 1991) used a comprehensive intervention program that included small group sessions facilitated by a trained leader with a similar demographic background and included individual counseling when needed. The intervention included information on (a) general knowledge of HIV and AIDS, (b) the importance of using coping skills effectively, and (c) resources available to adolescents (Rotheram-Borus et al., 1991). Findings from this study were that the number of sessions that adolescents participated in was associated with a reduction in high-risk behavior and an increase in consistent condom use.

More recently, a model for working with youths who are homeless has been suggested and includes strength-based case management (Nyamathi et al., 2005). This model includes frequent interactions between youths who are homeless and a designated case manager who provides intensive support. This type of case management may result in more appropriate, individualized services for youth, and the formation of a positive relationship may also function as an additional intervention (Haber & Toro, 2004). It is clear that limited outreach efforts may only serve as a band aid and not provide the level of support that youths who are homeless need. Gleghorn, Marx, Vittinghoff, and Katz (1998) found that higher levels of contact between the case workers and clients resulted in higher rates of follow-through on the part of the client and lowered rates of risky behavior. Thus, a consistent and sensitive outreach approach that provides ongoing information in many different formats on the risks of certain behaviors appears to be the best intervention option. Additional school-based interventions are presented later.

Family

To ensure that their children are receiving an appropriate education, parents need to know their children's rights within the educational system (National Coalition for the Homeless, 2006). The McKinney-Vento Homeless Assistance Act was enacted to attempt to alleviate barriers for school attendance for children who are homeless (Institute for Children and Poverty, 2003; National Coalition for the Homeless, 2006). According to this act, families of children who are homeless have the right to choose which school their children will attend, including the school their child attended before the family became homeless or the school closest to their temporary living conditions. Families also have the right to enroll their children in school even if they do not have current immunizations, proof of residency, or any school records (Institute for Children and Poverty, 2003; National Coalition for the Homeless, 2006). Although clear gains have been made since the 1980s when an earlier act was established, children who are homeless still encounter barriers. To obtain more specifics regarding their rights, parents could contact a local shelter, social service agency, or their school district.

In addition to knowing their children's rights to an education, families who are homeless need multiple supports. First, it is important that families and children have a safe and secure shelter facility that has a consistent routine and structure. Given that there is such a lack of affordable housing, many families stay in temporary facilities for quite some time. This provides the opportunity to intervene and support families through multifaceted approaches. It is critical that professionals also assist parents and children in managing the emotional distress associated with being homeless and help families achieve renewed hope and build on existing or create new social support systems. Two examples of approaches for building skills and renewing hope include *work plus housing* and the *multiple family group*.

In New York, the work plus housing model has already been established. The model includes continued education, life skills, and work skills for adults in families in order to prepare them for self-sufficiency. Shelters are communities where adults in families are expected to work and/or continue their education and children are nurtured in a stable environment and attend school. Partnerships could be built at the state, county, and district levels to financially support efforts to establish work plus housing in their communities (Institute for Children and Poverty, 2001). The multiple family group model has been implemented using weekly meetings and, more recently, has been executed within a weekend retreat (Davey, 2004). The content of the intervention is the same, regardless of the format. In this model, four to five families meet regularly with counselors to learn positive coping skills that focus on parenting, communication strategies, and how to deal with stress. Although some of the time is spent with the children in one group and parents in another, most of the time is spent with all of the children and parents together. Families are supported in recognizing their strengths, positively communicating with each other, and clarifying the roles that each member in a family serves. In general, parents found their experience to be beneficial for the entire family.

Another important goal for school and community professionals working with families is to remove barriers to receiving adequate health care. Community and school programs need to link families with the information they need regarding services they can access. For example, outreach programs, such as Healthcare for the Homeless, are available to provide health care for the uninsured (National Coalition for the Homeless, 1999a). Information on community resources for free immunizations can also be provided to families through outreach efforts.

School

School counselors' knowledge and sensitivity to serving homeless children in the schools make them the best coordinator of resources for these individuals. School counselors could coordinate efforts to educate teachers and administrators on the characteristics and educational needs of children who are homeless. According to a 2002 reauthorization of the McKinney-Vento Act, school districts need to have a person in charge of educating professionals and communities about homelessness (National Coalition for the Homeless, 2006). School counselors and this liaison could work together to provide in-service training for teachers on general information related to homelessness, children's characteristics, suggested classroom modifications, and ways to facilitate positive self-esteem and success in school. If we consider the children and youth from the case examples described earlier, it is easy to discern that they will have potential needs for support. Counselors should help teachers determine supports that are feasible for them to utilize, and then counselors could also provide support.

Academically, most children and youths who are homeless are behind in school. This is typically due, at least in part, to their lack of stable school attendance. One study found that 42% of children who were homeless attended at least two schools during the 2001–2002 school year and 51% of those children attended three or more schools (Institute of Children and Poverty, 2003). Some estimate that children lose 3–6 months of education every time they move (National Coalition for the Homeless, 2006). These disruptions contribute to the fact that 23% of homeless children repeat a grade in school, compared with 5% of children that are not homeless (National Center on Family Homelessness, 2004). Given these data, it is clear that most children and youths who are homeless will have significant gaps in their knowledge bases.

Accordingly, teachers, counselors, or school psychologists should administer quick, informal assessments to students who are homeless, and teachers should begin instruction in content areas at a place where the students can succeed (Bos & Vaughn, 2006; Stormont, 2007). Teachers should also be very systematic and not assume that students have gone through the curriculum with the same consistency as their peers. Instruction may need to be modified, and assignments may need to be adapted. Instruction modifications could include allowing completion of in-class assignments in groups and tailoring independent work according to students' interest areas. Teachers can also use technology, cooperative learning, and peer tutoring. The number of accommodations and modifications that could be used is beyond the scope of this chapter. The critical academic supports that both children and youth need include individualizing instruction and homework assignments according to their achievement levels, after-school environments, and personal learning styles and interests to support motivation to stay in school.

There are also many small changes a teacher can make in terms of homework assignments. If students have difficulty completing written work, a teacher can adjust the amount of work required by students or change the output requirements (e.g., recite a story into a tape recorder instead of writing it out). Teachers should modify homework assignments for students who have no place to study after school (Stormont, 2007). Modifications could include allowing early access to the library or classroom, work with peers, and after-school and weekend homework support at school or at a library. Teachers need to access family members, shelter professionals, and professionals in school who would be willing to assist with homework completion or other academic enrichment activities (Nabors et al., 2004).

In addition to academic needs, children and youths who are homeless have social, emotional, and behavioral needs. Counselors should take the lead to make sure that teachers are sensitive to students' well-being at all times. Teachers should be aware of the physical as well as emotional risk factors associated with homelessness. For younger children, teachers should use strategies that can promote social and emotional well-being. Teachers can make other arrangements if children celebrate their birthdays by bringing treats. They could enlist the support of the PTA or another parent to bring treats for children who are homeless if that would be a burden for their families. Conversely, teachers could work with counselors and lunch staff to utilize kitchen space to make treats for the class. It may also mean a lot to students if they have a consistent place in the classroom to work and to post their work.

Another strategy for supporting children who are homeless would be to develop a circle of friends for children to seek out if they need assistance and individuals who have specific responsibilities for supporting children in different settings (Turnbull, Turnbull, Erin, & Soodak, 2006). For example, an assistant principal (or another person) could be in charge of making sure a child arrives at school and could contact families when children are absent. They could then determine barriers to school attendance, and professionals could try to problem solve how to overcome barriers.

Another way to support both academic and social emotional needs is for school professionals to help children transition more smoothly from one school to another. Teachers could keep a work and assessment folder for children who are at risk for moving to save instructional time at their next school (Stormont, 2007). Making the transition to a new school smooth for children also helps to ensure that they feel welcome. This folder could have an introduction to the child written by his or her current classmates (e.g., including likes, dislikes, strengths) that the teacher at the new school could use to introduce the child to his or her classmates (Stormont, 2007). This folder should also include recent assessment data, work samples, and the sending teacher's phone number for consultation. This folder could be sent with the child's family and presented upon arrival at the new school.

For youths who are homeless, teachers and counselors should develop transition support plans to help students connect the content they are learning in school to work and life after school. Special education teachers and school psychologists could be accessed to help in this process. Transition plans are especially important for youths who are living in foster care. Programs that include vocational training, academic enrichment, and individual counseling are appropriate for older youths who are homeless given the complexities of their lives (Nabors et al., 2004). For youths who have mental health issues as well as limited education, job skills, and life skills, the probability that they will be able to break the cycle of homelessness without extensive support is dubious. Thus, a wraparound approach in which schools streamline the mental health services that students need while providing an appropriate education is critical for youth who are homeless (Nabors et al., 2004).

Community

Many of the strategies presented in this intervention section include community support. From a community perspective, resources in some areas may be rich, and partnerships among schools, businesses, and shelters could be quickly established and sustained to support children and youths who are homeless. Communities could then drive the establishment of after-school programs, day camps in the summer or on the weekends, and comprehensive and accessible mental and physical health services. In other communities, the school system is the most plentiful resource, and prevention and intervention efforts would need to come from the schools.

Most communities can and should support efforts to retain children and youths who are homeless in school. Community advocates could help identify those students who are not currently receiving an education. Community outreach representatives could begin by setting up networks with local shelters and emergency housing facilities. It is also important to have continuous lines of communication open with local shelters and churches that house students currently in school. Volunteers could be recruited to get parents and youths who are homeless involved and interested in education. Community volunteers could also be recruited to be mentors for children and youths who are homeless. Mentors could be responsible for meeting with young students at least once a week and could be a source of support and advocacy. Parent sponsors could also be solicited to provide resources for a particular child or youth who is homeless. These sponsors could provide, for example, birthday treats, school supplies, or clothing.

There are resources for schools and communities to access through local and state improvement grants (National Coalition for the Homeless, 2006). Local grant funds could help support outreach efforts for identification purposes, school attendance and transportation, local resource coordination, the establishment of after-school and summer programs, and the distribution of school supplies. State grants could help with professional development, technical assistance, and the development of educational materials for dissemination (National Coalition for the Homeless, 2006).

ADAPTATIONS FOR DIVERSITY

The primary focus of this chapter has been on children, families, and youth who are homeless. There are other groups of people who experience homelessness who have characteristics that need to be considered when designing appropriate supports, including single mothers and people from culturally diverse backgrounds.

Single Mothers

Research has shown that about 85% of homeless families are headed by a single female (National Center on Family Homelessness, 2004). It is clear that single mothers with children are a distinct subgroup within the population of the homeless with different psychological and demographic characteristics. The needs of mothers with small children are also very different from the needs of other homeless people (Buckner, Bassuk, & Zima, 1993). When compared with single women who are homeless but not caring for children, homeless mothers caring for children were younger, less educated, and had been homeless for shorter periods of time. Homeless mothers were also more likely to report greater degrees of psychological distress than single women.

The psychological distress for homeless mothers appears to be much greater than the distress of poverty alone. Thus, even though mothers caring for dependent children appear to have less major substance abuse and mental health problems than other homeless people, research has found that mothers living in shelters have substance abuse problems at high rates. In fact, 40% of homeless women report to have experienced drug or alcohol dependence during their lives (National Center on Family Homelessness, 2004). The psychological distress related to being a homeless mother may be due to the precipitating events to homelessness and/or the lack of outside support available once homeless.

One of the precipitating events to homelessness for mothers is domestic abuse. According to the National Coalition for the Homeless (1998c), studies have found that up to 50% of women are homeless because they are fleeing domestic abuse. Women who are homeless have also experienced more violence overall than other women. According to the National Center on Family Homelessness (2004, p. 3), "The frequency of violence in the lives of homeless mothers is staggering." For example,

- 63% have been violently abused by an intimate male partner.
- 27% have required medical treatment because of violence by an intimate male partner.
- 25% have been physically or sexually assaulted by someone other than an intimate partner.
- 66% were violently abused by a childhood caretaker or other adult in the household before reaching 18.
- 43% were sexually molested as children.

The lack of support that homeless mothers report is another major consideration for working with this diverse population. Almost 80% of mothers who are homeless receive financial support from the adults in their lives (National Center on Family Homelessness, 2004). However, mothers who are homeless appear to receive less emotional support from friends and family. In one study that included predominantly African American mothers, researchers documented that mothers in low-income housing saw and/or talked to more friends and relatives on a weekly basis than mothers who were homeless (Letiecq, Anderson, & Koblinsky, 1998). Furthermore, mothers who were homeless reported there were fewer people that they could count on in times of need and less family support in the last 6 months than mothers in low-income housing. Thus, another factor to consider for mothers who are not receiving much support from relatives and friends is that they may face a major child-care dilemma. The following quote eloquently describes the plight of single mothers with children:

> It is obvious that these mothers are extraordinarily stressed and are facing almost insurmountable problems of single parenting under the difficult circumstances of poverty, lack of extended family support, lack of affordable child care available to them if they could work, and are without a home. In reality, any smaller combination of these circumstances could render almost anyone immobilized, and it is highly unlikely that any improvement can occur without ongoing social assistance and interpersonal support. (Dail, 1993, p. 59)

Cultural Diversity

In addition to cultural differences related to marital status and gender, ethnicity and geographical location need to be considered when working with homeless children. There is extreme disparity between the percentage of cultural diversity in the general population and the percentage of people from culturally diverse backgrounds who are homeless. In fact, researchers have documented the percentage of homeless persons from culturally diverse backgrounds to be as high as 85% in certain areas (Danseco & Holden, 1998). Research that included a large sample of people who were homeless across the United States found that 61% were from African American backgrounds (Institute for Children and Poverty & Homes for the Homeless, 2005).

With this knowledge, preventative outreach approaches should target community and state-run services that serve minority groups, particularly African Americans, and support families who are teetering on the brink of homelessness. Once African American mothers become homeless, it is very important to provide linkages with social service organizations and other sources of support. Research has shown that this group may be particularly subject to alienation or a lack of support from family and friends (Letiecq et al., 1998). It is important to note that the triggers to homelessness also appear to be somewhat culturally related. Caucasians are more likely to have become homeless because of domestic abuse, and people from Hispanic backgrounds may be more likely to become homeless because of language barriers that cause difficulty accessing social services (Institute for Children and Poverty & Homes for the Homeless, 2005).

There is also a misconception in the general public that homelessness is an urban problem. Rural homelessness may be increasing at a faster rate than urban homelessness, and the demographic characteristics of the rural homeless are different from the urban homeless. Specifically, rural people who are homeless are more likely to be Caucasian than their urban counterparts (Herron & Zabel, 1995; National

Coalition for the Homeless, 2006). Native Americans and migrant workers who are homeless are also predominantly in rural areas (National Coalition for the Homeless, 2006). Another important consideration for working with homeless populations in rural areas is that it may be more difficult to identify rural families who are homeless because they may have a stronger support network and may be living in temporary residences with family and friends or because they may be living in wooded camp areas or other remote areas (Aron & Fitchen, 1996). Outreach efforts in rural areas should consider research by Vissing (1996) that has found that families represent the majority of people who are homeless in rural areas (National Coalition for the Homeless, 1999c).

Overall, it is important to remember to honor cultural diversity when working with all families. It is important to always be culturally sensitive without being stereotypic (Turnbull et al., 2006). Some examples of arrangements that professionals providing services to families who are homeless could make to be culturally sensitive include ensuring that the provider and the family have a language and cultural match, having flexible hours and accepting walk-ins, and using clergy or respected members of cultures in interventions (Turnbull et al., 2006; Watson, 1996).

SUMMARY

It is clear that children and youths who are homeless suffer physically, psychologically, socially, and academically. It is unconscionable that many of these children and youths are not being served when a portion of this population could be readily identified through homeless shelters, foster care, and other social agencies. Research on homeless children and youth is growing but still scarce despite the large numbers of homeless youth in the United States. More information regarding children and youth who are homeless and the barriers they face within and outside of the school system is needed. Additionally, state departments of education must recognize the prevalence of homelessness and fund programs designed to support coordinated outreach, prevention, and intervention efforts. Without more concentrated efforts for prevention and intervention, youths who are homeless will continue to be at risk for growing up uneducated, in poor health, and at risk for recreating the cycle of homelessness with their children.

REFERENCES

Anderson, J. E., Cheney, R., Clatts, M., Faruique, S., Kipke, M., Long, A., et al. (1996). HIV risk behavior, street outreach and condom use in eight high-risk populations. *AIDS Education and Prevention, 8,* 191–204.

Aron, L. Y., & Fitchen, J. M. (1996). Rural homelessness: A synopsis. In J. Baumchi (Ed.), *Homelessness in America* (pp. 81–85). Phoenix, AZ: Oryx Press.

Auerswald, C., & Eyre, S. L. (2002). Youth homelessness in San Francisco: A life cycle approach. *Social Science and Medicine, 54,* 1497–1512.

Boesky, L. M., Toro, P. A., & Bukowski, P. A. (1997). Differences in psychosocial factors among older and younger homeless adolescents found in youth shelters. *Journal of Prevention and Intervention in the Community, 15,* 19–36.

Bos, C. S., & Vaughn, S. (2006). *Strategies for teaching students with learning and behavior problems* (6th ed.). Boston: Pearson/Allyn & Bacon.

Buckner, J. C., Bassuk, E. L., & Zima, B. T. (1993). Mental health issues affecting homeless women: Implications for intervention. *American Journal of Orthopsychiatry, 63*, 385–399.

Burt, M., Aron, L. Y., Lee., & Valente, J. (2001). *Helping America's homeless: Emergency shelter or affordable housing?* Washington, DC: Urban Institute Press.

Cauce, A. M., Paradise, M., Ginzler, J. A., Embry, L., Morgan, C. J., Lohr, Y., et al. (2000). The characteristic and mental health of homeless adolescents: Age and gender differences. *Journal of Emotional and Behavioral Disorders, 8*, 230–239.

Center for Law and Social Policy. (2003). *Leave no youth behind: Opportunities for congress to reach disconnected youth.* Washington, DC: Author.

Chen, C., Dormitzer, C. M., Gutieerrez, U., Vittetoe, K., Gonzales, G. B., & Anthony, F. C. (2004). The adolescent behavioral repertoire as a context for drug exposure: Behavioral autarcesis at play. *Addiction, 99*, 897–906.

Children's Defense Fund. (2005). *The state of America's children.* Washington, DC: Author.

Dail, P. W. (1993). Homelessness in America: Involuntary family migration. *Marriage and Family Review, 19*(1–2), 55–75.

Danseco, E. R., & Holden, E. W. (1998). Are there different types of homeless families? A typology of homeless families based on cluster analysis. *Family Relations, 47*, 159–165.

Davey, T. L. (2004). A multiple-family group intervention for homeless families: The weekend retreat. *Health and Social Work, 29*, 326–329.

Embry, L. E., Stoep, A. V., Evens, C., Ryan, K., & Pollock, A. (2000). Risk factors for homelessness in adolescents released from psychiatric residential treatment. *Journal of the American Academy of Child and Adolescent Psychiatry, 39*, 1293–1299.

Fisher, M. (2005). *Why is U.S. poverty higher in nonmetropolitan than metropolitan areas?* Corvallis, OR: Rural Poverty Research Center. Retrieved October 1, 2006, from www.rprconline.org/WorkingPapers/WP0504.pdf

Gleghorn, A. A., Marx, R., Vittinghoff, R., & Katz, M. H. (1998). Association between drug use patterns and HIV risks among homeless, runaway and street youth in Northern California. *Drug and Alcohol Dependence, 51*, 219–227.

Greenblatt, M., & Robertson, M. J. (1993). Lifestyles, adaptive strategies, and sexual behaviors of homeless adolescents. *Hospital and Community Psychiatry, 44*, 1177–1183.

Haber, M., & Toro, P. A. (2003, June). *Parent–adolescent violence as a predictor of adolescent outcomes.* Poster session presented at the biennial conference on Community Research and Action, Las Vegas, NM.

Haber, M. G., & Toro, P. A. (2004). Homelessness among families, children, and adolescents: An ecological–developmental perspective. *Clinical Child and Family Psychology Review, 7*, 123–164.

Hammer, H., Finkelhor, D., & Sedlak, A. J. (2002). *Runaway/thrown away children: National estimates and characteristics.* Washington, DC: U.S. Department of Justice, Office of Juvenile Justice and Delinquency Prevention.

Heinze, H., Toro, P. A., & Urberg, K. A. (2004). Delinquent behaviors and affiliation with male and female peers. *Journal of Clinical Child and Adolescent Psychology, 33*, 336–346.

Herron, N. L., & Zabel, D. (1995). *Bridging the gap: Examining polarity in America.* Englewood, CO: Libraries Unlimited.

Institute for Children and Poverty. (2001). *A shelter is not a home: Or is it?* Retrieved from http://www.homesforthehomeless.com/PDF/reports/Shelter.pdf?Submit1=Free+Download

Institute for Children and Poverty. (2003). *Miles to go: The flip side of the McKinney-Vento homeless assistance act*. Retrieved from http://www.homesforthehomeless.com/PDF/merchandise/MilestoGo.pdf?Submit1=Free+Download

Institute for Children and Poverty. (2004). *Reports and statistics*. Retrieved from http://www.homesforthehomeless.com/index.asp?CID=3&PID=18

Institute for Children and Poverty & Homes for the Homeless. (2005). *Homelessness in America: Part 2. A statistical reader*. Retrieved from http://www.icpny.org/PDF/merchandise/HIA2%20final.pdf?Submit1=Free+Download

Kral, A. H., Molnar, B. E., Booth, R. E., & Watters, J. K (1997). Prevalence of sexual risk behavior and substance use among runaway and homeless adolescents in San Francisco, Denver, and New York City. *International Journal of STD and AIDS, 8*, 109–117.

Letiecq, B. L., Anderson, E. A., & Koblinsky, S. A. (1998). Social support of homeless and housed mothers: A comparison of temporary and permanent housing arrangements. *Family Relations, 47*, 415–421.

Lindholm, E. N. (1996). Preventing homelessness. In J. Baumohl (Ed.), *Homelessness in America* (pp. 187–200). Phoenix, AZ: Oryx Press.

Lloyd, G. A., & Kuszelewicz, M. A. (Eds.). (1995). *HIV disease: Lesbians, gays, and the social services*. New York: Haworth Press.

Lombardo, S., & Toro, P. A. (2004). *Risky sexual behaviors and substance abuse among homeless and other at-risk adolescents*. Unpublished manuscript, Department of Psychology, Wayne State University.

Maslow, A. H. (1968). *Toward a psychology of being* (2nd ed.). New York: Van Nostrand.

McCaskill, P. A., Toro, P. A., & Wolfe, S. M. (1998). Homeless and matched housed adolescents: A comparative study of psychopathology. *Journal of Clinical Child Psychology, 27*, 306–319.

McMorris, B. J., Tyler, K. A., Whitbeck, L. B., & Hoyt, D. R. (2002). Familial and "on-the-street" risk factors associated with alcohol use among homeless and runaway adolescents. *Journal of Studies on Alcohol, 63*, 34–44.

Milburn, N. G., Rotheram-Borus, M. J., Batterham, P., Brumback, B., Rosenthal, D., & Mallett, S. (2005). Predictors of close family relationships over one year among homeless young people. *Journal of Adolescence, 28*, 263–275.

Nabors, L. A., Weist, M. D., Shugarman, R., Woeste, M. J., Mullet, E., & Rosner, L. (2004). Assessment, prevention, and intervention activities in a school-based program for children experiencing homelessness. *Behavior Modification, 28*, 565–578.

National Center on Family Homelessness. (1999). *Homeless children: America's new outcasts*. Newton, MA: Author.

National Center on Family Homelessness. (2004). *Homeless children: America's new outcasts*. Newton, MA: Author. Retrieved September 6, 2006, from http://www.familyhomelessness.org

National Coalition for the Homeless. (1998a, May). *How many people experience homelessness?* (NCH Fact Sheet # 2). Retrieved from http://nch.ari.net/numbers.html

National Coalition for the Homeless. (1998b, May). *Who is homeless?* (NCH Fact Sheet # 3) Retrieved from http://nch.ari.net/who.html

National Coalition for the Homeless. (1998c, May). *Why are people homeless?* (NCH Fact Sheet # 1). Retrieved from http://nch.ari.net/causes.html

National Coalition for the Homeless. (1999a). *Health care and homelessness* (NCH Fact Sheet # 8). Retrieved from http://nch.ari.net/health.html

National Coalition for the Homeless. (1999b). *How many people experience homelessness?* (NCH Fact Sheet # 2). Retrieved from http://nch.ari.net/numbers.html

National Coalition for the Homeless. (1999c). *Who is homeless?* (NCH Fact Sheet # 3). Retrieved from http://nch.ari.net/who.html

National Coalition for the Homeless. (2006). *Homeless youth* (NCH Fact Sheet # 13). Retrieved September 6, 2006, from http://www.nationalhomeless.org

Nyamathi, A. M., Christiani, A., Windokun, F., Jones, T., Strehlow, A., & Shoptaw, S. (2005). Hepatitis C virus infection, substance use and mental illness among homeless youth: A review. *AIDS, 19,* 34–40.

Regan, P. (2003, April). *Youth homelessness and early intervention: The Reconnect experience.* Paper presented at the Third National Homelessness Conference, Beyond and Divide, Brisbane, Australia.

Rew, L., Fouladi, R. T., & Yockey, R. D. (2002). Sexual health practices of homeless youth. *Journal of Nursing Scholarship, 34,* 139–145.

Rew, L., Taylor-Seehafer, M., Thomas, N. Y., & Yockey, R. D. (2001). Correlates of resilience in homeless adolescents. *Journal of Nursing Scholarship, 33*(1), 33–40.

Robertson, M. J., & Toro, P. A. (1999). Homeless youth: Research, intervention, and policy. In L. B. Fosburg & D. L. Dennis (Eds.), *Practical lessons: The 1998 national symposium on homelessness research* (pp. 3.1–3.32). Washington, DC: U.S. Department of Housing and Urban Development and U.S. Department of Health and Human Services.

Rotheram-Borus, M. J., Koopman, C., Haignere, C., & Davies, M. (1991). Reducing HIV sexual risk behaviors among runaway adolescents. *Journal of the American Medical Association, 266,* 1237–1241.

Rotheram-Borus, M. J., Parra, M., Cantwell, C., Gwadz, M., & Murphy, D. A. (1996). Runaway and homeless youths. In R. J. DiClemente, W. B. Hansen, & L. E. Ponton (Eds.), *Handbook of adolescent health risk behavior* (pp. 369–391). New York: Plenum Press.

Stormont, M. (2007). *Fostering resilience in young children vulnerable for failure: Strategies for K–3.* Columbus, OH: Pearson/Merrill/Prentice Hall.

Sweeney, P., Lindegren, M. L., Buehler, J. W., Onorato, I. M., & Janssen, R. S. (1995). Teenagers at risk of human immunodeficiency virus Type 1 infection. *Archives in Pediatric Adolescent Medicine, 149,* 521–528.

Toro, P. A., & Goldstein, M. S. (2000, August). *Outcomes among homeless and matched housed adolescents: A longitudinal comparison.* Poster presented at the annual convention of the American Psychological Association, Washington, DC.

Turnbull, A., Turnbull, R., Erwin, E., & Soodak, L. (2006). *Families, professionals, and exceptionality: Positive outcomes through partnerships and trust* (5th ed.). Upper Saddle River, NJ: Pearson Merrill Prentice Hall.

Unger, J. B., Kipke, M. D., Simon, T. R., Montgomery, S. B., & Johnson, C. J. (1997). Homeless youths and young adults in Los Angeles: Prevalence of mental health problems and the relationship between mental health problems and substance abuse disorders. *American Journal of Community Psychology, 25,* 371–394.

Unger, J. B., Simon, T. R., Newman, T. L., Montgomery, S. B., Kipke, M. D., & Albornoz, M. (1998). Early adolescent street youth: An overlooked population with unique problems and service needs. *Journal of Early Adolescence, 18,* 325–348.

U.S. Conference of Mayors. (2005). *The United States Conference of Mayors: Sodexho hunger and homelessness survey.* Retrieved September 6, 2006, from www.usmayors.org/uscm/hungersurvey/2005/HH2005FINAL.pdf

Vissing, Y. (1996). *Out of sight, out of mind: Homeless children and families in small-town America.* Lexington: University of Kentucky Press.

Watson, V. (1996). Responses by the states to homelessness. In J. Baumohl (Ed.), *Homelessness in America* (pp. 172–178). Phoenix, AZ: Oryx Press.

Whitbeck, L. B., & Hoyt, D. R. (1999). *Nowhere to grow: Homeless and runaway adolescents and their families.* New York: Aldine de Gruyter.

Whitbeck, L. B., & Hoyt, D. R., & Ackley, K. A. (1997). Abusive family backgrounds and victimization among runaway and homeless adolescents. *Journal of Research on Adolescence, 7,* 375–392.

CHAPTER 17

■

"This Isn't the Place for Me": School Dropout

Lea R. Flowers and Mary A. Hermann

Concerns about at-risk youth and the national dropout rate have existed for decades. Dropping out of school presents a serious national, state, and local problem. Researchers, administrators, and educators have sought to gain a greater understanding of the causes of academic underachievement in hopes of identifying an effective course of prevention for youth at risk (Lynch, Hurford, & Cole, 2002). Campbell (2003) asserted that the United States has failed a vast majority of America's urban youth; such failure is evident in the public inner-city schools where there is a 1:1 ratio for the numbers of students graduating from high school versus the number of students dropping out of high school. The incidence of school dropout continues to climb to epidemic proportions. There are broad economic and social repercussions for today's society as a whole, as well as negative consequences related to the well-being of the youth at risk (Dunn, Chambers, & Rabren, 2004). Using data from the National Education Longitudinal Study, Manlove (1998) examined individual, family, and school characteristics associated with teenage pregnancy and birth among a nationwide school-age sample. Results revealed that White and Hispanic young women who dropped out of school were about 50% more likely to have a teenage birth than were those who remained in school; among Black adolescents in this study, however, dropping out of school had no significant impact on the risk of a teenage birth.

The current labor force is vastly different from those of past agrarian and industrial economies; the demands and complexities require an increased skill set and expertise (Harvey, 2001). Currently, we live in a growing global and technology-based economy; medium-income jobs for poorly educated workers have become more and more scarce. School dropouts are unprepared and cannot compete in the today's competitive workforce, which naturally results in a cycle of poverty and unemployment (Mayer, 2002, as cited in Campbell, 2003). On average the median income of high school dropouts age 18 and over was $8,247 less than the $20,431 median income of their direct age group peers who completed their education with a General Educational Development (GED) certificate (National Center for Education Statistics [NCES], 2006; U.S. Census Bureau, 2005). The Institute for Educational Leadership indicated that school dropouts cost the nation from $60 billion to $228 billion each year in welfare, lost revenue, unemployment expenditures, and crime prevention (Dunn et al., 2004; Grayson, 1998).

As of October 2000, 3.8 million young people between the ages of 16 and 24 had dropped out of school (NCES, 2002). This figure represents almost 11% of that age group. The NCES reported that 5% of students enrolled in high school in October 1999 had dropped out of school by October 2000. Based on these percentages, the incidence of school dropout seems to be worsening. Society suffers when students do not complete their education. Dropping out of school has been associated with substance abuse, crime, and other delinquent behaviors (Jimerson, 1999; Swaim, Beauvais, Chavez, & Oetting, 1997). Students who drop out of school are more likely to spend time in prison, earn low wages, and depend on public assistance (Dynarski & Gleason, 2002). Mortenson (1997) explained that since 1973, "the labor market has been brutally redistributing income among workers according to their educational attainment" (p. 94). Mortenson found a strong positive correlation between formal education and high income. People with the least formal education have experienced substantial declines in income and standard of living. Mortenson stated that this redistribution "clearly signals the end of the high wage–low skill labor economy" (p. 94). Thus, dropouts negatively affect the economy because they have limited resources and generally are not well-trained workers or lucrative consumers (Velez & Saenz, 2001).

The underlying causes of school dropout are complex and multidimensional (Christenson, Sinclair, Lehr, & Godber, 2001). Although the label *dropout* has been applied to large numbers of students who do not finish school, such a label fails to adequately represent the fact that youths who drop out of school are a diverse group who leave school for many different reasons. Bickel, Bond, and LeMahieu (1988) noted that the term *dropout* is potentially misleading because it implies that school dropout is an event instead of a process and that the student is the sole decision maker in the process. In actuality, these researchers suggested that some students do not really drop out but merely "fade out" after a period of feeling alienated from school, whereas other students may be subtly or not so subtly "pushed out" of school by school administrators who do not want to deal with the struggling student any longer. Still other students are "pulled out" by more important life demands on their time, such as parenting or having to work. Regardless of the reasons for school dropout, school personnel and counselors who work with these youths cannot afford to passively watch the levels of school attrition increase.

PROBLEM DEFINITION

The cause for student dropout cannot be measured in isolation of impeding factors. Numerous individual, family, and structural factors contribute to students' decisions to leave school (Newcomb et al., 2002; Velez & Saenz, 2001; Wayman, 2002b). Rumberger (1993) defined individual factors as factors that refer to the individual student's attributes, attitudes, and behaviors and family factors as the social, human, and cultural resources and experiences provided by the family. Structural factors range from school practices to economic and prevalent social conditions. Rumberger further explained that the individual, family, and structural factors that contribute to school dropout are interrelated. Students in certain subgroups, such as the economically disadvantaged and certain racial and ethnic groups, have historically graduated from high school at substantially lower rates than their peers.

Ethnicity

Although the majority of today's U.S. schoolchildren are Caucasian, there has been rapid increase in the number of immigrant and minority students within the last decade (Lunenburg, 2000). Based on the U.S. Census Bureau (1991, as cited in Lunenburg, 2000), it is predicted that nearly one in three U.S. schoolchildren will fall within the Census Bureau's designation of "minority" by the year 2010 (Lunenburg, 2000). Students' ethnic background has historically been correlated with risk for dropping out of school. Asian/Pacific Islanders were less likely dropouts than any other ethnic group. However, in major metropolitan areas such as New York City, the dropout rate for this group was much higher than the national dropout rate for this group. Researchers suggest as the Korean American population grows, the need for attention to at-risk Korean American students will also increase (Suh & Satcher, 2005). The NCES (2006) report indicated that the dropout rates for Caucasian youth remained lower than African American and Hispanic youth between the ages of 16 and 24. The gap between Caucasian and African American youth has consistently decreased since the 1970s and 1980s. From 1972 to 2002, the percentage of Hispanics ages 16–24 who were dropouts was consistently higher than that of Blacks and Whites. Within this 31-year period, dropout rates for Caucasian and African American youth have decreased by about half; the rates for African American youth declined from 21.3% to 10.9% and the rates for Caucasian youth declined from 12.3% to 6.3%. During this same period, Hispanic dropout rates have fluctuated considerably but also have demonstrated a long-term decline, falling from 34.3% to 23.5%. Hispanics born in the United States were less likely than immigrant Hispanics to drop out of school (NCES, 2006). These findings are consistent with the findings of McMillen, Kaufman, Hausken, and Bradby (1993), who reported that among Hispanics who speak English well, the dropout rate was 17%, compared with a dropout rate of 83% for Hispanics who spoke limited or no English at all. Rumberger (1993) hypothesized that such statistics may be due to the understandably high correlation between language proficiency and both academic achievement and grade retention, variables that have been directly correlated with higher dropout rates. Additionally, Velez and Saenz (2001) pointed out that Latino families typically move frequently to seek economic opportunities. As a result, Latino students often have to continually adapt to new school environments. This high frequency of relocation weakens the connection between the students and their schools, teachers, and communities, all of which contribute to the risk of school dropout.

In a qualitative study on Chicano/Latino students who dropped out of school, Aviles, Guerrero, Howarth, and Thomas (1999) reported the participants expressed that they believed school staff had low expectations of them and exhibited negative attitudes toward them. Furthermore, these students believed that they were disciplined more harshly than other students. Participants reported they were placed in English as a Second Language (ESL) classes seemingly on the basis of appearance or name, even if they were fluent in English. Being placed in special programs was a source of embarrassment for the participants. Participants also explained they were not encouraged and were often discouraged from participating in extracurricular activities. Themes that ran through the participants' perceptions of the school environment were marginalization, alienation, and discrimination.

Wayman (2002a) found that some students perceived differential treatment by teachers based on ethnic background. He noted school dropouts held this perception more than other students. Wayman explained that whether or not such bias existed, the perceptions of teacher bias based on ethnicity were real for the students who held these perceptions. Often such perceptions contributed to student disengagement and alienation, both of which hinder academic achievement.

Socioeconomic Status

Socioeconomic status has been correlated with school dropout (Alexander, Entwisle, & Kabbani, 2001; Rumberger, 1993; Vitaro, Larocque, Janosz, & Tremblay, 2001). Alexander et al. found that socioeconomic status had the strongest correlation to school dropout. Furthermore, Rumberger completed an extensive review of the literature and noted that when socioeconomic status was held constant, much of the difference in dropout rates among various racial/ethnic groups disappeared or was greatly diminished.

Educational researchers have concluded that low-income urban youth are at high risk for dropping out (Alexander et al., 2001; Rumberger, 1993). The increasing high dropout rate exacerbates inequalities between high-income and low-income children (Campbell, 2003). The NCES (2006) reported that in 2003 teenagers living in families with incomes in the lowest 20% of reported family incomes were five times as likely as teenagers living in families in the highest 20% to drop out of school. Velez and Saenz (2001) explained that socioeconomic status is related to quality of life and schools in the neighborhood. Students living in neighborhoods in poor areas may have to deal with inadequate housing and high crime rates. Schools in impoverished neighborhoods often have fewer resources and larger class sizes. Velez and Saenz found that in schools with a high student-to-teacher ratio, teachers cannot provide the individualized attention necessary to facilitate learning for all students.

School

There are numerous reasons why adolescents drop out of school, some of which include lack of interest in school, low grades, misconduct, low reading and math abilities, financial problems, personality problems, parental influence, family background, and other socioeconomic factors. The final decision to drop out of school, however, appears to be made over time. Many adolescents, by the time they do drop out, have lost all confidence in their ability to succeed in school (Beekhoven, & Dekkers, 2005) and have developed feelings of inferiority (Cairns, Cairns, & Neckerman, 1989, as cited in Wells, Miller, Tobacyk, & Clanton, 2002).

Baker et al. (2001) found that schools contribute to students' failure and to increase in dropout by overlooking the positive benefits of connecting with students and engaging them in the learning process. Students who are engaged in school are less likely to drop out (Alexander et al., 2001). Typically all students start school enthused, optimistic, and eager to learn, yet students who experience repeated failures in the school environment gradually disengage from the learning process (Alexander et al., 2001). Dropping out of school often results from a gradual disengagement from school activities; negative experiences as early as elementary school often begin the educational disengagement process, which later ends in the student dropping out of school completely (Garnier, Stein, & Jacobs, 1997).

Alexander et al. (2001) found that for most dropouts, the school environment was not a comfortable one, resulting in weak attachment to school. Life outside of school becomes more enjoyable than life in school because students can connect with and find a sense of belonging with other individuals who are not in school. Consequently, when students have conflicting demands on their time from work opportunities or other responsibilities, school becomes less important.

Retention

Jimerson, Anderson, and Whipple (2002) reviewed the literature and found that retaining students is one of the strongest predictors of school dropout. In their study of Baltimore school children, Alexander et al. (2001) found that 80% of students who repeated more than one grade dropped out of school, and 94% of students who repeated a grade in both elementary and middle school eventually dropped out. Students retained in early elementary school were at a much higher risk of dropping out than students who were promoted, and retention in any grade prior to high school increased the risk of student dropout. Alexander et al. also reported that even when socioeconomic status was held constant, significant differences were found based on whether the student was retained. These researchers reported that 75% of students from higher socioeconomic backgrounds dropped out when they were retained in middle school as opposed to 11% of students from higher socioeconomic backgrounds who were not retained.

Jimerson (1999) found that retained students were 20% to 25% more likely to drop out of school than low-achieving students who were socially promoted. He noted that any short-term benefits related to retention soon dissipated, and the overall effect of this remediation strategy was school withdrawal or dropout. Jimerson et al. (2002) stated that children who have been exposed to risk factors such as low socioeconomic status and low parental level of education are put at greater risk for retention. Jimerson clarified that retention is not the single event that causes dropout, but students who are retained are an increased risk for dropout. Thus, Jimerson concluded that student retention is not an effective remediation strategy for at-risk youth, and alternative remedial strategies should be explored.

Alexander et al. (2001) hypothesized that there are negative social ramifications to retaining students in the same grade. Gleason and Dynarski (2002) noted that students who have been retained are often 2 or more years older than classmates. Being older than one's classmates is particularly detrimental to the social development of students in middle school when self-consciousness is heightened and peer acceptance vital. Sustained feelings of failure and alienation from peers increase risk of school dropout. The transition into high school is a challenging period for most students. During this time students often experience deep feelings of fear and alienation. High schools are usually larger, more impersonal, and more academically challenging than middle schools. The transition period for high school students, particularly students who have experienced failure in school, can be even more difficult.

Disruptive Behaviors

Vitaro et al. (2001) found that disruptive behavior, even in early grades, was predictive of students dropping out of school. Students who followed school rules were less likely to drop out (Alexander et al., 2001). Velez and Saenz (2001) posited that not accepting societal goals and the resulting disruptive behaviors could be associated with an attempt to restore self-esteem that had been damaged by rejection from teachers and the educational system as a whole.

School factors associated with high dropout rates also include high absenteeism (Aviles et al., 1999; Gleason & Dynarski, 2002; Scanlon & Mellard, 2002). Aviles et al. (1999) conducted a qualitative study in which they interviewed 33 female and 39 male Chicano/Latinos who had dropped out of high school in the last 5 years. Participants offered the following reasons for their decision to drop out of school: receiving failing grades as a consequence of missing numerous days of school, not being able to catch up on or complete makeup work, and poor communication between the school and home. The participants explained the reasons for frequent absences as work schedules and lack of interest in schoolwork. Participants indicated that the following factors would have increased their decisions to remain in school: (a) flexible school times to accommodate their work schedules, (b) a clear explanation of the regulations related to attendance, and (c) school personnel who were more sensitive to the students' needs. Finally, the participants reported that there was a discrepancy in what they and their parents believed to be legitimate absences and what the school recorded as excused absences.

Some researchers argue that students at risk for educational failure are typically viewed from a perspective of personal deficit or from a standpoint of social inequity (Cassidy & Bates, 2005). These researchers identified the most common personal deficits that interrupt students' academic success as learning disabilities, poor motivation, or low intelligence. Likewise, environmental issues are often attributed to failure in school, factors such as living in a single-parent home, coming from a family with minimal education, or being part of a cultural group that does not value education (Cassidy & Bates, 2005).

Vitaro et al. (2001) reported that poor academic performance was predictive of dropping out. Furthermore, Newcomb et al. (2002) found that academic competence had the strongest correlation to completing high school. Students with higher grades are less likely to drop out of school (Keith & Schartzer, 1995; Velez & Saenz, 2001). Chinien and Boutin (2001) concluded that some students drop out of school because of the difficulties they encounter with schoolwork. They noted that these learning difficulties are exacerbated by a strong sense of rejection. The consequences of these feelings of rejection by the school environment include students eventually disengaging from the learning process. Each of these personal deficits can and often does have some influence on a student's decision to drop out of school. However, to suggest the root of the issue of school drop stems directly from individual deficits of the students and their families or perhaps their particular culture is short sighted. Campbell (2003) asserted that there are major flaws in this type of thinking, primarily because from this perspective, the impetus for change is on the victim, in other words, "blaming the victim." The difficulties experienced by individuals, families, and cultural groups are connected with larger social inequalities of poverty, marginalization, and disadvantage. The school system itself may reflect these disparities through discriminatory school practices and formulaic school policies (Deschenes et al., 2001, as cited in Campbell, 2003). As Campbell (2003) explained, the problem is that these students and their cultures are essentially categorized and perhaps even blamed for their expected failure without any acknowledgment of the systemic processes within the schools or larger sociopolitical experiences that occur externally that equally contribute to the student feeling alienated and isolated from succeeding in the academic environment. Hence, the students live down to the ex-

pectation set before them, and dropping out of school becomes a natural consequence. Researchers often agree that schools frequently fail to connect with the
lives and the worlds of the learners they are supposedly designed to serve (Cassidy
& Bates, 2005). Thus, the dropout problem is multifaceted; many students are "at
risk" or "pushed out" (Wotherspoon & Schussel, 2001, as cited in Cassidy & Bates,
2005) in school environments that are bound by bureaucratic regulations and policies that often do not understand or take into account the needs of the students,
which presents a quandary of whether students are at risk or whether the greater
issue is the school system's lack of effective interventions. Researchers have termed
this paradox as the "risk-inducing phenomena" for the schools (Gordon & Yowell,
1994, as cited in Cassidy & Bates, 2005).

No Child Left Behind Act

The public school systems in the United States are responsible for educating 48
million students, who will be the majority of the future workforce. Schools are designed to provide students with the skills needed to succeed, which is vital to the
nation's economic strength and ability to compete in a global economy. The No
Child Left Behind Act of 2001 (NCLBA) was passed in part to increase the likelihood
that all of the 48 million students in the nation's public school systems will graduate. The NCLBA holds states accountable by requiring states to use high school
graduation rates, along with test scores, to assess how much progress high schools
are making in educating their students. Graduation rates used in conjunction with
test scores provide a more complete picture of school performance than test scores
alone. It has been argued that school's test proficiency rates would be higher if
low-performing students dropped out and do not have their scores included with
their peers.

Family

Family variables related to school dropout include parental support for education
and stress levels in the family system. Alexander et al. (2001) found that almost
56% of students with low levels of emotional support from parents dropped out of
school compared with 27% of students with high levels of parental support.
Alexander et al. also found that the risk of dropout is increased by high levels of
stress in the family.

Multicultural variables have been linked to family variables in the studies of
school dropout. Keith and Schartzer (1995) examined family–school involvement
factors of Mexican American students in the 8th grade for their predictive value in
determining dropouts at the 10th-grade level. In terms of family involvement, these
researchers found that Mexican American students whose parents discussed school
activities with their children, expressed high aspirations for children, and were pro-
ficient in English were less likely to drop out.

Rumberger, Ghatak, Poulos, and Ritter (1990) found that parenting styles can influence dropout behaviors. These researchers found high school graduation rates related to an engaged, authoritative, and participatory parenting style. Parents of
students who completed high school were more likely to provide support for their
child's academic activities. These parents used encouragement, praise, and other
positive responses to school and academic work completed by their children.
Students were more likely to drop out of school if they had overly permissive parents, especially if the parents were not involved in their child's education and did

not provide guidance and support for their child's decision making. Rumberger et al. found that parenting that was too permissive also seemed to lead to increased influence, often negative, by the student's peer group. If students were involved with other students at risk for dropout, this effect could be particularly detrimental.

Peers

Mazza and Eggert (2001) found that adolescents at risk for school dropout were likely to engage in more social activities and less likely to do homework. Vitaro et al. (2001) noted that both association with deviant peers and rejection from conventional peers have been linked to dropping out of school. Lack of friendships with conventional peers can increase the possibility of disengagement from school. Thus, association with peers who do not value education has been understandably linked to school dropout.

Stress

Stress has been correlated with student dropout. Hess and Copeland (2001) found that ninth graders who eventually dropped out reported significantly more severe stress-related life events. Similarly, Velez and Saenz (2001) found that students who take on adult roles such as parenthood experience increased stress and are more likely to drop out of school.

CASE STUDY

Mark is a 15-year-old freshman from New Orleans, Louisiana. He and his family were displaced after losing their home in Hurricane Katrina. He now lives in inner-city Atlanta with his grandmother and mother. He helps around the house and takes care of his brothers when his mom goes to her night job. He feels pressure to do something to take care of his family in hopes that one day they can return home to New Orleans. He has made a plan to get a job so he can help out financially.

Mark's frustration is increasing with the difficulties he is having at school. He entered his new high school with reading and math achievement scores around the seventh-grade level. He reports that teachers treat him differently from other students and don't seem to care about him. He's frequently frustrated because his teachers and classmates tell him they cannot understand him when he speaks. He finds resolve, he says, by tuning everything out in class because he never understood lectures anyway and would rather think about his home and all his family that he misses in New Orleans. Although he does not have any history of delinquent or criminal behavior, he states whenever something bad happens at the school, he's "always one of the first they call to the office." The school is in an urban, inner-city neighborhood. It has a disproportionate amount of low-achieving students, insufficient resources, and overcrowded classrooms. The students are predominantly African American and Hispanic. Although Mark identifies as African American, because of his Creole, New Orleans heritage, his appearance seems more Hispanic. He confided that he feels like he really doesn't fit in with any of the groups of kids at his school; his complexion is too light to hang out with the African American students, and he is not Hispanic and doesn't speak Spanish, so the Hispanic students don't really accept him either.

Mark moved to Atlanta with his mother and two younger brothers. His mother has been divorced for 8 years. She works two part-time, minimum-wage jobs. She wants a better job to earn more money so that the family can move back and rebuild their home in New Orleans. But she is so busy with her current jobs and taking care of the three children that she has not had the time to look for a better job. She is also overwhelmed with trying to sort through the limited information and resources that have been available to help her and the family to return to their home in New Orleans. She feels unqualified for many jobs she finds in the newspaper because she dropped out of school when she was 15 to work full time. She doesn't believe she has any marketable skills for the job market in Atlanta. She said when she lived in New Orleans, she could always find work, and things weren't so bad because she had great family support. But now all that has changed; she and the children are in an unfamiliar city without any family support. This is their first time ever living or traveling outside of New Orleans.

Mark's mother tries to help her sons with their homework. She values education and wants them to complete high school so that they can "make something of their lives." She is dedicated and supportive of her children's academic success. She has missed work on occasion to attend PTA meetings at the high school. However, she leaves the meetings feeling discouraged because she doesn't feel that the teachers ever acknowledge her presence, and she is uncomfortable about speaking up or asking questions in the meetings among the other parents who seem to be more educated than her.

APPROACHES TO PREVENTION

Individual

The American School Counselor Association's (ASCA) position statement on at-risk students states that it is the professional counselor's role to collaborate with staff, schoolwide teams, parents, and the community to identify students who are exhibiting at-risk behaviors before such behaviors exacerbate to self-destructive behaviors (ASCA, 2004). The ASCA identifies seven possible ways the professional school counselor may intervene. The counselor may (a) provide classroom guidance lessons to increase students' knowledge and awareness of the dangers of at-risk behaviors and available resources to address students needs; (b) provide individual student planning sessions to address academic, personal/social, and career development needs; (c) provide responsive services, including short-term individual and group counseling; (d) collaborate with school staff to identify students in crisis; (e) provide referral services to appropriate support services and community agencies; (f) provide staff development to school and district staff; and (g) provide consultation and support to parents/guardians of students demonstrating at-risk behaviors.

The ASCA (2001a) takes the position that the school counselor acts as a resource person with expertise in developing discipline plans for prevention and intervention purposes. The stated position is clear: The role of the school counselor is not that of a disciplinarian, and thus the school counselor's role is not to give out punishment. The professional school counselor plays a participatory in the developmental aspects of discipline programs within state regulations and collaborates with school system personnel and other stakeholders to establish and maintain policies that encourage appropriate behavior so that schools can be a safe place where teaching and learning can be effectively accomplished. The counselor acts as a liaison, representative, and mediator to help create effective learning environment, keeping in mind students' diverse cultural, developmental, and emotional needs.

ASCA (2001b) states that professional school counselors make indispensable contributions to helping prevent school dropout. ASCA recognizes that the underlying reasons for students dropping out of school include personal and social problems, including low self-esteem, family problems, neglect, and abuse. School counselors can help students with these issues. School counselors can facilitate students' beliefs in their abilities through individual and group counseling. School counselors can help students learn to manage stress effectively. School counselors can also assist students in finding sources of support in school personnel, family, peers, and the community. Furthermore, school counselors can work closely with students to help them understand the lifelong, devastating effects of dropping out of school (ASCA , 2001b).

Consideration of students' attributes, attitudes, and behaviors is critical in designing prevention activities to reduce school dropout. Students' attributes include ethnicity, socioeconomic status, and IQ. Relevant attitudes are motivation and optimism. Behaviors linked to school dropout include students' classroom behaviors. Although some student attributes such as ethnicity and socioeconomic status cannot be altered, the impact of these variables can be diminished. Counselors can be at the forefront of prevention efforts aimed at reducing the impact of these variables. For example, one risk factor associated with ethnicity is language proficiency. Counselors can assist students with limited English proficiency by linking students with appropriate services within the school setting and throughout the community. Alienation is another risk factor associated with ethnicity. At-risk students are keenly aware of the overt and covert behaviors of the counselors, teachers, and administrators in their educational environment that signal a lower regard for their personal worth as learners. Often these students incorporate the low regard as a part of their personal identity as a result, and their behaviors exemplify the low expectations set before them (Acheson & Gall, 1998, as cited in Lunenburg, 2000). By establishing caring relationships with students and fostering the creation of a school environment that promotes inclusion for all ethnic groups, counselors also help minimize the potential negative impact of students' ethnicity. When students believe teachers and counselors care about them, they are more inclined to want to conform to the standards for achievement and behavior established by the school (Lunenburg, 2000).

Counselors' efforts can help lessen the likelihood that students like Mark in our case study will drop out of school. Mark seems to have significant adjustment issues combined with low self-esteem. He struggles academically and gets into trouble with his teachers. Neither he nor his mother believes the school personnel care about him. Experiencing a caring relationship with a school counselor, obtaining a peer mentor to help him acclimate to the new school environment, and participating in service project—perhaps a tangible activity geared toward the rebuilding efforts of his devastated city—would empower him and help him feel not only that he is valued but also that his situation is understood. The outcome is tremendous in terms of instilling hope and potentially developing a leader among his peers. The school counselor's input is integral in developing a discipline plan that considers

Mark's cultural, developmental, and emotional needs. A counselor could help locate the additional support, perhaps tutoring to address Mark's needs to overcome the learning challenges he is experiencing.

Family

Rumberger (1995) found that academic support from parents through activities like attending PTA meetings and volunteering at school events was strongly associated with students completing school. He also concluded that students were more likely to stay in school if parents talked with their children about school, helped them with their homework, and held high academic expectations. However, even when dealing with supportive families, school personnel need to reach out to parents and involve them in school activities. Children benefit when parents feel that the school is a partner in educating their children.

Lopez, Ehly, and Garcia-Vazquez (2002) explained that programs for parents can provide parents with support and ideas to assist them in advocating for their children in the school setting. Counselors can be at the forefront of the effort to provide these programs and workshops on parenting styles that are associated with children's school success. Counselors can also encourage parents to communicate with teachers, administrators, and other school personnel. Furthermore, counselors can help link families experiencing stress with community resources. According to ASCA, the school counselor is also expected to remain cognizant of students' diverse cultural, developmental, emotional needs as the counselor acts as a liaison and/or a mediator in creating effective learning environments.

When parents do attend school events, it is imperative that they do not feel marginalized. In our case study, Mark's mother missed work so that she could attend PTA meetings. It is clear that she is a mother who is concerned about her son's experience in school. Yet, she felt uncomfortable in the school setting and will probably not return. Counselors can help parents like Mark's mother feel more empowered in the school environment and become active participants in the school community. Parents like Mark's mother might appreciate the school counselor having an information table set up in a visible location where she could stop by and pick up handouts of information and talk to and feel welcomed by the counselor. The counselor in turn becomes a support for Mark's mother by connecting her to the teachers as well as fielding any questions that she may have in a nonthreatening manner.

School

Schools are partially responsible for the failure of their students (Baker et al., 2001). Alexander et al. (2001) stated that, according to the current accountability trend in schools, school policies can lead to students dropping out of school if they do not address the learning needs of all children. Of particular concern is the policy of student retention. Marcus and Sanders-Reio (2001) explained that school personnel need to be made aware of the high correlation between retention and school dropout. The ASCA's (2004) position statement on at-risk students states that the role of the professional school counselors makes a significant contribution toward academic, career, and interpersonal/social success of all students. Professional school counselors are to work in a leadership capacity in collaboration with parents and other student service professional, including social workers, psychologists, nurses, and staff, to identify students who are participating in behaviors that place them at risk. Student behaviors such as truancy, performing below academic potential, or participating in activities that are harmful to themselves or others (e.g., substance abuse, threats, or actual physical violence) are some of the many behaviors that have been identified as putting students at risk for dropout. Professional counselors should provide comprehensive school counseling programs that focus on the prevention and intervention of the behaviors that place students at risk.

Engaging Students in the Learning Process

To prevent school dropout, schools need to engage all students in the learning process and foster the enthusiasm that students have when they first start school. Researchers have identified five key ingredients that are necessary for effective student engagement: student participation, identification with school, social bonding, academic performance, and personal investment in learning (Lehr, Hansen, Sinclair, & Christenson, 2003). Teachers should include meaningful activities as well as activities that challenge students academically in curricula. Current research is positioning a shift in the conceptualization of at-risk students, steering focus from preventing dropout to promoting school completion (Lehr et al., 2003). The dropout problem is greater than simply keeping children in school (Christenson, Sinclair, Lehr, & Hurley, 2000, as cited in Lehr et al., 2003), thus engaging students in the learning process and increasing their enthusiasm involve more direct and purposeful support systems to help them meet the defined academic standards of their school. It is also important to address the underlying social and behavioral standards, with an added focus on understanding the intricate interplay between student, family, school, and community variables, as well as risk and protective factors that shape students' paths toward school withdrawal or completion (Hess & Copeland, 2001; Lehr et al., 2003; Valez & Saenz, 2001; Worrell & Hale, 2001). School personnel also need to promote attendance and make special efforts to bridge detrimental cultural, language, and procedural barriers related to attendance.

Culturally Diverse Students

The U.S. society is becoming increasingly diverse culturally. The statistics on minority students' high dropout rates are indicative of a school system that has been slow to respond to this cultural diversity. The failure of schools to respond to cultural diversity can also be viewed as a failure of schools to capitalize on the dynamic resources and opportunities for learning created by cultural pluralism. Wayman (2002a) explained that schools can respond to the reality of a pluralistic society by developing curricula that are more inclusive of minorities and promote cultural sensitivity within the school climate. These types of interventions would not only help minority students but could benefit all students by promoting tolerance for differences.

School Environment

Professional school counselors make a significant contribution toward the academic, career, and personal/social success of all students. Counselors can help create school environments that promote inclusion for all cultural groups. For example, counselors can play a role in raising the consciousness of teachers and administrators about cultural dynamics, and they can be proactive in helping schools create practices, procedures, and organizational structures that promote inclusion of all students. Furthermore, it is vital that school staff be trained in working with students who are ethnically and linguistically diverse (Lopez et al., 2002; Wayman, 2002a). Counselors can be at the forefront of this effort. Counselors can also help ensure that students with language barriers are receiving the services they need to succeed academically.

Counselors can assist students in building positive peer relationships. Lopez et al. (2002) postulated that social support is associated with academic achievement and prevention of dropout. Students who drop out often have a weak peer network or a peer network that includes peers who are disengaged from school and thus also at high risk for dropout (Marcus & Sanders-Reio, 2001). Marcus and Sanders-Reio suggested that the likelihood of school completion could be increased by fostering students' healthy attachment to other students. These authors advised school personnel to promote positive peer relationships and intervene against peer abuse and rejection, particularly in elementary and middle school. Counselors can also enhance social support for minority students by implementing multicultural support groups (Lopez et al., 2002). These groups could provide opportunities for students to meet with other students and to discuss issues related to peers, the school, and the community.

School and Class Size

Fostering the development of a sense of community at school includes advocating for smaller schools and structuring school activities to include ample opportunity for students to bond with adults and peers at school (Marcus & Sanders-Reio, 2001). Schools with low teacher/student ratios retain students until graduation more than schools with higher ratios (Baker et al., 2001). Large teacher/student ratios limit the ability of teachers to monitor student outcomes carefully and minimize the opportunity for the development of supportive teacher and student relationships. Counselors need to remain cognizant of the benefits of low teacher/student ratios and promote small class sizes.

Middle school students moving to high school experience increased academic demands as well as the developmental transitions associated with adolescence. When students transition to larger, unfamiliar school environments, this process can disrupt their relationships and social support (Baker et al., 2001). As in the case study with Mark and his mother's transition, counselors can help improve children's and parents' adjustment to new schools by interventions such as facilitating the building of positive relationships and fostering mutual respect among parents, teachers, and students.

Student Behaviors

Newcomb et al. (2002) found that deviant behavior was associated with high school dropout. These authors found tobacco use was the deviant behavior most highly to be correlated to school failure. The correlation between school failure and tobacco use was even higher than the correlation between school failure and students' use of alcohol or other drugs. Thus, although developmental guidance programming aimed at preventing alcohol and drug use is beneficial to students, Newcomb et al. advised early efforts in terms of the prevention of tobacco use.

ASCA (2001b) takes the position that school counselors are to provide comprehensive developmental counseling programs for all students, including students at risk for dropping out of school. Thus, programming designed to help keep students in school should be part of developmental guidance curricula. School counselors are also expected to work with other professionals such as social workers, psychologists, and other school personnel to help meet the needs of all students (ASCA, 2004). Furthermore, ASCA reiterates that school counselors need to work with parents to help foster each child's development.

In the case study, Mark struggles academically. He is a year older than most other ninth-grade students, so he was probably retained in at least one grade. He functions at about a seventh-grade level and has difficulty understanding what is going on in classes. Because of these factors, combined with his low socioeconomic status and his African American and Creole cultural background, he may be considered at risk for dropping out of school. Prevention efforts to minimize his risk for dropout could have included counselors working to make sure that his academic needs were addressed more adequately and fostering positive relationships between Mark and his teachers and peers. Counseling is vital for Mark to address any adjustment or loss issues he has had since his abrupt move to a new city and new high school. Creating an atmosphere within the school that embraced diversity and promoted multicultural activities could have been beneficial for all students, but particularly for students like Mark. Offering community support resources to Mark's mother may extend an expression of care and concern by letting her know that she is valued as a parent in the school.

Community

In the community, counselors can be advocates for schools and students. Counselors can promote the value of providing all students with a quality education. Counselors can also assist schools in obtaining human and financial resources from the community. For example, counselors can engage in collaborative relationships with community social service agencies so that appropriate referrals can be provided to students.

Counselors can encourage school–community collaboration by providing students with direct access to community and business leaders. This task can be accomplished through activities such as inviting professionals from the community to the school to talk to students about political issues or career opportunities in the community. Activities involving community members can help students see the value of staying in school. Providing a nontraditional career day that incorporates members of the community to discuss job opportunities relating to a skill or trade job (e.g., construction workers, beauticians, barbers, plumbers, HVAC technicians, artisans, mechanics, bakers) and their personal experiences with school and to offer advice on the importance of staying in school could be helpful for all students, particularly Mark. The career day could extend into job shadowing or mentorship opportunities. Students can gain relevant real-life experience for the tangible possibilities for completing school.

INTERVENTION STRATEGIES

Wang, Haertel, and Walberg (1994) studied resilience in terms of academic achievement and defined educational resilience as "the heightened likelihood of educational success despite personal vulnerabilities and adversities brought about by environmental conditions and experiences" (p. 46). Educational researchers examining resilience in at-risk student populations have identified factors that moderate the effects of students' individual and environmental vulnerabilities. For example, Wayman (2002b) described personal resilient factors as student attributes and attitudes that buffer the negative effects of a student's adverse situation. These attributes include positive self-concept and motivation. Developing a positive self-concept and optimistic attitude is particularly critical for minority students (Wayman, 2002b).

Wang, Haertel, and Walberg (1997) explained that educational resilience is the result of continual interaction between students and their environment. Wayman (2002b) described environmental factors that contribute to resilience as external influences that protect against negative influences facing at-risk youth. Wayman identified adult support as a factor that enables students to develop trust and learn from their challenges. Educational resilience has also been associated with family commitment to education as well as peer support (Gonzalez & Padilla, 1997; Horn & Chen, 1998).

Although Wayman's (2002b) work on educational resilience looked primarily at degree attainment after students drop out of school, his findings are relevant to intervention efforts with students at risk for dropping out of school. For example, protective factors identified in the educational resilience framework included students' self-confidence and positive attitudes about finishing school. Wayman argued that these factors are easier to change than socioeconomic status and students' academic capabilities, prevalent factors identified in previous research on school dropout. Furthermore, Wayman found that some of the negative effects from risk factors such as socioeconomic status became insignificant after the introduction of educational resilience factors. Thus, Wayman suggested that school personnel implement resilience-building strategies in their schools. Counselors can utilize resilience-building strategies in their work with students. Counselors can also provide training to teachers on effective resilience-building strategies.

The National Dropout Prevention Center/Network (NDPC/N) highlighted a model program, the Putnam City Academy, as a school of choice and second chances that voluntarily enrolls students and empowers them to set and reach their educational goals leading to graduation (NDPC/N, 2005b). This program was created to serve students who have not been successful in a regular school setting and who are at risk of dropping out of high school with the sole purpose of dropout prevention and dropout recovery through student achievement in an innovative, nontraditional learning community. The three goals of the program are to develop productive character and citizenship, improve academic skills and strategies, and develop resiliency through building assets (NDPC/N, 2005b).

Individual

Dynarski and Gleason (2002) studied the effectiveness of various dropout reduction interventions and described current interventions aimed at counteracting the numerous negative school experiences at-risk students encounter. These interventions included activities aimed at building students' self-esteem and increasing students' coping skills. Additionally, Dynarski and Gleason advocated for providing students with greater access to counselors to help students deal with challenges, including personal and family difficulties that are affecting success in school.

Hess and Copeland (2001) stated, "it is critical that we develop intervention programs that help students cope effectively with high levels of stress and create more extensive support systems to assist them with their emotional, social, and educational needs" (p. 403). These authors suggested providing interventions that focus on increasing students' engagement in school, improving students' problem-solving skills, strengthening family support systems, and helping students make good choices about friendships. Counselors can play a key role in these interventions.

Marcus and Sanders-Reio (2001) noted that attachment to peers promotes student achievement and engagement in school. Both association with deviant peers and rejection from conventional peers have been linked to dropping out of school (Vitaro et al., 2001). Lack of friendships can increase the possibility of disengagement from school. Thus, Vitaro et al. suggested that school personnel foster students' association with conventional peers.

The degree to which students persevere when they experience difficulties and optimism about the future may influence dropout (Gleason & Dynarski, 2002). Worrell and Hale (2001) found that hope in the future is a protective factor for students at risk for dropping out of school. Counselors can help create a school environment that promotes optimism in schools.

In the case study, Mark's counselors could provide interventions related to building self-esteem, enhancing his support system, and improving coping skills to help Mark overcome his academic challenges as well as effectively manage any stress he is experiencing because of his adjustment issues and responsibilities at home. Counselors could empower Mark and instill hope by reinforcing the belief in his ability to complete school. He needs to be able to perceive graduating from high school as a real possibility. Guidance is necessary to help Mark make the connection in his thoughts of how his behaviors and actions toward completing school relate to his success in the future.

Family

According to ASCA's position statement on at-risk students, school counselors are expected to consult with and support parents/guardians of students at risk (ASCA, 2004). Family members can play a role in intervening to prevent students from dropping out of school. For example, in 2005, the NDPC/N featured the Berkeley County School District as a model program because they developed a districtwide intervention plan to ensure that schools have a uniform response when students are truant and deemed at risk (NDPC/N, 2005a). The goal was to intervene as soon as possible. The focus of this intervention was on ninth-grade students at the three high schools with the highest percentage of dropouts. Activities included the development of a system for documenting unexcused absences, written contacts with parents, the creation of attendance intervention plans, access to a parenting program for parents of truant youth, makeup days on Saturdays and summer school, and a mentoring program in collaboration with local churches (NDPC/N, 2005a).

In the case study, Mark's mother tries to help her sons with their homework and stresses the value of an education. However, when she attempted to participate in a school–parent function, she felt uncomfortable. The Berkeley intervention plan offers many solutions that would be beneficial in collaborating community resources and garnering parental involvement with Mark.

School

Educational researchers have noted the importance of providing interventions to keep students engaged in active learning (Baker et al., 2001; Dynarski & Gleason, 2002; Worrell & Hale, 2001). Actively engaging students who are at risk for dropping out is particularly important (NDPC/N, n.d., para. 12).

Successful school programs incorporate teaching and learning strategies that provide students ownership in their learning. Technology offers some of the best opportunities for delivering instruction to engage students in authentic learning, addressing multiple intelligences, and adapting to students' learning styles (NDPC/N, n.d., para. 13). Researchers also advocate for smaller schools and flexible scheduling time during the school day for students to meet in small groups and work on academic skills with tutors or mentors to increase their academic competence. Peer tutoring and cooperative learning are other strategies found to be effective when working with students who are struggling academically.

Other effective strategies recommended by the NDPC/N might include individualized instruction that incorporates the students' unique interests and past learning experiences. Individualized instruction programs allows for flexibility in teaching methods and motivational strategies to consider these individual differences. Career and technical programs paired with related guidance programs are vital to all students, particularly students at risk. School-to-work programs recognize that youths need specific skills to prepare them to measure up to the larger demands of today's workplace (NDPC/N, n.d., para. 11). There are opportunities for counselors to collaborate with the community to identify mentors for students to pair with to begin the discovery process for work options. These strategies foster adaptable and creative ways to resolve conflicts and achieve success to become lifelong learners. When student feel engaged with lessons that are relevant with real-life applications and experiences, their behaviors will naturally be molded in more positive ways by challenging the way they think of their learning.

The integral key to effective intervention for at-risk students is professional development for teachers who work with this population (NDPC/N, n.d., paras. 14 & 15). Darling-Hammond (1999) suggested that the quality of teachers is one of the most important predictors of students' success. Therefore, teachers as well as counselors need to be supported and encouraged by their administrators to invest in training opportunities to hone their skills and develop techniques with current and innovative strategies. Newcomb et al. (2002) reiterated the critical role that academic remediation and support plays in preventing school dropout. They advised teachers to promote high school graduation as an achievable goal. Pianta (1999) advocated for providing at-risk youth with adequate support services before they fail. From an attachment perspective, these support services should be provided in a manner that preserves students' attachment to teachers and peers. Christenson et al. (2001) explained that successful interventions help students who feel marginalized by the school culture, school personnel, and other students become members of the school community.

Ineffective Intervention Approaches

Jimerson et al. (2002) suggested educators use great caution with utilizing retention as an academic intervention for students at risk. Unfortunately, teachers are often unaware of the research on the negative implications associated with retention (Haberman & Dill, 1993). It is important to increase the awareness of school personnel, parents, students, and the community of the detriments and the available alternative interventions for low-achieving students other than retention (Jimerson et al., 2002).

Another ineffective intervention is ability grouping. This approach involves placing low-achieving students in classrooms with other students struggling academically. Research has shown that placing low-achieving students together in the same classroom does not improve student achievement (Kulik, 1993; Lesters & McDill, 1995). In fact, ability grouping may worsen the situation because such placement negatively stigmatizes lower achieving students. Thus, students in these classrooms may experience shame and lowered self-esteem. Conversely, when lower achieving students are mixed with average and high-ability students, negative stereotypes are avoided, and students struggling academically often show more academic success.

Role of the School Counselor

One of the roles of school counselors is to work with other school personnel in identifying potential dropouts (ASCA, 2001b). The goal of the school counselor in this instance is to identify these students and intervene before the students engage in self-destructive behaviors such as dropping out of school. The school counselor is expected to work closely with these at-risk students and encourage them to stay in school. ASCA (2001b) explains that this task can be accomplished through providing responsive programs. These programs include components such as building self-esteem and improving decision-making skills. The school counselor is also expected to provide individual, group, family, and crisis counseling services to meet students' educational and career counseling needs. The school counselor may even need to help students find alternative means of completing their education (ASCA, 2001b).

In the case study, Mark could benefit from academic remediation and support services, individualized instruction, and peer tutoring to address the gap in his academic functioning. In efforts to invest in Mark's completion of school, a wise intervention plan may be to help him to identify a manageable community concern, either in his new community or an existing concern relating to the rebuilding of his home in New Orleans. This type of service learning project will foster a sense of belonging and acceptance for Mark as well as empower him to transform his view of self and circumstance. Mark could potentially be transformed to see himself no longer as the victim but a leader or change agent. Service learning projects can be developed to be completed in small groups utilizing technology, the student's unique learning styles, and previous learning experiences. The process and outcomes of these projects offer a meaningful connection and promotes personal and social growth as well as potential leadership development and civic responsibility. This is a powerful tool that could potentially generate effective school reform, beginning with the leadership of youth at risk.

Community

Alexander et al. (2001) noted that academic success and positive personal and family resources somewhat buffer at-risk students who live in impoverished communities, but these students are still extremely vulnerable. According to Aviles et al. (1999), school counselors can help students use inherent cultural strengths to overcome obstacles preventing academic success. Aviles et al. explained that counselors can also assist students in taking advantage of home and community resources. School counselors can act as a liaison between schools and the community.

ADAPTATIONS FOR DIVERSITY

Culture, ethnicity, students' learning differences, and family socioeconomic status can be considered risk factors for student dropout. However, these factors can also be viewed as attributes to the learning community. For example, fostering pride in students' cultural heritage can lead to increased self-esteem and tolerance for differences. Furthermore, utilizing the resources and social support inherent in many communities can benefit all students.

Counselors can help make school a comfortable place for every student. Workshops for school personnel on multicultural issues seem to be indicated. Counselors can also sponsor activities and clubs related to pride in diversity. Counselors can help make sure that students who need ESL classes or other academic support receive the services they need. Finally, counselors can take an active role in promoting home–school communication and increasing parents' involvement in school.

SUMMARY

School dropout is a serious social problem. Large numbers of dropouts place a burden on unemployment and welfare services as well as the criminal justice system. The correlation between ethnicity and student dropout is particularly disturbing considering that the Hispanic population is the largest minority population in the United States and remains one of the fastest growing U.S. populations (Velez & Saenz, 2001). Because the trend of increased school dropout is likely to continue, schools systems need to work harder to address the needs of all students.

Counselors can be instrumental in providing successful prevention and intervention efforts for students at risk for school dropout. Best practices for professional school counselors are to advocate for all students. Counselors can facilitate the development of self-esteem in students, and they can help increase the awareness of the negative implications of current school policies such as retention to school personnel, students, and their parents. Counselors should work collaboratively to encourage positive teacher–student interactions, foster family support and healthy peer relationships, and engage members of the community in school activities. Counselors can also help schools create environments that promote inclusion for all ethnic groups and academic success for all students. Furthermore, counselors can help students become more educationally resilient by providing interventions, such as promoting optimism, teaching students how to effectively manage stress, and helping students learn from the challenges they encounter. Professional school counselors make a significant contribution toward the academic, career, and personal/social success of all students. Professional school counselors work in a leadership role (ASCA, 2001b) with all entities relating to the betterment and well-being of the students.

REFERENCES

Alexander, K. L., Entwisle, D. R., & Kabbani, N. S. (2001). The dropout process in life course perspective: Early risk factors at home and school. *Teachers College Record, 103*, 760–822.

American School Counselor Association. (2001a). *Position statement: The professional school counselor and discipline.* Retrieved September 3, 2006, from http://www.schoolcounselor.org/content.asp?contentid=203

American School Counselor Association. (2001b). *Position statement: The professional school counselor and dropout prevention/students-at-risk.* Retrieved September 3, 2006, from http://www.schoolcounselor.org/files/positions.pdf

American School Counselor Association. (2004). *Position statement: The professional school counselor and the prevention and intervention of behaviors that place students at risk.* Retrieved September 3, 2006, http://www.schoolcounselor.org/content.asp?contentid=258

Aviles, R. D., Guerrero, M. P., Howarth, H. B., & Thomas, G. (1999). Perceptions of Chicano/Latino students who have dropped out of school. *Journal of Counseling & Development, 77*, 465–473.

Baker, J. A., Derrer, R. D., Davis, S. M., Dinklage-Travis, H. E., Linder, D. S., & Nicholson, M. D. (2001). The flip side of the coin: Understanding the school's contribution to dropout and completion. *School Psychology Quarterly, 16*, 406–426.

Beekhoven, S., & Dekkers, H. (2005). Early school leaving in the lower vocational track: Triangulation of qualitative and quantitative data. *Adolescence, 40*, 197–210.

Bickel, W. E., Bond, L., & LeMahieu, P. G. (1988). *Students at risk of not completing high school.* Unpublished manuscript, University of Pittsburgh.

Campbell, L. (2003). As strong as the weakest link: Urban high school dropout. *High School Journal, 87*, 16–28

Cassidy, W., & Bates, A. (2005). "Drop-outs" and "push-outs": Finding hope at a school that actualizes the ethic of care. *American Journal of Education, 112*, 66–99.

Chinien, C., & Boutin, F. (2001/2002, December/January). Qualitative assessment of cognitive-based dropout prevention strategy. *High School Journal,* 1–11.

Christenson, S. L., Sinclair, M. F., Lehr, C. A., & Godber, Y. (2001). Promoting successful school completion: Critical conceptual and methodological guidelines. *School Psychology Quarterly, 16*, 468–484.

Darling-Hammond, L. (1999). *Teacher quality and student achievement: A review of state policy evidence.* Seattle: University of Washington, Center of the Study of Teaching and Policy.

Dunn, C., Chambers, D., & Rabren, K. (2004). Variables affecting students' decisions to drop out of school. *Remedial and Special Education, 25*, 314–324.

Dynarski, M., & Gleason, P. (2002). How can we help? What we have learned from recent federal dropout prevention evaluations. *Journal of Education for Students Placed at Risk, 7*, 43–69.

Garnier, H. E., Stein, J. A., & Jacobs, J. K. (1997). The process of dropping out of high school: A 19-year perspective. *American Educational Research Journal, 34*, 395–419.

Gleason, P., & Dynarski, M. (2002). Do we know whom to serve? Issues in using risk factors to identify dropouts. *Journal of Education for Students Placed at Risk, 7*, 25–41.

Gonzalez, R., & Padilla, A. M. (1997). The academic resilience of Mexican American high school students. *Hispanic Journal of Behavioral Sciences, 19*, 301–317.

Grayson, T. E. (1998). Dropout prevention and special services. In F. R. Rusch & J. G. Chadsey (Eds.), *Beyond high school* (pp. 77–98). Belmont, CA: Wadsworth.

Haberman, M., & Dill, V. (1993). The knowledge base on retention vs. teacher ideology: Implications for teacher preparation. *Journal of Teacher Education, 44*, 352–360.

Harvey, M. W. (2001). Vocational-technical education: A logical approach to dropout prevention for secondary special education (statistical data included). *Preventing School Failure, 45*, 108.

Hess, R. S., & Copeland, E. P. (2001). Students' stress, coping strategies, and school completion: A longitudinal perspective. *School Psychology Quarterly, 16*, 389–405.

Horn, L. J., & Chen, X. (1998). *Toward resiliency: At-risk students who make it to college* (OERI Publication No. PLLI-98-8056). Washington, DC: U.S. Government Printing Office. (ERIC Document Reproduction Service No. ED419463)

Jimerson, S. R. (1999). On the failure of failure: Examining the association between early grade retention and education and employment outcomes during late adolescence. *Journal of School Psychology, 37*, 243–272.

Jimerson, S. R., Anderson, G. E., & Whipple, A. D. (2002). Winning the battle and losing the war: Examining the relation between grade retention and dropping out of school. *Psychology in the Schools, 39*, 441–457.

Keith, P. B., & Schartzer, C. L. (1995, August). *What is the influence of Mexican American parental involvement on school attendance patterns?* Poster presented at the annual meeting of the American Psychological Association, New York, NY. (ERIC Document Reproduction Service No. ED415450)

Kulik, J. A. (1993, Spring). An analysis of the research on ability grouping. *National Research Center on the Gifted and Talented Newsletter*, 8–9. (ERIC Document Reproduction Service No. ED367095)

Lehr, C. A., Hansen, A., Sinclair, M. F., & Christenson, S. L. (2003). Moving beyond dropout towards school completion: An integrative review of data-based interventions. *School Psychology Review, 32*, 342–365.

Lesters, N., & McDill, E. L. (1995). *Rising to the challenge: Emerging strategies for educating youth at risk* (Urban Monograph Series). Oak Brook, IL: North Central Regional Education Lab. (ERIC Document Reproduction Service No. ED397202)

Lopez, E. J., Ehly, S., & Garcia-Vazquez, E. (2002). Acculturation, social support, and academic achievement of Mexican and Mexican American high school students: An exploratory study. *Psychology in the Schools, 39*, 245–257.

Lunenburg, F. C. (2000). America's hope: Making schools work for all children. *Journal of Instructional Psychology, 27*, 39–41.

Lynch, S., Hurford, D. P., & Cole, A. (2002). Parental enabling attitudes and locus of control of at-risk and honors students. *Adolescence, 37*, 527–550.

Manlove J. (1998). The influence of high school dropout and school disengagement on the risk of school-age pregnancy. *Journal of Research on Adolescence, 8*, 187–220.

Marcus, R. F., & Sanders-Reio, J. (2001). The influence of attachment on school completion. *School Psychology Quarterly, 16*, 427–444.

Mazza, J. J., & Eggert, L. L. (2001). Activity involvement among suicidal and non-suicidal high-risk and typical adolescents. *Suicide and Life-Threatening Behavior, 31*, 265–281.

McMillen, M. M., Kaufman, P., Hausken, E. G., & Bradby, D. (1993). *Dropout rates in the United States: 1992*. Washington, DC: National Center for Education Statistics, U.S. Department of Education.

Mortenson, T. G. (1997). Postsecondary education opportunities: The Mortenson research seminar on public policy analysis of opportunity for postsecondary education, 1997. *Postsecondary Education Opportunity*, 93–98. (ERIC Document Reproduction Service No. ED416754)

National Center for Education Statistics. (2002). *Dropout rates in the United States: 2000*. Retrieved August 24, 2006, from http://nces.ed.gov/pubs2002/droppub_2001/

National Center for Education Statistics. (2006). *Dropout rates in the United States: 2002–2003*. Retrieved August 24, 2006, from http://nces.ed.gov/pubs2006/dropout/

National Dropout Prevention Center/Network. (n.d.). *Effective strategies*. Retrieved August 24, 2006, from http://www.dropoutprevention.org/effstrat/default.htm

National Dropout Prevention Center/Network. (2005a). *Model programs: The Berkeley County School District*. Retrieved August 24, 2006, from http://www.dropoutprevention.org

National Dropout Prevention Center/Network. (2005b). *Model programs: The Putnam City Academy*. Retrieved August 24, 2006, from http://www.dropoutprevention.org

Newcomb, M. D., Abbott, R. D., Catalano, R. F., Hawkins, J. D., Battin-Pearson, S., & Hill, K. (2002). Mediational and deviance theories of late high school failure: Process roles of structural strains, academic competence, and general versus specific problem behaviors. *Journal of Counseling Psychology, 49,* 172–186.

No Child Left Behind Act of 2001, Pub. L. 107–110 § 1425 (2002).

Pianta, R. C. (1999). *Enhancing relationships between children and teachers.* Washington, DC: American Psychological Association.

Rumberger, R. W. (1993). Chicano dropouts: A review of research and policy issues. In R. Valencia (Ed.), *Chicano school failure and success: Research and policy agendas for the 1990s* (pp. 64–89). Philadelphia: Falmer Press.

Rumberger, R. W. (1995). Dropping out of middle school: A multilevel analysis of students and schools. *American Educational Research Journal, 32,* 583–625.

Rumberger, R. W., Ghatak, R., Poulos, G., & Ritter, P. L. (1990). Family influences on dropout behavior in one California high school. *Sociology of Education, 63,* 283–299.

Scanlon, D., & Mellard, D. F. (2002). Academic and participation profiles of school-age dropouts with and without disabilities. *Exceptional Children, 68,* 239–258.

Suh, S., & Satcher, J. (2005). Understanding at-risk Korean American youth. *Professional School Counseling, 8,* 428–436.

Swaim, R. C., Beauvais, F., Chavez, E. L., & Oetting, E. R. (1997). The effect of school dropout rates on estimates of adolescent substance abuse among three racial/ethnic groups. *American Journal of Public Health, 87,* 51–55.

U.S. Census Bureau. (2005, March). *Educational attainment in the United States: 2003.* Retrieved August 17, 2006, from htttp://www.census.gov

Velez, W., & Saenz, R. (2001). Toward a comprehensive model of the school leaving process among Latinos. *School Psychology Quarterly, 16,* 445–467.

Vitaro, F., Larocque, D., Janosz, M., & Tremblay, R. E. (2001). Negative social experiences and dropping out of school. *Educational Psychology, 21,* 401–415.

Wang, M. C., Haertel, G. D., & Walberg, H. J. (1994). Educational resilience in inner cities. In M.C. Wang & E. W. Gorden (Eds.), *Educational resilience in inner-city America: Challenges and prospects* (pp. 42–72). Hillsdale, NJ: Erlbaum.

Wang, M. C., Haertel, G. D., & Walberg, H. J. (1997). Fostering educational resilience in inner-city schools. In M. C. Wang, G. D. Haertel, & H. J. Walberg (Eds.), *Children and youth* (pp. 119–140). Newbury Park, CA: Sage.

Wayman, J. C. (2002a, February/March). Student perceptions of teacher ethnic bias: A comparison of Mexican American and non-Latino White dropouts and students. *High School Journal,* 27–37.

Wayman, J. C. (2002b). The utility of educational resilience for studying degree attainment in school dropouts. *Journal of Educational Research, 95,* 167–178.

Wells, D., Miller, M., Tobacyk, J., & Clanton, R. (2002). Using a psychoeducational approach to increase the self-esteem of adolescents at high risk for dropping out. *Adolescence, 37,* 431–435.

Worrell, F. C., & Hale, R. L. (2001). The relationship of hope in the future and perceived school climate to school completion. *School Psychology Quarterly, 16,* 370–388.

Index

Tables and figures are indicated by *t* and *f* following the page number.

(Continued)

(Continued)